THE RAMAYANA OF TULSI DAS

THE RAMAYANA OF TULSI DAS

TRANSLATED FROM THE ORIGINAL HINDI

BY

F. S. GROWSE, B. C. S.

M.A., OXON; C. I. E.

GYAN

Published by

GYAN

Gyan Publishing House
5, Ansari Road
Daryaganj, New Delhi-110002
Phone: 011-47034999, 9811692060
E-mail: books@gyanbooks.com

Distribution Network
gyanbooks.com
India, USA, Canada, UK, Australia, France

ISBN : 978-81-212-9174-3 (PB)
First Published, 1914

2nd Impression 2023

Printed at: Gyan Press, Delhi.

THE RAMAYANA OF TULSI DAS
Translator: F. S. GROWSE

संवत सोरह सै इकतीसा
कहौं कथा हरि पद धरि सीसा

श्री श्री

THE

RAMAYANA

OF

TULSI DAS.

TRANSLATED FROM THE ORIGINAL HINDI
BY
F. S. GROWSE, B. C. S.;
M.A., OXON; C. I. E.;
FELLOW OF THE CALCUTTA UNIVERSITY.

SIXTH EDITION.
REVISED AND CORRECTED.

"The Rámáyan of Tulsi Dás is more popular and more honoured by the people of the North-Western Provinces than the Bible is by the corresponding classes in England."

GRIFFITH.

Allahabad:
RAM NARAIN LAL,
PUBLISHER & BOOKSELLER
1914.

मन करि विषय अनल बन जरहीं
होइं सुखी जे इहिं सर परहीं

राम चरित मानस यह नामा
सुनत श्रवन पाइय विश्रामा

होइहहिं राम चरन अनुरागी
कलिमल रहित सुमङ्गल भागी

जो यह कथा सनेह समेता
कहिहहिं सुनिहहिं समुझि सचेता

संवत सोरह सै असी असीगंग के तीर
श्रावण शुक्लासत्तमी तुलसी तज्यो शरीर

INTRODUCTION.

The Sanskrit Rámáyana of Válmíki has been published more than once, with all the advantages of European editorial skill and the most luxurious typography. It has also been translated both in verse and prose, and, in part at least, into Latin, as well as into Italian, French and English. The more popular Hindi presentment of the same great national Epic can only be read in lithograph or bazár print, [1] and – with the exception of a single Book—has never till now been translated in any form into any language whatever. Yet it is no unworthy rival of its more fortunate predecessor. There can, of course be no comparison between the polished phraseology of classical Sanskrit and the rough colloquial idiom of Tulsi Dás's vernacular ; while the antiquity of Válmíki's poem further invests it with an adventitious interest for the student of Indian history. But, on the other hand, the Hindi poem is the best and most trustworthy guide to the popular living faith of the Hindu race at the present day—a matter of not less practical interest than the creed of their remote ancestors—and its language, which in the course of three centuries has contracted a tinge of archaism, is a study of much importance to the philologist, as helping to bridge the chasm between the modern tongue and the mediæval. It is also less wordy and diffuse than the Sanskrit original and, probably in consequence of its modern date, is less disfigured by wearisome interpolations and repetitions ; while, if it never soars so high as Válmíki in some of his best passages, it maintains a more equable level of poetic diction, and seldom sinks with him into such dreary depths of unmitigated prose. It must also be noted that it is in no sense a translation of the earlier work : the general plan and the management of the incidents are necessarily much the same, but there is a difference in the touch in every detail ; and the two poems vary as widely as any two dramas on the same mythological subject by two different Greek tragedians. Even the coincidence of name is an accident ; for Tulsi Dás himself called his poem 'The

1 A handsome edition of the text was issued from the press of the Baptist Mission in Calcutta many years ago ; but it has long been out of print, and the only copy I have ever seen of it was the one in use at the college of Fort William in 1861. I had thus entirely forgotten the fact till reminded of it by Mr. Bate, a gentleman who has ably maintained the scholarly reputation of the Mission by his very useful Hindi Dictionary.

Rám-charit-mánas,' and the shorter title, corresponding in character to the 'Iliad' or 'Æneid,' has only been substituted by his admirers as a handier designation for a popular favourite.

However, the opinion that the more modern poem is a close adaptation, or *rifaccimento*, of the Sanskrit original is very widely entertained, not only by European scholars but also by Hindus themselves. For, among the latter, an orthodox pandit is essentially *homo unius libri*, to whom the idea of comparative criticism is altogether strange and unintelligible. Whatever is written in the one book, to which he pins his faith, is for him the absolute truth, which he positively declines to weaken or obscure by a reference to any other authority. It he can understand Válmíki's Sanskrit, he despises Tulsi Dás as a vulgarian and would not condescend to read a line of him; if he knows only Hindi, he accepts the modern poem with as implicit faith as if it were an immemorial shástra, and accounts a quotation from his Rámáyana an unanswerable argument on any disputed topic. Thus, in all probability, the only educated Hindus who have much acquaintance with both poems are the professors and students of Government colleges, whose views have been broadened by European influence. It may, therefore, be of interest to show a little more at length how great is the divergence between the two poems.

In both, the first Book brings the narrative precisely to the same point, *viz*, the marriage of Ráma and Síta. With Tulsi Dás this is much the longest book of the seven, and forms all but a third of the complete work; in the Sanskrit, on the contrary, it is the shortest but one, even after including the first four cantos, which are obviously a late addition. They give a table of contents, and explain how Válmíki learnt the story from Nárad, and taught it to Kusa and Lava; thus corresponding in no respect, with Tulsi Das's introduction. The actual poem commences at once, without any prelude, with a description of Ayodhyá and its King Dasarath and his ministers, and of his longing for an heir; and tells how Rishyasring, Vibhandak's son (whose previous adventures are recorded at length) was invited from the palace of his father-in-law, Lomapád, the king of Champa, to direct the ceremonies of a great sacrifice, which the childless Dasarath resolved to celebrate, in the hope of thereby obtaining his desire. The gods, being at that time sorely distressed by Rávan's persecution, had fled to Vishnu for succour; and he, in answer to their prayer, became incarnate in the four sons that were born to the king, while inferior divinities took birth as bears and monkeys. The four princes are named by Vasishta. They grow up, and the king is thinking where to find suitable brides for them, when Visvamitra comes, and, after a long colloquy, takes away with him Ráma and Lakshman to protect him at the time of sacrifice from the demons that persistently assail him. On the way they pass by the Anga hermitage, where the god of love had been reduced to ashes by Siva—a legend to which very brief allusion is made,—then though the forest of Táraká, whom Ráma meets in battle and slays, but not till her genealogy has been fully recorded. He is then invested by the saint with certain heavenly weapons and magical powers, and, arriving at Visvamitra's hermitage, he slays the demons Márícha and Subáhu. Being told of Janak's bow-sacrifice he resolves to attend it; and as he crosses the Son and the Ganges on his way thither, Visvamitra entertains him with a prolix account of his own descent from King Kusa, of the birth of Ganga, the legend of the sons of Sagar and his sacrifice, and how his descendant Bhagirath brougdt down the Ganges from heaven and concludes with the genealogy of the kings of Visála. As they draw near to Mithilá, Ráma delivers Gautam's wife Ahalyá, whose legend is given with all its circumstances. He is welcomed by Janak and by Ahalya's son, Satánanda, and the latter makes a long speech of eight hundred lines, in which he gives a complete history of the contention between Visvamitra and Vasishta, with an account of Trisanku and Sunahsepha and Ambarísha and of Visvamitra's final promotion to Bráhmanical rank. Janak shows Ráma the bow in its case, and he then and there takes it up and snaps it in pieces. The royal suitors had all tried in vain, and after fruitlessly besieging the city, with intent to carry off Síta by force, had returned discomforted to their own realms. Envoys are despatched to Ayodhyá for King Dasarath; Kusa-dhvaj, Janak's brother, is also summoned from Sankasya: and then in full conclave Vasishta proclaims Ráma's pedigree, after which Janak recites his own. The fourfold nuptials then take place, a hundred thousand cows being given to the Bráhmans in the name of each of the brides, and many precious gifts being bestowed in dowry. Dasarath then takes his way home with his sons and daughters, but is met by Parasurám with Vishnu's bow, which Ráma strings at once, and the son of Bhrigu acknowledges his supremacy. They then reach Ayodhyá, whence Bharat soon departs with his uncle, Yudhajit, on a visit to his mother's father, Kekaya.

On comparing the above sketch with my translation of the corresponding portion of the Hindi poem, it will be seen that the two agree only in the broadest outline. The episodes so freely introduced by both poets are, for the most part, entirely dissimilar; and even in the main narrative some of the most important incidents, such as the breaking of the bow and the contention with Parasurám, are differently placed and assume a very altered complexion. In other passages where the story follows the same lines, whatever Válmíki has condensed—as, for example, the description of the marriage festivities—Tulsi Dàs has expanded; and wherever the elder poet has lingered longest, his successor has hastened on most rapidly.

In the seventh, or last, Book, the divergence is, if anything, still more marked. It consists with Válmíki of 124 cantos, the first 49 of which are occupied by a dialogue between Ràma and the Rishi Agastya, who relates the story of Rávan's birth and his conquest of the world. In the 50th canto Ráma dismisses his monkey followers to their homes: and it in only is this one passage and in occasional reference to the glory and happiness of Ráma's reign that there is any coincidence with the Hindi 'Sequel.' The remainder of the Sanskrit poem relates the exile of Síta and the Asvamedh sacrifice; after which Ràma and his brothers ascend to heaven. All these topics are totally omitted by Tulsi Dás, who substitutes for them the story of Káka-bhusundi and a series of laboured disquisitions on the true nature of Faith.

The earliest notice of our author, as, indeed, of all the other celebrated Vaishnava writers who flourished about the same period, *viz.*, the 16th and 17th century A. D., is to be found in the Bhakt-Málá, or 'Legends of the Saints,' one of the most difficult works in the Hindi language. Its composition is invariably ascribed to Nábhá Jí, himself one of the leaders of the reform which had its centre at Brindá-ban; but the poem, as we now have it, was avowedly edited, if not entirely written, by one of his disciples named Náráyan Dás who lived during the reign of Sháh-jahan. A single stanza is all that is ordinarily devoted to each personage, who is panegyrized with reference to his most salient characteristics in a style that might be described as of unparalleled obscurity, were it not that each such separate portion of the text is followed by a *tika*, or gloss, written by one Priya Dás in the *sambat* year 1769 (1713 A. D.) in which confusion is still worse confounded by a series of the most disjointed and inexplicit allusions to different legendary events in the saint's life. The poem has never been printed, and though it is of the very highest repute among modern Vaishnavas, and is, therefore, not rare in MS. either at Mathurá or Brindá-ban, it is utterly unintelligible to ordinary native readers. The text of the passage referring to Tulsi Dás is, therefore, here given, and is followed by a literal English translation :—

॥ मूल ॥

कलि कुटिल जीव निस्तार हेत वाल्मीक तुलसी भयो ॥
त्रेता काव्य निबंध करिब सत कोटि रामायण ॥
इक अक्षर उद्धरै ब्रह्महत्यादि करि जिन होत पारायन ॥
अब भक्तनि सुख दैंन बहुरि वपु धरि लीला बिस्तारी ॥
राम चरन रसमत्त रटत अह निस व्रतधारी ॥
संसार अपार के पार को सुगम रूप नौका लियो ॥
कलि कुटिल जीव निस्तार हेत बाल्मीक तुलसी भयो ॥

Translation of the text of Nábhá Ji.

For the redemption of mankind in this perverse Kali Yug, Válmíki has been born again as Tulsi. The verses of the Rámáyana composed in the Treta Yug are a hundred crores in number ; but a single letter has redeeming power, and would work the salvation of one who had even committed the murder of a Brahman. Now again, as a blessing to the faithful, has he taken birth and published the sportive actions of the god. Intoxicated with his passion for Ráma's feet, he perseveres day and night in the accomplishment of his vow, and has supplied, as it were, a boat for the easy passage of the boundless ocean of existence. For the redemption of man in this perverse Kali Yug, Válmíki has been born again as Tulsi.

॥ टीका ॥

तिया सेा सनेह बिन पूछैं पिता गेह गई
भूली सुधि देह भजे वाही ठौर आप हैं ॥
बधू अति लाज भई रिसि सों निकसि गई
प्रीति राम नई तन हाड़ चाम छाप हैं ॥

सुनी अब बात मानों होय गयो प्रात वह
पाछे पछितात तजी कासीपुरी धाए हैं ॥
कियो तहाँ बास प्रभू सेवा लै प्रकास
कीनों दृढ़ भाव नैंन रूप के तिसाए हैं ॥
सौंच जल सेस पाय भूतहू बिसेस कोऊ
बोल्यो सुख मानि हनुमान जू बताए हैं ॥
रामायन कथा सो रसायन है कानिनि कों
आवत प्रथम पाछैं जात घृना छाए हैं ॥
जाय पहिचान संग चले उर आनि आए
बन मधि जानि धाय पाय लपटाए हैं ॥
करैं सीतकार कहि सकोगे न टारि मैं तो
जाने रससार रूप धर्‍यो जैसे गाये हैं ॥
मांगि लीजै बर कहि दीजे राम भूप रूप
अतिही अनूप नित्त नैंन अभिलाखिये ॥
कियो लै संकेत वाही दिन ही सों लाग्यो हेन
आई सोई समै चेंत कब छबि चाखिये ॥
आये रघुनाथ साथ लछिमन चढ़े घोरे
पट रंग बारे हरे कैसे मन राखिये ॥
पाछैं हनुमान आय बोले देखे प्रान प्यारे
नेकु न निहारे मैं तो भले फेरि भाखिये ॥
हत्या करि बिप्र एक तीरथ करत आयो
कहै मुख राम भिक्षा डारिये हत्यारे को
सुनि अभिराम नाम धाम में बुलाय लियो
दियो लै प्रसाद कियो सुद्ध गायो प्यारे कों ॥
भई द्विजसभा कहि बोलि कै पठाए आप
कैसें गये पाप संग लैके जेये न्यारे कों ॥
पोथी तुम बांचो हिये सार नहीं सांचो अजू
तातें मत काचो दूर करै न अंध्यारे कों ।

देखि पोथी बांच नाम महिमाहू कही सांच
ऐपै हत्याकरै कैसे तरै कहि दीजिये ॥
आवै जौ प्रतीत कहो योही याके हाथ जेवें
सिवजू को बैल तब पंगति में लीजिये ॥
थार में प्रसाद दियो चले जहां पन कियो
बोले आप नाम के प्रताप मति भीजिये ॥
जैसी तुम जानों तैसी कैसेंकै बखानों अहो
सुनिकै प्रसन्न पायो जै जै धुनि रीजिये ॥
आये निस चोर चोरी करन हरन धन
देखे श्यामघन हांथ चाप सर लिये हैं ॥
जब जब आवे बान सांधि डरपावै वे तो
अति मंडरावै ऐपैं बली दूरें किये हैं ॥
भोर आय पूछैं अजू सांवरो किसोर कोन
सुनि करि मौन रहै आंसू डारि दिये हैं ॥
दई सबै लुटाय जानी चौकी रामराय दई
लई उन्हें दीक्षा सीक्षा सुद्ध भये हिये हैं ॥
कियो तन बिप्र त्याग लागि चली संग तिया
दुरही तें देखि किया चरन प्रनाम है ॥
बोले यों सुहागवती मास्यो पति होउ सती
अब तो निकस गई ज्याऊं सेवो राम है ॥
बोलि कै कुटुंब कही जो पै भक्ति करो सही
गही तब बात जीव दियो अभिराम है ॥
भये सब साधु ब्याधि मेटी लै बिमुख ताकी
जाको बास रहै तो न सूझै स्याम धाम है ॥
दिल्लीपति पातसाह अहदी पठायो लैन
ताकों सो सुनायो सू वे बिप्र ज्यायो जानिये ॥
देखिवे की चाहै नीकैं सुख सों निबाहैं आप
कहि बहु बिनय गहि चले मन आनिये ॥

पहुंचे नृपति पास आदर प्रकास कियो
उच्च आसन लै बोल्यो मृदू बानियें ॥
दीजै करामाति जग ख्याति सब मात किये
कही झूठ बात एक राम पहिचानिये ॥
देखें राम कैसो कहि कैदि किये किये हियें
हूजिये कृपाल हनूमान जू दयाल हो ॥
ताही समय फैलि गये कोटि कोटि कपि नये
लोचें तन खैंचें चीर भयो यों बिहाल हो ॥
फोरें कोट मारें चोट किये डारें लोट पोट
लीजे कोन ओट जानि मानों प्रलै काल हो ॥
भई तब आंखैं दुखसागर को चाखैं अब
वेई हमें राखैं भाखैं वारों धन माल हो ॥
आय पाय लिये तुम दिये हम प्रान पावें
आप समझावें करामात नेकु लीजिये ॥
लाज दबि गयो नृप तब राखि लीयो कह्यो
भयो घर रामजू को बेगि छोड़ दीजिये ॥
सुनि तजि दियो और करयो लैके कोट नयो
अबहू न रहै कोऊ वामें तन छीजिये ॥
कासी जाय वृन्दाबन आय मिले नाभाजू सों
सुन्यौ हो कबित्त निज रीझि मति भीजिये ॥
मदन गोपालजू को दरसन करि कहि
सही राम इष्ट मेरे दृष्टि भाव पागी है ॥
वैसोई सरूप कियो लै दियो दिखाय रूप
मन अनरूप छबि देखि नीकी लागी है ॥
काहू कही कृष्ण अवतारोजू प्रसंस महा
राम अंस सुनि बोले मति अनुरागी है ॥
दसरथ सुत जानों सुन्दर अनूप मानों
ईसता बताई रति बीस गुनी जागी है ॥

Translation of the gloss (or supplement) by Priya Dás.

He had great love for his wife : without asking his leave she went home to her father's : he forgot all about himself and hastened there too. She was greatly ashamed, and went away in anger, saying :—"Have you no love for Ráma? My body is but a framework of skin and bone." When he heard these words, it was, as it were, the daybreak; he felt compunction and left her and sped to the city or Kási. There he made his abode, worshipping the lord publicly, making a rigid vow, and thirsting exceedingly for a vision.

A certain ghost, who had secured the remainder of the water he had used in washing,1 was grateful and told him of Hanumán. "A recitation of the Rámáyana has a special charm for his ears; he will be disguised in mean attire, but is always the first to come and the last to leave." Thus recognizing him as he left, he went with him in full confidence, and in the wood, knowing him to be in truth the god, ran and embraced his feet, crying with a shout of joy :—"You shall not escape me." Perceiving his intense devotion, he assumed the form in which he is famous, and said :—"Ask of me what you will." "I am ever craving to behold with my very eyes the incomparable beauty of King Ráma." He told him the place for meeting. From that day forth he was longing till the time came, thinking :—'When shall I behold his beauty? Raghunáth came, and with him Lakshman, both mounted on horseback, in green raiment (like huntsmen). Why should he notice them? Afterwards came Hanumán and said :—"Have you seen your dear lord?" "I did not give them even a glance; turn now and speak to them again."

A Brahman, who had committed a murder, came on a pilgrimage, crying —"For the love of Ráma give an alms even to me, a murderer." On hearing the delightful name, he called him into his own house, and gave him of the offerings to the god, and purified him and sang the praises of his Beloved. The Bráhmans met in conclave and summoned him before them, saying :—"How has his guilt been remitted that you could thus take and eat with him apart?" "Read your books; their real meaning has not penetrated your heart; therefore your faith is dull and your blindness has not been removed" "We have read and examined our books; the virtue of the name is truly as you have said; but can a murderer be absolved? Please explain that." "Tell me how I may convince you." They said :—"If Siva's bull will eat from his hand, then will we receive him into our company." He gave him of the temple offerings in a dish, and they returned to the place where he had made the vow. There he cried :—"Saturate their souls with the glory of thy name; thou knowest how the matter stands, what can I say?" On hearing those words he graciously accepted the offering: there was a joyous shout of Victory! Victory!

Some thieves came by night to thieve and plunder his goods, but beheld a cloud-dark form with bow and arrows in his hand. Whenever he approached with ready shaft, they were afraid; and though they went round and round, they could not get rid of this watchman. At daybreak they came and asked him :—"Sir, who is this dark-complexioned lad of yours?" On hearing this question, he remained silent and wept; then gave away all that he had, knowing that Ráma himself and been the watchman. They were initiated and received instruction, and became pure of heart.

A Bráhman had died; his wife was following him to the pyre. She saw him at a distance and made him obeisance He addressed her as a happy wife. She replied :—"My husband is dead, and I am about to perish with him." "The word has passed my lips; I will restore him to life; worsihp thou Ráma." Then he called her kinsfolk and said :—"But you must adopt

1 A ghost is supposed to suffer from perpetual thirst and to be glad to secure even a drop of water, however impure the purpose for which it has been used.

a religious life." They hearkened to his word, and he restored the man to the delights of life. They all became saints when he had taken away their sinful frowardness : none can see heaven in whom passion still lives.

The emperor of Delhi sent an officer to fetch him, explaining, "It is he, you must know, who brought the Bráhman to life again." "He is anxious to see you," they said, "so come; all will be well." They spoke so courteously that he agreed and went. They arrived before the king, who received him with honour, gave him an exalted seat, and said in gracious tones:—"Let me see a miracle; it is noised throughout the world that you are master of everything." He said :—"It is false ; know that Ráma is all in all." "How is Ráma to be seen?" he said, and threw him into prison. He prayed within himself : "O gracious Hanumán, have pity upon me." That very moment thousands upon thousands of sturdy monkeys spread all over the place, clawing bodies, and tearing clothes, and great was the alarm. They broke open the fort, wounding the men, destroying everything ; where could one fly for safety ? it seemed as though the end of the world had come. Then his eyes were opened by this taste of a sea of calamities, and he cried,—"Now I wager all my treasure it is he only who can save me." He came and clasped his feet : "If you give me life, I live ; pray speak to them." "Better watch the miracle a little." The king was overwhelmed with confusion. Then he stopt it all and said :—"Quickly abandon this spot, for it is the abode of Ráma." At the word he quitted the place and went and built a new fort, and to this day any one who abides there falls ill and dies.

After returning to Kási he came to Brindá-ban and met Nábhá Jí and heard his poetry, and his whole soul was filled with delight. On visiting the shrine of Madan Gopal he said :—"Of a truth Ráma is my special patron ; I would fain see him." Then appeared the god to him in that very form ; and he was glad on beholding his incomparable beauty. It was said to him ; —"The Krishna Avatár is of greatest renown; Ráma was only a partial incarnation." On hearing this he said :—"My soul was full of love for him when I took him only for the son of Dasarath and admired his incomparable beauty ; now that you tell me of his divinity, my love is increased twenty-fold."

Professor Wilson, in his most valuable and interesting "Essay on the Religious Sects of the Hindus," gives the following notice of Tulsi Dás, and adds that he had derived it from the Bhakt Málá :—"Having been incited to the peculiar adoration of Ráma by the remonstrances of his wife, to whom he was passionately attached, he adopted a vagrant life, visited Benares, and afterwards went to Chitrakut, where he had a personal interview with Hanumán, from whom he received his poetical inspiration and the power of working miracles. His fame reached Delhi, where Sháhjahán was emperor. The monarch sent for him to produce the person of Ráma, which Tulsi Dás refusing to do, the king threw him into confinement. The people of the vicinity, however, speedily petitioned for his liberation, as they were alarmed for their own security: myriads of monkeys having collected about the prison and begun to demolish it and the adjacent buildings. Sháhjahán set the poet at liberty and desired him to solicit some favour as a reparation for the indignity he had suffered. Tulsi Dás accordingly requested him to quit ancient Delhi, which was the abode of Ráma; and in compliance with this request the emperor left it and founded the new city, thence named Sháhjahánabád. After this Tulsi Dás went to Brindá-ban, where he had an interview with Nábhá Jí; he settled there and strenuously advocated the worship of Síta Ráma, in preference to that of Rádha-Krishna."

On comparing this sketch with the literal translation of the text from which it was derived, it will be seen that it is not very closely in accord with it. It omits many particulars and adds others, and was probably taken not from the genuine Hindi poem itself, but from some prose adaptation,[1] of which, in consequence of the difficulty of the original, there are very many in existence.

It is a curious illustration of the indifference to historical truth and the love for the marvellous, by which the Hindú mind has always been characterised, that although the *tika* even of the Bahkt-Málá was written less than a century after the poet's death, it still gives so little trustworthy information about the real incidents of his life and supplies so much that is clearly fictitious. That it was his wife who first persuaded him to exchange an earthly for a divine love and to devote himself to the service of Ráma may well be accepted as a fact. As to the other legends—of the ghost who introduced him to Hanumán, through whom he obtained a vision of Ráma and Lakshman: of the murderer whom he recognized as cleansed of his crime by the repetition of the holy name; of the widow on her way to the funeral pile, whose husband he restored to life; of the emperor's requiring him to perform some miracle and, on his refusal to produce the god to whom he ascribed all his power, throwing him into prison, from which he was delivered by Hanumán's monkey host; of the emperor's thereupon abandoning a spot which Ráma had made so peculiarly his own; of the

1 I was afterwards able to verify this conjecture, as Mr. Leonard, the Assistant Secretary of "the Calcutta Asiatic Society. was kind enough to lend me his copy of Price's "Hindi and Hindustani Selections," a work to which Professor Wilson refers more than once in the course of his essay. It was published in Calcutta in 1827, and has long been out of print. I find that as many as 50 pages of it are occupied with extracts from the Bhakt-Málá; but with the exception of some 18 stanzas from the *mul* of Nábhá Jí, all the rest is in simple narrative prose; and the compiler in his introduction specially mentions that the work itself was rarely to be met with in the Lower Provinces, and that his extracts were taken from a copy in Mr. Wilson's library. [Sanskrít and Hindi being two languages, as distinct as Latin and Italian, the above remarks were never intended (as a reviewer wrongly supposed) to detract in any way from the peculiar merits of one of the greatest Sanskrit scholars that England has ever produced and to whose works no one is more indebted than myself.]

thieves who were prevented from breaking into the poet's house by Ráma himself acting as watchman; of his visit to Brindá-ban and his interview with Nábhá Jí; and finally of his persistence in preferring the worship of Ráma to that of Krishna, though the latter assured him in person that there was no difference between the two—all these legends, as given in the Bhakt Málá, whatever their foundation, are still popularly accepted as verities and are indissolubly connected with the poet's name. A few further facts of more prosaic character may be gathered from his own works and from tradition; thus we learn from the prologue to the Rámáyana that he commenced its composition at Ayodhyá in the *Sambat* year 1631, corresponding to 1575. A.D., and that he had studied for some length of time at Soron. He was by descent a Bráhman of the Kanaujiya clan, and in the Bhakt-Sindhu—a modern poem of no great authority, the writér when at a loss for facts being as it seems, in the habit of supplying them out of his own imagination—it is stated that his father's name was Atma Rám and that he was born at Hastinapur. Others make Hájipur, near Chitrakút, the place of his birth. The greater part of his life was certainly spent at Benares, though he also passed some years in visits to Soron, Ayodhyá, Chitrakút, Allahabad, and Brindá-ban. He died in the *Sambat* year 1680 (1624 A.D.)

A complete copy of the Rámáyana in his own handwriting was once in existence at Rájapur, but it was stolen about the year 1800 by a devotee, who on being pursued threw it into the river. It was eventually recovered by a net, but not till it had been greatly damaged by the water; Book II, the Ayodhyá, which forms the centre of the volume, being the only part that remained legible. This fragment is still in the temple; but as every pilgrim is expected to make an offering of a cover for it, is it now enveloped in some 50 wraps and is quite lost to sight. The Mahárája of Benares is said to have employed a copyist to consult it before publishing his edition, which in that case represents the standard text; and a commentary written by Mahant Rám Charan in *Sambat* 1862, and published by Naval Kishore of Lucknow, professes to have been undertaken after 'handling' the original MS., which possibly was then complete. The 'handling,' however, may have been only from a motive of veneration and not for critical purposes.

In addition to his great work Tulsi Dás composed at least six other poems, all of them having the one object of popularizing the cultus of his tutelary divinity. They are the Rámgítávalí (which is one of the text-books in the Government examination for a Degree of Honour), the Dohávali, the Kabit-sambandh, the Binay Patriká, the Satsai and the Rám Agyá. All of these have been published, either at Lucknow or Benares, within the last few years, and all now for the first time, excepting the Binay Patriká, which was printed in good type by Sri Lallú Jí for the use of the college of Fort William as far back as the year 1826; but copies of this first edition are now very scarce. The list is not unfrequently extended by the addition of the following minor works, as to the genuineness of which there is considerable doubt, *viz.*, the Ráma-Saláká, the Hanumán Báhuka, the Jánaki Mangal, the Párvati Mangal, the Karká Chhand, the Rora Chhand and the Jhulná Chhand. An autograph MS. of the Rám Agyá was preserved in the temple of Sita' Rám at Benares, which Tulsi Dás had himself founded, till the Mutiny, but was then lost.[1]

His theological and metaphysical views are pantheistic in character, being based for the most part on the teaching of the later Vedantists as formulated in the Vedanta-Sára and more elaborately expounded in the Bhagavad Gíta, which is the most popular of all Sanskrit didactic poems. The whole visible world, as they maintain, is an unreal phantasm, induced by ignorance or illusion, and it is only by a concession to conventional speech that it can be said to exist at all. The sole representative of true existence is the supreme spirit, Brahm, conceived as absolute and unchangeable unity; invisible, eternal and all-pervading, but having no relation to the world—since that would involve a notion of dualism—and for the same reason void of cognition, will, activity and all other qualities; a potentiality, in the ordinary use of language, rather than an actual entity. All phenomena, whether material or spiritual, including even the gods of Vedic mythology, are simply fictions of the mind. But the worship of the inferior divinities and compliance with the external ritual of religion, are considered to purify and prepare the intellect for the reception of higher truths. They are therefore salutary and

1 For the information as to this and the Rajapur MS. I am indebted to Pandit Bháu Pratáp, Tiwari, of Chanár, who also tells me that he has in his possession a manuscript of the poem which professes to be copied from an original dated *Sambat* 1700; that is, only 20 years after the author's death. This he would gladly lend for collation, if a critical edition of the text—which is much required—should ever be undertaken. At present the best edition is Rám Jasan's, Benares, 1883.

even necessary practices during the early days of the soul's progress towards perfection. If a man is overtaken by death before he has advanced beyond this preliminary stage, he is born again either into this or into a higher world in some different form, the dignity of which is determined by the aggregate merit or demerit of all his actions in all his previous births.[1] The highest reward for devotion to any special god is the exaltation of the soul to his particular sphere in heaven. But this blessedness is not of permanent duration; on the expiry of a proportionate period the burden of mundane existence has again to be undergone. It is only on the attainment of perfect knowledge that final emancipation is complete and the individual soul is absorbed for ever into the Impersonal:

> "A spiritual star—wrought in a rose
> Of light in Paradise, whose only self
> Is consciousness of glory wide diffused."

Except to a theosophist, the promise of such an ultimate destiny is not a very attractive one, nor is it conducive to popular morality. For good deeds and evil deeds and the god that recompenses them, all alike belong to the unreal, to the fictitious duality, the world of semblances; while the so-called Supreme Being is no proper object of worship, being a mere cold abstraction, unconscious of his own existence or of ours, and devoid of all attributes and qualities. To correct this practical defect and supply some intelligible motive for withstanding temptation and leading a pure and holy life, the supplementary doctrine of Bhakti, or Faith, was developed. Some one of the recognized incarnations of the Hindu Pantheon was no longer regarded as a partial emanation of the divinity, but was exalted into the complete embodiment of it. A loving devotion to his personality was then enjoined as a simple and certain method of attaining to endless felicity; not the transitory sensual delights of Indra's paradise, nor the mere unconsciousness of utter extinction, but the conscious enjoyment of individual immortality in the immediate presence of the Beatific Vision.

The late introduction of this crowning dogma of Faith in an incarnate Redeemer and its marked similarity to Christian ideas have induced several scholars to surmise that the Bráhmans borrowed it from the early Christian communities in Southern India. The notion is favoured—if not,

[1] The absence of all recollection of acts done in former states of existence is not an objection to the theory of transmigration; for the continuity is not one of consciousness, but of that tendency or disposition which is the separate nature of each individual.

indeed, originated—by the fact that in the Bhagavad Gíta it is Krishna who figures as the embodiment of the Supreme Being, and both in the name and in the legends of Krishna there is a superficial resemblance to the name of Christ and to some of the incidents recorded of Him in the Gospels. As I have shown more fully elsewhere, there is no historical basis for the supposed connection, while the similarity of name is demonstrably accidental. The doctrine appears to have grown up as a natural sequel to the purely indigenous school of thought in which we find it established, and an exact parallel can be traced in the history of Buddhism, where the nihilism of Nirvána was practically abrogated by the gradual deification of its teacher.[1] In selecting Ráma as his ideal of the divine in preference to Krishna, Tulsi Dás has certainly improved upon the teaching of the Bhagavad.

The tendency of modern scientific thought is setting strongly in favour of the Vedantist theory; as declaring the existence from all eternity of a personal God to be simply unknowable, and referring all phenomena to a strange mysterious energy, or will, that pervades all nature, that produces all the work done on the face of the earth, and is probably at the roof of life itself; invisible and insensible, and exhibited only in its effects. Such a theory—as we see from our author's own case—is by no means incompatible with a belief in a divine incarnation: the difficulty is to establish by historical proof that such and such a character —Ráma or Krishna, or whoever it may be—was really born out of the ordinary course of nature, really performed the marvellous acts ascribed to him for the deliverance of the saints, the overthrow of the wicked and the establishment of righteousness, and having accomplished them was again taken up into the heaven from which he came. The whole of Tulsi Dás's Rámáyana is a passionate protest against the virtual atheism of philosophical Hindú theology. The problem that confronted him is the very same that now most exercises the thought of the nineteenth century. If the Supreme Being is a personal God, he must be limited by the conditions of personality, and can neither be omniscient nor omnipotent. If, on the other hand, the Deity is an omnipresent, all-pervading impersonality, how can any special relation be developed between such an abstraction

1 In a Chinese inscription, of the year 1021 A D., that has been discovered at Buddh Gaya, he is thus addressed: "O great master. merciful to the people, sympathizing with all creatures, although thou dost not manifest thyself, still thou art a most efficacious God."

and the individual soul? The difficulty is one that has its root in the nature of things; and no solution of the mystery can be found but in the recognition of faith and reason as two distinct human faculties, with the infinite and the finite as their separate provinces. In the words of Saint Ambrose *non in dialecticâ complacuit Deo salvum facere populum suum*. God would not be adorable if he were not incomprehensible: and a religion that does not transcend man's understanding is not, strictly speaking, a religion at all. A just discrimination of good and evil and a sound code of morality are not beyond the compass of natural intelligence: but the rites and mysteries of religion can only be learnt by a direct revelation from God and through the action of His grace. Their acceptance by faith, even when they seem to conflict with reason, is a part of our earthly probation and a meritorious confession of our dependence on the Supreme. The final purpose of the Incarnation, like the idea of any revelation whatever from God to man, is above comprehension. The fact of the divine message having been sent may be reasonably established by historical evidence, but the tenor of the message transcends argumentative discussion, and demands nothing short of implicit and absolutely unquestioning submission. For the dogmas of revealed religion must, *ex-hypothesi*, be incomprehensible mysteries. If they were ascertainable by the ordinary processes of reason it would not be consistent with the economy of the universe to communicate them by the special vehicle of revelation. A professedly revealed religion, which is demonstrable and intelligible throughout, stands self-convicted as a human invention.

The following passage from Book VII of the Bhagavad Gita, as freely rendered by Mr. Edwin Arnold in his 'Song Celestial,' is a very explicit summary of the accepted Vedantic doctrine:—

> "There be those, too, whose knowledge, turned aside
> By this desire or that, gives them to serve
> Some lower gods with various rites constrained
> By that which mouldeth them. Unto all such—
> Worship what shrine they will, what shapes in faith—
> 'Tis I who give them faith. I am content.
> The heart thus asking favour from its God,
> Darkened but ardent, hath the end it craves,
> The lesser blessing; but 'tis I who give.
> Yet soon is withered what small fruit they reap:
> Those men of little minds, who worship so,
> Go where they worship, passing with their Gods:
> But mine come unto me. Blind are the eyes
> Which deem the Unmanifested manifest,

> **Not comprehending Me in my true self.**
> **Imperishable, viewless, undeclared,**
> **Hidden behind my magic vail of shows,**
> **I am not seen by all ; I am not known—**
> **Unborn and changeless—to the idle world.**
> **But I, Arjuna, know all things which were,**
> **And all which are, and all which are to be,**
> **Albeit not one among them knoweth Me."**

The words "Blind are the eyes Which deem the Unmanifested manifest" emphatically condemn the worship of any incarnation, on the ground that it involes an inadequate conception of the Deity. Tulsí Dás, on the other hand, insists that they derogate from the divine perfection, who divest it of personality and reduce it to an abstraction. Against such theologians he hotly protests as when he cries (*VII Chhand* 5)—"Let them preach in their wisdom who contemplate thee as the Supreme Spirit, the Uncreate, inseparable from the universe, recognizable only by inference and beyond the understanding; but we, O Lord! will ever hymn the glories of thy incarnation." Nor does he want supporters even in this nineteenth century, who give the same answer to the old question 'Can the attribute of Personality be ascribed to the Absolute? Thus Lotze, in his *Outlines of the Philosophy of Religion*, argues as follows: "If all the predicates of unconditionateness are to be valid for the highest being then one condition of this validity lies precisely in the addition of a last formal predicate, *viz.*, that of personal existence. All hindrances of perfect personality we can imagine as not existent in the Infinite Spirit. On this account we conclude with the assertion -- which is exactly the opposite of the customary one—that Perfect Personality is reconcilable only with the conception of an Infinite Being; for finite beiugs, only an approximation to this is attainable."

The introductory portion of the first Book of the Rámáyana is curious as containing the author's vindication of his literary style as against his critics, the pedants. They attacked him for lowering the dignity of his subject by clothing it in the vulgar vernacular. However just his defence may be, it has not succeeded in converting the opposite faction: and the professional Sanskrit pandits who are its modern representatives, still affect to despise his work as an unworthy concession to the illiterate masses. With this small and solitary exception the book is in every one's hands, from the court to the cottage, and is read, or heard, and appreciated alike by every class of the Hindú community, whether high or low, rich or poor, young or old. The purity of its moral sentiments and the absolute avoidance of the slightest approach to any pruriency of idea—which the author justly advances among his distinctive merits—render it a singularly unexceptionable text-book for native boys. For several years I persistently urged its adoption upon the Education Department, [1] and —thanks to Rája Siva Prasád—extracts from it have been introduced into our primary schools; while it has always been prescribed as the principal test in the civil examinations for High Proficiency and a Degree of Honour. It is equally well adapted for these apparently incongruous purposes: for a Hindú child generally grasps at once the familiar idiom, and finds no great difficulty in even the most crabbed passage; while, on the other hand, both the terminology and the syntactic collocation of the words are in the highest degree perplexing to the European student, and severely try his knowledge of the language. As has been said of Spenser in the Faerie Queene, Tulsi Dás never scruples on his own authority to cut down or alter a word, or to adopt a mere corrupt pronunciation, to suit a place in his metre, or because he wants a rhyme. His treatment of words, on occasions of difficulty to his verse, is arbitrary in the extreme. He gives them any sense and shape that the case may demand. Sometimes he merely alters a letters or two; sometimes he twists off the head or the tail of the unfortunate vocable altogether. Such vagaries, being unconsciously regulated by the genius of the language, are no more puzzling to a Hindú than the colloquialisms of Sam Weller or Mrs. Gamp are to an English reader of Dickens. But they would seem inexplicable mysteries to any Anglo-Indian official, who knew only the language of the Courts and had never studied the vernacular of the people. For such neglect there was formerly much excuse, in the absence both of a dictionary and a grammar; but the latter want was most admirably supplied in 1876 by Mr. Kellogg, of the Allahabad American Presbyterian Mission, in a work that is to a remarkable degree both lucid and exhaustive; while Messrs. Hœrnle and Grierson's new Comparative Dictionary is not only more scientific in method and elaborate in execution than any

---

1 A writer in the *Calcutta Review* expressed his astonishment at my proposal. But he falls into the error which has wrecked so many well-intentioned schemes in this country, that of measuring Indian tastes and requirements by a purely English standard. Manuals of history, geography and physical science are all very well in their way, but correct information by itself is really the least part of education.

similar work that has ever before been attempted by Indian philologists, but it is further supplemented by a special Index to the Rámáyana, which exhibits every single word in the poem, and refers to all the passages in which it occurs. As yet only one part of this gigantic work has appeared, and some years must elapse before it is completed. Mr. Bate's dictionary, to which I have already referred, is scarcely intended for very advanced students, but it will be of much use to beginners, since it gives in alphabetical order all the archaic forms of inflection, which at the outset are found so perplexing.

The second Book is more generally read than any other part of the poem, and is the most admired by Hindú critics. The description of King Dasarath's death and the different leave-takings are quoted as models of the pathetic, and in a public recital there is scarcely one in the audience who will not be moved to tears. The sentiments that the poet depicts, and the figures that he employs to illustrate them, appeal with irresistible force to the Hindú imagination; and, if for no other reason than this, they would be interesting to the English student for the insight they afford into the traditional sympathies and antipathies of the people. The constant repetition of a few stereotyped phrases—such as 'lotus feet,' 'streaming eyes,' 'quivering[1] frame'—are irritating to modern European taste, though they find a parallel in the stock epithets of the Homeric poems, and a still more striking one in Klopstock's Messiah, where similar expressions are for ever recurring in wearisome reiteration. Everybody wonders and weeps and smiles and embraces everybody else and dissolves in tears, while every hair on their body stands on end; the last two performances being so specially Tulsian, that it ceases to be an exaggeration to describe the eyes of his *dramatis personæ*, in the words of Crashaw, as

> Two walking baths, two weeping motions,
> Portable and compendious oceans.

Again, the curiously artificial similes derived from the—frequently fabulous—habits of different birds and plants, which (like the oft-repeated refrain of a popular song) never

---

1 The *pulak*, which I generally translate by 'quivering' or 'throbbing, means strictly the bristling of the hair upon the body, which is a sign of violent mental agitation. The Munshi, with whom I read in Calcutta some twenty years ago, always, I remember, rendered it by 'horripilation'; a frightful word, which would destroy all the poetic effect of the most impressive passage, but which he greatly admired on account of its sesquipedalian proportions.

fail to elicit the applause of an appreciative audience, only repel a foreigner as frigid and unmeaning conventionalities. Such are the perpetual allusions to the lotus, that expands in the day and closes at evening; to the lily, that blossoms in the night and fades at sunrise; to the rice crop, that luxuriates in the rain, and to the *jawása* plant, that is killed by it; to the *chakwá*, that mourns its mate all through the hours of darkness; to the *chakor*, that is never happy except when gazing upon the moon; to the *chátak*, that patiently endures all the buffeting of the storm, in the confident expectation that the cloud will at last let fall the one auspicious drop for which it thirsts: to the swan, that knows how to separate milk from the water with which it has been mixed; and to the snake, that carries a precious jewel in its head, of which it is always afraid of being robbed. In Shakespear's time, who was contemporary with Tulsi Dás, many equally strange pieces of natural history were popularly accepted even in Europe, and were similarly worked up into poetical commonplaces. As, for instance, the maternal affection of "the kind life-rendering pelican;" the belief that the chameleon lives upon air; that the adder is deaf; that the swan sings before it dies; that crocodiles weep when they have done wrong; that bear's cubs are born formless and are licked into ursine shape by their mother; that some snakes have stings in their tail; and that the toad carries a jewel in its head which is an anidote to poison.

In spite of all drawbacks, the Hindi Rámáyana has many passages that are instinct with a genuine poetic feeling, which appeals to universal humanity, and which it is hoped will be dimly recognized even through the ineffectual medium of a prose translation. The characters also of the principal actors in the drama are clearly and consistently drawn; and all may admire, though they refuse to worship, the piety and unselfishness of Bharat: tho enthusiasm and high courage of Lakshman; the affectionate devotion of Síta, that paragon of all wife-like virtues; and the purity, meekness, generosity and self-sacrifice of Ráma, the model son, husband and brother, 'the guileless king, high, self-contained and passionless'—the Arthur of Indian chivalry.

In the later Books the narrative is generally more rapid than in the earlier part of the poem, and several incidents are so casually mentioned that, without the explanatory references to the Sanskrit Rámáyana, which I have given in the notes, a literal rendering would convey no meaning to the ordinary reader.[1] It is to some extent a literary defect that the rôle of poet is so often dropt for that of theologian; and the frequent hymns to Ráma, who is apostrophized under every conceivable name that can help to realize to the mind the mystery of incarnate divinity, soon become wearisome. But the object that Tulsí Dás had in view is his sufficient excuse. By the course that he has adopted, fitting his special doctrines of faith, individual immortality and the like into the familiar framework of ancient legend, instead of inculcating them by a more strictly didactic method, he has succeeded in popularizing his views to a far greater extent than any of the rival Hindu Reformers, who flourished about the same period. It was their object also to simplify the complications and correct the abuses of existing practice, but the only result of their preaching was to establish yet another element of dissension and augment the disorder which they hoped to remove. Tulsi Dás alone, though the most famous of them all, has no disciples that are called after his name. There are Vallabhachάris and Rádhá Vallabhis and Malúk Dásis and Prán Náthis, and so on, in interminable succession, but there are no Tulsi Dásis. Virtually, however, the whole of Vaishnava Hindúism has fallen under his sway; for the principles that he expounded have permeated every sect and explictly or implicitly now form the nucleus of the popular faith as it prevails throughout the whole of the Bengal Presidency from Hardwár to Calcutta.

In the year 1876, when I published the first instalment of my translation, I was still at Mathurá, in a congenial atmosphere of Hindú associations. After my transfer to Bulandshahr in 1877, I laboured under the serious disadvantage of writing in a thoroughly Muhammadanized district, where it was almost as difficult to obtain any assistance on subjects connected with Hindú literature or scholarship as it would have been in England. But by that time the familiarity I had acquired with my author was sufficiently long and intimate to enable me to complete my task unaided.

At the outset I was under the impression that as a translator, there was no one at all in the field before me; but

1 Of the two current recensions of the older poem, the one generally followed by Tulsi Dás is the Bengal, which is the text given by Gorresio in his handsome edition.

after making some little progress in the second book, I discovered that there was already in existence for that particular section of the poem an English version, published in 1871, by Adálat Khán, a Muhammadan Munshi of the College of Fort William in Calcutta. I at once procured a copy of it and it is only proper to acknowledge that it was of considerable assistance to me. It does not, however, encroach very largely upon the ground that I had intended to occupy. The Munshi appears to have written solely with a view to lighten the labours of his own pupils and of others who, like them, were preparing for a special examination. Despite not a few misapprehensions of the sense, such persons will probably find it quite as useful for their purpose as my translation, if not more so. But in the attempt to secure literal accuracy, and also, no doubt, from the fact that English was not the mother-tongue of the translator, the language employed is throughout so curiously unidiomatic that in many places it is absolutely unintelligible without a reference to the original, and this the general reader would not be in a position to make. As a specimen I give the *chaupái* following *dohá* 224 (with which may be compared my rendering, page 132, volume II).

"If he leaves me, knowing my mind wicked, and receives me, considering his servant, my sheltering-place then will be in the shoes of Rama: he is my good master; but the fault is in this servant. The *chaták* and the fish deserve the praise of the world; they are sincere in their usual vow and love. Thus having reflected in his mind, he went along the road, ashamed and overpowered with love. The sin committed by his mother was as if keeping him back; but the Bull of patience was walking by the power of his faith, and when he knew the nature of Rama, his feet fell on the ground hurriedly. The state of Bharat at that time was such as that of the bee in a current of water. Seeing the grief and love of Bharat, the pilot became stupefied at that moment."

The uncouthness of the Munshi's style will give some idea of what is certainly the main difficulty that has to be encountered in a prose translation from Hindi verse. No one who has not had practical experience in the matter can fully appreciate the amount of thought that has to be expended on almost every sentence before the peculiarities of Oriental expression can be adapted to the requirements of English idiom. Without the most delicate handling it is impossible to avoid either a sacrifice of accuracy in the letter, or a misrepresentation of the spirit by a baldness of rendering, which suggests only images of the ludicrous and grotesque, while the sentiments of the original in their native dress are felt to be both natural and pathetic.

F. S. GROWSE.

Post script. Under the patronage of Mr. Grierson, an enterprising Publisher of Patna (Babu Rám Din Sinh of the Kharg Bilás Press, Bánkipore), has now published a text of the Rám-charit-mánas, which is an exact reproduction of the original MSS. This must be a work of the highest interest to all Hindi Scholars; but it may be surmised that the variations from the received text are of more importance from the philological than from the literary point of view.

THE RAMAYANA

OF

TULSI DAS.

BOOK I.

CHILDHOOD.

Sanskrit Invocation.

I REVERENCE Sáradá and Ganes, the inventors of the alphabet and of phraseology, of the poetic modes and of metre. I reverence Bhavání and Sankara, the incarnations of faith and hope, without whom not even the just can see GOD, the Great Spirit. I reverence, as the incarnation of Sankara, the all-wise Guru, through whom even the crescent moon is everywhere honoured.[1] I reverence the king of bards[2] and the monkey king, of pure intelligence, who ever lingered with delight in the holy forest land of Ráma and Sítá's infinite perfection. I bow before Síta, the beloved of Ráma; the queen of birth, of life and death; the destroyer of sorrow; the cause of happiness.

I reverence, under his name RAMA, the lord Hari; supreme over all causes; to whose illusive power are subject the whole universe and every supernatural being from Bráhma downwards; by whose light truth is made manifest, as when what appeared to be a snake turns out a rope; and by whose feet as by a bark those who will may pass safely over the ocean of existence.

---

1. The crescent moon, being one of Sankara's (*i. e.* Siva's) constant symbols, is honoured on his account, though in itself imperfect: while the full moon is honoured for its own sake.

2. The king of bards, Válmíki, the reputed author of the Sanskrit Rámáyana. The monkey king is of course Hanumán, and the two are brought together more on account of the close similarity of name than for any other reason, *Kavisvara* and *Kapisvara* differing only by a single letter.

In accord with all the Puránas and different sacred texts, and with what has been recorded in the Rámáyana (of Válmíki) and elsewhere, I, Tulsi, to gratify my own heart's desire, have composed these lays of Raghunáth in most choice and elegant modern speech.

Sorathá 1.

O Ganes, of the grand elephant head; the mention of whose name ensures success, be gracious to me, accumulation of wisdom, storehouse of all good qualities! Thou, too, by whose favour the dumb becomes eloquent, and the lame can climb the vastest mountain, be favourable to me, O thou that consumest as a fire all the impurities of this iron age. Take up thy abode also in my heart, O thou that slumberest on the milky ocean, with body dark as the lotus, and eyes bright as a budding water-lily. O spouse of Umá, clear of hue as the jasmine or the moon; home of compassion, who showest pity to the humble; show pity upon me, O destroyer of Kámadeva. I reverence the lotus feet of my master, that ocean of benevolence, Hari incarnate, whose words are like a flood of sunlight on the darkness of ignorance and infatuation.[1]

Chaupái 1.

I reverence the pollen-like dust of the lotus feet of my master, bright, fragrant, sweet and delicious; pure extract of the root of ambrosia, potent to disperse all the attendant ills of life; like the holy ashes on the divine body of Sambhu, beautiful, auspicious, ecstatic. Applied to the forehead as a *tilak*, it cleanses from defilement the fair mirror of the human mind and gives it the mastery of all good. By recalling the lustre of the nails of the reverend guru's feet, a divine splendour illumines the soul, dispersing the shades of error with its sun-like glory. How blessed he who takes it to his heart! The mental vision brightens and expands, the night of the world with sin and pain

1. The persons addressed in this stanza are Ganes, Sarasvati, Nàràyan, Siva, and the poet's own spiritual instructor, or guru.

fades away, the actions of Ráma,[1] like diamonds and rubies, whether obvious or obscure, all alike become clear, in whichever direction the mine is explored.

Dohá 1.

By applying this collyrium as it were to the eyes, the student acquires both holiness and wisdom, and is able to understand his sportive career when on earth—on mountain, or in forest—and all the treasures of his grace.

Chaupái 2.

The dust of the guru's feet is a soft and charming collyrium, like ambrosia for the eyes, to remove every defect of vision. With this having purified the eyes of my understanding, I proceed to relate the actions of Ráma, the redeemer of the world. First I reverence the feet of the great Bráhman saints, potent to remove the doubts engendered by error. In my heart, as with my voice, I reverence the whole body of the faithful, mines of perfection; whose good deeds resemble the produce of the cotton plant in its austerity, purity, and manifold usefulness, and in its hiding the defects even of those by whom it has been most roughly treated: reverence to the saints, whatever the age or clime in which their glory was consummated. Their congregation is all joy and felicity, like the great *tírtha* Prayág endowed with motion: for faith in Ráma is as the stream of the Ganges; contemplation on Bráhma as the Sarasvati; and ritual, dealing with precepts and prohibitions for the purification of this iron age, as the sun-god's daughter, the Jamuná. The united flood of the Tribeni is represented by the legends of Hari and of Hara, filling all that hear with delight: the sacred fig-tree, by faith firm in its own traditions; and Prayág itself, by the assembly of the virtuous. Easy of access to all, on any day, at any place, curing all the ills of pious devotees, is this

1. The simple actions are compared to rubies, which may be picked up on the surface of the ground; the mysterious actions to diamonds, which have to be dug out of a mine.

unspeakable, spiritual chief *tírtha*, of manifest virtue and yielding immediate fruit.

Dohá 2.

At this Prayág of holy men, whoever hears and understands, and in spirit devoutly bathes, receives even in this life all four rewards.[1]

Chaupái 3.

In an instant behold the result of the immersion ; the crow becomes a parrot and the goose a swan. Let no one marvel at hearing this, for the influence of good company is no mystery. Válmíki, Nàrad and the jar-born Agastya[2] have told its effect upon themselves. Whatever moves in the water, or on the earth, or in the air ; every creature in the world, whether animate or inanimate, that has attained to knowledge, or glory, or salvation, or power, or virtue, by any work, at any time or place, has triumphed through association with the good ; neither the world nor the Veda knows of any other expedient. Intercourse with the good is attainable only by the blessing of Ráma and without it wisdom is impossible : it is the root of all joy and felicity ; its flowers are good works and its fruit perfection. By it the wicked are reformed: as when by the touch of the philosopher's stone a vile metal becomes gold. If by mischance a good man falls into evil company, like the gem in a serpent's head, he still retains his virtue. Bráhma, Visnu, Mahádeva, the wisest of the poets, all have failed to expound the

1. The four rewards are *káma, artha, dharma, moksha* ; that is, pleasure, wealth, religious merit and final salvation.

2. Válmiki confessed to Ráma that he had once been a hunter and taken the life of many innocent creatures, till he fell in with the seven Rishis, who converted him and taught him to express his penitence by constantly repeating the word *mára, mára*. As this contains exactly the same letters as the name Ráma, it acted as a spell and advanced him to the highest degree of sanctity.

Similarly Nàrad confessed to Vyása, the author of the Puráns, that he was by birth only the son of a poor slave-girl, and had become a saint simply by eating the fragments of food left by the holy men who frequented his master's house.

Agastya also declared to Mahádeva that by birth he was the meanest of all creatures, and had only attained to miraculous powers by the influence of good company.

pre-eminence of a saint: for me to tell it is, as it were, for a costermonger to expatiate on the merits of a set of jewels.

Dohá 3–4.

I reverence the saints of equable temperament, who regard neither friend nor foe, like a gracious flower which sheds its fragrance alike on both infolding hands.[1] Ye saints, whose upright intention, whose catholic charity, and whose ready sympathy I acknowledge, hear my child-like prayer, be gracious to me and inspire me with devotion to the feet of Ráma.

Chaupái 4.

Again, I would propitiate those wretches[2] who without cause delight to vex the righteous; with whom a neighbour's loss is gain; who rejoice in desolation and weep over prosperity; who are as an eclipse to the full-moon glory of Hari and Hara; who become as a giant with a thousand arms to work another's woe; who have a thousand eyes to detect a neighbour's faults but, like flies on *ghí*, settle on his good points only to spoil them; quick as fire, implacable as the god of hell; [3] rich in crime and sin as Kuver is in gold; like an eclipse for the clouding of friendship, and as dead asleep as Kumbha-karn[4] to everything good; if they can do any injury, as ready to sacrifice themselves as hailstones, that melt after destroying a crop; spiteful as the great serpent with a thousand tongues; and like Prithuráj[5], with a thousand ears, to tell and hear of others' faults: like the thousand-eyed Indra, too, ever delighting in much strong drink and in a voice of thunder.

1. Though the right hand is the one by which it has been plucked, and the left that in which it is held and preserved.

2. In the following lines the poet defends himself by anticipation against possible objections, and roundly abuses the whole army of critics.

3. Yama, the Hindu Pluto, is here called Mahishesa, from *mahisha* a 'buffalo,' that being the animal on which he is represented as riding.

4. Rávan's gigantic brother, Kumbha-karn, obtained as a boon from Bráhma, that whenever he had satisfied his voracious appetite the slumber of repletion might be of the longest and deepest, and that he might only wake to eat again.

5. It is not related that Prithuráj had really ten thousand ears, but only that he prayed that he might be as quick to hear whatever redounded to the glory of God as if his ears were so many.

Dohá 5.

I know when they hear of philosophers, who regard friend or foe as friends, they are enraged ; but I clasp my hands and entreat them piteously.

Chaupái 5.

I have performed the rôle of supplication, nor will they forget their part. However carefully you may bring up a crow, it will still be a crow and a thief. I propitiate at once the feet of saints and sinners, who each give pain, but with a difference : for the first kill by absence, while the second torture by their presence : as opposite as a lotus and a leech, though both alike are produced in water. Good and bad thus resemble nectar and intoxicating drink, which were both begotten by the one great ocean :[1] each by its own acts attains to pre-eminence ; the one in honour, the other in dishonour ; compare with the good, ambrosia, or the moon, or the Ganges ; and with the bad, poison, or fire, or the river Karmnásá. Virtue and vice are known to all ; but whatever is to a man's taste that seemeth him good.

Dohá 6.

The good aim at goodness, and the vile at vileness ; ambrosia is esteemed for giving immortality, and poison for causing death.

Chaupái 6.

Why enumerate the faults and defects of the bad and the virtues of the good ? both are a boundless and unfathomable ocean. Hence occasionally virtue is reckoned as vice, improperly and from want of discrimination. For

---

1 The churning of the ocean is one of the commonplaces of Hindú poetry, and the allusions to it in the Rámáyana are innumerable. With Mount Mandara as a churning-stick, the great serpent Vásuki as a rope, and Náráyan himself in tortoise form as the pivot on which to work, the gods and demons combined to churn the milky ocean. Thus were produced from its depth the moon ; the sacred cow, Surabhi or Kamá-dhenu ; the goddess of wine, Varuni ; the tree of paradise, Parijáta, or Kalpa-taru ; the heavenly nymphs, the Apsarás ; the goddess of beauty, Lakshmi or Sri ; and the physician of the gods, Dhanvantari. The cup of nectar which the latter held in his hand was seized and quaffed by the gods ; while the poison, which also was produced, was either claimed by the snake gods or swallowed by Mahádeva ; whence comes the blackness of his throat, that gives him the name of *Nil-kanth*.

God hath created both, but it is the Vada that has distinguished one from the other.[1] The heroic legends and the Puránas also, no less than the Vedas, recognize every kind of good and evil as creatures of the Creator: pain and pleasure ; sin and religious merit ; night and day ; saint and sinner ; high caste and low caste : demons and gods ; great and small ; ambrosia and life ; pôison and death ; the visible world and the invisible God ; life and the lord of life ; rich and poor ; the beggar and the king ; Kási and Magadhá ;[2] the Ganges and the Karamnásá ; the desert of Márwár and the rich plain of Málwá ; the Bráhman and the butcher : heaven and hell ; sensual passion and asceticism ; the Vedas and the Tantras, and every variety of good and evil.

Dohá 7.

The Creator has made the universe to consist of things animate and inanimate ; good and evil ; a saint like a swan extracts the milk of goodness and rejects the worthless water.[3]

Chaupái 7.

When the Creator gives men this faculty of judgment they abandon error and become enamoured of the truth ; but conquered by time, temperament, or fate, even the good, as a result of their humanity, may err from virtue ; but Hari takes their body—so to speak—and corrects it, and, removing all sorrow and sin, cleanses it and glorifies them. If the bad through intercourse with the good do good, their inherent badness is not effaced. An impostor of fair outward show may be honoured on account of his garb, but in the end he is exposed and does not succeed, like Kála-nemi, or Rávan, or Ráhu.[4] The good are honoured, notwithstand-

---

1. "I did not know sin, but by the law."—*St. Paul.*

2. Magadhá (Bihár) is taken as the opposite to Kási, in consequence of its being the birthplace of Buddhism.

3. To the swan (*ráj-hans*) is ascribed the fabulous faculty of being able to separate milk from water, after the two have been mixed together.

4. Kála-nemi by assuming the form of an ascetic imposed for a time upon Hanumán, as Rávan did upon Síta : and even Vishnu, at the churning of the ocean, was at first deceived by Ráhu, who appeared like one of the gods.

ing their mean appearance, like the bear Jámavant or the monkey Hanumán. Bad company is loss, and good company is gain ; this is a truth recognized both by the world and the Veda. In company with the wind the dust flies heavenwards ; if it joins water, it becomes mud and sinks. According to the character of the house in which a parrot or *maina* is trained, it learns either to repeat the name of Ráma or to give abuse. With the ignorant, soot is mere refuse ; but it may make good ink, and be used even for copying a Purána ; while water, fire, and air combined become an earth-refreshing rain-cloud.

Dohá 8—11.

The planets, medicines, water, air, clothes, all are good or bad things according as their accompaniments are good or bad ; and people observe this distinction. Both lunar fortnights are equal as regards darkness and light ; but a difference in name has been wisely made, and as the moon waxes or wanes the fortnight is held in high or low esteem. Knowing that the whole universe, whether animate or inanimate, is pervaded by the spirit of Ráma, I reverence with clasped hands the lotus feet of all gods, giants, men, serpents, birds, ghosts, departed ancestors, Grandharvas, Kinnaras, demons of the night—I pray ye all be gracious to me.

Chaupái 8.

By four modes of birth[1] are produced 84 laks of species inhabiting the air, the water and the earth. With clasped hand I perform an act of adoration, recognizing the whole world as pervaded by the spirit of Síta and Ráma. In your compassion regard me as your servant, and dissembling no longer, be kind and affectionate. I have no confidence in

[1] The four *ákaras*, or modes of birth, are named *pindaja*, or viviparous ; *andaja*, or oviparous ; *sweduja*, born in sweat, like lice ; and *udbhija*, produced by sprouting like a tree. The 84 lakhs of species are divided as follows : 9 lakhs of aquatic creatures, 27 lakhs of those attached to the earth, 11 lakhs of insects, 10 lakhs of birds, 23 lakhs of quadrupeds, and 4 lakhs of men. The literal meaning of *ákara* being a mine, *khàni*, which has the same primary signification, is used for it in *Chaupái* 44.

the strength of my own wisdom, and therefore I supplicate you all. I would narrate the great deeds of Raghupati, but my ability is little and his acts unfathomable. I am conscious that I have no skill or capacity ; my intellect in short is beggarly, while my ambition is imperial ; I am thirsting for nectar, when not even skim-milk is to be had. Good people, all pardon my presumption and listen to my childish babbling, as a father and mother delight to hear the lisping prattle of their little one. Perverse and malignant fools may laugh, who pick out faults in others wherewith to adorn themselves. Every one is pleased with his own rhymes, whether they be pungent or insipid ; but those who praise another's voice are good men, of whom there are few in the world ; there are many enough like the rivers, which on getting a rainfall swell out a flood of their own, but barely one like the generous ocean, which swells on beholding the fulness of the moon.

Dohá 12.

My lot is low, my purpose high, but I am confident of one thing, that the good will be gratified to hear me, though fools may laugh.

Chaupái 9.

The laughter of fools will be grateful to me ; the crow calls the *koil's* voice harsh, The goose ridicules the swan, and the frog the *chatak* ; so the low and vile abuse pure verse. As they have no taste for poetry nor love for Ráma, I am glad that they should laugh. If my homely speech and poor wit are fit subjects for laughter, let them laugh ; it is no fault of mine. If they have no understanding of true devotion to Lord, the tale will seem insipid enough : but to the true and orthodox worshippers of Hari and Hara the story of Raghubar will be sweet as honey. The singer's devotion to Ráma will by itself be sufficient embellishment to make the good hear and praise the melody. Though no poet, nor clever, nor accomplished ; though unskilled in every art and science ; though all the elegant devices of letters and rhetoric, the countless variations of metre, the infinite divisions of sentiment and style, and all the defects and excellences of verse, and the gift to distinguish between them are unknown to me. I declare and record it on a fair white sheet—

Dohá 13.

That though my style has not a single charm of its own, it has a charm known throughout the world, which men of discernment will ponder as they read—

Chaupái 10.

The gracious name of Raghupati; all-purifying essence of the Puránas and the Veda, abode of all that is auspicious, destroyer of all that is inauspicious, ever murmured in prayer by Umá and the great Tripurári. The most elegant composition of the most talented poet has no real beauty if the name of Ráma is not in it: in the same way as a lovely woman adorned with the richest jewels is vile if unclothed. But the most worthless production of the feeblest versifier, if adorned with the name of Ráma, is heard and repeated with reverence by the wise, who extract what is good in it, like bees gathering honey; though the poetry has not a single merit, the glory of Ráma is manifested thereby. This is the confidence which has possessed my soul; is there anything which good company fails to exalt? Thus smoke forgets its natural pungency and in incense yields a sweet scent. My language is that in vulgar use, but my subject is the highest, the story of Ráma, enrapturing the world.

Chhand 1.[1]

Though rapturous lays befit his praise, who cleansed a world accurst,
Yet Tulsi's rivulet of rhyme may slake a traveller's thirst.
How pure and blest on Siva's breast show the vile stains of earth!
So my poor song flows bright and strong illumed by Ráma's worth.

---

1 The *chhands* are generally somewhat enthusiastic outbursts, in which the oft-repeated rhyme is a little apt to run away with the sense. The better to indicate their special character, one-half of the 62 that occur in this book will be rendered metrically. The first line always repeats some emphatic word from the last line of the preceding stanza.

Dohá 14—15.

From its connection with the glory of Ráma, my verse will be most grateful to every one. Any wood that comes from the Malaya sandal-groves is valued; who considers what kind of wood it is? Though a cow be black, its milk is pure and wholesome, and all men drink it; and so, though my speech is rough, it tells the glory of Síta and Ráma, and will therefore be heard and repeated with pleasure by sensible people.

Chaupái 11.

So long as the diamond remains in the serpent's head, the ruby on the mountain top, or the pearl in its elephant's brow, they are all without beauty; but in a king's diadem or on a lovely woman they become beautiful exceedingly. Similarly, as wise men tell, poetry is born of one faculty, but beautified by another; for it is in answer to pious prayer that the Muse leaves her heavenly abode and speeds to earth; without immersion in the fountain of Ráma's deeds all labour and trouble count for nothing. An intelligent poet understands this, and sings only of Hari, the redeemer, and his virtues. To recount the doings of common people is mere idle beating of the head, which the Muse loathes. Genius is, as it were, a shell in the sea of the soul, waiting for the October rain of inspiration; if a gracious shower falls, each drop becomes a lovely pearl of poetry.

Dohá 16.

Then dexterously pierced and strung together on the thread of Ráma's adventures, they form a beautiful chain to be worn on a good man's breast.

Chaupái 12.

Men born in this grim iron age are outwardly swans, but inwardly as black as crows; walking in evil paths, abandoning the Veda,[1] embodiments of falsehood, vessels of impurity, hypocrites, professing devotion to Ráma, but slaves of gold, of passion, and of lust. Among them I give the first place to myself, a hypocrite, alas! of the very first rank; but were I to tell all my vices, the list would so grow that it would have no end. I have therefore said but very little, but a word is enough for the wise. Let none of my hearers blame me for offering so many apologies; whoever is troubled in mind by them is more stupid and dull of wit than I am myself. Though I am no poet, and have no pretensions to cleverness, I sing as best I can the virtues of Ráma. How unfathomable his actions, how shallow my poor world-entangled intellect! Before the strong wind that could uproot Mount Meru, of what account is such a mere fleck of cotton as I am? When I think of Ráma's infinite majesty I tremble as I write.

Dohá 17.

For Sarasvati, Sesh-nág, Siva and Bráhma, the Shástras, the Veda, the Puránas, all are unceasingly singing his perfection, yet fail to declare it.

Chaupái 13.

All know the greetness of the lord to be thus unutterable, yet none can refrain from attempting to expound it. For this reason the Veda also has declared many different modes of effectual worship. There is one GOD, passionless, formless, uncreated, the universal soul, the supreme spirit, the all-pervading, whose shadow is the world; who has become incarnate and does many things, only for the love that he bears to his faithful people; all-gracious and compassionate to the humble; who in his mercy ever refrains from anger against those whom he loves and knows to be

1 By the Veda, to which Tulsi Dás so frequently appeals, must be understood not the original Veda itself, with which he had absolutely nothing in common, but only the Upanishads, which are also popularly quoted as of Vedic authority. They are brief speculative treatises, over 200 in all, in a discursive and rhapsodical style and of an ultra-Pantheistic tendency. Though attached to the end of the Vedas, they are for the most part of much later date.

his own : restorer of the past ; protector of the poor ;[1] all-good, all-powerful, the lord Raghurāj. In this belief the wise sing the glory of Hari, and their song thus becomes holy and meritorious. I, too, bowing my head to Ráma's feet, am emboldened to sing his fame, following a path which has been made easy by the divine bards who have trodden it before me.

Dohá 18.

As when once a king has prepared a bridge over a broad stream, an ant, insignificant as it is, is able to cross without difficulty.

Chaupái 14.

In this manner re-assuring myself, I undertake to recount Ráma's charming adventures, as they have been reverently told by Vyása and the other great poets, whose lotus feet I adore, praying, Fulfil ye my desire. I reverence also the poets of these latter days, who have sung of Raghupati, bards of high intelligence, who have written in Prákrit and the vulgar tongue. All who have been in time past, or who now are, or who hereafter shall be, I bow to all in the utmost good faith and sincerity. Be propitious and grant this boon, that in assemblies of good men my song may be honoured ! If the good and wise will not honour it, the silly poet has had all his labour in vain. The only fame, or poetry, or power, that is of any worth, is that which like Ganges water is good for all. The incongruity between Ráma's glory and my rude speech makes me hesitate ; but by your favour all will turn out well ; for even coarse cloth, if embroidered with silk, becomes beautiful. Be kind enough to think of this, and my style will then match the excellence of my theme.

Dohá 19.

A clear style and an exalted theme are both commendable ; and when they are combined, an enemy even, forgett-

---

1 *Gharíb nawáz.* This is the first Persian word that has occurred in the poem.

ing his natural hostility, will repeat the strain. But such a combination is not to be acquired without genius, and genius I have none; so again and again I beg of you to bear with me while I sing the glory of Hari. The great poets are like the swans sporting in the Mánasa lake of Hari's deeds; look on me as a well-meaning child and make allowances.

Sorathá 2.

I reverence the lotus feet of the great sage who composed the Rámáyana, smooth strains on rough topics, and faultless, though a story of the faulty. [1] I reverence the Vedas which are like a boat in which to cross the ocean of existence, without ever dreaming of weariness, while recounting Ráma's excellent glory. I reverence the dust on the feet of Bráhma, creator of this ocean-like world, from which have been produced men, good and bad; as of old from the same source came at once ambrosia, the moon, and the cow Kámadhenu, and also poison and intoxicating liquor.

Dohá 20.

Reverencing with clasped hands gods, Bráhmans, philosophers, and sages, I pray—'Be gracious to me and accomplish all my fair desire.'

Chaupái 15.

Again I reverence the Sarasvati and the Ganges, both holy and beautiful streams cleansing sin by a single draught or immersion, whose name as soon as uttered or heard at once removes error. I adore as I would my guru, or my natural parents, Siva and Párvati, protectors of the humble,

---

1 In Hindi poetry it is considered a beauty if a phrase is so worded as to be capable of two or more different interpretations. It is sufficient to note this peculiarity once for all; but there are an immense number of passages in which, though the meaning which I have adopted seems to me, on the whole, the one most appropriate to the context, it by no means follows that other interpretations are not, from the grammarian's point of view, equally correct. Thus, the line rendered as above would literally stand thus—Rough, soft, beautiful, faultless, full of faults. And this conveys the general meaning which I have expressed. But there are two plays upon words; for *sakhara*, ordinarily 'rough,' and therefore contrasted with *sakomal*, 'soft,' is also intended to bear the meaning 'relating to the demon Khara'; and similarly *dúshan sahit*, 'full of faults,' can be forced into meaning 'with the demon Dushan.'

daily benefactors, servants and courtiers in attendance on Síta's lord and in every way Tulsi's true friends; who, in their benevolence and considering the degeneracy of the times, have themselves composed many spells in a barbarous language, incoherent syllables and unintelligible mutterings, mysterious revelations of the great Siva.[1] By his patronage I may make my story an agreeable one, and by meditating on Siva and Párvati may relate Ráma's adventures in a way that will give pleasure. It is only by his favour that my verse can be beautified, as a dark night by the moon and stars. Whoever in a devout spirit, with intelligence and attention, hears or repeats this lay of mine, he shall become full of true love for Ráma, and, cleansed from worldly stains, shall enjoy heavenly felicity.

Dohá 21.

Whether I am awake or dreaming, if Siva and Gauri grant me their favour, all that I say shall come true as to the effect of my song, though it be in the vulgar tongue.

Chaupái 16.

I reverence the holy city of Ayodhyá and the river Sarjú, cleansing from all earthly impurity. I salute also the inhabitants of the city, for whom the Lord had no little affection; seeing that he ignored all the sin of Sita's calumniator and set men's minds at rest.[2] I reverence Kausalya, eastern heaven, from which glory was diffused

---

1 The allusion is to the magic spells and mystical formularies of the Tantras, which are for the most part mere strings of uncouth and utterly unmeaning words, such as OM, AIN, HRIN SRIN, and again AN, HUN PHAT, two mantras recited during the ceremonies of the Durga Puja. They all purport to have been revealed by Siva himself to Pàrvati.

2 The calumniator was a washerman, whose wife had gone away, without asking his permission, to her father's house and had stayed there three days. On her return her husband refused to take her in, saying—'Do you think I am a Ráma, who takes back his Sita after she has been living for eleven months in another man's house?' When this came to Ráma's ears, he showed his respect for the delicacy of his subjects by dismissing Sita, and, instead of punishing the washerman, promoted him to honour. This incident would naturally find a place in the 7th canto of the poem; and from the allusion to it here, it may be presumed that Tulsi Dás orignally intended to relate it. But by the time he had written so far, the enthusiasm of his devotion had waxed too great to allow of his admitting that such an insinuation of evil had ever been made against the immaculate Sita.

over the whole world; whence Raghupati arose as a lovely moon, giving joy to the world, but blighting like a frost the lotus leaves of vice. To King Dasarath and all his queens, incarnations of virtue and felicity, I make obeisance in word, deed and heart, saying 'Be gracious to me as to a servant of your son, O parents of Ráma, that come of greatness, ye in whose creation the creator surpassed himself.'

Sorathá 3.

I reverence the King of Avadh, who had such true love for Ráma's feet that, when parted from his lord, his life snapped and parted too like a straw.

Chaupái 17.

I salute the King of Videha, with all his court, who had the greatest affection for Ráma; though he concealed his devotion under royal state, yet it broke out as soon as he saw him. Then, next, I throw myself at the feet of Bharat, whose constancy and devotion surpass description; whose soul like a bee thirsting for sweets was ever hovering round the lotus feet of Ráma. I reverence too the lotus feet of Lakshman, cool, comely and source of delight to their worshippers, whose glory is as it were the standard for the display of Ráma's pure emblazonment. Thou who to remove the terrors of the world didst become incarnate in the form of the thousand-headed serpent for the sake of the universe, be ever propitious to me, O son of Sumitrá, ocean of compassion, storehouse of perfection. I bow also to Ripusúdan (*i.e.*, Satrughna), the generous hero, Bharat's constant companion; and to the conqueror Hanumán, whose glory has been told by Ráma himself.

Sorathá 4.

The Son of the Wind, of profound intelligence, like a consuming fire in the forest of vice, in whose heart Ráma, equipped with bow and arrows, has established his home.

Chaupái 18.

The monkey lord, the king of bears and demons, Angad and all the monkey host, I throw myself at the benign feet of them all, for though contemptible in appearance they yet found Ráma. I worship all his faithful servants—whether birds, beasts, gods, men or demons—all his unselfish adherents. I worship Sukadeva, Sanat-kumára, Nárad, and the other sages of excellent renown, putting my head to the ground and crying: 'My lords, be gracious to your servant.' I propitiate the lotus feet of Jának's daughter, Jánki, mother of the world, best beloved of the Fountain of Mercy; by whose grace I may attain to unclouded intelligence. Again in heart, in word and deed I worship the all-worthy feet of Raghunáth; the glance of whose lotus eyes, like an arrow from the bow, rejoices his votaries by destroying all their misfortunes.

Dohá 22.

As a word and its meaning are inseparable, and as a wave cannot be distinguished from the water of which it is composed, the difference being only in the name; so with Ráma and Síta, the refuge of the distressed, whom I adore.

Chaupái 19.

I adore the name of Ráma as borne by Raghubar,[1] the source of all light, whether of the fire, or the sun, or the moon; substance of the triune god; vital breath of the Veda; the passionless; the incomparable; the source of all good; the great spell muttered by Mahádeva and enjoined by him as necessary to salvation even at Kási. By confessing its power, Ganes obtain the first place among the gods;[2] by its

---

1 For there are two other Rámas besides Ráma-chandra, *viz.*, Parasuráma and Balaráma.

2 According to the legend, the gods were disputing among themselves as to which of them should be accounted the greatest. To settle the matter Bráhma proposed that they all should race round the world. They started accordingly, each on the animal which he most delighted to ride; and Ganes being mounted, as was his custom, on nothing better than a rat, was of course, soon left far behind. In his distress the sage Nárad appeared to him and suggested that he should write the word Ráma in the dust and pace round that, for in it was virtually included all creation. This he did, and returned to Bráhma, who at once awarded him the prize.

power, though he muttered it backwards, the great poet Válmíki attained to purity; by its repetition, after she had heard from Siva that it was equal to a thousand names, Bhaváni was able to join her husband;[1] while he, Mahádeva, in his delight on beholding her simple faith, assumed the woman, making that ornament of her sex the ornament of his own body. Again, it was by the power of this name that the poison swallowed by Mahádeva was converted into ambrosia.

Dohá 23.

Devotion to Ráma is for the faithful Tulsi Dás like the rainy season for the rice-fields; the two glorious consonants in Ráma's name are like the months of Sáwan and Bhadon.

Chaupái 20.

Two sweet and gracious syllables, the eyes as it were of the soul, easy to remember, satisfying every wish, a gain in this world and felicity in the next; most delightful to utter, to hear, or to remember; as dear to Tulsi as the inseparable Ráma and Lukshman. My love is inflamed as I speak of these mystic syllables, as intimately connected as the universal soul and the soul of man; twin brothers like Nara and Náráyan; preservers of the world; redeemers of the elect; bright jewels in the ears of beauteous Faith; pure and beneficent as the sun and the moon; like sweetness and contentment, the inseparable attributes of ambrosia; like the tortoise and serpent, supporters of the world; like the bee and lotus of a pious soul; and as sweet to the tongue as Hari and Balaráma were sweet to Jasodá.

---

1 One day when Siva had finished eating, he called to his wife Párvati to come and take her food too before it got cold. She pleaded that she had not yet finished repeating, according to her daily wont, the thousand names of Vishnu: whereupon her husband instructed her that it would suffice if she said the mere name of Ráma once, for that had as much virtue as all the thousand. She at once believed him and complied; and the god was so pleased at her ready faith that in her honor he assumed the Ardhanári, or half male, half female form.

Dohá 24.

Like a royal umbrella and jewelled diadem over all the other letters of the alphabet shine the two consonants in Ráma's name.[1]

Chaupái 21.

A name may be regarded as equivalent to what is named, the connection being such as subsists between a master and servant. Both name and form are shadows of the lord, who, rightly understood, is unspeakable and uncreated. They are sometimes wrongly distinguished as greater and less, but the wise will understand my explanation of the difference between them. See, now, the form is subordinate to the name, for without the name you cannot come to a knowledge of the form; if the very form be in your hand, still without knowing the name it is not recognized; but meditate on the name without seeing the form, and your soul is filled with devotion.[2] The mystery of name and form is unspeakable and cannot be told, but delightful to those who have intuition of it; the name acting as a witness between the material and immaterial form of the deity, and being a guide and interpreter to both.

Dohá 25.

Place the name of Ráma as a jewelled lamp at the door

---

1 The allusion is to the form the letters *r* and *m* take when written above the line.

2 To the European reader all this panegyric of the Divine name will probably at first sight appear extravagant and absurd. But from the Hindu point of view it is reasonable enough, and *mutatis mutandis*, may be paralleled by many similar expressions in the writings of Catholic theologians, as for example the following:—

Sancta oratio, brevis ad legendum, facilis ad tenendum, dulcis ad cogitandum, fortis ad protegendum.—*Thos. á Kempis.*

Suo sanctissimo nomine, quod quinque literis constat, confert quotidie veniam peccatoribus.—*P. Pelbert.*

Nomen tuum devote nominari non potest sine nominantis utilitate.—*S. Bonaventura.*

Nomen solum sufficit ad medendum; nam pestis tam efficax nulla sic hæret, quæ ad nomen non cedat continuo.—*Ricardus de S. Laurentio.*

Spiritus maligni diffugiunt, audito nomine, velut ab igne.—*S. Bridget.*

Omnes dæmones verentur hoc nomen, et timent, qui audientes statim relinquunt animam de unguibus quibus tenebant eam.—*S. Bridget.*

Gloriosum et admirable est nomen; qui illud retinent, non expavescent in puncto, mortis.—*S. Bonaventura.*

Nomen plenum est omni dulcedine et suavitate divina.—*Honorius.*

of your lips and there will be light, as you will, both inside and out.

Chaupái 22.

As his tongue repeats this name, the ascetic wakes to life, his thoughts free from passion and all detached from the world; he enjoys the incomparable felicity of God, who is unspeakable, unblemished, without either name or form. Those who would understand mysteries, by repeating this name understand them ; the religious who repeat this name absorbed in contemplation, become workers of miracles[1] and acquire the power of rendering themselves invisible and the like ; those who repeat it when burdened with affliction are freed from their troubles and become happy. Thus there are in the world four kinds of Ráma-worshippers, all four good, holy, and beneficent ; but of these four sages they are the most dear to the lord who wisely rely upon his name. His name is great in the four Vedas and in all the ages of the world, but in this fourth age especially there is no other hope.

Dohá 26.

Free from sensual passions and absorbed in devout affection to Ráma, the soul disports itself like a fish in the ambrosial lake of his beloved name.

Chaupái 23.

The Supreme may be regarded either as unconditioned or as incarnate ; under either aspect it is unspeakable, unfathomable, without beginning and without parallel. To my mind the name is greater than both, for it has prevailed

---

1 The miraculous powers that can be acquired by perfect saints, or siddahs, are reckoned as eight in number, and are called *animá*, *mahima*, *garima*, *laghimá*, *prápti*, *prákámya*, *isitwa*, and *vasittwá*. These words denote the faculty—1st, of becoming infinitely small ; 2nd, of becoming infinitely great; 3rd, of becoming infinitely heavy; 4th, of becoming infinitely light; 5th, of obtaining whatever one wishes ; 6th, of doing whatever one wishes ; 7th, of absolute supremacy ; 8th, of absolute subjugation. Compare the four gifts of beatitude as enumerated by Catholic theologians : *viz.*—1st, Agility, by which the soul can in an instant descend from the height of heaven to earth ; 2ndly, Brightness, by which [according to S. Augustine] each blessed soul is so much more luminous than the sun as the sun is brighter than any other celestial body ; 3rdly, Subtilty, by which the soul can penetrate a mountain, in the same way as a ray of light passes through a crystal; and 4thly, Impassibility, by which it is exempt from suffering, disease, or death.

to bring both under its sway. My friends must not take this as an exaggeration on my part, for I say it confidently and with sincere devotion. This dual distinction of the Supreme is like the two kinds of fire, which is either potential in the wood or visible externally; each is in itself unapproachable but is easily approached by means of the name; and therefore I say that the name is greater than either Brahm or Ráma. For the one immortal, true, sentient, complete, and blissful Brahm is all-pervading ; yet though such an unchangeable lord is in our very soul, the whole creation is in slavery and wretchedness, till he is revealed in definite shape, and is energized by the name ; as a jewel is not valued till it is so called.

Dohá 27.

Thus the virtue of the name is infinite and transcends the Supreme, and in my judgment is greater that Ráma himself.

Chaupái 24.

From the love that he bore to his followers, Ráma took the form of a man and by himself enduring misery secured their happiness. By incessantly and devoutly repeating his name, all the faithful may attain to felicity. Ráma himself redeemed only one woman, the ascetic's wife ;[1] but his name has corrected the errors of millions of sinners. To gratify the Rishi Visvamitra, Ráma wrought the destruction of Suketu's daughter Táraká with her son Márícha and his army ; but as the sun puts an end to night, so his name has scattered all crime and pain and despair. In his own person Ráma broke the bow of Siva, but his glorious name has broken the fear of death ;[2] the Lord

1 Ahalyá, the wife of the Rishi Gautama, having been seduced by the god Indra, was cursed by her indignant lord, and doomed to remain alone and invisible in the forest for thousands of years, till Ráma should come and redeem her

2 Here is a play upon words which cannot be preserved in the translation, for in the first half of the couplet the word *bhava* is to be taken as a name of Siva, while in the second half it means life or rather death, since, according to Hindú ideas, all conscious life is merely a preparation for inevitable death. Compare Milton's expression :—" This earthly load of death called life, which us from life doth sever."

himself restored to life only the forest of Dandaka,[1] but his name has sanctified countless generations; the son of Raghu destroyed many demons, but his name has destroyed all the evil of the world.

Dohá 28.

Raghunáth conferred immortality on Savari and the vulture Jatáyu[2] and his other faithful servants; but his name, precious theme of the Vedas, has delivered innumerable wretches.

Chaupái 25.

Ráma, as all men know, extended his protection to Sugriva and Vibhíshana; but his name has protected countless supplicants, shining forth gloriously in the world and Veda. Ráma assembled a host of bears and monkeys, and even then had no little trouble to build his bridge; his name can dry up the ocean of life; meditate thereon, O ye faithful. Ráma killed in battle Rávan and all his family, and returned with Síta[3] to his own city, a king to Avadh, his capital, while gods and saints hymned his praises; but his servants, if only they affectionately meditate on his name, have no difficulty in vanquishing the whole army of error, and absorbed in devotion live at ease, without even a dream of sorrow.

Dohá 29.

The name is greater than either Brahm or Ráma, and is the best gift of the best giver; this Mahádeva knew when he selected it from the hundred *crores*[4] of verses in the Rámayaná.

---

1 Dandaka is the name of the pathless forest near the Godavari, where Síta was stolen away by Rávan.

2 The bird Jatáyu stopped the chariot in which Síta was being carried off by Rávan and was mortally wounded by the giant, but lived long enough to give Ráma tidings of his beloved. In return for his faithful services Ráma and Lakshman themselves performed his funeral rites.

3 Sugríva, the monkey chief, as told at full length later on in the poem, assisted Ráma in his search for Síta; and Ráma rewarded him by installing him as sovereign of Kishindhyá in the place of his brother Báli. Similarly, Vibhíshana was made king of Lanká in the room of Rávan.

4 Of these hundred crores it is said that Siva distributed 33 crores to each of the three worlds. The one crore that remained over he similarly divided into three sets of 33 lakhs each; the odd lakh into three sets of 33 thousand each; the odd thousand again into three sets of three hundred each; the odd hundred into three sets of thirty-three each, and finally the one remaining *sloka* into three sets of ten letters each. The two letters that remained over, being the two consonants in the name of Ráma, he kept for himself, as containing the gist of the whole matter.

Chaupái 26.

By the power of this name the blessed god of curst attire, even the great Siva, acquired immortality; by the power of this name Sukadeva, Sanat-kumára, and all saints, sages, and ascetics have enjoyed heavenly raptures: Nárad too acknowledged its power, himself as dear to Hara and Hari as Hari is dear to the world; by repeating this name Prahlád, through the Lord's grace, became the crown of the faithful.[1] Dhruva in his distress repeated the name of Hari, and was rewarded by a fixed and incomparable station in the heavens;[2] by meditating on his holy name Hanumán won and kept the affection of Ráma; by the power of Hari's name Ajámil[3] and the elephant and the harlot all three obtained salvation; why further extend the list? not even the incarnate Ráma could exhaust it.

Dohá 30.

The name of Ráma is as the tree of paradise, the centre of all that is good in this wicked world; and whoever

---

1 Prahlád, the pious son of the impious Hiranya Kasipu, who was destroyed by Vishnu in the Narsinh avatár, was made equal to Indra for life and finally united with Vishnu.

2 Dhruva, the son of Uttanapáda, being slighted by his step-mother, left his home with the determination of winning himself a name in the world. By the advice of the seven Rishis, he devoted himself to the service of Vishnu and was finally exalted by the god to the heavens, where he shines as the pole-star.

3 According to the history given in the 6th Skandha of the Sri Bhagavat, Ajámil was a Bráhman of Kanauj, of most dissolute and abandoned life. By a happy chance the youngest of the ten sons whom he had by a prostitute was named Náráyan, and the father when at the point of death happened to summon him to his side. But the god Náráyan, thus casually invoked, himself came in answer to the call and rescued the guilty soul from the demons that were about to carry it off to hell.

The story of the elephant is given in the 8th Skandha of the same Purána. An alligator had seized him by the foot while bathing, and though he struggled desperately for 2,000 years, he was unable to rid himself on his enemy, and at last was deserted by all his wives and children. He then began to give himself up for lost; but reflecting on the pertinacity of the alligator, he came to the conclusion that the creature must be the embodiment of all the sins he had committed in previous existences and that God alone could save him. He therefore addressed a fervent prayer to Náráyan, who thus invoked by name came down from heaven and with his discus Sudarsan cut off the alligator's head and delivered the suppliant.

The 8th chapter of the 11th Skandha gives the story of the penitent prostitute, Pingala.

meditates upon it becomes (says Tulsi Dás) transformed as it were from a vile hemp-stick into a sweet-smelling tulsi plant.

Chaupái 27.

In all four ages of the world; in all time, past, present, or future; in the three spheres of earth, heaven and hell; any creature that repeats this name becomes blessed. This is the verdict of the Veda, the Puránas and all the saints—that love of Ráma is the fruit of all virtue. In the first age, contemplation; in the second age, sacrifice; in the Dvápar age, temple-worship was the appointed propitiation; but in this vile and impure iron age, where the soul of man floats like a fish in an ocean of sin, in these fearful times, the name is the only tree of life, and by meditating on it all commotion is stilled. In these evil days neither good deeds, nor piety, nor spiritual wisdom is of any avail, but only the name of Ráma: his name is as it were the wisdom and the might of Hanumán to expose and destroy the Kálanemi-like[1] wiles of the wicked world.

Dohá 31.

As narsinh was manifested to destroy the enemy of heaven, Hiranya-kasipu, and protect Prahlad, so is Ráma's name for the destruction of the world and protection of the pious.

Chaupái 28

By repeating this name, whether in joy or in sadness, in action or in repose, bliss is diffused all around. Meditating upon it and bowing my head to Raghunáth, I compose these lays in his honour; he will correct all my defects, whose mercy is mercy inexhaustible. Thou art my good

1 Kálanemi was the uncle of Rávan, who commissioned him to kill Hanumán. Accordingly, he assumed the garb of a devotee and retired to a magic hermitage, where he was soon after visited by Hanumán. The latter accepted the hospitality of the holy man as he took him to be, but before eating went to a pond close by to bathe. As soon as he put his foot in the water, it was seized by a crocodile, which, however, he soon killed; when from its dead body sprung a beautiful nymph long under a curse, who informed him of Kálamemi's true character. Hanumán thereupon threw his tail round the demon's neck and strangled him. The incident is related in Book vi, dohás 55, 56.

lord, I thy poor servant; bear this in mind and graciously protect me. The world and scripture alike declare these to be the characteristics of a good master, that he hears prayer and acknowledges affection. Rich or poor, villager or citizen, learned or unlearned, pure or impure, good poet or bad poet, all according to their ability extol their king as being good, amiable, and gracious, lord of incomparable compassion; and he hears and accepts their honest attempts, recognizing in their words both devotion and a measure of ability. This is the way with earthly kings, and Ráma is their crown: he is satisfied with simple piety, though in one who is duller and feebler of intellect even than I am.

Dohá 32-33.

The merciful Ráma will regard the love and zeal of his poor servant, he who made a ship out of a rock and wise ministers out of monkeys and bears; although I am a byword, and every one says Ráma is exposed to ridicule, in that he, being such a lord, has such a servant as Tulsi Dás.

Chaupái 29.

My presumption is indeed very sad and villainous enough to disgust hell itself; I am quite aware of this and tremble to think of it; but Ráma never dreamt of taking notice. The lord listened and with his own eyes attentively considered my faith, and thereupon applauded my devout intention. Though my story is spoilt by the telling, Ráma is satisfied and accounts it good, since the will is good. The lord is not mindful of a chance fault, but on every occasion he considers the heart. Thus the very crime for which he like a huntsman killed Báli was in turn the sin of Sugríva, and again of Vibhíshan; but in their case Ráma did not dream of censure, but honoured them both at his meeting with Bharat and commended in open court.

Dohá 34-36.

The monkeys too that scrambled up in the boughs of the tree under which the lord sat, even these he held dear as himself: says Tulsi, there is no master so generous as Ráma. O Ráma, thy goodness is good to all, and if so, then good to Tulsi also. Thus declaring my merits and defects and again bowing my head to all, I proceed to tell the glorious acts of Raghubar, by the sound of which all the sin of the world is effaced.

Chaupái 30.

Now listen all in friendly wise while I relate the story as I have heard it, as it was communicated by Yájnavalkya to the great sage Bharadvája. It was first of all composed by Siva and graciously revealed to Umá, and again declared to Káka-bhusundi, known to be chief among the votaries of Ráma. From him Yájnavalkya received it and he recited it to Bharadvája. These listeners and reciters were of equal virtue and had an equal insight into Hari's sportive actions. Their intellect comprehended all time, as it were a plum in the palm of the hand. Other intelligent votaries of Hari have also in different ways heard, understood and spoken.

Dohá 37—38.

As for myself, I heard the story from my master at Sukár-khet (*i.e.*, Soron),[1] not understanding it, when I was quite a child and had no sense. How could such a dull creature, being both ignorant and eaten up with wordly impurities, understand so mysterious a legend and a dialogue between such sage interlocutors?

Chaupái 31.

But my master repeated it time after time, till at length I understood as much as could be expected; and I now put it down in the vulgar tongue for the better comprehension of my ideas; with a heart inspired by Hari and using all the little sense, judgment, and ability that I possess. The

1 Soron, the modern name, is a corruption of Súkara-gráma (Boar-town). The place is still much frequented by pilgrims, the principal concourse being on the festival of the Varáha (or Boar) avatár, Súkara-gráma = Súargáwn = Súaránw = Soron.

story that I have to tell clears my own doubts as it does every other error and delusion, and is a raft on which to cross the ocean of existence. The story of Ráma is a resting-place for the intellect; a universal delight; destroyer of wordly impurity; an antidote to the venom of passion; a match to enkindle the fire of wisdom; the cow of plenty in this iron age; an elixir to make good men immortal; a terrestrial stream of nectar; a destroyer of death; a snake to devour toad-like error; the annihilator of hell, like as Párvati on behalf of gods and saints annihilated the army of demons; like as Lakshmi was born of the sea, so conceived in the assembly of saints; immoveable as the earth that supports all the weight of creation; like the Jamuná, to put to shame the angel of death; like Kási, the saviour of all living creatures; as dear to Ráma as the pure tulsi; as dear to Tulsi Dás as his own heart's desire; as dear to Siva as the daughter of Mount Mekal (*i.e.*, the Narmadá), bestower of all perfection and prosperity; like Aditi, gracious mother of all the gods; the perfect outcome of love and devotion to Raghubar.

Dohá 39.

The story of Ráma is as the river Mandákini and a good intention like Mount Chitrakút, while sincere affection is the forest where Ráma and Sítá disported themselves.

Chaupái 32.

The legend of Ráma is like the delectable wishing stone; or as a fair jewel for the bridal adornment of saintly wisdom; His perfection is the joy of the whole world, fraught with the blessings of virtue, wealth, and eternal salvation: a true teacher of wisdom, asceticism and spiritual contemplation; like the physician of the gods to heal the fearful diseases of life; the very parent of devotion to Síta and Ráma; the seed of all holy vows and practices; the destroyer of sin, of pain, and of sorrow; our guardian in this world and the next; the Prime Minister and the

General of Kingly Counsel; a very Agastya,[1] to drink up the illimitable ocean of desire; a young lion in the forest of life to attack the wild elephants of lust, anger, and sensual impurity; as dear to Siva as the presence of a highly honoured guest; as an abundant shower to quench the fire of meanness; a potent spell against the venom of the world; effacing from the forehead the deep brand of evil destiny; dispelling the darkness of error like the rays of the sun; like a shower on a rice-field refreshing the aridity of prayer; like the tree of paradise granting every desire; like Hari and Hara, accessible and gracious to all servants; like the stars in the clear autumn sky of the poet's mind; like the richness of life enjoyed by Ráma's votaries; like the perfect felicity that is the reward of virtue; like the assembly of the faithful in benevolence and composure; like a swan in the pure lake of the believer's soul; like the abundant flood of Ganga's purifying stream.

Dohá 40—41.

Ráma's perfect merit is like a strong fire to consume the dry wood of schism and heresy, evil practices and worldly deceit, hypocrisy and infidelity. His acts are like the rays of the full moon that give pleasure to all, but are specially consoling to the souls of the pious like the lotus and the *chakor*.

Chaupái 33.

All the questions that Bhaváni asked, with Sankara's replies thereto, I now proceed to give in substance, with agreeable diversity of style. No one is to be astonished if he should happen not to have heared any particular legend before. A philosopher, on hearing for the first time any marvellous acts, will feel no surprise, reasoning thus with himself; I know well that there is no limit in the world to the stories about Ràma, for he has in various forms become

1 As Agastya was one day worshipping by the sea-side, a wave came and washed away some of his altar furniture, whereupon in three draughts he drank the whole ocean dry.

incarnate, and verses of the Rámáyana are some thousand millions in number; his glorious acts are of myriad diversity, and have been sung by sages in countless ways.[1] So indulge no doubts, but listen reverently and devoutly.

Dohá 42.

Ráma is infinite, his perfections infinite, and his legends of immeasureable expansion; men of enlightened and understanding will therefore wonder at nothing they hear.

Chaupái 34.

Having in this manner put away all doubt, I place on my head the dust from the lotus feet of my master, and with folded hand-making a general obeisance, that no fault may attach to my telling of the story, and bowing my head reverently before Siva, I proceed to sing of Ráma's excellent glory. In this *Sambat* year of 1631, I write with my head at Hari's feet, on Tuseday the 9th of the sweet month of Chait, at the city of Avadh, on the day when the scriptures say Ráma was born; when the spirits of all holy places there assemble, with demons, serpents, birds, men, saints, and gods, and there offer homage to Raghunáth, while the enlightened keep the great birthday festival and hymn Ráma's high glory.

Dohá 43.

Pious crows bathe in the all-purifying stream of the Sarjú and murmur Ráma's name, while his dark and beautiful form is imprinted on their hearts.

Chaupái 35.

The Vedas and Puránas declare that sin is cleansed by the mere sight or touch of this holy stream as well as by bathing in or drinking of it. Its immeasurable grandeur is indescribable even by the pure intelligence of Sarasvati.

---

1 "Truth has never been grasped on all sides, nor has ever been embraced entirely by the mind of man; and no one can gaze attentively on that truth which is always old, without discovering there beauties that are always new." These words of Abp. Dechamps express in abstract form the very same idea that the Hindú poet has presented in the concrete.

The city, exalting to Ráma's heaven,[1] beautiful, celebrated through all worlds, is so all-purifying that countless as is the number of animate species that result from the four modes of birth, yet every individual that is freed from the body at Avadh is free for ever. Knowing it to be in every way charming, a bestower of success and a mine of auspiciousness, I there made a beginning of my sacred song, which will destroy in those who hear it the mad phrensy of of lust; its mere name—lake of Ráma's acts—serves to refresh the ear, while the soul like an elephant escaping from a forest on fire with lust, plunges into it and gains relief; delight of the sages, as composed by Sambhu, holy and beautiful; consuming the three ill conditions of sin, sorrow and want; putting an end to the evil practices and impurities of the wicked world; first made by Mahádeva and buried in the deep lake of his own soul till at an auspicious moment he declared it to Umá; thus Siva looking into his own soul and rejoicing gave it the excellent name of Rám-charit-mánas.[2] And this is the blessed legend that I repeat: hear it, good people, reverently and attentively.

Dohá 44.

Now meditating upon Umá and upon him who has a bull emblazoned on his standard (*i.e.*, Mahádeva) I explain the connection, showing how it is a lake and in what manner it is formed, and for what reason it has spread through the world.[3]

Chaupái 36.

By the blessing of Sambhu a bright idea has come into the poet Tulsi's mind regarding the Rám-charit-mánas,

---

1 The compound may also mean—giving a home to Ráma—and probably both meanings are intended.

2 From this it will be seen that the name which Tulsi Dás himself gave to his poem was not 'the Rámáyana,' but the Rám-charit-mánas,' a name. which may be interpreted to mean either the lake or the soul of Ráma's acts. In the stanza above translated the word is first taken in the one sense and then in the other, and as there is no English word with the same double signification, some obscurity is unavoidable.

3 The words may also bear the following secondary meaning; I relate the whole history, showing how the great soul became incarnate, and why it dwelt in the world.

which I will state as well as I can, subject to the correction of those good people whose attention I invite. The heart is as it were a deep place in a land of good thoughts, the Vedas and Puránas are the sea, and the saints are as clouds, which rain down praises of Ráma in sweet, grateful and auspicious showers; the sportive actions related of him are like the inherent purity and cleansing power of rain-water; while devotion, which is beyond the power of words to describe, is its sweetness and coolness. When such a shower falls on the rice-fields of virtue, it gives new life to the faithful, and as its holy drops fall to the earth they are collected in the channel supplied by the ears, and flowing into the lake of the soul fill it and then settle down permanently, cool, beautiful and refreshing.

Dohá 45.

This pure and holy lake has four beautiful *gháts*, viz., the four charming dialogues contrived by divine wisdom.

Chaupái 37.

The seven Books are its beautiful flights of steps, which the eyes of the soul delight to look upon; the unqualified and unsullied greatness of Raghupati may be described as its clear and deep expanse; the glory of Ráma and Síta as its ambrosial water; the similes as its pretty wavelets; the stanzas as its beautiful lotus beds; the elegance of expression as lovely mother-of-pearl: the *chhands*, *sorathas*, and couplets as many-coloured lotus flowers: the incomparable sense, sentiment, and language as the pollen, filaments and fragrance of the lotus; the exalted action as beautiful swarms of bees; the sage moral reflections as swans; the rhythm, involutions, and other poetical artifices as diverse graceful kinds of fish; the precepts regarding the four ends of life, the wise sayings, the thoughtful judgments, the nine styles of composition,[1] the prayers, penance, abstraction

1 The nine poetical styles (or Indian Muses) are the Sringár-ras, or erotic; the Hásyaras, or comic; the Karuná-ras, or elegiac; the Bir-ras, or heroic; the Raudra-ras, or tragic; the Bhavának-ras, or melancholic; the Vibhatsa-ras, or satiric; the Shánt-ras, or didactic: and the Adbhut-ras, or sensational.

and asceticism, of which examples are given, are all beautiful living creatures in the lake; eulogies on the faithful, the saints and the holy name are like flocks of water-birds; the religious audience are like circling mango groves, and their faith like the spring season ; the expositions of all the phases of devotion and of tenderness and generosity are like the trees and cannopying creepers ; self-denial and holy vows are their flowers, and wisdom their fruit ; the love for Hari's feet as the sound of the Vedas : and all other stories and episodes as the parrots and cuckoos and many kinds of birds.

Dohá 46.

The hearer's emotion is some grove, garden or parterre, where sportive birds symbolise his delight and Piety the gardener pours a stream of devotion from the water-pot of his eyes.

Chaupái 38.

Those who diligently recite these lays are like the vigilant guardians of the lake; the men and women who reverently hear them, these excellent people are like its owners. Sensual wretches are like the cranes and crows that have no part in such a pond nor ever come near it ; for here are no prurient and seductive stories like snails, frogs and scum on the water, and therefore the lustful crow and greedy crane, if they do come, are disappointed. There is much difficulty in getting to this lake, and it is only by the favour of Ráma that any one reaches it. For bad company makes much steepness and difficulty in the road; their evil sayings are so many tigers, lions and serpents; the various entanglements of domestic affairs are vast insurmountable mountains; sensual desires are like a dense forest full of wild delusion ; and unsound reasoning is a raging flood.

Dohá 47.

For those who have not the support of faith, nor the company of the saints, nor fervent love for Raghunáth, for them this lake is very hard of access.

Chaupái 39.

Again, if any one laboriously makes his way to it, but becomes over-powered by sleep and feverishness, strange torpor and numbness settle on his soul, and though he is on the spot, the luckless wretch makes no ablution. Having neither bathed in the lake nor drunk of it he goes away in his pride, and when some one comes to inquire of him he abuses it. But no difficulties deter those whom Ráma regards with affection. They reverently bathe, are relieved from the fierce flames of sin, sorrow, and pain, and being sincerely devoted to Ráma will never abandon it. If, my friend, you would bathe in this lake, be diligent to keep company with the good. As for myself, having thus with the mind's eye contemplated it, my poetical faculty has become clear and profound, my heart swells with joy and rapture and overflows in a torrent of ecstatic devotion. My song pours on like a river flooded with Ráma's bright renown; like the river Sarju, fountain of bliss, with piety and theology for its two fair banks; a holy stream rejoicing the pious soul (*or* born of the Mánas lake,) sweeping away all worldly impurities like trees and roots on its bank.

Dohá 48.

The three kinds of hearers in the assembly are like the towns, villages, and hamlets on the river-side; while the saints are like the incomparable city of Avadh, full of all that is auspicious.

Chaupái 40.

The beautiful Sarju, as it were the glory of Ráma has united with the Ganges of devotion; and the magnificent river Son, like the warlike power of Ráma and his brother, has joined them as a third. Between the two, the Ganges stream of devotion shines clear in its wisdom and self-control, while the combined flood destroying the triple curse of humanity is absorbed in the mighty ocean of very Ráma. The united stream of the Mánas-born Sarju and the Ganges purifies the pious listener, while the various tales and episodes interspersed here and there are the groves and gardens on its opposite banks; the details of the marriage and wedding procession of Umá and Siva are like the innumerable fish in the water; the joy and gladness that attended Ráma's birth are like beautiful swarms of bees and the ripple of the lake.

Dohá 49.

The childish sports of the four brothers are like the goodly lotus flowers ; the virtuous king and queen and their court like the bees and water-birds.

Chaupái 41.

The charming story of Sítá's marriage like the bright gleam of the flashing river; the many ingenious questions like the boats on the stream; the appropriate and judicious answers like the boatmen; again, the argumentative discussions show like crowding travellers; the wrath of Bhrigunáth like the rushing torrent ; Ráma's soft speech like the well-arranged *ghats*; the marriage festivities of Ráma and Lakshman like the grateful swell of the tide; the thrill of pleasure that spreads through the delighted audience like the ecstatic feelings of the virtuous bathers; the auspicious preparations for marking Ráma's forehead with the *tilak* like the crowds assembled on holidays; and like river-mud is Kaikeyi's evil counsel, the cause of many calamities.

Dohá 50.

Like prayers and sacrifices effectual to remove every misfortune are Bharat's virtuous acts; while the corruptions of the world and sinful men and slanderers are like the scum on the water and the cranes and crows.

Chaupái 42.

This river of glory is beautiful in each of the six seasons, bright and holy exceedingly at all times. The story of the marriage of Siva with the daughter of the snowy mountains is like the winter; the glad rejoicings at the Lord's birth are like the dewy season; the account of the preparations for Ráma's wedding are like the delightful and auspicious spring; Ráma's intolerable banishment is like the hot weather, and story of the rough journeyings like the blazing sun and the wind; his encounters with fierce demons, by which he gladdens the hosts of heaven, are like the rains, that refresh the fields; the prosperity of his reign, his meekness and greatness are like the clear, bountiful and lovely autumn;[1] the recital of the virtues of Síta, that jewel of faithful wives, is as the undefiled and excellent water; the amiability of Bharat as its unvarying coolness.

Dohá 51.

Their looks and words at meeting, their mutual love and laughter, the true fraternal affection of the four brothers, are as the water's sweet odour.

Chaupái 43.

My suppliant address and self-depreciation and modesty correspond to the singular lightness of good water, which is anything but a defect. This marvellous lymph works its effect by the mere hearing, quenching the thirst of desire and cleansing the soul of impurity; it resuscitates true love to Ráma and puts an end to all the sin and sorrow of the world; draining life of its weariness; comforting with true comfort; destroying sin and pain and poverty and error; dispelling lust and passion and phrensy and infatuation, and promoting pure intelligence and detachment from the world. Those who reverently drink or bathe in this stream, from their soul is effaced all sin and distress; those who do not cleanse their heart in it are wretches whom the world has ruined, turning back, hapless creatures, like a panting deer that has seen a river in a mirage!

Dohá 52—54.

Thus I have declared to the best of my ability the virtues of this excellent water, and having plunged my own soul

1 The six Hindu seasons to which allusion is here made are Hemant, winter; Sisir, the early spring; Basant, the spring; Grishm, the hot weather; Vársha, the rains; and Sarad, the autumn.

in it, and ever remembering Bhaváni and Sankara, I proceed with my delectable story. I will first repeat in substance the original conversation, with the questions put by Bharadvája when he found the Muni Yájnavalkya; and laying my soul at the lotus feet of Raghupati and thus securing his patronage, I will sing the meeting of the two great saints and their auspicious discourse.

Chaupái 44.

At Prayág lives the saint Bharadvája, devoted beyond measure to Ráma's feet, a self-restrained ascetic full of sobriety and benevolence, supremely skilled in divine knowledge. In the month of Mágh, when the sun enters the sign of Capricorn, every one visits this chief of holy places; gods, demi-gods, *kinnars*, and men in troops, all devoutly bathe in the triple flood and worship the lotus feet of Mádhava while they have the happiness of touching the imperishable fig-tree. At Bharadvája's hallowed hermitage—so charming a spot that even the saint loved it—is ever a concourse of seers and sages come to bathe at the holiest of all holy places; and having with gladness performed their ablutions at break of day, they converse together on the glories of Hari.

Dohá 55.

Discussing the nature of the deity, the kinds of religious observance and the classification of primordial entities; and declaring faith in God to be the epitome of wisdom and spiritual detachment.[1]

Chaupái 45.

After thus bathing every day that the sun is in Capricorn, they again return each to his own cell, and every year there is a similar rejoicing when the saints meet for

1 This cuplet sums up the characteristics of the principal systems of Hindu philosophy : the Vedánta being chiefly concerned with and indeed defined as, *Bráhma Jijnasa*, 'an inquiry into the nature of God'; the Mimánsa being a system of ritualism and Vedic observances;' the Sánkhya 'a synthetic enumeration' of the primary germs, or elements, out of which creation has been evolved ; and the later eclectic Vaishnava school declaring that the only one thing needful is *bhakti*, 'religious faith.'

the annual ablution. On one occasion, when the bathing time was over, and all the holy men had left, Bharadvája clasped by the feet and detained the supremely wise saint Yájnavalkya, and having reverently laved his lotus feet and seated him on a pre-eminent throne, he with religious ceremony extolled the saint's glory, and finally thus addrest him in mildest of tones, "Sir, I have a great doubt, while in your grasp are all the mysteries of the Veda; I am afraid and ashamed to speak, but if I speak not, I lose a great opportunity.

Dohá 56.

This, sir, is a maxim of all the saints, and is also declared by the Vedas and Puránas, that there is no sound wisdom in his breast who conceals aught from his ghostly father.

Chaupái 46.

Remembering this, I lay bare my folly—take pity, my lord, on your faithful servant and dispel it. The might of Ráma's name is immeasurable; so tell the saints, the Puránas and the Vedic commentaries; the immortal Sambhu, who is the Lord Siva, the perfection of wisdom and goodness, is ever repeating it; though all the four groups of animate beings in the world attain to salvation if they die in his city Kási, yet O king of saints, it is by the virtue of Ráma's name; and therefore Siva in his compassion enjoins its use. I ask of you, my lord, who is this Ráma? be gracious enough to instruct me. There is one Ráma, the prince of Avadh, whose acts are known throughout the world who suffered infinite distress by the loss of his wife, and waxing wrath slew Rávan in battle.

Dohá 57.

Is it this Ráma, my lord, or another, whose name Tripurári is ever repeating? Ponder the matter well and tell me, O wisest and most faithful of men.

Chaupái 47.

Tell me the whole history in full, my master, so that my overpowering perplexity may be solved." Said Yájnavalkya with a smile,—"All the glory of Raghupati is known to you; you are a votary of his in heart, word and deed; I understand your stratagem. Wishing to hear the marvellous tale of Ráma's achievements, you have questioned me with an affectation of great simplicity. Listen then, my son, with devout attention while I repeat the fair legend, which vanquishes every monstrous error, as dread Devi vanquished the demon Mahishásur, but which is drunk in by the saints as the light of the moon by the *chakor*. When a similar doubt was suggested by Bhaváni, Mahádeva expounded the matter:

Dohá 58.

And I now, as best I can, repeat their conversation, noting both its time and occasion; on hearing it, my friend, all difficulties vanish.

Chaupái 48.

Once upon a time, in the second age of the world, Sambhu visited the Rishi Agastya; with him went the mother of the world, the faithful Bhaváni. The hermit made obeisance, for he recognized them as the sovereigns of the universe, and recited the story of Ráma, with which Mahádeva was delighted. The hermit then asked him about true faith in Hari; and Sambhu instructed him, for he saw him to be deserving. In such converse the mountain-lord Mahádeva passed some days there, but finally took his leave and returned home with the daughter of Daksha. Now at that time there had become incarnate, in the family of Raghu, Hari the detroyer of the burdens of the world, who at his father's word sorrowfully left the throne and wandered, immortal god though he was, in the Dandaka forest.

Dohá 59.

Siva kept pondering as he went, 'How can I obtain a sight of him? for every one knows that the lord has become incarnate secretly; if I visit him, every one will know who he is.'

Sorahtá 5.

In Sankara's heart was a great tumult, but Sati did not comprehend the mystery; says Tulsi, the hope of an interview filled his soul with agitation and his eyes with wistfulness.

Chaupái 49.

'Rávan has obtained the boon of death at the hands of man only and the lord has willed Bráhma's word to come true. If I do not go to meet him, I shall ever regret it': but all that he could do he could not hit upon a plan. At the very time that he was thus lost in thought, the ten-headed Rávan, taking with him the vile Márícha, all at once assumed the form of a false deer and treacherously in his folly carried off Síta, not knowing the lord's great power. When Ráma returned with his brother from the chase and saw the empty hermitage his eyes filled with tears; like a mortal man distressed by the loss of his mistress, he wanders through the forest in search of her, he and his brother; and he who knows neither union nor bereavement manifested all the pangs of separation.

Dohá 60.

Ráma's ways are most mysterious; only the supremely wise can comprehend them; the dull of soul and the sensual imagine something quite different.

Chaupái 50.

Then it was that Sambhu saw Ráma, and great joy arose in his soul. His eyes were filled with the vision of the most beautiful, but it was no fitting time to make himself known, and he passed on exclaming: 'Hail, Supreme Being, redeemer of the world.' But as he went on his way with Sati, his whole body thrilled with delight; and in Sati's soul, when she observed her lord's emotion, a great doubt arose,—'To Sankara, the universally adored and sovereign lord, gods, men and saints all bow the head; yet he has made obeisance to this prince, saluting him as the

Supreme God, and is so enraptured with his beauty that it is only to-day he has felt what love is.

Dohá 61.

What! the omnipresent and unbegotten God, the creator, who has neither parts nor passions, and is no respecter of persons, whom not even the Veda can comprehend,[1] has he taken the form of a man?

Chaupái 51.

According to what Siva says, though Vishnu in heaven's behalf assumes a human shape, he remains all-wise: yet here, as if quite at a loss, he is hunting for his wife, this fountain of wisdom, this lord of Lakshmi, this vanquisher of demons. Still Sambhu's words cannot be false, nor can his knowledge be gainsaid. Thus an infinite doubt has come into my mind, and there is no way of solving it.' Although Bhaváni did not speak out, Mahádeva can read the heart and knew her thoughts, and said,—"Listen to me, Sati; you are just like a woman, but you should not entertain these doubts; this is that Ráma, my special patron, whose story was sung by the Rishi Agastya; in whom I exhorted the saint to have faith, and who is ever worshipped by seers and sages.

Chhand 2.

Seers and sages, saints and hermits, fix on him their reverent gaze,
And in faint and trembling accents Holy Scripture hymns his praise.
He, the omnipresent spirit, lord of heaven and earth and hell,
To redeem his people, freely has vouchsafed with men to dwell."

Sorathá 6.

Though he spoke thus time after time, his words made no impression upon her; and at last Mahádeva, recognizing Ráma's deceptive power, smiled and said:

1 The reference is to such texts as the following in the Upanishads; "From whom words turn back, together with the mind, not reaching him" (Taittiriya, II, 9). "The eye goes not thither, nor speech, nor mind" (Kena, I, 3). "Unthinkable, unspeakable" [Mandukya, 7]. The process of Christian theology is similarly negative and agnostic: it sets forth what God is not, rather than what He is; since it is impossible for the lower nature to know the higher.

Chaupái 52.

"As the doubt in your mind is so great that it will not leave you till you have put the fact to the test, I will stay here in the shade of this fig-tree till you come back to me, after having evolved some device by which to satisfy your overpowering doubt." So Sati went by Siva's order, saying to herself,—'Come now, what shall I do?' while Sambhu reflected,—"There is mischief in store for Sati; her doubts will not yield to my arguments; truly no good can ever be brought about against the will of fate; whatever Ráma has ordained will come to pass, so why spin out any longer discussion?" So saying, he began the repetition of Hari's name, while Sati drew nigh to the Lord of grace.

Dohá 62.

After many an anxious thought she assumed the form of Síta and went and stood in the way where the king of heaven was coming.

Chaupái 53.

When Lakshman saw her in her disguise, he was much astonished and perplext. Wise as he was, he could say nothing, but discreetly waited for the revelation of the lord. He, the heavenly king, detected the deceit; for he sees all things alike and knows the heart, the all-wise lord Ráma, the mere thought of whom disperses error. Yet even him Sati attempted to deceive—see how inveterate woman's nature is. But Ráma, acknowledging the effect of his own delusive power, with a sweet smile and folded hands saluted her, mentioning both her own name and that of her father, and added,—'Where is Mahádeva, and why are you wandering alone in the forest?'

Dohá 63.

When she heard these simple but profound words, a great awe came upon her and she returned to Mahádeva, full of fear and distress.

Chaupái. 54.

'I would not listen to Sankara, but must go and expose my folly to Ráma ; now what answer can I give ?' Her distress was most grievous. Then Ráma, perceiving her vexation, manifested in part his glory, and as Sati went on her way she beheld a marvellous vision ; in front of her were Ráma, Síta and Lakshman ; when again she looked back, there too she saw the Lord with his brother and Síta in beauteous apparel ; whichever way she turned her eyes, there was the lord enthroned with saints and learned doctors ministering to him. Innumerable Sivas and Bráhmas and Vishnus, each excelling in majesty, bowing at his feet and doing homage ; all the host of heaven with their different attributes.

Dohá 64.

Sati too and Sarasvati and Lakshmi in marvellous multiplicity of form, according to the various appearances assumed by their lords, Bráhma, Vishnu and Mahádeva.

Chaupái 55.

Each separate vision of Ráma was attended by all the gods and their wives, and by the whole animate creation with all its multitudinous species. But while the adoring gods appeared in diverse dresses, there was no diversity of form in Ráma. Though she saw many Rámas, and with him an oft-repeated Síta, it was always the same Ráma, the same Lakshman, and the same Síta. Sati was awe-striken as she gazed ; with fluttering heart and unconscious frame she closed her eyes and sank upon the ground. When again she looked up, she saw nothing, and oft bowing her head at Ráma's feet, she returned to the spot where Mahádeva was waiting for her.

Dohá 65.

When she drew near, he smiled and asked if all were well, saying,—'Tell me now the whole truth, how did you put him to the test ?'

Chaupái 56.

Sati remembered the glory of the lord and in her awe concealed the truth from Siva, saying: 'O sir, I tried no test, but like you simply made obeisance. I was confident that what you said could not be false.' Then Sankara perceived by contemplation and understood all that Sati had done, and bowed to the might of Ráma's delusive power, which had been sent forth to put a lying speech into Sati's mouth. 'The will of heaven and fate are strong;' thus he reflected, in great distress of mind; 'as Sati has taken Síta's form, if now I treat her as my wife, my past devotion will be all cancelled, and it will be a sin to me.

Dohá 66.

My love is too great to be forgotten, yet to indulge it is criminal.' He uttered not a word aloud, but in his heart was sore distress.

Chaupái 57.

At last, having bowed his head at Ráma's feet and meditated on his name, he thus resolved and made a vow in his mind,—'So long as Sati remains as she is now, I will never touch her.' With this firm determination he turned homewards, repeating his Ráma rosary, and as he went there was a jubilant cry in the heaven,—'Glory to thee, Mahàdeva, for thy staunch devotion; who other but thou, O lord most strong in faith, would make such a vow?' Sati was troubled when she heard the heavenly voice and tremblingly asked Siva,—'Tell me, O true and gracious lord, what was the vow?' But though she asked once and again he told her not.

Dohá 67.

Then she guessed of herself,—'The all-wise has discovered it all, though I attempted to deceive him; silly and senseless woman that I am.'

Sorathá 7.

Water and milk if mixed together are both sold as milk; but see how like the union is to that of lovers; the introduction of a drop of acid, or of a lie, at once causes a separation.

Chaupái 58.

Deep in thought and reflecting on what she had done, no words could express her infinite sorrow, and she kept saying to herself,—'The gracious but impenetrable Siva has not openly mentioned my offence, but my lord has abandoned me.' Thus disturbed in soul by Sankara's sternness and thinking of her sin, she could say nothing, but all the more smouldered within like a furnace. When Mahádeva saw her so sorrowful, he began to amuse her with pleasant tales, relating various legends all the way till he came to Kailás. Then recalling his vow, he seated himself under a fig-tree in the attitude of contemplation and by an immediate control of all his members passed into a long and unbroken trance.[1]

Dohá 68.

There Sati dwelt in Kailás, sorrowing grievously; not a soul knew her secret, but each day that she passed was like an age.

Chaupái 59.

Ever growing more sick at heart, "When shall I emerge from this sea of trouble? I who put a slight upon Ràma and took my husband's word to be a lie. The Creator has repaid me and has done as I deserved. Now, O God, think not thus within thyself that I can live without Sankara. The anguish of my heart is beyond words; but I take comfort when I remember Ráma, whom men call the lord of compassion, and whom the Vedas hymn as

1 Literally translated, the above passage would stand thus:—"Vrisha-ketu, perceiving that Sati was distrest, began to amuse her with pleasant tales, relating various legends all the way till Visavnáth arrived at Kailás. Then recalling his vow, Sambhu seated himself under a fig-tree in the attitude of contemplation and by an immediate control of all his members Sankara passed into a long and unbroken trance." As the use of many different names, Vrisha-ketu, Visvanáth, Sambhu, and Sankara—all to designate the same person, viz., Mahadeva—is likely to perplex an English reader, I have in this and similar passages omitted them and simply substituted the personal pronoun.

remover of distress. Him I supplicate with folded hands. May this body of mine be speedily dissolved. As my love for Siva is unfeigned in thought, word and deed, and as his word cannot fail,

Dohá 69.

Do thou, O impartial lord, hear my prayer and speedily devise a plan by which I may die without pain and avoid this intolerable calamity."

Chaupái 60.

Thus sorrowing and weighed down by grievous and unutterable pain, the royal lady had passed 87,000 years, when the immortal Sambhu awoke from his trance and began to repeat Ráma's name. Then Sati perceived that he had returned to consciousness and went and bowed herself at his feet. He gave her a seat in his presence and began reciting the divine praises. Now at that time Daksha was reigning, and the Creator seeing him to be thoroughly fit had made him a king of kings. But when he had obtained great dominion he waxed exceeding proud. Never was a man born into the world whom kingship did not intoxicate.

Dohá 70.

By the priests' suggestion all began preparing a great sacrifice for Daksha, and the gods who accept oblations were all courteously invited to attend.

Chaupái 61.

Kinnars, serpents, saints, Gandharvas, all the gods and their wives, except Vishnu, Bráhma and Mahádeva, proceeded thither in their chariots. Sati saw the strangely beautiful procession going through the sky, with the heavenly nymphs singing so melodiously that any saint's meditation would be broken by the sound of it, and she asked Siva its reason; whereupon he explained. Then was she glad when she heard of her father's sacrifice and thought, —" If my lord will allow me, I will make it an excuse for going to stay a few days with him." It was such sore pain to leave her lord, that she long dare not speak, remembering her transgression ; but at last with soft and timid voice, overflowing with modesty and affection, she said :—

Dohá 71.

'There is great rejoicing at my father's house; with my gracious lord's permission I will duteously go and see it.'

Chaupái 62.

Said he, —'It would please me well ; but there is a difficulty, as you have not been invited. Daksha has summoned all his other daughters, but has left you out on account of his quarrel with me, for he took offence at my behaviour in Bráhma's court, and that is the reason he slights me to-day. If you go without being asked, there will be loss of temper, love and honour. One may go, no doubt, without an invitation to the house of a friend, or master, or father or confessor ; but no good can result from going where an enemy is present.' Thus Sambhu warned her over and over again ; but fate was too strong, she would not be convinced. Said the lord,—'To go unasked is not right, as I take it.'

Dohá 72.

When Mahadeva saw that no amount of talking would make her stay, he appointed his chief ministers as her escort and allowed her to depart.

Chaupái 63.

When Bhaváni came to her father's house, from fear of Daksha no one greeted her ; only her mother met her kindly and her sisters received her with a smile. Daksha uttered not a word of salutation and burned with rage to see her. When Sati went to look at the sacrifice, she could nowhere find anything for Sambhu: then Sankara's words came back into her mind, and her heart so burned within her at the slight upon her lord, that the former pain she had felt was not to be compared to her present emotion. There are grievous pains in the world, but nothing so bad as a family slight. The more she thought of it, the more furious she grew, though her mother tried hard to pacify her.

Dohá 73.

This insult to Siva could not be borne; her soul refused to be pacified: and thrusting away from her the shrinking crowd, she cried in wild accents: —

Chaupái 64.

" Hear, all ye elders of the assembly, who have talked over this slight upon Sankara. Speedily shall ye reap your due reward, and dearly shall my father rue it. Whenever blasphemy is spoken against the saints, or Sambhu, or Vishnu, the ordinance is either to tear out the blasphemer's tongue, if it is in your power, or else to close your ears and run away. The universal spirit, the great lord, Purári, the father of the world, the friend of all, he it is whom my besotted father has reviled. Therefore this body of mine, begotten of his seed, I hasten to abandon, and impress on my soul the image of him who bears the moon as his crest and a bull as his device." As she thus spoke, the flames consumed her body; a great cry of lamentation went up from the whole assembly.

Dohá 74.

When Sambhu's attendants heard of Sati's death, they began to destroy all the sacrificial offerings; but the great saint Bhrigu, seeing the destruction, came and saved them.

Chaupái 65.

When Sambhu got the news he sent Bírbhadra in his wrath, who went and scattered the sacrifice and requited all the gods as they deserved. Daksha's act is famous throughout the world as an example of hostility to Sambhu; and as the story is so well known, I have told it in brief. Sati at her death asked this boon of Hari, that in every successive birth she might show her love to Siva. On this account she was born in the form of Párvati, as the daughter of King Himálaya. From the time that she entered the house of the monarch of mountains, it was pervaded by fortune and prosperity, and hermits made their homes all about it, in fit places assigned them by the king.

Dohá 75.

Strange trees of many kinds, with never-failing flowers and fruits, appeared on the beautiful hills, and mines of jewels discoverd themselves.

Chaupái 66.

All the rivers flowed with the purest water; birds, deer and bees were all equally joyous; every animal forgot its instinctive antipathies and dwelt lovingly on the mountain, which was as glorified by Girija's coming as a man is glorified by the spirit of faith. Every day was some new delight in the king's palace, and Bráhma and all the gods vied in singing its praises. On hearing the news, Nárad went to visit the mountain king, who received him with high honour and bathed his feet and led him to a throne. The queen too bowed her head before him and sprinkled the whole house with the water sanctified by his use. Then the king told all his good fortune and summoned his daughter also to the presence and said;—

Dohá 76.

"Thou who knowest all time, past, present, or future, and who hast traversed the whole universe, tell me, best of saints, after well considering the matter, what there is good and what bad about my daughter."

Chaupái 67.

The saint replied with a smile, in soft but profound words,—"Your daughter is a mine of perfection, beautiful, amiable and intelligent, whether she be called Umá, or Ambiká, or Bhaváni; a maiden with every quality that endears a wife to a husband. Firm as a rock her good fortune, and in her her parents are blessed; she shall be worshipped throughout the whole world, and in her service shall be fruition of every desire. Through her name woman shall be enabled to walk the path of wifely duty, though it be like the edge of a sword. Such, O king, are thy daughter's merits; but you have now to hear two or three drawbacks.

A person who has neither beauty nor dignity, without father or mother, an ascetic with no thought for any one,

Dohá 77.

A mendicant recluse with matted hair, a celibate with naked body and hideous accoutrements—such a one shall be her lord, as I read by the lines on her palm."

Chaupái. 68.

When the father and mother heard the saint's words, and knew they must be true, they became sad ; but Umá rejoiced ; nor did Nárad even understand, for all seemed affected alike, though the cause was different.[1] All Girijá's attendants, and she herself and her father and her mother Maina, were trembling and had their eyes full of tears ; but Umá cherished the saint's words in her heart, saying, —'They cannot be false :' and her love for Siva's lotus feet revived ; though the doubt remained, How difficult to find him ! But as it was no fitting time for a disclosure, she suppressed her emotion and went back to the bosom of her playmates. They and the parents were distrest by the thought of the saint's infallible utterance, and the king, with an effort, cried aloud,—" O sir, tell me what remedy to devise."

Dohá—78.

Said the saint,—"Hear, O Himavant, what fate has written on the forehead, nor god nor demon, man, serpent, nor saint, is able to efface.

Chaupái 69.

Yet one mode of escape I will tell you, which by the help of heaven may avail. Umá's bridegroom will infallibly be such a one as I have described to you ; but all the bad points that I have enumerated I find to exist in Siva. If a marriage with him can be brought about, every one will account his vices as virtues. Though Hari takes a serpent for his couch, the wise hold it no fault in him ; though

---

1 That is to say, they all shed tears, but the parents wept for sorrow and Umà for joy.

fire and the sun devour anything they come across, no one therefore calls them blind; though its stream flows in one place pure and in another sullied, no one would call the Ganges impure. The powerful, my friend, are always faultless, like the sun, fire, or the Ganges.

Dohá 79.

The fool who in the pride of knowledge presumes to copy them, saying 'it is the same for a man as for a god,' shall be cast into hell for as long as the world lasts.[1]

Chaupái 70.

Though they know that wine is made with Ganges water, yet saints will never taste it; but the Ganges itself, wherever found, is always pure; and herein is seen the difference between mastery and subjection[2]. The lord Sambhu is all-powerful and an alliance with him is in every way auspicious. But it is hard to propitiate him; yet if penance is undergone, he is quickly satisfied. If, then, your daughter will practise penance, Tripurári will be able to erase the lines of fate; and though there may be many bridegrooms in the world, the only one for her is Siva, and none else. He answers prayer, relieves the distress of the faithful, is full of compassion and a delight to his servants; unless he is propitiated, no one will attain his heart's desire, though he practise infinite penance and authority."

---

1 A similar doctrine is inculcated in the Xth Book of the Bhágavata Purána: "The transgression of virtue and the daring acts which are withnessed in superior beings must not be charged as faults against those glorious persons. Let no one but a superior being ever even in thought practise the same. Seeing, then, that the saints are uncontrolled and act as they please, how can there be any restraint upon the Supreme, when he has voluntarily assumed a body." Granted those reasonable limitations which the Hindu mind, with its tendency to exaggeration, was unfortunately so prone to neglect, the sentiment is essentially true and is recommended by Catholic theologians Thus Cardinal Newman writes,—"It never surprises me to read anything unusual in the devotions of a saint. Such men are on a level very different from our own, and we cannot understand them. I hold this to be an important canon in the lives of the saints, according to the words of the apostle,—'The spiritual man judges all things, and he himself is judged of no one.' But we may refrain from judging, without proceeding to imitate. The sains are beyond us, and we must use them as patterns, not as copies.

2 The meaning is, wine, though made of Ganges water, is still impure but the Ganges itself is always pure, even though wine may have been poured into it.

Dohá 80.

So saying, and with his thoughts fixed on Hari, Nárad gave his blessing to the king and added,—'Now fear not, all will turn our well.'

Chaupái 71.

Having thus spoken, the saint returned to Bráhma's court. Hear now the end of the story how it came about. Maina finding her husband alone said to him,—"My lord, I do not understand the saint's meaning. If the bridegroom and his position and family are unobjectionable and such as befit your daughter, then conclude the marriage; but if not, let her remain a maiden: for, my lord, Umá is as dear to me as life If she does not get a husband worthy of her, every one will say the mountain-king is himself a mere block. Remember this, and so marry her that there may be no heart-burning hereafter." With these words she laid her head at his feet. The king affectionately replied,—"Sooner shall fire break out in the moon than Nárad's word be gainsaid.

Dohá 81.

Put away all anxiety, my dear, and fix your thoughts on the good God who has created Párvati and who will protect her.

Chaupái 72.

Now, if you have any love for your child, go and thus admonish her,—'Penance is the means of approach to Siva, and there is no other way of escaping sorrow. Nárad's words are pregnant and full of meaning; Mahádeva is in fact beautiful and accomplished; recognize this truth and doubt not; he is in every way irreproachable.'" When she heard her husband's words she was glad of heart and at once rose and went where Uma was. On seeing the girl her eyes filled with tears, and she affectionately took her in her lap and again and again pressed her to her bosom; but could not say a word for the choking in her throat. Then the mother of the universe, the all-wise Bhaváni, her mother's delight, said softly :—

Dohá 82.

"Listen, mother, to the vision I am about to tell you ; a fair and lovely Bráhman prince has thus instructed me :—

Chaupái 73.

Go, mountain-maid, and practise penance, reflecting that Nárad's words are infallibly true. Your parents, too, are pleased with the idea, for penance is full of peace and puts an end to pain and sin. By the virtue of penance the Creator made the world ; by the virtue of penance Vishnu redeems the world; by virtue of penance Sambhu destroys it. It is by the virtue of penance that the Great Serpent supports the burden of the earth, and in short the whole creation, Bhaváni, depends upon penance; do you then practise it." On hearing these words her mother was astounded, and sent for the king and declared to him the vision. Then, after consoling her parents in every possible way, Umá in gladness of heart commenced her penance; while they and all their loving dependants grew sad of face, nor could speak a word.

Dohá 83.

Then came Vedasiras[1] and instructed them all; and when they had heard of Párvati's glory they were comforted.

Chaupái 74.

But Umá, cherishing in her heart the feet of her dear lord, went into the forest and began her penance. Though her delicate frame was little fit for such austerities, she abandoned all food and became absorbed in prayer, her devotion so growing day by day that all bodily wants were forgotten, and her soul was wholly given to penance. For a thousand years she ate only roots and fruits; for a hundred years she lived on vegetables; for some days her only sustenance was water and air, and on some she

---

1 Vedasiras, a son of Márkandeya and Murdhanya was, by his wife Pívari, the Progenitor of the Bhárgava Bráhmans.

maintained a yet more absolute fast. For three thousand years she ate only dry leaves of the *bel*[1] tree that had fallen to the ground, and at last abstained even from dry leaves, whence she acquired the name of *aparna* ('the leafless'). At the sight of her emaciated frame, Bráhma's deep voice resounded through the heavens,—

Dohá 84.

"Hear, daughter of the mountain-king! your desire is accomplished; cease all these intolerable afflictions: Tripurári will soon be yours.

Chaupái 75.

Though there have been many saints, both resolute and wise, not one, Bhaváni, has performed such penance as this: submit now to my commands, knowing them to be ever true and ever good. When your father comes to call you, cease to resist and go home with him; and when the seven sages meet you, know this to be the test of the heavenly prediction." When she heard Bráhma's voice thus speaking from on high, Girijá thrilled with delight. Now with her we have done for a time, while we turn to Sambhu. From the day when Sati's spirit left the body he became a rigid ascetic, ever telling his beads in Ráma's name, and attending the public recitations in his honour:

Dohá 85.

Even he, Siva, the pure intelligence, the abode of bliss, exempt from lust, frenzy and delusion, wanders about on earth with his heart fixed on Hari, the joy of the whole world;

Chaupái 76.

Now instructing saints in wisdom, now expounding Ráma's praises, and though himself the all-wise and passionless lord god, yet saddened by the sadness of a bereaved disciple. In this way many ages passed, while his love for Ráma daily increased. Then the generous and merciful

1 The *bel* tree (*Ægle Marmelos*) is specially sacred to *Siva*.

god, full of grace and benignity, seeing his steadfastness and affection, and the unchangeable stamp of devotion on his soul, became manifest in all his glory and lauded him highly, for none other had ever accomplished such a vow. In diverse ways he instructed him, telling him of Párvati's birth and of her virtuous deeds, all at full length, in his infinite compassion.

Dohá 86.

"Now, Siva, if you have any love for me, listen to my request : go and marry the mountain-maid and do as I ask you."

Chaupái 77.

Said Siva,—"Though it is not what I approve, yet when a master speaks he must not be gainsaid. I must needs bow to your order, for obedience is the highest duty. If a man would prosper, he must do, without thinking, as he is told by his parents, or his confessor, or his superior ; you are in every way my benefactor, and I bow to your commands." The lord was pleased when he heard Sankara's reply so full of faith, knowledge, and religious feeling, and said,—"Hara, your vow has been kept ; attend now to what I have told you." So saying he vanished, but the vision remained impressed in Sankara's soul. Then came the seven Rishis to visit him, and he addressed them thus in pleasant wise :—

Dohá 87.

"Go to Párvati and make trial of her love, and then send her father to fetch her home and remove all his doubts."

Chaupái 78.

When the Rishis saw Gauri, she seemed to them like Penance personified, and they cried—Hear, O daughter of the mountain! Why practise such grievous self-mortification ? Whom do you worship and what do you desire ? Tell us the whole secret truly." When Bhaváni heard their speech, she replied in strangely moving terms,—"I greatly shrink from telling my secret, for you will smile at my folly when you hear it; but my soul is obstinately set and refuses to hear instruction, though I am like one building a house upon the water, or as one who would fly without wings, relying only on the truth of Nárada's prophecy. See, O saints, the extent of my madness. I long for the unchangeable Sankara as my husband."

Dohá 88.

The Rishis smiled on hearing her speech, and said :— "You are a true daughter of the parent rock; but tell me who has ever listened to Nárada's advice and had a home?

Chaupái 79

"Did he not advise Daksha's sons, and they never saw their father's house again? It was he, too, who ruined Chitraketu's family, and also Hiranya-kasipu's.[1] Whoever listens to Nárada's advice, be it man or woman, is certain to become a homeless beggar. Seemingly pious, but deceitful at heart, he would make every one like himself. And now you are led away by his words, and are longing to marry a very outcast, a worthless, shameless, tattered wretch, with a necklace of serpents and skulls, and without either family or house or even clothes. Tell me now—what pleasure is

---

1 It was by Nárada's advice that the sons of Daksha were dissuaded from multiplying their race and scattered themselves all over the world in the hope of acquiring knowledge. Not one of them ever returned, and the unhappy father, thus deserted by all his children, denounced as a curse upon Nàrada that he, too, should always be a homeless wanderer on the face of the earth.

King Chitraketu was childless, though he had a thousand wives. At last, by the blessing of a saint, one of them bore him a son; but when it was a year old they all conspired together and poisoned it. The king was weeping sorely with the dead child in his arms, when Nárada came and after much persuasion consented to restore it to life. It at once sat up and began to speak, saying that in a former state of existence it ha been a king, who had retired from the world into a hermitage. There one day a woman in charity gave him a cake of fuel, which he put on the fire without perceiving that there were in it a thousand little ants These innocent creatures all perished in the flames, but were born again in a more exalted position as Chitraketu's wives; while the woman who gave the fuel, and the hermit who used it, became the mother and the child, whom inexorable fate had thus punished for their former sinful inadvertence After finishing this explanation the child again fell back dead, and Chitraketu, giving up all hope of an heir, abandoned the throne and began a course of penance.

to be had from such a bridegroom as this? Better forget the ravings of the impostor. For he married Sati only because other people suggested it, and soon abandoned her and left her to die.

Dohá 89.

And now he never gives her a thought, but goes about a-begging, and eats and sleeps at his ease. What respectable woman could ever stay with such a confirmed solitary?

Chaupái 80.

To-day if you will hear my words, I have thought of an excellent bridegroom for you, so beautiful and honourable, so pleasant and amiable, that even the Veda hymns his praise—the faultless and all-perfect lord of Lakshmi, who reigns at Vaikuntha. He is the husband that I will bring you." On hearing this Bhaváni smiled and replied,—"You said true that I inherit a rock-nature, and would sooner die than yield. Gold, again, is another product of the rock that cannot be changed by any amount of burning. Nor will I change my faith in Nárada's word: whether my house be full or desolate, I fear not: whoever doubts the word of his spiritual adviser must never dream of obtaining either happiness or riches.

Dohá 90.

Mahádeva is full of faults, while Vishnu is all-perfect; but the heart concerns itself only about the object it happens to fancy.

Chaupái 81.

If, reverend sirs, I had met you sooner, I would have submitted to your advice; but now that I have given my life for Sambhu, it is too late to weigh his merits and

---

When Kayádhu, the wife of demon-king Hiranya-kasipu, was about to bring forth, she received instruction from the sage Narada, whose words reached even to the ears of the child in her womb. Accordingly from the moment he was born he devoted himself to the service of Vishnu, and thus provoked his impious father to the acts of persecution which resulted in his own destruction and the extinction of his royal line.

defects. If you are firmly resolved upon making a match, you need not stand idle; the world is full of young men and maidens : but as for me, though I hold out for a million lives, I will either wed Sambhu or remain a virgin. I will not forget Nárada's admonition, even though Mahádeva himself and again told me to do so. I, who am styled the mother of the world, fall at your feet and bid you return home; your time is lost." When the sages beheld her devotion, they cried--" Glory, glory, glory to the great mother Bhaváni,

Dohá 91.

United as Mayá to the god Siva, the parents of the universe!" then bowing the head at her feet and thrilling with rapture they left,

Chaupái 82.

And sent King Himavant, and with many entreaties brought Girijá back. When they returned to Siva and told him Umá's whole history, he was delighted to hear of her affection, and they went gladly home. Then the all-wise Sambhu, firmly directing his intention, began a meditation on Ráma. Now at that time was a demon Táraka, of gigantic strength of arm and high renown, who had subdued the sovereigns of every region and robbed the gods of all their happiness. Knowing neither age nor death, he was invincible; and the powers of heaven were vanquished in innumerable battles. At last they all went and cried to the Creator, and he seeing them so dismayed,

Dohá 92.

Re-assured them, saying,—" the demon shall die when a son is born of the seed of Sambhu, who shall conquer him in fight.

Chaupái 83.

Having heard what I say, devise a plan by which such a lord may arise and assist you. After Sati quitted the body at Daksha's sacrifice, she was born again as the daughter of the Himaláya, and has been practising penance in the hope of obtaining Sambhu to husband. He, on the other hand, has left all and sits absorbed in contemplation. Though it will be a difficult business, yet list to what I propose. Send Káma, the good of love, to Siva to agitate his soul, and then I will approach with bowed head and arrange the marriage, and in this way your object will be attained." All exclaimed that the plan was good, and heartily applauded it.' Then came the god with the five arrows and the fish-standard;

Dohá 93.

And they told him their distress. He heard, and after reflecting a little replied with a smile,—"Sambhu's displeasure will work me no good,

Chaupái 84.

Yet I will do you this service. The scriptures say charity is the highest of virtues, and one who gives his life for another is ever the praise of the saints." So saying he bowed, and took his leave, he and his attendant,[1] with his bow of flowers in his hand. And as he went he thought within himself,—'Siva's displeasure will surely be my death.' Therefore he hastened to exhibit his power, and for a time reduced to subjection the whole world. If Love is provoked, the stepping-stones of the law are swept away in a moment; religious vows and obligations, self-control, ceremonial observances, knowledge and philosophy, virtuous practices, prayer, penance, self-mortification, the whole spiritual army, is panic-stricken and put to flight.

Chhand 3.

Virtue's grand force is routed in panic and dismay,
And in dark nooks of holy books her champions skulk away.
Great god of fate! in this dread state what saving power is nigh?
'Gainst man's one heart Love's fivefold dart wins easy victory.

Dohá 94.

Every creature in the world, animate or inanimate, male or female, forgot natural restraint and became subject to love.

---

1 Kámadeva's attendant is Riturája, or Basanta, the spring season.

Chaupái 85.

In every heart was a craving for love: the tree bent its boughs to kiss the creeper; the overflowing river ran into the arms of ocean; lakes and ponds effected a meeting. And when such was the case with inanimate creation, what need to speak of man? Beasts on land and birds in the air, under the influence of love, were unmindful of time and season; all were agitated and blind with desire, and the swan regarded neither night nor day.[1] Gods, demons, men, *kinnaras*, serpents, ghosts, witches, goblins and imps were all at once enslaved by love; even saints and hermits, sages and ascetics, became again sensual under his influence.

Chhand 4.

When saints and hermits own his sway, why speak of serf and thrall,
God's whole creation, recreant grown, swore love was all in all;
Each jocund dame, each amorous swain, found heaven in love's embrace;
Two hours sped past, love still stood fast and reigned in Bráhma's place.

Sorathá 8.

None is so bold but love steals his heart, and only they whom Ráma protects can then escape.

Chaupái 86.

For two hours this triumph lasted, till Kámadeva drew nigh to Sambhu. On seeing him Love trembled, and the whole world returned to itself. Every living creature at once grew calm, as when a drunkard recovers from his drunkenness. When Love looked at Siva, the invincible and unapproachable god, he feared; then returned shame too strong for words and, resolved upon death, he formed his plan of attack. Forthwith lusty Spring stepped forth, and every tree broke into blossom; wood and grove, lake and pond, every quarter of the heaven, gladdened and overflowed as it were with love, and even the deadest soul quickened at the sight.

---

1 The male and female *chakwa* (swan, or rather Bráhmani duck) are doomed for ever to nocturnal separation, and are said to pass the night on the opposite banks of a river, vainly calling to each other to cross. During Love's brief triumph the curse was for once removed.

Chhand 5.

At love's touch the dead were quickened, blossomed all the wood so dark,
While a breeze soft, cool and fragrant, fanned the love-enkindled spark,
Laughs the lake with many a lotus, hum the bees with drowsy sound,
Swans and parrots chatter gaily, gladly dance the nymphs round.

Dohá 95.

Though he tried every trick and manifold device, yet he and his army were defeated; Siva's unbroken trance still continued, and Love grew furious.

Chaupái 87.

Seeing a mango tree with spreading boughs, he in his folly climbed up into it; then fitted a shaft to his flowery bow, and in his great passion taking aim and drawing the string home to the ear, he let fly and lodged the five arrows in his breast. Then the trance was broken and Sambhu awoke. In the lord's soul was great agitation; he opened his eyes, and looking all round saw Kámadeva in the mango tree. At his wrath the three worlds trembled. Then Siva unclosed his third eye, and by its flash Kámadeva was reduced to ashes. A confused cry went up through the universe from the gods in their dismay, from the demons in exultation; the rich were sad when they remembered love's delights, while saints and hermits felt relieved a of thorn.[1]

Chhand 6.

The saints were freed from torment : but Rati swooned for woe,
And in sad guise with weeping eyes at Siva's throne fell low,
Sore wailing and lamenting her dear lord's hapless fate :
Till quick to pardon spoke the god in words compassionate :

Dohá 98.

"Henceforth, Rati, your husband's name shall be called *Anang* (the bodiless), and thus etherealized he shall pervade all things. But hear how you will again find him hereafter.

---

1 With this whole narrative compare that in the *Kumára Sambháva* of Kálidása.

Chaupái 88.

When Krishna becomes incarnate in the family of Jadu to relieve the world of its burdens, your husband shall be born again as his son (Pradyumna) ; this my word shall not fail." On hearing this prophecy of Sankara's, Rati retired. I now turn to another part of my story. When Bráhma and the other gods heard these tidings they first went to Viakuntha, and thence, with Vishnu, Bràhma and all the rest, into the presence of the merciful Siva, and each of them separately sang his praises. Then the gracious power whose crest is the moon and whose standard a bull, said,—" Tell me, ye immortals, why ye have come." Said Bráhma,—" My lord, you can read our hearts, but as ordered I speak.

Dohá 97.

In the mind of all the gods is one idea. Sankara is love-smitten, and we would fain with our own eyes see his marriage.

Chaupái 89.

O destroyer of the pride of love, let us feast our eyes on this glad event. In granting a husband to Rati after Kámadeva had been consumed you have done well, O sea of compassion, in punishment remembering mercy ; the great have ever an easy temper. Accept now the interminable penance that Párvati has endured." On hearing Bráhma's speech and perceiving its purport, he exclaimed joyfully, " So be it ! " Then the gods sounded their kettle-drums and rained down flowers, and cried,—" Victory, victory to the King of heaven ! " Then, perceiving it was the proper time, the seven sages came and were despatched by Bráhma to the Himálaya where first they sought Bhaváni and addressed her in mild but deceptive terms :—

Dohá 98.

" You would not listen to us, but rather took Nárada's advice ; now again is your vow proved vain, for the god of love has been consumed by Mahádeva."

Chaupái 90.

Bhaváni replied with a smile,—"O wisest of sages, you have said well. Your words—'Love has been consumed by Mahádeva'—imply a belief that aforetime Sambhu was liable to change. But I know him to be from everlasting an ascetic, faultless, loveless, passionless: and if, knowing him to be such as he is, I have served him devotedly in heart, word and deed, so gracious a lord (be assured, O sages) will bring my vow to accomplishment. Your saying that Hara has destroyed Love betrays great want of judgment. Fire, my friend, has an unalterable nature, and ice cannot exist near it; brought near it must inevitably perish; and so must Love in the presence of Mahádeva." [1]

Dohá 99.

On hearing this speech and seeing her love and confidence the sages were delighted and bowed the head before her, and went to King Himáchal,

Chaupái 91.

And told him the whole history. When he heard of Love's annihilation he was much distressed, but was again comforted when told of Rati's promised husband. After pondering on the majesty of Sambhu, he reverently summoned the wise men, and at once had the day fixed according to Vedic prescription, selecting an auspicious date, and planet and hour. Then he gave the letter to the seven sages, humbly falling at their feet, and they took it to Bráhma, who could not contain himself for joy on reading it, but at once proclaimed it aloud. The whole company of heaven was delighted: there was music and a shower of flowers, and in every quarter festive preparations were commenced.

Dohá 100.

All the gods began adorning the different vehicles on

1 The line thus translated stands in the original *Asi Manmatha Mahesa ko nai.* There is an entirely different reading in some copies *jimi Sampáthi nij pachch ganwái*, 'like as Sampáthi lost his wings;' Sampáthi was the brother of Jatáyu, and in his pride flew so high into the heaven that his wings were consumed by the heat of the sun. See Book IV, *dohá* 27.

which they ride abroad, the Muses sung for joy, and all was bliss and happiness.

Chaupái 92.

Siva's attendants began to dress their lord, arranging his serpent-crest and crown of matted locks ; with snakes for his earrings and bracelets of snakes for his wrists ; his body smeared with ashes, and a lion's skin about his loins ; the moon on his brow, the lovely Ganges on the crown of his head, his eyes three in number, and a serpent for his Bráhmanical cord ; his throat black with poison ; a wreath of dead men's skulls about his breast. In such ghastly attire was arrayed the great god Siva. With trident in hand he advanced riding on a bull, while the drums beat and instruments of music were played. The female divinities all smiled to see him, and said, " The world has no bride worthy of such a lover." Vishnu and Bráhma and all the company of heaven followed in the procession, each on his own carriage. ' The gods make a fine sight, but still the procession is not worthy of the bridegroom.

Dohá 101.

So cried Vishnu with a smile and then commanded all the heavenly warders—" March separately, each one with his own retinue,

Chaupái 93.

Otherwise on going into a strange city they will laugh and say what a sorry procession for such a bridegroom."
The gods smiled to hear this speech, and marched separately, each at the head of his own followers. Mahádeva smiled too, not understanding Hari's joke, but taking it as a most friendly suggestion, and sent Bhringi to bring all his attendants. On receiving Siva's order they all came and bowed the head at his lotus feet. Then Siva laughed to see the host in their motley attire, riding every kind of vehicle; some with monstrous heads, some with no head at all; some with many hands and feet, and some with none ; some with great eyes, some with no eyes ; some very stout, some very slim.

Chhand 7.

All, stout or slim, or foul or trim, in gruesome panoply,
With skulls for wine-cups filled with blood, from which they quaffed with glee ;
With head of dog, or ass, or hog, a host no tongue can tell,
Ghosts, goblins, witches, every kind of denizen of hell.

Sorathá 9.

All the demons went singing and dancing with wonderful contortions, such as never were seen, and uttering all sorts of strange cries.

Chaupái 94.

Like bridegroom, like procession—an extraordinary sight as it went along the road. There King Himáchal erected a canopy more splendid than words can tell ; and every hill in the world, small and great, more than man can count, and every wood and sea, river, stream and lake, all were invited to attend ; and assuming forms of exquisite beauty, with all their retinue, male and female, they flocked to the palace singing songs of gladness. First of all the king had built a number of guest-houses, and so tastefully arranged them, that, after a glance at the beauty of the city, the Creator of the world seemed a contemptible architect.

Chhand 8.

Little seemed the world's Creator, and his skill of nothing worth :
Lake and fountain, grove and garden, shone more fair than aught on earth.
Wreaths and arches, flags and banners, made each house a goodly show ;
Gallant youth and lovely maidens set a saint's heart all aglow.

Dohá 102.

The city in which the great mother had taken birth surpassed description ; joy, prosperity and abundance were ever on the increase.

Chaupái 95.

When it was known that the marriage procession was close at hand, the stir in the city and the brilliancy of the decorations grew more and more. With numerous carriages and all due equipment the heralds started for the formal reception. When they saw the army of gods they were glad of heart, and yet more so when they beheld Hari. But when they perceived Siva's familiars, every beast they rode started back in affright. Grown men summoned up courage to stand, but the children all ran for their lives straight back home, and when their parents questioned them could only reply trembling all over,—"What can we say? it is beyond telling; it is no marriage procession, but the army of Death; the bridegroom, a maniac, mounted on a bull; with snakes and skulls and ashes to adorn him.

Chhand 9.

Skulls and snakes and streaks of ashes, matted locks and body bare,
Witches, imps, and frightful goblins, and appalling ghosts are there.
Happy man who sees such horrors nor dies at once of fright!"
So from house to house they babbled on Uma's wedding night.

Dohá 103.

The fathers and mothers smiled, for they recognized Siva's familiars, and reassured the children in every possible way, saying,—"Do not be afraid; there is no cause for fear."

Chaupái 96.

The heralds brought in the procession and assigned them all pleasant quarters. And Maina, having prepared an elegant sacrificial lamp, and lustrous water in a golden bowl, proceeded gladly to move it round over Siva's head while her attendants sang festive songs. When they saw his terrible attire, the women feared greatly and ran inside the house all of a tremble. Mahádeva advanced to the guest-room and Maina, sorely grieved at heart, called her daughter, and in the most loving manner took her in her lap, while her lotus eyes overflowed with tears,—"To think that the Creator should have made you so beautiful, and then give you such a raving fool for a bridegroom!

Chhand 10.

How can God send such a raving groom for such a lovely bride?
What a thorn bush is our wishing-tree, the fruit for which we cried!
From mountain-top, in sea or fire, I'll cast me down with thee;
Welcome disgrace, so they be gone; this wedding ne'er shall be."

Dohá 104.

All the ladies were distrest when they saw the queen so sad, who in her deep affection for her daughter began to weep and make great lamentation,—

Chaupái 97.

"What harm had I done to Nárada that he should make my home desolate and give Umá such advice, to undergo penance for the sake of a mad bridegroom? In good sooth he is fancy free and passionless, an ascetic who wants neither money, nor house, nor wife, and therefore in destroying another's home he has neither shame nor compunction; for what does a barren woman know of the pangs of child-birth?" When Bhaváni saw her mother's distress, she answered thus placidly and discreetly,—"Be not troubled, my mother, with these thoughts, for God's plans are unalterable. If fate decrees me a mad husband, then why should any one be blamed? Can you blot out the hand-writing of the Creator? Then refrain from profitless reproaches.

Chhand 11.

Cease from profitless reproaches, nor in vain bemoan my fate,
I must go where'er my destined joys and sorrows for me wait."
Hearing Umà's pious answer, all her ladies felt surprise.
Much they talked of God's injustice, while the tears bedewed their eyes.

Dohá 105.

At that time came Nárada, and with him the sages (for they had heard the news), and at once betook themselves to the king's palace.

Chaupái 98.

Then Nárada instructed them all, and recited in full the past history, saying,—"Hear, O Maina! my words are true; your daughter is Bhaváni, the mother of the world, the everlasting female energy; without birth or beginning; Sambhu's inseparable half; the creator, supporter, and destroyer of the universe; who at will assumes the semblance of human form. First she was born in Daksha's house,

Sati by name, of excellent beauty. Then as Sati she married Sankara, and her story is famous throughout the world, how once, with Siva, she met the sun of Raghu's lotus line (*i.e.*, Ráma), and in her infatuation was not obedient to Siva, but was beguiled into assuming the form of Síta.

Chhand 12.

For the crime of this assumption she was widowed many a day,
Till in the fire before her sire her sins were burnt away.
Now born your daughter, for her lord in penitence she stayed ;
And Siva aye shall be her lord ; know this, nor be dismayed."

Dohá 106.

On hearing Nárada's explanation the sadness of all was dispersed, and in a moment his words were spread from house to house throughout the city.

Chaupái 99.

Then Maina and Himavant were glad and fell again and again at Parvati's feet. All the people of the city, whatever their age, men and women alike, were equally delighted. Songs of joy began to sound in the streets; golden vases were displayed ; meats were dressed in various ways according to the rules of gastronomic science. But the banquet table in the palace inhabited by the great mother Bhaváni was altogether beyond description. The marriage guests—Vishnu, Bráhma and all the heavenly orders—were courteously entreated and took their seats line after line. Then the skilful servers began to serve and the women, when they found the gods were sat down, began to jest and banter in pleasant strain.

Chhand 13.

In pleasant strain with dark refrain they hint at love's delight ;
Charmed with the song, the gods sit long, nor heed the waning night,
With growing zest each jovial guest prolongs the festive hour :
At last they rise ; each bids adieu and seeks his separate bower.

Dohá 107.

Again the sages came and reminded Himavant of the marriage ; and he, seeing the time was fit, sent and summoned all the gods,

Chaupái 100.

Whom he courteously addressed, and assigned to each an appropriate seat. An altar was prepared according to Vedic ritual, while the women chanted festal strains; and a divinely beautiful throne was erected, the handiwork of a god, beyond description. Then Siva, after bowing to the Bráhmans, took his seat, remembering in his heart his own lord, Ráma. Then the sages sent for Umá, who was brought in by her handmaids, richly adorned. All the gods beholding her beauty were enraptured. What poet in the world could describe such loveliness! The divinities who recognized in her the universal mother, the spouse of Mahádeva, adored her in their inmost soul—Bhaváni, the crown of beauty—whose praises would still be beyond me even though I had a myriad tongues.

Chhand 14.

A myriad tongues were all too few to sing her matchless grace :
When gods and muses shrink abashed, for Tulsi's rhyme what place ?
With downcast eyes the glorious dame passed up the hall, and fell,
Bee-like, at Siva's lotus feet, the lord she loved so well.

Dohá 108.

At the injunction of the priests, both Sambhu and Bhaváni paid divine honours to Ganes. And let no one be perplexed on hearing this, but know well that they are gods from everlasting.

Chaupái 101.

The whole marriage ceremony was performed by the priests in accordance with Vedic ritual, and the father, with *kusa* grass in his hand, took the bride and gave her to Siva. When the two had joined hands, all the gods were glad of heart; the chief priests uttered the scriptural formulæ, and the cry went up of "Glory, glory, glory to Sankara!" all kinds of music began to play, and flowers were rained down from heaven. Thus was accomplished the marriage of Hara and Girijá amidst general rejoicing. The dowry given defies description—men-servants and maid-servants, horses, carriages, elephants, cows, raiment, jewellery, things of all sorts, and wagonloads of grain and golden vessels.

Chhand 15.

Thus great and more the dowry's store that King Himáchal brought ;
Yet falling low at Siva's feet he cried that all was nought.
The gracious lord cheered his sad sire in every way most meet,
Then Maina came, most loving dame, and clasped his lotus feet :

Dohá 109.

"Umá, my lord, is dear to me as my own soul ; take her as one of your servants, and pardon all her offences : this is the boon I beg of your favour."

Chaupái 102.

After Sambhu had in every possible way reassured his wife's mother, she bowed herself at his feet and went home, there called for Umá, and taking her into her lap gave her this excellent instruction,—" Be ever obedient to Sankara ; to say ' My lord and my god ' is the sum of all wifely duty." At these words her eyes filled with tears, and again and again she pressed her daughter to her bosom,—" Why has God created woman in the world, seeing that she is always in a state of subjection, and never can even dream of happiness ?" Though utterly distracted by motherly love, she knew it was no time to display it, and restrained herself. Running to her again and again, and falling on the ground to clasp her feet, in a transport of affection beyond all words, Bhaváni said adieu to all her companions, and then again went and clung to her mother's breast.

Chhand 16.

Still clinging to her mother's breast she cheered her weeping train,
Then with her handmaids sought her spouse, yet oft looked back again.
' Midst beggar's blessing, richly bought, forth rode the royal pair :
The glad gods rained down flowers, and sounds of music filled the air

Dohá 110.

Then went Himavant most lovingly to escort them, till with many words of consolation Mahádeva bid him return.

Chaupái 103.

Then he came speedily to the palace, called all the hills and lakes, entreated them courteously with words and gifts, and allowed them to depart. They proceeded each to his own realm, and Sambhu arrived at Kailása. How shall I tell its delights when thus occupied by Sambhu and Bhaváni, the father and mother of the world, and their attendants? They began to indulge in sport and dalliance, and every day was some new pleasure. Thus a length of time was passed and the six-headed child (Kartikeya) was born, who vanquished in battle the demon Táraka. His birth is sung by all the sacred books, and his deeds are known throughout the world.

Chhand 17.

All the world knows the story of the birth and the glory
of Mahádeva's six-headed son;
And this is the cause why so briefly I pause on the
generous deeds he hath done.
Man or maid, who shall tell, or sing true and well, how
Siva took Umá to wife,
Shall be happily wed, and, with blessings bestead, live
at ease all the days of his life.

Dohá 111.

The amorous doings of Girijá and her beloved are an ocean-like depth that not even the Veda can sound; how then can an ignorant clown such as Tulsi Dás succeed in describing them?

Chaupái 104.

When the sainted Bharadvája had heard all this pleasant and delectable history of Sambhu's doings, he was delighted and longed to hear yet more. With overflowing eyes and every limb thrilling, he was so mastered by love that his tongue could not utter a word. On seeing his condition the great sage was pleased,—"Blessed is thy birth, to whom Gauri's lord is dear as life. He who loves not Siva's lotus feet can never dream of pleasing Ráma: a guileless love for Siva's feet is the surest sign of faith in Ráma. For who is so faithful to Ráma as Siva, who for no fault thus left his wife Sati and made a vow, the pledge of unswerving fidelity? And whom does Ráma hold more dear than Siva?

Dohá 112.

I have begun by telling you of Siva's deeds, knowing well your secret, that you are are a true servant of Ráma, without any variableness.

Chaupái 105.

I understand your character and disposition; listen therefore while I proceed to recount Ráma's adventures. I cannot say how glad I am at this meeting with you to-day. Though Ráma's deeds are beyond measure, and not a myriad serpent kings could tell them all, yet I repeat the tale as it has been revealed, after fixing my thoughts on the god with bow in hand, who is the lord of the queen of speech. For Sarasvati is as it were but a puppet, and Ráma the manager who plays the hidden strings. When he finds a true believer, he graciouly sets her to dance in the courtyard of the poet's fancy. To him, the merciful Raghunáth, I bow before commencing the recital of his glory. Of all mountains the most beautiful was Kailás, since Siva and Umá had made it their home:—

Dohá 113.

Saints, hermits ascetics, gods, *kinnaras*, sages, and all pious souls came there to dwell and adore Mahádeva, the root of all good.

Chaupái 106.

But enemies of Hari and Hara, who had no love for virtue, could never even in a dream find their way to the place. On this mountain was an enormous *bar* tree, which no time nor season could rob of its beauty; ever stirred by soft, cool, fragrant breezes and a shade from the hottest sun; the *Vitap* tree famous in sacred song as Mahádeva's favourite haunt. Once on a time the lord had gone under it, and in an excess of delight spread with his own hands his tiger-skin on the ground and there sat at ease: his body as fair in hue as the jasmine or the moon, his arms of great length, a hermit's cloth wrapt about his loins, his feet like lotus blossoms, and his toe-nails like gleams of light to dispel the darkness of faithful souls; his face more splendid than the moon in autumn: and his decorations, serpents and streaks of ashes.

Dohá 114.

With his twisted coils of hair for a crown; with the Ganges springing from his head; with full-orbed eyes like the lotus, and with the crescent moon on his brow; the dark-throated god shone forth in all his brilliancy.

Chaupái 107.

So sat the enemy of Love, as it were Quietism embodied. Then Párvati, who is the great mother Bhaváni, approached, seeing her time. In recognition of her love he received her most courteously and enthroned her on his left side. Joyously she sat beside him and recalled her former life; and reckoning on his augmented attachment she spoke, being fain to hear the salutary tale,—"O lord of the world, my lord Purári, your greatness is known throughout all three worlds; things moving or motionless, serpents, men and gods, all do homage to your lotus feet.

Dohá 115.

You are the lord of all power and of all knowledge; the centre of art and science; the great storehouse of meditation, of wisdom and of asceticism; and your name is as the tree of life to the afflicted.

Chaupái 108.

If, O blissful being, I have found favour in your sight, and you know me to be your own devoted slave, then, my lord, disperse my ignorance by reciting to me the story of Ráma. How can he who dwells beneath the tree of paradise know aught of sorrow that is born of want? Consider, O moon-crowned god, and relieve my mind of this perplexity. The saints, who preach salvation, declare that Ráma is the uncreated god; Seshnág, Sarasvati, the Veda, the Purános, all sing his praises; you too, night and day, great conqueror of Love, reverently repeat his name. Is this Ráma the son of the King of Avadh, or some other uncreated, passionless, invisible Being?

Dohá 116.

If a king's son, and so distrest by the loss of his wife, then how the Supreme God? When I compare his acts that I see with the eulogies that I hear, my mind is completely distracted.

Chaupái 109.

Instruct me, my lord, with regard to him who is the passionless, all-pervading, omnipresent god. Be not wroth at my ignorance, but take steps to remove it. In the wood, though I was too awe-stricken to tell you, I beheld the majesty of Ráma, yet my mind was so dull that I did not understand, and I reaped a just reward. Again to-day I am in doubt, and with clasped hands I beg of you to compassionate me: be not angry, nor say you have been taught already; the past is past; my infatuation is gone, and I have a hearty longing to hear the sacred story of Ráma's virtuous deeds. Declare it, O glory of the serpent king, great lord of heaven.

Dohá 117.

Laying my head in the dust, I worship your feet, and with folded hands entreat you to tell me all Raghubar's excellent glory, as extracted from scripture and philosophy.

Chaupái 110.

Though a woman is not entitled to initiation, yet I am in a special degree your servant; further, the saints do not forbid mystic instruction to a woman in great distress, and it is in extreme distress that I call upon you, heavenly king, for an account of Ráma. First, weigh well and declare to me the cause why the invisible Brahm assumed a visible body. Then, my lord, tell me of his incarnation and his pretty actions when a child, and how he wedded Janaki, and for what fault he left his father's kingdom, and what he did when living in the woods, and how he slew Rávan, and how he amused himself when he recovered the throne ; tell me all about him, most amiable Sankara.

Dohá 118.

Then tell me, gracious lord, of his marvellous acts, and how with all his subjects the jewel of Raghu's line proceeded to his own abode.

Chaupái 111.

Next tell me, my lord what it all means ; explaining to me in full detail what is the intelligence that so absorbs the wisest saints ; what is faith, and wisdom, and supreme knowledge and detachment from the world. Tell me also, O lord of purest understanding, the many other mysteries connected with Ráma ; and if there be anything which I have omitted to ask, be kind enough not to suppress it. You, as the Vedas say, are the great teacher of the three worlds ; what can other poor creatures know ? " When Siva heard Umá's winning and guileless speech he was glad ; the whole of Ráma's acts thronged in upon his soul, his eyes were bedewed with tears and his very limbs thrilled with rapture; for the vision of Ráma filled his heart, and his ecstatic joy was beyond measure.

Dohá 119.

For a brief space Mahádeva was lost in contemplation ; then recovered himself and began with great joy to tell the tale of Ráma.

Chaupái 112.

" Not to distinguish between the false and the true is like mistaking a rope for a snake ; while as a dream vanishes away on awakening, so is it with those who look well and make sure. I reverence the child Rána, most easy of access to all who repeat his name. Come to me, O home of bliss and bane of woe, as when thou usedst to sport in Dasarath's courtyard." After thus paying homage to Ráma, Tripurári began his mellifluous recital,—" All blessings on thee, O daughter of the mountain-king, there is no such benefactor as thou art. Thou hast asked for Ráma's history as potent as the Ganges to sanctify the world ; and it is on the world's account that thou hast asked, being thyself full of love for Ráma's feet.

Dohá 120.

By the blessing of Ráma, O Párvati, not even in sleep can doubt, error, delusion, or distress enter into your mind ; this I know well :

Chaupái 113.

But you have so ordered your certainty as to benefit all who speak or hear. For the ears that hear not Rama's name are mere snake-holes ; the eyes that have not seen his true vision are like the false eyes in a peacock's tail ; the heads that have not bowed at the feet of Hari's priest are of no more worth than bitter pumpkins. They whose heart is not inspired with faith in Hari are mere animated corpses ; those who sing not his praises are like croaking frogs ; and hard and impenetrable as a thunderbolt is their breast who hear his deeds and take no delight in them. Listen O Girija, to the deeds of Ráma, which are to gods a delight and to demons a delusion ?

Dohá 121.

Who is the good man that will not listen to the story of Ráma, which is like the heavenly cow, that fulfils every desire of the gods who tend it.

Chaupái 121.

The story of Ráma is like a fair pair of cymbals to frighten away the birds of doubt, or like an axe at the root of the tree of sin; listen reverently, O daughter of the mountain-king. How sweet is the name of Ráma, and his ways and his deeds ; his lives and his actions are declared by the scriptures to be beyond number. And as there is no end to Ráma, so the legends about him and his glory are endless : yet, seeing the greatness of your love, I will attempt to tell them to the best of my ability and as the scriptures have revealed. Your inquiries, Umá, are most becoming and profitable, such as the saints approve, and I too am pleased to hear: but there was one thing I did not like, though you spoke under the influence of a delusion; for you said,—'Is there some other Ráma whom the Vedas sing, and whom sages love to contemplate?'

Dohá 122.

This is what is said by the vile wretches whom the demon of delusion has in his clutch: heretics, who are the enemies of Hari and know no difference between truth and falsehood.

Chaupái 115.

Ignorant, unlearned and blind reprobates; the mirror of whose mind is clouded by a film of sensuality; lustful, treacherous and desperately perverse, who have never even in a dream attained to a vision of true faith. They utter doctrines repugnant to the Veda, with no understanding of loss or gain; their glass is dim, their eyes are naught: how then can such hapless wights see the beauty of Ráma? Unable to distinguish between the material and immaterial, they jabber many lying words, and under Hari's delusive influence go utterly astray in the world; for whom no words are too strong. Windy, devilish, drunken, they can utter nothing to the purpose, and are so intoxicated with a strong delusion that no one should give ear to their ravings.

Soarthá 10.

Being thus assured in your heart, discard all doubt and fall in adoration at Ráma's feet. Listen, O daughter of the mountain-king, and the sun of my words shall disperse all the mists from your soul.

Chaupái 116.

There is no difference between the material and the immaterial; so declare saints and sages, the Veda and the Puránas. The formless, invisible and uncreated Immaterial, out of love for the faithful, becomes materialized. How can this be? In the same way as water is crystallized into ice.

But how can He be subject to sensual detusion whose very name is like the sun to disperse the darkness of error ? In Ráma, who is the Supreme Being and the sun of the world, the night of delusion can have no part whatever ; and in the Lord, who is himself true light, there can be no dawn of understanding ; neither joy nor sorrow, knowledge nor ignorance; neither personal piety, nor the sins of vanity and pride : but Ràma is the omnipresent God, the blissful Lord of all, the ancient of days ;

Dohá 123.

The Great Spirit, the glorious fount of light ; the Revealed, the Incomprehensible, the jewel of the family of Raghu, my own lord :", and so saying Siva bowed the head.

Chaupái 117.

"Fools do not perceive their own error, but senselessly attribute delusion to the lord ; like simple folk, who, seeing a clouded sky, say that the sun itself is dim, or who gaze at the moon through their fingers and fancy they see it doubled. O Umá, delusion affects Ráma in the same way as smoke, or a cloud, or dust affects the brightness of the heavens. The five objects of sense, the organs of sense, the gods of sense, as well as the soul, are all in their degree possessed of intelligence ; [1] but the great enlightener of them all is the eternal Ráma, the lord of Avadh. Whatever in the world is susceptible of enlightenment, Ráma enlightens ; every delusion is subject to him : in him centre all knowledge and virtue ; and by his truth the dulness of material creation shines bright as the Ideal, the senses contributing to the deception.

Dohá 124.

Though false as the gleam of a polished shell, or as a mirage caused by the sun's rays, yet no one, at any time, past, present or future, can rid himself of the delusion.

---

1 Even inanimate nature has an unconscious intelligence ; reason, order and activity pervade the material universe, the mineral as well as the animal and vegetable kingdoms.—*Mivart.*

Chaupái 188.

And such is the world in its connection with Hari : yet though unreal it can cause pain; in the same way as a man who dreams that his head is cut off, is in pain till he awakes. None can declare his beginning or his end, though holy scripture has hymned him as best it could. He moves without feet,[1] he hears without ears, and works in manifold ways, yet without hands. Without a mouth he enjoys all tastes, and without a voice is the aptest of speakers ; he can see without eyes, touch without limbs, and without a nose catch every scent. His actions are thus in every way supernatural, and his greatness is utterly beyond description.

Dohá 125.

He whom Scripture and Philosophy have thus sung, and whom the saints love to contemplate ; even the Lord GOD ; he is the son of Dasarath, the beneficent King of Kosala.

Chaupái 119.

By the power of his name I exalt to the regions of the blest any creature whom I see dying at Kási ; he is the sovereign of all creation, animate and inanimate, my lord Raghubar, who reads all hearts. By repeating his name the most abandoned of sinners cancels the accumulated crimes of many previous existences ; and by those who devoutly meditate upon him the ocean of life is as easily crossed as a puddle in the road. Ráma, O Bhaváni, is the Supreme Spirit, and the error to which you gave utterance on this point was most improper. Such doubt, when entertained in the heart, destroys knowledge, sobriety and every virtue." On hearing Siva's luminous exposition, the whole structure of heresy fell to pieces ; her love and devotion to Raghupati grew strong, and her sore incredulity passed away.

---

1 None hath beheld him, none,
Seen above other gods and shapes of things,
Swift without feet and flying without wings.
—*Swinburne.*

Dohá 126.

Again and again, clasping her lord's lotus feet and suppliantly folding her hands, her whole soul overflowing with affection, Girijá thus spoke and said,—

Chaupái 120.

"My grievous delusion, like the feverish heat of autumn, has yielded to the moon-like spell of your voice. In your compassion you have removed all my doubt, and I now understand the very Ráma. By my lord's mercy my distress is all gone, and I am made glad by his favour. Now regarding me as your own immediate servant, though I am but a poor ignorant woman, if I have really found grace in your sight, reply to those my former questions. If Ráma is the invisible and immortal God, without parts and passions, and whose temple is the heart, why did he take the form of a man? Declare and explain this to me." On hearing Umá's modest speech, and perceiving her sincere desire to be instructed in Ráma's history,

Dohá 127.

The all-wise Sankara, the destroyer of Kámadeva, was glad of heart, and with many words of praise was thus pleased to speak,—

Sorathá 11–13.

"Listen, Bhaváni, while I recite in auspicious strains the Rám-charit-mánas, or pure lake of Ráma's deeds, as of old Bhusundi[1] declared it in the hearing of Garur, the king of the birds. First I will relate the manner of their exalted converse, after which you shall hear of Ráma's incarnation and his all-glorious and sinless deeds. Hari's virtues and names are infinite, and his history and his manifestation beyond number or measure; I tell them as best I can; listen, Umá with respect.

1 Káka-bhusundi, originally a Sudra of Ayodhya, was by virtue of his birth in that holy place and the intercession of a saint of Ujjain born again as a Bráhman. His exclusive devotion to Ráma could not suffer him to listen to the Rishi Lomas when he made Brahm the theme of his discourse, and the sage was so annoyed that he changed him for a time into a crow (*Káka*). His story is told at length in Book VII.

Chaupái 121.

Listen, Girijá, to the grateful tale of Hari's great and holy acts, as they have been recorded in the scriptures. The cause of Hari's incarnation is not to be dogmatically defined; for to my mind, Bhaváni, Ráma is beyond the grasp of intellect, or soul, or speech; yet, as saints and sages, the Veda and the Puránas have partly and to the extent of their capacity explained the matter, so I, fair dame, will now declare to you the cause as I understand it. Whenever virtue decays, and evil spirits, waxing strong in pride, work iniquity that cannot be told, to the confusion of Bráhmans, cows, gods and earth itself, the compassionate Lord assumes some new bodily form; relieves the distress of the faithful;

Dohá 128.

Destroys the evil spirits; reinstates the gods; maintains the way of salvation; and diffuses the brightness of his glory throughout the world. Such are the motives of Ráma's incarnations.

Chaupái 122.

Singing his glory, the saints escape the waves of life, and it is for their sake only that the Compassionate assumes a body. The causes of Ráma's incarnations have been many and various, each more wonderful than the other. I will relate one or two of his previous births, if, Bhaváni, you are prepared to give me your devout attention. Hari had once two loving door-keepers, the famous Jaya and Bijaya: both brothers, in consequence of a Brahman's curse, were born again in the form of the malignant demons Hiranya-kasipu and Hiranyáksha, who became celebrated throughout the world as the tamers of the pride of the king of heaven. Incarnate as a Boar, he triumphed in battle over the first illustrious hero and destroyed him, and again, in the Narsinh avatár, slew the second; the fame of the faithful Prahlád is widespread.

Dohá 129.

Then the evil spirits went and took birth as the bold and powerful warriors Kumbha-karn and Rávan, who, as all the world knows, subdued even the gods.

Chaupái 123.

Though killed by the deity, they did not attain to salvation, for the Bráhman had doomed them to three births. They then were once the cause why the cherisher of the faithful assumed a body, and at that time his parents Kasyapa and Aditi were incarnate as Dasarath and Kausalya of glorious memory. Thus it was that in that age of the world he descended from heaven and wrought saving deeds on earth. In another age, seeing the gods distrest and waging ineffectual battle with Jalandhar, Sambhu warred against him times without number, but could not subdue the valiant giant, for the exceeding virtue of his wife protected him against Purári's every attack.

Dohá 130.

By a stratagem the Lord broke her vow and effected the will of the gods. When she discovered the deception, then in her wrath she cursed him.

Chaupái 124.

And Hari did according to her curse; for though the Lord God, he is full of playfulness and of mercy. So Jalandhar was born as Rávan, and being killed in battle by Ráma attained to high glory. This then was the cause of one birth and the reason why Ráma then assumed a human form. Each avatár has its legend, which the poets have sung in various ways and according to tradition. "On one occasion it was Nárad's curse that caused him to become incarnate." At this saying Girijá was astounded,—"Nárad is a wise saint and a votary of Vishnu's; what was his reason for uttering a curse? What offence had Lakshmi's lord committed? Tell me the whole story, Purári; it is passing strange that a saint should be subject to passion."

Dohá 131.

Then answered Mahádeva with a smile,—"There is neither wise nor fool; man is ever such as Raghupati will have him to be.

Sorathá 14.

I sing the glory of Ráma; listen devoutly, O Bharadvája; and do thou, O Tulsi, put away the intoxication of pride and worship Raghunáth, the destroyer of death.

Chaupái 125.

In the Himálaya mountains is a very sacred cave close to the holy Ganges. Seeing this pure and delightful hermitage, the divine sage Nárad was greatly pleased; and as he gazed upon the beauty of the rocks and the forest glades he was filled with love to God, and as he thought upon Hari the curse was broken[1] and his spotless soul fell all at once into a trance. When the king of heaven saw the sage's state he feared, and in terms of high respect addressed himself to Kámadeva,—"Go, I beg, with your assistant." He then, the god of love, went very gladly; but in Indra's mind was great alarm, for he thought,—'The saint would rob me of my kingdom.' All the world over, a gallant or a miser is as much afraid of interference as is a thievish crow.

Dohá 132.

Like a wretched dog that on seeing a lion runs away with the dry bone it has in its mouth, for fear it should be taken from him, so was Indra in his shamelessness.

Chaupái 126.

When Love reached the hermitage, his deceptive power created a false spring. All the trees broke out into many-coloured blossoms, there was a murmuring of cuckoos and a humming of bees. A delightful air, soft, cool and fragrant, sprung up, fanning the flame of desire; while Rambhá and the other heavenly nymphs, all well skilled in the art of love, began singing songs in every variety of

1 The curse had been pronounced by Daksha.

measure and disporting themselves in the dance with waving hands. When Love saw himself so well supported, he was glad and again manifested his creative power in diverse ways ; but his devices had no effect upon the saint ; and guilty Love began to tremble for himself. Who dare trespass on his bounds who has the great Ramápati for a guardian ?

Dohá 133.

In dire dismay both Kámadeva and his accomplice confessed themselves defeated, and went and clasped the holy man's feet, addressing him in accents of the deepest humility.

Chaupái 127.

There was no anger in Nárad's soul, who in friendly terms replied to Kámadeva and reassured him. Then, bowing the head at his feet and accepting his commands, they both retired, the god and his companion ; and repairing to Indra's court there related all their own doings and the saint's clemency. As they listened to the tale all were astonished, and bowing the head to Hari extolled the saint. Then went Nárad to Siva, greatly proud of his victory over Love, and told him all Love's doings. In acknowledgment of his affection Mahádeva gave him good advice,—"O great saint, again and again I beg of you never to repeat to Hari this story that you have now told me : should it happen to be brought forward, keep it as dark as possible."

Dohá 134.

Good as the advice was, it did not please Nárad. O Bharadvája, listen to the strange recital and see the strength of Hari's will.

Chaupái 128.

What Ráma wills to have done is done, and there is no one who can alter it. As Sambhu's words did not please the saint, he went straight to Bráhma's court, and, to the accompaniment of the famous lute that he had in his hand, sang right through the excellent song of Hari's praises.

Then he passed on to the milky ocean, where abides Vishnu, the glory of revelation. The Lord ran to meet him in great joy, and side by side they sat 'ogether. Said the sovereign of the universe with a smile,—'Reverend sir, 'tis long since you last did me this honour.' Then Nárad declared all Love's doings, though Siva had beforehand cautioned him; the deceptive power of Raghupati is so strong that there is no man living who can resist it.

Dohá 135.

Then spoke the great god, with an austere look, but in flattering terms,—"Self-delusion and the intoxicating arrogance of love shall perish at the rmembrance of your doings.[1]

Chaupái 129.

Know, O saint, that infatuation prevails in a soul that is devoid of wisdom and self-control; but what pain can Love cause to one so steadfast in asceticism as yourself?" Said Nárad in his pride,—'It is all your favour, my Lord.' The Compassionate saw into his heart and thought within himself,—"Pride like a huge tree has sprouted in his soul: I must at once tear it up by the roots; ever to relieve my servants is the vow that I have made. I will surely contrive some sportive device on behalf of the saint." Then Nárad bowed his head at Hari's feet and took his leave, swelling with pride; while Vishnu gave orders to the spirit of delusion. Listen now to his strange contrivance.

Dohá 136.

He constructed on the road a city a hundred leagues in circumference, with everything more perfect than even in Vishnu's own capital,

---

1 Siva's speech is so ambiguously worded that it really conveys a censure, while Nárad interprets it as a compliment. The hidden meaning is: Hereafter when you reflect upon this incident and all its consequences, you will take a lesson by it and be more humble, remembering your weakness; but the more obvious meaning of the words and that in which Nárad took them is: By meditating on your triumph over Love, other men will triumph too.

Chaupái 130.

And inhabited by such graceful men and women that you would take them all to be incarnations of Kámadeva and Rati. The king of the city, by name Sila-nidhi, had horses, elephants and troops beyond number ; his royal pomp like that of a hundred Indras ; himself a centre of power, policy and magnificence. His daughter Visva-mohani was so beautiful that even Lakshmi would be put to the blush and by Hari's delusive power was in every way so exquisite that no words could describe her. As the princess was selecting a husband, kings beyond number came as suitors. The saint, too, came to the fairy city and began making inquiries of the people. When he had heard all that was going on, he proceeded to the palace, where the king most respectfully gave him a seat,

Dohá 137.

And then brought his daughter for him to see, saying,—'Tell me, good sir, after consideration, all that is good or bad about her.'

Chaupái 131.

When Nárad saw her beauty, he forgot his vow of chastity and continued long gazing upon her. Her features quite fascinated him ; yet he would not in words express his heart's delight. "Her bridegroom must be one of the immortals, invincible in battle, reverenced by all creation ; such a one must Síla-nidhi's daughter wed." But, though he calculated her fortune thus correctly, he kept it to himself, and after saying something or other to the king, to the effect that his daughter would be of good fortune, he went away full of anxiety, considering,—" What scheme can I devise now, so as to make her marry me ? No time is this for prayers or penance ; good God, how am I to get the girl ?

Dohá 138.

I must on this occasion make myself exceedingly charming and beautiful, so that the princess may be pleased when she sees me and give me the wreath of victory.

Chaupái 132.

I will ask Hari for the gift of beauty; in going to him there will be much delay; but I have no other such friend, and this is an opportunity for him to help me." So he offered up a fervent prayer and the merciful Lord appeared to him in a vision. The saint's eyes brightened at the sight and he rejoiced in heart, saying,—' My object will be accomplished.' He then with the utmost humility told his tale, and added,—" O, my Lord, be gracious and assist me. Bestow on me beauty equal to your own; for in no other way can I get possession of her. Make haste to accomplish my success; for lo, I am your slave." When the Compassionate saw the mighty influence of the deception he had wrought, he smiled to himself:

Dohá 139.

"Hear, O Nárad; I will assuredly bring about your highest good—that and naught else; nor shall my words prove vain.

Chaupái 133.

If a sick man in the weariness of disease ask for what will harm, mark me, holy ascetic, the physician will not grant it. In the same way will I act as is best for you." So saying the Lord vanished. The saint was so demented by the power of the delusion that he did not understand Hari's hidden meaning, but hastened at once to the spot where the marriage arena had been prepared. The Rájas were seated rank upon rank, each with his retinue in grand attire. The saint thought joyfully within himself,—' My beauty is such that she will never leave me to wed another.' But the merciful God, the saint's true friend, had made him hideous beyond all description. Every one recognized him as Nárad and bowed the head, knowing nothing of what had taken place.

Dohá 140.

Now there were there two of Siva's attendants who knew the whole secret. Dressed like Bráhmans, they seemed to be spectators of the show, walking here and there and looking about.

Chaupái 134.

Both went and sat down in the same group with the saint so proud of his beauty; and in their Bráhmanical attire they attracted no notice. They say in jest so that Nárad might hear,—'Hari has given this man such excellent beauty that the princess will be charmed with his appearance and will certainly wed him, taking him for Hari himself.' The saint was so utterly subjugated by passion that Sambhu's servants could laugh and jeer as they liked, and though he heard their mockery, his intellect was too bewildered to understand it. No one perceived the transformation save only the princess, who, on beholding him just as he was with his monkey face and deformed body, was quite disgusted at the sight,

Dohá 141.

And with her handmaids glided like a swan through the long line of kings with the wreath of victory in her lotus hands.

Chaupái 135.

She would not let her eyes rest for a moment on the spot where Nárad was sitting in his pride. The saint in his anxiety kept fidgetting about, and Siva's attendants smiled to see the state he was in. Then entered the Compassionate, in form as a king, and gladly the princess cast on him the garland. Thus Lakshmi's lord carried off the bride, to the despair of the assembled kings. The saint was much disturbed; in his infatuation his reason was quite gone, like a diamond dropt out of a hole in a bag. Then Siva's attendants said with a smile,—'Get a glass and look at yourself'; and having so said both ran away in great alarm. The saint looked at his reflection in the water. When he saw himself, he was furious and cursed them with a grievous curse:

Dohá 142.

'Go false and guilty pair, and take birth as demons of the night. Be this your reward for mocking me; mock again a saint, if you dare.'

Chaupái 136.

Looking again in the water he saw himself in his proper form; yet still he was not content at heart, but his lip quivered with rage, and in haste he betook himself to Vishnu. 'Shall I curse him or kill myself, seeing that he has made a mock of me throughout the world?' On the way the conqueror of demons met him, and with him Ráma and the princess. With a smile and in gentle tones he said, —'Where goes the saint, like one distracted?' On hearing these words, his anger rose, and infatuation utterly mastered his reason, —"You never could bear to look upon another's prosperity; your envy and deceit are notorious; at the churning of the ocean you drove Siva mad and made the gods quaff the poisoned cup.

Dohá 143.

Intoxicating liquor was the demon's share, and the poison was for Mahádeva; but for yourself Ráma and the *Kaustubha* jewel. You have ever been selfish and perverse and treacherous in your dealings.

Chaupái 137.

Utterly self-willed, with no one over you, and bent on doing whatever comes into your mind; confounding the good and exalting the bad; with a heart incapable either of surprise or pleasure; trying every one with your tricks, without the slightest consideration and in mere lightness of heart. Neither good deeds nor bad in any way affect you, nor has any one up to the present ever succeeded in restraining you. Now for this fine treat that you have given me you shall receive a due return. Be born in the form in which you have now imposed upon me; this is my curse. And as you have made me like a monkey, you shall have monkeys for helpmates; and in the same way as you have sorely wronged me, so shall you be distrest by the loss of your wife."

Dohá 144.

The lord gladly accepted the curse, thus working the will of the gods, and in his compassion withdrew the influence of his deceptive power.

Chaupái 138.

When this was removed, there appeared neither Ramá nor the princess; and the saint fell in great fear at the feet of Hari, ever ready to heal the sorrows of a suppliant, crying,—" May my curse be made of no effect." Said the gracious god,—' It is my will.' Said the saint,—' I have spoken many injurious words; how shall my guilt be expiated?' " Go and repeat Sankara's hundred names, and your soul will at once be relieved. There is no one so dear to me as Siva; never let your faith in this truth be shaken. He on whom Siva will not show mercy shall never know true love to me. Think on this as you wander over the earth; the delusion haunts you no longer."

Dohá 145.

Having thus reassured the saint, the lord disappeared, and Nárad took his way to Paradise, chanting Ráma's praises as he went.

Chaupái 139.

Siva's two followers saw him on the road rejoicing and in his right mind. In great alarm they drew near, and clasping his feet made their supplication : " O great saint we are not Bráhmans, but servants of Mahádeva, and have reaped the fruit of our great sin : in your mercy remove the curse." Said the compassionate Nárad,—" You must both be born as demons of vast power, majesty and strength; but when you have subdued the universe by the might of your arm, Vishnu shall take upon him human form, and dying in battle at his hands you shall attain to salvation, nor ever be born again." After bowing their head at his feet, both went their way and in due course were born as demons.

Dohá 146.

In one age this was the reason why the lord became incarnate, to gladden the gods, to comfort the saints, and to ease earth of its burdens.

Chaupái 140.

Thus Hari's births and actions are many and various, but all of them glorious and beneficent. In every age he has manifested himself and wrought many excellent works; and on each occasion great saints have sung his acts in holy strains of choicest verse, relating marvellous histories of diverse kinds, which the wise hear without any amazement. For as Hari is without end, so are there endless verses about him, which are heard and repeated by scripture and the faithful. The delightful adventures of Rámchandra could not all be sung in a myriad ages. This story that I have now told, Bhaváni shows how Hari's deceptive power can infatuate even saints and sages. He, the lord, is sportive, gracious to suppliants, accessible to his servants, and a remover of all sorrow.

Sorathá 15.

There is neither god, man, nor saint whom unreality has not infatuated. Reflect upon this and worship the great master of the unreal.

Chaupái 141.

Hear, O daughter of the Himálaya, a second reason, which I will proceed to relate at full length, why the uncreated, the passionless, the incomparable Brahm became King of Kosala. The lord, whom you saw roaming in the forest with his brother in hermit's attire; at whose doings, Bhaváni, you in Sati's form lost your senses, and still to this day have a touch of disease; the recital of his adventures will heal all your sickness. All his sportive acts in that incarnation I am now about to tell as best I can." O Bharadvája, on hearing Sankara thus speak, the modest and affectionate Umá smiled for joy, while her lord continued,—" the cause of the incarnation.

Dohá 147.

I am now about to explain (listen, great saint, with attention to the delightful story of Ráma, which can cleanse all the stains of the world and bring man to heaven).

Chaupái 142.

Manu, the son of the self-existing, had to wife Satarúpa, and of them were born the whole human race ; even to this day the fame of their wirtue and conjugal fidelity is celebrated in the scriptures. Their son was King Uttánapáda, who begot Hari's faithful client Dhruva. The younger son, by name Priya-vrata, is mentioned with praise both by the Vedas and Puránas. Their daughter, Devahuti, became the devoted wife of Saint Kardama, and in her womb the eternal Lord God, in his mercy and compassion, planted Kapila, the author of the Sánkhya philosophy, the divine exponent of the theory of entities. This Manu reigned a long while, keeping all God's commandments.

Sorathá 16.

But in a palace complete detachment from the senses is impracticable. Old age came upon him, and he thought with grief,—' My life has been spent without any true devotion to Hari.'

Chaupái 143.

Then perforce he resigned the throne to his son, and with his queen repaired to the forest, to Naimisha, famous among all holy places as specially sacred and liberal of success. Glad of heart, King Manu sought the spot where dwelt the company of saints and sages ; and as the resolute pair passed along the way they seemed incarnations of Wisdom and Faith. On reaching the bank of the Gomati, they bathed with delight in the clear stream ; and there the inspired saints and sages came to meet them, recognizing in the king a champion of religion. Devoutly they took them to visit each different shrine, and with wasted body, clad in hermit's robes, they are ever in the assembly of the faithful listening to the Puránas.

Dohá 148.

Devoutly repeating the twelve-lettered charm[1], and with their whole soul directed to the lotus feet of Vásudevá.

Chaupái 144.

Meditating on the Supreme Brahm, they live on leaves and fruits and roots. Then doing penance as before Hari, they gave up roots and fruits for water only. In heart an endless craving,—" O that we might see with our eyes the very God, without parts or passions; without beginning or end; whom the preachers of salvation contemplate; whom the Vedas define as the unutterable; the pure spirit, without attributes and beyond all comparison; as part of whom are produced in various forms the lords Sambhu, Bráhma, and Vishnu. Yet so great a god submits to his own servants, and for their sake assumes in sport a body. If this be true, as the scriptures have declared, our desire will of a surety be accomplished."

Dohá 149.

In this way they spent six thousand years living only on water; and then seven thousand, living only on air.

Chaupái 145.

For ten thousand years they gave up even this and remained both standing on one leg. Now Bráhma, Hari and Hara saw this interminable penance and repeatedly came near to Manu and tempted him, saying,—' Ask your boon;' but for all their persuasion he was too steadfast to move. Though his body was reduced to a skeleton, there was not the least pain in his soul. Then the omniscient lord knew that the king and queen were his servants and had this single object in practicing such austerities. A solemn voice full of ambrosial grace sounded in the sky, saying: Ask, ask; a voice so blithe that it would wake the dead. As it dropped upon the ears of their soul, their bodies became again as comely and stout as if they had only that day left their home.

1 The twelve-lettered charm is *Om Namo Bhagavate Vásuderáya*.

Dohá 150.

As the ambrosial voice rung in their ears, their body quivered and thrilled; and falling on the ground in an irrepressible transport of love Manu thus spoke,—

Chaupái 146.

"Hearken, O thou that art as the tree of paradise or the sacred cow to thy servants; the dust on whose feet is ever worshipped by Bráhma, Hari and Hara; accessible to the faithful; bounteous of all good; protector of suppliants; lord of all creation: if, O friend of the friendless, I have found favour in thy sight, then in thy mercy grant me this boon: Let me with mine own eyes behold thee in that form in which thou dwellest in Siva's breast, which the saints desire to see; the swan in the lake of Bhusundi's soul; the sum and the negation of all attributes; the theme of the Veda: do me this grace, O thou that healest the woes of every suppliant." This gentle, submissive and affectionate speech of the wedded pair went to the heart of the generous and merciful god; and the sovereign of the universe manifested himself,

Dohá 151.

In hue as the lotus or the sapphire; dark as a raincloud; of such lustrous form that a myriad Loves could not be compared to it,

Chaupái 147.

With a face perfect in beauty like the autumnal moon; with lovely cheeks and chin and dimpled neck, red lips and gleaming teeth, and a nose and smile more radiant than a moonbeam; eyes bright as a lotus bud and a glance to fascinate the heart; brows surpassing Love's bow; on the forehead a sectarial mark and glistening star; golden fish in his ears and a bright crown on his head; crisp curling hair like a swarm of bees; on his breast the Srivatsa jewel and a long wreath of sweet wild flowers, and jewelled adornments about his neck; a waist like a lion, a comely Bráhmanical thread, and exquisite clasps upon his arms, long and round as an elephant's trunk ; with a quiver at his side and bow and arrow in his hand ;

Dohá 152.

His yellow apparel more lustrous than the lightning ; his body charmingly dimpled, and his navel like a bee hovering over the dark wave of the Jamuná ;

Chaupái 148.

His feet beautiful beyond description, lotus haunt of the bee-like souls of the saints. On his left side shines in equal glory the Primal Energy, queen of beauty, mother of the world ; of whose members are born countless Umás and Rámas and Bráhmanis, all alike perfect ; by the play of whose eyebrows a world flashes into existence, even Síta, enthroned at Ráma's side. As Manu and Satarúpa beheld this vision of Hari in all his beauty, gazing fixedly with open eyes, they adored his incomparable magnificence, nor could be satiated with the sight. Overcome with delight and transported out of themselves, they fell flat on the ground, clasping his feet in their hands. But the gracious lord putting his lotus hand upon their heads quickly raised them up,

Dohá 153.

And again said,—"Be assured that you have found favour with me : ask whatever boon you will, the largest gift you can think of."

Chaupái 149.

On hearing the lord's words they clasped their hands in prayer, and taking courage thus spoke in timid accents, —"O lord, we have seen your lotus feet, and our every object has been accomplished. Yet one longing remains, and I know not whether to describe it as easy or difficult of attainment. It is easy, my master, for you to give ; but so far as my meanness is concerned, it is difficult. Like a beggar who has found the wishing-tree, but trembles to ask for too good fortune, not realizing its full power, so my heart is troubled by doubt. O my god, you read all hearts and know what I wish ; grant me my desire."—" O king, fear not, but ask of me ; there is nothing I would not give you."

Dohá 154.

" O gracious lord, I will declare honestly the crowning boon ; for what concealment can there be ? I would have a son like you."

Chaupái 150.

On seeing his love and hearing his sincere words, said the Compassionate, " So be it. Where can I go to find your equal ? I myself, O king, will be born as your son." Then seeing Satarúpa with her hands still clasped, —" O lady, ask whatever boon you please." " O my lord, the boon my husband has wisely asked is what I too should most desire. But it is great presumption ; though in your clemency you have confirmed it. You are father of all the gods, the lord of the world, the supreme spirit, the omniscient ; and therefore my mind doubts ; and yet the Lord's words cannot fail. O my god, the bliss that is enjoyed and the future state that is attained by your own servants—

Dohá 155.

In your mercy grant to me even that bliss, that state, that devotion, that love to your feet, that knowledge, and that existence."

Chaupái 151.

Hearing this modest and deeply touching petition, the Compassionate gently replied :—" Fear not ; whatever your mind desires that I have granted. O mother, your supernatural wisdom by my favour shall never fail." Then again spoke Manu, bowing at his feet,—" I too have another petition, my lord. Is there any one who will not call me fool for devoting myself to your feet simply on account of a son ? As a snake's hood without a jewel, or a fish without water, so is my life dependent upon you." Begging this boon, he remained clasping his feet till the All-merciful said,—" Be it so: now, as I order, go and dwell at Indra's capital.

Sorathá 18.

There, father, enjoy yourself freely; and again, when some time has passed, be born as the King of Avadh, and I will be your son.

Chaupái 152.

Voluntarily assuming human guise, I will manifest myself in your house, father, and, with every element of my divinity incarnate will do great deeds for the consolation of my people. Blessed are they who listen reverently; quitting the vain conceits of self they shall pass over the ocean of life. Even the Primal Energy, by whom the visible world was created, that self-same shadow of me here present, shall also become incarnate. I will accomplish your desire; true is my promise, true, aye! true." Again and again thus saying, the compassionate lord vanished out of sight, and the wedded pair, full of faith in the All-merciful, stayed for a while at the hermitage, and then, when their time was come, passed painlessly out of the body and took up their abode in Amaravati, the city of the immortals.

Dohá 156.

Such was the pious legend which Siva related to Umá. Hearken now, O Bharadvája, to yet another motive for Ráma's incarnation.

Chaupái 153.

Listen, great saint, to the holy and hoary tale as it was repeated by Sambhu to Girijá. There is a world-famous country called Kekaya, and Satya-ketu was its king. A champion of religion; a storehouse of good policy; great in glory, magnificence, virtue and power. He had two gallant sons, staunch in fight, endowed with every good quality. The elder and the heir to the kingdom was named Pratápabhánu, and the other Ari-mardan, of unequalled strength of arm and like a rock to stand the brunt of battle.

The sympathy between brother and brother was perfect, and their mutual affection without either flaw or disguise.[1] To the elder son the king resigned the realm, and withdrew into the wood to devote himself to religion.

Dohá 157.

When Pratápa-bhánu became king, proclamation was made throughout all the land : Under a sovereign so skilled in sacred lore not a speck of sin will be allowed anywhere.

Chaupái 154.

The prime minister, Dharma-ruchi, a second Sukra,[2] was as devoted to the king as he was wise. With a prudent counsellor, valiant kinsmen, himself a glorious leader in war, with a countless host of horse and foot, and chariots and elephants, and fighting men beyond number, all eager for the fray, the king might well rejoice as he inspected his army 'mid the clash of tumultuous music. Having selected an auspicious day, he marched forth with a special force, bent on universal conquest. In all his numerous battles, wherever they took place, the pride of kings was abased ; all the seven continents were reduced by the might of his arm, and their princes escaped only on payment of tribute. At that time Pratápa-bhánu became the sole monarch of the whole round world.

Dohá 158.

Having thus subdued the universe by the might of his arm, he re-entered his capital and devoted himself in turn to business, duty, love and religion.

Chaupái 155.

The grateful earth, invigorated by Pratápa-bhánu's sway, became a very Kámadhenu, and all his subjects, both men and women, happy and free from all annoy, grew in

---

1 I read this couplet as follows : *Bháihi bháihi param samiti, sakal-dosh-chhal-varjita priti* : the penultimate syllable of *samiti* being lengthened *metri gratia* Such a license is of frequent occurrence ; but in this particular instance in appears to have troubled the copyists, who have made various substitutions all more or less injurious to the sense.

2 The regent of the planet Sukra (Venus) is the preceptor of the Daityas or Titans.

virtue and beauty. The minister Dharma-ruchi, devoted servant of Hari, lovingly instructed his lord in state policy; nor did the king ever fail in due reverence either to his spiritual teacher, or the gods, or the saints, or his departed ancestors, or the Bráhmans. All the duties which are enjoined upon kings in the Veda he carefully and gladly performed; every day he made large offerings and heard the scriptures read, both the Veda and the Puránas; and he constructed many baths and wells and tanks, flower gardens and beautiful orchards, handsome monasteries and temples, and also restored every ancient shrine.

Dohá 159.

For every single sacrifice enjoined in the scriptures or the Puráns the king in his zeal performed a thousand.

Chaupái 156.

In his heart there was no aiming after advantage, but such was his supreme knowledge and intelligence that he dedicated to God the whole merit of all his thoughts, words, and actions. One day he mounted his gallant steed and went, with his retinue equipt for the chase, into a dense forest of the Vindhyachal mountains and killed many fine deer. As he ranged the wood, he spied a wild boar, showing amid the foliage like Ráhu with the moon in his clutch; its orb too large to be contained in his mouth, though his rage will not suffer him to entirely disgorge it. The monstrous boar with its splendid tusks, as I have described them, and its vast limbs of immeasurable bulk, growled when he heard the tramp of the horse: it, too, at the sight started and pricked up its ears.

Dohá 160.

On seeing the huge boar, resembling some purple mountain-peak, the horse started aside, and it was only by much spurring and persuasion that the king could prevent it from breaking away.

Chaupái 157.

When it saw the horse coming on with speed, the beast took to flight swift as the wind, keeping close to the ground as it went, and ever regarding the shaft which the king had at once fitted to his bow. Taking steady aim he let it fly ; but the boar saved himself by his wiliness, and rushed on now well in sight, and now altogether hidden, while the king in much excitement followed closely on his track. At length it reached a dense thicket impenetrable by horse or elephant. Though alone in the wood and distressed by his exertions, still the king would not abandon the chase ; till the boar seeing him so determined slunk away into a deep cave. When the king perceived that there was no getting near him, he was quite sad, and moreover he had lost his way in this hunt through so great a forest.

Dohá 161.

Hungry and thirsty and exhausted with fatigue the king and his horse kept searching in much distress for a stream or pond, and were half dead for want of water.

Chaupái 158.

As he wandered through the forest, he spied a hermitage where dwelt a king in disguise of a holy man. He had been despoiled of his kingdom by Pratápa-bhánu, and had left his army on the field of battle, knowing that his adversary's star was in the ascendant and his own in the decline. Too proud to meet the king, too much mortified to go home, nursing the rage in his heart, he like a beggar, though a prince, took up his abode in the wood in the garb of an anchorite. He at once recognized King Pratápa-bhánu as he drew near ; but the latter was too tired to recognize him, and looking only at his dress took him to be a holy man, and alighting from his horse saluted him ; he was, however, too astute to declare his name.

Dohá 162.

Seeing the king to be faint with thirst, he pointed out

to him a fine pond, where he bathed and drank, both he and his horse, with much gladness.

Chaupái 159.

All his weariness passed away and he was quite happy again. The hermit took him to his cell and, as the sun had now set, showed him where he might rest; but yet enquired of him in courteous tones,—"Who may you be, and why, thus young and beautiful, do you risk your life by roaming alone in the forest? You have all the marks of a great sovereign, and at the sight of you I am quite moved" "Know then, reverend sir, that I am the minister of King Pratápabhánu; in pursuit of the chase I have lost my way, and by great good fortune have been brought into your presence. To get a sight of you was no easy matter, and I am satisfied that something good is about to befall me." Said the hermit,—"My son, it is now dusk, and your city is seventy leagues away.

Dohá 163-4.

The night is dark, the forest dense, and the road not easy to find. Tarry then here for to-day and start to-morrow at dawn." Says Tulsi—Fate is furthered in its own way; either you go to meet it, or itself comes and carries you off.

Chaupái 160.

"Very well, my lord, I obey your command;" and so saying the king tied up his horse to a tree and came and sat down. With many flattering speeches he bowed at his feet, extolling his own good fortune, and at last in modest and winning terms put the question,—"Regarding you, my lord, as a father, I make bold and beg of you to look upon me as your son and servant and to declare to me your name." Now the king did not recognize him, but he recognized the king, and was as false and crafty as the king was honest: moreover, being an enemy, and at the same time both a warrior by caste and of royal birth, he was bent on accomplishing his own ends, whether by fraud or by right. In his enmity he was grieved to see the king's prosperity, and his heart within him burned as with the fire of a furnace; but on hearing the prince's simple words he controlled his resentment and was glad at heart,

Dohá 165.

and uttered yet another smooth but false and artful speech, —"My name is now Bhikhári, a homeless beggar."

Chaupái 161.

Said the king,—"Philosophers like you, with whom all self consciousness has been extinguished, ever conceal their own personality, and are in every way blessed, though their outer garb be wretched. Therefore the saints proclaim aloud in men's ears that it is the poor whom Hari holds most dear. A poor and homeless beggar, such as you are, is an anxiety to Bráhma and Siva: at all events, I prostrate myself at your feet and beg of you to grant me your grace." When he saw the king's simple affection he waxed all the more confident, and won him over in every way, using words with a still greater show of friendliness,—"Hearken, O king, while I relate the truth of the matter. I have for a long time dwelt here,

Dohá 166.

and till now neither has any one come to me, nor have I spoken to any one; for worldly honour is like a fire, and penance a forest for it to consume."

Sorathá 19.

Says Tulsi:—Fools are deceived by fair appearances, but not wise men: though a peacock is fair to look upon and its voice is pleasant, [1] yet it devours the snake.

Chaupái 162.

"Therefore I live retired in the world, and, save Hari, have no care whatever. The Lord knows everything with-

1 The peacock's voice can scarcely be called pleasant in itself, but it may be so by association as a sign of the coming rains Thus Cowper:

"Sounds inharmonious in themselves and harsh,
Yet heard in scenes where peace for ever reigns,
And only there, please highly for their sake."

out being told ; so what is to be gained by conciliating the world ? But you are so good and sensible that I cannot but love you in return for the faith and confidence you have placed in me : and if I were to send you away, my son, it would be a very grievous sin on my part." The more the hermit talked of his detachment from the world, the more trustful grew the king ; till at last the false anchorite, seeing him completely in his power, said,—"My name, brother, is Ektanu" (one body). The king bowed and asked further,—"Tell me, I pray, the meaning of this name, for surely I am your servant."

Dohá 167.

"At the first dawn of creation my birth took place, and my name was Ektanu, for this reason that I have never taken any other body.

Chaupái 163.

"Marvel not in your mind, my son; for nothing is too difficult for penance. By the power of penance the Creator created the world ; by the power of penance Vishnu is the great redeemer ; by the power of penance Siva works destruction ; and to penance there is nothing in the world impossible." The king, as he listened, was charmed, for he commenced relating old-world stories ; many legends of pious deeds and holy lives ; examples of asceticism and divine wisdom ; tales of the birth, preservation, and destruction of the world, and innumerable other marvellous narratives. The king, as he listened, yielded completely to his influence, and proceeded to tell him his true name. Said the hermit,—"O king, I knew you ; though you tried to practise a trick upon me, I took it quite in good part.

Sorathá 20.

"Hear, O king ; it is a political maxim that on some occasions a king should not declare his name ; and when I observed your excellent sagacity I conceived a great affection for you.

Chaupái 164.

"Your name is Pratápa-bhánu, and your father is king Satyaketu. O sir, a spiritual man knows everything, there is no need of another's telling. Ah, my son, when I beheld your natural goodness, your faith and trustfulness, and your knowledge of state-craft, there sprung up an affection for you in my soul, and I told you my own story as you asked me. Now I am well pleased with you; doubt not, but ask whatever you will." On hearing these fair words the king was delighted, and clasping his feet entreated him suppliantly,—"O merciful saint, by the sight of you the four objects of human desire have all come within my grasp. Yet, as I see my lord so gracious, I will ask an impossible boon and be happy for ever.

Dohá 168.

May I die of old age, free from bodily pain; may I never be conquered in battle: may earth rid of every foe be all under my sole sway, and may my empire last for a hundred ages."

Chaupái 165.

Said the anchorite,—"O king, so be it; there is, however, one difficulty; hear it. The age shall bow down before you, with the sole exception of the Bráhmans. By the virtue of penance a Bráhman is ever powerful, and there is none who can deliver from his wrath. If you can reduce them to your will, Bráhma, Vishnu and Mahádeva will also be at your command. But against a Bráhman might is of no avail: with both arms raised to heaven I tell you this solemn truth. Hearken, O king, if you escape a Bráhman's curse, your destruction shall never be." On hearing his promise the king was glad,—"Then, my lord, my destruction will never be; by your favour, most gracious sir, I shall be prosperous for all time."

Dohá 169.

"Amen," said the false hermit, and added with crafty

intent,—"If you let any one know of your losing your way and your meeting with me, that will not be my fault.

Chaupái 166.

"For I warn you, sir, that it is most inexpedient to repeat the matter: if it come to a third pair of ears, I tell you true it will be your ruin. If you divulge this secret, or if a Bráhman curse you, you are undone, O Pratápa-bhánu. When Hari and Hara are wroth, wretched man has no other way of escape." "True, my lord," said the king, clasping his feet; "who can deliver from the wrath of a Bráhman or a spiritual director? The guru can save from Bráhma's anger, but if the guru himself be wroth, there is none in the world that can save. If I do not follow your advice, I have not the slightest doubt that I shall perish; but my soul is disturbed by one fear; the curse of a Bráhman is something most terrible.

Dohá 170.

"Of your great goodness, tell me in what way I can win over the Bráhmans; for except you, my gracious lord, I have no other friend."

Chaupái 167.

"Hearken, O king, there are diverse expedients among men, but hard to put in practice and of doubtful issue. There is, however, one very simple plan, though even this involves a difficulty. Its contrivance depends upon me, and for me to go to your capital is out of the question; for to this day from the time I was born I have never entered house or village. If I do not go, it will be a misfortune for you; and thus I am in a dilemma." The king replied in gentle tones,—"It is, my lord, a maxim of scripture that the great show kindness to the small; thus mountains ever bear tiny grasses on their head; the fathomless ocean bears on its front the floating foam, and earth on its head bears the dust."

Dohá 171.

Thus saying and embracing his feet, the king cried,—

"Be gracious, O my lord, ever pitiful to the faithful in distress, and take this trouble on my behalf."

Chaupái 168.

Perceiving that the king was altogether under his influence, the hermit, the arch-deceiver, said,—"Hearken, O king; I tell you truly there is nothing in the world I cannot do, and as you show yourself in thought, word and action to be devoted to me, I will assuredly accomplish your object for you. The power of magical devices, penance and spells works only when secrecy is maintained. If, O king, I act as cook and serve, without any one knowing me, whoever tastes the food so prepared shall become amenable to your orders; and, further, any one who eats in their house will, I tell you, be in your power. Go now and carry out this scheme: make a vow for a whole year,

Dohá 172.

and every day entertain a new set of a hundred thousand Bráhmans with their families; while I, as long as the vow lasts, will provide the daily banquet.

Chaupái 169.

"In this way, O king, there will be very little trouble, and all the Bráhmans will be in your power. They again will perform sacrificial services, and thus the gods, too, will be easily won over. And I will give you a sign. I will not come in this dress, but by my delusive power I will bring away your family priest, and by the virtue of penance will make him look like myself and keep him here for the year; while I in his form will manage everything for you. The night is far gone, so now take rest; on the third day we will meet again. While you are asleep I, by my penitential power, will convey you home, both you and your horse.

Dohá 173.

"I will then come in the form I have told you, and you will recognize me when I call you on one side and remind you of all this."

Chaupái 170.

The king, as ordered, retired to his couch, while the arch-deceiver took his wonted seat. Deep sleep came upon the weary king; but what sleep for the other, distraught with care? Then came the demon Kálaketu, who was the boar that had led the king astray, a great friend of the hermit king, and skilled in manifold ways of deceit. He had a hundred sons and ten brothers, unmatched in villainy, the torment of the gods; but they had all before this been killed in battle by the king, who saw the distress they had caused to the Bráhmans, saints and powers of heaven. The wretch, nursing this old quarrel, combined with the hermit king in devising a plot for the destruction of his enemy. The prince, overmastered by fate, knew nothing of it.

Dohá 174.

A powerful foe, even though surprised alone, is not to be lightly regarded; to this day Ráhu, though he has nothing left but his head, is able to annoy both sun and moon.

Chaupái 171.

When the hermit king saw his ally, he rose in great joy to meet him, and told his friend the whole story. The demon was glad and said,—"Hear, O king, I am ready to settle your enemy if you will take my advice. Free yourself of all anxiety and sleep quietly here: without taking any medicine God has cured your complaint. I will sweep away the enemy, root and branch, and in four days will be back again." Having thus cheered the hermit king, the arch-deceiver went away in his wrath, and conveyed to the palace Prátapa-bhánu still asleep, both him and his horse; the king he put to bed beside his queen, and the horse he tied up in the stall,

Dohá 175.

Again he carried off the king's family priest, and by supernatural power depriving him of his senses, kept him in a cave in the mountain,

Chaupái 172

While he himself assumed the priests form and went and lay down on his sumptuous couch. At daybreak the king woke and was astonished to find himself at home. Much impressed with the hermit's power, he rose and went out unperceived by the queen, and mounting his horse rode off to the wood without any of the people in the city knowing it. When it was noon he returned, and in every house there was rejoicing, with music and singing. When he saw the family priest, he looked at him in amazement, remembering the work in hand. The three days seemed like an age, so absorbed was he in expectation of the false hermit's coming. When the appointed time had come, the priest took the king and told him the whole plot.

Dohá 176.

The king was delighted to recognize the guru, and was too infatuated to have any sense left, but at once sent and invited a hundred thousand Bráhmans with their families.

Chaupái 173.

The priest superintended the cooking, and in accordance with sacred prescription concocted the six tastes in the four different ways,[1] preparing a most seductive banquet, with sauces and condiments more than any one could count. After dressing a great variety of meat, the wretch introduced into the dish some pieces of a Bráhman's flesh. He then summoned all the Bráhmans to the feast and washed their feet and politely showed them to their places. But directly they began to touch the food, a voice came from heaven,—"Up, up, all ye Bráhmans and return to your homes; though the loss be great, yet taste not the food; there is Bráhman's flesh in the dish." Up rose all the holy men, believing the heavenly voice; while the king, distracted and out of his senses, overmastered by fate, could not utter a word.

---

1 The six tastes are 'the sweet,' *madhur*; 'sour,' *amla*; 'salt,' *lavana*; 'pungent,' *katu*; 'bitter,' *tikta*; and 'astringent,' *kasháya*. The four ways in which food can be taken are *bhakkshya*, by mastication; *bhojya* by deglutition; *chashya*, by sucking, and *lehya*, by lapping.

Dohá 177.

Then cried the Bráhmans in their wrath, regardless of what must follow,—" O foolish king, take birth in demon's form, yourself and all your family.

Chaupái 174.

" O noble prince, you invited all this Bráhmanical company here simply to destroy us ; God has preserved our honour, and it is you and your race who are undone. You shall perish in the midst of your days, nor shall there be one left to offer libations to your ghost." When the king heard the curse he was terror-stricken. Again a voice came from heaven,—" The Bráhmans have uttered this curse without due consideration, the king has committed no crime." All the Bráhmans were astounded when they heard the heavenly voice. The king hastened to the kitchen ; there he found neither food nor Bráhmans cook, and he turned away in deep thought, declared the whole history to the Bráhmans, and in his terror and distress threw himself upon the ground.

Dohá 178.

" Though you, O king, are guiltless, what is fated fails not ; the past is unalterable : a Bráhman's curse is a terrible thing."

Chaupái 175.

So saying, all the Bráhmans went their way. When the people of the city heard the news, they were much vexed and abused Fate, who had begun upon a swan and ended in making a crow. The demon conveyed the family priest to the palace and told the hermit all the tidings. Then the wretch despatched letters in all directions ; a host of princes came in with their troops, and with blast of trumpets beleagured the city. Day after day there were battles of various kinds ; all his champions fell in fight, after doing valorously, and the king with his brother bit the dust. Not one of Satyaketu's family escaped, for a Bráhman's curse can never fail of accomplishment.

Triumphing over their foe, the chiefs refounded the city, and then, crowned with victory, returned to their own states.

Dohá 179.

Hearken, Bharadvája, whoever incurs the anger of heaven, for him a grain of dust becomes vast as Mount Meru, a feather like the angel of death, and every rope a snake.

Chaupái 176.

Hearken, reverend sir ; in due time this Rája, with his family, was born as a demon with ten heads and twenty arms, a formidable hero, by name Rávan. The king's younger brother, Ari-mardan, became the valiant Kumbha-karn, while the minister Dharma-ruchi became his half-brother, the world-famous Vibhíshan, the all-wise votary of Vishnu. As for the king's sons and servants, they were born a fierce demon crew ; wretches, taking various shapes at will : wicked, monstrous and devoid of knowledge ; merciless, injurious, criminal – a torment to all creation beyond what words can tell.

Dohá 180.

Though born in the incomparably pure and holy family of Pulastya,[1] yet on account of the Bráhmans' curse all were of hateful mien.

Chaupái 177.

The three brothers practised manifold penitential observances, severe beyond all description ; the Creator drew nigh to witness them, and said, – " Son, I am well pleased, ask a boon." The Ten headed suppliantly clasped his feet and cried,—" Hear, O lord of earth : I would die at the hand of none save man or monkey." Brahma and I granted him his boon, saying,—" So be it ; you have done great penance." Then the lord went to Kumbha-karn, and was astounded at his appearance, – " If this wretch is always

1 The patriarch Pulastya was the father of Visravas ; and the latter, by three handmaids, who had been given him by Kuver, begot (1) Rávan and Kumbha-karn, (2) Vibhíshan, and (3) Khara and Súrpa-nakhá.

eating, the whole world will be laid waste." So he sent Sarasvati to turn his head, and he asked for six months' slumber.

Dohá 181.

Then he went to Vibhíshan and said,—"Son, ask a boon :" and he asked for perfect love of God.

Chaupái 178.

After granting these boons Bráhma departed, and they went home rejoicing. Now Maya had a daughter by name Mandodari, of exceeding beauty, a jewel of womankind, whom her father brought and made over to Rávan ; and she became the demon's head-queen. Delighted at having obtained so good a wife, he next went and married his two brothers. In the middle of the ocean is a three-peaked mountain, by Bráhma's contrivance most difficult of access. Here the demon Maya had constructed a vast palace of gold and jewels, more beautiful and charming than Bhogavati, the city of the serpent kings, or Indra's capital Amaravati, and called it Lanká, a name famous throughout the world.

Dohá 182—83.

The deep ocean was its moat, washing its four sides ; and its massive walls were of gold, set with jewels in a way that defies description. In every age the Demon King, whom Hari predestines, lives there with his army, as a mighty and puissant chief.

Chaupái 179.

There had dwelt great demon warriors, but all had been slain in battle by the gods ; and now by Indra's commission it was occupied by a million guards of Kuver's. Rávan happened to hear of this, and at once marshalled his army and went and besieged the place. When the Yakshas saw the vast host of fierce warriors, they all fled for their lives. Thereupon Rávan inspected the whole of the city, and was so highly pleased with it that all his trouble was forgotten. Seeing that it was not only a beautiful, but also a naturally impregnable, site, he fixed the capital there, and assigning quarters to his followers according to their several deserts, made them all quite happy. Upon one occasion he sallied forth against Kuver, and carried away his chariot of flowers as a trophy.

Dohá 184.

Again, from mere lightness of heart, he went and overthrew Kailás, and after thus testing the prowess of his men of war, waxed yet more jubilant than before.

Chaupái 180.

His happiness and prosperity, the number of his sons, his army and his allies, his conquests, his might and his superior wisdom, all grew day by day more and more, in the same way as avarice grows with gain. Thus, too, his brother, the stalwart Kumbha-karn, was a champion without a match in the world. After drinking his fill he slept for six months, and at his waking the three worlds trembled. If he had taken a meal every day the whole world would soon have been stript bare: so unspeakably staunch in fight was he that no other hero could be compared to him. His eldest son was Meghnád, who held the first place among the world's champions; before whom none could stand in the battle; who was ever harassing the city of heaven.

Dohá 185.

And many other demons were there, each by himself able to subdue the whole world, such as the hideous Kumukh, the dauntless Akampan, Kulisa-radd with teeth like thunderbolts the fiery Dhumra-ketu, and the huge Atikáya;

Chaupái 181.

Taking form at will, skilled in every kind of fraud, without ever a thought of piety or pity. One day the Ten-headed was seated in court and reviewed his innumerable retainers, sons and grandsons, friends and servants, troops of demons, more than any one could count. On seeing the host, he swelled with pride, and in fierce tones said,— " Hearken, all ye demon troops, the host of heaven are my enemies, nor dare to stand up in open fight, but flee away at the sight of my great army. There is one way of effecting their death, which I will declare; now listen to it. Go ye and put a stop to all feasting of Bráhmans, to every sacrifice, oblation and funeral rite;

Dohá 186.

the forthwith the faint and hungry gods will come out to meet me, and whether I slay them or let them go, they will be equally in my power."

Chaupái 182.

Again he called for Meghnád and exhorted him to yet greater courage and resentment,—"The strong and warlike gods, who venture to confront you, you must vanquish and bring here in chains." Up rose the son to perform his father's commands. In this manner he ordered all, and himself sallied forth, club in hand. As he marched the earth shook, the heaven thundered, and pains of premature labour overtook the pregnant spouses of the gods. The gods themselves, on hearing of Rávan's wrathful approach, sought the caves of Mount Meru. As he approached in turn each of the eight quarters of the globe, he found it deserted by its guardian. Again and again he shouted the challenge to battle and vehemently scoffed at the gods, and mad with lust of blood traversed the whole universe in search of a foeman, nor could anywhere discover one.

An interpolation.

When Nárad met him, he said with a smile,—"Saint, where are the gods? show them to me." Nárad was not pleased to hear of his villainy, and forthwith sent him to White-land. When he crossed the ocean and arrived on the other side, he saw a company of women, and said to them,—"Go tell your husbands that the king of the demons is here; then I will conquer them in battle and take you away to my own home." On hearing this speech an ancient dame waxed wroth and ran and seized him by the feet and threw him up into the air; then after going a long way, scratching and clawing, she gave him a good shake and pitched him with great violence into the middle of the sea.

Dohá 187.

Senseless, but by the Bráhman's blessing still alive, he sank down into hell; then with a roar sprang up again all unhurt, with a soul unmoved either by joy or sorrow.

Chaupái 183.

After taking and pillaging the Nágas' capital, the enemy of heaven passed on to Bali's realm. When the Dwarf heard of Rávan's coming and how he had scoffed at Nárad the gods' teacher, the lord infused his own strength into all the children playing in the streets, who ran and seized him and brought him into the town, while every man and woman in the place flocked to see the sight,—"Where on earth can heaven have brought such a creature from, with its twenty arms and ten heads?" Though the guards bound him and vexed him sore, he would rather die than tell his name; in the Dwarf's presence he was much confounded, and the Merciful then had him set at liberty. Off at once rushed the demon king without the least shame or hesitation.

Dohá 188—189.

Shameless, pitiless, and ever bent on mischief, the ten-headed miscreant thought to conquer Ráma. Hearken, Bharadvája; if God is wroth with a man, his diamonds turn to bits of glass that are not worth a cowry.

Chaupái 184.

Where ever he found a stray god or Bráhman he frightened him into payment of ransom, and this is the way he went on day and night, the black-hearted ruffian. Then in haste he came to Pampapur, the seat of the monkey-king Báli, and beheld the beautiful lake that would charm the soul even of the greatest saint, where the monkey-king sat absorbed in contemplation. He smiled to see the Ten-headed, and Rávan shouted in a fury,—"You wretched, senseless, hypocritical ape, I no sooner heard your name then I came at once; have done with your cowardice and meet me in battle.

Dohá 190.

Unless you can vanquish me in combat your meditations are vain," said the demon king, gnashing his 320 teeth.

Chaupái 185.

Said Báli,—" Away, I want no fighting; be wise and take your ten heads home. Your valour, friend, is undisputed, for I hear of your victories all over the world." But Báli's reiterated advice had not the slightest effect; and at last the monkey-king sprang up in a rage and seized Rávan and nipped him tight under his arms, and then forgot all about him for the space of ten months. One day as he raised his hands to offer a libation to the sun, Rávan slipped out of his clutches and ran away. Next he went, being still without either shame or scruple, to where the thousand-armed Sahasrabhuj was sporting in the water.

Dohá 191.

Ocean was troubled at Rávan's might: the court began to sink, and Sahasrabáhu cried in a rage,—' What rival of mine is here to-day?'

Chaupái 186.

Then he went and saw where Rávan stood, by whose giant arms the water was agitated. Potent in artifice as in strength of limb, he with a loud cry seized the king of Lanká and kept him tied up for some days in his stable—a sight of wonder for his wives. He was ashamed to tell his name, though the wise king was ever asking, and Rambhá and her companions danced about him and set a lighted torch to each of his ten heads. The saint Pulastya came and set him free. Next he went and got cursed by Nala.

Dohá 192.

On the road he spied a most incomparably beautiful damsel, with sandal-wood and flowers and leaves in her hand, going to worship Tripurári.

Chaupái 187.

Urvasí was abashed at seeing him, but Rávan addressed her in gentle tones,—'Who are you lady, and where are you going?' She was too much overcome with modesty to give him an answer. Being mad with lust, he took no heed, but seized her by the hand, though she was the wife of Kuver's son. When he recognized her, there came upon him remorse and repentance for the evil deed,[1] and much troubled at heart the king of Lanká returned to his capital. Urvasí went sadly to Alaka and told Nala-Kúvra. In great wrath he uttered this curse,—'May the race of Rávan perish.' The curse went to Lanká, where Rávan was seated, and stood before him. He trembled with dismay at the sight.

Dohá 193.

Submitting to the curse, he thought within himself that he had never taken any tribute from the monks; so in a fury,

Chaupái 188.

he sent four messengers to a holy man's hermitage, who on seeing them forgot all about the Supreme Spirit and asked them of their welfare, saying, -'Tell me, is all well with Lanká's king?' "Reverend sir, all is well with him, and he wants your tribute-money." On hearing this speech he was much alarmed, and forgetful of his vow began to think within himself,—'It is ill going empty-handed to a court where justice is not, and where a pack of villains are banded together.' So he gave them a jar, which he had filled with blood taken from his own body, and made it over to the messengers, saying,—"Go tell the king,

Dohá 194.

If the jar is opened, death will come upon you and your family." The messengers in haste took the jar to the king's court at Lanká.

---

1 Rávan and Kuver were both sons, by different mothers, of one father, Visravas, and Urvasí was thus Rávan's niece by marriage. Hence in violating her he had been guilty not only of adultery but also of incest.

Chaupái 189.

Rávan was pleased at the sight of the jar, and the Messengers then told him what the saint had said. On hearing the curse his heart burned within him, and he said,—"Take the jar away to the north and carefully put it in the ground where no one can find it." They took it to Janak's dominions and there buried it in a field. There Janak, preparing for a sacrifice, was driving a golden plough: the offspring of the saint's blood sprung up out of the furrow and was carried off by Garur. Her blessed name was at first Jánaki, but Nárad afterwards came and directed that it should be Síta,[1] and explained all the circumstances as above related. The great saint then left; the messengers also returned to Lanká, and Lanká's lord, though worsted in four places, still greatly troubled the gods.

(*Here ends the interpolation*).

The sun and moon; the wind; Varuna and Kuver; fire, time and death, and every divine power; Kinnars, saints, men, gods and serpents, all were turned out of their course. From one end of earth to the other every living creature, whether male or female, was made subject to Rávan. All in turn do his bidding and crouch suppliantly at his feet.

Dohá 195—196.

By his mighty arm he subdued the whole universe and left not a single soul independent, but acting on his own counsel exercised dominion over the whole round world. And many were the lovely dames he wedded after conquest, daughters of gods and Yakshas and Gandharvas and men and Kinnars and Nágas.

Chaupái 190.

Whatever he told Indrajit to do was done in less time than it took to tell: hear now how the other chiefs acted to whom he gave orders. The whole demon crew, villainous at heart and foul of aspect, the torment of heaven, were

---

1 The word *Sita* meaning 'a furrow.'

ready for any outrage, disguising themselves by the assumption of various forms and acting in every way contrary to the Veda, in order to eradicate religion. Wherever they find a cow or a Bráhman, they at once set fire to the city, town or village : pious observances are no longer anywhere in existence ; no respect is paid either to scripture, or Bráhman, or spiritual instructor ; there is no faith in Hari, no sacrifice, no prayer, nor alms-giving, and no one would ever dream of listening either to Veda or Purána.

Chhand 18.

At a hint of prayer or of penance, of sacrifice, vigil or fast,
Not a moment's rest, but he hied on its quest, with a vow it should be the last.
The world was sunk in lawlessness ; all holy sounds were banned ;
To read a sacred text was death, or exile from the land.

Sorathá 21.

The fearful oppression that the demons wrought is beyond description : bent on mischief, there was no limit to their evil-doing.

Chaupái 191.

The wicked all throve ; such as thieves and gamblers, and those who coveted their neighbour's wife or goods, those who honoured neither father and mother nor the gods, and those who exacted service of better men than themselves. For people who act in this way, Bhávani, resemble demons. Seeing the general persecution of religion, earth was terror-stricken and dismayed,—' the weight of mountains, lakes and seas is nothing so heavy as this one tyrant.' She saw all faith perverted, and yet for fear of Rávan could say nothing. After some consideration she took the form of a cow and went to the spot where the gods and saints were gathered together, and with tears declared to them her distress. There was no help to be had from any one of them.

Chhand 19.

Gods and saints and heavenly minstrels, flocked they all to Bráhma's throne;
With them Earth, a horned heifer, making sad and piteous moan.
Pondered Bráhma in his wisdom,—'All vain is help of mine,
But a lord immortal is thy Lord, be he my help and thine.'

Sorathá 22.

"Take courage, Earth," said Bráhma, "and remember Hari; the Lord knows the distress of his servants, and will put an end to this cruel oppression."

Chaupái 192.

All the gods sat in counsel,—" Where can we find the Lord and make our cry to him? Said one,—' We must go to Vaikunth'; said another,—' His home is in the ocean. Nay, this is the way of the Lord, he is ever manifest to a faithful and loving soul.' Now, Girijá, I too was in the assembly and took occasion to say briefly,—" Hari is omnipresent everywhere alike, but, as I well know, is revealed by love. Tell me any place, time or quarter of the heaven where the Lord is not. Present in all creation, animate or inanimate, passionless and unbiased, he is revealed like fire by love." My words were approved by all, and Bráhma exclaimed,— ' Well said, well said.'

Dohá 197.

The Creator was glad at heart and thrilled with delight, while his eyes filled with tears, and clasping his immortal hands he thus composedly and deliberately chanted his praises:

Chhand 20–21.

" To the King of heaven be all glory given, refuge of creation in distress and care,
Priests and kine befriending, hell's brief triumph ending, best beloved of Lakshmi, Ocean's daughter fair.
Heaven and earth's upholder, who, than all men bolder, dares to scan the secret of thy strange mysterious way?

Ever kind and loving, humble souls approving, may thy gracious favour reach now to me, I pray.
Spirit all-pervading, fleshly sense evading, hail Mukund immortal, lord of blissfulness supreme,
Ever pure and holy, whom the Queen of Folly has no power to tangle in her world-deluding dream.
Glory, glory, glory, theme of endless story, sung by saints and sages in an ecstasy of love.
Daily, nightly gazing on the sight amazing, source of every blessing, Hari, lord of heaven above.
Triune incarnation, who at earth's creation, wert alone presiding, and other aid was none ;
Though in prayer unable, and my faith unstable, O great sin-destroyer, hear our hapless moan.
Life's alarms dispelling, all disasters quelling, comfort of the faithful, be our succour now ;
All the gods implore thee, falling low before thee, with unfeigned submission of body, soul and vow.
Lord God Bhagavána, Ved and eke Purána, Sáradá and Seshnág, and all the saintly throng,
Find the theme too spacious, only know thee gracious ; hasten then to help us in our hour of wrong.
In all grace excelling, Beauty's chosen dwelling, ark on life's dark ocean, home of all most sweet,
Gods and saints and sages, now this tempest rages, fly in consternation to clasp thy lotus feet."

Dohá 198.

Beholding the alarm of the gods and Earth, and hearing this devout speech, a dread voice came from heaven that removed all their doubt and anxiety,—

Chaupái 193.

" Fear not, Indra and ye saints and sages ; for your sake I am about to assume the form of a man, with every element of my divinity incarnate in the glorious Solar race. For the severe penance practiced by Kasyapa and Aditi I granted them the full boon they asked. In the form of Dasarath and Kausalyá they shall take royal birth in the city of Kosala. In their house shall become incarnate the four brothers, the pride of the family of Raghu. I will fulfil all that Nárad predicted, by myself descending from heaven with my eternal spouse, and will remove the whole of earth's burden." On hearing the heavenly voice in the air the gods turned and were consoled, and Bráhma exhorted Mother Earth, who forgot her fears in hopefulness.

Do h 199.

Then Bráhma proceeded to his own realm after thus instructing the gods,—'Go and worship Hari upon earth in form as monkeys."

Chaupái 194.

The gods went every one to his own abode, and with Earth had rest. All the orders that Bráhma had given they executed gladly and without delay. Taking birth on earth as monkeys of incomparable strength and dignity, warriors with rocks and trees and claws for weapons, they confidently awaited Hari's coming, swarming in every mountain and forest and divided among themselves into orderly troops, I have told you of their noble acts, and now you must hear of what was doing meanwhile elsewhere. The king of Avadh was named Dasarath, the jewel of the line of Raghu, well skilled in the Vedas, virtuous and wise, a defender of the faith, a sincere votary of Vishnu.

Dohá 200.

Kausalyá and his other loving queens were all of holy life, faithful and affectionate to their lord, and full of humble devotion to Hari's lotus feet.

Chaupái 195.

One day the king was sad that he had no son, and going in haste to his guru's abode fell at his feet with many entreaties and told him all his joys and sorrows. Vasishta in reply comforted him in every way,—"Take courage, you will have four sons, who will be famous throughout the three worlds and rid the faithful of all their fears." Then Vasishta summoned Saint Sringi to perform a sacrifice for the birth of a son. The saint devoutly offered the oblation, and the firegod appeared with the offering in his hand and cried in gracious tones,—"I am pleased more than I can say; whatever Vasishta has imagined in his heart is all granted for your good. Take this oblation, O king, and divide it in such proportions as is proper.

Dohá 201.

Then the fire-god vanished, after telling them all of all that had to be done. The king was transported with ecstasy and could not contain himself for joy.

Chaupái 196.

He at once sent for his loving wives, and Kausalyá and the others came. To Kausalya he gave a half share, and of the remaining half he made two portions, one of which he offered to Kaikeyi; what remained he again divided into two, which he placed in the hands of Kausalyá and Kaikeyi, and they gave them to Sumitrá, to her great delight. In this manner all the queens became pregnant, and they grew glad of heart with exceeding joy. From the day that Hari was conceived in their womb the whole world was fulfilled with happiness and prosperity, and the queens shone resplendent in the palace, full of beauty, virtue and glory. Some little time was thus happily spent, till the day arrived for the Lord to be revealed.

Dohá 202.

Auspicious was the conjunction of the planets in an auspicious house; auspicious the moment; auspicious the day of the week and of the month; and full of delight was all creation, animate and inanimate, when Rámá, father of delights, was born.

Chaupái 197.

On the ninth day of the sweet and holy month of Chait; in the bright lunar fortnight; under Abhijit, his favourite constellation; on a seasonable day neither hot nor cold, a holy time of rest for all; with soft, cool, fragrant breezes blowing; midst the delight of gods and heartfelt rapture of the saints; while the woods were full of blossoms as the hills with gems, and every river flowed a stream of nectar. When the Creator saw the time so fit, all the gods had their chariots equipped and came forth. The bright heaven was crowded with the host of them ; troops of Gandharvas chanted heroic lays ; flowers were rained down by handfuls ; the sky resounded with the beat of kettle-drums ; serpents, saints and gods hymned his praises, and each in his own fashion tendered him service.

Dohá 203.

Thus meekly did all the gods return to their several abodes when the Lord was revealed, who is the abode of the world, and in whom all the world finds rest.

Chhand 24—27.

From Kausalyá's blessed womb the great god at last has come, im response to a lost world's plaint,
And she gazes with what joy on the face of her dear boy, that would rapture the soul of a saint.
A vision of delight, with his eyes so large and bright, and his body as a cloud dark and grand,
By the garland on his breast and his four arms confest Kharári, with a weapon in each hand.
With fingers locked in prayer she cries,—"How may I dare, O lord god immortal, thy boundless praise to tell,
Far above the world's confusion and reason's vain intrusion, whom all the scriptures witness incomprehensible.
Whom saints and holy sages have hymned through all the ages, the fountain of compassion, the source of every grace.
Who aye with Lakshmi reignest, thou, even thou, now deignest to be my son and succour thy sore-tried chosen race.
Though we know by revelation, heaven and earth and all creation, in each hair upon thy body may be found,
In my arms thou sweetly dreamest, O mystery supremest, far beyond the comprehension of a sage the most profound."
Smiled the lord at her devotion and would fain have set in motion the magic that dazzles the crowd,
Telling all he had done and the triumphs he had won that his mother of her son might be proud.

But hurriedly she cried,—"My soul is terrified by these marvels, disperse them from my sight;

Let me see thee as a child, disporting free and wild, for in this is my greatest delight."

She spoke and he obeyed, and at once in fashion made as an infant began to cry.

Know that all who sing this lay, and in faith to Hari pray, shall in peace rest for ever when they die.

Dohá 204.

For the sake of Bráhmans, cows and gods and saints he took birth as a man, in a body formed at his own will, he who is beyond all form, or quality, or perception of the senses.

Chaupái 198.

On hearing the delightful sound of a baby's cries, all the queens came greatly agitated; their glad handmaids ran hither and thither and all the people of the city were drowned in joy. When Dasarath knew he had a son born, his joy was like that of the blest in heaven; with his soul full of love and his body quivering with delight he sought to rise, but could not till he had collected himself,—"The lord, whose very name it is bliss to hear, has come to my house." Thus rejoicing at heart the king sent for minstrels to play, and next summoned the *guru* Vasishta, who came to the court with a train of Bráhmans. He went and gazed upon the peerless babe, but its beauty and grace were beyond words to tell.

Dohá 205.

Then after performing the Nándi-mukh *Sráddh*[1] he completed every caste observance, and the king made offerings to the Bráhmans of gold, cows, plate and jewels.

Chaupái 199.

The city was full of flags and banners and festal wreaths arranged in a manner that defies description.

---

1 The *Nándi-mukh Sráddh* is a commemorative offering to the Manes preliminary to any joyous occasion, such as initiation, marriage, &c., in which nine balls of meat are offered to the deceased father, grandfather, and great-grandfather; to the maternal grandfather, great-grandfather, and great-great-grandfather; and to the mother, paternal grandmother, and paternal great grandmother.—*Monier Williams.*

Showers of flowers fell from heaven and every soul was rapt in bliss. There was a concourse of troops of women who had come running in their ordinary dress just as they were at the time, with golden vases and salvers laden with things of good omen, singing as they entered the king's court. After passing their offerings round and round over the child's head, they strew them on the ground, and again and again throw themselves at his feet, while bards and minstrels, singing men and choristers chant the solemn praises of Raghunáth. Every one made an offering of all that he had, and no one kept what was given him; while musk, sandal and saffron were thrown about in such profusion that the streets were muddy with perfumes.

Dohá 206.

In every house there was music and the jubilant shout,—"The fountain of joy has been revealed;" and all the men and women in the city were rejoicing everywhere.

Chaupái 200.

Both Kaikeyi and Sumitra too gave birth to a lovely boy. At that time the joy, the auspiciousness, and the crowds were more than Sarasvati or the serpent king could describe. The city of Avadh was as resplendent as it were Night going to meet her lord. The sun, abashed at the vision, faded into twilight, where the dusky clouds of incense were shot through with red gleams of *abír*: the piles of jewels in the temples were like stars, and the golden pinnacle of the palace as the gracious moon, while the murmuring sound of the muttered Veda in the house was like the evening song of garrulous birds. Gazing upon the spectacle the sun forgot himself, and a whole month passed without his knowing it.

Dohá 207.

The day was a month long, but the marvel was noticed of none—while the sun in his chariot stood still at gaze, how could there be any night?

Chaupái 201.

There was not one who observed the strange event, and at last the sun set still chanting Ráma's praises. The gods, saints and Nágas too, who had witnessed the spectacle, returned home, congratulating themselves on their good fortune. I will even tell you of a deception I practised myself; Hearken, Girijá, for I know your steadfast faith. Kákabhusundi and I were there together in human form, without any one knowing it. Full of rapture, love and delight, we roamed about the streets in ecstatic unconsciousness. Only one on whom rests the mercy of Ráma can attain to the knowledge of these acts of ours. At that time the king granted every one his heart's desire, whatever it might be that he had come for, bestowing on them elephants, carriages, horses, gold, cows, jewels and all sorts of apparel.

Dohá 208.

All were satisfied from their very heart and invoked blessings upon him, saying,—'May all the boys live long,' those lords of Tulsi Dás.

Chaupái 202.

In this manner some days were spent, without any one taking thought of noon or night, till the king, knowing the time had come for naming the children, sent and called the wise seer, and after reverently greeting him thus spake,—"Holy father, be pleased to declare the names upon which you have secretly determined." "Their names are many and wonderful; I will tell them, O king, to the best of my ability. The store-house of delights, the ocean of joy, by whose spray three worlds are gladdened, the very home of bliss, the Comforter of the universe, has for his name Rama ('delight'). The bearer and supporter of the world is named Bharat ('the supporter'), while he whose very thought brings victory over the foe is celebrated in the Veda by his name Satrughna ('destroyer of enemies')."

Dohá 209.

For the auspicious, the beloved of Ráma, the stay of the whole world, was reserved by Saint Vasishta the noble name of Lakshman (' of auspicious appearance ').

Chaupái 203.

After naming them the saint pondered in heart and said,—" O king, your four sons are the very Veda itself; the saint's treasure; the believer's all in all; the darling of Siva, who is delighted with their childish sports." Even from his earliest days Lakshman knew his dear lord and devoted himself to Ráma; while the affection of the two other brothers, Bharat and Satrughna, grew also as between master and servant. In both couples one was dark, the other fair; and their mother, as she gazed upon their loveliness, would break a blade of grass to avert the evil eye. Though all four were full of amiability, beauty and intellect, yet Ráma was a higher joy; his kindliness of heart was like the bright moon, which manifested itself in the radiance of a most winning smile; while now in the cradle, and now on her lap his mother fondled him and called him her own dear darling.

Dohá 210.

The omnipresent god, who has neither passion nor quality, nor sensation of pleasure, and who is from everlasting, lay a babe in Kausalya's arms, overcome by devout affection.

Chaupái 204.

With all the beauty of a myriad loves; dark of hue as the lotus or a heavy rain-cloud; the glistening nails on his rosy feet like clustered pearls on the leaves of the lily; the print of the thunderbolt, the flag and the elephant-goad distinctly to be seen; the tinkling of his anklets enough to charm a saint; with girdled waist and dimpled body and deep navel, such as no one could believe who had not seen; with long arms covered with many jewels and lovely set of tiger's claws upon his breast; with necklace of gems and sparkling amulet, and soul-ravishing print of the Bráhman's feet[1] with shell-marked neck and exquisite chin, and a face flushed with the beauty of all the loves ; with well-matched teeth and ruddy lips and nose and forehead-mark beyond description ; with beautiful ears and charming cheeks and lisping prattle most delightful to hear ; with eyes dark and full as the lotus, and heavy brows and a fair pendant on his forehead ; with lustrous curling hair that his mother was ever delighting to stroke ; with his body clothed in little yellow drawers, crawling on knees and hands upon the ground ; neither scripture nor Seshnág could do justice to his beauty, nor without a vision could any one imagine it.

Dohá 211.

The all-blissful god, who is above the reach of delusion and transcends all intellect, speech and perception of the senses, became subject to the strong love of his parents and sported like an innocent babe.

Chaupái 205.

In this way Ráma, the father of the universe, showed himself the delight of the people of Kosala ; and they who love their god, O Bhaváni, show themselves like his earthly parents. But his enemies, though they struggle for ever, will never extricate themselves from the bonds of existence. The delusive power that has subdued all life, whether in animate or inanimate creation, trembles before the Lord, who with the play of his eyebrows forces it to dance like a puppet. If we leave such a Lord, whom else can we supplicate ? Neither in thought, word nor deed be overwise ;

---

1 Rama is here identified with Vishnu, of whom the following legend is told in the *Bhágavat Puráṇa* :—The patriarch Bhrigu, being in doubt which of the three gods, Bráhma, Vishnu or Siva, was the greatest, determined to put the matter to the test. He first went to Bráhma and entered his court without making any obeisance, an affront at which the god showed himself exceedingly indignant. He then went to Siva and, treating him with a like want of respect, excited a yet more furious storm of passion. Lastly he went to Vaikunth, where finding Vishnu asleep in the embraces of his spouse Lakshmi, he struck him roughly on the breast with his foot to awaken him. The god started up, but seeing the saint, at once prostrated himself before him, and took and gently rubbed his foot with his hands, hoping it had not been hurt by striking against him. Thus Bhrigu learnt that in mercy and magnanimity, the highest attributes of the godhead, there was no other power that could be compared to Vishnu.

god is merciful only to those who pray. Thus the Lord sported as a child, to the delight of all the people of the city; and now his mother would take and dandle him in her arms, and now put him down and rock him in his cradle.

Dohá 212.

So lost in love that day and night succeeded one another unobserved, while in her fondness for her boy she kept singing to him nursery songs,

Chaupái 206.

One day his mother, after washing and dressing him, put him to sleep in his cradle, and prepared an offering for presentation to her partron divinity. When the service was over and she had made her oblation, she returned to the place where she had dressed the food; but when she came there she beheld Ráma in the act of eating. In a great fright she ran to the nursery and there found the child again sleeping; but coming back once more she still saw the boy. Then she trembled and was much disturbed in mind, for she saw two children, one here and one there and was utterly bewildered; saying,—'Are my senses at fault, or is this a miracle?' When Ráma saw his mother's distress, he broke out into a merry laugh,

Dohá 213.

and exhibited to her his whole marvellous form; with a myriad worlds gleaming on each individual hair of his body;

Chaupái 207.

With unnumbered suns and moons, Sivas and Bráhmas; with many mountains, rivers, oceans, lands and forests; with time, fate, merit, demerit nature and every power there manifested, even though unknown by name. When she beheld the awful vision she stood terror-stricken, with hands, clasped in prayer; for she saw both the life which Máya sets in motion and the faith that sets it free. With quivering body and speechless mouth she closed her eyes and bowed her head at his feet. Seeing his mother thus overpowered with amazement, Ráma again assumed the form of a child. But her terror left her not, while she hymned his praises, saying,—'I have regarded the great father as my own offspring.' Again and again Hari exhorted his mother,—'See, my mother, that you tell this to no one;'

Dohá 214.

and as often did Kausalyá meekly reply with clasped hands,—'See you too, my lord, that the delusive power of yours never again visits me,'

Chaupái 208.

Hari indulged in every kind of childish amusement, to the great delight of his attendants; and after a little time all the brothers grew to be big boys, gladdening every one about them. Then the guru came to perform the tonsure and again the Bráhmans received large offerings. The four lads run about and divert themselves in all sorts of pretty ways; and the lord, whose thoughts, works and acts transcend every human sense, plays in Dasarath's court-yard. If the king when at dinner called him, he would not leave his playmates and come, till Kausalyá herself went for him, when he would toddle along with her as fast as he could. He whom the scripture declares to be incomprehensible, of whom Siva could find no end, is picked up by his mother and carried off in a pet, and his father with a smile takes him in his lap, though grimy all over with dust.

Dohá 215.

Quickly glancing here and there during the meal, as soon as he got a chance, he would run away with a scream of delight, stuffing his mouth full of rice and curds.

Chaupái 209.

His pretty innocent childish sports have been sung by Sarasvati Seshnág Sambhu and the Vedas, and he whose soul does not warm to them has been brought into the world by God to no purpose. When the brothers were all grown up, the guru and their father and mother invested them with the sacred thread, and Ráma went to his guru's house to study. In a short time he mastered all knowledge. The four Vedas are but the breath of his mouth, and for him to study was a joke indeed. When they were proficient in scholarship and politeness and morality they began to practise all princely sports. With bow and arrow in hand they showed so fair that all creation was ravished at the sight, and as the brothers passed along the road every man and woman stopt to gaze at them.

Dohá 216.

Ráma was gracious to all; and not a soul in Kosala, man or woman, young or old, but held him dearer than life.

Chaupái 210.

Taking his brother with him as a companion, he would go to the forest to hunt; there selecting for death the noblest game, he every day brought and showed it to the king; and each beast, slain by his shaft, after death went straight to heaven. Taking his meals in company with his younger brother, ever obedient to his parents' commands, the gracious god omitted nothing that could please the people. He gave his mind to hear the Vedas and Puránas and then himself taught his brothers. Rising at break of day, he first saluted his parents and the priest, and then, after obtaining their sanction, busied himself with work in the city. The king was glad of heart when he saw his mode of life.

Dohá 217.

The all-pervading, indivisible, passionless, eternal God, who is without attributes, or name, or form, performs many wonders for the sake of his faithful people.

Chaupái 211.

I have now sung all these his doings; hearken attentively to the remainder of my story. The great and wise saint Visvamitra had chosen a fair hermitage in the forest, where he gave himself up to prayer, sacrifice and meditation. T demons Marícha and Subáhu, on beholding the preparati for sacrifice, feared greatly and hastened to disturb them. The saintly son of Gàdhi was pained and full of thought,—'There is no killing these accursed demons without Hari.' Then he reflected,—"The Lord has become incarnate to relieve earth of its burdens. I have now an excuse for going to visit him and after entreaty made will bring back with me the two brothers. Now I will feast my eyes with the sight of him who is the abode of all knowledge, piety and goodness."

Dohá 218.

His manifold longing brooked no delay on the road, and after bathing in the stream of the Sarju he proceeded to the king's court.

Chaupái 212.

When the Rája heard of the saint's arrival, he went to meet him with a retinue of Bráhmans, and prostrating himself reverently on the ground before him took and seated him on his own throne : then laved his feet and offered him religious honours, saying,—"There is no one so blest as I am to-day;" and had various kinds of food prepared for him. The great saint was highly pleased. Next, the king brought his four sons into the presence. On seeing Ráma the saint forgot his detachment from the world and was as enraptured with his lovely face as is the *chakor* with the full moon. Then said the glad king,—"Reverend sir, this favour is unparalleled ; what is the cause of your coming ? Tell me, and I will not delay to accomplish it." "There is a crew of demons that trouble me, and I am come to you, O king, with a request. Let me have Raghunáth and his brothers ; the demons' death is all I desire.

Dohá 219.

Give them, O king, gladly, without any selfish folly ; for you it will be a meritorious and honourable act, and it will also turn out well for them."

Chaupái 213.

When the king heard this cruel request, his heart beat

fast and all the brightness of his face grew dim,—"In my old age I have begotten four sons; O sir, you have spoken without consideration. Ask of me land, cattle, goods and treasure, and I will gladly give you all I have, at once. Nothing is dearer than the life of the body; but even that I would give in a minute. All my sons are dear to me as my own soul and, O sir, I cannot spare you Ráma. What is this pretty little boy of mine against a fierce and terrible demon?" On hearing the king's word so fraught with love, the wise saint was glad of heart. Then Vasishta much exhorted him, and the king's doubts were dispelled. Obediently he sent for the two boys and pressed them to his heart and fervently exclaimed,—"My two boys are my very life; but you, holy sir, are now their only father."

Dohá 200.

The king consigned the boys to the saint, again and again blessing them. Then they went to their mother's apartment and bowed the head at her feet.

Sorathá 23.

Glad to relieve the saint of his alarm, the two lion-hearted heroes set forth, oceans of compassion, resolute of purpose, the whole world's champions.

Chaupái 214.

Bright-eyed, broad-chested, long of arm, dark of hue as the lotus or the tamál tree; with quiver at side pendent from a yellow sash, and in either hand arrows and a comely bow, so marched the two brothers, one dark, the other fair, the treasure that Visvamitra had acquired,—"I recognize the lord god Bráhmanya-deva[1] in the child who thus on my account has left his own father." So thought the saint; and as he went he pointed out Táraká, who on hearing his voice rushed up in a fury. With a single arrow Hari took her life, but recognizing her submission gave her a place in his own heaven. Then the saint knew he had found his lord, but yet instructed him, the all-wise. As they travelled

1 Bráhmanya-deva is one of the epithets of Vishnu.

they felt neither hunger nor thirst; such their incomparable strength of body and glorious vigour.

Dohá 221.

After taking the Lord to his own hermitage, he made over to him every kind of weapon, and gave him herbs and roots and fruit to eat, knowing him to be ever gracious to men of holy life.

Chaupái 215.

At daybreak Raghurái said to him,—"Go and make ready the sacrifice, and fear not." The brotherhood began preparing the oblation, while he remained to guard the sacrificial fire. On hearing of this, the demon Márícha rushed up in a fury with his army to disturb the saint. Ráma smote him with a headless shaft, and he fell a hundred leagues the other side of ocean. Then he slew Subáhu with an arrow of fire, while his brother routed the whole demon host. When they had thus slain the demons and restored peace to the Bráhmans, the whole company of gods and saints began to hymn their praise. There Raghurái then stayed a few days and showed kindness to the hermits, who devoutly repeated to him many legends of the Puránas, though he knew them all before. Then the saint respectfully informed him,—"There is a sight, my lord, which is worth your going to see." When Raghunáth heard of the ordeal of the bow, he gladly accompanied the noble sage. On the way he spied a hermitage without bird, deer, or any living creature near it, and observing a remarkable stone inquired of the saint about it, who in reply gave him the whole history.

Dohá 222.

"Gautama's wife was by a curse turned into a hard rock, and is now longing for the dust of your lotus feet: O Raghubír, show mercy upon her."

Chhand 28 - 31.

At the touch so sweet of his hallowed feet, she awoke
from her long unrest,

And meekly adored her sovereign lord, awaiting his high behest.
With speechless tongue, limbs all unstrung, and eyes that streamed with tears,
She fell at his feet in rapture meet, far blest above all her peers.
Then bolder grown by the favour shown with a faith that himself had given,
She dared to raise her hymn of praise, —"Great Spirit, high lord of heaven,
Save me, O save, thy succour I crave, holy god, sinful wretch though I be,
Rávan's conquering foe, joy of all else below, who toil upon life's troubled sea.
Though the saint cursed me sore in the ill days of yore, now I hold it a blessing most sweet,
For my own eyes have seen my Redeemer, and I ween Siva only my rapture could mete.
Witless and weak, one only boon I seek; as the bee within the lotus loves to stay,
May my soul upon thy feet, O my god, I thee entreat, dwell in rapture never ending night and day:
Holy feet, the adoration of the lord of all creation, and source of the stream divine,
Which on Siva's head descended, this day have condescended to rest and on this vile head of mine."
Thus full of jubilation, with oft-renewed prostration, did Gautama's long lost bride,
With the boon she most had craved, thus graciously vouchsafed, return to her husband's side.

Dohá 223.

Thus the benevolent lord Hari is compassionate beyond our deserts, Worship him, says poor Tulsi Dás, and cease from all wrangling and hypocrisy.

Chaupái 216.

Ráma and Lakshman accompanied the saint to the world-purifying Ganges. Both the lord and his younger brother reverently saluted it, and Ráma was delighted beyond measure, as the son of Gádhi told him the legend how the heavenly stream had come down upon earth. Then the Lord and the hermits performed their ablutions and the Bráhmans received manifold gifts. The hermits' champion went on his way rejoicing, and quickly, drew near to the capital of Videha. When Ráma beheld the beauty of the city, he and his brother were delighted at the many ponds and wells and rivers and streams, with water of ambrosial purity and jewelled flights of steps; where the hum of bees, drunk with nectar, made a delicious sound and birds of all kinds were softly cooing: as the lilies expanded their many-coloured petals, and a cool, soft, fragrant breeze was ever delightful.

Dohá 224.

On all four sides the city was bright with flower-gardens, orchards and groves, the haunt of innumerable birds and full of fruit and flowers and verdure.

Chaupái 217.

The beauty of the city is not to be told; wherever one went there was something to charm the soul. Handsome bazárs and gorgeous balconies all studded with jewels, as though the Creator had fashioned them with his own hand; thriving bankers and traders, very Kuvers of wealth, sitting with all their various goods displayed; fine squares and beautiful streets, that were constantly sprinkled with fragrant waters; magnificent temples to all the gods, as bright as if they had been painted by Kámadeva himself; all the people of the city, both men and women, prosperous, well-dressed, virtuous, pious, intelligent and accomplished. But Janak's palace was such a masterpiece that the gods tired themselves with looking at it, and the mind was quite overcome by the sight of the Fort, for it seemed to have appropriated to itself all that was most beautiful in the world.

Dohá 225.

With glistening white walls and doors of gold with gems set in different devices, the exquisite mansion where Síta lived was far too lovely for words to describe.

Chaupái 218.

All the city gates were most massive with panels of adamant, and were thronged with princes and their retinues of mimists, bards and heralds. The vast and well-built stables were at all hours of the day crowded with horses, elephants and chariots : and the ministers, generals and warriors all had residences in the same style as the king. Outside the city, by pool and stream, the multitudinous princes had pitched their different camps. On seeing a fine mango grove, a most agreeable and convenient spot, the descendant of Kusika exclaimed,—"This is just what I like, let us stay here, Raghubír." "Very well my lord," answered the gracious god ; and there they alighted with all their hermit train. When the king of Mithilá heard the news that the great saint Visvamitra was come—

Dohá 226.

taking with him his ministers and many gallant fighting men and noble Bráhmans and the chief of his kinsmen,[1] in this fashion the king went forth rejoicing to meet the prince of sages.

Chaupái 219.

Bowing to the ground, he made obeisance, and the saint gladly gave him his blessing. Then the king respectfully saluted all the hermit train and congratulated himself on his good fortune. After making many inquiries as to his health and welfare, Visvamitra led the king to a seat, and at that very time arrived the two brothers who had gone to see the garden, one dark, the other fair, in childhood's tender bloom, the joy of all beholder's ravishing, the senses of the whole world. When Raghupati came, all rose and Visvamitra seated him by his side. All were charmed at the sight of the two brothers ; their eyes filled with tears and their body thrilled with rapture, and the

1 The words rendered, 'the chief of his kinsmen,' may also be taken to mean 'his *guru* (Satánand) and his kinsmen'.

king especially was beside himself with joy[1] on beholding their sweet and lovely appearance.

Dohá 227.

Though feeling himself overpowered with love, the king discreetly restrained himself, and bowing his head at the saint's feet, said in suppressed accents choking with emotion—

Chaupái 220.

"Tell me, my lord, who are these two lovely children. Are they the glory of a saintly family, or the bulwarks of a kingly line? or are they the twofold manifestation[2] of the Supreme Spirit, whom scripture declares to be unutterable. My mind, ordinarily free from wordly attachment, wearies itself with gazing upon them, as the *chakor* in gazing upon the moon. Therefore, sir, I beg you to tell me the truth and to conceal nothing. My love grows with looking, and my soul perforce is withdrawn from divine contemplation." Said the saint with a smile,—"You have spoken well, O king; your word is always true; there is not a living creature that does not love these boys." Ráma smiled to himself on hearing this. "They are the sons of Dasarath, the glory of the line of Raghu, and the king has sent them to help me.

Dohá 228.

Ráma and Lakshman by name, these two brothers, as strong as they are good and beautiful, with their companions, protected my sacrifice and vanquished all the demons in battle."

Chaupái 221.

Said the king,—"O saint, when I behold your feet I cannot tell how richly I am rewarded for any former good deeds. And these pretty twins have conferred a happiness

1 This line, *Bhayau* Videha *videha bisekhi*, contains a play upon words which cannot be preserved in a translation. A literal rendering would be; particular Videha (*i. e.*, Janak, the king of Videha) became really *videha* (*i. e.*, without a body).

2 The two manifestations are *nirgan* and *sagan*, the bodiless and the embodied.

upon you, the supremely happy. Their innocent mutual affection is indescribable in words ; a delight to the inmost soul. Hear me, sir, cried the king in his rapture, it is like the natural union between the universal soul and the soul of man." Again and again the king gazed upon the Lord with quivering body and heart bursting with emotion. Then with courteous phrase and bowed head he escorted the saint to the city and there assigned him apartments, which were bright and cheerful at all times of the day ; and finally, after further homage and proffers of service, the king took his leave and returned to the palace.

Dohá 229.

When Ráma and the hermits had taken food and rested a little, he went and sat down by his brother's side: now it still wanted an hour to sunset,

Chaupái 222.

and Lakshman had at heart a great longing to go and see Janak's city ; but again, for fear of his brother and respect for the saint, he said nothing out loud, but was smiling to himself. Ráma understood what was passing in his mind, and being ever considerate to his followers was glad and, with a most modest and submissive smile, after begging permission of his *guru* to speak, said,—" Sir, Lakshman wishes to see the city, but out of respect for you is afraid to speak. If you will allow me, I will show him the place and quickly bring him back again." The saint replied most affectionately,—" O Ráma how can you do aught but good ; the guardian of the bridge of religion, the loving benefactor of all faithful servants ?

Dohá 230.

Go, blessed pair of brothers, and see the city ; gladden the eyes of all the people by the sight of your beauty."

Chaupái 223.

After bowing at the saint's feet they went, these two brothers, the delight of the eyes of the whole world. When the children in the market-place saw their exceeding beauty their eyes and their very soul fastened greedily upon them. Clad in yellow apparel, with belt and quiver at their side, with graceful bow and arrows in hand, a lovely pair, one dark, the other fair of hue, with sandalwood *tilak* to match their complexion ; with lion-like waist and long arms, and breast adorned with strings of elephant pearls, with shapely ears and lotus eyes, and moonlike face to assuage the three kinds of pain ; with golden flowers for earrings, so beautiful as to steal the heart of every beholder ; with a bewitching glance and fair arched eyebrows, and a star on the forehead that seemed beauty's own stamp ;

Dohá 231.

With jaunty cap on comely head, with black curly locks the two brothers were all-beautiful from head to foot and exquisite in every part.

Chaupái 224.

When the citizens heard that the princes were come to see the town, they all left their business and started off like beggars to pillage a treasury. When they beheld the easy grace of the two brothers they were glad indeed, and their eyes were rewarded. The maidens peeping from the windows of the houses at once fell in love with Ráma's beauty, and in amorous strain addressed one another,—" They surpass in beauty a thousand loves : neither among gods, nor men, nor demons, nor serpents, nor deified stains has beauty such as theirs ever been heard of. As for Vishnu with his four arms, Bráhma with his four heads, and Purári with his five faces and wondrous attire, and all the other gods, there is not one in the whole universe whose beauty, my friend, can be compared to theirs.

Dohá 232.

Of tender age, the very home of beauty, equally lovely whether dark or fair, as though a myriad loves had been lavished on each individual limb of their body.

Chaupái 225.

Tell me, friend, is there any one in human form who would not be charmed at the sight of such beauty?" Said one in gentle loving tones,—"Hear, my dear, what I have been told. This pretty pair of young cygnets are the two sons of King Dasarath. They have protected the sacrifice of Saint Visvamitra and slain in battle the invincible demons. The lovely child with dark complexion and lotus eyes, who quelled the pride of Márícha and Subáhu and bears the bow and arrows in his hand, is the sweet son of Kausalyá, by name Ráma. The fair youth in gallant attire, who also has bow and arrows in hand and follows Ráma, is named Lakshman and is his younger brother. Sumitrá, you must know, is his mother.

Dohá 233.

After befriending the Bráhmans, and on the road setting free the sage's wife, the two brothers have come here to see the tournament." On hearing this all the ladies were delighted.

Chaupái 226.

Said one, after regarding Ráma's, beauty,—"Here is a bridegroom worthy of Jánaki. If the king does but see him, he will abjure his vow and insist upon a marriage with them." Said another,—"The king knows who they are and has received both them and the saint, with all honour. He has not, however, gone back from his vow, but mastered by fate persists in his folly." Said another,—"If God is good and is certain to reward every man according to his deserts, then here is the bridegroom Jánaki will wed. About this, my dear, there can be no doubt. When such a union is brought about by destiny, every one will be satisfied. O friend, I am deeply moved by the thought that if this marriage takes place he will come again some time;

Dohá 234.

otherwise there is no chance of my seeing him; it is only a

long accumulation of merit in previous existences that is rewarded by such intercourse."

Chaupái 227.

Said another,—"Friend, you have spoken well; this is a marriage that will please every one." Said another,—"Siva's bow is hard to bend, and this dark lad is of delicate frame; it is really a most unfair test." Hearing this, another soft-voiced maiden said,—"I have once and again heard say of them that though slight in appearance their strength is great. Touched by the dust of his lotus feet, the guilty Ahalya attained salvation: and he will never rest till he has broken the bow; this is a belief out of which I am no-how to be cheated. When the Creator fashioned Síta, he predestined for her this dark-complexioned bridegroom." On hearing these words all were glad and softly exclaimed,—"May it indeed prove so."

Dohá 235.

In their gladness of heart the bevy of fair-faced bright-eyed dames shower down flowers, and wherever the two brothers went there was all the joy of heaven.

Chaupái 228.

Now they reached the eastern quarter of the city, where the lists had been prepared for the tournament. In the midst of a fair and spacious paved area a spotless altar had been gorgeously adorned, with a broad golden paltform all around for the reception of the princes, and close behind another circular tier for the spectators, of somewhat greater height and elegantly decorated, where all the people of the city might come and sit. Close to this was another large and beautiful gallery of glistening white, painted in diverse colours, whence ladies might view the spectacle with due decorum, according to their family rank. The children politely show the two lords all the preparations, and with pleasant voice keep telling them what this is and that is;

Dohá 236.

thus, in their affection, finding a pretext for frequently touching their lovely person; while they thrill all over with delight as again and again they gaze on the twin brothers.

Chaupái 229.

When they perceived that Ráma was won by their devotion, they lovingly explain the different places, each according to his own fancy calling away the two brothers, who in their kindness are ever ready to come. Ráma shows Lakshman everything, still talking in light and merry tone: and he, in obedience to whose fiat Maya in a moment of time created the entire universe, out of compassion to his faithful people, feigns amazement at the sight of a tourney ground. When they had seen all the show, they returned to their guru in alarm at being so late: and he, by whose awe Terror itself is dismayed, thus manifests the transcendant virtue of devotion. With many kind and courteous phrases they reluctantly take bave of the children:

Dohá 237.

and meekly and submissively, with mingled awe and love, they bow the head at the guru's feet: nor sit down till they obtain his permission.

Chaupái 230.

When it was dusk the saint gave the word, and all performed their evening devotions, and in the recital of sacred legends spent two watches of the solemn night. Then the saint retired to his couch, and the two brothers began to shampoo his feet; they whose lotus feet the holiest of men longing to behold practise all kinds of penance and meditation, even they, these two brothers, mastered by love, affectionately shampooed their master's lotus feet. At last when the saint had so ordered again and again, Ráma himself retired to rest, while Lakshman pressed his feet to his heart and reverently caressed them with emotions of exquisite delight. Again and again the Lord said,—

'Sleep, my brother,' and at last he laid himself down, but with the divine feet still in his lap.

Dohá 238.

When the night was spent, at the first sound of cock-crow Lakshman arose; and next, before the saint, woke the lord of the universe, the all-wise Ráma.

Chaupái 231.

After performing all the customary acts of purification and going to bathe, they bowed before the guru, and by his permission went out to gather flowers, as befitted the time. As they went they spied a beautiful garden of the king's, where reigned perpetual Spring, planted with ornamental trees of every kind, and overhung with many coloured creepers, so rich in bud and fruit and flower that in its abundance it put to shame even the trees of paradise; while the peacocks danced responsive to the music made by the feathered choir of *chátak*, *koil*, parrot and *chakor*. In the midst of the garden a lovely lake shone bright with jewelled steps of varied designed : its pure expanse gladdened with many-coloured lotuses and the cooing of water-birds and the hum of bees.

Dohá 239.

Both the lord and his brother were delighted at the sight of the lake and the garden. What a charming pleasance must that have been which pleased even Ráma.

Chaupái 232.

After looking all about and asking leave of the gardeners they began in high glee to gather leaves and flowers. At that very time Síta too came there, having been sent by her mother to visit the shrine of Girijá. With her came all her young and lovely companions, singing glad songs. Now Girijá's shrine was close to the lake, beautiful beyond description, the delight of all beholders. When she and her attendants had bathed in the pool, she approached the goddess with a glad heart, and after adoration paid with much devotion begged of her a handsome and well-matched bridegroom. One of her attendant damsels, who had strayed away to look at the garden, chanced to see the two brothers and returned to Síta quite love-smitten.

Dohá 240.

When her companions observed what a state she was in, her body all in a tremble and her eyes full of tears, they asked in gentle tones,—'Declare the cause of this rapture.'

Chaupái 233

"There have come to see the garden two princes of tender age and charming in every way ; one dark of hue, the other fair, but how can I describe them ? Voice is sightless and eyes are dumb." All the damsels were delighted at her speech, and perceiving the intense longing in Síta's bosom, one of them exclaimed,—"My dear, they must be the king's sons, who, as I hear, arrived yesterday with the saint, who completely fascinated with their beauty and stole away the hearts of all the women in the city. Every one is talking of their loveliness ; we really must see them ; they are worth seeing." These words were most grateful to Síta, whose eyes were restless with longing. With her kind friend to lead the way, she followed, nor did any one know that it was an old love

Dohá 241.

Remembering Nárad's words, she was filled with holy devotion, and anxiously turned her gaze on every side, like a startled fawn.

Chaupái 234.

When he heard the sound of the golden bangles on her hands and feet, Ráma thought within himself, and then said to Lakshman,—"Imagine Love triumphant over the whole world to be now sounding the kettledrum of victory." So saying he again looked in that direction, and like the moon on the *chakor* flashed Síta's face upon his sight. His eyes became as immovably fixed as though Nimi, the winking god, had fled in confusion from his wonted post. Beholding her beauty he was enraptured; but his admiration was all within, and utterance failed him. As though the great Architect, after creating the world, had put before it in visible form all the skill with which he had fashioned it; or as if the Beautiful had been beautified into a temple of beauty and illuminated by a sudden flash of torchlight; but all the similes of the poets are stale and hackneyed; where can I find any likeness to Jánaki?

Dohá 242.

Dwelling in heart on Síta's beauty and reflecting on his own good fortune, the pure-souled god thus addressed his brother in terms appropriate to the occasion,—

Chaupái 235.

"Brother, this is the very daughter of king Janak for whom the tournament has been ordained. She has come with her attendants to worship Gauri, and a train of light marks her path through the garden. At the sight of her divine beauty, my ordinarily placid bosom is agitated; God alone knows the cause, but of a truth, brother, my lucky side is throbbing as though for coming good fortune. It has always been a mark of the race of Raghu that they never set their heart on evil courses; and thus I am confidently assured that all will be well; for I have never even in a dream looked upon another man's wife to long after her. And rare, indeed, in the world are the men who neither turn their back upon the foe in battle nor covet their neighbour's wife, and from whom no beggar meets a rebuff."

Dohá 243.

Thus discoursing to his brother, and with his soul enamoured of Síta's beauty, like a bee sucking honey from a flower, he drank in the loveliness of her face.

Chaupái 236.

Síta kept looking anxiously all round, in doubt as to where the princes had gone. Wherever fell her fawn-like glance, it seemed a rain of glistening lotus flowers. Then her companions pointed out to her under the shade of the creepers the two lovely youths, the one dark, the other fair of hue. Her eyes, on beholding their beauty, were filled with longing and with the gladness of one who has found a long-lost treasure. Wearied with gazing upon Ráma's charms, her eyelids forgot to wink, and her whole frame was fulfilled with desire, as is the partridge when it sees the autumnal moon. Receiving Ráma into her heart by the pathway of vision, she craftily closed upon him the doors of her eyelids. When her companions saw her thus overcome, they were too much abashed to utter a word.

Dohá 244.

Then emerged the twin brothers from the shade of the arbour, like two spotless moons from a riven cloud.

Chaupái 237.

Two gallant champions, the perfection of beauty, like a white lotus and a dark, with their hair parted like a raven's wing on their comely head, and here and there bedecked with bunches of flower-buds; their forehead bright with the *tilak* and beads of perspiration, and their graceful ears adorned with ornaments; with arched eyebrows and curly locks, and eyes bright as a lotus bud, with lovely chin and nose and cheeks, and a gracious smile enslaving every soul—such beauteous features as I could never describe; they would put to shame a myriad Loves. With a string of jewels on his breast, with exquisitely dimpled neck, and powerful arms, like the trunk of some young elephant in whom Kámadeva had become incarnate; with the flowers and cup of leaves in his left hand, the dark prince, O my friend, is beautiful exceedingly.

Dohá 245.

As her companions gazed upon the two glories of the Solar race, with their lion-like waist and bright yellow attire, very abodes of bliss and amiability, they lost all self-consciousness.

Chaupái 238.

Yet one summoning up courage, grasped Síta by the hand and said,—"You can at any time meditate upon Gauri; why not now look at the princes?" Then the modest Síta unclosed her eyes and saw before her the two scions of Raghu. As she gazed on Ráma, all beautiful from head to foot, and remembered her father's vow, she was greatly agitated. When her companions saw her thus overcome they all cried as if in alarm,—"It is getting late;" and one added with a meaning smile,—"We must come again at this time to-morrow." On hearing this clever hint Síta was abashed and said, as if in fear of her mother,—"It is late, indeed." Then summoning up resolution, she fixed the image of Ráma in her heart and turned to go; but again she thought how entirely it all depended upon her sire,

Dohá 246.

and under pretence of looking at a deer, or bird, or tree, again and again she turned her head, and each time that she beheld the beauteous Rghubír her love was augmented not a little.

Chaupái 239.

The thought of Siva's unyielding bow made her wild and as she went she kept in her heart the image of the darkhued swain. When the Lord perceived that she was going, he drew in his heart with the indelible ink of love a charming sketch of her infinite beauty and virtue and blissful devotion. Again she sought Bhaváni's shrine, and after embracing her feet, thus prayed with clasped hands,—"Glory, glory, glory to thee, O daughter of the mountain-king, as fixed in thy gaze on Siva's face as is the partridge on the moon; O mother of Ganes and Kartikeya; great mother of the world; whose body is lustrous as the lightning; of whom there is neither beginning nor middle nor end; whose infinite majesty is a mystery even to the Veda; cause of the birth, continuance, and ultimate destruction of all being; enchantress of the universe; delighting in thy own supremacy:

Dohá 247.

Among all faithful wives and true women, thy name, O mother, holds the first place; thy immeasurable grandeur is more than a thousand Sáradás and Seshnágs could tell.

Chaupái 240.

The four-fold rewards of life are easy of attainment by thy servants, O granter of boons, beloved of Tripurári; and all, O goddess, who adore thy lotus feet, are made happy, whether they be gods, or men, or saints. Thou knowest well my heart's desire, for in the heart of man thou ever dwellest: there is no need that I declare it aloud to thee." So saying, Síta embraced her feet. Bhavání was moved by her humility and devotion; the image smiled and a garland dropt. Reverently Síta clasped to her bosom the divine gift, and Gauri herself with a heart full of joy thus spoke,—"Hearken, Síta; my blessing is effectual; your heart's desire shall be accomplished. Nárad's words are ever truth itself; the bridegroom upon whom your soul is set shall, indeed, be yours.

Chhand 32.

The dark-complexioned youth, upon whose innate beauty your soul is set, shall indeed be yours. The All-merciful in his wisdom knows your loving disposition." On hearing Gauri pronounce this blessing, Síta and her companions were glad of heart, and in their delight (says Tulsi) returned again and again to the temple to adore the goddess.

Sorathá 24.

Finding Gauri so gracious, Síta was more glad of heart than words can tell; and as an auspicious omen, her left side, the seat of good fortune, began to throb.

Chaupái 241.

The two brothers returned to their guru, inwardly praising Síta's loveliness; and Ráma related to him all that had taken place, being simplicity itself and utterly devoid of all guile. The saint took the flowers and performed his devotions, and then imparted his blessing to the two brothers, saying,—"May your desire be accomplished." Ráma and Lakshman gladdened at the words. Then, after taking food, the saintly sage began the recital of sacred legends. When the day was spent, they first asked his permission and then went out to perform their evening duties. The glorious moon was rising in the eastern sky, and its orb reminded them of Síta's lovely face ; but afterwards they thus reasoned within themselves,—"The queen of night is not to be compared with Síta ;

Dohá 248.

for she was born of the restless Ocean, with poison for a brother, and by day she is dim and obscure, how then can such a poor feeble creature be matched with the lovely Síta.

Chaupái 242.

She waxes and wanes, is the curse of love-sick maids, and is devoured by Ráhu whenever the appointed time comes round ; she causes anguish to the *chakwa* and whithers the lotus ; O moon, thou art full of faults. It is a great sin and highly improper to compare Janak's daughter to thee." Thus, finding in the moon a pretext for extolling Síta's beauty, they returned to their guru, the night being now far advanced, and after bowing themselves at his feet and obtaining his permission they retired to rest. When the night was over, Raghunáyak arose and, looking towards his brother, thus began to say,—"See, brother, the day has dawned to the delight of the lotus, the *chakwa* and all mankind." Then said Lakshman in gentle tones and with folded hands, declaring the glory of the Lord,—

Dohá 249.

"At the dawn of day the lily fades and the brightness of the stars is dimmed, so at the news of your coming all the princes waxed faint ;

Chaupái 243.

for bright though they be as the planets, they cannot

master the night-black bow. The lotus, the *chakwa*, the bee, and every bird—all rejoice in night's defeat; and so, O lord, all your votaries will be glad when the bow is broken. Sunrise is an easy triumph over darkness: the constellations retire and light flashes upon the world. O Raghurái, the sun in its rising shows the chiefs in a figure the majesty of their lord, and your mighty arms are as it were the pass in the eastern mountain through which is manifested the spectacle of the broken bow." The Lord smiled to hear his brother's speech. The All-pure then performed the daily rites of purification and bathed and, after observance of the prescribed ceremonies, presented himself before the guru and bowed his comely head at his feet. Then Janak summoned Satánand and sent him in haste to Visvamitra. He came and declared his sovereign's message, and also called for the two brothers.

Dohá 250.

After reverently saluting Satánand, the Lord went and sat down by his guru, who said,—" Come, my son, Janak has sent for you.

Chaupái 244.

You must go and see Síta's nuptials, and who is the happy man whom heaven will honour." Said Lakshman,—" His will be the glory, my lord, upon whom your favour rests." The saints were glad to hear this seemly speech, and all with much effusion gave their blessing. Then the gracious god, attended by all the saintly throng, sallied forth to witness the tournament. No sooner had they reached the arena than the news spread all over the city, and every one put away his work and came thronging in, men and women, young and old, and even children in arms. When Janak saw the enormous crowd he gave orders to his practised servitors,—" Go round at once to all the people and marshal them to their proper seats."

Dohá 251.

With courteous phrase they respectfully seated them

all, both men and women, according to their respective rank, whether noble, burgher or churl.

Chaupái 245.

Then stept forth the two princes like beauty beautified, graceful and accomplished champions, one dark, the other fair, but both charming: resplendent in the assembly of princes like two full moons in a circle of stars. Every spectator seemed to see in them an embodiment of his own conception: the princes beheld a gallant warrior, as it were the Heroic incarnate: the wicked kings trembled at the sight of the Lord, as a visible presentment of the Terrible; the demons in their princely disguise thought they saw the image of Death: while the citizens regarded the twin brothers as the glory of manhood, a delight to the eyes.

Dohá 252.

The women with joy of heart saw what each loved most, as it were a bright vision of the Erotic in utterly incomparable form.

Chaupái 246.

By sages the Lord was seen in his divine majesty with many faces and hands and feet and eyes and heads. And how did he appear to Janak's family group? Like a noble kinsman and friend. The queen, no less than the king, regarded him with unspeakable love like a dear child: to mystics he shone forth as eternal Truth, the placid radiance of unruffled Quietism; while to the pious the two brothers, appeared as their own benignant patron saint. But as for Síta, when she gazed on Ráma, her love and joy were unspeakable; if she could not utter the emotion of her heart, how can any poet declare it? Thus according to the ruling passion of each individual spectator, were the Kosala princes seen by each—

Dohá 253.

Resplendent in the midst of the royal circle in their contrasted beauty, stealing the eyes of the whole universe.

Chaupái 247.

Both with such facile grace of form that a myriad Loves were all too mean a comparison: with beaming face, that would put to shame the autumnal moon, and irresistibly charming lotus eyes; with a glance so unspeakably winning that it would rob Love of all his pride; with rounded cheeks and ears adorned with pendulous gems; with beautiful chin and lips and sweet voice; with a smile more radiant than the light of the moon, and arched eyebrows and delicate nose; a broad forehead with glittering *tilak*, and clustering locks with which no swarm of bees could vie; with yellow turban on their shapely head, dotted here and there with flower-buds; with exquisite neck, marked with a triple line, enclosing as it were the bliss of the three spheres of creation.

Dohá 254.

Adorned with a necklace of elephant pearls[1] and a *tulsi* garland on their breast; with the shoulder of a bull and the gait of a lion, and long arms very models of strength.

Chaupái 248.

By their side a quiver slung from a yellow brace; with arrows in hand and bow on their left shoulder; with a charming Bráhmanical cord, also of yellow tint, and, in short, beautiful from head to foot, beauty all over. Every one who saw them was made happy, nor could for a minute take his eyes off them. Janak, too, rejoiced to behold the two brothers. Then went he to the saint and embraced his feet, and differentially related to him all his past history, and showed the hermits the place marked out for the games. Whenever the two gallant princes turned, all men's eyes were dazzled; each saw in Ráma what he himself most admired, without understanding that it was a special miracle. The saint told the king the arrangements were perfect, and the king was thereby highly gratified.

---

1 The *kunjara-mani*, as it is here named, or more commonly *gajamukta*, is a pearl supposed to be found in the projections on the forehead of an elephant.

Dohá 255.

There was one tier of seats bright, spacious and beautiful above all the rest, and here the Rája seated the saint and the two brothers.

Chaupái 249.

At the sight of the Lord all the chiefs grew sick at heart, like the stars at the rising of the full moon; for they felt inwardly assured that beyond all doubt Ráma would succeed in bending the bow; or even if he did not break the massy beam, that Síta would still bestow upon him the garland of victory. And so thinking, sir, they turned homewards, abandoning all glory of victory and pride of strength. There were other kings, blind and insolent fools, who mocked at such words and cried,—"To break the bow and win the bride is a difficulty,[1] but unless it be broken how can the bride be won? Should Death himself for once come forth against us, him too would we conquer in battle for Síta's sake." Hearing this there were other kings who smiled, good, pious and sensible men, and said,—

Sorathá 25.

Ráma will certainly marry Síta, to the discomfiture of those proud princes; for who can conquer in battle Dasarath's gallant sons?

Chaupái 250.

Why thus scoff and throw away your lives to no purpose; imagined sweets stop no man's hunger. Listen to this my solemn warning: be inwardly assured that Síta is the mother, and Ráma the father of the universe, and feast your eyes to the full on their beauty. These two brothers, so lovely, so gracious, so full of every excellence, have their home in Sambhu's heart. Why, when you have a sea of ambrosia at hand, should you leave it to run upon your death in pursuit of a mirage? But do ye what seemeth you good: we have to-day reaped our life's reward." So saying

1 The word *avagáha* in this line is explained in glossaries by *atháh* 'unfathomable,' as if from the root *gáh*, to dive into. Rather, however, it seems to be for *avagráha* (as *kohi* for *krodhi*), meaning an impediment or difficulty.

the good kings turned to gaze with affection on the picture of incomparable beauty; while in heaven the gods mounted their chariots to behold the spectacle, and showered down flowers and uttered songs of joy.

Dohá 256.

Then seeing the fitness of the time, Janak sent and summoned Síta; and obediently she came, with all her lovely and accomplished attendants.

Chaupái 251.

Her beauty is not to be told: seeing that she is the mother of the world, the perfection of all grace and goodness, every comparison seems to me unworthy of her and appropriate only to mortal woman. In describing Síta, to what can she be likened, or what can the poet name that will not rather do her dishonour? If I should liken her to other women, where is there on earth any nymph so lovable; or, if I look to the denizens of heaven, Sarasvati is a chatterer; Bhavâni has only half a body; Rati is in sore distress on account of her disfleshed lord; and as for Lakshmi, the twinbirth of poison and strong drink, how can Síta be compared to her? Even though the ocean of ambrosia were the Beautiful, and the tortoise Grace, the rope being Fascination, and Mount Meru the amorous sentiment, while Love with his own lotus hand played the part of churner;

Dohá 257.

Even then, though Lakshmi the source of all beauty end bliss, had thus been born, still the poet would shrink from saying that she could be compared to Síta.

Chaupái 252.

She came, and with her her attendant maids, singing sweet-voiced songs: the mother of creation, of incomparable beauty; her delicate frame veiled in a fair white robe, and with a profusion of brilliant and tasteful ornaments, with which her maidens had bedecked her every limb. When she set her foot within the lists, all beholders, men and women alike, were fascinated by her charms; the gods in their delight sounded their kettledrums and rained down flowers midst the singing of the *apsarasas.* The wreath of victory sparkled in her hands as she cast a hurried glance on the assembled kings, with anxious heart looking for Ráma. Not a king but was love-smitten. But by the saint sat the two brothers and on them she fell with her greedy eyes as upon a rich treasure.

Dohá 258.

Shrinking into herself from awe of the reverend fathers and at the sight vast assemblage, she turned her eyes upon her attendants, though at the same time she drew all Ráma into her soul.

Chaupái 253.

Not a man or woman, who beheld the beauty of Ráma and the loveliness of Síta, could close his eyes for a second: but all thought with dismay of the king's vow and in their heart made supplication to Bráhma,—"O God, quickly remove Janak's obstinacy and make him right-minded as myself. Let the king have no hesitation about breaking his vow and giving Síta in marriage to Ráma: the world will approve, and we all shall be pleased; but obstinacy, if persisted in, will at the last be as a consuming fire in his bosom." All were absorbed in the same ardent desire, saying,—"The dark youth is the match for Síta." Then Janak summoned the heralds, who as they came proclaimed his state and dignity, and bade them go and declare his vow. They went, but in their heart was little joy.

Dohá 259.

The heralds cried aloud,—"Hearken, all ye princes: we announce to you our sovereign's vow, and with upraised hands call heaven to witness it.

Chaupái 254.

Though your mighty arms be as the moon, yet Siva's famous bow is as terrible and unyielding as Ráhu. When Rávan and Bánásur saw it—albeit sturdy champions—they left it and went their way. Here is now the great god's massy beam, and whoever in this royal assembly shall to-day bend it shall be renowned in heaven and earth and hell, and at once without hesitation shall receive in marriage the hand of the king's daughter." When they heard the vow, all the kings were full of eagerness—insolent warriors, savage of soul—and girding up their loins they rose in haste, bowing their heads, ere they commenced, before their patron god. With flushed face and many a close look, they essay the divine bow: but though they put forth all their strength in a thousand different ways they cannot move it. Those, indeed, who had any sense at all did not go near it.

Dohá 260.

After straining at the bow—those foolish kings—without being able to stir it, they retire in confusion, as though it had gathered strength by in turn absorbing the force of each successive warrior.

Chaupái 255.

Next ten thousand kings all at once attempted to raise it, but it was not to be moved and yielding as little as a virtuous wife at the words of a gallant. All the princes appeared as ridiculous as a hermit who has no religion. Their mighty glory and renown and heroism were utterly worsted by the bow, and with much confusion of face and sadness of heart they went and took again each his own place in the assembly. When Janak saw the kings thus dismayed, he cried aloud as it were in anger,—"Hearing the vow that I had made, many kings have come from diverse realms, with gods and demons in human form, stalwart heroes, staunch in fight.

Dohá 261.

A lovely bride, a grand triumph and splendid renown are the prize, but God, it seems, has not created the man who can break the bow and win it.

Chaupái 256.

Tell me now who was dissatisfied with the guerdon or,

refused to try his strength on Siva's bow, but let alone lifting and breaking, sirs, there was not one of you who could stir it even a grain's breadth from the ground. Now let no proud warrior wax wroth if I assert there is not a man left on earth. Give up all hope and turn your faces homewards: it is God's will that Síta is not to be married. If I break my vow, all my religious merit is gone; the girl must remain a maid; what can I do? Had I known, sirs, that there were no men in the world, I would not have made myself a laughing-stock by recording such a vow." Every man and woman who heard Janak's words and looked at Jánaki were sad; but Lakshman was furious: his eyes flashed, his lips quivered and his brows were knit.

Dohá 262.

But for fear of his brother he could not speak, though the taunt pierced his heart like an arrow. Yet at last, bowing his head at Ráma's lotus feet, he thus spoke in dignified tones:—

Chaupái 257.

"May there never be repeated in any assembly, where even the lowest of the family of Raghu is present, such a scandalous speech as that now uttered by Janak in the presence of the greatest of the clan. Hearken, thou sun of the lotus-like solar race; I state the simple truth, without any vain boasting; if only I have thy permission, I will lift the round world with as much ease as a marble, and will break it in pieces like an ill-baked potter's vessel, and tear up Mount Meru like a potherb. Before thy infinite majesty, O my lord god, what is this wretched old bow? Only give me an order and see what an exhibition I will make. I will take up the bow as though it were a lotus stalk, and will run a hundred leagues with it to convince you.

Dohá 263.

Inspired by thy presence, my lord, I will snap it like the stick of an umbrella; or if I fail I swear by thy holy feet never to take bow in hand again."

Chaupái 258.

As Lakshman thus spoke in his wrath, earth shook and its elephant supporters tottered; the whole assembly and all the kings were struck with terror; Síta was glad of heart and Janak was ashamed; while the saint and Ráma and all the hermits were enraptured and quivered all over with excitement. Then Ráma with a sign checked Lakshman, and lovingly made him sit beside him, while Visvamitra, perceiving the fitness of the time, spoke in gentle and affectionate tones,—"Up, Ráma, break this bow of Siva's and relieve Janak, my son, of his affliction." On hearing the guru's words he bowed his head at his feet, and without joy or sorrow in his soul rose and stood upright in all his native grace, lordly in gait as a young lion.

Dohá 264.

As Raghubar ascended the stage, like the sun climbling the mountains of the east, the hearts of the saints expanded like the lotus, and their eyes were glad as bees at the return of day.

Chaupái 259.

The dark hopes of the kings vanished like the night and like the serried stars their vaunts waxed feeble: the arrogant shrivelled up like the lilies, and the false slunk away like the owls; saints and gods, like the *chakwa*, were relieved of their distress and rained down flowers in token of homage. After affectionately reverencing the guru's feet and asking permission of the holy fathers, the lord of all creation quickly stepped forth, with the tread of a majestic elephant when inflamed with love. As he moved, every man and woman in the city quivered all over their body with delight, worshipping the spirits of their ancestors and the gods, and recalling their own past good deeds, saying,—"If my virtuous acts be of any avail, O father Ganes, may Ráma snap the bow as it were a lotus-stalk."

Dohá 265.

After lovingly gazing upon Ráma, Síta's mother bade her attendants draw near, and thus spoke with affectionate anxiety,—

Chaupái 260.

" Girls, every one is bent on seeing the show, and as for saying what would be for my good, there is no one who will tell the king plainly :—These are two mere boys ; this excessive obstinacy of yours is wrong ; Rávan and Bánásur could not touch the bow, and the kings with all their pride were conquered by it ; how then give it into the hands of these boy-princes ? As well might a cygnet carry off Mount Meru. All the king's good sense is clean gone : Ah, girls, god's ways are inscrutable." A sharp-witted maiden gently answered,—" O queen, the glorious are never to be lightly regarded. Consider the weakness of Agastya and the boundlessness of ocean ; yet he drained it dry, and his fame has spread through the world. Again, the orb of the sun is small to look at, but—at its rising—darkness is expelled from heaven and earth and hell.

Dohá 266.

A charm is a very little thing, yet it overpowers Bráhma and Vishnu and Mahádeva and all the gods ; and a mere goad governs the mightiest and most furious elephant.

Chaupái 261.

Love, too, though his bow and arrows are but of flowers, has brought the whole world under subjection. Fear not then lady, but hearken to me—Ráma will assuredly break the bow." She took heart at these words of her attendant, her despondency ceased and her desire was enlarged. Then Síta, with her eyes fixed on Ráma, implored with anxious heart each god in turn, praying to them in her inward soul,—" Be gracious to me, O Mahádeva and Bhaváni, and reward my service by kindly lightening the weight of the bow O divine Ganes, granter of boons, it is with a view to to-day that I have done you service. Hearken to my oft-repeated supplication, and reduce the weight of the bow to a mere trifle."

Dohá 267.

Oft glancing at Raghubir's form, and taking courage from her heaven-ward prayers, her eyes were filled with tears of love, and her whole body was in a tremor.

Chaupái 262.

With fixed gaze she devoured his beauty, and then, as she remembered her father's vow, her soul was troubled,—"Alas, my father, for your cruel resolve, made without any regard to good or evil consequences; not a minister but was afraid to give advice—the more the pity—in the great conclave of counsellors. Here is a bow as firm as adamant, and here a little dark-hued prince of tender frame. O god, how can I maintain my faith?—Is it possible for a delicate *siris* flower to transpierce a diamond? The judgment of the whole assembly has gone astray; now, O bow of Sambhu, thou art the only hope left me; impart thy own heaviness to the crowd, and grow light thyself at once at the sight of Ráma." So great was the agitation of Síta's soul that an instant of time passed as slowly as an age.

Dohá 268.

As she looks, now at the Lord, and now at the ground, her tremulous eyes so glisten, as it were love's two fish disporting themselves in the orb of the moon.

Chaupái 263.

In her lotus mouth her bee-like voice lies bound; for modesty, like night, allows it not. In the corner of her eye stood a tear-drop, like a miser's buried hoard. Abashed by the consciousness of extreme excitement, she yet summoned up courage and confidence,—"If there is any truth in me at all and I am really enamoured of Raghupati's lotus feet, then the Lord God, who knoweth all men's hearts, will make me Ráma's handmaid; for wherever there is true affection of soul to soul, union will follow beyond a doubt."

With her eyes fixed upon the lord she recorded this loving vow ; and he, the most merciful, comprehended it all. After looking at Síta he cast a glance at the bow, as Garur might glance at a poor little snake.

Dohá 269.

When Lakshman perceived that the glory of his race had his eye fixed upon the bow, he thrilled with emotion, and striking the earth with his foot, cried thus aloud,—

Chaupái 264.

" Ye elephant warders, ye tortoise, serpent and boar, hold fast the earth with a will that it shake not, for Ráma is about to break the great bow ; hearken to my order and be ready." When Ráma drew near to the bow, the people all supplicated the gods by their past good deeds. The doubts and errors of the crowd, the arrogance of the foolish kings the proud pretentions of Parasurám the terror of all the gods and saints, the distress of Síta, the regrets of Janak, the burning anguish of the queens, were all heaped together on the bow as on a raft, while Ráma's strength of arm was the boundless ocean that had to be crossed, and with no helmsman to essay it.

Dohá 270.

Ráma first looked at the crowd, who all stood dumb and still as statues ; then the gracious Lord turned from them to Sìta, and perceived her yet deeper concern ;

Chaupái 265.

Perceived her to be so terribly agitated that a moment of time seemed an age in passing. If a man die of thirst for want of water, when he is once dead, of what use to him is a lake of nectar ? What good is the rain when the crop is dead ? or what avails regret when a chance has once been lost ? Thinking thus to himself as he gazed at Jánaki, the Lord was enraptured at the sight of her singular devotion, and after making a reverential obeisance to his *guru*, he took up the bow with most superlative ease ; as he grasped it in

R—24

his hand, it gleamed like a flash of lightning; and again as he bent it, it seemed like the vault of heaven. Though all stood looking on, before any one could see, he had lifted it from the ground and raised it aloft and drawn it tight, and in a moment broken it in halves; the awful crash re-echoed through the world.

Chhand 33.

So awful a crash re-echoed through the world that the horses of the Sun started from their course, the elephants of the four quarters groaned, earth shook, the great serpent, the boar and the tortoise tottered. Gods, demons and saints put their hands to their ears, and all began anxiously to consider the cause; but when they learnt that Ráma had broken the bow, they uttered shouts of Victory.

Sorathá 26.

All the deluded crowd who had gone on board 'the Siva's bow' were drowned in the waves of Ráma's might.

Chaupái 266.

The Lord tossed upon the ground the two broken pieces of the bow, and at the sight the multitude rejoiced. Visvamitra's love, like the clear unfathomed depth of ocean, swelled to the highest tide of ecstasy under the full moon influence of Ráma's presence. There was a jubilant noise of music in the sky; the heavenly nymphs danced and sang; Bràhma and all the gods and deified saints and sages praised and blessed the hero, and rained down wreaths of many-coloured flowers; the *kinnars* sung melodious strains; and the shout of 'Victory, Victory,' re-echoed throughout the world. The noise that followed the breaking of the bow defies description. Everywhere the people in their joy kept saying,—'Ráma has broken the great bow.'

Dohá 271.

Bards, minstrels and rhapsodists raise their loud-voiced pæans, and all the people lavish offerings of horses, elephants, money, jewels and raiment.

Chaupái 267.

There was a clash of cymbals, tabors, conches, clarions, sackbuts, drums, kettledrums and all kinds of music; and in every place were choirs of women singing auspicious strains. The queen with her attendants was as glad as a parched rice-field at a fall of rain; Janak was as pleased and free of care as a tired swimmer on reaching a shallow; the kings were as confounded at the breaking of the bow as a lamp is dimmed at dawn of day; but Síta's gladness can only be compared to that of the *chátaki*[1] on finding a rain-drop in October; while Lakshman fixed his eyes on Ráma as the *chakor* on the moon. Then Satánand gave the word and Síta advanced to Ráma.

Dohá 272.

Graceful in motion as a swan, and of infinite beauty in every limb; and with her came her fair and sprightly companions, who raise the glad marriage song.

Chaupái 268.

Resplendent in their midst as the Queen of Love among the loves, she held in her lotus hand the fair wreath of victory, enriched as it were with the spoils of world-wide triumph. With modest air, but rapture in her soul, her interior devotion was withdrawn from sight. As she drew near and beheld Ráma's beauty, she stood motionless like a figure on the wall, till a watchful attendant roused her, saying,—'Invest him with the ennobling wreath.' At the word she raised the wreath with both her hands, but was too much overcome by emotion to drop it; till as the lotus, flower and stalk, shrinks at the moonlight, so her hand and arm drooped in the glory of his moon-like face. At the sight of his beauty her handmaids break into song, while Síta let fall the wreath upon his breast.

---

1 The *chátaki* (Cuculus melanoleucos) is fabled never to drink, except it be such drops of rain as fall in the month of October, when the sun is in the same longitude as Arcturus, (*Swáti*), a time of the year when a shower is a very rare occurrence. The same precious drops if they fall into the sea, are transmuted into pearls, a belief to which allusion is made in page 11.

Sorathá 27.

When the gods saw the wreath resting on his breast they showered down flowers; and the kings all shrunk into nothing, like lilies at the rising of the sun.

Chaupái 269.

Both in the city and in heaven there were sounds of music; the bad were saddened, and the good were glad. Gods, kinnars, men, serpents and saints uttered blessings and shouts of victory. The heavenly nymphs danced and sung, and flowers fell in constant showers. In every place were Bráhmans muttering Vedic texts, and rhapsodists reciting lays of praise. Earth, hell and heaven were pervaded with the glad news,—'Ráma has broken the bow and will wed Síta.' The men and women of the city light votive torches and, regardless of their substance, scatter gifts in profusion. Síta by Ráma's side was as resplendent as if Beauty and Love had met together. Her companions whisper,—'Embrace your lord's feet;' but in excess of fear she dares not touch them.

Dohá 273.

She touches them not with her hands, remembering the fate of Gautama's wife; and Ráma smiled inwardly at this proof of her supernatural devotion.

Chaupái 270.

Then, as they looked on Síta, the kings were inflamed with desire, and waxed wroth of soul—frantic degenerate fools—and sprung up—the wretches—and donned their armour and began a general chorus of abuse,—"Come now, let us carry off Síta and overthrow and bind fast these two princes; though he has broken the bow, he has not yet gained his end; for who shall marry Síta while we still live? If the king give them any assistance, we will rout him in battle as well as the two brothers." When the good kings heard these words they answered and put the whole assembly to shame,—"The glory of your might and greatness of your strength were disgraced for ever at the breaking of the bow. Is that the might of which ye now boast, or have ye since acquired something new? Was it not thus that ye reckoned afore, when God so blackened your faces?

Dohá 274.

Cease from envy and arrogance and folly; feast your eyes upon Ráma; and be not like a moth in the fierce flame of Lakshman's wrath.

Chaupái 271.

Like a crow who would rob the king of the birds[1] of an offering; or a rat who would spoil a lion; as a man who is passionate without cause and yet wishes for peace of mind; as a reviler of Siva who wishes for happiness and prosperity; as a greedy and covetous man who wishes for fair fame, and as a gallant who would have no scandal; as an enemy of God who wishes to be saved; such is your desire, O ye kings." When Síta heard the tumult, she was afraid, and with her companions went away to the queen, while Ráma composedly joined the *guru*, talking to himself of Sita's affection. Síta and the queen were much distrest, saying,— "What is it God would have now?" And at the sound of the voices of the kings they looked helplessly up and down. For fear of Ráma Lakshman could not speak.

Dohá 275.

With fiery eyes and knitted brows he cast a furious look at the kings, like a lion's whelp watching to spring on a herd of wild elephants.

Chaupái 272.

Seeing the tumult, the people were all distrest and joined in reproaching the kings. Then it was that the sun of the lotus race of Bhrigu (Parasurám) arrived, for he had heard of the breaking of the bow. At the sight of him the kings all cowered down, as a partridge shrinking beneath the

---

1 The king of the birds—Garur—is here called *Vainateya*, that is to say, the son of Vinatà.

swoop of a hawk. Of pallid hue and well bestreaked with ashes; with the three horizontal lines sacred to Siva conspicuous on his broad forehead; with the hair on his head bound in a knot; and his moon-like face flushed with the furnace fire of smouldering wrath; with frowning brows and eyes inflamed with passion; he casts a quick and furious glance around. With bull-like shoulders and mighty chest and arms; with fair sacrificial cord and string of beads and deerskin with an anchorite's dress about his loins and two quivers slung by his side; with bow and arrows in hand, and his sharp axe upon his shoulder.

Dohá 276.

In his saintly attire and savage mien a figure beyond description, as though the Heroic had taken the form of a hermit; so he drew near to the kings.

Chaupái 273.

When they beheld his ghastly attire, they all rose in consternation, each mentioning his own and his father's name, and fell prostrate on the ground before him; and even those on whom he cast a kindly glance thought their life had come to an end. Then came Janak and bowed his head and called for Síta also to pay him homage. He bestowed upon her his blessing, and her glad companions escorted her back to her own appartments. Next came Visvamitra to salute him, and placed the two boys at his feet, saying,—"These are Ráma and Lakshman, Dasarath's sons." He admired the well-matched pair and blessed them, with his eyes long fixed upon Ráma's incomparable beauty, which would humble the pride even of Love himself.

Dohá 277.

Then he turned and said to Videha,—"Why all this crowd?" Asking as though he did not know, while his whole body was bursting with passion.

Chaupái 274.

Janak told him the whole history and the reason why

the kings assembled. After hearing his reply he again looked away and spied the fragments of the bow lying on the ground. In a mighty passion he cried in furious tones,—"Tell me now, Janak, you fool who has broken the bow? Show him to me at once, or this very day I will overthrow the whole of your dominion." In his excess of fear the king could give no answer: the wicked suitors were glad of heart; gods, saints, serpents and all the people of the city were full of anxiety and profound alarm; Síta's mother was lamenting,—"God has now undone all that had just been done so well;" and Síta when she heard of Bhrigupati's character felt half a minute pass like an age.

Dohá 278.

Seeing the people's consternation and Jánaki's anxiety, the imperturbable Raghubir thus spoke and said,—

Chaupái 275.

"My Lord, the bow has probably got broken by some one of your servants. What are your orders? Why not tell me?" At this the furious saint was yet more incensed and cried,—"A servant is one who does service, but he who does the deeds of an enemy must be fought. Hearken, Ráma, whoever it was who broke Siva's bow is as much my enemy as was Sahasrabáhu. Separate him from among the assembly, or else every one of these kings shall be killed." When Lakshman heard the saint's words, he smiled and said to him in a tone of contempt,—"O sir, I have broken many a bow as a child, and you were never before thus angry: why were you so fond of this bow in particular?" Parasurám replied in a fury,—

Dohá 279.

"Ah! death-doomed prince, is there no stopping your tongue? Would you compare to a common bow the great bow of Siva, that is famous throughout the world?"

Chaupái 276.

Said Lakshman with a smile,—"I thought, holy sir, that all bows were alike. What gain or what loss can there be in the breaking of a worn-out bow? Ráma by mistake took it for a new one, and directly he touched it, it snapped in two: but it was no fault of his; why then, reverend sir, be so angry for no cause?" He answered, with a glance at his axe,—"Fool, have you never heard of my temper? I do not slay you because, as I say, you are but a child. You in your folly take me for a mere recluse: and from my childhood an ascetic I am, but a fiery one and the terror of the whole Kshatriya race, as is known throughout the world. By the might of my arm I have made earth kingless, and time after time have bestowed her upon the Bráhmans. See here, you king's son, the axe with which I lopped of Sahasrabáhu's thousand arms.

Dohá 280.

Do not bring distress upon your father and mother: my cruel axe has ripped up even unborn infants in the womb."

Chaupái 277.

Lakshman replied with a quiet smile,—"Ah! holy sir, you think yourself a great warrior indeed, and keep brandishing your axe before me, as if with a mere puff of breath you could blow away a mountain. But I am not a *kumhar* blossom that droops as soon as it sees a finger raised against it. When I perceived your axe and quiver and arrows, I spoke a little haughtily; but now that I see by your Bráhmanical thread that you are of Bhrigu's line, say what you like and I will bear it patiently. In my family there is no waging battle against gods or Bráhmans, or devotees, or cows; for to kill them is a crime, and to be overcome by them a disgrace; and therefore I must throw myself at your feet, even though you strike me. Your curse is as awful as a million thunderbolts, and your axe and bow and arrows are unnecessary.

Dohá 281.

Pardon me, great and reverend sage, for anything improper that I said when I first saw you." The glory of Bhrigu's race cried furiously in his deep toned voice,—

Chaupái 278.

"Hearken, son of Kusika;[1] this child is demented; a perverse and death doomed destroyer of his own house; a dark spot on the moon-like brightness of the Solar race; utterly ungovernable, senseless and reckless. Another moment and he shall be a mouthful in the jaws of death, and I loudly protest it is no fault of mine. Take him away, if you would save him, and teach him my glory and might and the fierceness of my temper." Said Lakshman,—"So long as you live, father, who else can tell your fame so well? With your own mouth you have many times and in many ways declared your own doings. If you are not yet satisfied, tell them over again, and do not distress yourself beyond, endurance by putting any restraint upon your passion. But if you are really a resolute and dauntless warrior, there is no honour to be got by abuse.

Dohá 282.

Heroes perform valiant deeds in fight, but do not themselves publish them: cowards finding a foe before them in the battle talk very large, as you

Chaupái 279.

now would terrify me with your repeated cries of Death." On hearing Lakshman's rude speech he closed his hand upon his terrible axe,—"After this let no man blame me; this sharp-tongued boy deserves his death. I have spared him long on account of his being a child, but now of a truth he is as good as dead." Said Visvamitra,—"Pardon his offence; the wise regard not the faults or merits of children." "I have axe in hand and am pitiless in my wrath; he is moreover guilty: and has injured my *guru*. Yet though this be my answer, I will still spare his life, though solely out of regard for you, Visvamitra. But for you I had cut him in pieces with my terrible axe, and thus easily have paid my *guru* his due."

Dohá 283.

Said the son of Gádhi, smiling to himself,—"Everything

1 The son, or rather grandson, of Kusika is Visvamitra.

looks green to the saint's eyes;[1] though Ráma has to-day broken the bow as though it were a stick of sugarcane, still he has not the sense to understand."

Chaupái 280.

Said Lakshman,—"Is there any one, Father, ignorant of your honour? it is notorious throughout the world. You have well paid the debt you owed to your father and mother;[2] but it was a great distress to you to be still in debt to your *guru*. You have now transferred the account to me, but the interest by lapse of time has become very heavy. So you must bring forward the original creditor, and then, sir, I will at once open my purse." When he heard these bitter words he grasped his axe, and all the people cried—Alack, alack! "O Bhrigu-bar, you still keep showing me your axe, but, regicide as you are, I only spare you on account of your being a Bráhman. You have never yet met a real staunch fighting man, and, most reverend sir, you are a great man only in your own house." They all cried out,—'How very wrong;' and Ráma gave Lakshman a sign to be quiet.

Dohá 284.

Lakshman's words were like oil on the fire of Bhrigupati's wrath; till, seeing the flame increase, Ráma quenched it with the flood of admonition,—

Chaupái 281.

"My lord, have compassion on a child, and wreak not your wrath on such an unweaned infant: if he had any idea of your glorious power, how could he be so foolish as

---

1 The allusion is to a popular saying,—'A man who loses his eyesight in the month of Sáwan thinks everything is always green.' *Hariari*, 'green, may also be taken as two words *Hari* and *ari*, 'an enemy to Vishnu,' a light in which it would be the height of folly for Parasurám to regard Ráma, since Ráma was himself an incarnation of Vishnu, as also was Parasurám. The double interpretation was probably intended by the poet.

2 Every Hindu is said to be in debt by nature to three persons, *viz.*, his father, his mother and his *guru*. The two first debts had been paid by Parasurám in a notable fashion; for he had restored his mother Renuká to life again after he had first cut off her head in obedience to his father Jamad-agni's order; and again when his father had been slain by Sahasrabáhu, he avenged him by the slaughter of the whole Kshatriya race. It now remained for him to satisfy his *guru*, Mahádeva, for the outrage Ráma had done him in breaking his bow.

to put himself on an equality with you? When a child commits any naughtiness, its *guru* and father and mother are in raptures at it. Have pity then on the boy, who is really one of your clients; for thus it becometh a saint, so patient and wise as you are." On hearing Ráma's words he cooled down a little but again Lakshman said something with a smile, and seeing him smile he flushed all over with rage,—"Ráma, your brother is too wicked; though fair in outward hue, he is black at heart, and it is not mother's milk but poison that his lips have sucked. Perverse by nature, he neither takes after you nor regards me."

Dohá 285.

Said Lakshman with a smile,—"Hearken, O saint, passion is the root of sin; those who are under its influence do unseemly things and set themselves against every one.

Chaupái 282.

I am one of your followers, reverend sir; put away your wrath and show mercy upon me. Anger will not mend the broken bow; pray sit down, you must be tired of standing. If you were so very fond of it, devise a plan for getting it mended and call in some skilful workman." Janak was frightened at Lakshman's words,—'Be quiet; such frowardness is not right.' The citizens all shook and trembled: to think so small a boy could be so naughty. As Bhrigupati heard his fearless words his whole body was on fire with rage, and he became quite helpless, and in a tone of entreaty cried to Ráma,—"See if you can manage this little brother of yours; so fair without and foul within; he resembles a golden jar full of poison."

Dohá 286.

At this Lakshman smiled, but Ráma gave him a look of reproof and submissively approached the *guru*, putting away all petulance of speech.

Chaupái 283.

Clasping his two hands together and speaking in most

modest, gentle and placid tones, he said,—"Hearken, my lord, you were born a sage; pay no heed then to the words of a child. Boys are like gnats: no wise man will ever trouble himself about them. Nor is it he who has done the mischief; I, my lord, am the offender. Be pleased, your reverence, to visit everything on me, your servant, whether it be favour or anger, or death or bonds. Tell me quickly the means, O king of saints, by which your passion may be assuaged." Said the saint,—"O Ráma, how can my passion be assuaged? Your brother has to-day set me at nought, and yet I have not struck off his head with my axe: what then have I done in anger?

Dohá 287.

When they heard of the fierce doings of my axe, the proudest queens were seized with untimely pains of labour; my axe is still here, and yet I see this princeling, my enemy, alive.

Chaupái 284.

My hand moves not, though passion consumes my breast my regicide axe has become blunted. Fate is against me; my nature is changed: for when was I ever pitiful before? To-day by heaven's will I have suffered intolerable pain." On hearing this, the son of Sumitrá smiled and bowed his head,—"Even your pity is like a blast of wind and the words you speak would strip a tree of its blossoms. If a saint's body is thus parched even by pity, God help him when he is angry." "See now, Janak, keep this child away; he is bent in his folly on visiting the realms of death. Why do you not at once take him out of my sight, this little prince; so small to look at and yet so wicked?" Lakshman laughed and said to the saint,—'Shut your eyes and you will see nothing.'

Dohá 288.

Then said parasurám in tones of fury to Ráma,—"Wretch, after breaking Siva's bow do you now teach me?

Chaupái 285.

It is at your suggestion your brother utters these sarcasms, and your humility and folded hands are a mockery. Give me my satisfaction in combat, or forswear your name of Ráma. You enemy of Siva, have done with your tricks and meet me in battle, or I will slay both you and your brother too." Flushed with passion he raised his axe on high, but Ráma only smiled and bowed,— "Though the fault is Lakshman's your wrath is against me; it is sometimes a great mistake to be good and upright; for every one is afraid of the crooked, in the same way as Ráhu does not attack the crescent moon. Cease, O great saint, from your wrath." Said Ráma,—"Your axe is in your hand and my head is in front of you; do anything, sir, that will tend to pacify you, for I am your servant.

Dohá 289.

And how can a servant fight his master? O holy Bráhman, restrain your wrath; whatever the boy may have said, after looking at your dress, he meant no harm by it.

Chaupái 286.

For seeing you equipt with axe and bow and arrows, the child took you for a knight and challenged you; for though he knew your name, he did not recognize your person, and answered you according to ~~your~~ lineage. If you had come as a Religious, he would have put the dust of your Holiness's feet upon his head. Forgive the mistake of one who did not know you; a Bráhman's heart should be all mercy. What equality, my lord, can there be between you and me? We are as far apart as head and feet. I am called simply Ráma. You have the long name of 'Ráma of the axe.' I have only one string to my bow, while you have all the holy nine.[1] In every way I am your inferior: as a Bráhman, pardon my offence."

1 *Gun*, which is the name for a bowstring, means also virtue; and the cardinal virtues are said to be nine in number, though the list is a variable one.

Doha 290.

Again and again did Ráma intreat his namesake, addressing him by his titles of 'Saint' and 'Holy Bráhman,' till Bhrigupati exclaimed in his rage:—You are as perverse as your brother.

Chaupái 287.

You persist in taking me for a Bráhman ; I will tell you now what kind of a Bráhman I am. My bow is my sacrificial ladle, my arrow the oblation, and my wrath the blazing fire ; armies fully equipt with horses and chariots and elephants and footmen are the fuel, and mighty kings are the victims for oblation whom I have cut in pieces with this axe ; thus have I celebrated countless sacrifices of war all over the world. To you my glory is unknown, and you address me contemptuously, taking me for a mere Bráhman. Now that you have broken the bow, your pride has increased enormously, and you put yourself forward in your arrogance as universal conqueror," Said Ráma :—" O saint, think before you speak ; your anger is excessive ; my fault is a trifling one. The old bow broke at a touch. What reason have I to be proud ?

Dohá 291.

Hear the truth, O Bhrigunáth ; you say I set you at nought when I treat you with the respect due to a Bráhman ; but is there any warrior to whom I would bow my head in fear ?

Chaupái 288.

Any god, demon, king or warrior, whether my equal in strength or my superior, who will challenge me to combat, him would I gladly meet, or even Death himself. For one who is born of warrior caste and yet shirks the battle is a disgrace to his lineage and a contemptible wretch. I state what is only a characteristic of my race and make no idle boast ; there is not a descendant of Raghu who would fear to meet in battle even Death himself ; but so great is the power of Bráhmanical descent that he fears you, who fears nought else." On hearing this calm and profound speech of Ráma's, the eyes of the soul of the axe-bearer were opened :—" O Ráma, take and draw this bow of Vishnu's and let my doubts be ended." As he gave it, the bow strung itself of its own accord ; then was Parasurám amazed at heart.

Dohá 292.

He acknowledged the power of Ráma ; his whole frame quivered with excitement ; and his heart bursting with love, he thus spake with clasped hands :—

Chaupái 289.

"Glory to the Sun of the lotus race of Raghu, to the fire that consumes the serried ranks of the demons ; glory to the friend of gods, Bráhmans and kine ; glory to the dispeller of the delusions induced by pride, ignorance and passion ; glory to him whose piety, amiability, and compassion are fathomless as ocean ; glory to him who is unrivalled in the art of speech, the rewarder of service, the all-beautiful of form, more gracious of person than a myriad Loves. How can I with one tongue declare his praise, who is as it were the divine swan in the hyperboreal lake of Mahádeva's soul ? In my ignorance I have said much that was unseemly ; but pardon me, yet twin brothers, mercy's shrine." Still repeating as he went :—' Glory, glory, glory, to the mighty Ráma,' Bhrigupati withdrew to the forest to practise penance. The wicked kings were self-dismayed and trembled, and fled—the cowards—in all directions, without a word.

Dohá 293.

The gods sounded their kettledrums and rained down flowers on the Lord ; and all the people of the city rejoiced, now that the thorn of fear and error had been extracted from their heart.

Chaupái 290.

There was a tumultuous clash of instruments of music and a display of all things pleasant and auspicious. Troops of fair faced, bright-eyed maidens joined in song with voices of exquisite melody. Janak's delight was beyond description, as that of a born beggar who has found a treasure : and Síta relieved of her fears, was as glad as a young partridge at the rising of the moon. The king made obeisance before Visvamitra, saying :—"It is by my lord's favour that Ráma has broken the bow. These two brothers have gained me my purpose ; tell me now, reverend sir, what is becomes me to do." Said the saint :—"Hearken, wise king ; the marriage was dependent on the bow, and took effect directly the bow broke ; this is well known to every one, whether god, man or Nága.

Dohá 294.

Still, go and perform according to family usage whatever practices are prescribed in the Veda, after consultation with the Bráhmans and elders and your own guru ;

Chaupái 291.

and despatch a herald to Avadh to invite king Dasarath." The princes responded gladly :—"Tis well, gracious sir," and sent a messenger to Avadh that very moment. Then he summoned all the burghers, who came every one ofthem, and humbly bowing before him received the order :—"Decorate all the markets and streets and temples and shrines in all four quarters of the city." They returned in joy, each to his own house. Then he called up his own servants and instructed them :—"Have all kinds of pavilions made and erected." They obeyed in all gladness and sent word to the different artificers who were skilful in the construction of canopies and triumphal arches ; and they, after invoking Bráhma, set to work and made pillars of gold in the shape of plantain trees,

Dohá 295.

with leaves and fruit of emeralds and ruby flowers ; such a gorgeous show that the Creator was quite disconcerted at the sight.

Chaupái 292.

The rods all encrusted with emeralds, and so like in form

and colour,[1] that no one could tell them from real, with betel leaves fashioned in gold so bright and glistening that no one could look at them. Then they worked up the leaves into wreaths, with strings of beautiful perals inserted here and there, and after much cutting and graving and in laying made lotuses of mosaic with rubies, emeralds, diamonds and turquoises. Bees, too, they made and birds of varied plumage, which buzzed and whistled in the rustling breeze; and on the pillars they sculptured figures of the gods all standing erect with things of good omen in their hands. Squares were drawn on the ground and filled in with diverse devices made of elephant pearls[2] of exquisite beauty.

Dohá 296.

There were also made most lovely mango-boughs of graven sapphires with blossoms of gold, while clusters of emerald fruit glistened on silken cords.

Chaupái 293.

Next they made charming festoons as it were Love's own nooses and many golden vases with silken flags and banners and waving *chauris* and elegant lamps all studded with gems. It is impossible to describe the various pavilions and in particular the one intended for the royal bride; what poet would have the hardihood to attempt its description? while the canopy for Ráma, the bridegroom, the centre of all beauty and perfection, flashed its radiance through all three worlds. In every house throughout the city there was the same splendour as in Janak's palace; any one who then saw Tirhut there was nothing in the fourteen spheres[3] to compare with it, and the prosperous

---

1 Another reading, instead of *su-ras, sabarna*, is *saral sa-parva*, 'straight and knotted.'

2 For *sindhur*, 'an elephant,' another reading is *sindur*, 'vermilion,' but this cannot be correct, since the *chauks* or squares, to which reference is here made, are always marked out with some *white* material, ordinarily flour, though in a king's palace strings of pearls might be substituted.

3 The fourteen spheres are as follows, *viz.*, first. seven above the earth—Bhur-lok, Bhuvar-lok, Swar-lok, Mahar-lok, Jan-lok Tap-lok. and Satya-lok; and seven beneath the earth—Atal, Bital, Sutal, Rasátal, Mahátal, Talátal, and Pátál.

appearance of the very meanest house was enough to fascinate even the king of heaven.

Dohá 297.

For the magnificence of the city wherein dwelt the goddess Lakshmi, in disguise as a woman, was more than even Sáradá or Seshnág could tell.

Chaupái 294.

When the heralds arrived at Ráma's sacred birthplace, they rejoiced to see the beauty of the city. At the royal gate they sent in word, and King Dasarath at once summoned them to his presence. With a profound salutation they delivered the letter, and the king in his joy rose to receive it. As he read it his eyes filled with tears, his body quivered all over, and his heart seemed bursting. With Ráma and Lakshman in his soul and their dear letter in his hand, he could not utter a word either good or bad. At last, taking courage, he read the letter, and all the court rejoiced to hear the certain news. Now Bharat was playing about, and on hearing the tidings he, nay, the two brothers, came and with the utmost modesty and affection asked :—" Father, where has the letter come from.

Dohá 298.

Is all well with my two dear brothers ? Tell me what country they are in." On hearing these loving words the king again read the letter.

Chaupái 295.

On hearing it the two brothers trembled all over with irrepressible joy, and the whole court was charmed to see Bharat's wholy devotion. Then the king seated the messengers close by him and said in sweet and winning tones :—" Tell me, friend, are the two boys well ? Have you really seen them with your own eyes ? " " One is dark, the other fair ; both are equipt with bow and quiver, and are of tender age, and with them is Saint Visvamitra." Said the king again and again in his overpowering love :— You know them, it is clear ; tell me now of their state ;

for from the day that the saint took them away till now I have had no definite news of them. Tell me how Janak knew them." At these fond words the messengers smiled :—

Dohá 299.

"Hearken, O jewel and crown of kings ; there is no man so blest as you, who have for sons Ráma and Lakshman, who are the glory of the whole world.

Chaupái 296.

There is no need to ask your sons who they are ; lion-hearted heroes who irradiate the three spheres. Before their glory and renown the moon is dim and the sun is cold. Why say, my lord, how they were recognized? Does one take a lamp in his hand in order to see the sun? The countless kings at Síta's marriage, great warriors as they were, all shrunk away one after the other ; for not one of them could stir Sambhu's bow, but all failed, those mighty princes. The power of the haughtiest champions in the three worlds was crushed by it. Though Bánásur could uproot Mount Meru, even he confessed himself beaten, and retired after pacing around it ; and he who in sport uplifted Kailás (*i. e.*, Rávan) was worsted in this assembly.

Dohá 300.

Then Ráma, the jewel of Raghu's line (hearken, O sovereign lord), snapped the bow with as little effort as an elephant would put forth in breaking the stalk of a lotus.

Chaupái 297.

At these tidings Parasurám came in a fury, and after much brow-beating gave Ráma his own bow to test his strength, then suppliantly withdrew to the woods. Nor is Ráma more conspicuous in his unequalled might than is the all-glorious Lakshman, at sight of whom the kings tremble, as an elephant before a young lion. No one who sees your two sons, sir, can regard anything else on earth." At this eloquent and affectionate speech of the heralds, so loving, grand and heroic, the king and his court were much moved, and began to offer them lavish gifts ; but they closed their ears, crying,—" Not so, not so ; " and all were charmed to see their integrity.

Dohá 301.

Then the king rose and went and gave the letter to Vasishta, and after relating all the circumstances to the *guru* sent courteously for the envoys.

Chaupái 298.

After hearing them the saint was highly pleased and said :—" To a good man the world is full of happiness. As rivers run into the sea, though it has no greed for them, so joy and prosperity come unasked and of their own accord to a virtuous soul. Strict in the performance of your duties to your *guru* and to Bráhmans and kine and gods, and your queen Kausalyá no less devout than yourself ; you have no equals for piety in the whole world, either now or in the past, nor hereafter shall have. Who, O king, can be more blest than you, who have a son like Ráma ; nay, four heroic sons, all equally obedient, religious and amiable. Happy, indeed, are you for all time. Prepare the marriage procession to sound of music.

Dohá 302.

Go quickly." On hearing the saint's commands the king bowed in assent, and hastened to the palace, after assigning quarters to the heralds.

Chaupái 299.

Then he called all the ladies of the seraglio and read aloud to them Janak's letter—all rejoiced greatly at the news. He then told them all the verbal message ; and both himself and the queens were as enraptured with delight as a peacock at the sound of approaching rain. The *guru's* wives in their joy invoked the blessings of heaven, and the queen-mother was completely overwhelmed with ecstasy. They take the dear letter from one another, and press it to their bosom to cool as it were their burning heart. Again and again ere he turned to the door, the king repeated the glory and the exploits both of Ráma and Lakshman, adding,—"It is all by the saint's good favour." Then the ladies sent for the Bráhmans and joyfully made them offerings, for which the holy men returned their blessings.

Sorathá 28.

Next they called together the beggars and lavished every kind of gift upon them :—"May the four sons of the Emperor Dasarath live for ever :"

Chaupái 300.

Thus they shouted as they left, attired in raiment of many colours. There was a jubilant clamour of music and in every house, as the news spread among the people, there were joyous congratulations. The fourteen spheres were fulfilled with delight at the marriage of Raghubír with the daughter of Janak. When they heard the glad tidings, the citizens were enraptured and began decorating the roads and houses and streets; for although Avadh in itself was a charming place, and clean and pure as being Ráma's home, yet as the natural outcome of its love it garnished and adorned itself still more with festal decorations. Silken flags and banners and graceful *chauris* crested the gay bazár; and at every turn were golden jars and festoons of netted pearls and heaps of turmeric, *dúb* grass, curds, rice, and garlands of flowers.

Dohá 303.

Every one decorated his house; the streets were duly watered, and every square was filled in with some tasteful design.

Chaupái 301.

Troops of girls assembled at different places, who had practised all the sixteen kinds of female adornment,[1] brilliant

---

1 The sixteen *sringàr*, or modes of female adornment, are specified in the following rhymes :—

Prathama ang-suchi ek bidhi - Majjan dutiya bakháni,
Amal basan panirau tritiya -Yà ak chári sujáni.
Panchama kes-sanváriyo—Shashtahin máng-sindúr.

as the lightning, with moon-like face and fawn-like eyes, and beauty enough to rob even Love of his pride; singing auspicious strains with voice so melodious that the cuckoo was put to shame on hearing the sweet sound. How is the king's palace to be described? The pavilion they set up would dazzle the world. Everything beautiful and of fair omen was displayed, and every kind of music was heard. Here were rhapsodists chanting songs of praise; here were Bráhmans muttering Vedic spells; while lovely women carolled joyous songs, ever dwelling on the names of Ráma and Síta. The joy was so great that the palace was too small for it, and it overflowed on all four sides.

Dohá 304.

What poet can describe in full the magnificence of the palace of Dasarath, in which Ráma, the glory of highest heaven, had taken birth?

Chaupái 302.

The king next called Bharat:—"Go and prepare horses and elephants and chariots and start at once for Raghubír's marriage procession." When they heard this order, both brothers were full of excitement. Bharat sent for all the chief officers and issued his commands, and they rose in joy and haste to perform them. First they made gorgeous trappings for the horses. Of different colours were the gallant steeds, but all well-proportioned and mettlesome, touching the ground with their feet as lightly as though it were red-hot iron. I cannot tell all the various breeds; they would race the wind and outstrip it. The princes who mounted them were all like Bharat, graceful, and gorgeously attired, with bow and arrows in hand and well-filled quiver at their side.

Bhál-khauri saptama kahat—Ashtam chibuk til pur.
Mehndi kar pad rachan nava—Dasma argaja ang.
Gyárah bhúkhan nag-jatit—Bárah pushp prasang.
Básrág mukh terahi—Chaudah rangiyo dánt.
Adhar-rág gani panchadasa—Kajjal shodas bhánt.

Dohá 305.

Slim, elegant and lithesome youths, but expert warriors all ; and with each knight were two footmen well skilled in sword-play.

Chaupái 303.

Full of high resolve, the warriors staunch in fight sallied forth and halted outside the city, putting their well-trained steeds through all their paces and rejoicing in the clash of tabor and drum. The charioteers had made their cars equally gorgeous with flags and banners and jewelled adornments, with elegant *chauris* and tinkling bells, so as to outdo in splendour the chariot of the Sun. Innumerable were the black-eared horses,[1] which the grooms yoked to these chariots, and all were so beautiful and richly caparisoned that even a saint would be enraptured at the sight ; skimming the surface of the water like dry land, nor sinking even hoof-deep, so marvellous their speed. After completing their equipment of armour and weapons, the charioteers gave word to their masters,

Dohá 306.

who all mounted in turn, and the procession began to form outside the city ; all, whatever the object on which they were bent, were met by auspicious omens.

Chaupái 304.

On the magnificent elephants were splendid canopies, wrought in a manner beyond all description. As the mighty elephants moved, the bells clanged like the thunder from the clouds in the grateful month of Sáwan. And other vehicles were there of many kinds ; elegant *pálkis* and sedans and coaches, wherein were seated companies of noble Bráhmans, incarnations as it were of all the hymns of the Veda. The genealogists and bards and minstrels and rhapsodists were mounted on other cars according to their rank ; while mules and camels and oxen of every breed were laden with all sorts of baggage ; there were

1 A horse to be fit for sacrifice must have black ears.

also millions of porters with burdens slung across their shoulders; but who could enumerate such an endless list of things and the crowd of servants, each with his own set of appliances?

Dohá 307.

All were glad and fearless of heart, and were quivering with excitement in every limb, saying:—"When shall we feast our eyes with the sight of the two heroes, Ráma and Lakshman?"

Chaupái 305.

The elephants' bells clanged with a fearful din: on all sides there was a creaking of wheels and a neighing of horses; the drums would drown a tempest's roar, and no one could hear himself speak or any one else. At the king's gate was such an enormous crowd that the stone pavement was all trodden into dust. Women mounted on the upper story viewed the sight, with festal torches and salvers in their hands, and carolled melodious songs in an ecstasy of joy beyond description. Then Sumanta made ready two chariots and yoked them with steeds that would outrun the horses of the Sun, and brought them in all their beauty before the king—not Sáradá herself could do them justice—the one was for the royal retinue, but the other was still more splendid.

Dohá 308.

This the king first caused Vasishta to mount, and then himself ascended, with his thoughts fixed upon Hara, his guru, Gauri, and Ganes.

Chaupái 306.

By Vasishta's side the king shone forth as Purandara beside Vrihaspati. After performing every ceremony prescribed either by family usage or the Veda, and inspecting whatever had been done, he sallied forth to the blast of the conch shell, after obtaining the permission of his *guru*, and with his thoughts fixed on Ráma. The beneficent gods rejoiced to see the procession and rained down flowers.

There was a confused uproar, horses neighing, elephants trumpeting, and drums beating, both in the sky and on the line of march. Women and goddesses alike broke out in songs of joy, while tuneful clarions played in sweet accord.

There was an indescribable clamour of bells, both great and small. The foot soldiers leaped and danced as if challenging attack; the jesters practised all kinds of buffoonery, provoking laughter with facetious songs.

Dohá 309.

Gallant youths make their steeds curvet to the measured beat of tabors and kettledrums; accomplished dancers note with surprise that they never make a step out of time.

Chaupái 307.

But it is useless attempting to describe the procession. Every omen that occurred was fair and auspicious. On the left side a blue-necked jay was picking up food as if to announce the very highest good fortune; on a fair field on the right were a crow and a *mangús* in the sight of all; a grateful breeze breathed soft and cool and fragrant; a woman was seen with a pitcher and child; a fox showed himself winding about; and in front a cow was suckling its calf; a herd of deer came out on the right, an indication of everything good; a Bráhmani-kite promised all success: also a *syáma* bird perched on a tree to the left; a man was met bearing curds and fish; and two learned Bráhmans with books in their hands.

Dohá 310.

Every good and auspicious omen, and every bestower of desired reward, seemed all to have met at once as if to verify themselves.

Chaupái 308.

Every good and auspicious omen was ready at hand for him whose glorious son was the incarnate God, a bridegroom like Ráma, matched with such a bride as Síta, and with the pious Dasarath and Janak for the two parents. When they heard of the marriage, all the good omens began to dance and say:—"Now at last the Creator has really made us to be what our name denotes." In this manner the procession set forth, with noise of horses and elephants and beat of drums. When Janak, the glory of the Solar race, heard of its approach, he had all the rivers bridged, and at different stages had convenient rest-houses erected, which vied in splendour with the city of heaven and were supplied everything that one could desire—beds, food and linen. Ever discovering some new charm, all the travellers forgot their own home.

Dohá 311.

When it was known that the procession was close at hand, and the beating of the drums was heard, a deputation went out to meet it, with elephants and chariots and foot and horse.

Chaupái 309.

Beautiful golden vases and trays and salvers and costly dishes[1] of every kind, laden with cakes as sweet as nectar and of indescribable variety, with much luscious fruit and, in short, everything of the best, did the king in his gladness send as an offering. Ornaments, wearing apparel, jewels of all kinds, birds, deer, horses, elephants, carriages of every description, well-omened spices, delicious perfumes, these, too, did the king send, and there was a train of porters with their baskets full of curds and parched rice and other light entremêts. When the deputation saw the wedding guests, their soul was full of rapture and their body quivered with excitement; while the guests were no less charmed by the preparations made for their reception and beat their drums.

Dohá 312.

For a little they joined their ranks and marched in their joy as one body for the sake of company; like two oceans of bliss that had burst their bounds and come together.

1 For *bhájan*, 'dishes,' some copies read *bhojan*, 'food,' but incorrectly as the context shows.

Chaupái 310.

The nymphs of heaven rained down flowers and sang, the glad gods beat their drums. The offerings were all set out before the king, with a humble and affectionate address. The king graciously accepted them and bestowed them in charity on the poor. Then with religious honours and hymns of praise they conducted him to the guest-chambers. The cloths spread as carpets for King Dasarath to tread upon were so gorgeous that the god of wealth on seeing them could boast no longer. The gods rained down flowers and shouted Victory, Victory. The apartments assigned were most beautiful and supplied with every kind of comfort. When Síta knew that the procession had arrived in the city, she manifested her greatness to a slight extent, and with thoughtful heart called up the eight Siddhis, or wonder-working spirits, and sent them to arrange for the king's reception.

Dohá 313.

Obedient to her command, they repaired to the receptionhall, taking with them every kind of luxury and comfort and all the joys and delights of heaven.

Chaupái 311.

Each guest on going to see his apartment found it a veritable paradise; no, one, however, had an inkling of the mysterious power that had been exerted, but took it all as Janak's doing. Ráma alone recognized the influence of Síta and rejoiced at this proof of her love. When the two brothers heard of their father's arrival they could not contain themselves for joy, but were too modest to speak to their *guru*, though they longed greatly to see their sire again. Visvamitra perceived their humility, which filled his soul with contentment, and took the two brothers to his bosom with quivering body and eyes bedewed with tears. They went then to Dasarath's mansion, like thirsting travellers who have spied a pool.

Dohá 314.

When the king saw the saint coming with the two boys, he rose in joy and advanced to meet them, like one who feels his footing in a deep flood of bliss.

Chaupái 312.

He prostrated himself before the saint, again and again sprinkling on his head the dust of his feet. Visvamitra took him to his bosom and blessed him and enquired after his welfare. Then the two brothers prostrated themselves. The king on seeing them could not contain himself for joy, but took his boys to his heart, and forgetting the intolerable pain of the past seemed like a dead man restored to life. Then they bowed their head at Vasistha's feet, who also embraced them most affectionately; and in turn they saluted all the Bráhmans and received their welcome blessings. They greeted Bharat too and his younger brother Satrughna, who at once raised up Ráma and embraced him, and no less rejoiced to see Lakshman again. Thus they all met together with a display of the utmost affection.

Dohá 315.

The all-merciful and gracious lord had an appropriate greeting for all, whether citizens, or attendants, or kinsmen, beggars, or ministers, or friends.

Chaupái 313.

At the sight of Ráma the wedding guests were repaid for their toilsome journey, and their demonstrations of love were beyond all telling. Beside their royal father the four boys seemed as incarnations of the four great ends of life. All the people of the city were delighted beyond measure at the sight of Dasarath and his sons; the gods rained down flowers and beat their drums; the nymphs of heaven danced and sang. Satánand with the Bráhmans and ministers of state and the rhapsodists and bards and players and minstrels, who had come in deputation, after duly reverencing the king and the marriage guests, received permission to return.

The whole city was exceedingly delighted that the procession had come before the day fixed for the wedding, and were supremely happy, praying God to lengthen the days and nights :—

Doh 316.

"Ráma and Síta are the perfection of beauty, and the two kings the perfection of virtue :" thus would say all the people of the city whenever they happened to meet : –

Chaupái 314.

"Síta is the incarnation of Janak's merit and Ráma of Dasarath's : no one has equalled them in devotion to Síta, nor has any one obtained such a reward as they have. And all we must be everything that is good, seeing that we have been born into the world as Janak's citizens and have beheld the beauty of Jánaki and Ráma ; who is so superlatively blest as we are ? and we have yet to see Ráma's wedding, of all sights the best worth seeing." So, too, sweet-voiced maidens whispered to one another :—" This marriage, my dear, will be a great treat. God has brought about an event of signal felicity in lodging those two brothers in the guest-chambers of our eyes.

Dohá 317.

Many and many a time will Janak lovingly send for Síta, and the two brothers, beautiful as a myriad Loves, will come to fetch her.

Chaupái 315.

There will be all kinds of hospitable entertainments ; who, dear girl, would not rejoice in such a father-in-law ? Every one in the place will be delighted at the sight of Ráma and Lakshman ; and now two other lads, my friends, have come with the king, who are a match even for them ; one dark, the other fair, but beautiful in every limb, so says every one who has seen them." Said one in reply : " I saw them to-day, and thought God must have made them with his own hands. Ráma and Bharat are so much alike that neither man nor woman could without looking close tell one from the other; while again Lakshman and Satrughna are also one in appearance, perfectly beautiful in every limb from head to foot; the soul would fain express its rapture, but language fails it, for there is nothing comparable to them in all the three spheres of creation."

Chhand 34.

No poet, however ingenious, says Tulsi Dás, could find aught comparable to them; for so unbounded is their strength, their courtesy, their knowledge, their amiability and their beauty, that they have no peers but themselves. All the women in the city, spreading out their garments, made prayer to Bráhma,—"May all four brothers be married here, and may we sing their wedding song."

Sorathá 29.

Said the damsels to one another with streaming eyes and quivering body:—"Friends, the two kings are of such boundless religious merit that for their sake Mahádeva will bring it all about."

Chaupái 316.

In like manner they all expressed their desire, while their full heart overflowed with rapture. When the kings, who had come as Síta's suitors, saw the brothers, they all rejoiced and returned to their own homes, extolling Ráma's high and spotless fame. In this fashion several days were spent, to the joy alike of citizens and guests. At length the auspicious, day arrived, in the cold season, in the pleasant month of Aghan. The Creator himself had carefully fixed the date, when the sign of the zodiac, the age of the moon, the conjunction of the stars and the day of the week were one and all propitious. Of this he sent word through Nárad, and it was the very same that Janak's wise men had calculated. All the people on hearing this fact declared their astrologers to be very gods.

Dohá 318.

It was towards sunset,[1] the clearest and most delightful hour of the day, that the Bráhmans apprized Videha's king that the auspicious time had arrived.

Chaupái 317.

The monarch cried to the family priest:—"What is now the cause of delay? At once Satánand summoned the ministers, who all came bearing festal vases: conches, drums, and tabors sounded; all decked their vases in auspicious wise: graceful damsels sang songs, and holy Bráhmans murmured Vedic texts. In this manner they went with all ceremony to the visitors' camp, and on beholding the king of kosala's retinue it seemed to them that Indra was of much less glory. "The hour has come, be pleased to start." At this the drums gave a thundering beat. After consulting his *guru* and performing the family rites, the king and the saint sallied forth with all their host.

Dohá 319.

Bráhma and all the other gods, on beholding the pomp and magnificence of Avadh's king, began to extol him with a thousand tongues and declare their own life to have been wasted.

Chaupái 318.

Seeing the auspiciousness of the time, the deities rained down flowers and beat their drums. Siva and Bráhma and all the host of heaven mounted their chariots and came in

---

1 The word *dhenu-dhúli* stands for the more common *go-dhúli*—for *go* and *dhenu* are identical in meaning—and denotes the unfortunately very brief period of the day during which the Indian climate is thoroughly enjoyable. Professor Monier Williams in his Sanskrit dictionary explains the words as follows: "'dust of the earth'; a period of the day in the hot season when the sun is half risen; in the cold and dewy seasons when the sun is full but mild; and in the three other seasons, sunset; originally, a time at which mist seems to rise from the earth." I have always myself considered that the first part of the compound was used in its more ordinary sense of 'a cow,' and that *go-dhúli* would be literally rendered dust of cows,' not 'dust of the earth.' The word is still current in village use, and when I have been moving about in the district in the cold weather I have heard it applied by the country-people to the hour of sunset, when the cattle were all coming home from pasture, and raising dense clouds of dust along the narrow lanes; a fact to which the speaker was evidently referring, and which, I think, is the more correct explanation of the etymology.

crowds to see Ráma's wedding, their heart and every limb throbbing and quivering with excess of love. They were so charmed with Janak's capital that their own realms seemed to them as nothing worth. They gaze with astonishment at the pavilions and all the marvellous decorations; at the men and women so beautiful and well-formed, so good and amiable and intelligent, before whom all the gods and goddesses seemed like the stars at the rising of the full moon. Above all was Bráhma astounded at finding his own handiwork nowhere.

Dohá 320.

But Siva admonished them all:—"Do not give way to such surprise; recover yourselves and reflect that this is the marriage of Síta and Raghubír.

Chaupái 319.

The mere mention of whose name destroys all that is evil in the world; in whose hand are the four great ends of human life; such are Síta and Ráma, says Love's destroyer." When Sambhu had thus admonished the gods, he again urged on his noble bull. Beholding Dasarath march forth, their soul was full of joy and their limbs trembled. The crowd of saints and Bráhmans who accompanied him seemed like incarnate gods ministering to him. In the midst shone forth the beautiful boys as it were final Beatitude manifested in its four phases.[1] As they gazed on the pair, of golden and sapphire hue, the gods were moved with violent love, and especially were they delighted at the sight of Ráma, and glorified the king and rained down flowers.

Dohá 321.

Again and again as Umá and Mahádeva fixed their gaze upon Ráma, all-perfect in beauty from head to foot, their body trembled and their eyes filled with tears.

---

1 The four grades or phases of *apavarga*, *i. e.*, final beatitude, are *salokatá*, residence in the same heaven as god; *sarúpatá* being in the same form as god; *samápyata*, being in actual contact with god; and *sayujyatá*, complete absorption into god.

Chaupái 320.

On his body, dark as a peacock's glistening neck his bright raiment outshone the lightning; his wedding adornments of every kind were most exquisitely fashioned; his face more lustrous than a cloudless autumn moon; his eyes more brilliant than the lotus; his beauty, in short, so marvellous that no words can describe how it moved the soul. By his side shone forth his charming brother, making his mettlesome steed plunge and bound on the way, as also did all the attendant princes; while the family bards recited the glories of their line. As the king of the birds noted the action of the horse that Ráma bestrode, he blushed for shame; for its beauty was beyond all telling, as it might be Kámadeva himself in equine disguise.

Chhand 35.

As though Kámadeva himself in his love for Ráma had assumed an equine disguise, of such resplendent beauty as to charm all creation with his youth and vigour and form and points and paces. A saddle flashed its splendours on his back, thick set with pearls and rubies; bridle too and band gleamed bright with jewels that dazzled the gaze of men, saints and gods.

Dohá 322.

Obedient in every movement to the will of its lord, the gallant steed was as beautiful as a peacock, that dances in response to a thunder-cloud, whose dark mass is irradiated by the stars of heaven and the fitful lightning.

Chaupái 321.

But not Sáradá herself could do justice to the noble steed on which Ráma rode. Sankara was enchanted with his beauty, and congratulated himself on having fifteen eyes. When Hari affectionately gazed on Ráma he and Lakshmi were both equally charmed; while Bráhma rejoiced to behold his beauty, and regretted that he had only eight eyes. Kártikeya exulted greatly that in the matter of eyes he was half as well off again as Bráhma. When wise Indra looked at Ráma, he thought Gautam's curse a great blessing; and all the gods broke out in Indra's praise, saying:—'To-day there is no one like him.'[1] All heaven was delighted at the sight of Ráma, and there was joy above measure in the court of both the kings.

Chhand 36.

There was exceeding joy in both royal courts; the welkin resounded with multitudinous kettledrums; the gods rained down flowers and shouted in their joy,—Glory, glory, glory to Raghu's noble son." In this manner when they learnt that the procession was approaching, all sorts of music began to play, and the queen gave orders to her handmaids to prepare the auspicious materials for the lustral rite.

Dohá 323.

With many lights and torches and festal preparations of every kind, a bevy of graceful dames proceeded joyously to celebrate the lustral rite.

Chaupái 322

With fawn-like eyes and face of moonlike brightness, each one was beautiful enough to rob Rati of all self-conceit. Attired in costly garments of different colours, covered all over with ornaments and rendered beautiful in every limb, they sang more melodiously than the *koil* to the music of the bells on their wrists and waist and feet, as they moved, with all the undulating grace of a wild elephant. All kinds of music played, and there were rejoicings both in heaven and in the city. Indráni, Sáradá, Lakshmi and Bhaváni the wisests of all the queens of heaven, assumed the disguise of woman's form, and flocked to the king's seraglio, singing delightfully with divine voice; and for joy there was no one who recognized them.

Chhand 37.

In their ecstatic joy as they went to receive the bridegroom with melodious song and sweet music, who could

1 The reason being that Indra has a thousand eyes.

tell who was who? the gods showered down flowers and everything was delightful. As they gazed upon the bridegroom, the source of bliss, they were all glad of heart, their lotus eyes overflowed with tears and their every limb quivered with rapture.

Dohá 324.

The joy of Síta's mother on the beholding Ráma's gallant appearance was more than a thousand Sáradás and Seshnágs could tell in a hundred ages.

Chaupái 323.

Restraining her tears out of regard for the suspiciousness of the event, the queen with gladness of heart performed the lustral rite, and deligently completed the entire ceremony in accordance with Vedic prescription and family usage. The five kinds of music [1] were accompanied by festal chanting, and rich carpets of different sorts were spread upon the ground. After the lustral rite and the oblation Ráma proceeded to the pavilion. So great was the splendour and magnificence of Dasarath and his retinue that Indra was put to shame by it. From time to time the gods rained down flowers, while the Bráhmans repeated the appropriate propitiatory texts.[2] There was much jubilation on the earth and in heaven that no one could hear himself speak, much less any one else. In this manner Ráma entered the pavilion, where the libation was offered and he was conducted to his throne.

Chhand 38.

When the bridegroom was seated on the throne and the lustral rite was performed, all rejoiced at the sight, scattering around him jewels and raiment and ornaments

1 The five kinds of music are as follows; the *tàntri* or sitàra; the *tàl*; the *jhànjh*, or cymbals; the *nakára*, or kettledrum; and fifthly, the trumpet, fife or other wind instrument.

2 The prayer, or propitiatory text, ordinarily known by the name of *sànti* is as follows: *Om. Sanno Mitrah sam Varunah sanno bhavatvaryama sanna Indro Vrihaspatih sanno Vishnur urukramah namo Brahmane na maste Vayo twaneva pratyaksham Brahmàsitwam eva pratyaksham Bráhma vadishyami ritam vadishyàmi satyam vadishyàmi tan mám avatu tad vaktar am avatvavatu màm avatu vaktáram. Om. Sántis sàntis sàntih.*

in profusion, while women sang festal songs. Bráhma and all the other gods disguised as noble Bráhmans witnessed the spectacle, and as they gazed on the glorious sun of the lotus race of Raghu, reckoned it the happiest moment of their life.

Dohá 325.

The barber and torch-maker and singers and dancers, who gathered up the offerings that had been scattered about Ráma, [1] bowed their head and invoked blessings upon him from a heart that was bursting with joy.

Chaupái 324.

Janak and Dasarath joined most affectionately in the observance of every custom, whether religious or secular; and the royal pair were so glorious a sight that the poet, searching whereto to liken them and finding nothing, must acknowledge himself defeated and admit that they were comparable only to themselves. The gods beheld with delight the two fathers and rained down flowers and sang their praises :—' Since Bráhma first created the world, we have seen and heard of many marriages, but never till this day have we seen a match so perfect in all respects, and two such wellmatched fathers." At the sound of this voice from heaven so gracious and yet so true, there was on both sides a marvellous access of love. Janak led the way with due honours to the pavilion, offering libations and unrolling a carpet as he went.

---

1 The custom of distributing pieces of money among the crowd is still kept up by rich Muhammadan families at wedding festivals, and special coins for the purpose were struck by Jahángir and others of the Delhi Emperors. These are called *nisár*, while the word used by Tulsi Dàs here and in many other places, is *nichhàvari*. The resemblance is so close that the Hindi might easily be a corruption of the Arabic. But it seems improbable that such a thoroughly Indian custom should not have an indigenous name; and further, the derivation of *nichhàvari* would appear to be from the Sanskrit root *kship*, 'to throw,' with the prefix *ni*, 'down.' Mr. Bate, in his Hindi Dictionary forms it from *niyam plus kshay plus var*; but this can scarcely be accepted as a very plausible explanation. Anyhow the word does not look like a foreign importation. As to the etymology of *nisár*, I must leave Arabic scholars to speak; but if there is no connection between the two words, the coincidence in sound and meaning is at least curious. Should there be no earlier authority than Tulsi Dàs for *nichhávari* it might be a mere adaptation, such as has converted *intikàl* into *ant kál*; *bil ijmàl* into *Brij màl*, and has helped to popularize many other unintelligible terms of legal pharaseology.

Chhand 39.

Beholding the beauty of the manifold decorations of the pavilion, even the saints were astonished; but the wise Janak with his own hands conducted them all to their seats. Paying the same honour and respect to Vasishta as to his own patron divinity, he received his blessing; but the supreme devotion with which he greeted Visvamitra was of a kind that surpasses description.

Dohá 326.

With great joy the king did homage to Vámadeva too and the other saints, and gave them all exalted thrones and received their blessing.

Chaupái 325.

Again he did homage to the lord of Kosala, taking him to be the peer of Mahádeva, yea, none other; with clasped hands and in humble phrase extolling him and enlarging on his own marvellous good fortune. Then to all the wedding-guests he paid the same homage in every respect as to the bridegroom's father, and assigned them all appropriate seats. How can I with my one tongue describe all the pageant. With gifts and compliments and profuse apologies Janak did the honours to all his guests. Bráhma, Vishnu, Mahadeva, the eight guardians of the world[1] and the god of day, who knew Raghubir's glory, disguised themselves as learned Bráhmans and were delighted spectators of the festivities Janak, though he recognized them not, paid them homage as gods and led them to exalted seats.

Chhand 40.

Who could tell who was who, when there was no one who could answer even for himself. As they gazed on the bridegroom, the root of joy, joy was diffused on all sides. When

1 The guardians of the eight quarters of the world are Indra, of the east; Agni, of the south-east; Yama, of the south; Nirriti, of the south-west; Várma of the west; Váya or Marut, of the north-west; Kuvera, of the north; Isana, or Siva, of the north-east. Some lists substitute Súrya, 'the son,' and or Soma, 'the Moon,' for Nirriti and Isana: others again give the Sun and Chandra Moon and the Six Planets.—*Monier Williams.*

he saw the gods, the all-wise Ráma assigned them what seats they fancied ; and the heavenly powers were delighted to behold the gracious manner of their lord.

Dohá 327.

As the partridge drinks in the light of the moon, so their eyes reverently drank in the beauty of Rama's face with the utmost rapture.

Chaupái 326.

Perceiving that the time had arrived, Vasishta called, and Satánand came with ready obedience. "Go now and quickly bring the bride." On receiving this order the saint went gladly, and on hearing his message the queen with all her attendants was delighted, and sent for the Bráhman ladies and the elders of the tribe, and with songs of joy performed all the family rites. The goddesses, who were disguised as women, were all so amiable and lovely, in the first bloom of their youth, [1] that the ladies were charmed to see them, and, though not recognizing them, held them more dear than life. Again and again the queen did them honour accounting them equals of Umá, Ramá and Sáradá. After dressing Síta and forming in procession they joyously conducted her to the pavilion.

Chhand 41.

Reverently and with auspicious pomp her attendant ladies conducted Síta, each of them of lovely form and superbly adorned, moving with the voluptuous grace of a young elephant. At the sound of their melodious strains the saints forgot their meditations, the god of love and the *koil* were abashed ; while the bells on their anklets and gleaming girdless rang out with the cymbals a delightful accompaniment as they moved.

---

1 Hindus of the olden time had a perfect mania for classifying and defining, and have invented divisions and sub-divisions of every conceivable group of objects, with a definite technical name for each variety. Thus the word in the text, here translated 'in the bloom of youth,' is *syamá* which is strictly defined 'as a woman from eight to sixteen years of age, resembling in complexion the blossom of Priyangu and its slender stalk in shape.' There are many other varieties of the sex, that have their distinctive marks specified with equal minuteness.

Dohá 328.

Among her maidens Síta shines forth in native loveliness, like Bliss personified among the Graces.

Chaupái 327.

Her beauty is indescribable, so great is it and so little my wit. When the wedding guests saw her approach, so exquisitely charming and every way divine, they all did homage to her from their inmost soul. At the sight of her, Ráma was filled with love, and Dasarath and his sons were glad of heart beyond all telling. The gods did homage and rained down flowers; the saints gave their blessings in auspicious wise; there was a confused noise of singing and playing and general rejoicing throughout the city. In this manner Síta arrived at the pavilion, while the great saints joyously recited the set forms of prayer and the two family *gurus* performed all the due rites and ceremonies.

Chhand 42—43.

After the ceremonies the *gurus* directed the glad Bràhmans to worship Gauri and Ganes : the gods in visible form accepted the homage and gave their blessing, which they received with joy. Whatever dainty dish or condiment any holy man fancied at any time was at once supplied him by the table-attendants in plates and bowls of gold. Having reverently and dutifully performed all family rites in accordance with the Sun-god's prescription, and offered homage to the gods, they conducted Síta to her glorious throne. The mutual love with which Síta and Ráma regarded each other was too much to look upon; it exceeds all sense, or intelligence, or speech, or perception; how then can the poet express it?

Dohá 329.

At the time of the burnt sacrifice, the Fire-god in person most graciously accepted the oblation, and all the Vedas in the guise of Bráhmans uttered the marriage formularies.

Chaupái 328

What words can describe Janak's illustrious queen-consort, Síta's mother, in whose composition the Creator had combined the perfection of glory, piety, happiness and beauty? At the due time the saints called her, and she came responsive to the summons with her attendant maidens. Then shone forth Sunayana at Janak's left hand, as Maina beside Himálaya. With their own hands the glad king and queen take and place before Ráma golden vases and costly jewelled trays full of holy water and delicious perfumes. The saints with auspicious voice recite the Veda, and at the proper time the heaven rains flowers, while the father and mother of the bride look on in rapture and begin to wash the holy feet.

Chhand 44—47.

Their whole frame quivering with excess of love, they began to lave the lotus feet; while both in heaven and in the city there were singing and music and shouts of victory bursting forth and overflowing in all directions. The lotus feet that ever gleam in the lake of Siva's bosom; by meditating upon which for a single moment every impurity of the soul and defilement of this wicked world is removed; by whose touch the sage's guilty wife attained salvation; whose honeyed fragrance, as the gods declare, is ever present on Sambhu's head; on which the bee-like soul of saints and ascetics ever dwells ere they reach the heaven of their desire; these holy feet are bathed by Janak, 'midst the glad acclaim of all. The two family priests join the hands of the bride and bridegroom and recite their descent. The mystic union is completed, and at the sight Bráhma and all gods and men and saints were full of joy. As the bride's parents gazed on the gracious bridegroom, both their soul and body were raptured with delight; and having completed every family and scriptural observance, the glorious monarch gave his daughter to her lord. As Himálaya gave Girijá to Mahádeva, and as Ocean gave

Lakshmi to Vishnu, in like manner did Janak bestow Síta on Ráma, and creation was glorified anew. After stationing the happy pair on one spot (the bride so fair of hue, the groom so dark) and performing the sacrifice with all due rite, and tying the knot, the circumambulation commenced.

Dohá 330.

At the sound of the huzzas and minstrelsy and the recitation of the Veda and the auspicious chanting and the music, the all-wise gods were delighted and rained down flowers from the tree of paradise.

Chaupái 229.

The bride and bridegroom with measured paces performed the circumambulation, while all present feasted their adoring gaze on the spectacle. The beauty of the happy pair is not to be described ; whatever comparison might be suggested would fall short of the reality. The lovely images of Ráma and Síta were reflected in the jewelled pillars, and sparkled like incarnations of Kámadeva and Rati, who had come to witness Ráma's glorious wedding and, from mingled curiosity and bashfulness, at one moment showed themselves openly and at another retired out of sight. All the spectators were enraptured and like Janak forgot all about themselves. Joyously the saints bade them pace the circle round ; the rite was accomplished and the marriage offerings made. Ráma applied the vermilion to Síta's forehead, brilliant beyond all description ; and his arm seemed like a serpent thirsting for ambrosia, as it decorated her moonlike face with the red powder that filled his lotus hand. Then by Vasishta's direction the bride and bridegroom took their seat together.

Chhand 48–51.

When Ráma and Jánaki took their seat, Dasarath's soul wis rejoiced and his frame quivered with emotion, as again and again he fixed his gaze upon them and saw as it were his own virtue like the tree of paradise blossoming anew.

There was rejoicing all over the world at the news of Ráma's wedding, how can it be described? I have but one tongue in my head, while the joy had no bounds. Then Janak, having received Vasishta's order, provided all things necessary for the marriage ceremonial, and summoned the three maidens, Mándavi, Srutikírti, and Urmilá. After affectionately performing every rite, the king gave first to Bharat in marriage the beautiful and accomplished daughter of Kusaketu. Then next with all honour Janak bestowed upon Lakshman Janaki's lovely younger sister; and finally gave away to Ripu-súdan the bright-eyed and charming Srutikírti, no less amiable than beautiful. As bride and bridegroom modestly gazed on each other and noticed the contrast.[1] they were glad of heart; while every one delightedly applauded the beauty of the scene, and the gods rained down flowers. All equally beautiful, though diverse in hue, they shone resplendent in the pavilion, as though the four states of life with their several lords had met in one living soul.

Dohá 331.

The king of Avadh gazed with delight on his four sons and their brides; as though that jewel of monarchs had in them realized the four methods of religion and the four cognate ends of life.[2]

Chaupái 330.

All the princes were married with the same rites as I have described for Ráma. The enormous dowry was beyond description; the whole pavilion was full of gold and jewels. Shawls, robes and silks of kinds in the greatest profusion and of immense value; elephants, chariots,

---

1 Ráma and Bharat being dark were married to Jánaki and Mándavi who were fair; while the fair bridegrooms, Lakshman and Satrughna were wedded to the dark brides, Urmilá and Sruti-kírti

2 The *chár phal*, *i.e.*, the four fruits or ends of life, are, as has been before explained, *Dharma*, *Artha*, *Káma* and *Moksha*, which are here compared to Dasarath's four sons. The four brides are likened to the *chár kriya*, or four methods of religion, which are either *Sevá Sraddha*, *Tapasya* and *Bhakti*, that is to say, obedience, piety, penance and faith; or according to another enumeration, *anushthána*, religious ceremonial; *udyog*, diligence; *rati* love; and *virati*, detachment from the world.

horses, menservants, and cows with gilded horns and hoofs, as beautiful as the cow of plenty; things so many that no one could count them, nor credit their number if he had not seen them. At the sight the guardians of the world broke out into praises of the dowry, and Avadh's king received it all most graciously. To every one who asked was given whatever he desired, and what remained over was taken to the guests' quarters. Then with folded hands and bated breath Janak courteously entreated all the bridegroom's party.

Chhand 52–55.

After courteously entreating all the marriage guests with high ceremony, gifts, apologies and compliments, he joyfully proceeded with much devotion to do his humble homage to the saintly throng. With bowed head he propitiated the gods, and thus, with hands clasped in prayer, addressed them all, "Gods and saints desire only a good will; can Ocean's wants be satisfied by a libation of a few drops?"[1] Again with clasped hands Janak and his brother spoke to the king of Kosala, with winning words full of love and amiability:—"O king, I am greatly ennobled by your alliance; know that my realm and all that I have is freely yours to command. Take these girls as your handmaidens and graciously protect them, and pardon me my sin and presumption in inviting you." The glory of the Solar race in turn addressed his royal cousin in terms of highest honour; their courtesy was past all telling, and the love that overflowed their hearts. The deities rained down flowers as the monarch proceeded to the guest-chamber, midst the crash of kettledrums, the muttered recitation of the Veda, and glad rejoicings both on earth and in heaven. Then by the saint's command and singing auspicious strains as they went, the fair ladies of the court conducted to the marriage pavilion the bridegrooms and their brides.

1 Yet though it derives no benefit from a such scanty offering, it both demands and accepts it.

Dohá 332.

Again and again did Síta gaze upon Ráma with modest mien, but full of confidence at heart; and her eyes athirst with love outshone the fish in Kámadeya's blazon.

Chaupái 331.

Dark in hue and full of untaught grace, his beauty put to shame a myriad Loves; his lac-stained feet gleamed like some lotus, the haunt of bee-like saintly souls; his pure and lustrous yellow robe outshone the rising sun or lightning-flash; and the little bells on his waistbelt made delicious tinkling; long were his arms and clasped with glittering bangles; his yellow *janeo* set him off to perfection; his signet ring would ravish all hearts; lustrous were all his many wedding adornments and the stars and collars on his broad breast; across his shoulders a yellow scraf with fringe of gems and pearls; with lotus eyes and bright pendants from his ears and a face the very store-house of beauty; lovely brows and charming nose and on his forehead a most bewitching spot, while on his head the auspicious marriage-crown shone glorious with knotted pearls and gems.

Chhand 56—59.

The knotted gems and the crown and his comely person ravished all hearts; and not a woman or goddess in heaven or earth who did not break a blade of grass[1] at the sight of his beauty. After scattering round about him jewels and raiment and adornments they perform the lustral rite, singing auspicious songs, while the gods rain down flowers, and bards, minstrels and rhaposdists declare his glory. When the bride and bridegroom entered the marriage pavilion, great was the joy of the attendants, who with festive songs and in most lovingwise began to perform the accustomed observances. Gauri herself taught Ráma, and Sáradá told Síta how to manage the mess of rice-milk;

1 Either involuntarily from agitation and bashfulness, or as a charm to avert the evil eye, or to show how little they valued anything in the world in comparison with his beauty.

and all the ladies of the seraglio were so taken with the merry sport that they reckoned it the happiest moment of their lives. When Jánaki saw in the gems on her fingers the reflection of the all-beautiful, she dared not move her eyes or lithesome arm for fear of losing his presence. The rapture of delight, the ecstasy of love surpassed all telling; only those happy dames could comprehend it who escorted the bride and bridegroom to the guest-house. Then might be heard on all sides blessings and great exultation in heaven and on earth and a universal shout of joy:—'Long life to the four happy couples.'

Dohá 333.

Hermits, saints and sages, the gods too on beholding their lord, sounded their kettledrums and returned in gladness, each to his own realm, raining down flowers and crying 'Victory.' Then the four princes with their brides approached their father, and such was the glory, the felicity and the rapture that it seemed to overflow the court like a torrent.

Chaupái 332.

Again there was a magnificient banquet, to which Jának sent and invited all the visitors. Carpets of richest stuff were spread as the king sallied forth with his sons. After reverently washing his guests' feet, he seated them all according to their rank. First Janak bathed the feet of Avadh's lord with a loving devotion past all telling; then he bathed Ráma's lotus feet, feet ever enshrined in Mahádeva's heart; and, also with his own hands, bathed the feet of the three brothers, regarding them as Ráma's peers. To all the king assigned appropriate seats, and then gave his orders to the cooks, who with due ceremony set out the dishes, made all of jewels instead of leaves, and stitched with golden pins.

Dohá 334.

The quick and obsequious waiting-men passed round, and in a moment every guest was supplied with rice and condiments and fragrant butter, and everything luscious and savoury and nice.

Chaupái 333.

After making the five oblations,[1] they began to eat listening with delight the while to allusive songs. There were confections of many kinds, sweeter than nectar or than words can tell, which the well-trained waiters handed round, and such an infinite variety of sauces that no one could remember all their names, with food of the four kinds mentioned in the sacred books and an indescribable variety of each kind, and seasoning of the six flavours, and each flavour exhibited in a countless number of dishes. As the banquet proceeded, jests were bandied about in pleasant wise, and not a man or woman but heard his name brought in. Louder and broader grew the raillery of the festive hour, and the king and the whole assembly were moved to laughter as they listened. In this manner they all feasted, then punctiliously rinsed out the mouth :

Dohá 335.

And Janak in due form presented Dasarath and all his guests with *pán*, and the glorious king then retired to his own apartment.

Chaupái 334.

There was ever some new rejoicing in the city, and the whole day and night seemed gone like a minute. At early dawn the best of monarchs woke, and mendicants began to chant his praises. As he gazed upon the gallant princes and their brides, the rapture of his soul was beyond all telling. After performing his morning devotions he went to his *guru*, with his heart full of love and exultation and clasping his hands in prayer bowed before him and said with a voice of mellifluous sweetness :—" Hearken, king of saints ; it is by your favour that to-day my toils have been rewarded. Now holy father, summon the Bráhmans and present them all with cows with costly adornments." On hearing these words the *guru* much applauded the king, and sent to summon the whole saintly throng.

1 The five vital airs to which oblations are made are *prána*, *upána*, *smána*, *vyána* and *udana*.

Dohá 336.

Then came Vámadeva and Nárad and Válmíki and Jábáli and Visvamitra and all the other great saints and ascetics.

Chaupái 335.

The king threw himself upon the ground before them all and worshipped them, and then conducted them to seats of honour. Next he sent for 4,00,000 cows, all as gentle and beautiful as the cow of paradise, and after decorating them in every possible way bestowed them with great joy upon the saints, with many a phrase of studied humility, declaring it to be the happiest day of his whole life. On receiving their blessing the king, the pride of the solar race, rejoiced, and next sent for all the begging fraternity and gave them, according as each desired, gold, or apparel, or jewels, or horses, or elephants, or chariots. They all left loudly telling and singing his praises :—'glory, glory, glory, to the lord of the Sun-gods's race.' Such were the rejoicings at Ráma's wedding; beyond all that could be told even had I a thousand tongues.

Dohá 337.

Again and again the lord bowed his head at Visvamitra's feet :—"All this happiness, O king of saints, is the result of your benignant regard."

Chaupái 336.

King Dasarath spent the whole night extolling Janak's affection[1] and amiability and magnificence; every day on rising he asked permission to return home, but Janak would lovingly detain him. There was constantly some new fête in his honour, and every day a thousand different kinds of entertainment. The rejoicings in the city never flagged, and no one liked to think of Dasarath's departure. In this manner many days were spent, and the guests were fast bound by the cords of love, till Visvamitra and Satánand went and told Videha's lord :—"You must now let Dasarath take his

---

1 The line, which I translate, stands thus: *nrip sab ràti saràhat biti* Another reading is *nrih sab bhánti saráh bibhúti.*

leave, even though you cannot part with your love for him." The king replied :—'It is well,' and summoned his ministers, who came and bowed the head crying :—'All hail!'

Dohá 338.

"Make it known in the palace that Avadh's lord wishes to depart." At these words the ministers, Bráhmans, counsellers and princes were greatly moved.

Chaupái 337.

When it was noised in the city that the guests were leaving, every one anxiously asked his neighbour if it were a fact. When they heard they were actually going all were as unhappy as a lotus that fades in the evening. Every place where the visitors had put up on their arrival was crowded with parting presents,[1] fruits and confections of every kind, and dishes too various for description. A multitude of porters laden with wearing apparel[2] and cooks beyond number were sent by Janak with 1,00,000 horses and 25,000 chariots all exquisitely finished throughout, with 10,000 powerful elephants duly caparisoned, at sight of which earth's guardian elephants would feel ashamed of themselves, besides wagons full of gold and raiment and jewels; buffaloes also and cows, and things of all kinds.

Dohá 339.

The dowry, moreover, given by Videha's king was immeasurable and beyond all telling; and Indra, had he seen it, would have thought the riches of the universe as nothing in comparison.

Chaupái 338.

When the whole equipage had been thus arranged, Janak despatched it to Avadh. On hearing that the guests were about to start, all the queens were as unhappy as fish when water falls. Again and again they clasped Síta to their bosom and blessed and exhorted her, saying:

1 The word *sidh* probably stands for *sidhya* 'auspicious,' though it might be for *sidhu*, wine.

2 For *basan* 'wearing apparel,' some copies read *basah*, 'oxen.'

"May you ever be beloved by your husband, and with him live a long and happy life; this is my blessing. Be obedient to your new father and mother and guru, and regarding your lord's displeasure[1] do as he bids." Her sweet-voiced companions, too, in their overpowering affection reminded her of woman's crowning duty. Again and again after thus duly admonishing them the queens clasped the four brides to their bosom, and time after time, in the midst of their maternal embraces, exclaimed :—'Why has God made women?'

Dohá 340.

Then came the joyous Ráma, the glory of the Solar race, with his brothers, to Janak's palace to take leave.

Chaupái 339.

All the people of the city, whether men or women, ran to see the four brothers so lovely and so unaffected. Said one :—'To-day they have made up their mind to go, and Janak has completed all the preparations for their departure; so feast your eyes on their beauty for the last time. All four princes have been most welcome visitors; who can say; friend, what we have done to deserve that god should bring our eyes such guests. Like a man at the point of death who is given ambrosia; or as one who has been hungry all his life and discovers the tree of paradise; or as one of the damned in hell who approaches Hari's feet, so am I after seeing them. Gaze upon Ráma's beauty and treasure his image in your heart, as it were the jewel in a serpent's hood." In this manner the princes gladdened the eyes of all as they proceeded to the palace.

Dohá 341.

The ladies all rose in their joy as they beheld their exquisite beauty; and the mothers of the brides, in token of their delight, pass the lustral lamp around their heads and scatter gifts.

1 In this line *rukh* may be the Persian word meaning 'face;' but it is more probably the Sanskrit *rush*, 'displeasure.'

Chaupái 340.

Full of love at the vision of Ráma's beauty, they affectionately fall at his feet again and again, nor are conscious of shame, so rapt is their soul in devotion and an involuntary attachment beyond all description. After bathing him and his brothers and rubbing his body with cosmetics, they lovingly entertain him at a banquet of the six flavours. Then seeing that the time had come, Ráma said to them in the most amiable, loving and modest tone: "The king is desirous of starting for Avadh and has sent us to take leave of you. O mother, be pleased to give me your commands and ever regard me with affection as your own child." At these words the queens grieved sore and were too overcome by love to speak a word, but clasped their daughters to their bosom and then meekly gave them to their lords.

Chhand 60.

Meekly her mother surrendered Síta to Ráma, crying again and again with hands clasped in prayer:—"Ah, my son, you, I ween, are all-wise, and to you are apparent the thought of all men. Know well that Síta is dear as life to the king and myself, nay, to all her kinsfolk and all the people of the city; consider her amiability and her affection and accept her as your own servant.

Sorathá 30.

You are the fullness of desire, the crown of wisdom, the beloved of the universe, quick to recognize merit in your votaries, destroyer of evil, Ráma the all merciful."

Chaupái 341.

So saying, the queens still clung to his feet and their voice seemed lost as it were in the quicksands of love. On hearing their most affectionate address, Ráma showed them the highest honour, and with clasped hands begged his congê again and again making them obeisance. When he had received their blessing, he bowed once more and then with his brothers took his leave. Treasuring up his sweet and gracious image in their heart, the queens at first seemed paralyzed by excess of love: but summoning up courage they called their daughters and again and again gave them a maternal embrace: then leading them a few steps would take them to their arms yet again with ever-growing mutual love. Time after time they left their attendants for yet one more last embrace, as a heifer not yet weaned from the cow.

Dohá 342.

Every one in the palace, attendant and all, were so overpowered by emotion that it seemed as though they had made the city of Videha the very home of piteousness and lovers' partings.

Chaupái 342.

The pet parrots and *mainas*, that Jánaki had kept in golden cages and taught to speak, cry in their agitation:—'Where is the princes?' and, on hearing, which of them was not robbed of all peace of mind? When birds and beasts were thus distrest, how can the feelings of the people be told? Then came Janak with his brother (Kusa-dhvaja) overflowing with love and his eyes full of tears. As he gazed upon Síta, all his courage deserted him and his eminent asceticism lasted but in name. As he clasped Jánaki to his bosom the stronghold of his stern philosophy was broken down. All his wise counsellors admonished him; and seeing the unfitness of the time he recovered himself, and again and again taking his daughter to his heart he ordered a gorgeous pálky to be got ready.

Dohá 343.

The whole court was overpowered with emotion, when the king, perceiving that the auspicious moment had arrived, seated the bride in the pálki, with his thoughts intent upon Ganes, the author of success.

Chaupái 343.

The monarch gave his daughter much advice and instructed her in the whole duty of women and in family customs. He bestowed upon her many men-servants and maid-servants and all her own favourite attendants. As she went on her way the citizens were in distress, but all good signs and auspicious omens were forthcoming. Bráhman's and ministers with all their retinue joined company to escort the Rája. The wedding-guests made ready their chariots and elephants and horses, and there was a tumultuous noise of music. Then Dasarath called up all the Bráhmans and gratified them with gifts and compliments, and putting the dust of their lotus feet upon his head rejoiced—great king as he was—to obtain their benison. As he set forth on his way with his thoughts on Ganes, every omen of good occurred.

Dohá 344.

The gods rained down flowers, the heavenly nymphs sang for joy, as the king of Avadh set forth for his capital 'midst the clash of jubilant music.

Chaupái 344.

Courteously the king dismissed the burghers and reverently bade all the mendicants approach and bestowed upon them ornaments and clothes and horses and elephants, and affectionately cherishing them made them stand up before him. After again and again reciting his praises they turned home with Ráma in their heart. Though Kosala's lord spoke time after time, Janak in his exceeding love would not turn back. Once more said the king in gracious tones:—'I beg you to turn back, sire; you have come a great distance.' At last he dismounted and remained standing, his eyes overflowing with love's torrent. Then said Videha's lord with folded hands and in a voice fraught with the ambrosia of affection:—" How can I fitly express my unworthiness, on whom my lord has conferred such high honour?"

Dohá 345.

Kosala's king in return showed the profoundest respect to the father of the bride and his retinue; and as braced with mutual courtesy their heart could not the love they felt.

Chaupái 345.

Janak bowed his head to the throng of saints and received a blessing from all. Next he reverently saluted his sons-in-law, the four brothers, each a treasure of beauty, amiability and accomplishments: and clasping his gracious lotus hands he cried in accents begotten of love:—"O Ráma how can I tell thy praise; swan of the Mánas lake of the saints and Mahádeva's souls; for whose sake ascetics practise their asceticism; devoid of anger, infatuation, selfishness and pride; the all-pervading Brahm, the invisible, the immortal, the supreme spirit, at once the sum and negation of all qualities; whom neither words nor fancy can pourtray; whom all philosophy fails to expound; whose greatness the divine oracles declare unutterable, and who remainest the selfsame in all time, past, present, or future?

Dohá 346.

Source of every joy, thou hast revealed thyself to my material vision; for nothing in the world is beyond the reach of him to whom God is propitious.

Chaupái 346.

Thou hast magnified me in every way, and recognizing me as one of thy servants hast made me thy very own. Not ten thousand Sáradás and Seshnágs, though they kept up their count for a myriad ages, could tell all my good fortune or thy perfections; know this, O Raghunáth; yet I have somewhat to say - for I have this ground of confidence that thou art easily appeased by the slightest evidence of affection—and therefore time after time I implore with clasped hands that never may my soul be deluded into deserting thy feet." On hearing these excellent sentiments, the true birth of devotion, even Ráma, in whom all pleasure ever dwells, was pleased and with much courtesy saluted his father-in-law, holding him equal to his own sire, or Visvamitra, or Vasishta. Next he bowed himself before Bharat and affectionately embraced him and gave him his blessing.

Dohá 347.

Then the king embraced and blessed both Lakshman and Satrughna, and all again and again bowed the head, being overpowered with mutual love.

Chaupái 347.

At last, after many courtesies and flattering speeches, Ráma and his brothers proceeded on their way. Then went Janak and clasped Visvamitra by the feet and put the dust of his feet on his head and eyes:—"Hearken, O greatest of saints; now that I have seen you, I am persuaded that nothing is beyond my attainment. Such bliss and glory as the sovereigns of the universe might desire, though they would be ashamed to express their longing, has all, my lord, been brought within my reach, for all prosperity follows upon seeing you." After again and again humbly bowing the head, the king received his blessing and took leave. The marriage procession set forth to the sound of music, and the whole populace, great and small, were all enraptured and, as they gazed upon Ráma and feasted their eyes upon him, were happy for life.

Dohá 348.

Halting at convenient stages on the road, to the great delight of the people, the procession, on an auspicious day drew near to Avadh.

Chaupái 348.

'Midst the beat of kettledrums and noise of many tabors and sackbuts and conches, and a din of horses and elephants, and clash of cymbals and drums and sweet-tuned clarions, when the citizens heard the procession coming, they were all in a tremor of delight, and every one began to decorate his own house and the markets and streets and squares and gates of the city. The whole roadway was watered with perfumes; on every side were festal squares filled in with elegant devices; the show in the bázar was beyond all telling, with wreaths and flags and banners and canopies.

Trees of the areca-nut and the plantain and the mango, the *málsari*, the *kadumb* and the *tamála*, were transplanted all laden with fruit, and grew into fine trees as soon as they touched the soil, being set in jewelled screens of exquisite workmanship.

Dohá 349.

In house after house festal vases of every kind were ranged in order, and Bráhma and all the gods were delighted as they gazed upon the city of Ráma.

Chaupái 349.

At that time the king's palace was so resplendent that the god of love was distracted by the sight of such magnificence. It was as though everything auspicious and of good omen and all beauty, all plenteousness and prosperity and joy and felicity and gladness had come in bodily form to visit King Dasarath. There was a universal longing to get a sight of Ráma and Jánaki. Troops of fair women were crowding together, each exceeding in loveliness the Lovegod's queen, all with festal offerings and torches and singing, as it were so many Sarasvatis. The rejoicings in the palace at that glad time are beyond all description. Rám's mother Kausalyá and the other queens were too overcome with love to think about themselves.

Dohá 350.

They bestowed large gifts upon the Bráhmans, after worshipping Ganes and Mahádeva, and were as rejoiced as Poverty would be on finding the four great prizes of life.

Chaupái 350.

Each royal mother was so overcome with love and delight that her feet refused to walk and the whole body was paralyzed. Greatly longing for a sight of Ráma, they all began preparing the lustral lamps. Instruments of music were played in various modes, as the glad Sumitrá arranged her auspicious offering of turmeric, *dúb* grass, curds, sprigs and flowers, *pán*, betelnut and well-favoured roots, rice, blades of wheat, yellow pigment, parched grain, and bunches of the graceful *tulsi* in embossed golden vases, so exquisitely beautiful that they seemed like nests made for Love's own birdlings. The auspicious offerings and the perfumes were beyond all telling ; there was nothing of good omen which each one of the queens had not prepared. With lustral lights arranged in various devices they sing for joy melodious festal strains.

Dohá 351.

With golden salvers in their lotus hands, laden with their offerings, and their body quivering with emotion, the queens go forth with joy to perform the lustration.

Chaupái 351.

The heaven was darkened with the fumes of incense, as though overhung with Sávan's densest thunderclouds : the gods rained down garlands of flowers from the tree of paradise which seemed to the beholders as cranes in graceful flight ; the lustrous jewelled festoons resembled the rainbow ; the maidens on the house-tops, now in sight and now out of sight, were like the fitful flashes of lightning ; the beat of the drums was as the crash of thunder ; the beggars as clamorous, as the cuckoos and the frogs and peacocks ; the sweet perfumes were as copious showers of rain. and all the people of the city like the freshened pastures. Seeing that the time had arrived, the *guru* gave the word, and the glory of Raghu's line made his entry into the city, mindful at heart of Sambhu and Girjá and Ganes, and exulting greatly, he and all his retinue.

Dohá 352.

Every omen was auspicious ; the gods beat their drums and rained down flowers, while the heavenly nymphs danced for joy and sang jubilant songs of triumph.

Chaupái 352.

Bards, minstrels, rhapsodists, mimes and players chanted his glory that irradiates the three spheres. In all ten regions of the heaven might be heard loud shouts of victory intermingled with the religious intoning of the Veda. All kinds of music played, and gods in heaven and men on earth were alike enraptured. The magnificence of the procession was past all telling, and the joy was more than heart could contain. The citizens made a profound obeisance to the king, and then were gladdened by a sight of Ráma. They scatter around him jewels and vestments, with their eyes full of tears and their body all tremulous with excitement. Their wives move over his head the lustral lights and rejoice greatly to behold the four noble princes; but when they lifted the curtain of the well-appointed pálki and saw the brides, they were still more glad.

Dohá 353.

In this manner, to the delight of all, they arrived at the gate of the palace, where the glad queens waved the lustral lights over the princes and their brides.

Chaupái 353.

Time after time they perform the ceremony in a rapture of love that is beyond all words. They scatter around in boundless profusion gold and silver ornaments and gems and silks of every kind, and as they gaze on their four sons and their brides, are overwhelmed with the bliss of heaven. Again and again as they regard the beauty of Ráma and Síta, they think with joy that this is the happiest moment of their life. As her companions look again and again into Síta's face they sing and exult over their good fortune. Every moment the gods rain down flowers, midst dancing and singing and obsequious homage. Seeing four such charming couples, Sáradá looked up all her similes, but not one would do; all seemed unworthy, and she could only stand at gaze enchanted with their loveliness.

Dohá 354.

After performing all the rites prescribed by the Veda or family usage, they conduct their sons and their brides to the palace; sprinkling lustral water, spreading carpets in the way, and waving torches.

Chaupái 354.

After seating the brides and their grooms on four thrones so magnificent that they seemed as if made by Love's own hands, they proceeded reverently to lave their sacred feet and to do them homage—all holy as they were—with incense and lights and oblations in accordance with Vedic ritual. Time after time they pass the torch around and wave over their head gorgeous fans and *chauris* and scatter profuse gifts; for each royal mother was as full of exultation as a devotee who has obtained beatitude; or a man sick all his life who has gotten an elixir; or a born beggar who has found the philosopher's stone; or a blind man restored to sight; or a dumb man endued with eloquence; or a warrior who has triumphed in battle.

Dohá 355-56.

Greater by a hundred million times than their joy was the rapture of the queens, when Ráma and his brothers returned home married. As the royal matrons performed the accustomed ceremonies, the brides and their grooms were much confused, but Ráma smiled to himself on beholding their joy and delight.

Chaupái 355.

In due fashion they did homage to the gods and the spirits of their ancestors, and every imagination of the heart was satisfied. Humbly they begged of all the highest boon, namely, the prosperity of Ráma and his brothers, and the gods unseen conferred their blessing. The matrons in their joy took them to their bosom, while the king sent for all who had joined in the procession and gave them carriages and raiment and jewels and ornaments. Then, on receiving permission, and still cherishing the image of Ráma in their heart, they returned in joy each to his own abode. All the people of the city, both men and women, were clad in festal attire, and in every home was a noise of jubilant music. Anything that a beggar begged was at once bestowed upon him by the glad king, and every attendant and every minstrel band was overwhelmed with gifts and compliments.

Dohá 357.

All profoundly bowing invoke blessings upon him and sing his praises, as the king with his *guru* and the Bráhmans proceeded to the palace.

Chaupái 356.

Under Vasishta's directions he reverently performed every ceremony prescribed either by usage or the Veda. The queens, on seeing the throng of Bráhmans, thought themselves most highly favoured and rose to greet them. After bathing their feet and doing them all due homage, the king feasted them at a banquet and loaded them with affectionate civilities and gifts. Greatful at heart, they blessed him at parting. To the son of Gádhi he paid special homage, saying:—'My lord, there is no man in the world so blest as I am;' and with many other flattering speeches both he and his queens took of the dust of his feet. Next he assigned him a splendid apartment within the palace; the king and his royal consorts alike watching his every wish. Again he adored his lotus feet with the greatest humility and devotion.

Dohá 358.

The princes and their brides, the king and his royal consorts, again and again did reverence to the guru's feet and received the holy man's blessing.

Chaupái 357.

With humility of heart and deep devotion he placed before him his sons and everything that he possessed. But the great saint asked only for the accustomed offering, and invoking upon him every blessing set out with joy on his homeward way, with the image of Ráma and Síta impressed upon his heart. Then were summoned the Bráhman dames and the elders of the tribe and invested with fair robes and ornaments; and next the younger ladies of the house,[1] who too were presented with dresses such as each most fancied. Every person with any claim to be remembered received from the jewel of kings suitable remembrance according to his taste, while more dear and honoured friends were overwhelmed with courtesies. The gods, who witnessed Raghubír's marriage, rained down flowers as they applauded the spectacle,

Dohá 359.

and with beat of drum returned each to his own realm; all highly delighted and talking to one another of Ráma's glory with irrepressible rapture.

Chaupái 358.

The king showed every one all possible honour, and with a heart full to overflowing of gladness proceeded to the private apartments, and then gazing upon the princes and their brides took them to his bosom in a rapturous embrace and with a joy beyond all telling. Seating his little daughters in his lap in a most affectionate manner, he again and again caressed them with gladness of heart. All the ladies of the harem were charmed at the sight, and their soul was filled with happiness and exultation, while they listened with delight to the king's account of the marriage and his praises of King Janak's virtue and amiability, and the kindness of his reception and his generous magnificence. The king told it all like a hired encomiast, and the queens were enraptured when they heard of all that had been done.

Dohá 360.

After bathing with his sons the king summoned his guru's kinsmen and entertained them at a sumptuous banquet till five hours of the night were spent.

Chaupái 359.

Lovely women sang joyous songs, and the night was

1 The *suasini* in a Hindu marriage take much the same place as a bridesmaid in the west; and the word might be so translated, were it not that it is essential for the *suasini* to be herself married and with her husband alive.

one of exquisite happiness. As they rose from their seats, all were presented with *pán* and decorated with beautiful and sweet-scented garlands ; then after one more look at Ráma and bowing the head they received the royal permission to retire each to his own abode. The display of love and rapturous delight and the beauty of the court at that time was more than could be told by a hundred Sáradás or Seshnágs or by the Veda, or Bráhma, or Mahádeva, or Ganes : how then can I tell it, any more than an earthly serpent could support the world on its head ? After showing every one the highest honour, the king in gentle tones addressed the queens : —" The brides are but children, and have come to a strange house ; watch over them as closely as the eyelid guards the eye.

Dohá 361.

Go and put them to bed, for they are tired and sleepy." And so saying he retired to his own couch with his thoughts intent on Ráma's feet.

Chaupái 360.

On hearing the king's kind words, they made ready the bed, which was of gold and set with gems, with various rich coverings as soft and white as the froth of milk, and pillows finer than words can tell. In the jewelled chamber were sweet-scented garlands, and a beautiful canopy flashing with lustrous gems which defied description ; no one who had not seen it could imagine it. When they had prepared this exquisite couch, they took up Ráma and lovingly laid him down upon it, who again and again had to tell his brothers to leave him before they too retired to rest. On seeing his dark little body, so soft and delicate, the fond mothers cried :—" O my son, how could you kill on the way the terrible monster Táraká ?

Dohá 362.

How were you able to slay those savage demons, those ferocious warriors, who in battle held no man of any account, the vile Máricha and Subáhu and all their host ?

Chaupái 361.

It was by the saint's favour, I vow, my son, that God averted from you countless calamities, while you and your brother guarded the sacrifice ; and by your guru's blessing you acquired all knowledge. At the touch of the dust of your feet the hermit's wife attained to salvation : the whole world is filled with your glory : in the assembly of princes you broke Siva's bow, though hard as a tortoise-shell or a thunderbolt ; you have won universal glory and renown and Jánaki for your bride, and have now with your brothers returned home married. All your actions are more than human ; it is only by Visvamitra's good favour that you have prospered. To-day my birth into the world has borne fruit, now that I see your moon-like face, my son. The days that were spent without seeing you, God ought not to take into account at all."

Dohá 363.

Ráma in most modest phrase reassured the royal dames, and meditating on the feet of Sambhu and his *guru* and all Bráhmans, he closed his eyes in sleep.

Chaupái 362.

As he slept, his pretty and piquant little mouth gleamed like a red lotus, half closed at eventide. In every house women kept vigil and jested with one another in auspicious wise. The city was so brilliant, nay, so brilliant the night itself that, the queens cried "See, girls, see." The matrons slept with the beauteous brides enfolded in their arms, as lovingly as a serpent would clasp to his bosom the precious jewel from inside its head. At the holy hour of dawn the lord awoke, ere Chanticleer had well begun to crow. Minstrels and bards, proclaimed his praises and the citizens flocked to the gate to do him homage. The four brothers saluted the Bráhmans, the gods, their *guru*, and their father and mother, and gladly received their blessing and while the queens reverentially gazed upon their face advanced with the king to the door.

Dohá 364.

Pure though they were in themselves, they performed all the customary ablutions and bathed in the holy river and completed their morning devotions ere they returned to their sire.

Chaupái 363.

The king on seeing them took them to his bosom. Then at his command they gladly seated themselves. The whole court was rejoiced at the sight of Ráma, and accounted their eyes supremely blest. Then came saints Vasishta and Visvamitra and were conducted to exalted thrones. Father and sons reverently adored their feet, and both the holy men rejoiced as they gazed on Ráma. Vasishta recited sacred legends, while the monarch and his queens listened. He told with joy in diffuse strain of all the doings of Gádhi's son which surpass even the imagination of the saints. Cried Vámadeva :—" The tale is true ; its fame has become renowned through the three worlds." All who heard were glad, but in Ráma and Lakshman's heart there was exceeding joy.

Dohá 365.

Thus passed the days in perpetual delight, happiness and festivity ; and the whole of Avadh was full to overflowing with bliss that was ever on the increase.

Chaupái 364.

After calculating an auspicious day, they loosened the string on the wrist[1] with no little solemnity and rejoicing. The gods, beholding the constant succession of delight, were in raptures and begged of Bráhma that they might be born at Avadh. Visvamitra was always wishing to take leave, but was persuaded by Ráma's affectionate entreaties to stay on. Day after day, seeing the king's devotion and the excellence of his nature, the great saint was loud in

1 A few days before marriage the wrist is bound round with a piece of cloth containing particles of different things that are supposed to possess a hidden virtue; and this is not taken off again till after the marriage is completed.

his praises. When he asked permission to go, the king was greatly moved and with his sons stood before him in the way, saying:—"My lord, all that I have is yours, and I, my sons, and my wives are your servants; be ever gracious to these boys and allow met to see you." So saying the king with his sons and his queens fell at his feet, and speech failed his tongue. The Bráhman invoked upon him every kind of blessing and set forth amidst a display of affection that is past all telling, Ráma and his brothers lovingly escorting him till they received orders to return.

Dohá 366.

The moon of Gádhi's race went on his way rejoicing and praising to himself the beauty of Ráma, the piety of the king and the magnificence of the marriage festivities.

Chaupái 365.

The Vámadeva, the learned *guru* of the house of Raghu, again told the story of Gádhi's son. As he listened to the saint's high fame, the king thought to himself how efficacious his own good deeds had been. At his command the crowd dispersed, while the king and his sons entered the palace. Everywhere the glory of Ráma's wedding was sung, and his holy fame was diffused through the three worlds. From the day that Ráma brought his wife home, all delight made its home at Avadh. The rejoicings attendant on the lord's marriage were more than the tongue of the serpent king could tell, but knowing the praises of Ráma and Síta to be a mine of auspiciousness and the very life and salvation of the race of poets, I too have tried to sing them, in the hope of thus sanctifying my song.

Chhand 61—62.

For the purpose of sanctifying his song has Tulsí told of Ráma's glory; but the acts of Raghubír are a boundless ocean that no poet can traverse. All pious souls, that devoutly hear or recite the auspicious festivities that accompanied Ráma's investiture with the sacred thread and his marriage, shall by his and Vaidehi's favour attain to everlasting felicity. Blessing on the lord of Himálaya's daughter, from whom have learnt my song : all who hearken to Hari's deeds acquire a constant access of devotion and incomparable faith. The love of Raghubír's feet, like a flood, extinguishes at once the fire of covetousness; and in this assurance Tulsi Dás devotes his every thought and word and act to Hari's praise.

Dohá 367.

The times are evil; the body is stained with filth; there is but one remedy; be only is wise who so thinketh and in faith meditates upon Hari.

Sorathá 31 32.

Have a hearty love for Hari's feet, discarding all vanities; much time has been spent in sleep; awake from the darkness of delusion.) Whoever with love and reverence listens to the tale of Ráma and Síta's marriage shall be happy for ever, for Ráma's praises are an unfailing joy.

———o———

[*Thus endeth the book entitled* CHILDHOOD, *composed by Tulsi Dás for the bestowal of pure wisdom, continence and contentedness: being the first descent into ' the holy lake of Ráma's deed's, that cleanses from every defilement of the world.*]

BOOK II.

AYODHYA.

AYODHYA.

Sanskrit Invocation.

MAY he on whose left side shines resplendent the daughter of the mountain-king; on whose head is the river of the gods; on whose brow the crescent moon; on whose throat the poison-stain; on whose breast a huge snake; whose adornments are streaks of ashes; the chief of divinities; the eternal lord of all; the complete, the omnipresent, the moon-like Siva, the holy Sankara; may he protect me.

May he who neither rejoiced when anointed king, nor was saddened by painful exile in the woods; the holy son of Raghu of the lotus face; may he ever vouchsafe to me success and prosperity. Him I adore, with his body dark and soft as the lotus, with Síta enthroned on his left side, with graceful bow and arrows in hand, even Ráma, the lord of the race of Raghu.

Dohá 1.

Cleansing the mirror of my soul with the sand from the lotus feet of the holy *guru*, I sing Ráma's spotless fame, the giver of all good things.

Chaupái.

From the time that Ráma returned home with his bride there was a constant succession of joys and delights. The fourteen spheres were like the great mountains, where clouds of virtue fall in showers of happiness; wealth, affluence and prosperity were bounteous rivers, which overflowed into Avadh as into the ocean; while the noble citizens, men and women alike, were its brilliant pearls, all precious and of perfect beauty The magnificence of the capital was beyond description, it seemed the *chief d'œuvre* of the Creator. Gazing on Rámchandra's moon-like face, the people were perfectly happy; the queens and all their attendants were enraptured to see their heart's desire bear fruit; and still more enraptured was the king, as he heard tell and saw for himself Ráma's beauty and accomplishments and amiability.

Dohá 2.

In every heart was one desire, which they expressed in their prayers to Mahádeva : " O that the king in his own lifetime would entrust Ráma with the regency."

Chaupái.

One day the monarch sat enthroned in court with all his nobles. Himself the incarnation of every virtue, he was delighted beyond measure to hear of Ráma's renown. All kings were solicitous for his patronage, and the very gods desired his friendship. No man so blest as Dasarath in the three spheres of the universe, or in all time—past, present or to come. Words fail to describe his blessedness, who had for his son Ráma, the source of every bliss. The king happened to take a mirror in his hand, and looking at his face in it set his crown straight. Close to his ear was a white hair like old age whispering :—" O king, make Ráma regent, and thus accomplishment the purpose of your life."

Dohá 3.

Having thus considered and settled it in his mind, the king on an auspicious day and at a fitting time, his body quivering with emotion and his soul full of joy, went and declared his purpose to his *guru.*

Chaupái.

Said the king : Hearken, great saint ; Ráma is now perfect in every accomplishment. Servants, ministers, the whole body of citizens, whether my enemies or friends or indifferent to me, all hold Ráma as dear as even I do, and regard him as a glorious incarnation of my lord's blessing. The Bráhmans and their families, reverend sir, have the same love for him as you have. They, who put on their head the dust from the feet of their spiritual father, obtain as it were the mastery over all dominion. There is no man my equal ; but all that I have flows from the worship of your holy feet. I have now a desire at heart; it can only be accomplished, my lord, by your good favour." The saint was pleased to witness his sincere devotion and said: "O king give me your commands.

Dohá 4.

Your name and glory, sire, provide for every wish; on every desire of your soul, O jewel of kings, success follows naturally."

Chaupái.

When he saw the *guru* so amiably disposed, the king replied smilingly in gentle tones: "My lord, invest Ráma with regal powers; be pleased to direct the necessary arrangements to be made. Let this happy event take place in my lifetime, that the eyes of all people may be gladdened by the sight. By my lord's blessing Siva has brought everything happily to pass, but I have still this one desire at heart. It will then be a matter of no concern whether I remain in the body or depart hence, if I have nothing on this score whereof, to repent." When the saint heard Dasarath's noble words, he experienced the greatest delight: "Hearken, O king; the lord whose averted face all creatures lament, and to whom one must pray for removal of all distress, has been born your son even the holy and compassionate Ràma.

Dohá 5.

Quick, O king, let there be no delay, but at once make all the preparations: happy and auspicious indeed the day when Ráma is proclaimed regent."

Chaupái.

The glad king proceeded to the palace and summoned his servant, the minister Sumanta. He bowed the head, crying 'All hail,' and the king then declared to him the glad news: "To-day to my great joy the *guru* has charged me to install Ráma as heir to the throne. If the proposal seems good to the council, prepare with gladness to impress the royal mark on Ráma's brow." The minister was rejoiced to hear these gracious words, which fell like a shower of rain on the young plant of his desire. With clasped hands he made his petition: "O lord of the world, live for ever; the deed you propose is good and beneficent; haste, my lord, let us have no delay." The king was delighted by his minister's assent, like a creeper that spreads apace when it has once clasped a strong bough.

Dohá 6.

Said the king: "Whatever orders the saint may give with regard to Ráma's coronation, see that you perform with all speed."

Chaupái.

In gentle accents the glad saint spoke and said: "Bring water from all holy places, and all kinds of herbs, roots, fruits and flowers (enumerating by name every auspicious variety) with *chauries* of different sizes apparel of all sorts, both of wool and silk and every other material, with jewels and all the auspicious things that there are in the world, that are fit for a king's installation." Then after repeating all the forms prescribed in the Veda, he said: "Erect in the city a number of pavilions, and plant the streets in every quarter with fruit-bearing[1] mangoes and trees of betel-nut and plantains, and fashion bright and beautiful jewelled squares, and have all the bazárs speedily decorated, and do reverence to Ganes and your *guru* and your family god, and diligently serve the Bráhmans.

Dohá 7.

Make ready flags and banners and wreaths and vases, horses too, and chariots and elephants." All were obedient, to the holy sage's words and busied themselves each in his own special work.

Chaupái

Whatever the order that any one had been given by the saint, that he regarded as the very first thing to be

1 For *sa-phal*, 'fruit-bearing,' some MSS. read *panas*, 'the jack-fruit or Artocarpus integrifolia'.

done. The king worships Bráhmans, saints and gods, and does everything to promote Ráma's prosperity. On hearing the glad news of Ráma's installation, all Avadh resounded with songs of jubilee. Good omens declared themselves in the body, both of Ráma and Síta by a sudden quiver of the lucky side, and they said affectionately to one another : " This betoken, Bharat's return. We have greatly missed him for many a long day. This good sign assures us of a friend's approach, and in the whole world there is no friend so dear to us as Bharat : this good omen can have but one meaning." Every day Ráma is as lovingly anxious about his brother as a turtle for its eggs in the sand far away.

Dohá 8.

At that time the ladies of the court were as delighted to hear these most glad tidings as the waves of ocean swell with joy on beholding the moon in its glory.

Chaupái.

First they took care that those who brought the news were richly guerdoned with jewels and robes; then with a body all quivering with emotion and soul full of love, they proceeded to make all festal preparations. Samitrá filled in a lovely square with exquisite gems of every kind ; Ráma's mother, drowned in joy, sent for a crowd of Bráhmans and loaded them with gifts ; then worshipped the local divinity and the gods and the serpents, and vowed them future sacrifices, praying ; " In your mercy grant me this boon, that Ráma prosper." Auspicious strains are chanted by moonfaced, fawneyed damsels, with voice sweet as that of the *koil.*

Dohá 9.

On hearing of Ráma's installation, all good women were glad of heart and began diligently to make festal preparations, thinking God to be gracious to them.

Chaupái.

Then the monarch summoned Vasishtha and sent him to Ráma's apartments to inform him of the coming event. When Raghunáth heard of the *guru's* approach, he came to the door and bowed his head at his feet, and after reverently sprinkling lustral water, conducted him in and paid him honour in the sixteen[1] prescribed modes. Then after again with Síta clasping his feet, Ráma thus spoke his lotus hands folded in prayer: "For a lord to visit his servant's house is a source of great joy, a cure for all distress; yet it had been more fitting, sir, and more in accordance with custom, had you kindly sent to say you wanted me. Since my lord has graciously waived his prerogative, my house has to-day become highly blest. Let me know, holy father, what are your orders; it is for a servant to do his master service.

Dohá 10.

On hearing these affectionate words the saint extolled Raghubír: "O Ráma, glory of the Solar race, it is like you to speak thus."

Chaupái.

After eulogizing Ráma's high qualifications and amiable character, the great saint with much emotion explained: "The king has prepared for a royal installation, and wishes to confer upon you the dignity of regent. To-day, Ráma, you should devote yourself to practices of devotion, that God may bring the matter to a happy issue." Having

1 The 16 modes of showing honour are as follows: (1) *ásin*, a seat; (2) *argha*, lustral water; (3) *pádya*, water for the feet; (4) *snán*, a bath; (5) *áchaman*, water for rinsing the mouth; (6) *gandhákshat*, perfumes and rice, the former only being offered to Vishnu, the latter to Mahádeva; (7) *vastra*, raiment; (8) *dhúp*, incense; (9) *dip*, lights; (10) *naivedya*, temple offerings; (11) *mukhahasta-jal*, water for the face and hands; (12) *támbúla*, betel-leaf; (13) *puga-phal*, betel-nut; (14) *dakshiná*: a gift; (15) *pradakshiná*, circumambulation; and (16) *niráján*, lustration. As some of these ceremonies take place at the reception of a guest and some at his departure, they would never be all performed at once. But here, as in many other paralled phrases, a difinite number, the highest that could under any circumstances be predicated of the subject, is used to express merely the general idea of completeness.

thus admonished him, the *guru* returned to the king; while Ràma's heart was all amazement: "My brothers and I were all born together, and together have we ate and slept and played in childhood; the piercing of our ears, the investiture with the sacred thread, our marriage, in short all our rejoicings have taken place together. This is the one flaw in a spotless line that the eldest only should be enthroned without his younger brothers." These gracious regrets on the part of the lord remove all unworthy suspicion from the mind of his votaries.[1]

Dohá 11.

Then came Lakshman, full of love and joy, and was welcomed with words of affection by the moon of the lily-like Solar race.

Chaupái.

There was a noise of music of every kind, and the delight of the city was beyond description. All prayed for Bharat's return, that he might come quickly and like them enjoy the spectacle. In every street and lane and house and market and place of resort, men and women were saying to one another: "When will to-morrow come and the auspicious moment in which God will accomplish our desire; when, with Síta by his side, Ráma will take his seat on the golden throne and all our wises be gratified." They were all saying: "Whe will to-morrow come?" But the envious gods prayed that difficulties might arise; the rejoicings at Avadh pleased t em as little as a moonlight night pleases a thief. So they humbly called in Sáradá and again and again threw themselves at her feet:

Dohá 12.

"O mother, regard our great distress and make haste to relieve it. It Ráma refuses the throne and retires into the forest, all will be well with us."

---

1 If Ráma had at once and gladly accepted the proffered dignity, it might have been urged by objectors that he had taken an unfair advantage of his brother Bharat's absence.

Chaupái.

On hearing this prayer of the gods, she stood still thinking sadly : " I am like a winter's night to a bed of lotuses." The gods seeing her hesitate cried yet once more : " O mother, not the least blame will attach to you ; for Raghu-ráo—you know his nature well—is exempt from sorrow as from joy ; and (as for his people) they, like all other creatures, have their share in pain or pleasure, under the law of necessity : go therefore to Avadh and befriend us gods." Time after time they clasped her feet, till she yielded and went, though still thinking to herself : " the gods are meanspirited crew ; though they dwell on high, their acts are low ; and they cannot endure to see another's prosperity." Again reflecting on the future, that the ablest poets would do her will,[1] she became cheerful of heart and flew to the city of Dasarath, as it were some intolerably inauspicious aspect of the planets.

Dohá 13.

Now Kaikeyi had a wicked handmaid, by name Mantherá. Her ideas Sáradá first distorted and made her a very storehouse of meanness and then went her way.

Chaupái.

When Mantherá saw the preparations in the city, the joyous festivities, the music and the singing, she asked the people : " What mean these rejoicings ? " When she heard of Ráma's inauguration, her soul was afire and she plotted, wicked wretch that she was, how that very night to defeat it ; like a crafty hillwoman, who has spied a honeycomb hanging from a tree and schemes how to get hold of it. So she went crying to Bharat's mother. " What is wrong now ? " the queen smiled and said. She gave no answer, but drew a deep sigh and, like a woman, began shedding a

1 If Ráma goes into exile, his adventures will form an inexhaustible theme for the poets of all time, who will therefore be always invoking my aid and propitiating my good will.

flood of tears. Said the queen laughing: "You were always an impudent girl, and Lakshman, I suspect, has been giving you a lesson." Still the wicked handmaid said not a word, but breathed hard like some venomous serpent.

Dohá 14.

Said the queen with a nervous smile: "Is Ráma not well, or the king, or Bharat, or Lakshman, or Satrughna?" These words tortured the heart of the hump backed girl.[1]

Chaupái.

"Why, O lady, should any one give me a lesson, and who is there to encourage me in any impudence? With whom again is it well to-day if not with Ráma, whom the king is now associating with himself on the throne? God has been very gracious to Kausalyá; and after seeing her, who else can have any pride left? Why not go and see all the magnificence, the sight of which has so agitated me? Your son is away and you take no heed, making sure of your influence with the king, and not observing his treachery and wiliness so drowsy are you and so anxious for your bed and pillow." On hearing this affectionate address, the queen—who knew well her froward mind—cried: "Peace, have done. If you speak to me again in this way, you mischief-maker, I will have your tongue pulled out."

Dohá 15.

But remembering that the one-eyed, the lame and the hump-backed are ever vicious and vile, more especially if they be women to boot, and slaves, Bharat's mother smiled and added:

Chaupái.

"I have only given you kind advice and am not the least bit angry. If what you say is true, it is the best and happiest of days. It has ever been the custom in the Solar

---

1 Because the fact that the queen asked first of all about Ráma's welfare showed her intense love for him.

race that the eldest-born should be the lord, and the younger brothers his servants. If Ráma is really to be crowned to-morrow, ask of me, girl, what you will and I will give it you. There is no difference between Kausalyá and the other royal mothers. Ráma is equally fond of all: in fact he has a special affection for me, as I have often tested. If I am born again, God in his goodness grant that Ráma and Síta be again my son and daughter! Ráma is dearer to me than life; why then should you be troubled at his being crowned king?

Dohá 16.

I adjure you in Bharat's name, tell me the truth without any fraud or concealment; declare to me the reason why you are in distress at such a time of gladness."

Chaupái.

"I have been satisfied once already; have I a second tongue that I should speak again? I deserve to have my head broken on the funeral pile, wretch that I am, since I pain you by my well-meant words. Those who make the false appear true are the people who please you, my lady; while I offend you. Henceforth I too will speak only as my mistress pleases, or else will remain silent day and night. God has given me a deformed body and made me a slave: we must all reap as we have sown and take as we have given. Whoever is king, what do I lose? Shall I cease to be a servant and become a queen? It is only my worthless character that I cannot bear to see your disgrace, and hence I gave utterance to a word or two; but pardon me, mistress, it was a great fault on my part.

Dohá 17.

On hearing these affectionate words, so deep and crafty, the queen, being only a weak-minded woman and under the influence of a divine delusion, really believed her enemy to be a friend.

Chaupái.

Again and again in kindly terms she questioned her, like a fawn bewitched by the song of a huntress. Her reason veered as fate would have it so; and the slave-girl rejoiced at the success of her scheme: "You ask, but I am afraid to reply, now that you have given me the name of mischief-maker;" thus spoke the malignant star[1] of Avadh, trimming and fashioning her speech in every way to win confidence: "You spoke, O queen, of Síta and Ráma as your friends; and true enough Ráma did love you once, but now those days are past; in time friends become foes. The sun invigorates the lotus, but burns it to ashes if it have no water: the rival queen would tear you up by the root: take care of your garden and hedge it about.

Dohá 18.

Thinking yourself the king's favourite and that he is quite in your power, you notice nothing; but however fair his words, his heart is black; but you are so good-natured.

Chaupái.

Ráma's mother, on the contrary, is deep and crafty; and having found the means has played her own game. The king has sent away Bharat to his grandmother's by her suggestion, and because he is your son; for she said all the other queens are well disposed to me, but Bharat's mother presumes on her influence with her lord. You, lady, are the thorn in Kausalyá's side; she is too deep and crafty for you to fathom; the king has greater love for you than for any one else, and like a rival she cannot bear to see it. For her own ends she has worked upon the king and got him to fix a day for Ráma's inauguration. Now Ráma's promotion is a good thing for the family: all are pleased at it, and I too like it well. But I am alarmed when I consider the consequences; heaven make them recoil on her own head!"

---

1 *Sárh-sáti*, literally '7½,' is a name for the malignant star Saturn, one of whose revolutions occupies a period of 7½ years.

Dohá 19.

With innumerable crafty devices she planned her cunning tale, telling story after story of jealous wives, whereby to increase her resentment.

Chaupái.

Overmastered by fate, the queen was persuaded at heart, and adjured her by the love she bore her to speak out. "What is it you would ask ? still do you not understand : even the brute beasts know what is good or bad for them. For the last fortnight the preparations have been going on, and it is only to-day that you learn the news from me. I am clothed and fed in your service, and I must therefore speak the truth at any cost. If I invent a word of falsehood, may God repay me for it ! Should Ráma be crowned to-morrow, God will have sown you a crop of misfortunes. I draw this line on the ground, O lady, and declare most emphatically that you will be like a fly in a milkbowl. If you and your son will submit to be servants, you will be able to stay ; but on no other conditions.

Dohá 20.

As Kadru tormented Binatá[1] so will Kausalyá treat you Bharat will be a slave in bonds, under Ráma and Lakshman".

Chaupái.

When she heard these cutting words, —Kekaya's[2] daughter could say nothing; she was all in a fever for fear: her limb, were bathed with perspiration ; and she trembled like a

---

1 Kadru and Binatá were the two wives of the patriarch Kasyapa. the former being the mother of the serpent race and the latter of the birds. A discussion arose between them regarding the colour of the horses of the sun. Binatá insisting that it was white, and Kadru that it was black. It was agreed that whichever of the two was proved to be in the wrong should become the servant of the other. Kadru then contrived to fasten one of her black snakes on to the horse's back and Binatá, taking it to be the animal's real tail, admitted herself defeated.

2 The name of Kaikeyi's father was Asva-pati, but he is often called Kekaya from the country over which he ruled, supposed to be part of the Panjáb. The Bráhmana of the white Yajur Vedá mentions Asva-pati, king of Kekaya. as nearly contemporary with Sítá's father, Janak : an interesting act noted by Prof. Monier Williams.

plantain stalk. Then Humpback bit her tongue[1] and with innumerable crafty speeches kept consoling the queen saying 'courage,' courage,' till with her ill-teaching she warped her like a seasoned plank, which there is no bending straight again.[2] By a turn of fate the vile became a favourite, as though a beautiful flamingo should flatter an ugly crane. "Hearken, Manthará, your words are true; my right eye is always throbbing and every night I have some ill dream; but in my folly I did not tell you. What can I do, friend? I am such an innocent that I cannot myself tell right from left.

Dohá 21.

Up to this day I have never of my own accord done an unkindness to any one: for what offence has heaven all at once put me to such intolerable distress?

Chaup i.

Rather would I go and spend all my days in my father's house than live a servant of a rival wife. Whomever God creates the dependent of an enemy, it is good for him to die rather than live." Many such lamentable speeches did the queen utter, and Humpback, on hearing them, formed a thorough woman's device: "Why speak thus, as though patient of disgrace? Your honour and wedded joy shall yet increase daily, and may he who has plotted you this misfortune in the end reap the fruit of it himself? Since your servant, my lady, first heard the bad news, I could neither eat by day or sleep at night. I consulted the astrologers and they declared positively: 'Bharat shall be king, this much is certain.' If, madam, you will only act upon it, I can tell you a way: for the king is under an obligation to you."

Dohá 22.

"I would throw myself down a well if you told me to do so, or even abandon my husband and son. Speak, then:

---

1 Meaning probably to remind herself that she must be careful in what she said.

2 This couplet appears to be an interpolation, as it is said not to be in the Rájapur MS.

you see how great is my distress: why should I not do what will be for my good?"

Chaupái.

Taking Kaikeyi as a victim for the slaughter, the Humpback whetted the knife of treachery on her heart of stone; and the queen, like a sacrificial beast that nibbles the green sward, saw not the approaching danger. Pleasant to hear, but disastrous in their results, her words were like honey mingled with deadly poison. Says the handmaid: "Do you or do you not, my lady, remember the story you once told me of the two boons promised you by the king?[1] Ask for them now and relieve your soul: the kingdom for your son, banishment to the woods for Ráma; thus shall you triumph over all your rivals. But ask not till the king has sworn by Ráma, so that he may not go back from his word. If you let this night pass it will be too late; give heed to my words with all your heart."

Dohá 23.

Said the wretch, having fully contrived her abominable design: "Go to the sulking-room; make all your arrangements circumspectly, and do not yield too readily."

Chaupái.

The queen thought Humpback her best friend, and again and again extolled her cleverness, saying: "I have no such friend as you in the whole world: I had been swept away by the flood but for your support. To-morrow if God will fulfil my desire I will cherish you, my dear, as the apple of mine eye." Thus lavishing every term of endearment on her handmaid, Kaikeyi went to the dark room; her evil temper being the soil in which the servant-girl, like the rains, had

1 Aforetime Dasarath had marched into the south to Vijayanta, a city in the Dandaka forest, to wage war against its king Timi-dhwaja, or Sambara, who had revolted against Indra. The battle lasted till night, and Dasarath, wounded and senseless, would have been left for dead on the field, had not Kaikeyi taken him up into her chariot, inserting her own arm in the place of its broken axle-tree, and speedily driven him away out of reach of the enemy. The grateful monarch, thus restored to life by his wife's devotion, promised to grant her any two boons she might ask; and she had prudently reserved them both till such time as she might require them.

sown the seed of calamity, which, watered by treachery, took root and sprouted with the two boons as its leaves, and in the end ruin for its fruit. Gathering about her every token of resentment, she undid her reign by her evil counsel. But meanwhile palace and city were given over to rejoicing, for no one knew of these wicked practices.

Dohá 24.

All the citizens in their delight were busied with festive preparations, and the royal hall of audience was crowded with a continuous stream of people passing in and out.

Chaupái.

Delighted at the news, not a few of Ráma's boyish friends went to congratulate him, and the Lord, sensible of their affection, received them graciously and politely asked of their welfare. At his permission they roam through the palace discussing his praises : " Is there anyone in the whole world so kind and amiable as Raghubír? Whatever future births fate has in store for us, God only grant us this, that we may always be the servants of Síta's lordly spouse: we ask for nothing more." This was the desire of every one in the city; only Kaikeyi's heart was in a flame; for who is not spoiled by evil communications? There is no profit in taking counsel with the vile.

Dohá 25.

At eventide the happy king repaired to Kaikeyi's apartments, as it were Love incarnate visiting Obduracy.

Chaupái.

He was dismayed when he heard of the chamber of wrath and could scarcely put his feet to the ground for fear. He, under whose mighty arm the Lord of heaven dwells secure, and upon whose favor all monarchs wait, was in a fever at hearing of an angry woman ; see how great is the power of love. The bearers of trident, thunderbolt, and sword are slain by the flowery shafts of Rati's spouse. Anxiously the king approached his beloved and was terribly distressed to see her condition, lying on the ground in old and coarse attire with all her personal adornments cast away : her wretched appearance according with her wretched design, as if in mourning for her instant widowhood. The king drew near and asked in gentle tones : " Why are you angry, my heart's delight ?

Chhand 1.

Why so angy, my queen ? " and touched her with his hands. She put away her lord and flashed upon him a furious glance like an enraged serpent, with her two wishes for its double tongue, and the boons for fangs, spying out a vulnerable point. Under the influence of fate, says Tulsi, the king took it all as one of love's devices.

Sorathá 1.

Again and again the king cried : " Tell me the cause of your anger, O beautiful, bright-eyed dame, with voice as melodious as the *koil*, and gait as valuptuous as the elephant.

Chaupái.

Who is it, my dear, who has vexed you ? Who is it with a head to spare and so enamoured of death ? Tell me what begger I should make a king, or what king I should banish from his realm. I could slay even an immortal, were he your enemy ; of what account then are any poor worms of men and women ? O my love, you know my sentiments and how my eyes ever turn to your face as the partridge to the moon. O my beloved ! my life, my son, and everything that I own, my palace, my subjects are all at your disposal. Could I tell you a word of untruth, lady, at least an oath by Ráma must be binding. Ask with a smile whatever you desire ; adorn your lovely person with jewels ; consider within yourself what an hour of torture this is for me, and at once, my darling, put away this unseemly attire."

Dohá 26.

On hearing this and considering the greatness of the oath, the wicked queen arose with a smile and resumed her royal attire, like a huntress who sets the snare on marking the chase.

Chaupái.

Thinking her reconciled, the king spoke again in soft and winning accents, his whole body quivering with love; "Your heart's desire, lady, has come to pass; there is joy and gladness in every house in the city; to-morrow I give Ráma the rank of Regent; so, my love, make ready for the festival." At the sound of these untoward words she sprang up with a bound, like an over-ripe gourd that bursts at a touch; with a smile on her lips, but with such secret pain at heart as a thief's wife who dare not cry openly.[1] The king could not penetrate her crafty schemes, for she had been tutored in every villainy by a master; and skilled as he was in statesmanship, the abyss of woman's ways was more than he could fathom. Again she cried with a further show of hypocritical affection and a forced smile in her eyes and on her lips:

Dohá 27.

"Ask, ask, indeed; but tell me, sir, when has it come to giving and taking? you once promised me two boons, and yet I doubt my getting them."

Chaupái.

The king replied with a smile: "I see what you mean, you are very fond of a little quarrel. You kept my promise in reserve and asked for nothing, and as my way is, I forgot all about it. Do not tax me with the guilt of a lie, but for two requests make four and you shall have them. It is an immemorial rule in the Raghu family to lose life rather than break a promise. No number of sins is eqaul to a lie; in the same way as myriads of *ghunchi* seeds will not make a mountain. Truth is the foundation of all merit and virtue, as the Vedas and Puránas declare and as Manu[2]

1 On seeing her husband suffer punishment, lest she too should be made to suffer with him. Such at least seems to me the most obvious meaning of the comparison, though some of the Hindu commentators explain it differently.

2 Some manuscript for *Manu* read *Muni*, "the saints;" but the former may well stand, as the great lawgiver in many passages of his Code insists very strongly on the merit of truth. Thus in VIII., 81-83—"A witness, who states the truth in evidence, obtains a high place in heaven and the grea-

has expounded. Moreover I have sworn by Ráma, the chief of our house, the perfection of all that is good and amiable." When she had thus bound him to his word, the wicked queen smiled and cried—loosing as it were the bandage from the eyes of her hawk-like plot.

Dohá 28.

The King's desire being as a pleasent forest, and the general happiness as a flock of birds, at which as a huntress she sent forth the cruel falcon of her speech :

Chaupái.

" Hear, my beloved, what is the desire of my heart. Grant me for one boon Bharat's installation ; and for the second (I beg with clasped hands, O my lord, accomplish my desire) may Ráma be banished to the woods for 14 years there to dwell in the penitential garb of a hermit." At these words of the queen the king's heart grew faint, as the *chakwa* is troubled by the rays of the moon : he trembled all over, nor could he utter a sound, like a partridge in the wood at the swoop of a falcon ; the mighty monarch was as crestfallen as a palm-tree struck by lightning ; with his hands to his forehead and closing both his eyes, as it were Grief personified, he began his moan : " My desire, that had blossomed like the tree of paradise, has been stricken and uprooted as it were by an elephant at the time of bearing. Kaikeyi has desolated Avadh and laid the foundation of everlasting calamity.

Dohá 29.

What a thing to happen at such a time ? I am undone by putting trust in a woman ; as at the time of heavenly reward for penance an ascetic is destroyed by ignorance."

Chaupái.

In this manner the king burned within himself, and the

test reputation on earth : such a statement is held in reverence even by Bráhma himself By truth a witness is purified from sin ; by truth justice is advanced ; therefore the truth should be spoken by witnesses of every caste." I have often thought that if these four lines were printed or engraved in bold characters in the Sanskrit original and set up in our courts of justice they might have a wholesome effect.

wicked woman, seeing his evil plight, thus began : "What, then, is Bharat not your son too, but a slave even as I am, bought for a price ? If my words, thus like arrows, pierce you to the heart, why did you not think before you spoke ? Answer now, say either yes or no, most truthful lord of Raghu's truthful line. Refuse me the boon you promised, break your word and be publicly disgraced. When you engaged to grant the boon, you were loud in your praises of truth, imagining, no doubt, that I should ask for a handful of parched grain. When Sivi,[1] Dadhíchi[2] and Bali,[3] made a promise; they gave life and wealth to keep their word." Kaikeyi's speech was as stinging as salt applied to a burn.

Dohá 30.

The righteous king took courage and opened his eyes,

---

1 King Sivi (or Saivya), the son of Usinara, had already offered 92 great sacrifices, and was hoping to complete the full number of a hundred, a feat which would have exalted him to the highest dignity in heaven, when Indra, jealous of his own supremacy, determined to prevent him. Himself assuming the form of a hawk and changing Agni, the god of fire, into a dove, he chased it through the air till it flew into the temple and took shelter in Sivi's bosom, who thereupon promised that he would protect it from all harm. The hawk followed close behind and protested that the dove was his lawful spoil, and that it was unjust of the king to rob him of food which he had fairly won, and without which he would die of starvation. The king offered him anything else that he liked to name : but the hawk would be satisfied with nothing but an equal weight of the king's own flesh. Scales were brought, the dove was put in the one balance, and the monarch began to hack and hew pieces of his own body and cast in the other ; but still the dove weighed heavier. At last, when all had been cut away and only his bones were left, he threw himself in. The gods then came and restored him to life and bore him off in triumph to heaven.

2 When Indra and the other gods were hard pressed by the demon Vritra, Vishnu told them that there was a great saint named Dadhíchi practising penance in the Naimisha forest, and that if he would let them have his bones they could be made into weapons, before which no enemy could stand. Dadhíchi, as soon as he heard what they wanted, at once devoted himself to death, and out of his bones the gods made thunderbolts, with which they won an easy victory.

3 King Bali, the son of Virochana, had so extended his empire that he had acquired dominion over the three worlds. Indra, to rid himself of so dangerous a rival, applied to Vishnu who assuming the form of a dwarf, as the son of Kasyapa, appeared before Bali and begged an alms. The king promised to give him whatever he asked. He said he only wanted as much land as he could pace in three steps. This modest request was granted without hesitation ; whereupon he at once developed himself into a giant, and with the first stride covered the whole earth, and with the second the heaven. For the third step he planted his foot on Bali's head and crushed him down into the infernal regions, of which he became the sovereign.

and beating his head gasped out: "She has pierced me in the most vital part."

Chaupái.

He saw her standing before him burning with passion, as it were Fury's own sword drawn from the sheath, with ill-counsel for its hilt and cruelty for its sharp edge whetted on the Humpback grindstone. The monarch saw her stern and terrible: "She will rob me either of life or honour;" but stilling his heart he cried in suppliant tones which she regarded not: "Bharat and Ráma are as my two eyes. I tell you truly and call Siva as my witness. O my beloved, what is this ill word that you have uttered, destructive of all order, confidence and affection? I will not fail to despatch a messenger at daybreak and as soon as they hear the news both brothers will come. Then after fixing an auspicious day and making all due preparation. I will solemnly confer the kingdom on Bharat.

Dohá 31.

Ráma has no greed of empire and is devotedly attached to Bharat: I made my plans according to royal usage, thinking only of their respective ages.

Chaupái.

I swear by Ráma that I tell you true of his mother, that she never said a word to me. I arranged it all without asking you, and this is how my scheme has failed. Put away your displeasure, assume a festal garb; yet a few days and Bharat shall be Regent. There was only one thing that pained me, your second petition, really an unreasonable request. To-day your bosom burns with unwonted fire; is it anger, or do you jest, or is it all really true? Tell me calmly Ráma's offence. Every one says that he is amiability itself. Even you used to praise and caress him, and I am quite perplexed at what I now hear. His pleasant ways would charm even an enemy; how then can he have vexed his own mother?

Dohá 32

Have done, my beloved, with this, be it raillery or

displeasure ; make a just and reasonable request, that I may rejoice in the sight of Bharat's installation.

Chaupái.

Rather might a fish live out of the water, or a wretched serpent live without its head-jewel—I tell you my true case without any deception—but there is no life for me without Ráma. Consider well, my dear, my prudent wife, my very existence depends upon my seeing Rama." On hearing this soft speech the wicked woman blazed up like the fire on which has fallen an oblation of *ghi* : "You may devise and carry out any number of plans, but your subterfuges will not avail with me. Either grant my request, or refuse me and be disgraced ; I do not want any long discussion. Ráma is good, you too are good and wise, and Ráma's mother, as you have discovered, is also good. The benefit that Kausalyá devised for me is the only fruit that I now in turn give her.

Dohá 33.

At daybreak, if Ráma does not assume the hermit's dress and go out into the woods, my death will ensue, O king, and your disgrace ; be well assured of this"

Chaupái.

So saying, the wretch rose and stood erect, as it were a swollen flood of wrath that had risen in the mountains of sin, turgid with streams of passion, terrible to behold, with the two boons for its banks, her stern obduracy for its current, and her voluble speech for its eddies, overthrowing the king like some tree torn up by the roots, as it rushed on to the ocean of calamity. The king perceived that it was all true, and that death, in fashion as a woman, was dancing in triumph on his head. Humbly he clasped her by the feet and begged her to be seated, crying : "Be not an axe at the root of the Solar race. Demand of me my head and I will give it at once, but do not kill me by the loss of Ráma, be it in any way you will, or your heart will be ill at ease all your life long."

Dohá 34.

Seeing that his disease was incurable, the king fell upon the ground and beat his head, sobbing out in most lamentable tones, " O Ráma, Ráma,"

Chaupái.

The king's whole body was so broken down by distress that he seemed like the tree of paradise that some elephant had uprooted. His throat was dry, speech failed his lips, like some poor fish deprived of water. Again Kaikeyi plied him with biting taunts, infusing as it were poison into his wounds: " If you meant to act thus in the end, what compulsion was there to say, ask, ask? Is it possible, sire, to be two things at once? To laugh and jest and at the same time mourn; to be called the munificent, and yet be miserly; to live without anxiety, and yet be a king? Either break your word or show more fortitude, do not, like a woman, appeal to compassion. It is said that life, wife, sons, home, wealth, nay the whole world, all are but as a straw compared to the ocean of truth."

Dohá 35.

On hearing these fatal words the king exclaimed: " It is no fault of yours; my evil destiny, like some demoniacal delusion, has possessed you and bids you speak.

Chaupái.

Bharat has never dreamed of desiring the royal dignity but by the decree of fate evil counsel has lodged in your breast. All this is the result of my sins. I can do nothing; God is against me. Hereafter beautiful Avadh shall flourish again under the sway of the all-perfect Ráma; all his brethren shall do him service and his glory shall spread through the three spheres of creation; your disgrace also and my remorse, though we die, shall never be effaced or forgotten. Now do whatever seemeth you good; only stay out of my sight and let your face be veiled: with clasped hands I ask but this, speak not to me again so long as I live. You too will repent at the last, O miserable woman, who aiming at the tiger have thus shot dead the cow."

Dohá 36.

The king fell to the ground crying again and again: "Why have you wrought this ruin?" But the perfidious queen spoke not a word, like a funeral pile that is ever burning.

Chaupái.

The king in his distress sobbing out "Ráma, Ráma," was like some luckless bird clipped of its wings. In his heart he was praying: "May the day never break nor any one go and tell Ràma. Rise not great patriarch of the Solar race, for at the sight of Avadh your breast will be consumed with anguish." The king's affection and Kaikeyi's cruelty were both the most extreme that God could make. While the monarch was yet lamenting, day broke and the music of lute and pipe and conch resounded at his gate. Bards recited his titles, minstrels sung his praises; but like arrows they wounded the king, as he heard them. All tokens of rejoicing pleased him as little as the adornment of a widow who ascends the funeral pile. That night no one had slept, from the joyous anticipation of beholding Ràma.

Dohá 37.

At the gate was a crowd of servants and ministers, who exclaimed as they beheld the risen sun: "What can be the reason why to-day of all days our lord awaketh not?

Chaupái.

He was always wont to wake at the last watch; to-day it strikes us as very strange. Go Sumanta, and rouse him and obtain the royal order to commence the work." Sumanta entered the palace, but as he passed on was struck with awe and dismay at its appearance, as though some terrible monster were about to spring upon him and devour him; it seemed the very home of calamity and distress. Asking, but with no one to answer him, he came to the apartment where were the king and Kaikeyi; with the salutation

"Live for ever" he bowed the head and sat down. On beholding the king's condition he was much distressed, for he was fallen on the ground crushed and colourless, like a lotus broken off from its root. The terrified minister could ask no question; but she, full of evil and void of all good, answered and said:

Dohá 38.

"The king has not slept all night: God knows why. He has done nothing but mutter 'Ráma, Ráma,' even till daybreak; but he has not told me the reason.

Chaupái.

Go at once and send Ráma here, and when you come back you can ask what the matter is." Perceiving it to be the king's wish, Sumanta went; but he saw that the queen had formed some evil design. So anxious was he that his feet scarcely touched the ground as he wondered to himself: 'What will the king have to say to Ráma?' Composing himself as he reached the gate, when all observed his sadness and asked the cause, he reassured them and proceeded to the prince's abode. When Ráma saw Sumanta coming, he received him with the same honour that he would have shown to his own father. Looking him in the face, he declared the king's commands and returned with him. Remarking the state of disorder in which Ráma accompanied the minister, the people began to be a little anxious.

Dohá 39.

When the jewel of Raghu's race had come and beheld the king's miserable condition, like some aged and pain-stricken elephant in the power of a tigress, his lips became parched and his body all aflame, like a poor snake that has been robbed of the jewel in its head. Seeing the furious Kaikeyi near, like death counting the minutes, the pitiful and amiable Raghunáth, though he now for the first time saw sorrow, and had never before heard its name even, composed himself as the occasion required and in pleasant tones asked his mother : " Tell me, mother, the cause of my father's distress, that I may endeavour to put an end to it." " Listen, Ráma : the sole cause is this : the king is very fond of you ; he has promised to grant me two requests, and I have asked for what I wanted ; but he is disturbed on hearing them and cannot get rid of a scruple on your account.

Dohá 40.

On the one side is his love for his son ; in the other his promise ; he is thus in a strait. If it lies in your power, be obedient to his commands and so terminate his misery."

Chaupái.

She sat and spoke stinging words so composedly that Cruelty itself was disturbed to hear her. From the bow of her tongue she shot forth the arrows of her speech against the king as it were some yielding target ; as though Obduracy had taken form and become a bold and practised archer. Sitting like the very incarnation of heartlessness, she expounded to Raghupati the whole history. Ráma, the sun of the Solar race, the fountain of every joy, smiled inwardly and replied in guileless terms, so soft and gracious that they seemed the very jewels of the goddess of speech : " Hearken, mother ; blessed is the son who obeys his parent's commands ; a son who cherishes his father and mother is not often found in the world.

Dohá 41.

I have a particular wish to join the hermits in the woods and now there is also my father's order and your approval, mother.

Chaupái.

Bharat, moreover, whom I love as myself, will obtain the kingdom ; in every way God favours me to-day. If I go not to the woods under these circumstances, then reckon me first in any assembly of fools. They who desert the tree of paradise to tend a castor-oil plant, or refuse ambrosia to ask for poison, having once lost their chance, will never get it again ; see, mother, and ponder this in your heart. One special anxiety still remains, when I see the king so exceedingly disturbed. I cannot understand, mother, how my father can be so much pained by such a trifling matter. He is stout-hearted and a fathomless ocean of piety[1] : there must have been some great offence on my part, that he will not say a word to me : I adjure you to tell me the truth."

Dohá 42.

Though Raghubar's words were as straightforward as possible, the wicked queen gave them a perverse twist ;[2] like a leech, which must always move crookedly, however smooth the water be.

Chaupái.

Seeing Ráma's readiness, the queen smiled and said with much show of false affection : "I swear by yourself and Bharat, there is no other cause that I know of. There is no room for fault in you, my son, who confer such happiness both on your parents and your brother. All that you say, Ráma, is true ; you are devoted to the wishes of your father and mother. Remonstrate, then, solemnly with your sire, that he incur not sin and disgrace in his old age. Having been blest with a son like you, he cannot properly disregard your advice" These fair words in her false mouth were like Gaya and the other holy places that are in Magadha : but Ráma took his mother's speech in good part, like the Ganges, which in its course receives and hallows any stream.

Dohá 43.

At the remembrance of Rama, the king's swoon left him and he turned on his side. Taking advantage of the opportunity, the minister humbly informed him of Ráma's arrival.

1 Being so stout of heart, why should he be thus dismayed at the mere thought of losing me ? And being so pious, how is it possible that he can hesitate for a moment about keeping his word ? There must be something else in the background. I fear I have done wrong and displeased him.

2 The queen thought to herself : By his praises of a hermit's life he hopes I may be persuaded to send Bharat to the woods instead of himself, *or* by his ready compliance, he hopes to wheedle me out of my resolve.

Chaupái.

When the king heard that Ráma had come, he summoned up courage and opened his eyes. The minister supported his sovereign to a seat, where the king saw Ráma falling at his feet. In an agony of affection, he clasped him to his bosom, like some snake that has recovered the jewel it had lost. As the monarch continued gazing upon Ráma, a flood of tears came into his eyes, nor in his sore distress could he utter a word, but again and again he pressed him to his heart. Inwardly he was praying God that Raghunáth might not be banished to the woods; and remembering Mahádeva humbly begged: "Immortal Siva, hear my petition; thou art easily satisfied, compassionate and generous; recognize then in me a poor suppliant and remove my distress.

Dohá 54.

As thou directest the hearts of all, give Ráma the sense to disregard my words and stay at home, forgetful for once of his filial affection.

Chaupái.

Welcome disgrace and perish my good name; may I sink into Hell rather than mount to Heaven; be it mine to support the most intolerable pain rather than have Ráma taken from my sight." Thinking thus to himself, the king spoke not a word, while his soul quivered like a *pipal* leat. Perceiving his father to be thus overpowered with love, Raghupati spoke again with a view to his mother, in modest and thoughtful phrase, as the place, the time, and the circumstances demanded: "Father, if I speak a little wilfully, forgive the offence by reason of my childish years. You are troubled about a very little matter; why did you not speak and let me know of this at the first? After seeing you, sire, I questioned my mother, and on hearing her explanation my fear subsided.

Dohá 45.

Put away, father, the anxiety which at this time of rejoicing your affection has caused you, and give me your commands : " so spoke the Lord with heartfelt joy and a body quivering with emotion.

Chaupái.

" Blessed is his birth into the world whose father is rejoiced to hear of his doings. He has in his hand all the four rewards of life, who holds his parents dear as his own life. By obeying your orders, I attain the end of my existence. If then it be your command, I can soon come back, and after taking leave of my mother, I will throw myself once more at your feet and then start for the woods." Having thus spoken, Ráma departed, while the king in his anguish answered not a word. The bitter news spread through the city, like the sting of a scorpion that at once affects the whole body. Every man or woman that heard it was as distrest as the creepers and bushes when a forest is on fire. Wherever it was told, every one beat his head, and the grief was too great to be endured.

Dohá 46.

Their lips were parched, their eyes streamed, their heart could not contain their sorrow ; it seemed as though the Pathetic, in battle array and with beat of drum, had marched into Avadh and taken up quarters there.

Chaupái.

"It was a well-contrived plan, but God has spoilt it." In this fashion they kept abusing Kaikeyi : " What could this wicked woman mean by thus setting fire to a new-thatched house ; who tears out her eyes with her own hands, and yet wishes to see ; who throws away ambrosia and prefers the taste of poison ; cruel stubborn, demented wretch, a very fire among the reeds of Raghu's line ; who sitting on a branch of the tree has hacked down the stem ; and in the midst of joy has introduced this tragedy ? Rama used ever to be dear to her as life ; for what reason has she now taken to such perversity ? The poets say truly that a woman's mind is altogether inscrutable, unfathomable and beyond comprehension. Sooner may a man catch his own shadow in the glass than grasp the ways of a woman.

Dohá 47.

What is there that fire will not burn; what is there that ocean cannot contain; what cannot a woman do in her strength; or what is there in the world that death does not devour?

Chaupái.

God first ordained one thing, but now ordains something quite different, and what he would show us now is the very reverse of what he showed us then." Said one: "The king has not done well, and without consideration has granted the wicked woman her request. He has wilfully brought all this misery upon himself, and in yielding to a womàn has lost all good sense and discretion." Another wisely recognized the king's supreme virtue and would not blame him, as they repeated to one another the legends of Sivi, Dadhíchi, and Harischandra.[1] One suggested Bharat's connivance, another was distressed at the mention of such a thing; while a third stopping his ears with his hands and biting his tongue exclaimed: "Such words are false; you damn yourself by saying such things. Bharat is Ráma's dearest friend.

Dohá 48.

Sooner shall the moon rain sparks of fire, or ambrosia have the same effect as poison, than Bharat ever dream of doing anything to injure Ráma."

---

1 For the legends of SIVI and DADHICHI see notes to page 19.

HARISCHANDRA, the son of Trisanku, was king of Ayodhya and the twenty-eighth in descent from Ikshváku, the founder of the solar dynasty. In order to satisfy the claims of Visvamitra. who wanted to make trial of his integrity, he sold his kingdom and all that he had, together with his wife Satyavati and his only son, and hired himself out as the servant of a man who kept a burning ghat. Whenever a corpse was brought, ha had to take the fee and make it over to his master. One day a woman brought her dead child and he recognized them as his own wife and son. She had no money and he was so zealous in his employer's interests that he would not allow the body to be burnt till the regular fee was paid. As the only way to satisfy his demand, she was stripping off the one poor rag that covered her nakedness, when the gods interposed and restored the king to his throne and all his former prosperity.

Chaupái.

One reproached the Creator, who had promised ambrosia but given poison. The whole city was agitated and every one so sad that the intolerable pain in their heart utterly effaced all the previous rejoicing. The venerable and highborn Bráhman matrons, who were Kaikeyi's chief friends, began to give her advice and praise her good disposition; but their words pierced her like arrows: You have always said, as every one knows, that Bharat was not so dear to you as Ráma: show him, then, your wonted affection; for what offence do you now banish him to the woods? You have never shown any jealousy of the rival queens; your love and confidence in them were known throughout the land. What has Kausalyá done wrong now that you should launch this thunderbolt against the city?

Dohá 49.

What! will Síta desert her spouse, or Lakshman remain here at home? Will Bharat enjoy the dominion of the state, or the king survive without Ráma.

Chaupái.

Reflect upon this and expel passion from your breast, nor make yourself a stronghold of remorse and disgrace. By all means make Bharat the king's coadjutor; but what need is there for Ráma to be banished to the woods? Ráma is not greedy of royal power; he is righteous and averse to sensual pleasures. Let him leave the palace and go and live with his guru; ask this of the king as your second petition. A son like Ráma does not deserve banishment; what will people say to you when they hear of it? If you do not agree to what I tell you, nothing will prosper in your hands. If this is only some jest of yours, speak out clearly and let me know. Up quickly and devise a plan to avert future remorse and disgrace.

Chhand 2.

Devise a plan to avert remorse and disgrace and save your family. Be instant in diverting Ráma from going to the woods, and labour for nothing else. As the day without the sun, as the body without life, as the night without the moon, so (says Tulsi Dás) is Avadh without its lord; I beg you, lady, to consider this."

Sorathá 2.

Pleasant to hear and beneficial in result was the advice her friends gave; but she paid no heed to it, having been tutored in villainy by Humpback.

Chaupái.

She answered not a word, but raged with irrepressible fury like a hungry tigress that has spied a deer. Perceiving her disease to be incurable, they left her, saying as they went: 'Demented wretch! Fate has destroyed her in her pride; she has acted in such a way as no one has ever acted before." Thus all the men and women of the city were lamenting and heaping countless abuse on the wicked queen. Burning with intolerable fever they sob out: "What hope of life is there without Ráma?" Agonized by his loss, the people were as miserable as creatures of the deep when water fails. Great was the distress of all, whether man or woman: but the saintly Ráma went to his mother, with joy in his face and fourfold joy in his soul, fearing only that the king might detain him.

Dohá 50.

The Glory of Raghu's line resembled some young elephant with kingship for its chain: the news of banishment was as its breaking: at which he rejoices exceedingly.

Chaupái.

With folded hands the Crown of Raghu's line bowed his head blithely at his mother's feet. She gave him her blessing and clasped him to her bosom, and scattered around him gifts of jewels and raiment. Again and again she kissed his face, with tears of joy in her eyes and her body all quivering with emotion. Then seating him in her lap, she pressed him once more to her heart, while drops of affection trickled from her comely breasts. Her rapture of love was past all telling, like that of a beggar made all at once rich as Kuver. Tenderly regarding his lovely features, his mother thus addressed him in sweetest tones: "Tell me, my son, I adjure you as your mother, when is the happy moment to be; you are such an exquisite paragon of piety, amiability and good fortune, that in you Avadh has reaped the full fruition of its existence:

Dohá 51.

For whom the people long as anxiously as a pair of thirsting *chátaks*, in the season of autumn, for the rainfall of Arcturus.

Chaupái.

Go at once, my darling, I beg of you, and bathe and take something nice to eat, such as you like, and then, dear boy approach your father: I, your mother, protest there has been too much delay.' On hearing his mother's most loving speech, which seemed as the flower of the paradisal tree of affection laden with the fragrance of delight and produced from the stem of prosperity, Ráma's bee-like soul was not distracted by the sight, but in his righteousness he distinguished the path of virtue, and thus in honeyed tones addressed his mother: "My father has assigned me the woods for my realm, where I shall have much in every way to do. Give me your orders, mother, with a cheerful heart, that I too may cheerfully and in auspicious wise set out for the forest. Do not in your affection give way to causeless alarm; my happiness, mother, depends on your consent.

Dohá 52.

After staying fourteen years in the woods, in obedience to my sire's command,[1] I will come back and again behold your feet; make not your mind uneasy."

Chaupái.

Raghubar's sweet and dutiful words pierced like arrows through his mother's heart. At the sound of his chilling

1 *Or*, and thus making good my father's vow.

speech she withered and drooped like the *jawása*[1] at a shower in the rains. The anguish of her soul was past telling, as when an elephant shrinks at the roar of a tiger. Her eyes filled with tears and her body trembled all over, like a fish overtaken by the scour of a flooded river.[2] Summing up courage, she looked her son in the face and thus spoke, in faltering accents : " My son, you are your father's darling and it is a constant delight to him to watch your doings. He had fixed an auspicious day for giving you the sceptre ; for what offence does he now banish you to the woods ? Tell me my boy, the upshot of it all ; who is the destroying fire of the Sun-god's line ? "

Dohá 53.

After a look at Ráma's face the minister's son explained to her the reason. On hearing his account she was struck dumb : words fail to describe her condition.

Chaupái.

She could neither detain him, nor yet say Go ; either way her heart was distraught with cruel pain: as though for 'moon' one had written 'eclipse': God's hand is ever against us all. Duty and affection both laid siege to her soul ; her dilemma was like that of a snake with a musk-rat.[3] "If I keep my son, it will be a sin ; my past virtue will go for nothing and my friends will abhor me. If I order him into exile, it will be a sad loss." In this distressing strait the queen was sore tried. Again reflectingdiscreetly on her wifely duty and remembering that Ráma and Bharat were both equally her sons, the queen in the sweetness of her

1 A popular Hindi couplet says that every creature in the world rejoices at the coming of the rains, except four, *viz.*, the *ák* and *jawása* plants, which flourish only on dry soil, and the saltpetre manufacturer and the carter, who cannot ply their trade :

Ák, jawása, ágara, chauthe gáriwán,
Jyon jyon chamake bijli, tyon tyon taje prán.

2 the line, as I translate it, stands thus : *Manja Manahun min kahan vyápi.* As to the meaning of the word *mánjá* see the note on page 86 ; the Commentators explain it as a sickness that prevails at the beginning of the rains ; or, as the scum raised on the water when the rains first break ; or, as the juice of a plant. Another reading is *Mánjá-hi khai min janu mápi*, where *mápi* would be for *máti*, drunk."

3 If it swallows the rate, it dies ; if it disgorges it, it goes blind ; such is the popular belief.

disposition summoned up courage and, spoke these woful words : " May I die, my son, but you have done well ; a father's command is the most paramount duty.

Dohá 54.

Though he promised you the kingdom : and now banishes you to the woods I am not the least sad or sorry : but, without you, Bharat and the king and the people will all be put to terrible distress.

Chaupái.

Yet, boy, if it is only your father's order, then go not ; hold your mother still greater.[1] If both father and mother bid you go, the forest will be a hundred times better than Avadh, with its god for your father, its goddess for your mother and birds and deer to wait upon your lotus feet. At the end of life retirement to the woods is the proper thing for a king, but I am troubled at heart when I consider your tender age. How blest the forest and how wretched Avadh if you abandon it, you, the crown of Raghu's line. If, child, I say 'take me with you,' there may be some hesitation in your mind ; O my son, all hold you most dear, life of our life ; if you say 'mother, I go alone to the woods,' on hearing your words I sink down in despair.

Dohá 55.

Being thus minded I do not press my suit with a show of love beyond what I really feel ; agree to your mother's request ; or if you go alone, at least I pray you not to forget me.

Chaupái.

May all the gods and the spirits of your ancestors guard you, noble boy, as closely as the eyelids guard the eyes. The term of banishment is like the water of a lake in which the fish are your friends and relations ; you are all-merciful and righteous ; remember then to make your plans so that you may find them all alive when you come again. Go in peace to the woods—ah ! woe is me !—leaving your servants, your

---

1 For *jáni bari mátá*, the words that I translate, some copies read *jái bál mátá*.

relatives, the whole city in bereavement; to-day the fruit of all their past good deeds has gone, and awful death confronts them." Thus with many mournful moanings she clung to his feet, accounting herself the most hapless of women. Cruel and intolerable pangs pierced her heart through and through, and the burden of her misery was past all telling. Ráma raised his mother and took her to his bosom and consoled her with many soothing words.

Dohá 56.

At that moment Síta, who had heard the news, rose in great agitation, and having reverenced her mother's lotus feet, bowed her head and sat down.

Chaupái.

In tender accents her mother gave her her blessing, and at the sight of her delicate frame was more distressed than ever. With drooping eyes Síta, the perfection of beauty, model of wifely devotion, sat and thought: "The lord of my life would go to the woods, how can I merit to accompany him? Whether in the body or only in the soul, go I must; but God's doings are inscrutable." With her lovely toe-nails she wrote upon the ground, while the music of her anklets, like the poet's honeyed song, rang out the passionate prayer: 'Never may we be torn from Síta's feet.' Seeing her let fall a flood of tears from her lovely eyes, Ráma's mother cried: "Hearken, my son; Síta is very delicate; she is the darling of your father and mother and all your kindred.

Dohá 57.

Her own father is Janak, jewel of kings; her father-in-law is the Phœbus of the solar race; her lord, the perfection of beauty and virtue, is as it were the moon of the lily-like progeny of the sun-god;

Chaupái.

I again have found in her a dear daughter, amiable, beautiful and accomplished. She is like the apple of my eye and my affection has so grown that it is only in Jánakí that I have my being.[1] I have tended her as carefully as the tree of paradise and watered her growth with streams of affection. When she should have blossomed and borne fruit, God has turned against me, and there is no knowing what will be the end. Or ever she left her bed or seat, I cradled her in my lap, and never has Síta set her foot on the hard ground. I cherished her as the very source of my life, and never bade her so much as even to trim the wick of a lamp. And this is the Síta who would follow you to the woods; what are your orders, O Raghunáth? Can the partridge, that drinks in with delight the rays of the moon, endure to fix its gaze on the orb of the sun?

Dohá 58.

Elephants, lions, goblins, and many fierce animals roam the wood: ah, my son, is the charming tree of life fit to set in such a deadly pasture?

Chaupái.

God has created for the forest Kol and Kirát women, who care not for bodily delights. Of nature as hard as the stone insect, the woods are no trial to them. A hermit's wife again is fit for the woods, who for the sake of penance has renounced all pleasures. But how, my son, can Síta live in the woods, who would be frightened by even the picture of a monkey? Can the cygnet that has sported in the lovely lotus-beds of the Ganges find fit abode in a muddy puddle? First ponder this, and then, as you order, I will instruct Jánaki. If she remain at home (and call me mother) she will be the support of my life." Raghubír on hearing his mother's speech, which was drenched as it were with the ambrosia of grace and affection,

Dohá 59.

replied in tender and discreet terms for his mother's consolation, and began to set clearly before Jánaki all the pleasures and troubles of forest life,

1 In the original is a play upon words which it is impossible to preserve in a translation; *ján Prán*, the ordinary expression for the 'breath of life,' being presented to the eye by the conjunction of *prán* with the first syllable of Síta's name Jánaki.

Chaupái.

speaking diffidently as in the presence of his mother, and considering well within himself the requirements of the time: "Hearken, lady, to my instructions; nor from any different fancies in your mind. If you desire your own good and mine, agree to what I say and remain at home. My order is this: the service of a mother-in-law is in every way, madam, a blessing to a family. There is no other duty so paramount as reverential submission to a husband's parents. Whenever my mother recalls me to mind and is distracted by affectionate solicitude, do you, my love, console her with old-world tales and tender speeches. I speak from my heart and confirm it with a hundred Oaths: it is for my mother's sake, beloved, I leave you here.

Dohá 60.

The reward of virtue can be obtained without trouble by submission to Scripture and one's spiritual director; through their obstinacy Gálava[1] and king Nahusha[2] were subjected to all sorts of trouble.

Chaupái.

I shall soon fulfil my father's words and come back again; hearken, fair and sensible dame. The days will quickly pass away; listen, love, to my advice. If, my spouse, you persist in your affectionate obstinacy, you will rue it in the end. The forest is exceedingly toilsome and terrible, with awful heat and cold and rain and wind; the path is beset with prickly grass and stones, and you will

1 Gálava was a pupil of Visvamitra's. When he had completed his studies, he asked his tutor what fee he ought to pay. He was told there was no fee. However, he still persisted in asking, till at last Visvamitra was annoyed and, to get rid of him, said he would be satisfied with nothing less than a thousand black-eared horses. After a long search and many inquiries, Gálava discovered three childless rájas who had each 200 horses of the kind that he required, and they agreed to let him have them, but only on this condition, that he got each of them a son. Gálava then went to Yayáti, whose daughter had the miraculous gift of bearing a son for any one she wished, and yet herself remaining a virgin. By her means each of the three kings became a father. The 600 horses were made over to Gálava, and he presented them to Visvamitra, who as an equivalent for the other 400 horses, wanting to make up the thousand, had himself two sons by the same mysterious birde.

2 For the legend of king Nahusha.

have to walk without protection for your feet: and your lotus feet are so soft and pretty, while the road is most difficult: and there are huge mountains, chasms and precipices, streams, rivers and torrents, deep and impassable, terrible to behold; while bears and tigers, wolves, lions and elephants make such a roaring that the boldest is dismayed.

Dohá 61.

[1] The ground will be your couch, the bark of trees your raiment, and your food bulbs, wild fruits and roots; nor, think that even they will be always forthcoming every day, but only when they are in season.

Chaupái.

There are man-eating demons who assume all sorts of deceptive forms; the rainfall on the hills is excessive, and in short the hardships of the forest are past all telling. There are terrible serpents and fierce wild birds and gangs of goblins that steal both man and woman. The bravest shudders at the thought of the dense forest; while you, my fawneyed wife, are timid by nature. Ah! delicate dame, you are not fit for the woods; people will revile me on hearing of such a thing. Can the swan that has been nurtured in the ambrosial flood of the Mánas lake exist in the salt sea? Can the *koil*, that roves with delight through the luxuriant mango groves, take pleasure in a jungle of *kar*í*l*, bushes? Ponder this, my fair bride, and stay at home; the hardships of the forest are too great.

Dohá 62.

Whoever with a view to her own good does not at once accept the advice given by a friend, or a *guru*, or her husband shall assuredly have a surfeit of repentance and gain no good."

1 Yet take good hede, for ever I drede that ye coude not sustain
The thorney wayes, the deep valleys, the snow, the frost, the rain,
The cold, the hete, for dry or wete, we must lodge on the plain,
And us above, none other roof, but a brake, bush or twayne,
For ye must there in your hande bere a bowe ready to drawe,
And as a thief, thus must ye lyve, ever in drede and awe.

The Nut-browne maid.

Chaup i.

On hearing the tender and winning words of her husband, Síta's lotus eyes filled with tears, and his soothing advice caused her as burning pain as the autumn moon causes the *chakwi*. In her distress no answer came to her lips: 'So great is his love that he would leave me behind.' Perforce restraining her tears and summing up courage, Earth's daughter embraced her mother's feet, and with folded hands thus spake: "Pardon me, lady, my great presumption: my dear lord has thought me what is all for my own good; but I look to my feelings, and conclude that no sorrow in the world is so great as separation from one's beloved.

Dohá 63.

O my dear lord, most compassionate, beautiful, bounteous and wise, the moon of the lilies of the Raghu race, heaven without you would be very hell.

Chaupái.

Dear are father and mother, sisters and brothers; dear are my companions and my many friends; but father-in-law and mother-in-law, spiritual director, generous associates, and even sons, however, beautiful, amiable and affectionate, nay, my lord, all love and every tie of kindred, to a woman without her husband, are a greater distress than the sun's most burning heat. Life, wealth, house, land, city and empire are but accumulated misery to a woman bereft of her lord. Ease is disease, her jewels a burden, and the world like the torments of hell. Without you, O lord of my soul, there is nothing in the whole world that could give me any comfort. As the body without a soul, as a river without water, so, my lord, is a woman without her husband. With you, my lord, are all delights, as long as I can behold your face that vies in brightness with the autumn moon.

Dohá 64.

The birds and deer will be my attendants, the forest my city, and strips of bark my glistening robes; with my lord a hut of grass will be as the palace of the gods, and all will be well.

Chaupái.

The sylvan nymphs and gods will of their grace protect me like my own lord's parents ; my simple litter of grass and twigs will with my lord become a sumptuous marriage-couch ; bulbs, roots and fruits will form an ambrosial repast, and the mountains resemble the stately halls of Avadh. Every moment I gaze on my lord's lotus feet, I shall be as glad as the *chakwi* at the dawn. You have recounted, my lord, the numerous hardships of the forest, its terrors, annoyances and many discomforts ; but, O fountain of mercy, all these united will not be comparable to the pain of bereavement. Consider this, O jewel of wisdom, and take me with you, abandon me not. Why make long supplication ? my lord is full of compassion and knoweth the heart.

Dohá 65.

Do you think, if you keep me at Avadh, that I can survive till the end of your exile ? O most beautiful, help of the helpless, fountain of grace and of love,

Chaupái.

as I go along the road I shall never weary, every moment beholding your lotus feet. In every way I shall minister to my beloved, and relieve him of all the toil of the march. Seated in the shade of some tree, I shall lave your feet and rapturously fan you, and gazing on your body stained with sweat and blackened by the sun, what thought, my dearest lord, shall I have for my own hard times ? Spreading grass and leaves on the level ground, your slave will all night shampoo your feet, and ever gazing on your gracious form, nor heat nor wind will ever vex me. Who will look at me when I am with my lord, except as a hare or jackal furtively regards a lioness ? Am I to be dainty and delicate, while my lord roams the woods ? Is penance to be your portion and enjoyment mine ?

Dohá 66.

My heart will burst at the mere sound of so cruel a sentence, and never will my miserable existence survive the anguish and torture of bereavement."

Chaupái.

So saying, Síta was overwhelmed with distress, nor could endure the word 'separation.' On seeing her condition, Ráma made sure, 'If I insist upon leaving her, I leave her dead.' Then said the compassionate lord of the Solar race: "Have done with lamentation and come with me to the woods. There is no time now for weeping; at once make your preparations for the journey." Having consoled his beloved with these tender words, he embraced his mother's feet and received her blessing: "Return quickly and relieve your subjects' distress, nor forget me your hard-hearted mother.[1] Who knows but God may change my lot, and my eyes may see you both again. Ah! my son, when will arrive the happy day and moment that I shall live to see your moon-like face once more?

Dohá 67.

When again shall I call you 'my child,' 'my darling' noblest and best of Raghu's line,' 'my own son,' and fondly bid you come to my arms that I may gaze upon your features?"

Chaupái.

Seeing that his mother was so agitated by affection that she could not speak and was utterly overwhelmed with distress, Ráma did everything to console her, and the pathos of the scene was beyond description. Then Jánaki embraced her mother's feet: "Hearken, mother, I am of all women most miserable. At the time when I should have been doing you service, fate has banished me to the woods and has denied me my desire. Cease to sorrow, but cease not to love me; Fate is cruel, I am blameless." On hearing Síta's words her mother was so afflicted that her state was past all telling. Again and again she took her to her breast and summoning up courage thus blest and admonished her: "May your prosperity be as enduring as the streams of Gangá and Jamuná!"

Dohá 68.

When her mother had repeatedly blessed and admonished

1 That is to say, I must be hard-hearted, for, if not, I should die at once.

Sita, she took her leave, after again and again affectionately bowing her head at her lotus feet.

Chaupái.

When Lakshman heard the news, he started up in dismay with a doleful face, his body all of a tremble and his eyes full of tears, and ran and clasped his feet in an agony of affection. He could not speak, but stood and stared aghast, like some poor fish drawn out of the water, thinking within himself: "Good God, what will happen? All my happiness and past good deeds are gone for ever. What will Raghunath tell me to do? Will he keep me here, or take me with him?" When Ráma saw his brother with folded hands renouncing life and home and all, he address him thus—the all-righteous Ráma, fountain of grace, love, and perfect bliss: "Brother, do not afflict yourself with love, but reflect that all will be well in the end.

Dohá 69.

They who submit without reserve to the commands of their father and mother, their spiritual director or their lord, or born into the world to some purpose: otherwise their birth is in vain.

Chaupái.

Consider this, brother, and hearken to my advice, wait upon the feet of your father and mother. Neither Bharat is at home, nor Ripu-súdan: the king is old and sorrowing for me. If I go to the woods and take you with me, Avadh be completely masterless, and an intolerable weight of affliction will fall upon priest and parents, subjects, family and all. Stay then to comfort them; if not, brother, it will be a great sin. The king, whose faithful subjects endure distress, is of a truth a prince of hell. This is sound doctrine, brother; ponder it and stay." Lakshman was grievously distrest on hearing this, and his body became as dead and shrivelled as a lotus that has been touched by the frost.

Dohá 70.

Overmastered by love, he could not answer, but clung

in anguish to his feet: " O my lord, I am your slave and you my master: leave me, then what can I do?

Chaupái.

You have given me, good sir, excellent advice; but in my confusion I find it impracticable. Valiant leaders of men and champions of the faith can master such abstruse doctrine, but I am a mere child, nurtured by your affection; can a cygnet uplift Mount Mandar or Meru? I know no *guru*, nor father, nor mother? believe me, my lord, I speak from my heart: all the love in the world, all claims of kin, all affection, sympathy, wisdom and skill are for me centred in you, my lord, the protector of the humble, the reader of the heart. Expound questions of theology to one who aims at fame and glory and high estate; I am in heart, word and deed devoted only to your feet; and am I, gracious lord, to be discarded?"

Dohá 71.

The compassionate lord, on hearing the tender and modest words of his good brother, took him to his bosom, and seeing him so affectionately dejected thus consoled him:

Chaupái.

" Go, brother, and take leave of your mother, and then come and set out for the woods." On hearing Raghubar thus speak, he was overjoyed; his triumph was great, his sorrow all gone. He approached his mother as glad of heart as a blind man who has recovered his sight, and while he bowed his head at her feet, his heart was away with Raghunandan and Jánaki Seeing his agitation his mother inquired the cause, and Lakshman told her the whole history. On hearing his cruel speech she trembled like a fawn that sees the forest on fire all around it. Lakshman reflected: " Everything goes wrong to-day: her very love will work me harm." Timidly and hesitatingly he asked her permission to go, thinking " Good God, will she let me go or not?"

Dohá 72.

After reflecting on the beauty and amiable disposition

of Ráma and Síta and considering the king's affection, Sumitra beat her head and exclaimed: "That wicked woman is at the bottom of this bad business."

Chaupái.

But perceiving the time to be untoward, she took patience and in her kindness of heart answered gently: "Your mother, child, is Vaidehi, and Ráma is your most loving father; where Ráma dwells, there is Avadh; and wherever is the light of the sun, there is day. If Ráma and Síta go to the woods, you have no business at Avadh. A *guru*, a father and mother, brethren, the gods and our master are all to be tended as our own life; but Ráma is dearer than life, is the soul of our soul, and the disinterested friend of all; our dearest and most honoured friends are to be accounted those of Ráma's household. Thinking thus to yourself, go with them to the woods, and receive, my son, the fruition of your existence.

Dohá 73.

You have become the receptacle of the highest good fortune, and I too—ah, woe is me!—if from an unfeigned heart you have made Ráma's feet your home.

Chaupái.

A mother indeed is she who has a son devoted to Raghubar; if not, it is better to be barren, she has given birth in vain; a son who is Ráma's enemy is a curse. It is your good fortune that Ráma goes to the woods; and other reason is there none; this, my son, is the highest reward for all good deeds, to have a sincere affection for the feet of Ráma and Síta. Never give way even in thought to lust, or passion, or envy, or pride, or delusion; but put aside all changeableness and serve them in heart, word and deed. For you the poorest is a place of joy, since Ráma and Síta your father and mother, will be there with you. Take heed, my son, that Ráma be put to no trouble; this is my admonition.

Chhand 3.

This is my admonition, my son; see that Ráma and Síta

live at ease and in the woods forget to remember their father and mother, their friends and relations and all the pleasures of the city." Having given her son such instruction and commands (says Tulsi) she again invoked upon him her blessing: "May your love for Síta and Raghubír be constant and unsullied and ever renewed!"

Sorathá 3.

Having bowed his head at his mother's feet, he left in haste with trepidation of heart, as flies a hapless deer that has burst a perilous snare.

Chaupái.

He went to Jánaki's lord, and his soul rejoiced to recover his dear society. After reverencing Ráma and Síta's gracious feet, he proceeded with them to the king's palace. The citizens say to one another: "How goodly a plan God made and now has marred!" With wasted frame, sad soul and doleful face, they were in as great distress as bees robbed of their honey; wringing their hands, beating their heads and lamenting, like wretched birds that have been clipt of their wings. There was a great crowd in the royal hall: grief immeasurable, beyond all telling. The minister raised the king and seated him, as Ráma advanced with loving address. When he saw Síta and his two sons, the king's agitation was profound.

Dohá 74.

Again and again turning his troubled gaze on Síta and his two fair sons, he clasped them to his bosom time after time in an agony of love.

Chaupái.

In his agitation he could not speak; grief overmastered him and wild anguish of heart. After most affectionately bowing his head at his feet, Raghunáth arose and begged permission to depart: "Father, give me your blessing and commands; why so dismayed at this time of rejoicing? From excessive attachment, sire, to any beloved object, honour is lost and disgrace incurred." At this the love-sick king arose and taking Raghupati by the arm made him sit down: "Hearken, my son; the sages say that Ráma is the lord of all creation, animate or inanimate; that God, after weighing good and bad actions and mentally considering them, apportions their reward, and the doer reaps the fruit of his own doings: this is the doctrine of the Scriptures and the verdict of mankind.

Dohá 75

But for one to sin and another to reap its reward—the ways of God are most mysterious; who is there in the world who can comprehend them?

Chaupái.

The king in his anxiety to detain Ráma tried every honest expedient, but when he saw that he was bent on going—righteous, brave and wise as he was—he took and pressed Síta to his bosom and gave her much most affectionate advice, telling her of all the intolerable hardships of the forest, and reminding her of the happiness she might enjoy with her parents-in-law or at her father's house. But Síta's heart was set on Ráma's feet, and neither home seemed to her attractive nor the woods repulsive. Every one else too warned her with stories of all the many miseries of the desert. The minister's wife and the *guru's*—prudent dames—affectionately urged her in gentle tones: "He has not sent you into exile. You should do as you are told by your parents and your *guru.*"

Dohá 76.

This advice, friendly and kind and tender and judicious as it was, was not pleasing to Síta to hear; in the same way as the *chakwi* is distrest by the rays of the autumn moon.

Chaupái.

She was, however, too modest to reply; but Kaikeyi on hearing them started up in excitement and, bringing a box of anchorite's dresses and ornaments, placed it before her and said in whispered tones: Raghubír, you are dearer than life to the king; he cannot rid himself of his too great kindness and love, and will never tell you to go, though he forfeit his virtue, his honour and his hope of heaven. Think of this and act as seems to you good." Ráma was glad to hear his mother's suggestion, but her words pierced the king like arrows: 'Will my miserable life never leave me?' In his distress he fainted outright, and no one knew what to do. But Ráma quickly assumed the hermit's dress and bowing his head to his father and mother went forth.

Dohá 77.

Having completed his full equipment for the woods, the lord set forth with his wife and brother, after reverencing the feet of the Bráhmans and his *guru*, and leaving them all in bewilderment.

Chaupái.

He came out and stood at Vasistha's gate; the beholders were consumed as with fire by the anguish of parting. With kindly words Raghubír consoled them all and, summoning the Bráhmans, begged his *guru* to give them a year's maintenance. Many gifts he bestowed with respectful courtesy, satisfying the mendicants with largesse and civilities, and his personal friends with demonstrations of affection. Next he called up his men-servants and maid-servants and made them over to his *guru*, saying with clasped hands: "O sir, be to them as their own father and mother, and cherish them all." Again and again did Ráma with clasped hands and in gentle tones address each one of them: "He is my best friend in whom the king finds comfort.

Dohá 78.

So act, all thoughtful and considerate citizens, that my mother be not distrest by my absence."

Chaupái.

When Ráma had thus exhorted them all, he cheerfully bowed his head at his *guru's* lotus feet, and invoking Ganes, Gauri, and Mahádev, and receiving their blessing, sallied forth. As he went, there was great lamentation and a mournful wailing throughout the city, terrible to hear.

In Lanka omens of ill, in Avadh exceeding distress: while mingled joy and sorrow possessed the hosts of heaven. When his swoon had passed, the king awoke and sent for Sumanta and thus began: "Ráma has gone to the woods, and yet my life flits not; what good does it hope to get by still remaining in my body?" What more grievous tortures can there be, to force it from my frame? Again taking patience, he added: "friend, take you the chariot and go;

Dohá 79.

the two boys are young and delicate, and Janak's daughter a delicate girl; take them up into the chariot and show them the forest, and come back in a day or two.

Chaupái.

Both brothers are brave, and Raghurái is the very ocean of truth and staunch to his word; if they will not turn, do you with clasped hands humbly entrèat him: 'Send back, my lord, the daughter of Mithila's king.' When Síta is alarmed by the sight of the forest, take the opportunity of telling her my instructions, saying: 'This is the message sent by your father-in-law and mother-in-law; come back, daughter; there are many perils in the desert. You can stay at your pleasure now with your own father, now with your husband's parents.' In this manner try every way you can; if she comes back, it will be the succour of my life; if not, it will end in my death; what can I do? God is against me." So saying, the king fainted and fell to the ground, crying: "O that you could bring them back to me, Ráma, Lakshman and Síta!"

Dohá 80.

Having received the king's commands, he bowed his head and in haste made ready the chariot, and went to the place outside the city where were Síta and the two brothers.

Chaupái.

There Sumanta declared to them the king's message and respectfully made Ráma ascend the chariot. When Síta and the two brothers had mounted and drove away, they mentally bowed the head to Avadh. As the bereaved city saw Ráma depart, all the people began confusedly to follow him. The gracious lord said everything to console them, and they turned homewards, but again came back overmastered by their affection. Avadh appeared to them as gloomy and oppressive as the dark night of death ; the citizens looked with trembling at one another like so many wild beasts : their home seemed like the grave, their retainers like ghosts, and their sons, friends and neigbbours as the angels of death. The trees and creepers in the gardens all withered ; the streams and ponds were fearful to behold.

Dohá 81.

All the horses, elephants and tame deer, the town-cattle, the cuckoos and the peacocks, the *koils*, swans, parrots, *mainas*, herons, flamingoes and partridges,

Chaupái.

All stood aghast at Ráma's departure, dumb and motionless as statues. The whole city resembled some dense forest in which the agitated people were as the birds and deer, while Kaikeyi had been fashioned by God as some wild woman of the woods, who had set all in a fierce blaze. Unable to endure the burning pain of Ráma's departure, the people all flocked after him in their bewilderment, each one thinking to himself : "There is no happiness apart from Ráma, Lakshman and Síta. Everything can be had where Ráma is, and Avadh without Raghubír is of no account." With this settled idea they bore him company, abandoning halls of delight that the gods might envy. For what influence can the pleasures of sense have upon men who are devoted to Ráma's lotus feet ?

Dohá 82.

Young and old, all left their homes and followed him ; and on the bank of the Tamasá Ráma made his first day's halt.

Chaupái.

When Raghupati saw his people overpowered with love, his kind heart was greatly troubled. The merciful lord Raghunàth, being quickly touched by the grief of others, spoke to them many words of tenderness and affection and did his best to comfort them, admonishing them much of their religious duty. But in their fondness they could not tear themselves away. As there was no means of overcoming their innate affection, Raghurái was reduced to perplexity. Worn out with grief and toil the people fell asleep —a divine delusion helping to beguile them —and when two watches of the night were spent Rama affectionately addressed his Minister: "Father drive the chariot so as to efface the tracks of the wheels; there is no other way of settling the business."

Dohá 83.

Ráma, Lakshman and Síta then mounted the car, after bowing the head to Sambhu's feet, and the minister drove it speedily hither and thither, confusing the tracks.

Chaupái.

At day break the people all woke, and there was a great cry, that Raghubír had gone. They could no how distinguish the tracks of the chariot, though they ran in all directions, crying Ráma, Ráma, like as when a ship is sinking at sea all the merchants are in terror. One suggested to another: Ráma left us on seeing our distress.' They revile themselves and envy the fish[1] crying: "A curse on our life away from Raghubír: as god has robbed us of our Beloved, why has he not granted us our prayer to die?" With many such lamentations they returned to Avadh full of heaviness: the anguish of parting was beyond description, and it was only the hope of his return kept them alive.

Dohá 84.

Men and women alike began to fast and make vows to secure his return, like the poor *chakwá* and the lotus when bereft of the sun.

1 That die at once when withdrawn from their natural element.

Chaupái.

Síta with the Minister and the two brothers arrived on their way at the city of Sringavera. On beholding the river of the gods, Ráma alighted and with much joy made it his obeisance. The Minister, Lakshman and Síta saluted it also, and Ráma was as glad as any of them; for the Ganges is the source of all bliss and beatitude, the author of all happiness, the destroyer of every sorrow. Many were the stories and legends that Ráma repeated as he gazed upon its flood, instructing the Minister, his younger brother, and his bride in the majesty and grandeur of the heavenly stream. They bathed and all the fatigue of the march was removed; they drank of the holy water and their soul was gladdened. It is only in vulgar phrase that fatigue is ascribed to him by whose remembrance all the burdens of the world are lightened.

Dohá 85

Ráma, the champion of the Solar race, is the holy God of supreme wisdom and bliss, the bridge over the ocean of existence,[1] though he acts like an ordinary man.

Chaupái.

When Guha, the Nishád, heard the news, he was glad and called together his friends and relations, and taking a great quantity of fruits and vegetables as a present, went out to meet him with infinite joy of heart. With a profound obeisance he put down his offering before him and gazed upon the lord with the utmost devotion. Raghurái with his natural kindliness asked him of his health and seated him by his side. "The sight of your lotus feet, sire, is health indeed; I am most highly favoured, as all

---

1 *Sansriti-ságara-setu* : The 'transmigrations'-*sansriti*—through which the soul has to pass would be endless, a limitless ocean (*ságara*) from which none could escape, were it not that Ráma has given himself to be the bridge, *setu*, over the abyss. *Anukarat* here means simply 'like.' It is almost impossible to translate this and similar phrases at once literally, concisely and intelligibly : for birth and life, which we are taught to regard as blessings, are to the Hindu theologian a curse. Compare Milton's—

. . . . "This earthly load
Of death called life, which us from life doth sever."

will admit. My land, my house, my fortune are yours, my lord; I and mine are your poor vassals Do me the favour of entering my abode; treat me as one of your servants and I shall be the envy of all men." "All that you say, my good friend, is very true; but my father has given me other commands.

Dohá 86.

For fourteen years I must dwell in the woods and adopt the rules, the dress, and the diet of a hermit; to stay in a village is forbidden." On hearing this, Guha was much grieved.

Chaupái.

Seeing Ráma, Lakshman and Síta to be so beautiful, the citizens affectionately protested: "What kind of parents can they be, friend, who have banished such children to the woods?" Said one: "The king has done well to give our eyes such a treat." Then the Nishád chief on reflection decided upon a beautiful sinsapa[1] tree, and took Raghunáth and showed him the place, who declared it to be most excellent. The citizens after paying him their respects went home, and Ráma proceeded to the performance of his evening devotions. Guha made and spread for him a charming bed of grass and soft leaves, and brought him leaf-made bowls filled with all such fruits and vegetables as he knew to be sweet and wholesome and good.

Dohá 87.

After he had partaken of the fruits and herbs with the Minister and Síta and his brother, the jewel of Raghu's line lay down to sleep, while Lakshman shampooed his feet.

Chaupái.

When he knew his lord to be asleep, he arose and softly bade Sumanta take rest, while he himself fitted an arrow to his bow and took up the position of a marksman at a little distance, there to watch. The affectionate Guha, having summoned trusty sentinels and stationed them

1 The *sinsapa* is either the asoka, or the shisham tree.

round about, went himself and sat down by Lakshman, with his quiver at his back and an arrow fitted to his bow. When the Nishád saw Ráma asleep, his soul was troubled with excess of love, his body thrilled with emotion, his eyes flowed with tears, and he thus in tender accents addressed Lakshman: "The king's palace is altogether beautiful, nor can the courts of heaven be compared to it; its charming pavilions, inlaid with precious stones, seem to have been adorned by Love's own hands.

Dohá 88.

Rich and luxurious are its beds, sweet with odorous flowers and perfumes, with jewelled lamps and appliances of every description,

Chaupái.

with all kinds of coverlets and pillows, and matresses as soft and white as the froth of milk, where Síta and Ráma reposed at night and put to shame with their beauty both Rati and Kámadev, who now sleep on a pallet, weary and naked, pitiful to behold. The Ráma whom his father and mother, his own family and all the people of the city, his companions and associates, his men-servants and maid-servants, all cherished as tenderly as their own life, is now sleeping on the bare ground. The Síta, whose father is Janak of world-wide fame; whose father-in-law is Dasarath, the friend of the King of heaven; whose spouse is Rámchandra; is now sleeping on the ground; is not God against us all? Are Síta and Ráma fit dwellers of the desert? Well do men say, 'Fate is supreme.'

Dohá 89.

The foolish daughter of Kekayá has wrought sad mischief by bringing this trouble on Ráma and Jánaki on their day of rejoicing.

Chaupái.

She has become the axe at the root of the tree of the Solar race, and through her wickedness has plunged the whole world in woe." Seeing Ráma and Síta asleep upon the ground, the Nisháđ became sad exceedingly; but Lakshman addressed him in sweet and gentle tones that were full of the essence of wisdom, sobriety and faith: "No man is the cause of another's joy or sorrow; all is the fruit of one's own actions, brother. Union and separation, pleasure, good and evil, friendship, enmity and neutrality are snares of delusion. Birth, death, all the entanglements of the world prosperity and adversity, fortune and destiny, earth, home, wealth, city and family, heaven, hell and all human affairs; all that you can see, or hear, or imagine in your mind, all is delusive and unreal.

Dohá 90.

In a dream a beggar becomes a king, and the lord of heaven a pauper; but on waking the one is no gainer, nor the other a loser; this is the way in which you should regard the world.

Chaupái.

Reasoning thus, be not angry with any one, nor vainly attribute blame to any. All are sleepers in a night of delusion and see many kinds of dreams; in this world of darkness they only are awake who detach themselves from the material, and are absorbed in contemplation of the Supreme; nor can any soul be regarded as aroused from slumber till it has renounced every sensual enjoyment. Then ensues spiritual enlightenment and escape from the errors of delusion, and finally devotion to Ráma. This, friend, is man's highest good, to be devoted to Ráma in thought, word and deed. Ráma is God, the totality of good, imperishable, invisible, uncreated, incomparable, void of all change, indivisible, whom the Veda declares that it cannot define.

Dohá 91

In his mercy he has taken the form of a man and performs human actions, out of the love he bears to his faithful people and to Earth and Bráhmans and cows and gods. On hearing them, the snares of the world broken asunder.

Chaupái.

Having thus reflected, friend, give no place to deceits, but fix your affections on Síta and Ráma's feet." While he was yet speaking of Ráma's virtues, the day dawned and the joy of the world awoke. After performing every purificatory rite he bathed, the all-pure and wise, and called for some milk of the *bar* tree, and bound up the hair of his head into a knot, as did also his brother. On seeing this, Sumanta's eyes filled with tears. Sore pained at heart, with doleful face and clasped hands he made this humble speech : " The king of Kosala, my lord, thus enjoined me : 'Take the chariot and go with Ráma ; let them see the forest and bathe in the Ganges, and then speedily bring them home again, both the brothers, Lakshman and Ráma and Síta too, bring them back, settling all their doubts and scruples.'

Dohá 92.

Thus spoke the king, sire ; but woe is me ! I can do only as you tell me." He fell in supplication at his feet weeping helplessly as a child.

Chaupái.

" Have pity, my son, and so act that Avadh be not left a widow." Ráma raised the Minister and thus exhorted him : " Father, you know the path of virtue. Sivi, Dadhíchi and king Harischandra, for the sake of their religion, endured countless afflictions. Rantideva[1] and wise king Bali kept their faith through many trials. There is no virtue equal to truth, as the Vedas, Shástras, and Puránas declare. I have reached this virtue by an easy road : if I abandon it, my disgrace will be published in earth, heaven and hell : and disgrace to a man of honour is pain as grievous as a million deaths. But why say all this to you, father ? I only incur sin by answering you.

Dohá 93.

Fall humbly at my father's feet and with clasped hands beg of him not to distress himself in any way on my account.

1 Rantideva, the son of Sanskriti, was a king famous for his great liberality. He offered so many cattle in sacrifice that their blood formed a river, said to be the Chambal.

Chaupái.

You, again, are equally dear to me as my father, and I implore you, sire, to do everything that will prevent the king from grieving about me." On hearing this conversation between Raghunáth and the Minister, the Nishád and his people were sad and Lakshman spoke a little angrily. But the lord stopt him, knowing it to be altogether out of place, and nervously adjured Sumanta, by the love he bore him, not to repeat his words. Sumanta then proceeded with the king's message : Síta is not able to bear the hardships of the desert ; you should try and persuade her to return to Avadh, otherwise I shall have no prop left, and must die as inevitably as a fish out of water.

Dohá 94.

She has a happy home both with her own mother and with her husband's parents, and she can live when she pleases at either, till these troubles are overpast.

Chaupái.

The piteousness of the king's entreaties and the earnestness of his affection are more than I can express. On hearing his father's message, the All-merciful tried in every way to persuade Síta : " Only return ; and the affliction of your parents, your *guru*, and all your friends and relations will be at an end." Replied Vaidehi to her husband's words : Hearken most dear and loving lord, full of compassion and infinite wisdom ; can a shadow exist apart from its substance ? Where is the sunlight without the sun, or the radiance of the moon when the moon is not ? " Having uttered this affectionate prayer to her husband, she turned to the Minister with these winning words : " You are as much my benefactor as my own father or my father-in-law, and if I answer you, it is the height of impropriety.

Dohá 95.

Yet, sire, take it not ill of me if in my grief I withstand you : away from the lotus feet of my lord's son all my kindred are nought.

Chaupái.

I have seen my father's luxury and magnificence and his foot-stool thronged with the jewelled crowns of kings, yet though his palace be such a blissful abode, I have no pleasure there without my spouse. My Imperial father-in-law, the sovereign of Kosala, is of such glorious renown throughout the fourteen spheres that the king of heaven would advance to meet him and cede him half his throne; yet though he be so great and Avadh his home, and though the whole of his family be dear to me and my mother-in-law as my own mother, I could not find pleasure in a single thing for a moment, away from the lotus flowers of Ráma's feet. Though the forest road be rough, and the country mountainous, full of elephants and tigers, boundless, lakes and streams, wild Kols and Kiráts, and beasts, and birds; all is delightful, if my dear lord be with me.

Dohá 96.

Fall at the feet of my father-in-law and my mother-in-law and tell them humbly from me not to grieve on my account, for I am perfectly happy in the woods.

Chaupái.

With the sovereign of my soul and my dear brother, stoutest of champions, bearing bow and quiver, the toilsome wanderings of the march will not trouble me at all; be not then the least anxious about me." On hearing Síta's chilling speech, Sumanta became as distressed as a serpent at the loss of its headjewel. With eyes that saw not and ears that heard not, and unable to utter a word, he was completely confounded. Ráma said everything to console him, but his heart refused to be comforted. Earnestly he begged that he too might accompany him; but Raghunandan returned an appropriate answer to all he urged. "Ráma's commands cannot be withstood; Fate is against me, I can do nothing." Bowing his head at the feet of Ráma, Lakshman and Síta, he turned away like a merchant who has lost his all.

Dohá 97.

The very horses of his chariot, as he drove, continued whinnying and looking back upon Ráma ; and the Nishád at the sight gave way to his grief and beat his head and moaned :

Chaupái.

"When even brute beasts are so distrest at his loss, how can his subjects and his father and mother exist without him ?" Having thus perforce dismissed Sumanta, Ráma went on his way and came to the bank of the Ganges. When he called for the boat, the ferryman would not bring it, saying : "I know your magic power : every one says that the dust of your lotus feet is a charm for making man. A rock on which it fell became a beautiful woman, and wood is not so hard as stone. Should my boat in like manner be turned into a saint's wife, the ferry will be closed and the boat lost, which is the support of my whole family. I have no other means of living. If, my lord, you are bent on crossing, you must allow me first to wash your feet.

Chhand 4.

After bathing your lotus feet I will take you on board but I will not accept any toll. I tell you the truth, O Ráma, swearing by yourself and Dasarath—Lakshman may shoot me with his arrows, but I will not take you across, gracious lord, until I have bathed your feet."

Sorathá.

On hearing the ferryman's rude but loving speech, the All-merciful smiled[1] and looked at Jánaki and Lakshman ;

Chaupái.

then gaily cried : "Do anything to save your boat, bring water at once and bathe my feet ; time has been lost ; take me across." The gracious lord thus made request of a boatman ; even he by one thought on whose name mankind is transported across the boundless ocean of existence, and for

1 As much as to say : We thought the Nishád king a pattern of piety, but even he is outdone by this rude ferryman.

whose three strides the whole universe did not suffice.[1] The Ganges rejoiced on beholding his toe-nails,[2] and the sound of his words was relieved of all anxiety. On receiving Ráma's commands, the ferryman brought a basin full of water and in an ecstacy of joy and love proceeded to bathe his lotus feet. All the gods rained down flowers and uttered their congratulations : " Never was any one so meritorious !"

Dohá 98.

After laving his feet, and drinking of the water, both himself and his family, and thus redeeming the souls of his fathers, he joyfully conveyed his lord across to the other side.

Chaupái.

They landed and stood on the sands of the Ganges, Síta, Ráma Lakshman and Guha. The ferryman landed too and made his obeisance. The lord was ashamed that he had nothing to give him. Síta knew what was passing in the mind of her beloved and cheerfully drew a jewelled ring from off herfinger. Said the All-merciful : " Take your toll." The ferryman in distress clasped his feet : " What have I not already received, my lord ? sin, sorrow, poverty and all their attendant ills have been removed I have laboured for a length of years, but today God has given me my wages in full. Now, gracious lord, I ask for nothing but your favour ; at the time of your return, whatever you bestow upon me I will thankfully accept."

Dohá 99.

Lakshman and the lord both pressed him much, but the ferryman would take nothing; the All-merciful then dismissed him with the gift of unclouded faith, best of all boons.

Chaupái.

Then the lord of Raghu's line bathed and bowed his head in adoration to Mahádeva :[3] while Síta with clasped

---

1 Ráma is here indentified with Vishnu who in the form of a dwarf outwitted king Bali : see note to page 19, Volume II.

2 From beneath which it had issued at its birth.

3 The word in the text is *Párathi*, or in some manuscripts *Párthiva*, a derivative of *prithi*, ' the earth,' meaning ' a king,' and here – it would seem—denoting Máhadeva.

hands thus addressed the sacred stream: "O mother, accomplish my desire that I may return in safety with my husband and his brother and again adore you." On hearing Síta's humble and affectionate speech, a favourable response came from the holy flood: "Hearken, Vaidehi best beloved of Raghubír; who is there in the world who knows not your glory? they who behold you become as the sovereigns of the spheres, and all the powers of magic meekly do you service. In the petition that you have deigned to address to me, you have graciously paid me all too high an honour; yet, lady, unworthy as I am, I bestow upon you my blessing, in order to prove my utterances true.

Dohá 100.

You shall return in safety to Kosala with your beloved and his brother; your every wish shall be accomplished, and your renown shall be spread throughout the world."

Chaupái.

On hearing Gangá's gracious speech, Síta was delighted to find it so propitious. Then said the lord to Guha: "Return home." At this his face grew wan and his bosom burned, and with clasped hands and in suppliant tones he cried: "Noblest of the sons of Raghu, hearken to my prayer. Let me remain with my lord to show the road and do him service for a day or two, and make a shapely hut of twigs for him in the wood where he goes to stay. After that I swear by Raghubír to do as he shall command me." Seeing his unfeigned affection, he took him with him, to Guha's delight, who there upon called all his kinsmen and dismissed them with kind assurances.

Dohá 101.

Then directing his intention to Ganes and Siva, and bowing his head to the Ganges, the lord with his companion and his brother and Síta took his way to the woods.

Chaupái.

That day he halted under a tree, and Lakshman and his attendant supplied all his necessities. At dawn, having performed his morning ablutions he proceeded to visit the king of Sanctuaries. A king with Truth for his minister, Faith for his cherished consort, the god Mádhava[1] for his friend and favourite ; his treasury stored with the four great prizes of life, and all holy places for his fair dominion ; with an impregnable domain and magnificent forts, so strong that no enemy could ever dream of taking them ; with an army of shrines of such virtue and power as to rout the whole army of Sin ; with the meeting of the rivers for his glorious throne and the Akhaya-bat for his royal umbrella, dazzling even the soul, of a saint ; with the waves of the Ganga and Jamuná for his *chauries*, a vision to disperse all sorrow and distress :

Dohá 102.

His attendants pure and holy anchorites, guerdoned with all they desire : his heralds, the Vedas and Puráns, to declare his immaculate virtue.

Chaupái.

Who can tell the power of Prayág, a lion to destroy the elephantine monster Sin? On beholding the beauty of this king of sanctuaries, Raghubar, the ocean of delight, was delighted, and with his holy mouth he discoursed on its greatness to Síta, his brother and his companion. After making it an obeisance he visited the woods and groves, dilating on their virtue with the utmost devotion. So he came to the Tribeni – the mere thought of which confers all happiness—and after gazing upon it, rapturously bathed and paid homage to Siva and to the divinity of the spot in all due form. Then came the lord to Bharadvája ; as he prostrated himself at his feet, the saint took him to his breast in an ecstacy of joy past all telling, as though he had realized the perfect bliss of heaven.

Dohá 103.

The patriarch gave him his blessing with as much joy of heart as though God had set before him in visible form the reward of his virtue.

1 Veni-Madhava is the name of the god worshipped as the tutelary divinity of the Tribeni, the confluence of the three streams, at Prayág.

Chaupái.

After enquiring of his welfare, he conducted him to a seat and indulged his affection in doing him honour. Then he brought and presented roots, fruits and herbs, all sweet as ambrosia, of which Ráma, with Síta, Lakshman and their attendant, partook with much pleasure and content. Ráma was refreshed and all his fatigue forgotten. Then cried Bharadvája in complacent tones : " This day my penance, my pilgrimages, and my vigils have been rewarded ; my prayers my meditations and my detachment from the world have to-day borne fruit ; yea, all my pious practices have to-day, Ráma, been rewarded by the sight of you. This and nought else is the height of gain, the height of happiness ; in beholding you my every desire is satisfied. Now of your favour grant me this one boon, a life-long devotion to your lotus feet.

Dohá 104.

Until a man in heart, word and deed, and without reserve, becomes wholly yours, he cannot even dream of happiness, despite all that he may do."

Chaupái.

On hearing the saint's words, Ráma was confused, yet revelled with delight in so exquisite a display of faith. Then proceeded he to declare unto them all in countless ways the saints illustrious renown : " Great indeed and highly endowed is he, Holy Father, whom you are pleased to honour." Thus they bowed to one another, the saint and Raghubír, and were filled as they conversed with indescribable happiness. When the people of Prayág heárd the news, all the religious students, ascetics, monks, hermits and anchorites flocked to Bharadvája's cell to see the glorious son of Dasarath. All made their obeisance and rejoiced that their eyes had been so highly favoured. They blessed him and returned with exceeding joy, extolling his beauty.

Dohá 105.

Ráma rested for the night. At daybreak he bathed at Prayág, and then, after bowing his head to the saint proceeded joyfully on his way with Síta, Lakshman and his attendant.

Chaup i.

Ráma had affectionately asked the saint: "Tell me, my lord, by what road we shall go." The saint replied with a smile: "All ways are easy to you," but called his disciples to go with him. They came with joy, some fifty in number, all in their boundless love for Ráma declaring that they knew the road. The saint selected four students, who in many previous existences had done many good deeds. Then having bowed to the saint and received his permission to depart, Raghurái went forth rejoicing. When they had come out near to the village, the men and women who all flocked to see them found in the sight of their lord the fruition of their life, and sadly turning home, sent their heart after him.

Dohá 106.

Courteously Ráma dismissed the disciples, who returned with their heart's desire obtained; then alighted and bathed in the stream of Jamuná, dark as his own body.

Chaupái.

The dwellers on the bank, when they heard of his arrival, left whatever they were doing and ran to see him. On beholding the beauty of Lakshman, Ráma and Síta, they congratulated themselves on their good fortune, and all with longing heart began diffidently to ask their name and home. The sage elders of the party had wit enough to recognize Ráma, and related his whole history, and how he had come into the desert by his father's order. At this, they were all sad and complained: 'The king and queen have done ill.'[1] Men and women alike, on beholding the beauty of Ráma, Lakshman and Síta, were agitated with love and pity: "What kind of father and mother must they be, friend, who have sent such children into the wood?"

---

1 Here in some copies is found a whole additional stanza, which is said to exist also in the Rájapur MS. It may, therefore, have been written by Tulsi Dás: but if so, was probably afterwards cancelled by him. The lines contain nothing of any interest, and they fit in very awkwardly with the context, I therefore, like most of the native editors, prefer to omit them.

Dohá 107.

Then Raghubír urgently exhorted his guide, who in submission to his commands took his way home.

Chaupái.

Again with clasped hands Síta, Ráma and Lakshman made renewed obeisance to the Jamuná, and as they went on their way their talk was all of the daughter of the Sun and her glory. Many travellers met them on the way, and exclaimed, after gazing with affection at the two brothers: "You have all the marks of royalty on your person; on seeing them we are troubled at heart, for you go your way on foot, and the astrologers methinks are false. The road is difficult; the mountains and forests are very great; yet you have with you a delicate girl. Elephants and tigers make the woods too terrible to contemplate; with your permission, we will accompany you, will escort you as far as you please, and then make our bow and return."

Dohá 108.

As they proffered this request, their body trembled all over with excess of love, and their eyes filled with tears; but the All-merciful gently and courteously dismissed them.

Chaupái.

All the towns and villages along the road where the envy of the cities of the Serpents and the Gods: 'At what an auspicious moment and by what a holy man must they have been founded, to be so happy and blessed and altogether highly favoured!' Whatever spot was trodden by Ráma's feet Paradise was not to be compared to it. The dwellers by the wayside, of high desert, where the praise of the denizens of heaven, as they feasted their eyes on Síta and Lakshman and Ráma dark of hue as a storm-cloud. The ponds and river in which Ráma bathed were the envy of the lake and river of heaven; the trees under which the Lord sat were magnified by the tree of life; and Earth, touched by the dust of Ráma's lotus feet, thought her good fortune complete.

Dohá 109.

The clouds gave him shade, the exultant hosts of heaven rained down flowers, as Ráma proceeded on his way looking at the rocks and woods and birds and deer.

Chaupái.

Whenever Síta, Lakshman and Raghurái came out near a village on the way, every one,—young and old ; man and woman—came directly they heard the news, forgetting their own private affairs, and as they gazed on their beauty obtained the fruition of their eyes and were made happy for ever. At the sight of the twó heroes their eyes filled with tears, their body quivered with emotion, and they became all-enraptured, their state of mind as indescribable as though a beggar had discovered a pile of heavenly jewels. Every one was telling his neighbour : " Now is the time to prove the value of sight.'' One in his delight to see Ráma would go with him, gazing as he went ; another, drawing his beautiful image into his heart by the way of his eyes, was utterly overpowered in body, soul and speech.

Dohá 110.

One, seeing a fine shady fig-tree, would spread under it soft grass and leaves and cry ; " Rest a little after your fatigue, and proceed again either at once or at daybreak."

Chaupái.

Another brought a jar full of water and tenderly besought him 'Drink' my lord." On hearing, their affectionate speech and seeing their great devotion, the compassionate and most amiable Ráma, who moreover perceived that Síta was wearied, rested for a while in the shade of the fig-tree. All were enraptured with his beauty—men and women alike—and their soul was enamoured of his incomparable loveliness. Like a circle of partridges about his moon-like face, so fixed was their gaze. At the sight of his body, dark in hue as a young *tamál* tree, a myriad Loves were fascinated ; while Lakshman, all comely from head to foot, charmed the soul with his fair limbs, bright as the lightning; in his anchorite's dress, with his tightly-fitted quiver and bow, and arrows gleaming in his lotus hand.

Dohá 111.

With their hair done up in a knot as a crown upon their graceful heads, with broad chest, strong arms, and large deep eyes, with face like the autumnal full moon, glistening with beads of moisture,

Chaupái.

the loveliness of the two brothers is past all telling; it is boundless, and my wit is scant. With every faculty of mind and soul, they all gaze upon the beauteous trio; man and woman thirsting and faint with love, like deer dazed by a light. The village women drew near Síta with tender and bashful enquiries, and again embracing her feet, in their simplicity whispered the question:—"Noble lady, we have a petition, but, like women, are afraid to make it. Pardon our presumption, madam, and be not offended by our country manners. These two charming young princes, from whom emerald and gold might borrow splendour,

Dohá 112.

the one dark, the other fair, but both beautiful and homes of delight, with face like the autumn moon, and eyes like the lotuses of autumn,

Chaupái.

that would put to shame a myriad loves, say, fair lady, how stand they to you." On hearing their pleasant and loving speech, Síta smiled in modest confusion, and looking first at them and then at the earth was abashed—the pretty maid—with a double abashment. But drooping her fawn-like eyes, and with a voice sweet as the *koil's*, she lovingly replied: "The fair youth, so easy and graceful, is by name Lakshman, my younger brother-in-law; while he, the dark complexioned, with the large eyes and arms, the all-beautiful with the gentle voice:" here veiling her moon-like face with the border of her robe she looked towards her husband, and her eyebrows with a side-long glance like a pretty *khanjan*[1] thus by signs indicated to them her lord. All the village women were as delighted as beggars who have robbed a pile of jewels.

Dohá 113.

Falling at Sítas feet in their great affection, they invoked upon her every blessing : May your happy wedded life last as long as Earth rests on the serpent's head.

Chaupái.

May you be as dear to your lord as Párvati to Siva. Yet, lady, cease not to have some regard for us : again and again with clasped hands we beseech you, if you return by this road, remember us your servants, and allow us to see you." Finding them all so athirst with love, Síta comforted them with many soothing words, as the lily is cheered by the moonlight. Then Lakshman, perceiving Raghubír's wish, gently asked the people the way. At his words they became sad, their limbs trembled, their eyes filled with tears, their joy was extinguished, and they were troubled at heart : " God has given us a treasure only to take it away again !" Then reflecting on the ways of Fate and taking courage, they fixed upon the easiest road and explained it to them.

Dohá 114.

Raghunáth took his way to the woods, and with him Lakshman and Jánaki ; and they all returned home, but with many fond speeches, and in heart accompanied them.

Chaupái.

Men and women alike on their way back lamented exceedingly and imputed blame to Fate, saying sadly to one another : " God's doings are all perverse. He is utterly uncontrollable, cruel and remorseless ; who has made the moon sickly and spotted, the tree of paradise a lifeless block, and the ocean all salt, and who now has sent these princely boys into the wilderness. If the woods are their proper abode, then for whom has he intended ease and pleasure ? If they are to wander on their way barefooted, it is to no purpose that he has invented so many kinds of

1 The *khanjan* is a species of wagtail.

carriages. If they are to lie on the ground littered only with grass and leaves, for whom has God created comfortable couches? If he makes them live under the trees, why has he taken such pains to erect splendid palaces?

Dohá 115.

If such lovely and delicate children wear the rough dress and matted locks of anchorites, it is to no purpose that the great artificer has made so many kinds of dress and ornament.

Chaupái.

If they are to eat only fruits and herbs, all the delicacies of the world are thrown away." Said one: "They are so beautiful, they must have been spontaneously produced and not made by God at all. In all the works of God of which the Vedas speak, that either the ears can hear, or the eyes see, or the mind imagine, or the tongue tell--search and examine the whole fourteen spheres—where is there such a man, and where such a woman? When he saw them, God was so pleased that he essayed to make their match: but after much labour, nothing came of it, and thus in spite he has sent and buried them in the woods" Said another: "I am no great scholar, but I account myself supremely happy; nay, blessed are all, in my opinion, who see him, or have seen him, or shall see him."

Dohá 116.

With such affectionate discourse their eyes filled with tears: "How can they, who are so délicate, traverse so difficult a road."

Chaupái.

All the women were made as uneasy by their love as is the *chakwi* at evening time. As they thought upon their tender lotus feet and the hardness of the road, they were distrest at heart and cried in plaintive tones: "At the touch of their soft and rosy feet, the very earth shrinks, as shrinks our heart. If the great God must send them to the woods, why did he not strew their path with flowers? If there be one boon that we may ask of Heaven and obtain, let it be, friend, that we keep them ever in our eyes." All the people who had not come in time, and thus had missed seeing Síta and Ráma, when they heard of their beauty, asked anxiouly 'How far, brother, will they have got by this time ?' They who were strong ran on and saw them, and returned with joy, having obtained the fruition of their eyes.

Dohá 117.

The women and children and the aged wrung their hands and lamented. In this manner, wherever Ràma went, the people were smitten with love.

Chaupái.

In every village was similar rejoicing at the sight of the moon of the lilylike solar race. Some who had learnt by hearsay of what had been going on imputed blame to the king and queen. One said : "It was very good of the king to give our eyes such a treat." Said others among themselves in simple and loving phrase : "Happy the father and mother who gave them birth and happy the city from whence they came ? Happy the hills, and plains, and woods, and towns, and every spot which they visit. Even the Creator who made them is pleased—nay, is absolutely in love with them." The delightful history of Ráma, Lakshman and Sita thus spread over every road and forest.

Dohá 118.

In this manner the Sun of the lotus-like solar race gladdened the people on the road, as with Síta and the son of Sumitrá he proceeded on his travels through the woods,

Chaupái.

Ráma walked in front and Lakshman behind, conspicuous in the hermit's dress they wore ; and between the two Síta shone resplendent as Mayá who connects the life of God with the life of the world. Or, to describe her beauty by another fancy, she seemed like Rati between Spring and Love ; or, to ransack my mind for yet another simile, like the constellation Rohiní[1] between Budha and the Moon.

1 Rohiní is the ninth lunar asterism personified as the daughter of Daksha and the favourite wife of the Moon. Budha is the planet Mercury.

As she went along the way, Síta carefully planted her feet between the footprints of her lord; while Lakshman, avoiding the footprints of them both, set his feet as he went to their right and left. The charming affection of all three was beyond all telling; how can I declare it? Birds and deer were fascinated at the sight of their beauty, and Ráma the wayfarer stole their heart.

Dohá 119.

All who beheld the dear travellers, Síta and the two brothers, joyously and without fatigue arrived at once at the end of the toilsome journey of life.

Chaupái.

And to this day any soul in which the vision of the wayfarers, Ráma, Sita and Lakshman abides, finds the path that leads to Ráma's home, path that scarce a saint may find. Then Raghubír, knowing that Sita was tired, and observing a fig tree close at hand and cool water, there rested and took some roots and fruits to eat, and after bathing at dawn again went on his way. Admiring the beauty of the woods and lakes and rocks, he arrived at Válmíki's hermitage. He found the saint's dwelling a charming spot, a lovely wooded hill with a spring of clear water, lotuses in the pond, the forest trees all in flower, with a delightful hum of bees drunk with sweets, and a joyous clamour of birds and beasts feeding happily and in peace together.

Dohá 120.

The Lotus-eyed was glad as he gazed upon the bright and fair retreat, and the saint on hearing of his arrival came forth to meet him.

Chaupái.

Ráma prostrated himself before him, as the holy man gave him his blessing. At the sight of Ráma's beauty, his eyes were rejoiced and he conducted him with all honour to his cell; there gave him a choice seat as a guest dear to him as his own life, and sent for herbs and sweet fruits, of which Síta, Lakshman and Ráma ate. Great was the joy of Válmíki's soul as his eyes beheld the image of bliss. Then folding his lotus hands, Ráma thus spoke in words to charm his ears : " King of sages, all time, past, present and future, is in your ken, and the universe is like a little plum in the palm of your hand." So saying, the lord related to him the whole history and how the queen had banished him.

Dohá 121.

" My father's promise, my mother's schemes, my brother Bharat's coronation, and my own meeting with you, my lord, are all blessings that only past merit can have won for me.

Chaupái.

In beholding your feet, holy sir, all my good deeds are rewarded. Now, wherever it may be your order, and no anchorite be troubled—for those monarchs burn, even though there be no fire, who vex either saint or ascetic : the satisfaction of a Bráhman is the root of all happiness, while his wrath consumes a thousand generations—tell me then some place to which I can go with Síta and Sumitrá's son, and there build a pretty hut of grass and twigs and rest awhile, kind sir." On hearing his ingenuous speech, the allwise, seer exclaimed : " True, true ! It is only natural for you so to speak, pride of the Raghu line, guardian of the eternal bridge of Revelation.

Chhand 4.

Guardian of the bridge of Revelation, you, O Ráma, are the lord of the universe, and Jánaki is Mayá, who at your gracious will creates, preserves, or destroys the world. And Lakshman is the thousand-headed serpent lord, the supporter of the world with all that it contains, living or lifeless, who in behalf of the gods has taken a kingly form and goes forth to rout the demon host.

Sorathá 4.

Your semblance, O Ráma, transcends speech and is beyond conception, all-pervading, unutterable, illimitable, undefinable even by the Scriptures.

Chaupái.

You look on at the drama of life, and Bráhma, Hari and Sambhu are your puppets. Even they know not your secret, and who else could discover you? He only knows you to whom you have vouchsafed knowledge; and he who knows you becomes one with you. It is by your grace, O Raghunandan, that your votaries learn to know you, soothing sandal-wood of the devout soul. Your body is pure intelligence and bliss, devoid of change, as they know who have found you. In behalf of the saints and the gods you have taken a human body and speak and act like an ordinary king. Fools are bewildered, but the wise rejoice, as they see or hear of your doings; whatever you say or do is true, and we can only play such parts as you set us.

Dohá 122.

You ask of me 'Where can I stay?' but I ask with trembling, tell me where are you not, there will I assign you a place."

Chaupái.

On hearing the sage's affectionate words, Ráma was abashed and smiled to himself. Again Válmíki cried gaily in tones of honeyed sweetness: "Hearken, Ráma; I will now tell you the places where you and Síta and Lakshman should abide. They whose ears are like the ocean to catch the blessed streams of your traditions, and though ever replenished are never filled to the full, their heart shall be your chosen abode. They whose eyes long for your presence, as passionately as the chátak for the rain-cloud, and scorning the water of river, lake or sea, quench their thirst only in your beauty, their hearts are your glorious mansion; there abide, O Raghunáyak, with Lakshman and Síta.

Dohá 123.

Whose tongue, like the swan in the clear hyperboreal lake of your renown gathers up the pearls of your perfections; in his heart, Ráma, fix your home.

Chaupái.

They who ever reverentle inhale the sweet and blessed odour of the offerings to their lord; who feed upon what has been offered to you; who wear only raiment and adornments first offered to you; who bow their heads when they see a god, a *guru*, or a Bráhman, and treat them with all honour and affection; whose hands are ever engaged in paying Ráma worship; who have no other hope but Ráma in their heart; and whose feet ever bear them to his shrines; be their soul, Ráma, your dwelling-place. They who are ever repeating your holy name, and adoring you with their family; who perform the varied rites of oblation and sacrifice; who feast Bráhmans, and give them liberal donations; who regard their own *guru* even more than you, and serve him with all honour and affection,

Dohá 124.

who ask of all one only boon, devotion to Ráma; be their heart your temple wherein to abide, O Sita and you two brothers.

Chaupái.

Who so is unmoved by lust, anger, pride or arrogance, and is without covetousness, excitement, partiality or malice without fraud, hypocrisy or heretical delusion; dwell in his heart, Raghuráya. They who are all men's friends, and are friendlyto all; to whom pleasure and pain, praise and abuse are alike; who are careful to say what is both true and kind; who, whether sleeping or waking, place themselves under your protection and have no other way of salvation but you; in their heart, Ráma, abide. Thoy who look upon another man's wife as their own mother, and another man's wealth as the deadliest poison, who rejoice to see a neighbour's prosperity and are grieved for his misfortunes; and to whom you, O Ráma, are dear as their own life: be their heart your auspicious abode.

Dohá 125.

To whom, my son, you are at once master and companion,

father, mother and spiritual guide; be their heart your temple, ye brothers twain, wherein with Síta to abide.

Chaupái.

They who pick out all men's good points and leave their bad; who endure troubles on behalf of Bráhmans and kine; and who are of note in the world for soundness of doctrine; in their heart be your chosen home. They who understand your righteousness and their own defects and fix all their hopes on you, and have an affection for all your worshippers; in their heart dwell, you and Síta. He who has left all tribe, sect, wealth, hereditary religion, worldly advancement, friend, relations, home and all, and given himself wholly to you; in his heart take up your abode, Raghurái. To whom heaven and hell and release from transmigration are all alike, if only they can behold the god with his bow and arrows; and who in heart, word and deed are your faithful slaves; be their heart, Ráma, your tabernacle.

Dohá 126.

They who never ask for anything but simply love you; in their heart abide for ever, for that is your very home."

Chaupái.

Such were the dwelling-places the sage indicated, and his loving speech pleased Ráma's soul. The saint continued: Hearken, lord of the solar race; I will tell you a hermitage suitable for your present wants. Take up your abode on the hill of Chitra-kút;[1] there you will have every convenience. It is a beautiful hill finely wooded, the haunt of elephants,

1 The sacred hill of Chitra-kút is one of a small group that forms the last spur of the great Vindhyan range. It is situated in the modern district of Bánda, close to the town of Karwi and about 60 miles from Prayág (Allahabad). A river flows at its base, now called the Paisuni (the Sanskrit Payoshni; 'warm as milk'), which has some fine waterfalls before it joins the Jamuná. The Mandákiní, so frequently mentioned, is only a small tributary stream which enters the Paisuni near the village of Sitápur, where are a number of handsome temples The hill is about three miles in circumference, and a narrow paved path runs the whole way round. This was constructed about 150 years ago by one of the Rájas of the neighbouring state of Panna for the convenience of pilgrims performing the ceremony of circumambulation. The two principal fête days are the Rám-navmi (Ráma's birthday) in the month of Chait, and the Diwáli in Kartik. About 20 miles from Chitra-kút on the bank of the Jamuná is the town of Rájapur, which was founded by Tulsi Das, where he lived for several years, and

tigers, deer and birds. It has a sacred river mentioned in the Puránas, which the wife of Atri brought there by the power of penance.[1] It is called the Mandákini, and is a branch of the Ganges, as quick to drown sin as a witch to strangle and infant. Atri and other sages live there, engaged in meditation and prayer and wasting their body with penance. Go and bless their labours, Ráma, and confer dignity on the mountain."

Dohá 127.

All the glories of Chitra-kút did the great saint tell and declare. The two brothers and Síta proceeded to bathe in the sacred stream.

Chaupái.

Said Ragubar, " It is a good place, Lakshman; now make arrangements for our stopping somewhere here." Lakshman then spied out the north bank: " The ravine bends round it like a bow, with the river for its string, asceticism and charity for its arrows, and all the sins of this evil age for its quarry, while Mount Chitra-kút is the huntsman of unerring aim striking at close quarters." So saying, Lakshman showed the spot; when he had seen it, Raghupati was pleased. The gods learnt that Ráma was well content, and came with Indra at their head. In the garb of Kols and Kiráts they came and put up neat huts of boughs and grass, two of them; both prettier than words can tell, the one of larger size, the other a nice little cottage.

Dohá 128.

In his rustic cell the Lord, attended by Lakshman and

---

where a manuscript of the Rámayana in his own handwriting is still preserved. He imposed some curious restrictions upon the inhabitants of the place, which are still to this day religiously observed No private houses, however wealthy the owners may be, are allowed to be built of any material but mud and wood, stone being reserved exclusively for the temples: and no barber, potter or dancing-girl may live within the limits of the town; when their services are required, they have to be called in from some other village.

1 Ansúya, the wife of Atri, was one of Daksha's 24 daughters. She practised severe penance for ten thousand years, and by virtue of the religious merit that she had thus acquired she created the river Mandákini, and by its waters maintained the fertility of the country through a ten years drought.

Jánaki, shone forth as beautiful as Love in the dress of a hermit between Rati[1] and Spring.

Chaupái.

Then flocked to Chitra-kút gods, serpents, Kinnars and Digpáls. All the immortals bowed low before Ràma and gazed with joy on that most longed-for vision. Showering down flowers and exclaiming "At length, O Lord, we have found our Lord," the heavenly host in piteous wise declared their intolerable distress, and joyfully started for their several homes. As soon as they heard the news of Raghunandan's stay at Chitra-kút, the saints sallied forth; seeing the holy company draw near, Ráma prostrated himself before them: but they all took him to their bosom, and invoked upon him blessings,[2] knowing that they would be accomplished. As they beheld the beauty of Ráma and Sita and Sumitra's son, they accounted all their good deeds to have been well rewarded.

Dohá 129.

After all due honours paid, the Lord dismissed the saintly throng to practise contemplation, prayer, sacrifice and penance at pleasure in their own retreats.

Chaupái.

When the Kols and Kiráts got the tidings, they were as glad as if the nine treasures[3] had come to their house. With leaf platters full of herbs, roots and fruits, they ran like beggars scrambling for gold. Those among them who had already seen the two brothers were questioned about them by the others on the road. Telling and hearing Ráma's perfections, all came and saw him. Laying their offering before him and making obeisance, their love increased exceedingly as they gazed upon their Lord. Motionless as

1 Ráti is the Indian Venus.

2 Their blessing could do Ráma no good, but its fulfilment would redound to their own credit, as showing them to be true prophets.

3 The nine *Nidhis* or heavenly treasures of Kuvera, the god of wealth, are thus enumerated: the Padma, Mahá-padma, Sankha, makara, Machchhapa, Makunda, Níla, Nanda and Kharba; but their nature is not exactly defined, though some of them appear to be precious gems. According to the Tántrik system they are personified and worshipped as demi-gods, attendant either upon Kuvera, who is sometimes called *Nidhinàm Adhipah*, 'lord of the Nidhis,' or upon Lakshmi, the goddess of prosperity.—*Williams.*

figures in a picture they stood about anyhow, their body thrilling with emotion and their eyes filled with tears. Ráma, perceiving that they were overwhelmed with affection, spoke to them words of kindness and received them with honour. Again and again bowing low before the Lord, the addressed him in humble strain with folded hands :

Dohá 130.

"Now at length that we have seen our Lord's feet, we have all found a protector : O prince of Kosala, what a blessing for us is your arrival.

Chaupái.

Happy land and forest and road and hill, where thou, my lord, hast planted thy foot ; happy the birds and deer and beasts of the forest, whose life has been crowned by thy sight ; happy we and all our kin, who have filled our eyes with thy vision. Thou hast chosen an excellent spot whereon to take up thy abode ; here at all seasons of the year thou wilt live at ease. We will do thee service in every way, by driving away elephants, lions, snakes and tigers. The thickets, ravines, mountains, chasms and caves have all, my lord, been explored by us foot by foot; we will take you to the different haunts of game, and point out to you the lakes and waterfalls and every other place. We and our people are thy servants ; do not hesitate to command us."

Dohá 131.

The lord, whom the Veda cannot utter nor the saints comprehend, in his infinite compassion listened to the words of the Kiráts, as a father to the vice of a child.

Chaupái.

It is only love that Ráma loves ; understand this, ye who are men of understanding. He charmed all the foresters by his tender loving[1] speeches. Having taking leave and bowed the head, they set forth, and discoursing on the way of their Lord's perfections they reached their homes. In this

1 *Pariposhe,* 'abounding with,' 'fraught with,' is for the Sanskrit *paripushta.*

fashion the two brothers and Síta dwelt in the forest, delighting gods and saints. From the time that Raghu-náyak took his up his abode there, the wood became bounteous in blessing; every kind of tree blossomed and bore fruit; luxuriant creepers formed pleasant and beautiful canopies; as though the tree of paradise in all its native loveliness had abandoned the groves of heavan. Strings of bees made a greatful buzzing, and a delicious air breathed soft, cool and fragrant.

Dohá 132.

Jays, cuckoos, parrots, *chátaks*, *chakwás*, *chakors*, and birds of every description charmed the ear and ravished the soul with their notes.

Chaupái.

Elephants, lions, monkeys, boars and deer forgot their animosity and sported together. Enraptured above all were the herds of deer who beheld the beauty of Ráma as he tracked the chase. All the forests of the gods that there are in the world were envious at the sight of Ráma's forest. The Ganges, the Sarasvati, the sunborn Jamuná, the Narmada, daughter of Mount Mekal, and the sacred Godávari, every river, stream and torrent discoursed of the Mandákini. The mountains of the rising and the setting sun, Kailás, Mandar, Meru, home of all the gods, the crags of Himálaya, and all the hills there be, sang the glory of Chitra-kút. The delight of the gods was more than their soul could contain, to think it had won such renown without an effort.

Dohá 133.

"Of highest merit and blessed indeed are all the birds, deer, creepers, trees and grasses of Chitra-kút," so day and night cried the gods.

Chaupái.

All creatures with eyes, who looked on Ráma, felt with delight that now they had lived to some purpose. Things without life, touched by the dust of his feet, were gladdened by promotion to the highest sphere. The woods and rocks, all charming in themselves, were so blissful, so entirely the holiest of the holy, that how can I declare their glory, when they became the abode of the infinitely blessed, and when leaving the Milky Ocean[1] and deserting Avadh, Síta, Ráma, and Lakshman came there to dwell? The delights of the forest would be past telling even by a hundred thousand Seshnágs. How then can I describe them, any more than a common hole tortoise could uplift Mount Mandar? In every thought, word and act Lakshman does him service, with an amiability and devotion more than can be told.

Dohá 134.

For ever gazing on the feet of Síta and Ráma and conscious of their love for him, not even in his sleep did Lakshman dream of absent kindred, or father or mother, or home.

Chaupái.

In Ráma's company Síta lived so happy that she lost all memory of city, family and home. Ever watching the moonlike face of her beloved, she rejoiced like the partridge at night, and seeing her lords affection daily increase she was as happy as the cuckoo by day. Her heart was so enamoured of him that the forest was a thousand times as dear to her as Avadh; dear was the cottage with her love's society, dear were the fawns and birds, now her only attendants: like her husband's father and mother were the hermits and their wives, and sweet as ambrosia the wild fruits and roots. Shared with her lord, a litter of leaves[2] was a hundredfold more delightful than Cupid's own couch. How can material delights beguile him, the mere sight of whom confers the sovereignty of the spheres?

Dohá 135.

Remembering Ráma, men discard as no more worth than a blade of grass all the pleasures of sense; no wonder then in Síta's case, Ráma's own beloved, the mother of the world.

---

1 Here Sita, Ráma, and Lakshman are all three regarded as incarnations of Vishnu, whose eternal home is the Milky Ocean.

2 *Sáthari* is for the Sanskrit *Sastara*, 'made by strewing,' a bed of leaves.

Chaupái.

Anything that would please Síta and Lakshman, that would Raghunáth do, exactly as they suggested. He would recite legends and tales of olden times, in the hearing of which Lakshman and Sita took great delight. If ever he made mention of Avadh, his eyes filled with tears; as he called to mind his father and mother, his family and his brother, with all Bharat's affection and amiable attention, the compassionate Lord grew most sad, but restrained himself knowing that the time was out of joint. At the sight Síta and Lakshman became distressed also, like the shadow that follows a man. When Raghunandan noticed the emotion of his spouse and his brother, being self-restrained and tender and as soothing to his votaries as sandal-wood when applied to the breast, he would begin to relate some sacred story to divert them.

Dohá 136.

Ráma and Lakshman with Síta in their leafy hut were as resplendent as Indra in the city of heaven with his spouse Sachi and their son Jayanta.

Chaupái.

The Lord was as watchful over Síta and his younger brother as the eyelids over the pupil of the eye; while Lakshman was as careful of Síta and Raghubir as a fool of his own body. Thus happily the Lord lived in the woods, gratify alike birds beasts and pious ascetics. I have now told the story of Ráma's excile to the woods; here how Sumanta reached Avadh. The Nishád returned after escorting his Lord, and came in sight of the Minister and the chariot. No words can tell the distress with which he found the Minister to be agonized. Crying out "Ráma, Ráma, Síta, Lakshman," he had fallen to the ground utterly overpowered, while the horses kept on looking to the south[1] and neighing as piteously as a bird that has lost its wings.

1 Hoping, as Ráma had gone to the south, to get the first glimpse of him coming back again from that direction.

Dohá 137.

They would neither eat grass nor drink water, and their eyes shed tears. At the sight of Ráma's horses all the Nishâds were deeply grieved.

Chaupái.

At length summoning up courage the Nishád said: "now, Sumanta, cease mourning; you are a learned man and a philosopher, submit patiently to adverse fortune." With such kindly expostulations he made him mount the chariot, whether he would or no; but he was so unstrung by grief that he could not drive, his heart ached so grievously for Ràma's loss. The horses reared and would not go; you would think they were wild deer put in harness, jibbing, lying down and turning to look behind them, being overcome by sore pain for Ráma's loss. If any one mentioned the name of Ráma, Lakshman, or Síta, the horses would at once neigh and look at him; the way in which they declared their grief is not to be described, like a snake that has lost its head-jewel.

Dohá 138.

The sight of the Minister and the horses made the Nishád very sad. He told off four trusty grooms and with them a charioteer.

Chaupái.

After making over the charioteer, Guha returned home, more sorry at leaving than words can tell. The Nishád's drove off to Avadh; sunk every moment in deeper distress, Sumanta, tortured by regrets, a prey to woe, cried: "A curse for life without Raghu-bír! This vile body must perish at last; it lost all glory when bereft of Raghu-bír and became a sink of infamy and crime; why does it not take its departure? Ah! fool that it is, it missed its opportunity, seeing that to-day my heart has not broken in twain," Wringing his hands and beating his head in his remorse he went his way like a miser robbed of his pelf, or like a warrior of high renown, some famous champion, who has had to flee from the battle-field.

Dohá 139.

The Minister's grief was like that of some learned Bráhman well read in the Vedas, a man of good repute, of integrity and birth, who has been entrapped into drinking.

Chaupái.

Or like some well-born, virtuous and discreet lady, who is entirely devoted to her lord, but whom Fate has forced to desert him ; such was the cruel torture that racked the Minister's heart. His eyes so full of tears that he could scarcely see ; his ears deaf, his senses all confused, his lips dry his tongue cleaving to his palate, the breath of life only restrained by the bar of Ráma's promise to return ; all the colour gone from his face, he looked like one who had murdered his father and mother. His soul was so possessed with the greatness of his loss and his remorse that he might be some grievous sinner trembling at the gate of death. Words would not come, but to himself he moaned : " How can I look Avadh in the face ; when they see the chariot and no Ráma in it, they will turn in bewilderment to me.

Dohá 140.

When the agitated citizens run to question me and I have to answer them, my heart will be cleft asunder as by a thunderbolt.

Chaupái.

When the piteous queen-mothers ask of me, Good God ! what shall I say to them ? When Lakshman's mother questions me, what good news can I tell her ? When Ráma's mother comes running, like a cow mindful of its now weaned calf, and questions me, I can only answer, 'Ráma, Lakshman and Síta have gone into the forest.' Whoever asks, I must answer so : this is the treat I shall have at Avadh. When the sorrowful king, whose life hangs upon Ráma, questions me, with what face can I answer him, 'I have seen the princes safe to their journey's end and have come back.' When the king hears the news of Lakshman, Síta and Ráma, he will discard his life as not worth a straw.

Dohà 141.

My heart bereft of its beloved is like clay drained of water, but it cracks not : now I know how capable of torture is this body that God has given me."

Chaupái.

Thus bemoaning himself as he went, he quickly arrived in his chariot at the bank of Tamasá. There he courteously dismissed the Nisháds, who after falling at his feet turned sorrowfully away. The Minister was as downcast on entering the city as one who had killed his own spiritual guide or a Bráhman, or cow. He passed the day sitting under a tree, and at eventide took the opportunity to enter Avadh in the dark. He slunk into his house, leaving the chariot at the gate. All who heard the tidings came to the king's door to see the chariot, and having recognized it and observed the distress of the horses, their body melted away like hail in the sun. All the citizens were as woebegone as fish when the waters are dried up.

Dohá 142.

When they heard of the Minister's arrival, all the ladies of the court were agitated. The palace struck him with as much dread as a haunted chamber.

Chaupái.

All the queens questioned him in great excitement ; no answer came, his voice was all broken. With no ears to hear, nor eyes to see, he could only ask every one he met, 'Tell me where is the king.' Seeing his confusion, the handmaidens conducted him to Kausalya's apartments. On entering, Sumanta found the king in such state as the moon shows when all its lustre has waned. Fasting, sleepless, stript of every adornment, he lay on the ground in utter wretchedness, sighing as piteously as Yayáti[1] after he had been

1 Yayáti as a reward for his many sacrifices was exalted to heaven. There Indra met him, ceremoniously conducted him to the throne, and then craftily drew him out to speak of all the meritorius acts he had done. The more he boasted, the more his virtue evaporated, till at last he was left without any merit at all. The gods then turned him out of heaven and Indra was able to resume the vacant throne.

hurled from heaven, his heart every moment bursting with grief, like Sampáti[1] falling with singed wings, fondly crying 'Ráma, Ráma, Ráma', and again 'Ráma Lakshman, Síta.'

Dohá 143.

The Minister on seeing him cried 'All hail!' and bowed to the ground. At the sound of his voice the king started up hurriedly and exclaimed 'O Súmanta, where is Ráma?'

Chaupái.

The king clasped Sumant to his bosom, like a drowning man who has caught hold of some support. He seated him affectionately by his side, and with his eyes full of tears asked: "Tell me, kind friend, of Ráma's welfare: where are Raghunáth, Lakshman and Síta? Have you brought them back, or have they sought the forest?" At these words the Minister's eyes streamed with tears. Overpowered by anxiety, the king asked again: "give me tidings of Síta, Ráma and Lakshman." Calling to mind Ráma's beauty and amiability, he sorrowed yet more: "I promised him the kingdom and then imposed exile; he obeyed with soul unmoved either by joy or sorrow. Breft of such a son I yet can live: who so guilty a monster as I?

Dohá 144.

Take me, my friend, to the place where Ráma, Síta and Lakshman are. If not, I tell you the very truth, my soul will take flight at once."

Chaupái.

Again and again he implored him: "Friend, tell me of my son. Hearken, comrade; contrive some means for speedily showing me Ráma, Lakshman and Síta." Summoning up courage the Minister gently replied: "Sire, your majesty is a scholar and philosopher, a model of courage and endurance, and a constrant attendant of holy assemblies. Life and death; pleasure, pain and all enjoyments; loss and gain; the society of friends and their bereavement; all, sir, are governed by time and fate as unalterably as the succession of night and day. Fools triumph in prosperity, and are downcast

1 See Chaupái of Kishkindhya after Dohá 26.

in adversity; wise men account both alike. Consider the matter wisely and take courage; the good of all depends upon you; cease vain regrets.

Dohá 145.

Their first halt was at the Tamasá; their second on the bank of the Ganges, where the two heroes and Síta bathed and stayed to drink water.

Chaupái.

The boatmen showed them great courtesy and they passed the night at Sringavera. At daybreak they called for milk of the fig-tree and fastened up the hair of their head into a crown-like top-knot. Then Ráma's friend called for the boat, and after putting his beloved on board, Ráma himself followed, and after him by his Lord's permission, Lakshman too claimed the boat equipt with bow and arrows. Seeing my distress, Raghu-bír restrained his emotion and addressed me thus kindly: 'Father, give my salutation to my father, and again and again embrace his lotus feet. There at his feet entreat him with all humility, saying, Father, mourn not for me; my banishment to the forest is pleasant and profitable to myself, and on your part is a grace, a favour, and a meritorious deed.

Chhand 5.

By your favour, father, I go to the forest, there to enjoy complete happiness. After fulfiling your command, I shall return again in safety to behold your feet.' Next falling at the feet of each of the queen mothers, console and implore them to make every effort that Kosala's king may live happy.

Sorathá 5.

Again and again clasping the lotus feet of my spiritual instructor, give him this my message: 'So exhort the king that he may cease to sorrow on my account.'

Chaupái.

Bowing down before all the citizens and the people of the court make known to them, sir, this my petition: 'He is my best friend who ensures the king's happiness.' Say to

Bharat, too, when he comes,' Now that you have obtained the royal dignity, forget not sound polity. Cherish your subjects in word, thought and deed, and be obedient to all the queen-mothers without partiality. Fulfil your duty, brother, as a brother, and in dutifulness to father, mother and kindred, and take such care of the king, sir, that he may never regret me. 'Lakshman gave vent to some angry words, but Ráma checked him, and begged of me again and again, adjuring me by himself, not to mention his childishness.

Dohá 146.

Síta sent her reverence, and would have said more, but was unable; her voice faltered, her eyes filled with tears, and her body quivered with emotion.

Chaupái.

Then it was that at a sign from Rahugbar the boatman propelled the boat to the opposite side. In this manner the Glory of Raghu's line went his way, and I stood looking on with a heart as of adamant. How can I describe my own anguish, who have come back alive, bearing Ráma's message?' With these words the Minister stopped speaking, being overpowered by affection, remorse and distress. When he had heard Sumanta's speech, the king fell to the ground, heartbroken with grief, and in a wild phrenzy of soul writhed like a fish in the scour of a turbid stream.[1] All the queens wept and made lamentation; how can I describe so great a calamity? at the sound of their wailings. Sorrow itself grew sorrowful and Endurance could no more endure.

---

1 This simile, as noted at page 33 has puzzled many of the commentators, who are ordinarily grammarians rather than observers of nature. It is well illustrated and explained by a letter in the *Pioneer* of August 5th, 1878, from a correspondent at Mirzapur. He writes as follows :—" We observed a curious phenomenon here which seems worth recording. Early on Friday morning huge quantites of fish of every description were seen coming to the surface all along both banks of the river gasping and dying. The people living near the sides flocked down and clubbed and secured very many..... Before many hours all the fish susceptible to whatever influence was at work seem to have perished and in the afternoon they rose to the surface and floated past in a state of decomposition. The river is in high but not full flood. The water, probably on account of the prolonged drought, is intensely and abnormally turbid. It is to this peculiarity I attribute the death of the fish. The particles of earth held in suspense have impregnated the gills and stopped breathing."

Dohá 147.

Avadh was in a tumult at the sound of the outcry in the king's palace: as when a cruel thunderbolt has fallen at night in some dense forest full of birds.

Chaupái.

The breath of life flickered at the king's mouth, forlorn as a snake robbed of its jewel; all his senses as heavy smitten as the lotuses in a lake that has been drained of its water. When Kausalyá saw the king's misery—the Sun of the solar race setting as it were at noon—Ráma's mother summoned up courage and spoke in words befitting the occasion: "Consider, my lord, and reflect that Ráma's exile is like the vast ocean, you are the helmsman of the good ship Avadh, and your friends are the merchants, its passengers; if you have courage you will get across: if not the whole family will be drowned. Take to heart this entreaty of mine, my spouse, and you will yet see again Ráma, Lakshman and Síta.

Dohá 148.

Hearing these tender words from his beloved, the king opened his eyes and looked up, writhing like some hapless fish when sprinkled with cold water.

Chaupái.

The king with an effort sat up: "Tell me, Sumanta, where is my generous Ráma? Where is Lakshman? Where my loving Ráma? Where my dear daughter-in-law, the princess of Videha?" Thus miserably moaning, the night seemed an age long and as though it never would end. The blind hermit's curse[1] came back to his mind,

---

1 The incident to which such brief allusion is here made is told at full length in the Sanskrit Rámayana, where it occupies nearly 200 lines. One day, when Dasarath was still a youth, he was out shooting, and had taken up a position near the bank of the Sarju, where he hoped to get a shot at some tiger or buffalo as it came down in the evening to the river to drink. Hearing a splash in the water, he left fly an arrow. From the cry that followed, he learnt to his dismay that he had shot a young hermit, who had been filling his pitcher for the use of his blind and aged parents. His dying words were to implore the king that he would carry the water to the hermitage and inform the bereaved couple of their son's sad fate. He did so, and was told that as a punishment for his crime he, too, should hereafter die of grief for the loss of a son. The time should be far distant, because the blow was dealt unwittingly, and his confession had further lightened his guilt: had he concealed the deed, he and the whole of his line had perished for ever.

and he told the whole story to Kausalyá. As he related the circumstances his agitation increased: "Bereft as I am of Ráma, I have done with life and hope; why should I cherish a body that has failed to fulfil my love's engagement? Ah Raghunandan, dearer to me than life, already I have lived too long without you. Ah, Jánaki and Lakshman! Ah, Raghubar the raincloud of a fond father's *chatak*-like heart."

Dohá 149.

Crying 'Ráma, Ráma!' and again 'Ráma!' and yet once more 'Ráma, Ráma, Ráma!,' the king's soul, bereft of Raghubar, quitted his body and entered heaven.

Chaupái.

Thus Dasarath reaped his reward both in life and death, and his spotless fame has spread through countless cycles of creation. In life he saw Ráma's moon-like face, and dying for his loss had a glorious death. All the queens bewept him in an agony of grief, and spoke of his beauty, his amiability, his power and majesty. They made manifold lamentation, throwing themselves upon the ground again and again. Men-servants and maid-servants sadly bemoaned him; and there was weeping in every house throughout the city: "To-day has set the sun of the solar race, the perfection of justice, the treasury of all good qualities." All reviled Kaikeyi, who had robbed the world of its very eyes. In this manner the night was spent in lamentations till all the great and learned sages arrived.

Dohá 150.

Then the holy Vasishtha recited many legends befitting the time, and checked their grief by the wisdom that he displayed.

Chaupái.

After filling a boat with oil and putting the king's body in it, he summoned messengers and thus addressed them: "Hasten with all speed to Bharat, and say nothing to anybody about the king; only tell Bharat when you arrive. 'The guru has sent for you two brothers.'" On receiving the saint's orders, they ran off at once with speed that would shame the fleetest of horses. Directly these troubles had begun at Avadh, Bharat was visited with evil omens; he saw fearful visions in his sleep by night, and on awaking formed all sorts of ill conjectures. He daily feasted Bráhmans and gave alms, and with elaborate ritual poured water over the emblem of Mahádev, and with heartfelt prayers implored the god for the prosperity of his parents, his family and his brethren.

Dohá 151.

In this state of anxiety was Bharat found by the heralds on their arrival. As soon as he had heard his guru's commands he offered up a prayer to Ganes and started.

Chaupái.

They went with the speed of the wind, urging on their horses over rivers, rocks and trackless forests. So great was his distress of mind that nothing pleased him; he thought to himself, 'O that I had wings to fly!' A moment seemed like a year. In this manner Bharat drew near to the city. On entering he was met by evil omens. Gruesome noises sounded in uncanny places, asses and jackals uttered presages of ill, which pierced him to the heart as he listened. Even the lakes and rivers, groves and gardens, seemed forlorn; while the city struck him as more melancholy still. Birds, deer, horses and elephants were painful to look at, as though the loss of Ráma were some dreadful disease that had destroyed them. The citizens were as downcast as if they had all lost everything they had in the world.

Dohá 152.

The people who met him did not speak, but bowed and passed on. For the fear and dismay in his mind Bharat could not ask 'Is all well?'

Chaupái.

The market-places and streets were as dreary as though the city had been the prey of a general conflagration. When Kaikeyi heard of her son's approach, the moon of the lotus-like solar race rejoiced. She sprang up gladly and ran with lamp in hand and met him at the door and brought him in. Bharat saw all the household as woe-begone as a bed of lotuses when smitten by the frost, his mother as jubilant as a wild hill-woman who has set the forest in a blaze. Seeing her son sad and distressed, she asked 'Is all well in my mother's house?' Bharat assured her that all was well, and then asked after the welfare of his own family: "Say, where is my father and where the other queen-mothers? where is Síta and my dear brothers, Ráma and Lakshman?"

Dohá 153.

On hearing her son's loving speech, the guilty woman's eyes filled with false tears, and she replied in words that pierced Bharat's ears and soul:

Chaupái.

"My son, I had arranged everything with the help of poor[1] Manthará, but God somehow spoilt my plan half-way. The king has gone to heaven." On hearing this Bharat was overcome with distress, like an elephant at the roar of a lion. Crying "My father, my father, alas, my father!" he fell upon the ground in grievous affliction. "I could not see you ere you left, nor did you my father, commend me to Ráma." Again, with an effort, he collected himself and got up: "Tell me, mother, the cause of my father's death." On hearing her son's words Kaikeyi replied, as one who drops poison into a wound, and with a glad heart, vile wretch that she was, recounted all that she had done from the very beginning.

Dohá 154.

Bharat forgot his father's death when he heard of Ráma's banishment, and knowing himself to be the cause he was staggered and remained speechless.

Chaupái.

Seeing her son's distress she comforted him, in such a manner as when one applies salt to a burn: "The king, my

---

1 *Bichàri* is here for the Persian word *bechara*. The Hindu commentator explains it by *chara rahita?*

boy, is no fit subject for lamentation; he won glory and renown and lived happily. In his life he reaped all life's rewards, and in the end has entered the court of heaven. Regard the matter in this light and banish grief; in state assume the sovereignty of the realm." The prince shrunk exceedingly at her words, as though cautery had been applied to a festered wound; then collecting himself he gave a deep sigh: Wretched woman, the ruin of us all! if this was your vile desire, why did you not kill me at my birth? After cutting down a tree you water the branches and drain a pond to keep the fish alive.

Dohá 155.

Born of the solar race, with Dasarath for my father and Ráma and Lakshman for my brothers, I have had you, mother, for a mother: what can be done against Fate?

Chaupái.

Wretch! when you formed such an evil design in your mind, how was it your heart did not break in pieces? When you asked the boon, your soul felt no pain, your tongue did not burn, nor your mouth fester? How could the king trust you? his hour of death had come, and God had robbed him of his senses. Not even God knows the ways of a woman's heart; such a mine is it of all deceit, crime and sin. The king was so simple, good and pious, what did he know of woman's nature? Is there any living creature in the world who loves not Raghunáth like himself? Yet he was your special enemy. Tell me the truth, what are you? Whatever you may be, you have blackened your own face; up, hence out of my sight.

Dohá 156.

God has created me out of a womb hostile to Ráma; who so guilty a wretch as I? but it is useless for me to say anything to you."

Chaupái.

When Satrughna heard of his mother's wickedness he burned all over, his anger was beyond control. At that very moment Humpback came up, dressed out in fine attire and many jewels. On seeing her, Lakshman's young brother was filled with passion, like fire upon which butter has been poured. He sprung forward and struck her such a blow on her hump that she fell flat on her face and screamed aloud. Her hump was smashed, her head split, her teeth broken, and her mouth streamed with blood. "Ah! my God! what harm have I done? this is an ill reward for all my services!" Then Satrughna, seeing her so all vile from head to foot, seized her by the hair of the head and began dragging her about, till the merciful Bharat rescued her. Both brothers then went to Kausalyá.

Dohá 157.

In sordid attire, pale, agitated, with wasted frame and soul opprest with woe, she seemed some lovely creeper or golden lotus smitten by the frost.

Chaupái.

When the queen saw Bharat she sprang up in haste, but fell swooning to the ground overtaken with giddiness. At this sight Bharat was grievously distrest, and threw himself at her feet, forgetting his own condition: "Mother, let me see my father; where is Síta, and where Ráma and Lakshman, my two brothers? Why was Kaikeyi born into the world? or if born, why was she not barren instead of bearing me to disgrace the family, a very sink of infamy, the curse of my home? Who in the three spheres is so wretched as I am, on whose account, mother, you have been brought to this plight? My father dead, Ráma banished, and I alone the cause of all this calamity! Woe is me, a very fire amongst the reeds, fraught with intolerable torment, anguish and offence."

Dohá 158.

Hearing Bharat speak so tenderly, his mother again took courage and arose and lifted him up and clasped him to her bosom, while she wiped the tears from his eyes.

Chaupái.

Simple and kind, she took him to her heart as lovingly

as though Ráma himself had come back. Then Lakshman's young brother was also embraced, while her soul overflowed with sorrow and affection. All who witnessed her kindness said: "She is Ráma's mother, it is natural to her." Seating Bharat in her lap she wiped away her tears and said soothingly; Now, my child, I adjure you to compose yourself; reflect that the times are evil and cease to lament. Think no more of your loss and vexation; remember that the course of time and fate is unalterable. Do not attach blame to any one my son: it is God who has set himself against me. He has made me live through such distress: who knows what may be his pleasure with me now?

Dohá 159.

At his father's command Raghubír put aside his ornaments and ordinary attire and assumed the bark dress without either dismay or exultation.

Chaupái.

With a cheerful countenance and a soul unmoved by anger or attachment, he did all in his power to comfort us. Síta hearing he was off to the forest, went too; in her devotion to Ráma's feet she could not stay. Lakshman also, when he heard the news, rose up to accompany him, and for all Ráma's persuasions would not remain behind. Then Raghupati bowed his head to all in turn and set out accompanied by Síta and his younger brother. Ráma, Lakshman and Síta went thus into exile. I neither joined them nor sent my spirit after them. All this took place before my eyes, and yet—wretch that I am - life did not leave my body. I felt no shame, for all my love, with such a son, as Ráma and myself his mother. The king knew well the time to live and the time to die, but my heart is a hundredfold harder than adamant."

Dohá 160.

Hearing Kausalyá's words, Bharat and all the seraglio made woeful lamentation; the palace seemed the very home of affliction.

Chaupái.

Bharat, nay, both brothers, wept piteously. Kausalyá clasped them to her bosom, and comforted Bharat in every way with words of excellent wisdom. With appropriate maxims from the Puránas and Vedas all the queens reasoned with Bharat. And he, pure, guileless and sincere, made fitting answer thus with clasped hands: "The crime of slaying father, mother or guru; of burning cows in their stalls or a city of Bráhmans; the crime of murdering wife or child; of poisoning a friend or a king; every mortal or venial sin, of thought, word and deed, as enumerated by the seers; may all these sins be mine, O God, if this, mother, was a plot of mine.

Dohá 161.

May God award me the fate of those who forsake the feet of Hari and Hara and worship abominable demons, if, mother, this was any plot of mine.

Chaupái.

Those who sell the Veda and trade on piety; backbiters, who talk of others' faults; the treacherous, the perverse, the litigious, the violent; the revilers of the Veda, the enemies of all creation; the covetous, the lecherous, the fickle, the boastful,[1] who covet their neighbour's wealth or their neighbour's wife; may I come to a like ill end with them if, mother, this plot had my consent. The wretches who have no regard for the example of the good, who reject the way of salvation, who worship not the incarnation of Hari and take no delight in the glory of Hari and Hara, who abandon the path of Scripture and follow a contrary road, who by knavish disguise impose upon the world; may Sankara allot me a fate like theirs if, mother, I knew of this plot.

Chhand 6.

Hearken, mother; in all my thoughts, word and deeds I am the slave of the All-merciful. The omniscient Ráma dwells in my heart and discerns perfectly between true

1 For the two words *lolá*, *lawárá*, it would seem preferable to read, *lolupawárá*, if there were any manuscript to support it.

affection and feigned." As he thus spoke, his eyes streamed with tears, his body quivered, and his toes drew lines upon the ground. Again his mother took and clasped him to her bosom, knowing him to be indeed a votary of Ráma's

Dohá 162.

Hearing Bharat's true and honest and generous words, his mother exclaimed : "Son, you have ever in thought, word and deed been Ráma's friend.

Chaupái.

Ràma is the very life of your life, and you are dearer than life to him. The moon may drop poison, ice distil fire, fish avoid water, a sage persist in folly; but you could never become Ráma's enemy. If any one in the world says this was of your contriving, he shall never even in his sleep have any peace or happiness." With these words his mother took Bharat to her arms while her breasts dropped milk and her eyes filled with tears. As they sat and made such long lamentation, the whole night was spent. Saints Vámadeva and Vasishtha came and summoned all the Ministers and nobles and did everything to console Bharat by appropriate discourse on religious topics.

Dohá 163.

"Son, take heart and perform the duties of the day." Bharat arose at the guru's command and ordered everything to be done.

Chaupái.

As directed in the Veda, he had the body of the king washed and a sumptuous funeral car prepared. Then clasping the feet of each of the queens he bid them stay.[1] They stayed in the hope of seeing Ráma. Many loads of sandalwood and aloes were brought and immense quantities of sweetscented spices. The pile was raised on the bank of the Sarju like a fair ladder reaching to heaven. So all the rites of cremation were accomplished; the prescribed bathing,

1 That is to say, he would not allow them to ascend the funeral pile with the body of the king and perish with him as Satis.

the oblation of sesamum seeds, the ceremony of the ten balls of rice,[1] which Bharat performed after due study of the Vedas, the Puranas and the Code or Ritual. Whatever order was given at any time by the great sage was thereupon executed accordingly a thousand times over. For his purification he gave abundant gifts; cows, horses, elephants, all kinds of carriages,

Dohá 164.

thrones, jewels, robes, grain, lands, money, and houses did Bharat take and present to the Bráhmans: their every wish was gratified.

Chaupái.

All the ceremonies that Bharat performed on his father's account were more than a million tongues could tell. Then came the great sages, after determining an auspicious day, and summoned all the nobles and ministers, who went and sat down in the royal council chamber, where they sent and summoned Bharat and his brother. Vasishtha seated Bahart by his side and addressed him in words full of wisdom and piety. First the holy man repeated the whole history of Kaikeyi's monstrous doing and extolled the king for his piety and faithfulness to his promise, who by his death had manifested his love. As he spoke of Ráma's good qualities and amiable disposition the saint's eyes filled with tears and his body quivered with emotion. As he went on to tell of the affection shown by Lakshman and Síta, the ascetic sage was drowned in love and grief.

Dohá 165

"Hearken, Bharat"—thus sadly spoke the prince of sages—"Fate is overstrong; loss and gain, life and death, honour and dishonour are in God's hands.

Chaupái.

Having so considered, why blame any one, or why be angry with any without cause? Ponder this in your heart,

---

1 One ball is offered on the first day, two on the second, and so on till the tenth, when the ceremony is complete.

my son ; king Dasarath is not to be pitied. Pitiable the Bráhman who is ignorant of the Veda and has abandoned his faith and become absorbed in the delights of sense; pitiable the king who knows not the principles of government and to whom his subjects are not as dear as his own life ; pitiable the merchant, miserly and rich, who regards not the duties of hospitality nor the service of Mahádev ; pitiable the Súdra who insults a Bráhman, who is boastful, ambitious and proud of his knowledge ; pitiable again the wife who deceives her own husband, and who is perverse, quarrelsome and self-willed ; pitiable the religious student who breaks his vows and obeys not the commands of his *guru*,

Dohá 166.

pitiable the householder who, overcome by delusion, forsakes the path of religion ; pitiable the ascetic who is enamoured of the world and has lost his judgment and self-governance ;

Chaupái.

pitiable the anchorite who has given up penance and takes delight in pleasure ; pitiable the backbiter and the angry without a cause, the enemies of their own parents, their spiritual guide and their kinsmen ; pitiable in every way is the malevolent who cherishes self and is utterly merciless ; pitiable in every way is he who does not eschew guile and become a follower of Hari ; but the king of Kosala is not to be pitied ; his glory is spread abroad through the fourteen spheres. Their neither has been, nor is now, nor shall be hereafter, a king like your father, Bharat. Bráhma, Vishnu, Siva, Indra and all the Regents of the air sing the virtues of Dasarath.

Dohá 167.

Tell me, my son, in what way can any one magnify him, who has such noble sons as Ráma, Lakshman, you and Satrughna ?

Chaupái.

The king is altogether fortunate ; it is vain to lament on

his account. Thus hearing and considering, cease from grief; obediently submit to the royal commands. The king has given you the throne, and you must needs fulfil your father's word. The monarch who for the sake of his word abandoned Ráma, though in the anguish of separation from Ráma he lost his life, and thus held his word dearer than life, is a father, my son, whose word must be obeyed. Bow your head to the royal command; it will be in every way for your good. Parasurám, to obey his father's order, slew his own mother, as all the world bears witness; and Yayáti, son gave him up his youth;[1] in a father's order there can be no sin nor disgrace.

Dohá 168.

They who cherish their father's words, without discussing right or wrong, they are vessels of honour and glory and dwell in the palace of the king of heaven.

Chaupái.

You must certainly make good the king's word; cherish your subjects and cease to grieve. He will receive comfort in heaven; for you it will be a merit and an honour, and no fault. It is laid down in the Veda, and approved by all men, that he takes the crown to whom the father gives it. Reign then, nor further distress yourself, but accept my advice as the best for you. Ráma and Síta will rejoice when they hear of it and no wise man will call it wrong. Kausalyá and all the queens will be happy in the happiness of the people. Ráma knows your secret thoughts and will take it quite in good

---

1 The legend of Yayáti is thus given in the Vishnu Purána, IV., 10:—He was the second son of king Nahusha, and succeeded to his father's throne. He had two wives, Devayáni, the daughter of Usanas (also called Sukracharya, the preceptor of the Daityas), and Sarmishtha, the daughter of Vrishaparvan, king of the Danavas. Having been cursed by Usanas, whose daughter had complained to him of her husband's infidelity, he became old and infirm before his time, but was allowed to transfer his decrepitude to any one who would consent to take it. Four of his sons, to whom he successively applied for relief, refused to grant it, and received in consequence their father's curse, that none of their posterity should possess dominion. But when he made the same request of his fifth and youngest son, Puru, he at once consented to give up his youth and receive in exchange his father's infirmities. After some years of enjoyment Yayáti himself withdrew to a hermitage in the woods and resigned the throne to Puru, whom he appointed supreme monarch of the world, making his elder brothers his viceroys under him.

part ; on his return you can deliver up the throne and serve him with cheerful affection."

Dohá 169.

The ministers with clasped hands exclaimed : " You must needs obey your guru's command : when Raghupati returns, you can then do as shall seem good."

Chaupái

Kausalyá took courage and cried : " My son, you have your father's and your guru's commands, which you must respect and affectionately carry out. Cease to lament, knowing it to be the will of Fate that Ráma is in banishment, the king in heaven, and you in such perplexity. You, my son," continued his mother, " are the sole refuge of your family, your people and the ministers of state. Seeing God against us and the fates untoward, summon up resolution. I, your mother, adjure you, obediently comply with your guru's command ; cherish your people, relieve the affliction of your family." The guru's speech and the ministers' approval had been as grateful to Bharat's hearing as sandal perfumes, but when he heard his mother's tender appeal fraught with the pathos of sincere affection—

Chhand 7.

when he heard his mother's pathetic appeal, Bharat was overcome ; his lotus eyes rained with tears that bedewed the fresh shoots of desolation in his soul. All who then beheld his condition entirely forgot about themselves—ah, Tulsi!—and reverently extolled him as the very perfection of true love.

Sorathá 6.

Clasping his lotus hands, Bharat, the champion of honour, stoutly made answer to them all in noble words that seemed as if dipped in nectar.

Chaupái.

" The guru has given me good advice, which has been approved by ministers, people, and all. My mother, too, has given me proper commands, and I must needs bow and obey. The injunctions of a guru, a father or mother, or master, or friend, should be cheerfully performed as soon as heard, and as all for the best; to deliberate whether they are right or wrong is a failure of duty and involves grievous sin. You have now given me honest advice, which it will be good for me to follow; yet, though I understand this clearly, my soul is still discontent. Hearken then to my prayer, and according to my circumstances so instruct me, forgiving my presumption in answering you: when a man is in distress good people do not reckon up his merits and demerits.

Dohá 170.

My father is in heaven, and Síta and Ráma in exile, and you tell me to be king; is it my gain or your own advantage that you expect to result from this?

Chaupái.

My gain is to serve Síta's lord, and of this I have been robbed by my mother's wickedness. After reflecting and searching my thoughts I find no other way of happiness than this. Of what account is a throne with all its cares, if I cannot see the feet of Lakshman, Ráma and Síta? Without clothes a mass of jewels is of no use; of no use is asceticism without divine meditation; of no use is any enjoyment to a diseased body; prayer and penance go for nought without faith in Hari; without life, beauty of body is nought; and all is nought to me without Ráma. Permit me to join Ráma; this is one word is my only happiness. If again in making me king it is your own advantage that you desire, you speak under the influence of foolish affection.

Dohá 171.

In your infatuation you hope for happiness from the reign of such a wretch as I, Kaikeyi's son, of wicked nature, Ráma's enemy, and lost to shame.

Chaupái.

I speak the truth; hearken all and believe; in a king is required a righteous disposition. If you persist in giving the crown to me, earth will sink into hell. What guilty wretch is equal to me, for whom Síta and Ráma have been exiled ? The king banished Ráma, but died in losing him. I, the miserable cause of all this wrongdoing, sit and listen to it all unmoved. I see the palace with no Ráma there, yet live to endure the world's jeers. Holy Ráma eschews all pleasures of sense, and I, a greedy king, am hungering after enjoyment. In what words can I tell the hardness of my heart, which surpasses even adamant?

Dohá 172.

That every result is harder than its cause is no fault of mine ; the thunderbolt is harder than bone,[1] and iron more stiff and unbending than the rock from which it is quarried.

Chaupái.

If my worthless life can cling to a body born of Kaikeyi it will have a surfeit of misery : if, bereaved of my beloved, life is still dear to me, I shall have much hereafter to see and hear. Kaikeyi has banished Lakshman, Ráma and Síta, and for her own advantage has caused the death of the king ; she has taken upon herself widowhood and disgrace and has caused the people sorrow and affliction, has allotted me glory and honour and dominion and has settled everybody's business. What good is this now to me? and yet you too cry out to make me a king. I have been born into the world from Kaikeyi's womb, and all this is only my due ; God has fashioned all my destiny ; but why should my people combine to give a helping hand?

Dohá 173.

Stricken as I am by fate, overcome by organic disease,[2] and then stung by a scorpion, you give me wine to drink ; tell me, tell me what kind of treatment is this?

---

1 The thunderbolt is said to be made from the bones of the Rishi Dadhíchi, who devoted himself to death in order that the gods might be supplied with arms against the Kàlakeya Asuras, by whom they were oppressed. When his bones had been fashioned into thunderbolts by Tvashtri (the Vedic Vulcan) Indra hurled them against his enemies and slew their leader, the cloud demon Vritra.

2 According to Hindu physicians all organic disorders of the human frame arise from derangements of the blood or one of the three humors of the body, *kapha*, phlegm, *vàyu*, wind, or *pitta*, bile. The vitiated humor which is specified in the text is wind, *bát*.

Chaupái.

The wise Creator has ordained for me everything that befits a son of Kaikeyi. That I am also Dasarath's son and Ráma's younger brother is an honor which God has bestowed upon me to no purpose. You all tell me to allow myself to be crowned, for kingly power is desired by all men. How and whom shall I answer? You talk at random as the fancy takes you. Apart from myself and my unhappy mother, tell me who will say that I have acted rightly? excepting myself, who else is there in the whole animate or inanimate creation that does not love Síta and Ráma as their own life? That a universal calamity should be my great gain, this is my illfortune and no blame to any one. You are moved by anxiety, kindness and affection, and anything you say is all for the best.

Dohá 174.

Ráma's mother is so utterly guileless and bears me such great love that she speaks from natural amiability, on seeing my remorse.

Chaupái.

The guru, as all the world knows, is an ocean of wisdom, and the universe is like a plum in the palm of his hand. He too is making ready for my coronation: when God is against me, every one is against me. Except Ráma and Síta there is not any one in the whole world who will not say this was a scheme of mine, and I must listen and bear it patiently: wherever there is water, there at last will be mud. I am not afraid of the world calling me vile; I have no thought for heaven: the one great intolerable anguish of soul is this, that through me Síta and Ráma have been rendered unhappy. Well has Lakshman reaped his life's reward who left all and clave to Ráma; while my birth has been the cause of Ráma's banishment. Wretch that I am, why thus lament in vain.

Dohá 175.

I declare before you all my grievous distress; unless I see Ráma's feet, the fire in my soul cannot be quenched.

Chaupái.

No other remedy can I discover: without Raghubar what care I for life? This wish alone is stamped upon my soul; at daybreak let me follow my lord. Although I am a guilty wretch, and all his trouble is on my account, still when he sees my suppliant mien he will in his great mercy forgive me all. Raghuráo is so meek and utterly guileless of disposition, such a home of mercy and tenderness, that he would never injure even an enemy: while I, bad as I am, am his son and his servant. Be pleased, sirs, then to give me your blessing and permit me to depart, knowing it to be for my good; so Ráma will come again to his kingdom, after hearing my prayers and considering my devotion.

Dohá 176.

Though born of a wicked mother, and myself evil and ever doing wrong, still I am confident of Raghubír that he will know me for his own, and not abandon me."

Chaupái.

Bharat's words pleased all, imbued as they were with the nectar of piety. The people suffering from the baneful poison of separation revived as if at the sound of a healing charm. The queen-mothers, the ministers, the guru and all the men and women in the city were agitated by the vehemence of their affection and kept on telling Bharat's praises: 'His body is the very personification of devotion to Ráma; ah, my lord Bharat, how can we say otherwise, seeing that Ráma is as precious to you as your life? If any churl in his folly ascribe to you your mother's sin, the wretch, with all who are his from generation to generation, shall have their abode in hell for hundreds of ages. The jewel is not infected with the guilt and villany of the serpent (in whose head it is found), but is an antidote to poison and subdues pain and poverty.

Dohá 177.

By all means let us follow Ráma to the woods; Bharat

has given good advice ; sinking as we all were in an ocean of despair, you have held out help to us.'

Chaupái.

There was as great joy in the hearts of all as when the *chátak* and peacock hear the sound of thunder. To start to-morrow seemed an excellent resolution ; Bharat was to every one dear as his own life. After reverencing the sage and bowing the head to Bharat, they all took leave and went to their several homes, praising as they went his affectionate disposition, whose life was a blessing to the whole world. Exclaiming to one another, 'what a glorious idea !' they all went to make their preparations. Whoever was left with orders to keep watch at home felt it like his death-stroke, and one would cry : " No one ought to be told to stay : who does not desire life's best reward?

Dohá 178.

Perish property, house, fortune, friends, parents, kinsmen and all, that does not help to bring one to Ráma."

Chaupái.

In every house carriages of all kinds were making ready, and the start to-morrow was a heart-felt joy. Bharat pondered on going home : 'The city, with its horses, elephants palaces and treasuries, and all its wealth, is Ráma's. If I recklessly go and leave it, in the end it will not be good for me ; to injure[1] one's own lord is a crowning sin. A good servant acts for his master's interests, however much others may abuse him." So thinking, he called such faithful servants as would never dream of failing in their duty, and after declaring to them his intention and instructing them in their work, he told them off for the posts for which they were severally fit. When he had thus diligently posted the guards he proceeded to visit Ráma's mother.

Dohá 179.

Understanding the ways of love, he sympathized with a

---

1 *Dohái* here would seem to be not for *duhai*, 'lamentation,' but for *droha*, 'injury.'

mother's anxiety and ordered to be got ready convenient palanquins and seated carriages.

Chaupái.

The men and women of the city like the *chakwa* and *chakwi* were anxious at heart for the dawn, when they might start. The whole night had been spent in watching, when Bharat summoned his wise counsellors and said to them: "Take all materials for the coronation, and there in the forest, sirs, invest Ráma with the sovereignty: start at once." At his word they bowed and speedily made ready horses, carriages and elephants. The king of sages (Vasishtha) first mounted his chariot and led the way with his spouse Arundhati and all the materials for sacrifice. A host of Bráhmans renowned for their asceticism, followed in vehicles of different kinds, and next the citizens on their own conveyances all set forth for Chitra-kút. The elegance of the palanquins in which the different Ránis were seated is beyond description.

Dohá 180.

After making over the city to his faithful servants and ceremoniously starting the procession, Bharat himself with his brother started too, his thoughts fixed on Ráma and Síta.

Chaupái.

All the people were as eager for a sight of Ráma as when a herd of elephants makes a rush for a stream Reflecting within themselves that Síta and Ráma were in exile, Bharat and his brother went on foot. The people were moved by their affection and themselves dismounted and left horses, elephants and carriages. But Ráma's mother stopped her palanquin by his side and softly said: "My son I entreat you to mount your chariot, or all your people will be sufferers; if you walk, they will all walk, and they are so wasted with sorrow that they are not fit for the journey." Obedient to her commands he bowed his head to her feet, and with his brother mounted the chariot. They halted the first day at the Tamasá,[1] and the second on the bank of the Gomati.[2]

Dohá 181.

Out of devotion to Ráma, some vowed to drink only water, some to eat nothing but fruit, others to make only one meal and that at night, and they forswore all luxuries of dress and food.

Chaupái.

After resting at the Sai[3] they started at dawn and drew near to the city of Sringavera.[4] When the Nishád heard the news he thought sadly to himself: "For what reason is Bharat going to the forest? he has some evil design at heart. If he had no wrong intention, why should he bring an army with him? He thinks to kill Ráma and his brother, and then to reign in ease and security. Bharat has not taken to heart the maxims of sound polity; there was disgrace already, and now there will be loss of life. If all the gods and demons were to combine to fight, they would never conquer Ráma in battle. What wonder that Bharat should act thus; fruits of ambrosia do not grow from a poison stock."

Dohá 182.

Having thus reflected, Guha cried to his kinsmen: "Be on the alert, up and sink the boat and close the ferry.

Chaupái.

Make ready and blockade the pass, equip yourselves with every instrument of death. Take up arms against Bharat, and never let him cross the Ganges alive. To die in the battle and on the Ganges bank; in Ráma's cause to lay down this frail body; and mean as I am to join battle

---

1 The Tamasá, 'the dark-coloured' (more commonly spelt Tons) is a branch of the Ghogra (the Sanskrit Gharghara, 'the roaring'), which leaves that river about 10 miles above Ayodhyá, and after passing the town of Azamgarh falls into the Sarju [Sarayu].

2 The Gomati [the name meaning 'rich in cattle'] rises in a lake near Pilibhit, and after a course of 482 miles, in which it passes the cities of Lakhnau, Sultánpur and Jaunpur, falls into the Ganges.

3 The Sai is a river in Audh, which rises about midway between the Gomati and the Ganges, and after a course of some 230 miles falls into the former, 10 miles below the city of Jaunpur.

4 The site of the ancient Sringavera is marked by a village bearing the same name, under the modernized form Sangraur, 22 miles to the north-west of Allahabad. The river has changed its course, and only a small branch now flows through the old channel.

with a king like Bharat; all this is a great gain for me, even if I meet my death. If I war and fight on my lord's behalf, I reap brilliant renown throughout the fourteen spheres. If I lose my life for Ragunáth, I shall have both hands full of luscious sweets. Whoever is not numbered among the just, nor counted among Ráma's votaries, is all the time that he lives only a burden to earth, and an axe at he foot of the tree of his mother's youth."

Dohá 183.

The Nishád king thus fearlessly excited the ardour of his followers, and mindful of Ráma called in haste for quiver and bow and coat of mail.

Chaupái.

"Hasten, brethren, to complete your equipment, and after hearing my command let no one hesitate." All cheerfully responded, "'Tis well, my lord," and mutually encouraged each other's zeal. Bowing again and again before the Nishád all the gallant warriors, eager for the fray, invoking the sandals of Ráma's lotus feet, girt themselves with quiver, slung on the bow, donned their coats of mail, put helmet on head, and furbished up axe and bludgeon and spear – some so expert in the use of shield and sword that they seemed when they sprung into the air as though they had left the earth for good. When each and all had completed their full arrangements, they went and bowed before king Guha. Seeing his gallant warriors so fit and ready, he addressed them each by name with courteous phrase.

Dohá 184.

"Do not play me false, my brethren; this is a great day's work for me." At this they cried with vehemence, "Fear not, captain.

Chaupái.

By Ráma's favour and your might, my lord, we will leave the enemy without a single fighting-man or horse. While life lasts, we will never draw back our foot, and will make the earth one heap of corpses and skulls." When the Nishád lord had inspected his gallant band he cried "Beat the drum for the onset." When he had so said, some one sneezed on the left. The soothsayers exclaimed, "A prosperous issue to the battle!" One old man thought over the omen and said "Bharat must be met, but there will be no fighting. He is going to make entreaty to Ráma, the omen says thus; there will be no battle." On hearing this, Guha said: "The elder has spoken well; fools act in haste and repent. Unless we ascertain Bharat's temper and disposition, we may do ourselves harm by fighting without knowledge.

Dohá 185.

Close up, my men, and stop the pass, and all join to discover the mystery. When we know whether he is a friend, an enemy, or a neutral, we can then lay our plans accordingly.

Chaupái.

We shall soon test his devotion and honest intent; hatred and love are not to be concealed." So saying, he began to make ready a present, and sent for bulbs, roots and fruits, birds and beasts, with the finest of fish, large *páthíns*,[1] which were brought by the fishermen in basketsful. When everything was arranged they went out to meet him, and had the most auspicious omens of good fortune. As soon as he saw the great sage afar off, he declared his name and prostrated himself before him. Vasishtha, knowing him to be a friend of Ráma's, gave him his blessing, and told Bharat about him. He, on hearing that he was Ráma's friend, left his chariot and advanced on foot to meet him with exuberant affection. Guha declared his home and race and name, and making obeisance laid his forehead to the ground.

Dohá 186.

But Bharat, seeing him about to prostrate himself, took him to his bosom with as much uncontrollable rapture as though it were Lakshman he had met.

Chaupái.

Bharat received him with the very greatest affection,

1 The páthín is a kind of she-fish, the *Silurus Pelorius* or *Boalis*.

and the people extolled the manner of his love. There was a jubilant cry of 'Glory, Glory', as the gods applauded and rained down flowers upon him. "Though this man is in every way vile, both by custom of the world and by scriptural prescription, so that contact with his shadow requires ablution, yet Ráma's brother has embraced him in his arms and thrilled all over with delight at meeting him. One who cries 'Ráma, Ráma,' even in a yawn, a multitude of sins will not rise up against him. Here is one whom Ráma had clasped to his bosom and thereby purified him and all his family. If water of the Karmnása falls into the Ganges, tell me who will refuse to reverence it? again, it is known throughout the world that Válmíki was made equal to Bráhma simply for repeating Ráma's name backwards.

Dohá 187.

Even a Chandál,[1] a Savara, a Khasiya, a stupid foreigner, an outcast, a Kol, or a Kirát, by repeating the name of Ráma becomes most holy and renowned throughout the world.

Chaupái.

It is no wonder, it has been so for ages; who is there whom Raghubir cannot exalt?" As the gods told the greatness of Ráma's name, the people of Avadh listened and were glad. Bharat affectionately greeted Ráma's friend and asked him of his health and welfare. At the sight of Bharat's affectionate disposition, the Nishád was at once utterly overpowered; so great was his confusion, his love and his delight, that he could only stand and stare at Bharat. Collecting, himself, he again embraced his feet and with clasped hands made this loving speech: "When I beheld his blessed lotus feet I accounted myself blessed for ever. Now, my lord, by your high favour my prosperity is secured for thousands of generations.

---

1 The word translated 'Chandál' is in the original *Swa-pach* literally 'a dog-cooker,' *i.e.*, either one who feeds on dog's flesh, or who cooks food for dogs 'a dog-keeper.' A Savara is a wild mountaineer. The Khasiya is a native of Khasa, a hill tract in Northern India. The word for 'foreigner' is Jaman, *i.e.*, Yavan, which originally denoted specially a Greek, an Ionian, and then came to mean any foreign barbarian. Accustomed as our ears are to the division of mankind into Greeks, and Barbarians, it is a little strange to find the Greek selected as the typical barbarian.

Dohá 188.

Reflecting on my past deeds and my descent and again considering the greatness of the Lord, any man in the world who adores not the feet of Raghubír must be under supernatural delusion.

Chaupái.

False, cowardly, low-minded and low-born as I am, an utter outcast by the laws both of God and society; since the time that Ráma took me for his own, I have become the glory of the world." After witnessing his devotion and hearing his graceful humility Lakshman's younger brother next embraced him. Then the Nishád introduced himself by name and respectfully saluted the royal dames, who received him even as they would Lakshman and gave him their blessing: "May you live happily for millions of years." The citizens too were as glad to see him as if he had been Lakshman and cried: "Here is one who has lived to some purpose; whom Ráma's our brother has taken to his arms and embraced." When the Nishád heard them thus magnify his good fortune, he was glad at heart as he showed them the way.

Dohá 189.

At a signal all his attendants, having learnt their master's will, went on and made ready tents under the trees and rest-houses by the ponds, gardens and groves.

Chaupái.

When Bharat beheld the city of Sringavera, he was overcome by emotion and was unnerved in very limb. As he leant upon the Nishád, it was as goodly a sight as though embodied Humility and Love had met together. In this manner Bharat with all his army went to see the earth-purifying stream of the Ganges. As he made his obeisance to the ford where Ráma had crossed, he was as entranced as though he had met Ráma himself. The citizens bowing low gazed upon the divine stream with rapture, and after bathing prayed with clasped hands; "May our love to Rámchandra's feet never grow less." Bharat exclaimed:

"Thy sands, O Gangá, are the bestowers of all happiness, the very cow of plenty to thy votaries: with folded hands I beg this boon, unalterable devotion to Síta and Ráma."

Dohá 190.

When Bharat had thus bathed and knew that all his mothers had bathed too, he received the *guru's* permission and took them to their tents.

Chaupái.

Wherever the people had pitched their tents, Bharat took every care of them all. After paying homage to the *guru* and obtaining his permission, the two brothers went to Ràma's mother. Then Bharat, after kissing their feet, with many tender phrases did reverence to all the queens, and having left them to the dutiful care of his brother, went away with the Nishád. Hand-in-hand they went, his body fainting with excess of love, as he begged his companion to show him the spot—that the fierce longing of his eyes and soul might be a little assuaged—where Síta, Ráma and Lakshman had spent the night. As he spoke, his eyes overflowed with tears, and the Nishád in great distress at his speech led him at once to the place,

Dohá 191.

where Raghubar had rested under the sacred *sinsipa* tree. With great reverence and devotion Bharat postrated himself.

Chaupái.

When he spied the delectable grassy couch, he again made obeisance and reverently paced round it. He put upon his eyes the dust of the foot-prints, with an enthusiasm of devotion beyond all telling. And seeing two or three golden spangles, he placed them upon his head as relics of Síta. With streaming eyes and aching heart he thus in gentle tones addressed his companion: "They are dim and lustreless through Síta's absence, and all the people of Avadh are equally woe-begone. To whom can I compare her father, Janak, who was conversant at once with all life's pleasures and all philosophy? Her father-in-law, the sun-like monarch of the solar race, was the envy of even the lord of heaven. Her husband is the beloved Raghunáth, by whose greatness alone it is that any one is great.

Dohá 192.

I gaze on the couch of Síta, that devoted wife, that jewel of good women, and my heart breaks not with agitation; surely it is harder than a thunderbolt.

Chaupái.

Lakshman so young and comely and made to be fondled; never was there such a brother, nor is there, nor will be: so beloved by the people, the darling of his father and mother, and dear as their own life to Ráma and Síta; the picture of delicacy, the daintiest of striplings, whose body has never been exposed to the hot wind, how can he bear the hardships of the forest? O my heart would shame for hardness a million thunderbolts! Ráma at his birth was the light of the world, an ocean of beauty, of virtue, and all good qualities. Ráma's amiability was the delight of his subjects, his household, his *guru*, his father and mother, and all. Even enemies would praise Ráma: his courtesy of speech and manner stole every heart. Not a million Sarasvatis, not a hundred million Seshnágs, could reckon up all my lord's virtues.

Dohá 193.

The image of bliss, the jewel of the family of Raghu, the storehouse of all auspicious delights, slept on the ground on this littered grass: how wonderful are the ways of Providence!

Chaupái.

Ráma had never heard mention of pain, the king cherished him like the tree of life, and day and night all his mothers guarded him as the eyelids guard the eyes, and as a serpent guards the jewel in its head. And now he is roaming on foot through the woods, with nothing to eat but wild roots and fruits. A curse on thee, Kaikeyi, root of all evil, thou hast undone my best beloved : cursed be my wretched self, that ocean of iniquity, on whose account all these calamities have come to pass. God created me to disgrace my family, and my wicked mother has made me the ruin of my lord." Hearing these words the Nishád affectionately implored him : " Why, my lord, make these vain laments ? Ráma is dear to you, and you are dear to Ráma ; even she is blameless : the blame rests with adverse fate.

Chhand 8.

The ways of adverse fate are cruel ; it has made your mother mad. That every night Ráma again and again broke out into respectful praise of you. There is no one so dearly beloved by Ráma as you. I declare this on oath : be assured that all will be well in the end, and take comfort to your soul.

Sorathá 7

Ráma is omniscient, full of meekness, tenderness and compassion ; of this make firm assurance in your heart ; and come, take rest."

Chaupái.

Hearing his companion's speech he took comfort and with his thoughts directed to Raghubír went to his tent. When the citizens were informed, heavy with woe they too came to see. Having reverently paced around, they made obeisance and cursed Kaikeyi to their hearts' content. Their eyes streamed with tears as they reproached the cruelty of fate. One would praise Bharat for his devotion, another would say the king had sown the greatest love ; they reproached themselves and praised the Nishád : who can describe their agitation and distress ? In this manner they all kept watch throughout the night and at daybreak began the passage. First the *guru* was put on a fine handsome boat, and then all the queens on another boat newly built. In an hour and a half all had crossed over ; as they came to land Bharat took count of them all.

Dohá 194.

After performing his morning rites and reverencing his

mother's feet and bowing the head to the *guru*, he sent the Nishâds on ahead and started the host.

Chaupái.

He made the Nishád king lead the van and started all the queens in their palanquins. He charged his younger brother with their escort, and made the *guru* go with the Bráhmans. He himself bowed reverently to the Ganges, and invoking Ráma, Síta and Lakshman, set forth on foot, while his horse was led by the bridle. Again and again his faithful servants cried : " Be pleased, my lord, to mount your horse." " Ráma," he answered, " has gone on foot, and are chariots, elephants and horses made for me ? It would be right for me to walk on my head ; a servant's work should always be the hardest." When they saw his behaviour and heard his tender speech, all his servants melted away for pity.

Dohá 195.

At the third watch of the day Bharat entered Prayág, crying ' O Ráma, Síta ; Ráma, Síta ! ' with irrepressible affection.

Chaupái.

The blisters on his feet glistened like drops of dew on a lotus bud. The whole company were distressed, when they heard that Bharat had made the day's march on foot. After ascertaining that all the people had bathed, he went and did homage to the threefold stream. All who had dipped in the parti-coloured flood gave alms and did honour to the Bráhmans. As Bharat gazed on the commingling of the dark and white waves, his body throbbed with emotion and he clasped his hands in prayer : " O queen of the holy places, bounteous of every blessing, whose power is declared in the Vedas and renowned throughout the world, I abandon my proper calling and make myself a beggar : is there anything so vile that a man in distress will not do it ? As I know you to be all-wise and beneficent, accomplish the prayer of thy suppliant.

Dohá 196.

I crave not wealth nor religious merit, nor voluptuous delights, nor deliverance from transmigration; but only that in every new birth I may persevere in love to Ráma; this is the boon I beg, and nought else.

Chaupái.

Ráma knows my wickedness; the people call me the ruin of my lord and master; through your favour may my devotion to the feet of Síta and Ráma increase more and more every day. Though the cloud neglects her all her life, and while she begs for rain, casts down upon her thunder and hail, yet were the *chatak* to cease her importunity, she would be despised; she perseveres in her affection, and is much honoured. Again, as the quality of gold is refined by the fire, so may my vow to the feet of my beloved endure through all tribulation." In answer to Bharat's speech there came a soft and auspicious voice from the midst of the Tribeni: "Son Bharat, you are altogether upright; your love to Ráma's feet is unfathomable; you distress yourself without cause; there is no one so dear to Ráma as you are."

Dohá 197.

As he heard the river's gracious speech, Bharat's body quivered with heartfelt gladness; the heaven resounded with shouts of applause, and the gods rained down flowers.

Chaupái.

The inhabitants of Prayág, aged anchorites and boy students, householders and celibates, were all enraptured and said to one another as they met in groups: "Bharat's affection and amiability are thoroughly genuine." Still hearing of Ráma's many charming qualities, Bharat approached the great saint Bharadváj. When the saint saw him prostrate himself upon the ground, he looked upon him as his own good angel incarnate, and ran and raised him up and took him to his arms and gave him the blessing he desired, and made him sit down. He bowed his head and sat, shrinking into the inmost recesses of shamefacedness; greatly distrest lest the saint should ask any question. Seeing his confusion the saint said: "Hearken, Bharat; I have heard everything; God's doings are beyond our power.

Dohá 198.

Be not distrest at heart by the thought of what your mother has done. Son, it is no fault of Kaikeyi's; it was Sarasvati who stole away her senses.

Chaupái

If you say thus, 'No one will excuse me;' I reply, Scripture and the practice of the world are both accepted as authorities by the wise; and your glory, my son, will be sung unsullied, while the Veda and custom will both be honoured, for every one admits that this is according both to custom and the Veda that he takes the throne to whom his father gives it. The truthful king summoned you to confer upon you the honour of sovereignty and its higher duties. Ráma's banishment is a monstrous wrong, which the whole world is grieved to hear of: but the queen was demented by the power of Fate, and in the end she has repented of the evil she has done. You are not the least in fault; whoever says you are is a vile and ignorant wretch. Had you reigned, it would have been no sin, and Ráma would have been pleased to hear of it.

Dohá 199.

But now, Bharat, you have done still better; your present purpose is excellent; devotion to the feet of Raghubar is the root of every blessing in the world.

Chaupái.

This is your wealth and the very breath of your life; is there any one with good fortune equal to yours? Nor, my son, is it strange that you should act thus; you are a son of Dasarath's and Ráma's own brother. Hearken, Bharat; in Raghupati's heart there is no one upon whom so much love is lavished as upon you. Lakshman, Ráma and Síta are all most fond of you ; they spent the whole night in your praises. I learnt their secret when they came here to Prayág to bathe; they were overwhelmed with love for you. Raguhbar has as great affection for you as a fool has for a life of pleasure. And this is no great credit to Raghurái, who cherishes all his suppliants and their kin ; while you, Bharat, as it seems to me, are the very incarnation of love to him.

Dohá 200.

That which seems a reproach[1] to you, Bharat, is a lesson to all of us ; it is an event which inaugurates a new flood of passionate devotion.

Chaupái.

Your glory, my son, is a newly created and spotless moon ; its lotuses and partridges are Ráma's servants ; it is ever rising and never sets, nor wanes in the world its heaven, but increases day by day ; the three spheres, like the *chakwas* are exceedingly enamoured of it, and the sun of Ráma's majesty never robs it of splendour, but by day as well as night it is ever bountiful to all, and Kaikey's evil deeds cannot eclipse it. Full of the nectar of devotion to Ráma, and unsullied by any stain for wrong done to the *guru*,[2] you are saturated with the nectar of faith, and have brought this nectar within the reach of the whole world. King

1 Your disobedience to the wishes of your mother and the commands of your *guru* in refusing to accept the throne.

2 There is a popular legend that Vrihaspati, the *guru* of the gods, on one occasion when he returned from his bath in the Ganges, found his wife in the embraces of the Moon-god. He was not able to seize the adulterer, but threw his dripping bathing robe at him and hit him in the face, thus causing the spots that are still to be seen there. Throughout this stanza Bharat's glory is compared to a newly-created moon, which is in every respect superior to the ordinary moon which we see in the heavens. The one sets and wanes, the other is always on the increase ; the one mainly delights only lotuses and partridges, the other is the joy of Ráma's faithful servants ; the one shines only by night, the other by day as well ; the one yields nectar, it is true, but none can get at it ; the other is impregnated with the nectar of faith, which is brought within the reach of all ; the one is branded with the marks of Vrihaspati's indignation, the other is spotless ; though Bharat too offended his *guru* by refusing to reign at his command, the one is stamped only with the figure of a hare [the man in the moon of European nurseries], the other is inscribed with love to Ràma.

Bhagiratha brought down the Ganges,[1] whose invocation is a mine of all prosperity; but Dasarath's virtues are past all telling ; why say more ? He has no equal in the world.

Dohá 201.

Through his devotion and humility Ráma was made manifest, whom the eyes of Siva's heart are never wearied of beholding.

Chaupái.

You have created an incomparable moon of glory, in which for the figure of the hare is stamped love to Ráma. Cease, my son, from lamentation ; you have found the philosopher's stone and yet fear poverty ! Hearken, Bharat ; I tell no falsehood ; a hermit and ascetic dwelling in the forest, I obtained a glorious reward for all my good deeds when I beheld Ráma, Síta and Lakshman ; the fruit of that fruit is the sight of you : Prayág and I are both highly favoured. Bharat, I congratulate you ; you have achieved universal renown." So saying the saint was overwhelmed with emotion. As they hearkened to his words, the whole assembly rejoiced ; the gods applauded his goodness and rained down flowers. Shouts of 'Glory, Glory,' resounded in heaven and in Prayág ; Bharat was lost in rapture at the sound.

Dohá 202.

With quivering body, with his heart full of Ráma and Síta, and his lotus eyes flowing with tears, he bowed to the saintly assembly and thus spoke in faltering accents :

Chaupái.

" In a conclave of saints and in this so holy a place, truth must needs be spoken ; any oath is superfluous and vain if in such a spot I were to say anything false, no sin or vileness would equal mine. You are all-wise, and

---

1 Bhagiratha, the son of king Dilípa, after a thousand years spent in austerities, brought down the Ganges from heaven to earth, and with its vivifying flood watered and restored to life the ashes of the sixty thousand sons of his great-grandfather, Sagara, who had been destroyed by the Rishi Kapila. This was a great achievement, but Dasarath's was a greater, by whom Ráma was begotten into the world.

therefore I speak honestly; Ráma, too, knows the secrets of the heart. I am not grieved for what my mother has done, nor pained at heart lest the world deem me caitiff. I have no dread of the loss of heaven, no sorrow for my father's death, whose good deeds and renown are glorious all the world over, who had such sons as Lakshman and Ráma, and who, as soon as he lost Ráma dropt his fragile body; why make long mourning for the king? But Ráma, Lakshman and Síta, without shoes to their feet, in hermit's dress, are wandering from wood to wood;

Dohá 203.

clad in deer-skins, feeding on wild fruits, sleeping on the ground on a litter of grass and leaves, under trees, ever exposed to the inclemency of cold and heat and rain and wind.

Chaupái.

This is the burning pain that is ever consuming my breast, so that I cannot eat by day nor sleep by night. For this sore disease there is no remedy; I have searched in mind the whole world over. My mother's evil counsel, the root of all calamity, like a carpenter fashioned an axe out of my advantage, made a handle of the ill-wood of Resentment, and fixed the term of banishment as it were a horrible spell. To me she applied this infamous contrivance and has hurled me down in wide-spreading ruin. These disasters will cease when Ráma returns to live in Avadh; there is no other remedy." When the saints heard Bharat's speech, they were glad and all gave him high praise: "Son, grieve not so sorely: at the sight of Ráma's feet all sorrow will pass away."

Dohá 204.

The great saints comforted him and said: "Be our welcome guest: accept such herbs and roots and fruits as we can offer, and be content."

Chaupái.

On hearing the saints' words Bharat was troubled at heart: the time was not one for feasting, and yet he was very loth to decline. At last, reflecting that a *guru's* command is imperative, he kissed his feet and replied with clasped hands : "I must needs bow to your behest, for this, my lord, is my highest duty." The great saint was pleased at Bharat's words and called up all his trusty servants : "An entertainment must be provided for Bharat : go and gather herbs, roots and fruits." They bowed the head and said 'Certainly, my lord,' and gladly set about each his own work. But the saint thought to himself : "I have invited a distinguished guest, who should be treated like a god." At his command Animá and the other good Fairies came : "What are your orders, master, and we obey."

Dohá 205.

"Bharat and his brother and all their host are distrest by the loss of Ráma ; show them hospitality and ease them of their toil ;" thus cheerily spoke the great saint.

Chaupái.

The Fairies bowed to his commands and thought themselves most highly favoured, saying one to another : Ráma's brother is indeed a guest beyond compare." Then kissing the saint's feet, "To-day we will do such things that the whole of the king's party shall be pleased." So saying, a number of such charming pavilions were erected, that the equipages of the gods were put out of countenance at the sigh of them. They were furnished with so much luxury and magnificence that the immortals beheld them longingly. Men-servants and maid-servants with every appliance were in attendance and gave their whole mind to their work. In an instant of time the Fairies completed all the arrangements though no dream of heaven was ever so beautiful. First the people were assigned their quarters, all bright and pleasant and in accordance with their taste.

Dohá 206.

Then, as the saint had ordered, Bharat and his family had theirs assigned them, which astonished even the Creator by their magnificence; so great the power of the holy ascetic's penance.

Chaupái.

When Bharat beheld the saint's power, the realms of all the rulers of the spheres seem to him as trifles. The luxuries that had been prepared cannot be described; any philosopher would forget his self-restraint on seeing them. Thrones, couches, drapery and canopies; groves and gardens; birds and beasts; sweet-scented flowers, fruits like nectar, and many a lake of limpid water; with luscious food and drinks of innumerable kinds, so that the people were quite put out of countenance by what they saw, as though they had been ascetics. Each one had as it were his own cow of plenty and tree of paradise. Indra and Sachi grew covetous at the sight. The season, spring; the air soft, cool, and fragrant; all the great objects of life ready at hand: garlands, perfumes, dancing-girls and delights of every kind to charm and astonish the spectator.

Dohá 207.

Affluence, like the *chakwi*,[1] and Bharat as her mate, by compulsion of the saint's order were prisoned together that night, as by a fowler, in the cage of the hermitage, till dawn broke.

Chaupái.

Then he bathed at the holy place and with his host bowed the head to the sage. Having submissively received his commands and blessing, he prostrated himself and made much supplication. Then taking guides well acquainted with the road, he set out resolutely for Chitrakút; supported on the arm of Ráma's friend, he seemed, as

1 According to Hindu belief the *chakwa* and his female mate, the *chakwi*, are doomed for ever to nocturnal separation. Even though they may be caught and imprisoned together in one cage they cannot enjoy each other's society till the break of day. In the same way Bharat, though detained for the night by the saint's order at the hermitage in the midst of luxury, could not enjoy it by reason of his vow. Válmiki represents him as less abstemious, and, in describing the banquet, makes mention of wine and flesh meat of various kinds—venison, wild boar, peafowl and partridges—all of which Tulsi Dás has omitted in concession to modern prejudices.

he went, the very incarnation of Love. With no shoes and no shelter for his head, in the fulfilment of his loving vow and his unfeigned intagrity, he asked his companion for a history of the wanderings of Ráma, Síta and Lakshman. In soothing accents he told it. When he saw the tree where Ráma had rested, his heart could not contain its emotion. At the sight of his condition, the gods rained down flowers, and the path that he trod grew smooth and pleasant.

Dohá 208.

" The clouds afford him shade and the air breathes soft and refreshingly : Ráma's road was not thus, as it is now for Bharat.

Chaupái.

All created things, whether living or lifeless, that saw the Lord, or were seen by him, were rendered fit for salvation, and the sight of Bharat has now healed them of the curse of transmigration ! This is no great thing for Bharat, whom Ráma is mindful to remember. A single mention of the name of Ráma on earth makes a man safe and a saviour of others But Bharat is Ráma's beloved and own brother ; why should he not bring a blessing on the road he treads ? As saints, sages and hermits thus reasoned and gazed upon Bharat, they rejoiced at heart. Indra was troubled by the sight of his power : " In the world things turn out well for the good and badly for the bad." Then turning to his *guru* (Vrihaspati), "Something must be done, sir, to prevent the meeting between Ráma and Bharat.

Dohá 209.

Ráma is so modest and sympathetic, and Bharat such an ocean of affection ; our scheme threatens to be spoilt ; we must bestir ourselves and devise some new stratagem."

Chaupái.

Hearing the speech, the teacher of the gods smiled, to find the thousand-eyed so blind, and said : " Leave tricks alone ; it will be all trouble in vain ; any deception here would be absurd. O king of heaven, any delusion practised on a servant of the lord of delusion must recoil on the contriver. I interfered once, knowing it was Ráma's wish, but any underhand work now would only do harm. Listen, O king: it is Ráma's nature never to be angry at any sin against himself, but whoever sins against one of his servants is consumed in the fire of his wrath. Popular tradition and the Vedas abound in such legends; Durvásas[1] knows well this great trait in his character. And is there any one so faithful to Ráma as Bharat, who is ever repeating Ráma's name and Ráma his?

Dohá 210.

Think not, lord of the immortals, to injure any servant of Raghubar's, unless you would suffer the pain of disgrace in this world, sorrow in the next, and a daily increasing burden of regret.

Chaupái.

Hearken to my advice, king of the gods: Ráma has the greatest love for his servants; he is pleased at any service done to a servant, while enmity to a servant is the height of enmity to himself. Although he is ever the same, without either passion or anger, and contracts neither sin nor merit, virtue nor defect; and though he has made fate the sovereign of the universe, and every one has to taste the fruit of his own actions, still he plays at variations according as hearts are faithful or unfaithful. Though without attributes or form, illimitable and impossible, Ráma has yielded to the love of his followers and taken a material form. He has always regarded the wishes of his servants, as the Vedas and Puránas and gods and saints bear witness. Knowing this, refrain from naughtiness and show fitting devotion.

Dohá 211.

Any worshipper of Ráma is zealous for the good of others, sorrows with the sorrowful, and is full of compassion;

[1] King Ambarísha was a devout worshipper of Vishnu [with whom Ráma is here identified] and thereby excited the jealousy of the irascible sage Durvásas, the most intolerant of all the adherents of Siva. On some trivial pretext he cursed the king, who at once fell senseless to the ground, but Vishnu was ready at hand to succour his faithful follower and sent his fiery discus upon Durvasas, which chased him all over the world and up into heaven, where the gods said nothing could be done for him till he went back and humbly begged pardon of Ambarísha.

then fear not Bharat, O king, who is the crown of worshippers.

Chaupái.

The lord is an ocean of truth and a well-wisher of the gods, and Bharat obeys his orders. You are troubled by your own selfishness ; there is no fault in Bharat : it is a delusion on your part.[1] " When the great god heard the words of the heavenly preceptor he got understanding and his anxiety passed away. In his joy he rained down flowers and began to extol Bharat's good qualities. In this manner Bharat went on his way, while saints and sages looked and praised. Whenever he sighed Ráma's name, it seemed like the bubbling over of love. Thunderbolts and stones melted at his words ; as for the people, their emotion is beyond description. Encamping half-way, he came to the Jamuná, and as he gazed on its water his eyes filled with tears.

Dohá 212.

As he and his retinue gazed on the lovely stream, the colour of Ráma's body, he was plunged into a sea of desolation, till he climbed the boat of discretion.

Chaupái.

That day he halted on the bank of the Jamuná, giving every one time for what they had to do. In the night boats came from all the ghâts in greater number than could be counted. At daybreak all crossed in a single trip. The good service of Ráma's companion pleased him greatly. After bathing and bowing to the river, he again set forth with the Nishád king and Satrughna. First of all in his glorious car went the great saint, followed by all the royal host; after them the two brothers on foot; their dress, apparel and ornaments all of the very simplest. With them their servants and friend and the Minister's son, invoking Lakshman, Sita and Ráma. Any spot wherever Ráma had encamped or rested they lovingly saluted.

1 In the Sanskrit poem there is nothing that corresponds to this colloquy between Indra and Vrihaspati. It is introduced by Tulsi Dás a peg on which to hang a theological exposition.

Dohá 213.

At the news, the dwellers by the roadside left their household work and ran after them ; seeing his form, they were overcome with love and joy and had their life's reward.

Chaupái.

Lovingly one said to another : " Friend, are they Ráma and Lakshman, or not ? In age, figure, complexion and beauty they are the same, dear girl, and resemble them in an equally affectionate disposition. But their dress is not the same, friend, nor is Síta with them, and before them marches a vast host of horse and foot, elephants and chariots. Nor are they glad of countenance, but have some sorrow at heart ; from this difference, friend, a doubt arises." The women were persuaded by her arguments and cried : "There is no one so clever as you." After praising her and admiring the truth of her remarks, another woman spoke in winning tones, and lovingly related the whole history, how Ráma had lost the delights of empire ; and again set to praising Bharat for his affectionate disposition and happy nature.

Dohá 214.

" He travels on foot, feeding only on wild fruits, and abandoning the crown given him by his father, is going to Ráma to persuade him to return ; is there any one at the present day like Bharat ?

Chaupái.

To tell and hear of Bharat's brotherly devotion and his course of action dispels all sin and sorrow. Anything that I can say, friend, is all too little ; he is Ráma's brother ; how could he be different from what he is ? All of us who have seen him and Satrughna have truly become blessed among women." Hearing his virtues and seeing his forlorn state they lamented : " He is not a fit son for such a mother as Kaikeyi." One said : " It is no blame to the queen that God has been so kind to us. What are we, outcasts from the world and the Veda, women of low birth and mean livelihood, whose home is a wretched hovel in some poor village of this miserable country, that we should have such a vision, a sufficient reward for the highest religious merit?" There was the same delight and wonder in every town, as though the tree of paradise had sprung up in the desert.

Dohá 215.

At the sight of Bharat, the good fortune of the people by the wayside manifested itself in like manner, as though by the will of providence Prayág had been made accessible to the people of Lanká.

Chaupái.

Hearing these praises of his own and Ràma's many virtues, he went on his way, ever mindful of Raghunáth. Whenever he spied any holy place, or hermitage, or temple, he bathed and reverently saluted it, praying in his heart of hearts for this one boon, perseverance in devotion to the feet of Síta and Ráma. If there met him a Kirát, or Kol, or other dweller in the woods, anchorite or student, hermit or ascetic, whoever he might be, he saluted him and asked in what part of the forest were Lakshman, Ráma and the Vid ehan princess. They told him all the news of the lord, and at the sight of Bharat reaped their life's reward. If any person said 'We have seen them well,' they were counted as dear as Ráma and Lakshman themselves. In this manner asking courteously of every one, he heard the whole story of Ráma's forest life.

Dohá 216.

Halting that day, Bharat started again at dawn, invoking Raghunáth: all who were with him being equally desirous with himself for a sight of Ráma.

Chaupái.

Every one had auspicious omens; lucky throbbings in the eyes and arm; Bharat and the host rejoiced, "Ráma will be found and our sore distress will be at an end." Each indulged his own fancy, and as they marched all seemed intoxicated with the wine of love, their limbs relaxed, their feet unsteady on the ground, and the accents of their voice inarticulate from excess of emotion. Then was the time that Ráma's guide pointed out the monarch of mountains in all its beauty, near which on the river's bank the two heroes and Síta were dwelling. All at the sight fell to the ground with cries of 'Glory to Ráma, the life of Jánaki!' The royal host was as overwhelmed with emotion as though Ráma had come back to Avadh.

Dohá 217.

Bharat's love at that time was such that not Seshnág could describe it: it is as far beyond the poet as the bliss of heaven is beyond a man stained by selfishness and sensuality.

Chaupái.

Being all unmanned by their love for Raghubar, they had gone but two *kos* by the close of day, then scanning land and water they halted. When the night was past, the beloved of Raghunáth sallied forth again. On the other hand Ráma while it was yet dark, awoke, and Síta told him what she had seen in a dream: "Methought Bharat had come with an army, being tortured in body by the fever of separation from his lord; all were sad, wretched and downcast, and the queens consort were greatly altered." On hearing Síta's dream, the healer of sorrows grew sorrowful and his eyes filled with tears: "This dream, Lakshman, bodes no good: we shall hear of something that we by no means wished." So saying, he and his brother bathed, worshipped Purári and propitiated the saints.

Chhand 9.

After propitiating the gods and reverencing the saints, the lord went and sat down with his gaze to the north. The dust in the air and the many birds and deer taking to flight disquieted him and he returned to the hermitage. He stood up and looked, anxious in mind as to the cause. Then came Kiráts and Kols and told him all the news.

Sorathá 7.

When he heard the glad tidings his heart was full of joy and his body quivered all over: white his eyes, like the autumnal lotus, were filled with the moisture of affection,

Chaupái.

Again Síta's lord became anxious: 'What can be the cause of Bharat's coming?' Then came one and said: 'There is with him no small army in full equipment.' Hearing this, Ráma was greatly disturbed; on the one hand was his father's injunction, on the other his regard for his brother. Thinking to himself over Bharat's disposition, the lord's mind found no sure standing-point; but at last he calmed himself with the reflection: 'Bharat is said to be good and sensible.' Lakshman saw that his lord was troubled at heart, and spoke out as he thought the occasion demanded: "I speak, sire, before I am asked; but sometimes impertinence in a servant is not impertinent. You, master, are the crown of the wise; I a mere retainer, but I say what I think.

Dohá 218.

You, my lord, are kind and easy, a storehouse of amiability; you love and trust every one, and think them all like yourself.

Chaupái.

A worldly man, who has got power, becomes mad and infatuated and so betrays himself. Bharat was well-taught, good and clever, and, as every one knew, was devoted to his lord's feet; but now that he has become king, he breaks down in his course all the bounds of duty. A wicked and ill-disposed brother having spied out his time, and knowing that Ráma is alone in the forest, he has taken evil counsel and equipt an army, and has come to make his sovereignty secure. After plotting all sorts of wicked schemes, the two brothers have assembled their army and come. If he had no treacherous malpractice at heart, why should he affect chariots and horses and elephants? But why reproach Bharat? all the world goes mad on getting dominion.

Dohá 219.

The Moon-god debauched his *guru's* wife: Nahusha mounted a palanquin borne by Bráhmans; and who fell so low as Vena, the enemy of established usage and the Veda?

Chaupái.

Sahasra-báhu, Indra, Trisanku; all were brought to disgrace by the intoxication of kingly power.[1] Bharat has planned this clever scheme, so as not to leave himself a single enemy in the field; but in one point he has made a mistake, in despising Ráma as if he had no friends; he will discover this to-day with a vengeance, when he sees Ráma's indignant face in the battle." So saying, he forgot all prudence, and his whole body, so to speak, bristled with pugnacity. Falling at his lord's feet and putting the dust of them upon his head, he cried in tones of natural and honest vehemence: "My lord, think it not wrong of me; Bharat has tried me not a little; how long shall I endure to remain quiet, my lord being with me and my bow in my hand?

---

1 The pride of kings and its ruinous results are here illustrated by reference to six famous mythological personages. The first is the great Moon-god, who in the wantonness of power robbed his own spiritual instructor, Vrihaspati, of his bride Tàrà, and had by her a son named Budha, the regent of the planet Mercury. Of this legend mention has already been made in a note after *dohá* 201. For punishment, he bears for ever in his face the marks of the brand set upon him by the injured husband.

NAHUSHA was the grandson of Purú-ravas, the founder of the lunar race of kings, who reigned at Pratishthána on the Ganges opposite Prayág. When Indra had temporarily abdicated his throne in heaven Nahusha was selected to fill it. But not satisfied with this dignity, he demanded also Indra's queen. She agreed to receive him, if he came to her in a pàlki borne by Bráhmans. At his request the seven great Rishis agreed to do him this service. But he was so inflamed with arrogance and lust that they could not walk fast enough for him, and at last, disgusted with his violence and abuse, they threw down the pàlki and cursed him and he was turned into a serpent.

VENA, the son of Anga, as soon as he had been proclaimed monarch of the whole world, forbade any gifts to be given to Bràhmans or sacrifice offered to the gods, for that he was sole lord of all and none else was entitled to worship. The holy sages implored him to desist from such impiety, but he would not listen to them. They then struck him with the light blades of grass that had been consecrated by their prayers, and he immediately fell dead.

KARTAVIRYA was a mighty conqueror, who, among other boons granted him by the sage Dattatreya, obtained also this one, that he should have a thousand arms; whence he is here called Sahasra-bàhu. One day, when out hunting in the woods, he was hospitably entertained by Jamadagni in his hermitage. But instead of making any proper return for this kindness, he carried off his host's sacrificial cow. Jamadagni's son, Parasuràm, was away at the time, but when he returned and heard of what had been done, he followed after kàrtavirya and cut off his thousand arms and slew him. The king's sons, to avenge their father's death, attacked Jamadagni in his hermitage; and in consequence of this, Parasurám made his famous vow to extirpate the whole Kshatriya race.

INDRA, the king of heaven, became enamoured of Ahalyà, the wife of

Dohá 220.

Am I not of warrior descent, a scion of the house of Raghu, and known throughout the world as Ráma's brother? What is so low as the dust? Yet if stirred by a kick it rises and falls upon your head." [1]

Chaupái.

As he stood with clasped hands and sought permission, he seemed like Heroism itself aroused from slumber, binding up his hair in a knot, girding on his quiver by his side, trimming his bow, and taking arrows in hand. "To-day I shall distinguish myself as Ráma's servant and will give Bharat a lesson in fighting. Reaping the fruit of their contempt for Ráma, both brothers shall sleep on the couch of battle. It is well that the whole host has come; to-day I shall manifest my wrath and have done with it. As a lion tears in pieces a herd of elephants, or as a hawk clutches and carries off a quail, so will I lightly overthrow upon the field Bharat and his brother and all their host. If Siva himself should come to their aid, in Ráma's name I would worst him in battle."

Dohá 221.

Lakshman spoke so furiously that the regents of the

---

the sage Gautama, and visited her disguised as her husband. The sage saw him as he left her room and cursed him with perpetual loss of virility. Ahalyà was changed into a stone till Ràma should come and deliver her, see Book I. pp. 21, 145.

TRISANKU was a king of Ayodhyá, who in his pride aspired to celebrate a great sacrifice and by its merit ascend to heaven in person. He first requested Vasishtha to conduct the ceremony; but the saint saw through his motives and refused him. He then applied to Vasishtha's sons, but they, thinking that he only wished to bring about a quarrel between them and their father, cursed him, so that he became a Chandàl. While in this low estate he killed Vasishtha's cow; and for these three sins, pride, mischief-making, and cow-killing, three great horns grew out of his forehead. He then put himself under the protection of Visvamitra, who engaged to perform the sacrifice and invited all the gods to it They, however, declined to come; whereupon Visvamitra created new gods, completed the sacrifice, and translated Trisanku to the skies. But no sooner had he arrived there than the gods hurled him down again: and falling headlong he was suspended midway, where he is still to be seen, as the constellation in the southern hemisphere called Trisanku. The saliva that dropped from his mouth forms the river Karmnàsà, which flows between Banàras and Bihàr and which it is considered a pollution to touch.

1 The general meaning of the passage would seem to be: Bharat has given such provocation that the meanest creature in the world would resent it; much more should I, who am a warrior by birth.

spheres, beholding and hearing his solemn oath, looked on in terror and longed to flee away.

Chaupái.

The world was entranced ; a voice was heard in the air, declaring the mighty power of Lakshman's arm : "Son, who can tell, or who can understand your might and majesty? but any business, whether right or wrong, should be done deliberately ; so every one agrees. They who act rashly and afterwards repent, the Vedas say are anything but wise." On hearing this voice from heaven Lakshman was abashed, and both Ráma and Síta addressed him courteously : "What you have said, brother, is sound wisdom : the intoxication of power is the worst of all : the merest taste of it maddens any king who has not been trained in the school of philosophy. But hearken, Lakshman ; in the whole of God's creation I have never seen nor heard of any one so good as Bharat.

Dohá 222.

He would never be intoxicated with power, even though he sat upon the throne of Bráhman, Vishnu and Siva. What ! can a few drops of *kánji* curdle the milky ocean ?

Chaupái.

The sun may grow dim at midday ; yea, sooner may the pure ether be absorbed in cloud ; sooner may Agastya[1] be drowned in the puddle of a cow's footprint, or earth forget to be long-suffering ; sooner may the buzz of a mosquito puff away Mount Meru, than kingly pride, my brother, touch Bharat. O Lakshman, I swear by you and by our father, there is none so true a brother as Bharat. The Creator has fashioned the world by mixing the milk of goodness with the water of evil ; Bharat is the swan in the lake of the Solar race, who from the day of his birth has known to distinguish between the good and the evil ; choosing the milk of goodness and discarding the water of evil, he has illumined the whole world with his glory." As Raghurài thus recited Bharat's virtues and amiable disposition, he became drowned in a sea of love.

---

1 Who swallowed up the ocean.

Dohá 223.

The gods, hearing his speech and seeing his affection for Bharat, all applauded Ráma, saying: "Who so compassionate as the Lord?

Chaupái.

If Bharat had not been born into the world, who was there on earth to be the champion of all right? Bharat's good qualities are more than all the poets could describe; who save you, Raghunath, could comprehend them?" When Lakshman, Ráma and Síta heard these words of the gods they were more glad than can be told. Now Bharat and all his host bathed in the sacred Mandákini. Then leaving the people on the bank and having asked permission from his mother, his *guru* and the Minister, he set out to visit Síta and Raghurai with the Nishád king and his brother. As he thought upon his mother's deeds he was abashed, and formed a thousand ill-conjectures in his mind: "What if Ráma, Lakshman and Síta, on hearing my name, should leave the place and go elsewhere?

Dohá 224.

Taking me to be my mother's accomplice, nothing that he might do would be too much. If, again, he overlooks my sin and folly, and receives me kindly as his well-wisher;

Chaupái.

whether he spurns me as a black-hearted wretch, or welcomes me as his servant, my only refuge is at Ráma's feet; he is the best of masters, the fault is all his servants. The *chátak* and the fish are celebrated throughout the world for the thoroughness and constancy of their vows of love." With these thoughts in his mind he went on his way, his whole body rendered powerless by excessive love and trepidation; his mother's sin, as it were, turning him back, while his strong faith, like some sturdy bull, dragged him forward. Whenever he thought of Ráma's good nature, his feet moved swiftly along the way; his course was like that of a water-fly carried about by the stream. Seeing Bharat's anxiety and affection, the Nishád was transported out of himself.

Dohá 225.

Auspicious omens began to occur, and the Nishád after hearing them and making a calculation said : " Sorrow will pass away, joy will succeed ; but in the end there will be distress again."

Chaupái.

Knowing his servant's words to be all true, he went on and drew near to the hermitage. When Bharat saw the vast woods and rocks, he was as glad as a hungry wretch on getting a good meal. Like people afflicted by every calamity,[1] worn out with troubles,[2] ill-fortune and pestilence, who rejoice on escaping to a prosperous and well-governed country, so were Bharat's feelings. The forest where Ráma dwelt was as bright and happy as people are happy who have got a good king ; with Asceticism for King Wisdom's Minister of State ; with the beautiful and sacred groves for his realm ; with Continence and Faithfulness for champions, and the rocks for his capital ; with Peace and Good-will for his virtuous and lovely queens ; a king perfect at all points ; a suppliant at Ráma's feet, and therefore easy in mind,

Dohá 226.

Royal Wisdom, having conquered King Delusion with all his host, held undisputed sway in his capital : all was joy, happiness, and prosperity.

Chaupái.

The frequent hermits' cells about the woods were his cities, towns, villages and hamlets ; the many birds and beasts of all descriptions were his innumerable subjects. The hares, elephants, lions, tigers, boars, buffaloes and wolves, a wonder to behold, forgetting their antipathies, grazed together, like a duly marshalled army complete in all its parts. The roar of the mountain torrents and the cries of mad elephants were like the din of kettle drums ;

1 Public calamities. or visitations of God, *iti*, are reckoned as seven in number, *viz.*, droughts, floods, locusts, rats, parrots, tyranny, and invasion.

2 Trouble (*táp*) is of three kinds, specified in Book VII. *dohá* 21 as *daihika*, *daivika*, and *bhautika*, physical, casual and spiritual.

the *chakwas, chakors, chatakes,* parrots and cuckoos made a delightful concert ; swans were in their glory ; the bees buzzed and the peacocks danced like the festive *entourage* of some Rája, while the creepers, trees and grasses, with the flowers and fruits, formed his brilliant court.

Dohá 227.

Beholding the beauty of Ráma's hill, Bharat's heart was overpowered with love, like as an ascetic is overjoyed when he completes his vow and reaps the fruit of his penance.

Chaupái.

Then the pilot mounted a height and reaching out his hand cried to Bharat : " See, my lord, those huge trees *pákar*, *jáman*, mango and *tamálá*,1 in the midst of which is conspicuous a *bar* tree, so beautiful and grand that the soul is charmed at the sight, with dense dark shoots and red fruit, affording a pleasant shade in all seasons of the year, a mass of black and purple, as if God had brought together all that was lovely to make it. Under this tree, near the river, sir, where Ráma has roofed in his sylvan hut, are many graceful shrubs of Tulsi, planted, some by Síta sten and some by Lakshman, and in the shade of the *bar* tree Síta with her own lotus hands has reared a charming altar.

Dohá 228.

There the well-instructed Síta and Ràma are ever wont to sit in the midst of the hermits, listening while sacred legends are read and all the Vedas, Shástras and Puránas,"

Chaupái.

As he listened to his friend's speech and gazed upon the tree, Bharat's eyes overflowed with tears. The two brothers advanced reverently ; Sáradá would fail to do justice to their love. When they saw the prints of Ráma's feet they rejoiced like some beggar on finding the philosopher's stone, a applied the dust to their head, heart and eyes, with as mu

1 The *Pahr* is the Ficus venosa ; the *jáman*, the Eugénia jambola the *tàmala*, the Xanthochymus pictorius ; the *bar*, or banyan, the F Bengalensis.

delight as if they had found Ráma himself. Seeing Bharat's utterly indescribable condition, birds, beasts and all created things, whether animate, or inanimate, were absorbed in devotion. The guide in his excitement lost the way, but the gods showed it to him and rained down flowers. Saints and sages gazed in rapture and burst out into praises of his sincere affection : 'Who in all the world is like Bharat, who makes fools wise and the wise fools ?'

Dohá 229.

Raghu-bír, the ocean of compassion, after churning the depths of Bharat's soul with the Mount Meru of bereavement, brought out from it the nectar of love.

Chaupái.

The two fair brothers and their guide were not visible to Lakshman, by reason of the dense shade of the forest; but Bharat could see his lord's sacred hermitage, the charming home of everything delightful. As he entered it his burning grief was assuaged, as when an ascetic is rewarded with salvation. He saw before him Lakshman affectionately conversing with his lord, his hair fastened in a knot, a hermit's robe girt about his loins, his quiver slung, arrows in his hand, and his bow on his shoulder. By the altar an assembly of saints and sages, among whom Síta and Ráma were conspicuous in hermit's attire, with matted hair and body darkened by exposure; like Rati and Kámadeva in saint's disguise. He, who with one smiling glance can dispel every anguish of soul, had bow and arrows ready in his lotus hands.[1]

Dohá 230.

In the midst of the circle of saints, Síta and Ráma shone forth as fair as Faith and the Supreme Spirit incarnate in the council chamber of wisdom.

Chaupái.

He, his brother and their guide were so absorbed that

1 The idea would seem to be that Ráma, though the benefactor of the whole world, was obliged in the forest to go armed, to protect himself against attack.

joy and sorrow, pleasure and pain were all forgotten. Crying ' Mercy, mercy, O lord and master ! ' he fell flat on the ground, like a log. Lakshman recognized his loving cry and made obeisance, knowing that it must be Bharat. On the one hand he was moved by brotherly affection, but on the other was the stronger claim of obedience to his lord. Unable to embrace him and yet loth to refrain ; what poet could describe Lakshman's state of mind ? Though obedience was the weightier, and therefore he stayed, he was like a child pulling against a kite high in the air. Bowing his head to the ground, he said affectionately : " It is Bharat, O Raghunáth, who greets you." On hearing this, Ráma started up in loving agitation, his robe flying in one direction and his quiver and bow and arrows in another.

Dohá 231.

Whether he would or no, the All-compassionate took and raised him up and clasped him to his bosom. Those who witnessed the meeting of Bharat and Ráma lost all self-consciousness.

Chaupái.

How can such an affectionate meeting be described? Their thoughts, words and actions were beyond any poet. Both brothers were filled with the utmost love ; self, reason, knowledge and understanding were all forgotten. Tell me who can pourtray such perfect love ? by what shadow can the poet's mind attain to it ? If the poet has a model, he can work out his meaning by the force of words, and players dance when they have an accompaniment ; but the love of Ráma and Bharat is unapproachable, beyond the conception even of Bráhma, Vishnu and Siva ; how then can I describe it ? If an instrument is only strung with grass,[1] can it make sweet music? When the gods saw the meeting of Bharat and Raghubar they were alarmed and trembled all over ; but

1 I know no other instance of the use of the word *gádari* in the sense of "grass," which is the meaning that the best Hindu commentators give it here. It ordinarily means ' a sheep.'

when Vrihaspati had spoken to them, they awoke from their folly and rained down flowers and applauded.

Dohá 232.

After affectionately embracing Satrughna, Ráma greeted the pilot; and then Lakshman too as a brother courteously greeted Bharat.

Chaupái.

When he had fondly embraced his younger brother, Lakshman next took the Nishád to his bosom. Then the two brothers, Bharat and Satrughna, after reverencing all the saints and joyfully receiving from them the desired blessing in a rapture of love, placed on their head the dust of Síta's lotus feet. As they again and again prostrated themselves she raised them up, and with a touch of her lotus hands motioned them to be seated; in her heart invoking a blessing upon them, and so absorbed in affection as to lose all self-consciousness. When he saw Síta so thoroughly propitious, he became free from anxiety and all fear passed away. No one made any remark nor asked any question; the soul was so full of love that it ceased to act. Then the pilot took courage and bowing with clasped hands made humble petition:

Dohá 233.

"Distressed by your absence, my lord, there have come with the great sage your mothers and all the people of the city, your servants, captains and ministers."

Chaupái.

When the Ocean of amiability heard the *guru* had come, he left Satrughna with Síta and went off in haste that very minute; he Ráma, the steadfast, the righteous, the all-merciful. On seeing the *guru*, he and his brother were delighted and fell on their faces to the ground. The holy man ran and raised them up and embraced them, and greeted both brothers with the utmost affection. The pilot, quivering with emotion, gave his name and prostrated himself afar off; but the Rishi must needs greet him as a friend of Ráma's, as though love had been spilt upon the ground and he stopped to pick it up. Faith in Ráma is the root of all goods; in heaven the gods applauding rained down flowers: "There is no one so utterly vile as he, nor any one in the world equal to the great Vasishtha:

Dohá 234.

yet the king of saints on seeing him was overjoyed and embraced him before Lakshman; so glorious in their manifestation are the effects of faith in Síta's lord."

Chaupái.

Finding all the people sad, Ráma, the all-merciful and all-wise God, gave every one his wish in the way he most desired: in an instant he and his brother embraced them all and at once removed the sore anguish of their pain. This was no such great thing for Ráma to do; similarly the sun is reflected at once in a thousand water-jars. All the citizens with rapturous affection embraced the pilot and praised his good fortune. Seeing his mothers as woe-begone as the sprays of some delicate creeper smitten by the frost, Ráma first of all saluted Keikeyi, softening her will by his gentleness and piety. Falling at her feet he soothed her with many words, attributing all the blame to Fate, Destiny and Providence.

Dohá 235.

Raghubar embraced all his mothers and consoled them, saying: 'Mother, the world is subject to God; there is no one to blame.'

Chaupái.

The two brothers kissed the feet of their *guru's* wife; as also of the Bráhman ladies who had accompanied her, paying the same honour to them as to Ganga and Gauri; and they with gentle voice gladly gave them their blessing. When he embraced Sumitrá, after clasping her feet, he was like a beggar who has picked up a fortune. Then both brothers fell at the feet of queen Kausalyá and their whole body was convulsed with love; the mother took them tenderly to her bosom and bathed them with tears of affection. How can any poet describe the mingled joy and grief of such a time, any more than a dumb man can express the sweetness that he tastes? After embracing their mother, Ráma and his brother requested the *guru* to accompany them, and at his command the citizens crossed over, admiring the scenery as they went.

Dohá 236.

Taking with them the Bráhmans, the Minister, the quens, the *guru*, and some others chosen out of the people, Bharat, Lakshman and Raghunáth proceeded to the holy hermitage.

Chaupái.

Síta came and embraced the saint's feet and received the precious blessing that her soul desired. The affectionate manner in which she greeted the *guru's* wife and the Bráhman ladies is beyond description. Again and again she kissed all their feet and received their benediction rejoicing her heart. When the queen-mothers looked at Síta, they closed their eyes and shuddered to see her so delicate, like some cygnet fallen into the clutch of a fowler; what a cruel thing God has done! As they gazed at her, they became distrest beyond measure, that she should have to bear all that Fate had put upon her. Then Janak's daughter summoning up courage, while her dark lotus eyes were suffused with tears, went and embraced all her mothers-in-law; and that moment Earth reeked with piteousness.

Dohá 237.

Again and again kissing all their feet, Síta most tenderly embraced them: and from their heart came the loving benediction 'May you long live a happy wife!'

Chaupái.

Síta and the queens being thus agitated by emotion, the learned *guru* bade them all be seated. First he expounded to them the instability of the world and spoke a little of the joys of heaven, and then announced the king's death. At the news Raghunáth was grievously distrest; thinking he had died out of love for him, the firmest of the firm was sore shaken. On hearing the sad tidings, which fell upon them like a thunderbolt, Lakshman, Síta and all the queens broke out into lamentations, and the whole assembly was as much agitated as if the king had died only that very day. Then the great sage exhorted Ráma and directed him and all the people to bathe in the sacred stream. All that day the lord fasted even from water; and though the saint allowed them, no one else would drink either.

Dohá 238.

At daybreak, according to the order given him by the saint, the lord Raghunandan reverently and devoutly performed his father's funeral obsequies.

Chaupái.

Having celebrated every rite as prescribed in the Veda, he became pure, even he, the Sun to annihilate the night of sin, whose name, is a fire that consumes the cotton of wickedness, and which if merely invoked is the source of all prosperity. He became pure, in like manner as, theologians say, a bather in the Ganges who invokes other *tiraths* is purified.[1] After his purification, when two days had passed, Ráma said affectionately to the *guru*: " My lord, all the people are much inconvenienced by having nothing to take but water and the wild produce of the woods. When I look at Bharat and his brothers, the Minister and all the queens, a minute seems to me like an age. Return, I pray, with all of them to the city: for you are here, the king is in heaven, and there is no one left at Ayodhya. I have said too much and have presumed greatly: but do, sir, as you think best."

Dohá 239.

" O Ráma, bulwark of righteousness, home of compassion, it is but natural for you to speak thus: the people are wearied, let them rest for two days and enjoy your presence."

---

1 In the Ganges are concentrated the virtues of all holy places: any one who bathes in it is purified, and it is therefore a work of supererogation for him to invoke any other power. He cannot make himself cleaner than he had become already; nor could Ráma, the all-pure, become purer by any act of ceremonial purification.

Chaupái.

On hearing Ráma's words, the assembly was in dismay, like a ship tossed on the ocean ; but when they heard the saint's auspicious speech, it was as if the wind had turned in their favour. At the three set times they bathed in the sacred stream, the mere sight of which destroys any multitude of sins ; and ever feasting their eyes on the incarnation of blessedness, and again and again prostrating themselves before him, they looked and rejoiced. Then they went to see Ráma's hill and wood where all was good and nought evil: the torrents flowing with streams of nectar ; the air so soft, cool and fragrant that it soothed every pain of mind or body ; the trees, creepers and grasses of infinite variety ; the many kinds of fruits, flowers and sprays ; the magnificent rocks and the pleasant shade under the trees, all made the forest beautiful beyond description.

Dohá 240

The ponds were gay with lotuses, the haunt of cooing waterfowl and buzzing bees, while forgetful of mutual antipathies, beasts roamed in the forest and birds of varied plumage.

Chaupái.

The Kols, Kiráts and Bhíls, the inhabitants of the woods, brought delicious honey sweet as nectar, and piled up leafy bowls with herbs, roots, fruits and flowers daintily arranged. With humble salutations they offered them to all telling the taste, character, quality and name of each. The people offered a liberal price, but they would not accept it, and begged them for Ráma's sake to take it back, saying in gentle tones in the depth of their affection : " The good accept what they know to be of love. You are holy, and we low Nishads ; by Ráma's favour we have been admitted into your presence, an honour as difficult of attainment for us as for the desert of Máru to be watered by the Ganges. Ráma is merciful and the Nishads' patron ; as is the king, so should be his family and subjects.

Dohá 241.

Consider this in your mind, and without more demur recognize our affection and make friends with us; accept these fruits and herbs and flowers and so render us happy.

Chaupái.

You have come to the forest as our welcome guests, though we are all unworthy to do you service. And what is it, sirs, that we offer you? Fuel and fodder are a Kirát's tokens of friendship, and our greatest service is not to steal and run off with your clothes and dishes. We are a rude people, often taking life, of vile nature and vile pursuits, low-minded and low-born, who day and night commit sin, without either clothes for the body or food to satisfy the belly; how could we possibly have ever dreamt of the knowledge of virtue, but for the effectual apparition of Ráma? Since we beheld our lord's lotus feet, our sore distress and sin have both been removed." On hearing this speech, the citizens were much affected and broke out into praises of their good fortune.

Chhand 10.

All began to praise their good fortune and addressed them in loving terms, being delighted to find in their speech and attitude such devotion to the feet of Síta and Ráma. Every one, man or woman, thought little of his own devotion, on hearing the language of the Kols and Bhíls; through the mercy of the jewel of Raghu's line (says Tulsi) a boat floats, even though laden with iron.

Sorathá 9.

Day after day all the people felt as great delight, as they roamed through every part of the forest, as the frogs and peacocks when invigorated by a shower at the beginning of the rains.

Chaupái.

The citizens of Ayodhyá were so absorbed in excess of love that a day was gone in a minute. Síta, assuming as many forms as she had mothers-in-law, waited reverently upon them all with equal attention. No one but Ráma noticed the miracle ; for Síta is the very power of delusion, and he Delusion's lord. Síta won over all the queens by her services, and they being pleased gave her both instruction and benediction. Looking at Síta and the two noble brothers, the wicked queen repented bitterly : and Kaikeyi now prays in her heart : "Is there no escape for me ? Does God refuse me even death ? as it is declared in the Vedas and by popular tradition, and as the poets also have sung, that if Ráma be against you, not even in hell can you find a restingplace." Now this was the question in every one's mind : "Good God, will Ráma return to Avadh or not ?"

Dohá 242.

Bharat was so anxious and sorely perplext that he could neither sleep by night nor eat by day, like as a fish sunk in the last of the mud is in trouble about water.[1]

Chaupái.

"It was Fate in my mother's form that did me this injury, as when a ricefield ripening for the harvest is smitten by hail. In what manner can Ráma's coronation be secured ? There is nothing now left for me to do. He would certainly return in obedience to an order of the *guru*; but then the saint will only order what he knows Ráma to wish. At his mother's bidding, too, he would return, but Kausalyá would never insist upon anything. Of what account am I, who am only his vassal, and am fallen upon evil times, and have God against me. If I resist him, it would be a grievous sin ; for the duty of a servant to his master outweighs Kailás." Without being able to settle a single plan in his mind, Bharat spent the whole night in thought. At daybreak he bathed, bowed his head to his lord, and was sitting down when he was sent for by the Rishi.

1 The fish thinks to himself, 'There is now only a little mud left, in which I can just manage to live ; if that too dries up, what on earth am I to do for water ?' In like manner Bharat was thinking 'The two days are now nearly over ; when they are gone and I am left without Ráma, how shall I be able to survive ?

Dohá 243.

After saluting the *guru's* lotus feet and receiving his permission, he took his seat: while all the Bráhmans, nobles and ministers of state came and assembled in council.

Chaupái.

The great sage addressed them in words appropriate to the occasion: "Hearken, ye counsellor, and you, wise Bharat. The champion of righteousness, the sun of the Solar race, king Ráma, the autocratic, the lord God, the ocean of truth, the protector, the bulwark of scripture, has taken birth for the benefit of the whole world. Obedient to the word of his *guru* and his father and mother; destroying the armies of the wicked and befriending the gods; in policy and devotion, in all things that pertain to this life or the next, there is no one equal to Ráma in the knowledge of what is right. Bráhma, Vishnu and Siva; the sun, the moon, the guardians of the spheres; Delusion, life, Fate, and this Iron age; the sovereigns of hell, the sovereigns of earth and all the powers that be; magic and sorcery and every spell in the Vedas and the Tantras—ponder it in your heart and consider well—all are obedient to Ráma's commands.

Dohá 244.

If we observe Ráma's pleasure and commands, it will be well for us all; now, wise sirs, think it over, and all resolve to do whatever may be decided.

Chaupái.

Ráma's coronation will be agreeable to all, as a sure source of happiness and the one way to felicity. How is he to be brought back to Avadh? Think before you speak, and upon that plan we will act." All listened respectfully to Vasishtha's speech, full as it was of justice, religion and worldly wisdom; but no answer was forthcoming: every one was dumbfounded, till with bowed head and clasped hands Bharat spoke: "In the Solar race there have been many kings, each one greater than the other; all owed their birth to their parents, but their good or ill fortune was the gift of God. And, as all the world knows, it was through your blessing that they triumphed over sorrow and attained complete prosperity ; whatever the course of fate that you, sir, marked out for them, none could alter it ; it was fixed immoveably.

Dohá 245.

And yet now you ask advice of me : such is my ill fate." When the *guru* heard this affectionate speech, love sprung up in his heart.

Chaupái.

" My son, this is a true saying, it is all Ráma's mercy ; without Ráma no one can ever dream of happiness. There is one way, my son, though I am ashamed to propose it ; but a wise man will sacrifice the half when he sees the whole going ; do you two brothers go into exile, then Lakshman, Síta and Ráma will come back." On hearing this favourable speech, the two brothers rejoiced and their whole body thrilled with excitement ; they were as pleased at heart and as radiant all over as if king Dasarath had been restored to life and Ráma were already enthroned. The people gained much and sacrificed little ; but the queens all wept, for their pain was equal to their joy.[1] Said Bharat : " What the saint has proposed is already as good as done ; he has granted me the one thing above all others that I most desired. I will stay all my life in the forest ; there is nothing I should like better.

Dohá 246.

Ráma and Síta know my heart and you are full of knowledge and wisdom ; if, my lord, you mean what you say, make your word good."

Chaupái.

Hearing Bharat's words and seeing his love, the saint and the whole assembly were transported out of themselves. Bharat's vast generosity was like a sheet of water and the saint's proposal like a woman standing on its brink, anxious to cross and trying different ways, but unable to find either

1 For, though they recovered two of their sons, they lost the other two.

ship, boat, or raft. Who can describe Bharat's magnanimity? Can the ocean be contained in a river-shell? The saint was inwardly at heart charmed with Bharat, and accompanied by the assembly went to Ráma. The lord saluted him and led him to a seat of honour and on receiving the saint's permission all sat down. Then spoke Vasishtha in well-considered words, according to the circumstances of the place and time: "Hearken, Ráma; you are omniscient and wise, a store-house of piety, prudence, virtue and intelligence;

Dohá 247.

you dwell in the hearts of all and know what they really wish or do not wish: now advise what will be best for your subjects, your mothers and Bharat.

Chaupái.

A man in pain talks wildly, and a gambler watches only his own play."[1] " On hearing the saint's speech, Raghurái replied: "My lord, the remedy is in your own hands. To attend to your wishes will be best for all. Only give the order, and cheerfully, I assure you, whatever you commands may be, I answer for myself in the first place, those instructions I will dutifully obey; and after me, each, as he has his orders, will hasten to do his service." Said the saint: Ráma, you say truly; but Bharat's affection has disturbed calculation; therefore I say again and again my judgment is overcome by Bharat's piety; in my opinion, Siva be my witness, whatever will please Bharat is the best thing to be done.

Dohá 248.

Listen respectfully to Bharat's prayer; reconsider the matter; and after weighing well the duties of a king and the texts of Scripture, take the advice given you both by philosophers and men of the world."

Chaupái.

Seeing the *guru's* love for Bharat, Ráma's heart rejoiced

---

1 Therefore we come for advice to you, being too much excited and having too great a personal interest in the matter to judge for ourselves calmly and impartially.

exceedingly, for he knew Bharat to be a champion of righteousness, and in thought, word and deed his own faithful servant. In obedience to the *guru's* commands, he made this sweet, gentle and excellent reply : "I swear by you, my lord, and by my father's feet that in all the world there has been no brother like Bharat. All who love the lotus feet of their *guru* are highly blessed : so say both the world and the Veda. But who can tell Bharat's blessedness, to whom such love has been shown by you ? When I look at him, my younger brother, my senses are abashed, as I thus praise him to his face. Whatever Bharat says, that will be good for us to do." Having so said Ráma remained silent.

Dohá 249.

Then the saint said to Bharat. "Put aside all diffidence, my son, and tell the Ocean of mercy, your own dear brother, what you really have at heart."

Chaupái.

Hearing the saint's address, and having already received Ráma's consent, he was satisfied of the good-will both of his *guru* and his master ; but seeing the weight of the whole business put upon his head, he could say nothing and remained lost in thought, as he stood in the assembly, quivering all over his body, and his lotus eyes filled with the moisture of affection : "The king of saints has already spoken for me : what more is there for me to say ? I know my lord's amiable disposition, that he never shows displeasure even to the guilty ; and for me he has a special tenderness and love ; even in play he never gave me an angry look. From a child I have never left him, and never at any time has he wounded my feelings. I have observed my lord's gracious ways ; when beating me in any game he would allow me to win.

Dohá 250.

I am too much overcome by affection and modesty to say a word before him ; to this day my eyes, thirsting for his love, have not been satiated with the sight of him.

Chaupái.

God could not endure my fondness, and cruelly interposed an obstacle by means of my mother. In saying this now I do myself no honour. Who is made good by his own good estimation? To get into my mind that my mother is a wretch and I myself good and upright is a thousand times worse. Can rice be produced from stalks of *kodo*,[1] or the shells of a pond sweat pearls? Not a shadow of blame or wrong-doing attaches to any one; it is my ill-luck, like some fathomless ocean. Not perceiving that it is the fruit of my own sins, I revile my mother, to my own undoing. I search my heart, but am beaten all round. In one matter only am I really fortunate; with Vasishtha for my *guru* and Síta and Ràma for my masters, things must come right in the end.

Dohá 251.

In this honourable assemblage, in the presence of my lord and my *guru* and in this holy place, I speak my true sentiments; the saint and Ráma know whether my affection is sincere or feigned, and my words true or false.

Chaupái.

The whole world is witness to the king's death, the result of his uncompromising love, and to my mother's wickedness; the queens are so woe-begone that I cannot bear to look at them; the citizens are consumed by intolerable anguish; and I am the cause of all their troubles; and yet though I hear and feel all this, I can still endure the torment. When I heard that Raghunath had taken with him Lakshman and Síta, and in pilgrim's weeds had set out for the woods, without shoes and walking on foot, be Sunkara my witness, how I survived the misery. Again, when I saw the Nishád's devotion, my heart must have been harder than adamant not to break. And now I have come and with my own eyes have seen everything; surely in this life my wretched soul has borne all that can be borne. The serpents

1 The *kodo* (Sanskrit *kodrava* is the *Paspalum frumentaceum or scrobiculatum*, which bears a small grain of inferior quality, eaten only by the boor.

and scorpions on the road at the sight of them forget their virulent venom and savage viciousness;

Dohá 252.

but to her Ràma, Lakshman and Síta appeared as enemies; and how can God spare her son, or on whom would he rather inflict intolerable pain?

Chaupái.

On hearing these lamentable words of Bharat's, fraught with distress and love, humility and discretion, the whole assembly was lost in sorrow and anxiety, as when the frost smites a bed of lotuses. The learned sage comforted Bharat by reference to various ancient legends, and Ráma, the moon of the liles of the solar race, spoke thus in seemly wise; "Brother, grieve not your heart in vain; know that the ways of life are in God's hands, To my mind, brother, all the men of highest renown for virtue in all time, past, present or future, and in the three spheres of creation, fall short of you Whoever even imagines wickedness in you shall perish both in this life and in the next. It is only fools, who have never studied in the school of philosophy and religion, who ascribe blame to your mother.

Dohá 253.

Sin, Delusion and the burden of every ill are destroyed by the invocation of your name, glory is own in this world and eternal happiness in the world to come.

Chaupái.

Be Siva my witness; I state the fact truly: the world, Bharat, exists by your support. Do not, brother, entertain evil surmises to no purpose; love and hatred cannot be hid: birds and beasts come up close to a saints, but flee at the sight of a fowler, though he tries to stop them. If beasts and birds can distinguish between friends and enemies, how much more man, whose body is a vessel of virtue and intelligence. I know you thoroughly, brother; how can I do anything that would be discordant with your spirit? The king, to keep his word, abandoned me and, to keep his vow of love, discarded life ; if I now break his word, I shall be heartily grieved ; and yet my respect for you is greater ; the *guru* moreover has given me his commands ; in short, whatever you say, that I am ready to do.

Dohá 254.

Set your mind at ease ; cease this timidity and speak out ; I will do it at once." When they heard Ráma, the ocean of truth, speak thus, the assembly rejoiced.

Chaupái.

But the king of heaven and all the gods were alarmed and began to think 'Things will all go wrong.' Though they took counsel together, nothing came of it ; mentally[1] all had recourse to Ráma for protection. After again considering, they said to one another : Ràma is moved by the faith of the faithful" Remembering the story of Ambarísha and Durvásas, Indra and the gods were greatly dejected. 'Long time the gods endured distress, till at last Prahlád revealed Narsingha.'[2] They beat their heads and whispered in the ear : "Now our only chance lies with Bharat there is no other plan, sir, that I can see. Ráma accepts service done to one of his servants; do you all with loving heart do service to Bharat, and he will subdue Ráma to his own temper."

Dohá 255.

When the *guru* of the gods heard this their plan, he said : Well done, you are in great good fortune ; devotion to Bharat's feet is the source of every good in the world.

Chaupái.

The service of the servant of Síta's lord is as good as a thousand Kámadhenus. Now that you are resolved to put faith in Bharat, cease to have any anxiety ; God has provided

---

1 If they had gone to him in person their whole scheme would have been frustrated, for Rávan would have heard of it and thus have become aware of Ràma's divinity.

2 The legends of Ambarisha and Prahlád show how ready Vishnu (*i.e.*, Ràma) has always been to hear the prayers of his followers, and how fierce is his indignation against those who persecute them ; it was therefore useless for the gods to think of opposing Bharat ; their only plan was to win him over to their side.

a way. See, Indra, the extent of Bharat's power; he has subdued Ráma with the greatest ease. Make your mind easy, sir, never fear, knowing that Bharat is Ráma's shadow." the Lord, who knows the heart, was disturbed when he heard the plans and fears of Vrihaspati and the other gods. Bharat, knowing that the whole responsibility rested upon him, was raising a thousand different arguments in his mind. After much deliberation, he came to the conclusion that his happiness consisted in obeying Ráma. "He is breaking his own vow in order to satisfy me, and in this is showing me no little love and affection.

Dohá 256.

Síta's lord has in every way done me great and unbounded favour." Then bowing low, and with his lotus hands clasped in supplication, Bharat thus spoke:

Chaupái.

"All-merciful and omniscient lord, what now can I say myself or have others to say for me? My *guru* is pleased and my master kind: the imaginary torments of my troubled soul are all over. I feared disgrace, but my fear was unreasonable; it is no fault of the sun's sir, if a man mistake the points of the compass.[1] My ill-luck, my mother's wickedness, God's adverse action, and the malignity of fate set themselves firm and combined to overthrow me; but the protector of suppliants has maintained his character. This is no strange procedure of his; it is declared both by Scripture and tradition, and is no secret. The world is evil; the Lord only is good; tell me by whose goodness is he good save by his own? Your attributes, sire, are those of the tree of paradise, which is never either for or against any one in particular.

Dohá 257.

All who draw near and acknowledge that its shade

1 Your mercy is as sure as the course of the sun; but even with sun for his guide, a man may lose his way by mistaking the points of the compass: in like manner I was alarmed through my ignorance of the course that your mercy was taking.

relieves every sorrow, high or low, rich or poor, ask and obtain the fruit that they desire.

Chaupái.

Now that I have seen the affection of my *guru* and my master, my anxiety is gone: my mind is freed from doubt. Now, O Mine of compassion, do whatever will be for the good of your servant, without being a trouble to the soul of my lord. The servant who worries his master and seeks only his own advantage is a base-minded varlet. A servant's gain is to do his master's service, to get him every comfort, and not be greedy. If my lord returns to Ayodhya, every one will be a gainer; but obedience to orders will be a thousand times greater gain; it is the highest good in this world, and in the next it is the fruit of all well-doing and the ornament of beatitude. Listen, sire, to this my one request, and then do as you think proper. I have brought with me all the requisites for the coronation; if you approve, my lord, have them brought into use.

Dohá 258.

Send me and my brother into the woods, and give the people back their king; or else let Lakshman and Satrughna return and let me accompany you:

Chaupái.

or all three brothers go into the woods, and only you and Síta return. O most merciful lord, do whatever is most pleasing to yourself. You have cast the whole burden upon me, sire, who am unversed both in politics and theology; I make all my proposals on the ground of worldly interest: but when a man is in distress he cannot reason. A servant who hears his master's orders and answers him is one that Shame herself would be ashamed to look at: and yet though I do this and am a fathomless ocean of faultiness, still my master in his kindness praises me as good. Now, O merciful one, that plan best pleases me which will cause my lord's soul the least vexation. By my lord's feet I swear that I speak the truth; there is only one scheme for securing the world's happiness.

Dohá 259.

If my lord cheerfully and without reserve will only give each one of us his orders, they will be reverently obeyed, and all this trouble and perplexity,[1] will be at an end."

Chaupái.

On hearing Bharat's guileless speech the gods were glad of heart and extolled his generosity and rained down flowers; the people of Avadh were overwhelmed with uncertainty, and the hermits and all the dwellers in the woods were greatly rejoiced. Raghunáth maintained an anxious silence. Seeing his state, the whole assembly became disturbed. At that very moment arrived messengers from Janak[2]. Saint Vasishtha on hearing of it sent for them at once. They made obeisance and looked towards Ráma. At the sight of his attire they were exceedingly grieved. The great saint asked the embassy the news: 'Tell me is all well with the king of Videha?' At this question the noble heralds with a deprecating air bowed their heads to the ground and with clasped hands replied: "Your courteous enquiry, sire, makes all well;

Dohá 260.

otherwise, my lord, welfare died with the king of Kosala; the whole world is in bereavement, but especially Mithilá and Avadh.

Chaupái.

When Janak and his court heard of king Dasarath's death, every one was mad with excess of grief. All who at that time saw Videha thought that name a truly appropriate one[3]. As he listened to the tale of the queen's wickedness, the monarch became as helpless as a serpent without its headjewel. Bharat king, and Ráma in exile! Janak's soul

1 *Avareva*, which I translate 'perplexity,' is explained by the Hindu commentators as meaning the same as *ghát* or *pench*. The word is not given in Dr. Fallon's or any other Hindustani-English Dictionary that I have seen. *Anat* is for *ánt*.

2 Janak's visit and the long discussions that follow it, which occupy almost all the remainder of this book, are the invention of Tulsi Dás, and find no counterpart in the Sanscrit poem.

3 *Videha*, meaning literally 'out of the body,' and Janak being out of his mind, beside himself, as we should say, for grief.

was sore distrest. He enquired of all his wise men and ministers, 'Consider and tell me what ought now to be done.' Reflecting on the state of Avadh and the double difficulty, if he went or if he stayed, no one gave any answer. After reasoning with himself, the king resolved to send four clever spies to Avadh, to discover whether Bharat meant well or ill, and return in haste without being seen.

Dohá 261.

The spies went to Avadh, ascertained Bharat's movements and saw what he was doing, that he had started for Chitra-kút, and then went back to Tirhút.

Chaupái.

On their arrival, they announced in Janak's court to the best of their ability all Bharat's doings. The *guru*, the citizens, the ministers and the king were all agitated with grief and love at the report. Restraining his emotion and glorifying Bharat, he summoned his warriors, and captains,[1] and having stationed guards for the palace, city, and realm and made ready horses, elephants, chariots and conveyances of every description, all in less than an hour, the king set out and halted nowhere on the road, but this morning at daybreak bathed at Prayág. The host has begun to cross the Jamuná and we, my lord, have been sent on ahead for news." So saying, they bowed the head to the ground. The saint at once gave them an escort of six or seven Kiráts and allowed them to take leave.

Dohá 262.

The people of Avadh were all delighted to hear of Janak's arrival; but Raghunandan was greatly disquieted and Indra overwhelmed with alarm:

Chaupái.

the wicked Kaikeyi was sinking with remorse, 'to whom shall I be able to speak or whom can I blame?' while the people were delighted with the thought that now they had got

1 *Sáhani*, which I translate 'captains,' is a word not given in any dictionary.

another day or two to stay. In this manner the day was spent. On the morrow all bathed and after their ablutions worshipped Ganes, Gauri, Siva and the Sun; then reverenced the feet of Lakshman's lord and offered up their prayers, the men[1] raising their joined hands, the women holding out the skirt of their dress: "With Rama our king and Jánaki our queen, may Avadh, our capital, the centre of all delights, be gloriously re-peopled, court and all, and Ráma install Bharat as heir-apparent. Revive us all, O lord, with this ambrosial bliss and grant the world its life's desire.

Dohá 263.

May Ráma sway the state, assisted by his *guru*, the council and his brothers; and may we die with Ráma still Avadh's king." This was the universal prayer.

Chaupái.

When they heard the citizens' loving words, the wisest saints thought little of their own penance and austerities. When the people had in this manner performed their daily devotions, with much joy they went and saluted Ráma. High and low and of middle estate, men and women, all looked up to him as their own special patron, and he discreetly received them all with due honour. Every one extolled his inexhaustible generosity: "From a child it was said of Raghubar that he cherishes all in whom he recognizes sincerity and affection; with his bright face, bright eyes and guileless ways, he is a very ocean of amiability and gentleness." Thus affectionately telling Ráma's good qualities, all began to magnify their own good fortune. "There are few people in the world who can have been so meritorious as we, whom Ráma has thus accepted for his own."

Dohá 264.

At the time when all were thus absorbed in love, they heard of the approach of the king of Mithilá: the Sun of the lotuses of the Solar race rose in haste, he and the whole assembly.

---

1 That is to say, in the attitude of beggars; the women holding out the skirt of their dress to catch whatever may be thrown into it, the men holding out their hands.

Chaupai.

Raghunáth led the way, accompanied by his brothers, the *guru*, the Minister and the people. As soon as king Janak saw the holy hill, he dismounted from his chariot and saluted it. In their eagerness and excitement to see Ráma, no one felt the slightest fatigue from the toilsome journey, for their soul was with Ráma and Síta ; and who without a soul can be conscious of bodily pain or pleasure ? In this manner Janak and his host advanced, drunken with the drunkenness of love. When they came near and in sight, they lovingly and reverentially began mutul salutations. Janak kissed the feet of the hermits, and Ráma with his brothers, having first reverenced the king's spiritual advisers, embraced him, and led the way for him and his army.

Dohá 265.

Ráma conducted the host to the hermitage, as it were a river of pitifulness flowing into an ocean full of the pure water of tranquillity ;

Chaupái.

flooding the banks of wisdom and asceticism : with sorrowful speeches for its tributary streams and torrents ; with sighs and lamentations for the wind and waves that break the stout trees of Resolution on its bank ; with grievous anguish for its rapid current, and terror and delusion for its many eddies and whirlpools ; with sages for ferrymen and wisdom for the huge boat, which can no-how be got across ; while the poor Kols and Kiráts of the woods are the forlorn travellers wearied with waiting. When it reached the hermitage, it was as though ocean had been agitated with a sudden rush of waters. The two royal-hosts were so overcome with grief that they had no sense, courage or shame left. Extolling king Dasarath's majesty, virtue and amiability, they sorrowed like men drowned in a sea of sorrow.

Chhand 11.

Drowned in a sea sorrow, they sorrowed, men and women alike, in utter bewilderment, all angrily and reproachfully exclaiming. 'What is this that cruel fate has done?' Gods, saints, anchorites, ascetics and sages witnessed Janak's condition, but his love—says Tulsi—was like a broad river that no one could get over.

Sorathá 10.

When all the people and the great sages had exhausted ever topic of consolation, Vasishtha thus addrest Videha: "King of men, be comforted.

Chaupái.

By the sun of your wisdom the darkness of the world is dispelled, and in the light of your speech saints expand like the lotus: how then can the power of delusion affect you? This is the marvellous result of love for Síta and Ráma. There are three classes of beings, whom the Vedas term wise in their generation, the sensual, the sorcerer and the saint: amongst the pious the highest honour is for him whose soul is full of love for Rama: but without knowledge love for Ráma is imperfect, like a boat without a helmsman." When the saint had finished his exhortation to the king, all the people bathed at the Ramghát. Every one, men and women alike, were so agitated with grief that they spent the day without drinking water: even the cattle, birds and deer would eat nothing; much less would his own kindred think of doing so.

Dohá 266.

At daybreak the royal son of Nimi[1] and the royal son of Ragu having bathed with all their retinue went and sat under the *bar* tree, sad at heart and wasted in body.

Chaupái.

The Bráhmans from Ayodhyá, as also those from the capital of the king of Mithilá: Vasishtha, the *guru* of the Solar race, and Satánand, Janak's family priest, who while on earth had explored the path of heaven, began long exhortations full of religion, morality, asceticism and philosophy. Then Visvamitra eloquently admonished the assembly with

1 *Nimi* was a former king of Videha and one of Janak's ancestors.

many a reference to ancient legend ; till Raghunáth suggested to him : " Sire, every one since yesterday has gone without water." Said the saint : " Ráma has spoken in season ; two-and-a-half watches of the day are now spent." Understanding the saint's pleasure the king of Tirhút replied : " It is not good for us to eat bread here."[1] The king's word pleased every one, and having obtained his permission they went to bathe.

Dohá 267.

At that very moment arrived the people of the woods, bringing large baskets laden with fruits, flowers, leaves and roots of every description.

Chaupái.

By Ráma's favour the mountain had become a granter of desires : merely to look at it removed sorrow. The ponds, streams and glades were bursting as it were with joy and love ; all the creepers and trees broke out into blossom and fruit : the birds and beasts made a most melodious concert. In short, the gladsomeness of the forest was surpassing ; the air, soft, cool and fragrant, was delightful to every one ; and the beauty of the scene was beyond description, as though Earth herself had prepared Janak's reception. When each and all of the people had finished bathing and had received permission from Ráma, Janak and the saint, they gazed with rapture on the magnificent trees and threw themselves down here and there ; while leaves and fruits, flowers and roots of every kind, fresh and fair, and sweet as nectar,

Dohá 268.

were courteously sent to all, in baskets full, by Ráma's *guru* ; on which they made their repast, after reverencing their ancestors, the gods, their guests and the *guru*.

Chaupái.

In this manner four days were spent, in which the people saw Ráma and were happy. In both camps there was

1 This refers to the custom which forbids a Hindu ever to take food in the house of his son-in-law.

this desire at heart : " It is not good for us to return without Síta and Ráma. Life in the woods in their society is a thousand times better than heaven. If any one, in his longing for home, would desert Lakshman, Ráma and Síta, his fate is an unlucky one : it is the height of good fortune for us all to dwell in the forest near Ráma, bathing three times a day in the Mandákini, seeing Ráma, which will be a constant delight, rambling about on the sacred hill and among the hermitages in the wood, and feeding on sweet herbs and roots and fruits, so contentedly that the fourteen years will pass like a minute, without our knowing how they go.

Dohá 269.

We are not worthy of so great happiness" they all exclaimed. " What luck can be like it ?" Such was the spontaneous devotion to Ráma's feet in both camps.

Chaupái.

In this manner as all were expressing their hearts' desire in affectionate words, which it ravished the soul to hear, Síta's mother sent a handmaid, who ascertained that it was a convenient time and returned. On learning that Síta's mothers-in-law were at leisure, Janak's queen and her attendants came to visit them. Kausalya received them with due honour and gave them such seats as circumstances allowed. On both sides there was such love and tenderness, that the most rigid thunderbolt would have melted, could it have seen and heard. Their body quivering and unnerved, their eyes full of tears, and all lost in grief, they drew lines with their toes on the ground, each a separate incarnation of love to Síta and Ráma, or as it were tearful Sympathy repeated in many forms. Said Síta's mother: "God's judgment has gone astray, using the thunderbolt for a chisel to break up foam !

Dohá 270.

We hear of ambrosia but see only venom ; all his doings are hard ; crows, owls and cranes are everywhere, but swans only in the inaccessible Mánas lake."

Chaupái

Upon this, queen Sumitrá said sadly: "God's ways are contrary and unaccountable. He creates and cherishes, and then destroys: his purposes are as idle as child's play." Said Kausalyá: "It is no one's fault; pain and pleasure, loss and gain are governed by actions: the effects of action are inscrutable; God only knows them, who awards its own fruit to every act, whether it be good or bad. The Lord's decree dominates over all, whether for rising, staying or falling, whether for poison or ambrosia. It is vain, madam, to give way to sorrow; God's schemes are, as I have said, unchangeable and from everlasting. Consider the question of the king's life or death; look now, friend, and think whether it was a loss to him or gain." Síta's mother replied: "Noblest of noble women, consort of Avadh's kings, your eloquent words are true.

Dohá 271.

If Lakshman, Ráma and Síta stay in exile, all will be right in the end and no harm done." "But" (said Kausalyá with a troubled heart) "I am anxious about Bharat.

Chaupái.

By God's favour and your blessing, my son and his wife[1] are both pure as Ganges water. Though I have never yet sworn by Ráma, I now invoke him to witness, friend, that I speak truly. The greatness of Bharat's generosity, goodness and humility, his brotherly affection, faith, hope and charity, even Sarasvati's eloquence would fail to declare; can the ocean be ladled out with a shell? I have always known that Bharat was the glory of his house, and the king repeatedly told me so. Gold is known by assay and precious stones by the test; a man's temper is tried by fortune. It is not right for me now to have spoken thus; but sorrow and love have left me little reason." On hearing these words, as pure as Ganges stream, all the queens were overcome with emotion.

1 For *suta-badhú*, 'a son's wife,' might be better to read *su-bandhu*, 'a good brother.'

Dohá 272.

Kausalyá continued: "Hearken to me, queen of Mithilá, and take courage. Who is able to advise you, the consort of the wisest of men?

Chaupái.

Having found a fitting opportunity, speak, madam, to the king as if of yourself, and suggest that he should stop Lakshman and let Bharat go to the forest. If the king agrees to this proposal, I will then devise and carry out some proper plan. I am greatly disturbed about Bharat, for his love is so profound that if he stays I surmise evil." When they saw her generosity and heard her frank appeal, they were all overpowered with sympathy. There was a shower of flowers from heaven with cries of Glory 'Glory;' saints, ascetics and sages grew faint with love. The queens, despite their fatigue, still looked and waited; till Sumitrá made bold to say: "Madam nearly an hour of the night is gone." At this Kausalyá rose and affectionately

Dohá 273.

said, "Pray return at once to your tent; of a truth now our help is in God and the king of Mithilá."

Chaupái.

Seeing her affection and hearing her modest speech, Janak's queen clasped her holy feet: "Madam, this modesty on your part is only natural, since you are Dasarath's wife and Ráma's mother. Monarchs give honour to the lowest of their servants; in the same way as fire tops itself with smoke and a hill with grass. King Janak is your servant in thought word and deed, and Mahádev and Bhaváni are your constant auxiliaries. Who is there on earth who can act as your supplement? Does the sun shine by the help of a torch? After going into exile and assisting the gods, Ráma will hold undisputed sway at Ayodhyá. Through the might of his arm gods, serpents and men will all dwell in peace, each in his own place. This has all been foretold by Yajnavalkya; and the words of a saint, madam, can never be false."

Dohá 274.

So saying, she fell at her feet and affectionately made request for Síta ; permission was accorded and Síta set out with her mother.

Chaupái.

Síta embraced all her old domestics in such manner as in each case was most befitting. When they saw her in hermit's dress, they were all distrest with exceeding sorrow. Janak, on receiving the permission of Ráma and the *guru*, came to the tent to see his daughter and clasped her to his bosom, the sanctifying guest of the soul of love. His bosom swelled with a flood of affection and his royal soul resembled Prayág; with his love for Síta conspicuous as the spreading *bar* tree, on which devotion to Ráma appeared like the child, clutched for support by the king's bewildered senses as by the sage Chiranjív when on the point of drowning.[1] Videha was so overwhelmed by his feelings that he had no sense left; such is the power of love for Síta and Raghubar.

Dohá 275.

Síta could not bear to see her father and mother so overcome by affection, but calling to mind both the time and her own duty, Earth's daughter summoned up courage.

Chaupái.

When Janak looked at her in her anchorite's dress, he was filled with love and consolation : " Daughter, you have sanctified both families ; everybody in the world proclaims your brilliant renown. The stream of your fame excels the Ganges and has spread over millions of universes. The Ganges has only three great sites[2] on earth, but the congregations of saints that have been made by you are innumerable." At her father's sincere and loving eloquence Síta was abashed and shrank into herself. Again her father and mother took

---

1 The sage Markandeya had the presumption to ask Náráyan to show him a specimen of his delusive power. The god in answer to his prayer drowned the whole world in a sudden flood. Only the Akhay-bar, or imperishable fig-tree at Prayág, raised its head above the waters, with a little child seated on one of its topmost boughs, that put out its hand and rescued the terrified saint as he was on the point of sinking.

2 They are Hari-dwár, Prayág, and Ságar.

her to their arms and gave her kind instructions and invoked rich blessings upon her. Síta could not speak out, but was anxious at heart: "It is not well for me to spend the night here." The queen saw her wish and explained it to the king, inwardly praising the excellence of her disposition.

Dohá 276.

After again and again embracing her, they graciously gave her leave to depart. Having now an excellent opportunity, the discreet queen adroitly mentioned Bharat's going.

Chaupái.

When the king heard of Bharat's conduct, brilliant as gold, refreshing as sweet perfumes, consolatory as ambrosia or the soft light of the moon, he closed his tearful eyes and his body thrilled with rapture, as he broke out into ecstatic praises of his glory. "Mark me well, fair-faced and bright-eyed dame, the legend of Bharat is effectual to loosen the bands of existence. According to my ability, I too have mastered somewhat of theology, statecraft and spiritual meditation; but whatever my ability, if I would tell Bharat's greatness, I cannot make a pretence of reaching even its shadow. Bráhma, Ganes, Seshnág, Siva, Sarasvati, the inspired poets and the sages most renowned for wisdom, when they hear or meditate upon Bharat's doings, his glory, his vigour, his piety, his temper, his virtues and his spotless dignity, all are enraptured; it has a flavour of purity like the Ganges, surpassing ambrosia,

Dohá 277.

His perfection is limitless; he is the incomparable protoplasm; I know none like Bharat but himself. Can Mount Meru be weighed in any balance? The wit of the whole race of poets is at fault.

Chaupái.

He is, fair dame, as impossible to describe as it is impossible for a fish to walk on dry land. Hearken, lady; Ráma knows, but even he cannot describe Bharat's illimitable greatness. If Lakshman returns and Bharat goes to the forest, every one will imagine it to be good for all: but, madam, Bharat's love and confidence in Ráma are past all telling. Bharat is the perfection of love and devoted attachment, but Ráma is the lord of impartiality. Bharat's mind has never even dreamt of all the felicities of this world and the next; only his love for Ráma's feet has brought him success. This, as I consider, is Bharat's belief.

Dohá 278.

He would never be beguiled into thwarting an order of Ráma's; do not then in your affection give way to sorrow;" said the king, and sighed as he spoke.

Chaupái.

As the wedded pair thus affectionately discoursed of Bharat's excellences, the night passed like a minute. At daybreak both the royal camps awoke and bathed and worshipped the gods. After bathing, Ráma approached his *guru*, embraced his feet, and on receiving permission spoke thus: "My lord, Bharat and the people and my mothers are distrest and inconvenienced by their sojourn in the woods. The king of Mithilá too and his retinue have been enduring hardships for many days; be pleased to do, my lord, as seems to you good; the happiness of all is in your hands." So saying, Ráma was greatly abashed. The saint thrilled with delight on seeing his disposition. "Without you, Ráma, the greatest bliss would seem to both camps like hell.

Dohá 279.

O Ráma, you are the soul of their soul, the life of their life, the joy of their joy. Any one, my son, who would desert you for the sake of the pleasure of home has destiny against him.

Chaupái.

Perish the happiness, life and religion, in which is no love for Ráma's lotus feet! That piety be impiety, and wisdom unwisdom, in which love for Ráma is not supreme! Through you men are made happy, and without you they are unhappy; you know the heart of every one. Your commands rule all, and every motion is thoroughly manifest to your benignity. Return now to the hermitage." The king of saints was over-powered with love. When Ráma had bowed and retired, the *guru* composed himself and went to Janak, and repeated to him what Ráma had said, enlarging upon his amiability, affection and excellent disposition: "Now, sire, do what-ever will be for the advantage of all without prejudice to religion.

Dohá 280.

O king of men, you are the wisest among the most wise, the champion of true piety; who save you can at this time end these troubles?"

Chaupái.

Janak was so moved by the saint's address and by the sight of his agitation that all his philosophy and asceticism were forgotten. Faint with love, he reasoned to himself: "I have not done well in coming here. Dasarath ordered Ráma into exile, but himself gave the best proof of his affection; I have now sent him from one wood to another and return in triumph forsooth with increased reputation for wisdom." Seeing the agitation of the anchorites, saints and Bráhmans, the king was still more overcome with emotion; but considering the circumstances he made an effort, and with his retinue set forth to visit Bharat. Bharat advanced to meet him and gave him the best seat the time allowed. "Son Bharat," said the king of Tirhút, "you are well acquainted with Ráma's character.

Dohá 281.

He is devoted to truth, a zealot in religion; out of kindness, he endures inconvenience without murmuring; but if you have any orders to give, speak."

Chaupái.

At this Bharat's whole frame quivered and his eyes filled with tears; but putting a strong restraint upon himself he replied: "My lord, I love and revere you as my father, and hold you as dear as my own family *guru*; father and mother I have none. Here are Visvamitra and the other sages, and all this assembly; you too yourself, an ocean of wisdom; I am your obedient son and servant: regard me in this light, my lord, and instruct me. In this assembly and at this holy place you enquire of me, and I am to answer, though besmirched of soul and demented. Can I speak great words out of my little mouth? Pardon me, father; the fates are against me. It is declared in the Vedas, Tantras and Purânas, and all the world knows, that loyal service is difficult. Duty to a master conflicts with self-interest; the deaf and blind cannot show their love.

Dohá 282.

Have regard to Ráma's wishes, so pious as he is, and remember that I am but a servant; do as all approve and as will be best for all, but forget not their love."

Chaupái.

When the king heard Bharat's speech and witnessed his generosity, he and his court burst out into praises. Simple but profound; soft and delicate but severe; pregnant with meaning in a small compass; his speech was as mysterious as the shadow of a face in a glass, which no hand can grasp. The king, Bharat, the saint, and all the venerable assembly went to Ráma, by whom the gods were made as glad as the lilies by the moon. On hearing the news all the people were as distrest as fish in unaccustomed waters. The gods, seeing first the emotion of the family *guru*, and then Janak's exceeding affection, and Bharat so full of devotion to Ráma, were sorely anxious and began to despond in their relfishness. The sight of Ráma's kindness made the company of heaven unspeakably dismayed.

Dohá 283.

Indra cried sadly: "Rama is overcome by love and modesty: we must combine to devise some scheme, or else we shall be undone."

Chaupái.

The gods invoked Sáradá in flattering terms: "Protect,

O goddess, the gods your suppliants. Exert your power of delusion and change Bharat's purpose; by some deceptive artifice rescue the host of heaven." When the wise goddess heard their prayer, she understood their stupid selfishness and said: "You tell me to change Bharat's purpose; you have a thousand eyes and yet cannot see Mount Meru. The delusive power of Bráhma, Vishnu and Siva is exceedingly great, but it cannot see through Bharat's purpose, and yet you tell me to pervert it. What! can the moonlight rob the moon? Bharat's heart inhabited by Síta and Ráma; can darkness invade the splendour of the sun?" So saying, Saradá withdrew to Bráhma's heaven, and the gods were as downcast as the *chakwa* at the approach of night.

Dohá 284.

The self-seeking gods were troubled at heart and devised evil projects and schemes, creating by strong delusion artifices of fear, error, sorrow and vexation.

Chaupái.

Indra practised this villainy, thinking "Success or defeat is all in Bharat's hands." When Janak approached Ráma, the glory of Raghu's line received them all with honour. Then spoke Vasishta in terms appropriate to the time, the assembly and the principles of religion, mentioning the conversation between Janak and Bharat and eloquently repeating all that Bharat had urged. "Son Ráma, any order that you may give, all will obey; this is my conclusion." Upon this Raghunáth, clasping his hands, made truthful and guileless reply in gentle tones: In the presence of yourself, sir, and the king of Mithilá, for me to speak is altogether out of place. Whatever command you may be pleased to give I swear by yourself I am ready to comply."

Dohá 285.

On hearing Ráma's oath, the saint and Janak and the whole assembly were confounded: and fixed their eyes on Bharat's face helplessly and without power to answer.

Chaupái.

Bharat saw the distress of the assembly, and being Ráma's brother, put a strong restraint upon himself. Seeing the unfitness of the time, he subdued his emotion, in the same way as Agastya bowed down the Vindhya mountain.[1] Grief like Hiranyáksha carried away his soul as it were the Earth; but at once from his spotless perfection like the womb of the universe came forth the mighty Boar[2] of discretion and wrought immediate deliverance. Clasping his hands, he bowed reverentially to all, to Ráma, the king, the *guru*, and the saints: "Pardon me if to-day I act most unbecomingly and with the tongue of a child speak stubborn words." As he mentally invoked the gracious Sáradá, from the depths of his soul there came to his lotus mouth a swan-like strain fraught with pure intelligence, piety and righteousness.

Dohá 286.

With the eyes of his mind, Bharat saw that the assembly was faint with love; bowing low and invoking Síta and Ráma he thus spoke;

Chaupái.

"My lord is my father and mother, my friend, my *guru* and my master; object of my adoration, my best benefactor, reader of my heart; the kindest of patrons, the perfection of amibility, the protector of the humble; the all-learned, the all-wise; the powerful befriender of suppliants; quick to appreciate merit and to ignore demerit and wickedness; my sovereign, my god-like God; while no servant can be so bad as I am. In my infatuation I have come here at the head of an army, in defiance of the commands of my lord and my father. In the world there are good and vile, high and low, ambrosia and heaven, poison and death; but

1 Agastya is said to have compelled the Vindhya mountains to prostrate themselves before him; and when once down, they were never able to rise again. This he did to oblige the sun, who found the range so high that he could with difficulty climb it in his daily passage from east to west.

2 The allusion is to the third Avatár, when Vishnu in the form of a Boar rescued the earth, which had been seized by the demon Hiranyaksha and carried off into the depths of the ocean.

never have I seen or heard of any one who even in thought could cancel an order of Ráma's. Yet I have been thus contumacious, and my lord in his kindness has taken it as service.

Dohá 287.

Out of his own mercy and goodness he has made me good; my errors have become adornments and my fair fame has been spread all around.

Chaupái.

Your mode of procedure, your gracious speech, and generosity are known throughout the world; they are sung in the Vedas and Tantras. The cruel, the perverse, the vile, the low-minded, the outcast, the base, the ill-conditioned, the godless, the reckless, so soon as you hear that they have come before you as suppliants and have made a single prostration, are all reckoned as friends. Though you see faults, you never take them to heart; and if you but hear of virtues you proclaim them in the assembly of the saints. What other master is there so kind to his servants, so perfect in all points, who never dreams of reckoning up what he has done himself, and is heartily vexed at any embarrassment of his servants. He is my sovereign lord, and there is none other, with arms upraised, I declare on oath. A beast may dance and a parrot be a clever talker; but all depends upon the music of the dancing-master and the method of the teacher,

Dohá 288.

who now has corrected his servant and treated him with honour, and made him the crown of the head of the just. Who is there, save the all-merciful, who, whether we will or no, maintains our fair fame?

Chaupái.

Whether it was from grief and affection or from mere childishness that I came here in despite of your commands, you in your compassion have looked upon me as a friend and in every way taken it in good part. Seeing your blessed feet and knowing my lord's natural benignity, I look upon this great assembly as a piece of good fortune, and my great sin as evidence of my lord's kindness ;[1] for by his gracious favour he has satisfied my whole being and his compassion has exceeded everything. Out of the goodness of his own disposition my good lord has made sure of my fidelity. I have now displayed great audacity in discarding respect for this august assembly and speaking boldly or humbly, just as the fancy moved me ; but pardon me, sire, for I am in grievous perplexity.

Dohá 289.

It is a great mistake to say too much to a true friend or really wise man or good master. Be pleased, sire, to give your commands and set me all right.

Chaupái.

I swear by the dust of my lord's lotus feet, the glorious consummation of truth, virtue and happiness ; with an oath I protest that the desire of my soul, whether waking, sleeping or dreaming, is to serve my lord with spontaneous devotion, without any regard to self-interest, fraud, or my own ends in this life or the next. There is no duty so imperative as submission ; let your servant, sire, obtain this favour."[2] So saying he was utterly overwhelmed with emotion ; his body quivered, his eyes filled with tears, and in great agitation he clasped his lord's lotus feet. So pathetic a scene defies description. The Ocean of compassion honoured him with gracious words and took him by the hand and seated him by his side ; while himself and all the assembly were faint with love, after hearing Bharat's prayer and seeing his noble nature.

Chhand 12.

Raghuráo himself, the august assembly, the saint, the king of Mithilá, all were faint with love, and mentally applauded the exceeding greatness of Bharat's brotherly

---

1 The meaning would seem to be : the greater my sin, the greater his kindness in forgiving it, and the greater the assembly, the greater my glory in having so many witnesses to his love.

2 That is to say, favour him with some order, that he may show how good a servant he is, by his immediate submission to it.

affection and devotedness. The gods too commended Bharat and ranied down flowers, though with a heavy heart. Every one, says Tulsi, was as distrest by what he had heard, as the lotus that withers at the approach of night.

Sorathá 11.

Seeing every man and woman in both assemblies so grieved and downcast, Indra,[1] vile wretch, still sought his own happiness, killing as it were the already dead.

Chaupái.

Though king of the gods, there is no limit to his deceitfulness and villainy; he loves another's loss and his own gain; Pákaripu's[2] ways are like those of a crow—crafty, disreputable and with no faith in any one. Having in the first instance formed an evil design and accumulated deceits, he piled up trouble on the heads of all. Every one was infatuated by the god's delusive power; their love for Ráma was so violent that they would not be separated from him. They were all distracted; with nothing settled in their mind; at one moment longing for the woods, at another anxious to return home. The people in their

1 Though Tulsi Dás constantly appeals to the authority of the Vedas, it is clear that like 999 out of 1,000 of the most educated of his countrymen at the present day, he had not the faintest idea of their contents; otherwise he would not have spoken thus disrespectfully of Indra, who is one of the principal Vedic divinites, while Siva, whom he places in a much higher sphere and regards as one of the manifestations of the Supreme Spirit—while Indra and the others are mere demi-gods—is a power for whose cultus the Vedas, though searched from beginning to end, would fail to supply any authority. If a Bráhman were now to set up a temple at Muthurà or Banáras to Indra, or Mitra, or Varuna, or any other Vedic divinity, he would be thought as eccentric as an Englishman who should rededicate a shrine to Diana in the precincts of St Paul's churchyard in the city of London. Perhaps more so; for the characters of the old Greek and Roman Pantheon are still thoroughly familiar to modern Europeans and have considerable influence upon art and literature; while the Vedic mythology has utterly perished, and scarcely a single name in it would be recognized by any native of India except a professed Pandit. Nor is this very surprising, inasmuch as the Vedas were not really composed by Hindus, nor have Hindus in any past time ever adopted them as a religious standard. To regard them in that light now is—as the founders of the Bráhma Samaj soon discovered—an impracticable absurdity. Dating from a time when neither Englishman nor Hindu had yet come into existence, they are the common inheritance of all nations of Aryan descent. Their intrinsic value is *nil*; the only interest they possess is due to the fact that they are the earliest surviving record of the first semi-inarticulate utterances of nascent humanity

2 *Pákaripu*, 'Páka's enemy.' is one of Indra's names, in consequence of his having destroyed a demon called Páka.

distress had the current of their ideas as divided as the water at the confluence of a river with the sea. Thus wavering in mind they got no comfort in any quarter; no one told another his secret thoughts. Seeing this, the, Ocean of compassion smiled to himself and said: "Indra is like a dog in his ways."

Dohá 290.

Excepting Bharat, Janak, the saints, the ministers and the more intelligent nobles, the heaven-sent delusion took effect upon all, according to the circumstances of the individual.

Chaupái.

The Ocean of compassion saw the people distrest by their love and by Indra's potent deception; the assembly, the king, the *guru*, the Bráhmans and the ministers, all with their hearts under the spell of Bharat's devotion; motionless as pictures, gazing upon Rama, nervously uttering words which they seemed to have learnt by rote. The eulogy of Bharat's affection and constant humility is delightful to hear, but difficult to pronounce. Seeing only the tiniest morsel of his devotion, the saints and the king of Mithilá were absorbed in love; how then can I, Tulsi, tell its greatness? It is only by the blessing of faith that the ambitious design of my heart has prospered. I am little; I know the enormous greatness of my subject, and I shrink in confusion before a crowd of other poets; unable to utter the vehemence of my passionate love for his perfection, the motions of my fancy are like the stammerings of a child.[1]

Dohá 291.

Bharat's bright fame is as the bright moon rising in the bright sky of a faithful heart, ever intently watched by my daring fancy as by an unfledged partridge.

---

1 Most readers of the original will agree with the poet that his powers of expression have here been scarcely adequate to the intensity of his feelings All this part of the poem abounds with obscure and involved passages, the precise interpretation of which is often very difficult to determine, and I cannot flatter myself that I have invariably succeeded in hitting upon it.

Chaupái.

Bharat's generosity is scarce fathomable by the Vedas; pardon, ye poets, the frivolities of my poor wit. Who, that hears or tells of Bharat's perfect nature, does not become enamoured of the feet of Síta and Ráma? Whoever invokes Bharat and still finds love for Ráma a difficult matter is a monster without a parallel. Seeing the state that every one was in, the merciful and all-wise Ráma, who knows their devotion to him, being the staunch champion of religion, a master of policy, an ocean of truth and love and amiability and everything good, having considered the place and circumstances, the time and assembly, Raghuráj, the maintainer of justice and affection, delivered a speech, the quintessence of eloquence, grateful as ambrosia at the time of hearing, and salutary also in the end: "Brother Bharat, you are the champion of righteousness, perfectly conversant with all the laws of the world and the Vedas;

Dohá 292.

for purity of thought, word and act, your only equal, brother, is yourself. In this venerable assembly and in such distressing circumstances how can all the virtues of my younger brother be told?

Chaupái.

Brother, you know the custom of the Solar race and the renown and the affection of our father, that ocean of truth; the circumstances of the time and of this assembly, the reverence due to these venerable personages, and the secret thoughts of all men, whether they be indifferent, or friends, or unfriends, are understood by you, as also your own highest gain and mine and the requirements of religion. I have entire confidence in you and yet I speak as the circumstances suggest. My words, brother, in the absence of my father, have been kept straight only by the favour of our *guru*; otherwise all my subjects, together with the citizens, the people of the palace and myself, would have been undone. If the lord of day sets at the wrong time, tell me, will not the whole world be in confusion? Such trouble, brother, fate had ordained; but the saint and the king of Mithilá have averted it.

Dohá 293.

The State; our honour and fair name; Religion; our land, wealth and homes; all have been defended by the power of the *guru*; and everything will be well in the end.

Chaupái.

My followers and yours, the palace and the forest, are both protected by his favour. The order of a father or mother, a *guru* or a master, is like Seshnág, the supporter of a whole world of righteousness. Obey it yourself, brother, and let me obey it, and thus become a protector of all the Solar race. Obedience is the one means for the attainment of every success, a triple flood of Glory, Salvation and Power. Having thus reflected, endure the grievous burden and make your people and family happy. I have distributed my afflictions amongst you all; but upon you is the full weight of the greatest difficulty. I know your tenderness, though I speak so harshly; the times, brother, are out of joint; the fault is not mine. In an emergency a brother is used for a shield, in the same way as the stroke of a sword is parried by the hand."

Dohá 294.

A servant is like a hand, or foot, or eye; a master is like the head. Hearing this description of love, say Tulsi, the greatest poets are full of admiration.

Chaupái.

When they heard Raghubar's speech, imbued as it were with the nectar of an ocean of tenderness, the whole assembly became lost in an overpowering trance of love. Sáradá herself was struck dumb at the sight of them. Bharat was immensely consoled by the graciousness of his lord and his putting away of every trouble and wrong-doing. Cheerful of aspect and with the grief of his soul effaced, he seemed like a dumb man who has received the gift of speech. Affectionately bowing again and again and folding his lotus hands, he thus spoke: "My lord, I am as happy as if I had gone with you; I have reaped the reward of being born into the world. Now, O merciful sire, whatever may be your order, that will I dutifully and reverently obey. But, sire, grant me some support, by the help of which I may struggle on to the end of the time.

Dohá 295.

In compliance with the *guru's* command, sire, I have brought here water from all holy places for the purpose of your royal inauguration: what are your orders concerning it?

Chaupái.

I have one great desire at heart, but for fear and shame I cannot tell it." "Tell me what it is, brother," Upon this his lord's command, he replied in affectionate and winning terms: "With your permission I would go and see Chitrakút with all its hermitages, shrines and woods, its birds and beasts, its ponds and streams, its waterfals and rocks, and the spot[1] so specially marked with the prints of my lord's feet." "Certainly, brother: only obtain Atri's permission, and then wander without fear through the woods. It is the saint's blessing, brother, that makes the forest so auspicious, holy and exquisitely beautiful. In whatever place the king of sages may direct, there deposit the holy water." On hearing his lord's words, Bharat was glad and joyfully bowed his head to the saint's lotus feet.

Dohá 296.

The selfish gods, when they heard this most delightful conversation between Bharat and Ráma, praised the whole family and rapturously showered down flowers upon them.

Chaupái.

"Blessed be Bharat and glory to our lord Ráma." cried

---

1 One of the temples of Chitra-kút bears the name of Charan-páduka, and has been erected over a rock which is said to bear the impression of Ráma's foot. Supposing there were any truth in the legend, it would seem rather from the name that it ought to commemorate the place where Ráma gave Bharat his sandals.

the gods in their irrepressible delight. The saint, the king of Mithilá and every one in the assembly rejoiced on hearing Bharat's speech. King Videha broke out into ecstatic praises of the many virtues and the affection both of Bharat and Ráma; master and servant of equally charming disposition, their fidelity and love the purest of the pure. The ministers too and all the spectators effectionately extolled them, as each best could. In both camps there was blended joy and sorrow, when they heard the conversation between Ráma, Bharat and the saint. Ráma's mother, feeling pleasure and pain equally balanced, exhorted the queens, reckoning up both good and evil. One would magnify Ráma, another would praise Bharat's amiability.

Dohá 297.

Then said Atri to Bharat: "There is a fine well near the hill; there deposit the holy water, pure, unsullied, incomparable."

Chaupái.

On receiving Atri's command, Bharat despatched all the water vessels, and himself with Satrughna, the saint and elders, went to the deep well.[1] There he poured out the holy water on that sacred spot; and Atri in a rapture of affection thus spoke: "Son, this has been a holy place from all eternity; but time had obscured it, and it was known to no one, till my servants, seeing the spot to be a desirable one, made this great well for the sake of a good supply of water. By the decree of fate the whole universe has been benefited, and a merit most difficult to compass has been rendered easy. People will now call it Bharat's well, hallowed in a special degree by the combination in it of the water of all holy places. Every one who lovingly and religiously bathes in it, will be made pure in thought, word and act."

1 Válmíki makes no mention of this well. Under the name of 'the Bharat-kúp', it is now one of the seven principal stations visited by the pilgrims to Chitra-kút.

Dohá 298.

All then went to Raghunáth, telling the virtue of the well; and Atri explained to him the blessed efficacy of holy places.

Chaupái.

The night was pleasantly spent in loving discourse on matters of religion and sacred legends until it was dawn. After performing their daily duties, Bharat and his brother, having received permission from Ráma and Saint Atri, attended by all their retinue in simple attire, proceeded on foot to visit Ráma's wood. Earth, in confusion of heart at being trodden by their delicate and unshod feet, smoothened herself, and cleared away all the spiky grass and thorns and stones and ruts and everything rough and unpleasant. Earth made the way delightfully easy for them ; they were refreshed by soft, cool and fragrant breezes ; the gods rained down flowers ; the clouds afforded shade ; the trees gave blossom and fruit ; the grass made a soft carpet ; the deer with their timid glances, and the birds with their sweet song, all recognized Ráma's friends and did them homage.

Dohá 299.

And what great matter is this for Bharat, Ráma's dearest friend? when any ordinary person finds the highest success easy of attainment, if he merely repeats Ráma's name when he yawns.

Chaupái.

In this manner Bharat roamed the woods, and the saints, who saw his faith and love, were abashed. Seeing all so divine, he asked about the sacred ponds and various localities, the birds and deer, the trees and grasses, the hills, woods and orchards, beautiful and varied and pre-eminently holy; and in reply the great saint with gladness of heart gave him the history of each, with its name, virtues and spiritual efficacy. Bathing at one place, prostrating himself at another ; here admiring the beauty of the wood, here sitting down to rest as the saint directed, he meditated on Síta and the two brothers. Seeing the goodness of his disposition, his love and faithfulness in service, the gods of the wood were charmed and gave him their blessing. The third watch of the day was half spent when he returned to gaze upon the lotus feet of his lord.

Dohá 300.

In five days Bharat visited every shrine and holy place. The day was spent in discourse on the glory of Hari and Hara until the evening.

Chaupái.

On the morrow, after bathing, the whole assembly was gathered together—Bharat, the Bráhmans and the king of Tirhút. Ráma new at heart that the day was an auspicious one, but in his kindness hesitated to say so. He looked at the *guru*, the king, Bharat, and the assembly, and then in confusion turned his eyes to the ground. All the spectators admired his generosity, thinking. 'Never was there a master so considerate as Ráma is!' Bharat in his wisdom understood Ráma's wish. He stood up and, lovingly putting the greatest restraint upon himself, bowed low, and with clasped hands thus spoke : " My lord has granted my every desire. For me he has borne, every affliction and has himself experienced every kind of trouble. Now, sire, give me your royal permission to go and serve at Avadh till the appointed time.

Dohá 301.

But, O merciful and compassionate king of Kosala. teach me some way by which your servant may see your feet again when the time is over.

Chaupái.

Your citizens, your kinsmen, and all your subjects, sire, are true and real, and bound to you by ties of affection. The sorrows of this miserable life, borne by your command are a delight ; without my lord, highest heaven is a worthless gain. The all wise master knows the fancies, the desires, the habit of mind of all his servants : the protector, of suppliants will be our protector, and both in this world and the next will secure our deliverance. I have thus the most perfect confidence ; not a particle of anxiety disturbs my calculations. My own distress and my lord's forbearance have combined to make me thus presumptuous. Pardon, my lord, this my great offence, and shrink not from instructing your servant what to do." All who heard Bharat's prayer applauded it ; like a swan it had separated the milk of truth from the water of error.

Dohá 302.

The all-wise Ràma, the brother of the meek, on hearing his brother's meek and guilelss speech, replied in terms appropriate to the place, the circumstances and the time :

Chaupái.

" The *guru* and the king, brother, take thought for you, for me and our people, whether at home or in the forest. So long as Visvamitra, Vasishtha, and Janak direct us, neither you nor I can dream of trouble. For us two brothers, both for me and you, obedience to our father's command is the highest object we can have, our greatest gain, our glory, our duty and our salvation. A king's good is a good thing both in the Vedas and in the estimation of the world. Whoever observes the injunctions of *guru* or father and mother, or master treads an easy path and never stumbles. Remember this, and putting aside all regrets, go and reign at Avadh for the appointed time. The burden of the realm, the treasury, the people and the family will weigh no heavier than the dust of the *guru's* feet. Observe the instructions of the saint your mother and the Minister, and protect your country, your subjects and your capital."

Dohá 303.

A chief should be like the mouth, which alone (says Tulsi) does all the eating and drinking, and yet supports and nourishes to a nicety each separate member of the body.

Chaupái.

A king's duty includes everything, in the same way as every latent desire exists potentially in the mind. In various ways he consoled his brother ; but without some memento his mind would not be satisfied nor at rest. The *guru*, the minister and the whole assembly were like-minded with Bharat ; and Ráma overpowered with modesty and affection, took compassion upon him and gave him his sandals, which Bharat reverently received and placed upon his head. Not these the mere foot-gear of the All-merciful, but rather twin guardians of his people's life ; a casket to contain the jewel of Bharat's love ; the two letters[1] of the alphabet for which the soul struggles ; the folding-doors that guard the house ; the hands for holy work ; the pure eyes of service and righteousness Bharat was as glad to receive this memento as if Ráma and Síta had themselves stayed.

Dohá 304.

As he bowed and begged permission to depart, Ráma took and clasped him to his bosom. Wicked Indra finding a sad opportunity made the people weary.

Chaupái.

But his villainy was a good thing for all ; the hope that the time of exile would soon be over was the life of their life. Otherwise the separation from Lakshman, Síta and Ráma would have been such a blow that all would have died of it. The mercy of Ráma solved this difficulty, and the hostile gods became serviceable allies. Ráma closed his arms around Bharat with a burst of affection that cannot be described. Body, soul and speech overflowed with love ; the firmest of the firm lost all firmness, and his lotus eyes streamed with tears. The assembled gods were grieved to see his condition : the saints and *gurus* who were as firm as Janak, the gold of whose soul had been tested by the fire of wisdom, and whom the Creator had created as unimpressionable by the world as the leaves of the lotus by the water ;

1 The two letters are the consonants in the name Ráma : for a panegyric on which see Dohá 24, Book 1, page 18.

Dohá 305.

even they, seeing the unparalleled and boundless affection of Ráma and Bharat, were overwhelmed in body, soul and speech, lost all reason and restraint.

Chaupái.

If Janak and Vasishtha were dumbfounded, the emotion of ordinary persons is not worth speaking about. People would think any poet harsh when they heard him describe the parting of Ráma and Bharat; Eloquence herself, remembering the unspeakable pathos of the scene, would be struck dumb with confusion. Raghubar first embraced and consoled Bharat and then rejoiced to take Satrughna to his arms. Knowing Bharat's wishes, his servants and ministers began each to set about his own work. In both camps there was sore distress at the news, as they commenced their preparations for the march. The two brothers, after reverencing their lord's lotus feet and submissively receiving his commands, set out on the way, bowing to the saints, the hermits and forest gods and again and again showing them respect.

Dohá 306.

Lakshman, too, they embraced, and making obeisance, placed on their head the dust of Síta's feet, and received her affectionate blessing, the source of happiness.

Chaupái.

Ráma and his brother bowed the head to the king with many expressions of modesty and praise: "In your kindness, sire, you have suffered great inconvenience, you and your retinue, by coming to the forest; now grant me your blessing and return to the city." The monarch mastered his emotion and went. After reverencing the saints, Bráhmans and nobles, and taking leave of them as though they were the equals of Hari and Hara, the two brothers approached their mother-in-law, and came back after kissing her feet and obtaining her blessing. Then they took leave of Visvamitra, Vámadeva and Jábáli ;[1] the people of the court, the citizens, the good ministers and all ; with courteous speech and address, as was most befitting. The Ocean of compassion respectfully dismissed them all, men and women, high, middle-class and low.

Dohá 307.

With sincere affection the Lord kissed the feet of Bharat's mother and embraced her, and escorting her to the pálki that he had in readiness, effaced all her alarm and distress.

Chaupái.

After saluting her father and mother and the court, Síta came back purified by the love of her beloved. Reverently she embraced all her mothers-in-law, with an affection which the poet's soul shrinks from describing. Hearkening to their instruction and receiving the blessing she desired of them, Síta stood burdened with conflicting love. Having sent for elegant pálkis, Ráma with words of consolation escorted each of his mothers to their carriage. Again and again both brothers embraced them and led each by the hand with equal affection. When the horses, elephants and different vehicles were ready, the king and Bharat started the host. Their hearts full of Ráma, Síta and Lakshman, all the people went disconsolate; even the bullocks, horses, elephants and cattle were out of heart and went only by force and against their will.

Dohá 308.

The Lord with Síta and Lakshman kissed the feet of the *guru* and the *guru's* wife, and turned and came back to their leafy hut with mingled pleasure and amazement.

Chaupái.

The Nishád was dismissed with honour and departed; sorely grieved at heart to leave. The Kols, Kiráts and

---

1 In the Sanskrit Rámayana Jábáli is represented as being, or professing to be, an atheist. In this character he alone openly advised Ráma to return to Ayodhyá as king; for as there was no life after death, the wisest plan was to get as much enjoyment as possible out of the present life while it lasted.

Bhíls, the people of the woods, turned again and again, after they had been dismissed, to make yet one more obeisance. The lord with Síta and Lakshman sat under the shade of the fig-tree and sorrowed for the loss of their dear friends. Ráma, overpowered with affection, discoursed to his spouse and brother in eloquent terms on Bharat's love and generosity, and with his own blessed mouth declared that faith and devotion were in his every thought, word and deed. At that time the birds, deer and fish, every creature at Chitra-kút, whether animate or inanimate, were all woe-begone. The gods, seeing Raghubar's state, rained down flowers and told him of what was doing in their several spheres. The lord bowed and reassured them ; they went away glad, without a particle of anxiety in their mind.

Dohá 309.

With Síta and his brother the Lord shone forth in the leafy hut as resplendent as Faith, wisdom and Ascetism incarnate.

Chaupái.

Vasishtha, the Bráhmans and Visvamitra, Bharat and the king were all in evil case at leaving Ráma and paced the road in silence, counting up in their mind all Ráma's virtues. After crossing the Jamuná they passed that whole day without food. The next day they crossed the Ganges, where Ráma's friend made every arrangement for them. Then they crossed the Sai, bathed in the Gomati, and on the fourth day reached Ayodhyá. Janak stayed four days in the city, settled the entire administration of the state, committed the government to the Minister, the *guru* and Bharat, and then with all his retinue set out for Tirhút. All the people, in compliance with the *guru's* directions, settled down quietly in Ráma's capital,

Dohá 310.

fasting and praying to see him once again, discarding all personal adornments, pleasure and enjoyment, and living only in the hope of his return.

Chaupái.

Bharat exhorted his ministers and trusty servants, and they executed his orders, each in their appointed sphere. Then he spoke and gave instructions to his younger brother, and entrusted to him the care of the dowager queens. He also with folded hands spoke to the Bráhmans, bowing low and using humble supplication: "Give your orders and hesitate not, to high or to low, in great matters or in small." Next he summoned the people of the palace, of the city, and all his subjects, and set their minds at rest and appointed them places to live in. After this he, with his brother, went to the *guru's* house, and after prostrating himself and joining his hands in prayer said thus: "With your permission I will now live a life of penance." The saint thrilled with rapturous affection and replied: "Whatever you think, or say, or do, is always best."

Dohá 311.

On receiving his command and his blessing, he sent for a great astrologer and fixed the day, and then devoutly placed upon the throne his lord's sandals.

Chaupái.

After bowing his head at the feet of Ráma's mother and the *guru*, and receiving the commands of his lord's sandals, the champion of righteousness made for himself a hut of leaves at Nandigráma, [1] and there abode, with his hair gathered up into a knot on his head, attired in hermit's dress, and his couch of grass spread in a cave in the earth, lovingly practising the austerities of religious life in food, dress, posture, fasting and prayer; discarding in thought, word and deed, as of no more value than a broken blade of grass, all clothes and adornments and every luxury and enjoyment. The city of heaven envied the capital of Avadh, and the god-of riches was confounded at the sight of

1 Nandigráma, now contracted to Nandgánw, is a few miles from Ayodhyá.

Dasarath's wealth; yet in that city Bharat dwelt as indifferent as a bee in a garden of *champa* trees.[1] A man so highly blest as to be enamoured of Ráma spurns like vomit all Lakshmi's delights.

Dohá 312.

This is no such great achievement for Bharat, the very shrine of the love of Ráma; even the *chátak* and the swan are models in their way, the one of marvellous constancy, the other of discrimination.

Chaupái.

Day by day his body grew thinner, but his lustre and vigour were not diminished, and the beauty of his face remained the same. Nourished by an ever-increasing devotion, his virtue waxed stronger and his soul was unclouded: as the waters decrease in the brightness of the autumn, but the reeds spring up and the lotuses blossom. His tranquillity, self-control, piety, fasting and prayer were like stars in the pure heaven of Bharat's soul: his faith like the pole-star, the return from exile as the full moon, his constant remembrance of the Lord as the glistening milk-way, his devotion a fixed and unsullied moon shining ever clear amidst a galaxy of stars. All the greatest of poets would fail to describe Bharat's composure, wisdom and magnanimity, his faith, his impassibility, and the perfect splendour of his virtues; not even Seshnág, Ganes and Sarasvati could attain to them.

Dohá 313.

Paying daily homage to his lord's sandals, his affection was greater than his heart could contain: he constantly referred to them in the disposal of all matters of state,

Chaupái.

his body quivering with emotion, Síta and Ráma in his heart, their names upon his tongue, and with tears in his eyes. Ráma, Lakshman and Síta dwelt in the forest, but

---

1 Though the *champa* bears a very sweet-scented flower, it is said that no bee ever sucks it.

Bharat dwelling in the palace endured the bodily penance. Every one after considering both sides said that Bharat was in every way praiseworthy. The religious were abashed who heard of his fasting and penance; the king of saints, who saw his condition, was put to shame. Bharat's mode of life was utterly holy, sweet and charming, and the cause of every blessing; it removes the grievous distress of this sinful age: is the sun to disperse the darkness of the great delusion; the lion to quell the elephant host of sin: the pacifier of every kind of affliction; the joy of the faithful: the liberator from the burden of existence the essence of the ambrosia of Ráma's love.

Chhand 13.

If Bharat had never been born, full of the ambrosia of devotion to Ráma and Síta who would have practised such self-restraint and penance, such composure, patience and rigorous fasting, transcending every imagination of the saints? Who in legendary disguise would have removed our burning sorrows and poverty, our arrogance and sin? What poor wretch like Tulsi now in this iron age would have ventured to set Ráma before you?

Sorathá 12.

All, says Tulsi, who make a vow and listen with reverence to Bharat's acts shall assuredly acquire a great devotion to the feet of Síta and Ráma and a distaste for the pleasures of life.

———o———

[*Thus endeth the book entitled* AYODHYA, *composed by Tulsi Dás for the bestowal of pure wisdom and continence being the second descent 'into the holy lake of Ráma's deeds,' that cleanses from every defilement of the world.*]

BOOK III.

THE FOREST.

THE FOREST.

Sanskrit Invocation.

I REVERENCE the Bráhmanic race; the very root of the tree of piety; the full moon of the sea of intelligence; the joygiver; the sun of the lotus of asceticism; the destroyer of sin; the dispeller of darkness; the healer of distress; the most auspicious conjunction in the high heaven of wisdom, which scatters the thick clouds of delusion; the sin cleansing; the beloved of king Ráma.

I worship him, whose body resembles a cloud teeming with abundant delights; the yellow-apparelled; the beautiful; the hero with bow and arrows in hand and well-fitted quiver gleaming by his side; with the large lotus eyes; the long tresses of whose hair are bound into a knot on his head, all glorious to behold; the way-farer accompanied by Sita and Lakshman, the charmer of charmers.

Sorathá 1.

O Umá, the saints, who are learned in Ráma's mysterious qualities, enjoy peace of mind; but fools, who are Hari's enemies and have no love for religion, reap only delusion.

Chaupái.

I have sung to the best of my ability the incomparable and charming affection shown by the citizens and Bharat: hearken now to the all-holy acts of the Lord, that he wrought in the forest, to the delight of gods, men and saints. Once upon a time Ráma picked some lovely flowers and with his own hands made a wreath, with which he reverently decked Síta. As she sat in her glory on the crystal rock, the son of the king of the gods[1] took the form of a crow and wickedly thought to make trial of Ráma's might, like an ant so imbecile of mind as to attempt to sound the depths of ocean. With its beak it bit Síta in the foot and flew away, the foolish crow, in its utter

1 Jayanta, the son of Indra.

stupidity. The blood flowed; Raghunáyak saw it and made ready his bow and arrow, fashioned merely of reeds.[1]

Dohá 1.

The All-merciful Ráma, ever full of compassion for the poor, even he it was upon whom the wicked wretch came and played this trick.

Chaupái.

The divine arrow, winged with a charm, sped forth; the crow in terror took to flight and assuming his proper form went to his father, who would not shelter him, as he was Ráma's enemy. He was in despair, and as panicstricken in soul as was the Rishi Durvásas by the terror of Vishnu's discus. Weary and worn with fear and remorse, he traversed the realm of Bráhma, the city of Siva and every other sphere; but no one even asked him to sit down; who can befriend an enemy of Rama's? Hearken Garur: his own mother becomes his death; his father is changed as it were into the king of the infernal regions;[2] ambrosia turns to poison; a friend does him all the harm of a hundred enemies; the Ganges is converted into the Vaitarani,[3] and all the world burns hotter than fire—mark me, brother—when a man opposes Ráma. When Nárad saw Jayanta's distress, being tender-hearted and good, he took pity on him and sent him straight to Ráma. There he cried 'Save me, O thou that art the suppliant's friend!' In terror and confusion he went and clasped his feet, crying "Quarter, quarter, O merciful Raghurái! Thy might is immeasurable, and immeasurable thy majesty; in ignorance of mind, I knew thee not. I have reaped the fruit of my own actions; now my Lord, succour me, for to thee I have come for refuge." When the Merciful heard

1 In the Sanskrit Râmâyana this incident of the crow forms the subject of the 105th canto of the Ayodhyâ Kând, Gorresio's edition.

2 *Samana*, 'the destroyer,' here denotes Yama, the Indian Pluto.

3 The Vaitarani is the Hindu Styx, or river of hell, which the dead have to cross before entering the infernal regions. It is represented as an impetuous and filthy torrent, full of blood, hair and bones and every kind of impurity.

this most piteous appeal, he dismissed him, Bhaváni, with the loss of one eye.

Sorathá 2.

Although in his infatuation he had committed such an offence that death was his due, the Lord had compassion upon him and set him free; who is so merciful as Raghubír?

Chaupái

Ráma stayed on at Chitra-kut and performed many acts that were like the scriptures or ambrosia for excellence. At last, he thought to himself—"There will be a crowd here, now that every one knows of me." So the two brothers with Síta took leave of all the saints and went on their way. When the Lord drew near to Atri's hermitage, the holy man was rejoiced at the news, and quivering in every limb he sprang up and ran to meet him. On seeing him, Ráma advanced hurriedly and was falling to the ground before him, but the saint took him to his bosom. Both wept tears of affection. At the sight of Ráma's beauty, his eyes were gladdened and he reverently conducted him to his cell, where doing him every honour he addressed him in gracious terms and offered him roots and fruits such as his soul relished.

Sorathá 3.

As the Lord took his seat, the great saint supremely wise, gazed with streaming eyes upon his beauty, and joining his hands in supplication he thus hymned his praise:—

Chhand 1.

"I reverence thee, the lover of the devout; the merciful, the tender-hearted; I worship thy lotus feet, which bestow upon the unsensual thine own abode in heaven. I adore thee, the wonderously dark and beautiful; the mount Mandar to churn the ocean of existence; with eyes like the full blown lotus; the dispeller of pride and every other vice; the long-armed hero of immeasurable power and glory; the mighty Lord of the three spheres, equipped with quiver and bow and arrows; the ornament of the Solar race ; the breaker of Siva's bow ; the delight of the greatest sages and saints ; the destroyer of all the enemies of the gods ; the adored of Kámadev's foe (*i. e.*, of Siva) ; the reverenced of Bráhma and the other divinities ; the home of enlightened intelligence ; the dispeller of all error : Lakshmi's lord ; the mine of felicity ; the salvation of the saints. I worship thee with thy spouse and thy brother, thyself the beloved younger brother of Sachi's lord.[1] Men, who unselfishly worship thy holy feet, sink not in the ocean of existence, tost with the billows of controversy. They who in the hope of salvation, with subdued passions, ever delightedly[2] worship thee, having discarded every object of sense, are advanced to thy own sphere in heaven. I worship thee, the one, the mysterious Lord, the unchangeable and omnipresent power, the eternal governor of the world, the one absolute and universal spirit ; the joy of all men day after day. I reverently adore thee, the king of incomparable beauty, the lord of the earth-born Síta ; be gracious to me and grant me devotion to thy lotus feet." They who reverently repeat this hymn, full of faith in thee, will undoubtedly attain to thy heaven.[3]

Dohá 2.

Again with bowed head and folded hands the saint made supplication and cried, 'Never, O Lord, may my soul abandon thy lotus feet.

Chaupái.

The amiable and modest Síta clasped Anasúyá[4] by the feet with frequent embraces. The soul of the Rishi's wife was filled with joy ; she gave her her blessing and seated her by her side. Then arrayed her in heavenly robes and

---

1 This epithet is a peculiar one ; but it would seem to be intended simply as a periphrasis for Upendra, 'the lesser Indra,' a well-known title of Vishnu, who, in the dwarf incarnation, was born as a son of Kasyapa ; Indra, here called 'Sachi's lord,' being accounted the eldest of Kasyapa's sons.

2 *Mudá* is here the instrumental case of *mud*, 'delight.'

3 The whole of this Chhand is in loose and occasionally ungrammatical Sanskrit, like the language of the Gàthàs in Buddhist literature.

4 The interview with Atri and Anasùyà is narrated at the end of the Ayodhyà Kànd in one recension of the Sanskrit Ràmayana.

jewels which remained ever bright and beautiful. In simple and affectionate phrase the saintly dame spoke and instructed her in matters of wifely duty. "Hearken, royal lady; mother, father, brethren and friends are all good in a limited degree; but a husband, Vaidehi, is an unlimited blessing; and vile is the woman who worships him not. Courage, virtue, a friend and a woman are four things that are tried in time of adversity. Though her lord be old, diseased, impotent and poor, blind, deaf, passionate and utterly vile, yet even so the wife who treats him with disrespect shall suffer many torments in hell. Her one duty, her one fast and penance consist in a devotion of body, word and thought to her husband's feet. There are four kinds of faithful wife in the world, as the Vedas, Puránas and saints all say. The best is so firmly settled in mind that she could not even dream of there being any other man living: the next regards another's husband as her own brother or father, or son; she who is restrained by thought of duty and consideration for her family is said in the scriptures to be a woman of low character; but reckon her the very lowest of all, who is restrained only by fear and want of opportunity. She who deceives her husband and carries on an intrigue with another man shall be cast for a hundred ages into the hell called the terrible. Who such a wretch as she, who for a moment's pleasure considers not the torment that shall endure through a hundred million lives? Without any difficulty a woman attains to salvation, if only without guile she adhere to her duty as a faithful wife; while she, who lives to despite her spouse, becomes a widow while still a girl.

Sorathá 4.

An utterly wicked woman who is faithful to her husband has a happy fate when she dies; so sing the four Vedas and so too in these days sings Hari's poor friend, Tulsi. Hearken, Síta; a woman will be kept faithful, if she invoke your name; for you love Ráma like your own life; these words that I say are for the good of the world."

Chaupái.

On hearing this Jánaki was overjoyed and reverently bowed her head at her feet. Then the All-merciful said to the saint, "With your permission I would go to some other wood. Continue to be ever gracious to me and knowing me to be your servant, cease not your kindness." On hearing this speech of the Lord, the champion of righteousness, the wise saint affectionately replied: "O Ráma, you are he whose favour is desired by Bráhma, Siva, Sanat-kumara, and the other gods and by all the preachers of salvation; the passionless, the kindly, the friend of the helpless, who thus modestly bespeak me. Now I understand the cleverness of Lakshmi who has left every other god and worships you alone. Of a truth there is none your equal; how then could your goodness be other than it is? How can I, my lord, tell you what wood to visit? Say, master, for you read the heart." Having thus spoken, the saint strong-minded as he was, trembled in every limb and his eyes streamed with tears as he gazed upon the Lord.

Chhand 2.

Trembling exceedingly in every limb he fixed his loving eyes upon his lotus face: "It is the reward of prayer and penance that I have beheld the Lord, who transcends the senses and every faculty of thought and reason." By prayer and meditation and religious observances, men attain to the crowning virtue of faith; therefore day and night Tulsi Dás sings the holy acts of Raghubír.

Dohá 3.

Ràma's praises remove the pollution of this wicked age, subdue the soul, are the source of beatitude; and Ráma continues gracious to all who reverently hear them.

Sorathá 5.

Grievous is the burden of the sin of the world; nor religion, nor knowledge, nor meditation, nor penance avails against it; they are wise who discard trust in all else and worship Ráma only.

Chaupái.

The Lord of gods and men and saints, after bowing his head at the lotus feet of the sage, proceeded to the wood. Ráma first and after him his brother, in the garb of hermits all full and complete. Between the two the incarnation of Lakshmi shone forth like Máya between God and the soul. The rivers and thickets and precipitous and mountain-passes all recognized their lord and made the way smooth for him. Wherever the divine Raghurái passed, the clouds made a canopy in the heaven. As they went along the road the demon Virádha met them. While he was yet coming Raghubír overthrew him, then at once he assumed beauteous form; and Ráma seeing him sorrowful dismissed him to his own sphere.[1] Then the All-beautiful with his brother and Jánaki visited the sage Sarabhanga.

Dohá 4.

At the sight of Ráma's lotus face the bee-like eyes of the saint reverently drank thereof; blessed indeed was Sarabhanga to have been born.

Chaupái.

Said the saint: "Hearken, gracious Raghubír, the swan of Sankara's lake. I had taken my departure to the halls of the Creator,[2] but I heard say that Ráma is coming into the forest. Day and night I have been watching the road; now I have seen my lord and my heart is at rest. I am deficient my lord, in all that is good, but you have graciously acknowledged me as your humble servant. Now, sire, I have no request to make; I have accomplished my vow, O ravisher of the soul of the faithful, to wait in expectation of the suppliant's friend till I saw you and then to discard my body. I have practised meditation, sacrifice, prayers, penance and fasting, and have received the gift of faith as a boon of the lord. In this manner with his funeral pile all

1 The encounter with Virádha, which is here so very baldly told, occupies more than a hundred lines in Válmíki's poem.

2 Válmíki represents Indra as having come with his chariot and horses to carry off the sage to Bráhma's sphere at the very time of Ráma's arrival.

ready prepared, saint Sarabhanga has sat and waited, with a heart freed from every attachment.

Dohá 5.

May the Lord, whose body is dark of hue as a sombre raincloud, incarnate in form as the divine Ráma, dwell for ever in my soul together with Síta and his brother !"

Chaupai.

When he had thus said, the fire of his devotion consumed his body, and by Ráma's favour he ascended to Vaikunth.[1] The saint was not absorbed into the divinity for this reason, that he had already received the mysterious gift of faith.[2] When the assembled Rishis saw the great saint's translation, they were mightily rejoiced at heart and all broke forth into hymns of praise, 'Glory to the champion of the humble, the fountain of mercy.' Then Raghunáth went on further into the forest, and a great company of holy men with him. Seeing a heap of bones, he asked the saints about them and was moved with much compassion. "I know, but why ask, Master ? You are all-seeing and know even our thoughts. These are all saints whom the demon hosts have devoured." On hearing this, Raghubír's eyes filled with tears.

Dohá 6.

He raised his arms and vowed to rid the earth of demons : then gladdened the saints by visiting them all in turn at their hermitages.

Chaupái.

Saint Agastya had a learned disciple, by name Sutíkshna devoted to God ; in thought, word and deed one of Ráma's faithful servants, who had never even dreamt of any other hope or divinity. When he heard of the Lord's approach, he rushed out hurriedly, full of longing desire : "O God,

---

1 According to Válmíki it was not Vaikunth, but Bráhma's sphere, to which he was translated III 9. 36.

2 The reward of faith (*bhakti*) is the admission to the actual presence of the divinity in the sphere where he specially reigns Absorption into the divinity implies the extinction of individual existence and individual consciousness, and therefore, though the *summum bonum* of many Hindu sects, it is not so of those who cherish a personal love for any particular incarnation a love which can only be satisfied by a consciousness of the presence of the beloved.

the compassionate Raguhrári will be gracious to even a wretch like me. The holy Ráma and his brother will receive me as their own servant. I have no assured confidence of heart, no faith, nor command over self, nor wisdom of intellect; no communion with saints, no practice in meditation, prayer, or vigil, and no steadfast devotion to his lotus feet; only the promise of the All-merciful: 'He is my friend who goeth to none other.' To-day my eyes will be blest with the sight of the lotus-faced, the deliverer from the bondage of existence." The saint, philosopher as he was, was so utterly overwhelmed with love that his state, Bhaváni, was beyond all discription. He could not see his way either in this direction or in that, nor remember who he was, or where he was going; at one time he would turn and go back, at another would dance and sing songs of praise. The saint's love and faith waxed yet more vehement as the Lord watched him stealthily from behind a tree. Then Raghubír, who removes all the troubles of the world, after witnessing his exceeding devotion, manifested himself in his soul. The saint was struck motionless in the middle of the road, and his body bristled like the jack-fruit with every hair on end. Then Raghunáth drew near, rejoicing to witness the emotion of his servant, and tried many ways to rouse him; but he neither awoke nor derived any happiness from the vision; till Ráma doffed his kingly guise and mentally revealed himself as the four-armed god. The saint thereupon started up in alarm, like a poor snake that has been robbed of its jewel; but seeing before him the dark-hued Ráma with Síta and his younger brother, the abode of delight, he fell like a log at his feet, drowned in love and supremely happy. With his strong arms he took and lifted him and clasped him to his bosom with the utmost affection. As he embraced the saint, the All-merciful showed forth like a *tamála* tree clasped by a tree of gold: and the saint as he gazed on Ràma's face stood so still that you would take him for a figure painted in a picture.

Dohá 7.

At last the saint growing bolder at heart, after again and again clasping his feet, conducted the Lord to his hermitage and did everything in his honour.

Chaupái.

Said the saint: "Hearken, Lord, to my supplication; but how can I hymn thy praise? Thy greatness is immeasurable and my wit is scant, as ineffectual as a fire-fly in the presence of the sun, I adore without ceasing the divine Raghubír, with body dark of hue as a string of lotuses, with his knotted hair for a crown and an anchorite's dress for his robe, with bow and arrows in hand and quiver by his side. A fire to consume the dense forest of delusion, a sun to animate lotus growth of the saints, a lion against the elephant herd of demons, hawk to scatter the birds of metempsychosis, may he ever protect us with eyes bright as the lotus; apparelled with glory; the moon of Síta's partridge-like eyes; the swan in the lake of Siva's soul; the broad-chested, strong-armed Ráma, him I adore. A Garúr to devour the serpents of doubt; the queller of violence, wrangling and pain; the conqueror of death; the delight of the company of heaven: the home of compassion, may he ever protect us. At once bodiless and embodied, like and unlike, endowed with form and formless; transcending all thought, speech and perception; pure, all-pervading, faultless, illimitable, Ráma, the loosener of earth's, burdens, him I adore. A forest of trees of Paradise for his faithful people; the dispeller of passion, avarice, pride and lust; the All-beautiful; the bridge to cross the ocean of life, the champion of the Solar race, may he ever protect us. With unlimited might of arm, the home of strength; the true disperser of the manifold impurities of this iron age; the shield of righteousness; the giver of delights, the assemblage of all good qualities; may he, my Ráma, ever grant us prosperity. Though he be passionless, all-pervading, eternal, and ever dwelleth in the hearts of all; yet in his character of the wood-roaming conqueror of Khara, with his brother and bride, may he abide in my thoughts. They who understand, know him to be the Lord, though embodied, the bodiless ruler of the soul, the lotus-eyed sovereign of Kosala; then make thy abode in my heart, O Ráma. Never be this sentiment forgotten; I am his servant and Raghupati is my Lord." Ráma was pleased at heart on hearing the sain't speech, and in his delight pressed him again to his bosom: "Know, O Saint, that I am highly gratified: ask any boon and I will grant it you." Said the saint: "I have never begged a boon, nor can I discern between true and false. Whatever seems good to you, O Raghurái, that bestow upon me, for you are your servant's benefactor." "I give you steadfast faith, self-control, and wisdom, and make you a storehouse of all virtue and knowledge." "I have received, my lord, the boon that you have given, now grant me my own wish.

Dohá 8.

O my lord Ráma, with your brother and Jánaki, yourself equipt with bow and arrows, for ever abide like the moon in the heaven of my soul."[1]

Chaupái.

'So be it,' said Lakshmi's lord, as he joyously started on his visit to the Rishi Agastya. "It is a long time since I last saw my *guru*, and since I came to live in this hermitage; now, my lord, I will go and see him with you; I am not putting you under any obligation." The Fountain of

---

1 Tulsi Dás's theory as the principal that should regulate man's prayers to Heaven is enforced by the example of the famous sages and ascetics, whom he so frequently brings before his readers and whose aspirations refer exclusively to spiritual blessings. An exact parallel is afforded by the teaching of the great English moralist of the last century as inculcated in the following lines:—

> "Yet when the scene of sacred presence fires,
> And strong devotion to the skies aspires,
> Pour forth thy fervour for a healthful mind,
> Obedient passions and a will resigned,
> For love which scarce collective man can fill,
> For patience, sovereign o'er transmuted ill,
> For faith, that—panting for a happier seat—
> Counts death kind nature's signal of retreat."

Detachment from the world, subjugation of the passions, love for the divinity, patience under suffering, and, to crown all, an unhesitating faith are the highest boons that man can secure; the last being followed after death by the beatific vision of the godhead, a joy for all eternity, an everlasting harmony, in which God will know Himself, and all will know God.

mercy saw through the saint's craftiness, and both brothers smiled as they took him with them. Discoursing on the excellence of faith in himself, the king of the gods arrived at the saint's hermitage. Sutíkshna at once went to the guru and after prostrating himself thus addressed him: "My lord, the son of the sovereign of Kosala, the refuge of the world, has come to see you, even Ráma, with his brother and Vaidehi, to whom, sir, you make your prayer night and day." As soon as he heard this, Agastya started up and ran, and at the sight of Hari, his eyes filled with tears. The two brothers fell at the saint's holy feet, but he took and clasped them to his bosom with the utmost affection. After courteously enquiring of their welfare, the holy sage conducted them to a seat and then again did all homage to his lord, saying: 'There is no other man so blessed as I am.' So long as the other hermits stayed, their delight was to gaze upon the root of joy.

Dohá 9.

As he sat in their midst with their eyes all fastened upon his person, they seemed like a bevy of partridges gazing on the autumnal moon.

Chaupái.

Then said Raghubir to the saint: "My lord, nothing is hid from you; you know why I have come, and therefore, sire, there is no need to inform you. Give me now some charm by which I may destroy the persecutors of the saints." The sage smiled when he heard the lord's speech: "You ask me, sire; but what do I know? By virtue of my devotion to you, O destroyer of sin, I understand a little of your greatness. Your delusive power is a vast fig[1] tree, its clustering fruit the countless multitude of worlds, while all things animate and inanimate are like the insects that dwell inside, and think their own particular fig the only one in existence. This fruit is devoured by harsh and inexorable fate, but even he

1 The word in the text is *dunri* which represents the Sanskrit *udumbara*, the *ficus glomerata*. It bears large clusters of fruit, and every single fig in every cluster is always full of insects.

trembles in fear of you. You, sire, are the sovereign of all the spheres, and you ask of me, as though you were only a man. O fountain of mercy, I beg this boon; dwell in my heart Lakshmi and your brother, and grant me steadfast faith, pity, fellowship with the saints, and unbroken love for your lotus feet. Though you are supreme spirit, indivisible and eternal, beyond the reach of perception, the adoration of the saints, yet I declare and recognize your incarnation, and again and again adore the embodiment of Brahm and Rati. You always exalt your own servants, and this, Raghurái, is the reason why you consult me. There is, my lord, a very charming and holy spot called Panchavati. Sanctify the whole Dandaka forest, in which it is, and relieve it of the saint's grievous curse,[1] by taking up your abode there, Rama; and thus show mercy to all the saints." On receiving his permission, Ráma set out and quickly arrived at Panchavati.

Dohá 10.

After meeting the king of the vultures [2] and warmly renewing old friendship, Ráma stayed near the Godávari, where he made himself a thatched cottage.

Chaupái.

From the time that Rama took up his abode there, the saints lived happily and without fear. The mountains, woods, rivers and lakes were suffused with beauty and day by day grew yet more exceedingly lovely. The many birds and deer were full of joy and the bees added a charm by their sweet buzzing. Not even the serpent-king would be able to describe the forest, in which the glorious Ráma had manifested himself. One day, as the Lord was sitting at ease, Lakshman most humbly addressed him thus: " Sovereign of gods, men and saints, and of all animate and

---

1 The curse had been pronounced by Bhárgava, whose daughter Abjá had been violated by Danda, son of Ikshavâu, who was then king of country. His populous realm at once became a wild forest waste, inhabited only by wild beasts and demons.

2 The interview with the vulture-king Jatâyu, thus briefly despatched in two lines, occupies the whole of the 20th canto in the Sanskrit Aranyakând. It was on this occasion that he made the promise to protect Síta which subsequently cost him his life.

inanimate creation, I have a question to ask of you as of my own special master. Speak, sire, and answer it for me, for I have left all to serve the dust of your feet. Explain to me knowledge, self-governance, and the delusion of Máya ; tell me what is that faith to which you extend mercy.

Dohá 11.

Instruct me, my lord, in all the difference between God and the soul, that I may be entirely devoted to your feet and free from grief, ignorance and error."

Chaupái.

"I will explain the whole matter in brief; hearken, brother, with attention of mind and soul. It is from egoism and distinctions between mine and thine, that the illusion is produced which has subjugated all classes of existence. The senses and the objects of the senses, as far as the mind can reach, are all a delusion, brother; understand that. Now learn its divisions: they are two, *viz.*, knowledge and ignorance ; the one utterly bad and calamitous, which forces the principle of life down into the pit of transmigration ; the other, the power by virtue of which the world is created, being sent by God, and having no strength of itself. Knowledge, in which there is no particle of self-consciousness, sees the supreme spirit equally in all things; and he, brother, is to be reckoned chief of stoics, who abandons fortune, and the three elements of which the universe, is composed as if of no more account than a blade of grass.

Dohá 12.

That is to be called soul which, through the power of delusion, does not recognize itself as being really God ; [1] God the giver of bondage and of deliverance, the head of all things, the sender forth of delusion, the one goal.

Chaupái.

After piety, asceticism ; and after ascetic meditation knowledge : and knowledge, as the Vedas declare, is the

1 Or it may be thus translated : 'That is to be called soul, which doubts regarding itself whether it be a delusive manifestation or really God.'

giver of salvation. But that at which I melt more quickly, brother, is faith, which is the blessing of my votaries ; it stands by itself without other support, and is above all knowledge whether spiritual or profane. Faith, brother, is an incomparable source of happiness, and only to be acquired by the favour of a saint. But I will explain the means towards it, the easy path by which men may find me. In the first place, an exceeding devotion to Bráhmans and in every action a close adherence to scriptural prescription. Secondly, the fruit of this will be detachment from the world, and then will spring up a delight in my worship. The nine kinds of faith as exercised by the ears, &c., will strengthen ; there will be an exceeding love in the soul for my manifestations, a great affection for the lotus feet of the saints, a persistency in prayer—in deed and in heart as well as in tongue—and faithfulness in service done to one's guru, or father and mother, or family, or loads and masters, knowing it to be really done to me. While singing my praises the body quivers, the voice trembles, the eyes flow with tears ; and neither lust, pride, nor deceit, finds a place in the soul ; I am ever, brother, at the command of such a one as this.

Dohá 13.

I take up my abode for ever in the lotus heart of those who in thought, word and deed make their fervent prayer to my incarnation.

Chaupái.

On hearing the doctrine of faith and devotion,[1] thus expounded, Lakshman was greatly rejoiced and bowed his head at his lord's feet. In this manner several days were spent in discourses on asceticism, wisdom, virtue and

1 *Yoga*, the word here rendered 'devotion,' is one of the system of Hindu philosophy. Its chief aim is to teach the means by which the human soul may attain complete union with the Supreme Being. It is defined by Patanjali, the founder of the school, as 'the prevention of the modifications of thought by the practice of self-mortification and by keeping the mind constantly unaffected by all external influence.' The final beatitude, which is held out as the reward of such devotion, consists in the cessation of all idea of self and of any distinction between matter and spirit.

morality. One day Rávan's sister, Sùrpa-nakhá, foul-hearted and venomous as a serpent, came to Panchavati and was excited by the sight of the two princes. A woman, Garúr, must needs look after a handsome man, whether he be brother, father or son.[1] In her excitement she could not contain herself, life the sun-stone that melts at the sight of the sun. Having assumed a beautiful form, she went to the Lord and with many smiles thus addressed him : " There is not another man like you, nor a woman like me ; here is a match that God has taken some pains to make. I have searched the three spheres, but have not found anywhere in the world a man with beauty to equal mine. And for this reason I have till now remained a virgin, but now that I have seen you I am fairly satisfied." The Lord looked at Síta and said in reply : " My younger brother is a bachelor." The demon's sister took the hint and went to Lakshman. He looked to his lord and said in gentle tones : " Hearken, fair lady, I am his servant ; it is not right that you should be in subjection to any one. My lord is the mighty king of Kosala, and whatever he does is all done at his own pleasure. A servant who expects to take his ease, a beggar who expects honour, a spendthrift who hopes for wealth, a profligate who hopes for heaven, or an avaricious man who expects renown, these are four dreamers, men who would expect milk from milking the air." Again she turned and came to Ráma, but he sent her back once more to Lakshman. Said Lakshman, " The bridegroom for you must be a man lost to all sense of shame." Then in a fury she went to Ráma, revealing herself in a shape of terror. Raghurái, seeing that Síta was frightened, made a sign to his brother ;

Doha 14. ३१

And Lakshman with the greatest ease struck off her nose[2] and ears : her hands he sent to Rávan in defiance.

---

1 That is to say apparently, whatever his age may be, whether he be of the same age or old enough to be a father, or young enough to be a son.

2 The traditionary scene of this event is laid at Násik, which is supposed to derive its name from Násika, 'a nose.' The suburb on the Opposite bank of the river Godávari is still called Panchavati.

Chaupái.

Without nose and ears she was as hideous to look upon as a mountain flowing with torents of red ochre. She went moaning to Khara and Dúshan ; " A curse, a curse, I say, on your manhood and strength, brother." They questioned and she told them all. When they heard, the demons gathered an army, and a swarming multitude of fiends rushed forth like so many winged mountains of darkness, on diverse vehicles, of diverse shapes, armed with diverse weapons, terrible and beyond number. At the head went Súrpa-nakhá in hideous guise, without ears and nose. Many fearful omens of ill occurred, but the host heeded them not, being all death-doomed. They shouted, they defied the enemy, they leaped in the air, their captains inspected the ranks and rejoiced exceedingly. Said one, ' Capture the two brothers alive and then take and kill them and carry off the bride.' The vault of heaven was filled with the dust of them. Ráma called his brother and said: " Take Jánaki away to some mountain-cave ; a terrible array of demons has come; remain on your guard." Obedient to his lord's command he took his bow and arrows in hand and led Sita away. When Ráma saw that the hostile force had drawn near, he smiled as he strung his massive bow.

Chhand 3.

As he strung his massive bow and bound up his long hair in a knot on his head, he seemed as it were a sapphire rock encircled with flushes of lightning and with two snakes entwining its summit. As the Lord girded up his quiver by his side and clasped the bow in his mighty arm and fitted the arrow to the string, he glared with the glance of a lion on a herd of elephants.

Sorathá 6.

The warriors came on with a rush, shouting ' seize him, seize him,' for they saw that he was alone: the demons closed round upon him, but he stood as the rising sun,

Chaupái.

and at the sight of his majesty they could not discharge

their arrows; the whole demon host became powerless. Khara and Dúshan summoned their ministers and said: "This ornament of the human race must be some king's son. Nágas, demons, gods, men and saints of all sorts I have seen, conquered and slain; but in the whole of my life—mark me my brethren all—I have never seen such beauty. Though he has disfigured my sister, so incomparable a hero is not worthy of death. 'At once put away and surrender your bride and return home alive, you and your brother.' Declare to him this that I have said and quickly come back with his answer." The heralds went and told Ráma. He smiled to hear them and said: "I am a warrior by caste and am hunting this wood; wretches like you are the game that I am tracking. I am not dismayed at the sight of the enemy's strength, but am ready to do combat with death himself. Though a man, I am the exterminator of the race of demons; and though a mere child I am the protector of the saints and the destroyer of the wicked. If there is no strength in you, turn and go home; I will never turn my back upon the battle. If you have come up to fight, show now your cunning and dexterity; mercy to an enemy is the height of weakness." The heralds immediately went and repeated all this: Khara and Dúshan's heart was on fire when they heard it.

Chhand 4.

Their heart was on fire and they cried: "Rush upon him and seize him, ye mighty demon warriors, with your bows and arrows, clubs, pikes, spears, scymetars, maces and axes." The lord gave his bow one twang; in a moment, at the awful and terrible sound the demons were deafened and dismayed, they had no sense left in them.

Dohá 15.

When they had recovered themselves they made a rush, for they knew the strength of their foe; and shafts and weapons of all kinds began to rain upon Ráma. But Raghubír cleft them in twain, making them of no more account than so many sesamum seeds, and then drawing the bowstring to his ear he let fly his own arrows.

Chhand 5–6.

Then the terrible arrows sped forth, hissing like many serpents. The holy Ráma waxed wrath in battle; his arrows flew of exceeding sharpness. When they saw his shafts so keen, the demon leaders turned to flight; but the three brothers became furious: 'Whoever runs from the field I will slay with my own hand; let him stay then and make up his mind to die.' Weapons of diverse kinds beat upon him from the front, and the Lord perceiving that the foe was exceedingly furious fitted an arrow to his bow. He let fly the huge bolts; the hideous demons were cut to pieces; bodies, heads, arms, hands and feet were scattered about all over the ground. The shrill arrows struck; like mountains the bodies fall. The leaders had their frames cut into a hundred pieces, yet they stood up again by power of magic. Many arms and heads flew through the air and headless trunks ran to and fro. Kites, crows and Jackals made an awful and horrible wrangling.

Chhand 7.

Jackals wrangled; ghosts, goblins and demons made cups of the skulls; more warlike devils clashed skulls together for music, and witches danced. Raghubír's mighty arrows smote off the leaders' bodies, arms and heads; they fell on every side, but stood up again to fight with terrible cries of 'strike, strike.' Vultures flew away with men's entrails in their claws, goblins scampered off with hands that they had seized; one might fancy all the children of Battle-town were flying kites. The mighty champions lay dead and vanquished, with mangled bodies. Seeing their army routed, Khara and Dúshan, with Trisira and the other champions, stood at bay, and all at once demons innumerable hurled furiously against Raghubír arrow and spear, club, axe, javelin and dagger. In the twinkling of an eye the Lord had warded off all his enemies' missiles and sent forth his own arrows, slaying all the demon leaders with ten shafts planted in the breast of each of them. Though they fell to the ground, they rose again in their valour and joined in the fray, and would not die, but made the strangest sight. The gods feared, when they saw the demons fourteen thousand in number, and the king of Avadh alone ; till the Lord perceiving alarm of goods and saints, and having power over all illusion, wrought a prodigy, and while they were yet looking at one another he finished the battle, and the army of the enemy all perished fighting,

Dohá 16.

crying 'Ráma, Ráma,' as their soul left their body; they thus attained beatitude. In a moment the Fountain of mercy slew all his enemies by magic. The gods in their joy rained down flowers, instruments of music sounded in the áir, and with cries of 'Glory, glory,' they all departed, each in his own splendid carriage.

Chaupái.

When Raghunáth had vanquished his foes in the battle, gods, men and saints were all relieved from fear. Lakshman then brought back Síta. As she fell at her lord's feet, he took and rapturously clasped her to his bosom, and she fixed her gaze upon his dark and delicate form, but so vehement was her love that her eyes could never be satisfied. Thus the blessed Ráma stayed at Panchavati, delighting gods and saints by the deeds that he did. But Súrpanakhá, when she saw the death of Khara and Dúshan, went and called Rávan. In tones full of fury she cried: "You have lost all thought of realm and treasure ; you drink and sleep day and night and do not consider that the enemy is at your gate. A kingdom without policy, wealth without religion. good works without consecration to Hari, knowledge without discretion, these all bring no fruit save trouble to the student, the doer, or the possessor. An ascetic is quickly undone by attachment, a king by ill-counsel, wisdom by conceit, modesty by drinking, friendship by want of consideration, and good sense by pride; so goes the saying.

Sorathá 7.

An enemy, sickness, fire, sin, a master and a serpent are never to be accounted trifles." So saying and with much lamentation beside she set to weeping.

Dohá 17.

In her distress she threw herself down in the midst of the assembly with many tears and cries, "O Rávan, to think that you should live and see me thus treated!"

Chaupái.

When they heard this, the assembly rose in confusion and took her by the hand and lifted her up and consoled her. Said the king of Lanká: "Why do you not tell me what has happened? who has cut off your nose and ears?" "The sons of Dasarath, the lord of Avadh, very lions of men, have come to hunt the forest. I understood what they were about; they would rid the earth of demons. Relying on the might of their arm, O Rávan, the saints roam the woods without any fear. They are children to look at, but in fact resistless as Death himself, the most intrepid of archers, with many strings to their bow.[1] Both brothers are glorious with incomparable might, and have devoted themselves to the extermination of the wicked and the relief of gods and saints. Ráma—for such is his name—is the very perfection of beauty, and with him is a young girl, whom the Creator has made the loveliest of the sex: a hundred million Ratis would be no match for her. It is his younger brother who cut off my ears and nose and made a mock of me, when he heard I was your sister. When Khara and Dúshan were told of this, they gave him challenge; but in an instant he slew the whole of their army." When he heard of the defeat of Khara, Dúshan and Trisira, the Ten-headed was on fire all over.

[1] In the word *guna-nana*, *guna* is intended to be understood in its two senses of, 1st, a virtue, 2ndly a bowstring.

Dohá 18.

After consoling Súrpa-nakhá and forcing himself to say much to her, he went to his palace in a great state of anxiety and had no sleep all night.

Chaupái.

" Among gods, men and demons, serpents and birds, there is none who can withstand my servants ; and Khara and Dúshan were my own equals in strength ; who can have killed them, unless it be God himself ? If God has become incarnate, in order to rejoice the saints and relieve earth of its burden, then if I go and fight against him and lose my life by an arrow of the Lord's, I shall escape further transmigration ; prayer will not do for one like me of demon form ; this is the plan upon which I am absolutely determined. If he is only some earthly king's son, I shall conquer them both in battle and carry off the bride." He mounted his chariot and went off alone to the spot where Márícha was living by the sea-shore. Hearken now, Umá, to the delectable account of the device that Ráma invented.

Dohá 19.

When Lakshman had gone into the wood to gather roots, fruits and herbs, the gentle and joyous god said with a smile to Janak's daughter :

Chaupái.

" Hearken, most lovely and amiable of faithful wives, I am going to act a fantastic human part. Be you absorbed into fire until I have completed the destruction of the demons." As soon as Ráma had finished speaking she pressed her lord's feet to her heart and entered into the fire, leaving only an image of herself, of exactly the same appearance and the same amiable and gentle disposition. Lakshman did not know this mystery or that the god had taken any action. The Ten-headed approached Márícha and bowed his head, the selfish and contemptible wretch. When a mean creature bends, it is only to give more pain, like an elephant-goad, a bow, a snake, or a cat; the friendly speech of a churl is as portentous, Bhavání, as flowers that blossom out of season.

Dohá 20.

After doing him homage, Máricha respectfully enquired of him his business : " What is the cause, my son, that you have come so disturbed in mind and all alone ? "

Chaupái.

Rávan put the whole matter before him and added presumptuously--the wretch—" Do you for the purpose of deception assume the form of a deer, and by this means, I shall be able to carry off the princess." He replied :— " Hearken, Rávan ; though in form as a man, this is the lord of all animate and inanimate creation ; there is no fighting against him, my son ; if he kills, you die ; and if you live, it is he who gives you life. He is the prince Raghupati, who when he went to protect the saint's sacrifice, smote me with a pointless arrow, and in an instant I was driven a distance of a hundred leagues :[1] it is not well to quarrel with him. Wherever I look, I see these two brothers, and my senses are utterly bewildered like a fly fascinated by a spider. Even if he be only a man my son, he is a tremendous hero, and opposition to him will do no good.

Dohá 21.

But can he possibly be a man, who was strong enough to vanquish Táraka and Subáhu, who broke Síva's bow and slew Khara, Dûshan and Trisira ?

Chaupái.

Consider the welfare of your family and go home." When he heard this, he was furious and abused him soundly : " You fool, you take upon yourself to teach me, as if you were my master ! Tell me where is there in the world any warrior my equal ? " Máricha then thought to himself : " There are nine whom it is not good to make enemies ; an armed man, an accomplice, a king, a man without principle, a rich man, a physician, a panegyrist, poet or any person of special ability." Either way he saw he must die ; but he reflected that Ráma would be his sanctuary. So he answered : " You will be the death of me, poor wretch ;

1 See Book I, *chaupai* 211.

for how can I escape when smitten by Raghupati's shaft ?" With these thoughts at heart, he accompanied Rávan, staunch in his devotion to Ráma's feet and with an exceeding gladness of heart that he would not show : "To-day I shall behold my best beloved.

Chhand 8.

My eyes will be rewarded with the sight of my best beloved, and I shall be happy. I shall imprint upon my soul the feet of the All-merciful with Síta too and his brother. Hari, the ocean of beatitude, whose very wrath confers salvation, who gives himself up entirely to the will of his worshippers, will with his own hands fit an arrow to the string and slay me.

Dohá 22.

As he runs after me to seize me with his bow and arrows, I shall ever and again turn and get a sight of my lord : there is none else so blessed as I am."

Chaupái.

When the Ten-headed drew near to the wood, Máricha took the form of a deer, so beautifully spotted as to defy description, with a body of gold, all bespangled with jewels. When Síta saw the wonderously beautiful creature clothed with loveliness in its every limb, she cried : "O Raghubír, hearken, kind sir, this deer has a most charming skin ; I pray you, shoot it, most amiable lord, and bring me the hide." Thereupon Ráma, who understood the meaning of it all, arose with joy to execute the purpose of the gods, Having marked the deer, he girded up his waistbelt, took his bow in his hand and trimmed his shapely arrows. Then the lord cautioned Lakshman : "Many demons, brother, roam the forest ; take care of Síta with all thought and consideration and with force too, if occasion require it." The deer seeing the Lord, took to flight : Ráma pursued with ready bow : even he, to whom the Veda cannot attain, nor Siva is able to contemplate, hastened in pursuit of a mimic deer. Now close at hand, now fleeing at a distance, at one time in sight, at another hid, alternately showing and concealing itself and practising every kind of wile, in this manner it took the Lord far away. At last Ráma aimed and let fly the fatal shaft; the deer fell to the ground with a terrible cry, first calling aloud to Lakshman, but afterwards mentally invoking Ráma. As life ebbed, he resumed his natural form and devoutly repeated the name of Ráma, who in his wisdom recognizing his inward love, gave him such a place in heaven as saints can scarcely attain to.

Dohá 23.

The gods rained down abundant flowers and hymned the Lord's high virtue: "Raghunáth, the suppliant's friend, raises to his own sphere even a demon!"

Chaupái.

As soon as he had slain the monster, Raghubír returned; the bow gleaming in his hand and the quiver by his side. When Síta heard the agonizing cry, she called to Lakshman in the greatest alarm: "Go in haste, your brother is in some sad strait." Lakshman answered with a smile. "Hearken, mother; he, by the play of whose eyebrows the world is annihilated, cannot be imagined as having fallen into any difficulty." But when Síta urged him with taunting words, Lakshman's resolution—for such was Hari's will—was shaken; he made over charge of everything to the forest and its gods, and went after the Ráhu of the moon-like Rávan. When the Ten-headed saw the ground vacant he drew near in the guise of an anchorite. He, for fear of whom gods and demons trembled and could neither sleep by night nor eat food by day, even that Rávan came looking this side and that, as furtively as a cur bent on thieving. After he had turned his steps, Garúr, to this vile course, not a particle of his majesty, or intellect, or strength of body was left in him. After repeating a variety of legends and moral sentiments, he had recourse to threats and blandishments. Said Síta, "Hearken, reverend Father; what you say is hateful to me." Then Rávan showed himself in his proper form ; and she was terror-stricken when he declared his name. But plucking up all her courage she said: "Wretch, stay as you are; my lord is at hand. Like as a hare that would wed a lioness, so have you wooed your own destruction, O demon king." On hearing this speech the Ten-headed was furious, though in his heart he delighted to adore her feet.

Dohá 24.

Rávan angrily seized her and seated her in his chariot. As he took his way through the air, he was so agitated with fear that he could scarcely drive.

Chaupái.

"Ah! gallant Raghurái, sovereign of the universe, for what fault of mine have you forgotten mercy? Ah! reliever of distress, health-giving sanctuary, sun of the lotuses of the Raghu race. Ah! Lakshman! this is no fault of yours; I have reaped the fruit of the temper I showed." Manifold were the lamentations that she uttered. "My affectionate and loving lord is far away; who will tell him of my calamity; that an ass is devouring the oblation intended for the gods!" At the sound of Síta's woeful lament every created being, whether animate or inanimate, was made sad. The vulture-king, too, heard her piteous cry and recognized the wife of the glory of Raghu's line, whom the vile demon was carrying away, as it were the famous dun cow that had fallen into the hands of some savage. "Fear not, Síta my daughter, I will annihilate this monster." The bird darted forth in its fury, like a thunderbolt launched against a mountain. "Stop you villain, how dare you go on thus and take no heed of me." Seeing him bearing down upon him like the angel of death, Rávan paused and considered: "Is it mount Maináka[1] or the king of the birds! anyhow they both know my might, as also do their lords."[2] When he

1 Maináka is the only peak which is said to have retained its wings when Indra clipped those of the other mountains.

2 Maináka's lord is the Ocean, which Rávan and the other demons had churned; and Garúr, 'the king of the birds,' has Vishnu for his lord, with whom Rávan had always been at war.

perceived that it was poor old Jatáyu, he cried, "he shall leave his body at the shrine of my hands."[1] At this, the vulture rushed on in a fury, crying: "Hearken, Rávan, to my advice; surrender Jánaki and go home in peace; if not, despite your many arms, it will turn out thus; Ráma's wrath is like a fierce flame, and your whole house will be consumed in it like a moth." The warrior demon gave no answer. Then the vulture rushed wildly on and clutched him by the hair and dragged him from his chariot so that he fell to the ground. Again, having sheltered Síta, the vulture turned and with his beak tore and rent his body. For nearly half an hour the demon was in a swoon, then gnashed his teeth with rage and drew his monstrous sword and cut off Jatáyu's wings. The bird fell to the ground, calling upon Ráma, and doing marvellous feats of courage. Then Rávan again seated Síta in the chariot and drove off in haste in no little alarm. Síta was borne through the air lamenting, like a frightened fawn in the power of a huntsman. Seeing the monkeys sitting on the rocks, she cried out Hari's name and dropt her scarf. In this manner he went off with Síta and put her down in the Asoka forest.

Dohá 25.

Though he tried every kind of threat and blandishment, the monster could not succeed, and at last after exhausting all his devices he left her under the Asoka tree. With Ráma's beauteous form impressed upon her heart, as he appeared when pursuing the mimic deer. Síta was incessantly invoking his name, O Hari, Hari!"

Chaupái.

When Raghupati saw his brother coming, he was seized with a new and greater fear: "O brother, have you left Síta alone and come here against my order, though so many demons roam the forest? My mind misgives me that Síta is not at the hermitage." Lakshman clasped his lotus feet and cried with folded hands: "Hearken, my lord, it is no

---

1 That is to say, 'as a man goes to a place of pilgrimage in order to die there, so has he come to me to die by my hand.'

fault of mine." When he found the hermitage bereft of Síta, he was as agitated as any commom man. "Alas! Jánaki, my precious Síta, so beautiful and amiable, so divinely pious and devoted!" Lakshman did all he could to comfort him. As he went along, he questioned all the trees and flowers by the way: "O ye birds and deer, O ye swarms of bees, have you seen the fawn-eyed Síta? The wagtails, parrots, and pigeons; the deer and fish; swarming bees and clever cuckoos: the jasmine and pomegranate flowers; the lightning, the lotus, the autumn moon; the gliding serpent; the meshes of Varuna, the bow of Kámadeva; the swan, the elephant and the lion can now hear themselves praised; the cocoanut, the champa, and the plantain can now rejoice, without any doubt or misgiving at heart.[1] Hearken, Jánaki, now that you are away, they are all as glad as if they had gotten a kingdom. How can I endure this cruelty at your hands; why do you not at once disclose yourself, my beloved?" In this manner the lord searched and lamented, like a fond lover distressed by separation. Ráma who has no wish unsatisfied, the perfection of bliss, the uncreated and the everlasting, acted the part of a man. Further on he saw the vulture-king lying, with his thoughts fixed on the prints of Ráma's feet.

Dohá 26.

The compassionate Raghubír laid his lotus hands upon his head. At the sight of Ráma's lovely face all his pain was forgotten,

Chaupái.

and the vulture recovered himself and spoke as follows. "Hearken Ráma, remover of life's troubles. My lord, this is Rávan's doing; he is the wretch, who has carried off Janak's daughter. He took her away, sire, to the south, crying as

1 The different objects here mentioned from the Hindu poet's stock in trade upon which he invariably draws for comparisons when he wishes to describe the charms of a lovely woman: with clustering hair like swarms of bees, teeth white as buds of jasmine, lips like the pomegranate, eyes bright as flashes of lightning, breasts swelling like cocoanuts, waist like a lion's, a gait like an elephant's &c., &c. Now that Síta is gone, who excelled each of them in the very point on which they most prided themselves, they may again hear themselves quoted as perfect.

piteously as an osprey. I have kept alive, my lord, only to see you ; now, O most merciful, I would depart." Said Ráma : "Remain alive, father." He smiled and answered : "He, by the repetition of whose name at the hour of death the vilest sinner, as the scriptures declare, attains salvation, has come in bodily form before my eyes ; what need is there, sire, for me to live any longer ?" Raghurài's eyes filled with tears as he replied : "Father, it is your own good, deeds that have saved you. There is nothing in the world beyond the reach of those who devote their soul to the good of others. When you pass out of the body, father, ascend to my sphere in heaven. What more can I give you ? your every wish is gratified." Dropping the form of a vulture, he appeared in all the beauty of Hari, bedecked with jewels and in gorgeous yellow attire, with dark-hued body and four mighty arms, and with his eyes full of tears he chanted this hymn of praise :

Chhand 9.

"Glory to Ráma of incomparably beauty ; the bodiless, the embodied ; the veritable source of every bodily element ; who with mighty arrows has broken the might of the arm of the ten-headed demon ; the ornament of the earth With his body dark as a rain-cloud, with his lotus face and his eyes large as the lotus flower, I unceasingly worship Ráma the merciful, the mighty-armed, the dispeller of all life's terrors ; of immeasurable strength ; without beginning and unborn ; the indivisible ; the one ; beyond the reach of all the senses ; the incarnate Govinda ; the annihilator of duality ; the profound in wisdom ; the supporter of the earth ; an everlasting delight to the soul of the saints, who practise the spell of Ráma's name. I unceasingly worship Ráma, the friend of the unsensual, the destroyer of lust and every other wickedness. He, whom the scriptures hymn under the name of the passionless Brahm, the all-pervading, the supreme spirit, the unbegotten ; to whom the saints attain after infinite study and contemplation, penance and abstraction ; he the all-merciful, the all-radiant, the unapproachable, has now become manifest for the delight of the world. He who is at once inaccessible and accessible, like and unlike, the essentially pure, the unfailing comforter, whom ascetics behold only when they have laboriously subdued their mind and senses; even Ráma, the spouse of Lakshmi, who is ever at the command of his servants, though the lord of the three spheres, may he abide in my heart, the terminator of transmigration, whose praises make pure."

Dohá 27.

After asking the boon of perfect faith, the vulture departed for Harí's sphere. Ràma with his own hands performed his funeral rites with all due ceremony.

Chaupái.

The tender-hearted and compassionate Rághunáth, who shows mercy even on the undeserving, bestowed upon a vulture, an unclean flesh-eating bird, such a place in heaven as the greatest ascetics desire. Hearken, Uma; the most miserable of men are they who abandon Hari and become attached to objects of sense.

The two brothers in their search for Síta visited and examined many woods, tangled with creepers, dense with trees, and swarming with birds, deer, elephants and lions. As they went on their way they overthrew Kabandha, who declared the whole history of the curse. "Durvásas[1] cursed me, but now that I have seen my lord's feet, my sin has been blotted out." Hearken, Gandharva; those who trouble Bráhmans are displeasing to me.

Dohá 28.

They who without guile in thought, word and deed do

1 The reference to Durvásas is obscure. According to the legend as told by Vàlmíki, Kabandha had been a beautiful youth by name Danu, who as a reward for penance abtained from heaven the boon of a long life. On the strength of this promise he ventured to challenge Indra to battle, who launched his thunderbolt against him and drove his head and shoulders down into his body, which was thus made a horrible headless shapeless trunk. To keep him from starving, since he needs must live, his arms were made a league long; and a huge mouth was opened in his belly In the text as translated by Griffith, there is mention of a sage Sthúla-Siras (Great-head) who had been annoyed by Danu and therefore cursed him; but the passage has rather the air of an interpolation, and does not appear in Gorresio's edition. The meaning of the word *kabandha* is 'a headless trunk.'

service to (the gods of earth,) subdue unto themselves Bráhma, Síva, myself and every other divinity.

Chaupái.

A Bráhman, though he curse, beat and abuse you, is still an object of reverence; so declare the saints. A Bráhman must be honoured, though devoid of every virtue and merit; but a Súdra never, though distinguished for all virtue and learning." So saying, he instructed him in his doctrine and was pleased to see his devotion to his feet. When the beneficent Ráma had given him beatitude, he passed on to the hermitage of Savari.[1] When she saw that Ráma had come to her abode, she remembered the saint's promise and was glad of heart. With lotus eyes, mighty arms, hair fastened up in a knot on their head, and a garland of wild flowers upon their breast, one dark of hue, the other fair, stood the two brothers. Savari fell and embraced their feet. She was so drowned in love that no speech came to her lips, but again and again she bowed her head at their lotus feet, then reverently brought water and laved their feet and finally conducted them to a seat of honour.

Dohá 29.

Then she brought and presented to Ráma the most delicious fruits and herbs and roots, and the lord graciously ate of them, again and again thanking her.

Chaupái.

She stood before him with folded hands and as she gazed upon the Lord her love waxed yet more vehement. "How can I hymn thy praises, seeing that I am of meanest descent and of dullest wit: the lowest of the low and a woman to boot; nay among the lowest of woman the one who is of all most ignorant, O sinless god." Said Raghupati: "Hearken, lady, to my words: I recognize no kinsmanship save that of faith; neither lineage, family, religion,

1 *Savara*, is the feminine *savari*, is, strictly speaking, not the distinctive name of any one particular person, but of a whole savage tribe. The word is probably connected with *sava*, 'a corpse.'

rank, wealth, power, connections, virtue, nor ability. A man without faith is of no more account than a cloud without water. I will explain to you the nine kinds of faith ; hearken attentively and lay them up in your mind. The first step in faith is communion with the saints ; the second a love for the legends relating to me :

Dohá 30.

The third,—an incalculable step—devotion to the lotus feet of the guru ; the fourth, singing my praises with a guileless purpose.

Chaupái.

The fifth, as the Vedas have expounded, prayer and the repetition, with an assured confidence, of mystic spells : the sixth, self-governance, kindness, detachment from the world and in every action a loving and persevering piety ; the seventh, seeing the whole world full of me, and holding the saints in yet greater account than myself ; the eighth, contentment with what one has, without ever a thought of spying out fault in others ; the ninth, a guileless simplicity towards all, and a hearty confidence in me without either exultation or dejection. Verily, lady, whoever possesses any one of these, whether he be man or woman, rational or irrational, is my friend ; and you have them all in the highest degree. The heavenly prize, which the greatest ascetics scarcely win, is to-day within your easy reach. The result of seeing me is something most marvellous ; every creature at once attains its proper consummation. But lady, have you any tidings of Jánaki ; tell me, fair dame, all that you know." "Go, Raghurai, to the lake Pampá ; there make friends with Sugriva ;[1] he will tell you all. You know it already my god Raghubir, yet have the patience to ask him." After again and again bowing her head at the Lord's feet, she lovingly repeated the whole story.

Chhand 10.

After repeating the whole story, as she gazed on Hari's

1 According to the Sanskrit Rámáyana it was not Savari, but Kabandha, who directed Ráma to apply to Sugriva.

face and imprinted his lotus feet on her heart, she left her body in the sacrificial fire and became absorbed in Hari's feet beyond return. O men, abandon all your religious observances, which are unrighteousness, and your many sects, which yield only sorrow, and with all confidence (says Tulsi Dás) lovingly embrace the feet of Ráma.

Dohá 31.

He gave salvation to a woman of such low descent and so altogether born in sin as even this Savari was: foolish indeed are they who desire peace of mind after forgetting such a lord.

Chaupái.

When they had left this wood, they went on their way Ráma and his brother, two lions among men, of immeasurable strength. The Lord, like a bereaved lover, kept making lamentation and turning his discourse to many topics: "Observe, Lakshman, the beauty of the forest; whose heart is not moved to see it? The birds and deer, all accompanied by their mates, seem to laugh and jeer at me. When the deer see me and would scamper away, he does cry; 'Have no fear, enjoy yourselves, for you are genuine deer, and it is only a golden deer that these people have come to look for.' The female elephants, as they take aside their lords, seem to be giving me this caution; 'The scriptures, however well studied, must be read over and over again; a king, however well served, is never to be depended upon; and a woman like the scriptures and the king, though you cherish her in your bosom, is never thoroughly mastered.' See, brother, how beautiful the spring is; yet to me without my beloved it is frightful.

Dohá 32.

Love, finding me tortured by separation, powerless and absolutely alone, has made a raid upon me with the bees and birds of the forest. His spy has seen me with only my brother, and on his report the amorous god has, as it were, resolutely encamped against me with his army.

Chaupái.

The huge trees and tangled creepers are as it were the diverse pavillions that he has spread ; the plantains and stately palms his pennons and standards, that none but the stoutest could see without amazement ; the many kinds of different flowering shrubs are his warriors, arrayed in all their various kinds of panoply; the magnificent forest-trees, that stand here and there, are the separate encampments of warrior chiefs ; the murmuring cuckoos are his infuriated elephants, and the herons his bulls, camels and mules ; the peacocks, chakors and parrots are his war horses ; the pigeons and swans his Arab steeds ; the partridges and quails his foot soldiers ; but there is no describing the whole of Love's host. The mountains and rocks are his chariots, the waterfalls his kettle-drums, the *chataks* the bards that sing his praises, the garrulous bees are his trumpets and clarions, and the three kinds of wind his scouts. With an army complete in all its four branches, he goes about and exhorts every one. O Lakshman, they who can see Love's battle-array and stand firm, they are men of mark in the world. His greatest strength lies in woman ; any one who can escape her is a mighty champion indeed.

Dohá 33.

Brother, there are three evils of surpassing strength, love, anger, and greed : in an instant they upset the souls of the wisest philosopher. The weapons of greed are desire and pride ; of love, nothing but woman ; while anger's weapon is harsh speech ; so thoughtful sages have declared."

Chaupái.

O Umà, Ráma is without attributes, the lord of all animate and inanimate creation, and knows all secrets ; yet he exhibited all the distress of a lover no less than the detachment and steadfastness of a philosopher. Anger, love, greed, pride, delusion, all are dissipated by the grace of Ráma, and the only man superior to all this jugglery is he to whom the great conjuror has shown favour.[1] I tell you,

---

1 That is to say, whom he has taken behind the scenes.

Umá, what is my conclusion; the worship of Hari is real and all the world is a dream.

The Lord went on from there to the shore of the deep and beautiful lake called Pampá; its water as clear as the soul of the saints; with charming flights of steps on each of its four sides; where beasts of different kinds came as they listed, to drink of the flood, like crowds of beggars at a good man's gate.

Dohá 34.

Under its cover of dense lotus leaves the water was as difficult to distinguish as is the unembodied supreme spirit under the veil of delusive phenomena. The happy fish were all in placid repose at the bottom of the deep pool, like the days of the righteous that are passed in peace.

Chaupái.

Lotuses of many colours displayed their flowers; there was a buzzing of garrulous bees, both honey-makers and humble-bees; while swans and waterfowl were so noisy you would think they had recognized the Lord and were telling his praises. The geese and cranes and other birds were so numerous that only seeing would be believing, no words could describe them. The delighted voice of so many beautiful birds seemed as an invitation to the wayfarers. The saints had built themselves a house near the lake with magnificent forest-trees all round, the *champa*, the *málsari*, the *kadamb* and *tamála*, the *pátala*, the *kathal*, the *dhák* and the mango.[1] Every tree had put forth its new leaves and flowers and was resonant with swarms of bees. A delightful air, soft, cool and fragrant, was ever in delicious motion, and the cooing of the cuckoos was so pleasant to hear that a saint's meditation would be broken by it.

Dohá-35.

The trees laden with fruit bowed low to the ground; like

---

1 The *champa*, or *champaka*, is the Michelia champaka, a handsome tree with sweet-scented golden flowers.

a generous soul whom every increase of fortune renders only more humble than before.

Chaupái.

When Ráma saw this most beautiful lake, he bathed in it with great delight, and then with his brother sat down in the shade of the magnificent trees. There all the gods and saints came once more to hymn his praises and then returned each to his own home. The All-merciful rested in supreme content and addressed his brother in edifying discourse. When Nàrad saw the Lord God thus sorrowing for the loss of his beloved, his soul was much disturbed. "In submission to my curse[1] Ráma endures all this weight of woe. I must go and visit so noble a lord, for I may never have such an opportunity again." Having thus reflected, Nárad with his lute in his hand,[2] approached the spot where the lord was sitting at ease. In dulcet tones he sang his acts, affectionately dwelling upon them in all detail. As he prostrated himself, Ráma took and lifted him up, and again and again clasped him to his bosom and asked him of his welfare and seated him by his side. Then Lakshman reverently laved his feet.

Dohá 36.

Perceiving that his lord was well pleased, Nárad made much supplication and clasping his lotus hands addressed him in these words:

The *málsari*, called in the text by another of its Sanskrit names, *vakula*, is the Mimusops elengi. Its fragrant star-shaped flowers are much used by Hindus for garlands and supply the native silversmiths with a very favourite pattern.

The *kadamb* is the Nauclea cadamba, a large and handsome forest tree, which grows wild in the Mathurá district and figures in many of Krishna's pastoral adventures.

The *tamàla* is a tree with dark bark and white blossoms.

The *patála* is the Bignonia or Stereospermum suaveolens, a large tree common in South India, with dark dull-crimson, exquisitely fragrant flowers.

The *kathal*, called in the text by its Sanskrit name *panasa*, is the Artocarpus integrifolia, or jack-tree. The fruit is an important article of food in South India and Ceylon.

The *dhák*, called in the text by its Sanskrit name *palása*, is the Butea frondosa, a tree with scarlet flowers, which precede the new leaves, and when in full bloom make a striking sight, like a fire on the horizon Hence the vernacular name, *dhák*, from the Sanskrit *dagha*, 'on fire.'

1 For the explanation of Nárad's curse see Book 1, *chaupài* 143.

2 Nárad is the reputed inventor of the vína, or India lute.

Chaupái.

"Hearken, most generous Raghu-náyak, beautiful and beneficent, at once unapproachable and easy of approach, grant me, my lord, the one boon that I ask; though you know it without my asking, since you know the secrets of all hearts." "Reverend father, you understand my character; can I ever turn away my face from any one of my worshippers? There is nothing I hold so dear that you, most excellent of saints, may not ask it of me. There is nothing of mine that I would refuse to a believer; never allow yourself to abandon this confidence in me." Then Nárad was glad and said: "This is the boon that I presume to ask. Though my lord has many names, each more glorious than the other, as declared in the scriptures, may the name Rama, sire, surpass all names, exterminating the whole brood of sin, as when a fowler ensnares an entire flock of birds.

Dohá 37.

May your name Ráma be as the moon in the bright night of cloudless faith, and your other names as brilliant stars in the heaven of the believer's soul." Raghunáth, the ocean of mercy, said to the saint, 'so be it.' Then was Nárad's soul rejoiced exceedingly and he bowed his head at his lord's feet.

Chaupái.

Seeing Raghunáth so gracious, Nárad spoke again in winning tones: "O Ráma, when you sent forth your delusive power and infatuated me—hearken, O Raghurái—I was anxious to accomplish a marriage, why was it, my lord, that you did not allow me to do so?" "Hearken, O saint, and I will tell you, if you will not be angry: If men will abandon all other hope and worship me only, I always keep watch over them as a mother over her infant child. If an infant child run to lay hold of the fire or a snake, the mother at once rescues it; when her son has grown up, the mother does not show her affection to him in the same way as before. The wise are, as it were, my grown up sons and humble worshippers my infant children. The latter are protected by my strength, the former by their own, and both have to fight against love and anger. Philosophers know this and worship me, and though they have acquired wisdom, still they do not discard faith.

Dohá 38.

Lust, anger, greed and all other violent passion form a rushing torrent of deception; but among them all the most formidable and the most calamitous is that incarnation of vanity, woman.

Chaupái.

Hearken, O saint, to the teaching of the Puránas, the Vedas and the saints: Woman is like the season of spring to the forest of infatuation; like the heat of summer to dry up the pools and waterfalls of prayer, penance and devotional exercises; like the rains to rejoice the gnats[1] and frogs of lust, anger and pride; like the autumn to revive the lily-like growth of evil propensities; like the winter to distress and deaden all the lotus beds of piety; and lastly, like the dewy season[2] to foster the *jawása* weeds of selfishness. Woman, again, is like a dark and murky night, in which owls and deeds of darkness delight, or like a hook to catch the fish of sense and strength and honour and truth; so say the wise.

Dohá 39.

Wanton woman is the root of all evil, a source of torment, a mine of all unhappiness; therefore, O saint, knowing all this, I prevented your marriage."

Chaupái.

As the saint listened to Raghupati's delightful discourse, his body quivered with emotion and his eyes filled with tears. "Tell me, is there any other lord, whose wont it is to be so kind and considerate to his servants? All, who will

---

1 *Matsara*, translated 'gnats,' also means 'selfishness,' and may be intended in that sense here, as both meanings suit the context equally well.

2 *Sisira*, 'the dewy season,' consists of the months, Mágh and Phálgun, that come between the winter and the spring.

not abandon their errors, nor worship such a lord as this, are indeed dull and witless fools." Nárad the sage reverentially enquired further : "Hearken Ráma, versed in all wisdom : tell me, my lord Raghubír, lightener of earth's burdens, what are the marks of a saint?" Listen, reverend sir, and I will tell you what are the qualities of the saints, by virtue of which they hold me in their power. They have overcome the six disturbing influence[1] ; are sinless, passionless, and imperturbable ; have no worldly goods, but live a life of chastity and contentedness ; their wisdom is immeasurable ; they are without desires and temperate in enjoyment ; oceans of truth, inspired bards, practised in meditation ; circumspect ; void of pride and arrogance ; persevering and eminently wise in the mystery of salvation :

Dohá 40.

Mines of virtue, free from the troubles of the world and with all their doubts solved ; who, rather than abandon my lotus feet, account neither life nor home precious ;

Chaupái.

Who are abashed when they hear themselves praised, and exceedingly glad to hear the praises of others ; who are always equable and calm, consistent in virtuous practice ; honest and kindly disposed to all men ; distinguished for prayer, penance, religious observances, temperance, self-denial, and performance of pious vows ; for devotion to their guru, to Gobinda and to Bráhmans ; for faith, forbearance, charitableness and compassion ; for a rapturous love of my feet ; a superiority to all material delusions ; an absolute composure, discrimination, humility and knowledge ; and for doctrine in strict accordance with the Vedas and Puránas ; who never display ostentation, arrogance, or pride, nor ever by any chance set their foot on the way of wicked-

1 According to the Sánkhya philosophy there is an original eternal germ, or primal source of all things, except soul, which is called Prakriti. From it are evolved certain *vikáras*, or productive products, or modifications, which occasion all the diversity of material phenomena, and which may therefore be designated 'disturbing influences.'

ness ; who are always either hearing or singing my acts and have no selfish object, but are devoted to the good of others ; in short, reverend sir, the characteristics of the saints are so numerous that not even Sáradá or the scriptures could tell them all.

Chhand 11.

Not Sáradá nor Sheshnág could tell them." Hearing this, Nárad clasped his lotus feet, crying, "Thus the friend of the suppliant, the all-merciful, has with his own mouth declared the characteristics of his worshippers." After again and again bowing his head at his feet, Nárad returned to the city of Bráhma. Blessed, says Tulsi Dás, are all they who abandon other hope and attach themselves to Hari.

Dohá 41.

People who hear or recite the sanctifying praises of Rávan's foe, even without asceticism, prayer and meditation, are rewarded with steadfast faith in Ráma. Woman is like the flame of a candle; let not your soul be as the moth, but discard love and intoxication, worship Ráma and hold communion with the saints.

[*Thus endeth the book entitled* "THE FOREST" *composed by Tulsi Dás for the bestowal of pure wisdom and continence; being the third descent 'into the holy lake of Ráma's deeds,' that cleanses from every defilement of the world*].

BOOK IV.

KISHKINDHYA.

KISHKINDHYA.

Sanskrit Invocation.

BEAUTIFUL as the jasmine or the lotus, of surpassing strength, store-houses of wisdom, all glorious and accomplished bowmen, hymned by the Vedas, benefactors of cows and Bráhmans, may they who appeared in the form of mortal men as the two noble sons of Raghu, the champions of true religion, the wayfarers intent on their search for Síta, may they grant us faith.

Blessed are the pious souls, who ever imbibe the nectar of holy Ráma's name ; nectar, the product of no ocean, but of Brahm himself, the utter exterminator of all the impurities of this sinful age, the imperishable, the quintessence of the beauty of blessed Sambhu's moonlike face, the ever glorious, the remedy for all the diseases of life, the exquisitely sweet, the life of blessed Jánaki.

Sorathá 1.

How is it possible not to reverence Kásí, the home of Sambhu and Bhaváni, knowing it to be the earthly birthplace of salvation, a treasury of knowledge and the destroyer of sin. Dull indeed of soul is the man who worships not him, who when all the hosts of heaven were in distress, drank up the deadly poison; who is so merciful as Sankara?

Chaupái.

Ráma again proceeded on his way and drew near to the mountain Rishyamúka.[1] There Sugriva dwelt with his ministers, who, seeing them approach in all their immeasurable strength, was exceedingly alarmed and cried : "Hearken, Hanumán ; take the form of a young Bráhman student and go and see who these two heroes are, of such remarkable strength and beauty, and when you have ascertained make some sign by which I may know also. If that wretch Báli has sent them, I must leave the hill and flee at once."

1 The mountain Rishyamúka derives its name from *Rishya*, a kind of antelope.

The monkey assumed the form of a Bráhman and went to the place; there bowed his head and thus questioned them: "Who are you two knights of warrior mien, who roam this wood, one dark of hue, the other fair? The ground is rough for your soft feet to tread. What is the reason, my masters, that you visit this forest? Your body is too delicate and exquisitely beautiful to be exposed to the intolerable sun and wind of these wild regions. Who are you? A Person of the Trinity; or the two great gods Nara and Naráyan?[1]

Dohá 1.

Or has the lord of all the spheres become incarnate in your human form, for the good of the world, to bridge the ocean of existence and relieve earth of its burdens?"

Chaupái.

"We are the sons of Dasarath, the king of Kosala, and have come into the forest in obedience to our father's command; Ráma, the name of one brother, and Lakshman of the other. With us was my young and beautiful bride, the daughter of the king of Videha. But some demon here has stolen her away; and it is she, O Bráhman, whom we are trying to find. We have told you our affairs, tell us now your own story." He recognized his lord and fell and clasped his feet with a joy, Umá, beyond all description. His body thrilled with emotion and all words failed his tongue, as he gazed upon the fashion of their ravishing disguise.

1 Nara, the original or eternal Man, the divine imperishable spirit that pervades the universe, is always associated with Náráyana, which, as a patronymic from Nara, means 'the Son of the original Man.' In Manu, I. 10, Nara is apparently identified with Náráyana: the waters, it is said, being called Nárá, as produced from Nara, the eternal Spirit, or Paramátmá, which is also styled Náráyana, as having its first place of motion on the waters. In the more systematic theology Nara and Náráyana are distinct, the former being regarded as a sage or patriarch, while the latter is a god. In epic poetry they are the sons of Dharma by Murti, or Ahinsá, and are emanations of Vishnu, Arjuna being identified with Nara, and Krishna with Náráyana. In some places Nara and Náráyana are called *devau*, 'the two gods'; or *purva-devau* 'the two original gods'; or rishi, 'the two sages'; or *puranau rishi—sattamau*, 'the two most ancient and best of sages; or *tapasau* 'the two ascetics; or *maha-muni*, 'the two great munis.—*Monier Williams*, sub verbo.

At last he collected himself and burst forth into a hymn of praise, with great joy of heart, for he had found his lord. "I asked, sire, in my ignorance; but why should you ask, as though you were a mere man. Under the influence of your delusive power I wandered in error, and therefore I did not at once recognize my lord.

Dohá 2.

In the first place I was a bewildered dullard, ignorant and perverse of soul, and then my gracious Lord God himself led me astray.

Chaupái.

Although, sire, my faults are many, yet a servant cannot anyhow be above his master. All created things are first fettered by your delusive power and then again set free by your grace. Therefore I make my cry to Raghubír, and know no other saving mode of prayer. As a servant has confidence in his master, or a child in its mother, so all dwell secure under the protection of the Lord." So saying, he fell in much agitation at his feet, and the love that filled his soul showed itself in every part of his body. Then Raghupati raised him up and took him to his bosom, while his own eyes were flooded with tears of joy. "Hearken, O monkey; do not account yourself vile; you are second to Lakshman only in my affection; every one says that I have no respect of persons; any servant is beloved of me, and has a rank in heaven second to none.

Dohá 3.

For he, Hanumán, is second to none who never wavers in this faith, that he is the servant of the Lord God who is manifested in creation."

Chaupái.

When the Son of the Wind (*i.e.*, Hanumán) saw his lord so gracious, he rejoiced at heart, and every anxiety was at an end. "The king of the monkeys, sire, lives on this rock, Sugriva by name, a servant of yours. In return for his submission you should make friends with him and set his mind at rest. He will have Síta tracked; for he will despatch millions of monkeys in every direction." In this manner he told them all the particulars and took them both with him and gave them stools to sit upon. When Sugríva saw Ráma, he thought it a great blessing to have been born. He reverentially advanced to meet him and bowed his head at his feet; and Raghunáth and his brother returned his courtesy. The monkey's mind was occupied with this thought, 'If God would only give me such allies!'

Dohá 4.

Hanumán then explained the circumstances of both sides; holy fire was made a witness, and a firm alliance concluded.

Chaupái.

When the alliance had been concluded, nothing was kept in reserve; Ráma and Lakshman told all their adventures. Sugríva's eyes were full of tears as he replied — "The daughter of the king of Mithilá will be recovered. One day when I was sitting here with my ministers deep in thought, I saw some one flying through the air, with a woman in his power, who was weeping piteously and crying 'Ráma, Ráma, O my Ráma!' When she saw me, she dropped her scarf." Ráma at once asked for it; he gave it him; he pressed the scarf to his bosom in the deepest distress. Said Sugríva; "Hearken, Raghubír; be not so distressed; take courage. I will do all in my power to serve you and recover Jánaki."

Dohá 5.

The All-merciful and Almighty rejoiced to hear his friend's speech. "Tell me, Sugriva, the reason why you are living in this forest."

Chaupái.

"My lord, Báli and I are two brothers; our mutual love was past all telling. The son of Maya, Máyávi by name came to our town. In the middle of the night he shouted at the city-gate. Báli endures no enemy to set him at defiance and sallied forth. Seeing this he fled. Now I too accompanied my brother, and when he had gone into one of the caves of the mountain, Báli said to me : 'Wait for me a fortnight, and if I do not come then, conclude that I have been killed. I stayed there a whole month, Kharári ; a tremendous stream of blood then flowed out ; I made sure that Báli had been defeated and that the enemy would come and kill me too. I therefore closed the mouth of the cave with a rock and fled away. When the ministers of state saw the city without a master, they forced the government upon me, whether I would or no. When Báli, who had slain the foe, came home and saw me, he was greatly set against me and gave me a severe beating, as he would an enemy, and took from me everything that I had, together with my wife. For fear of him, O merciful Raghubír, I wander forlorn all over the world. The curse[1] prevents him from coming here, and yet I am ill at ease in mind." When the friend of the suppliant heard of his servant's troubles, his two mighty arms were uplifted with a convulsive motion.

Dohá 6.

" Hearken, Sugríva ; I will slay Báli with a single arrow ; though he take refuge with Bráhma even, or Rudra, he shall not escape with his life.

Chaupái.

They, who are not distressed at the sight of a friend's distress, are guilty of grievous sin. They, who do not think it the most natural thing possible to regard as a mere grain of sand their own mountain-like troubles, while a friend's trouble, though really no bigger than a grain of sand, seems to them as weighty as mount Meru ; such men are churls, upon whom it is useless

1 When Báli had slain the demon Dundubhi, who had attacked him in the form of a bull, he hurled the body away, and a drop of blood fell in the hermitage of the Rishi Matanga, who thereupon pronounced a curse upon Báli, that if ever he came that way he should at once die.

to press friendship. To restrain from evil paths and to direct in the path of virtue ; to publish all good qualities and conceal the bad ; to give and take without any distrust of mind ; to be always ready to assist with all one's power, and, in time of misfortune to be a hundred times more affectionate than ever ; such the scriptures declare to be the properties of a true friend. But one who speaks you fairly to your face, but behind your back is an enemy in the viciousness of his soul, whose mind, brother, is as tortuous as the movements of a snake, such a man is a bad friend, whom it is well to let alone. A dishonest servant, a miserly king, a false wife, and a treacherous friend, are four things as bad as the stake. Cease to distress yourself, friend ; I will put forth all my strength to do your business for you." Said Sugriva : " Hearken, Raghubír ; Báli is very strong and most resolute in battle," and he showed him Dundubhi's bones and the palm-trees.[1] Without an effort, Raghubír tossed them away. At this exhibition of boundless strength the affection of the monkey king was increased and he made sure of killing Báli. Again and again he bowed his head at his feet, in the greatest delight, knowing him to be the Lord. Knowledge sprung up in his soul, and he spoke and said : " By my lord's favour my mind is set at rest ; I will abandon pleasure, fortune, home, grandeur and all, to do you service ; for all these things are hindrances to faith in Rámá, as the saints declare who are devoted to the worship[2] of your feet. All the friends and enemies, joys and sorrows of the world, are effects of

1 This mention of 'palm-trees' would not be intelligible without a reference to the Sanskrit Rámáyana. There it is told how after Ráma by a slight touch of his foot had sent flying a hundred leagues through the air the giant Dundubhi's enormous skeleton, Sugriva still doubted whether he were a match in strength for Báli, who had hurled the body an equal distance, while it was still clothed with flesh and therefore of much greater weight. To convince him, Ráma shot an arrow from his, which cleft seven palm-trees that stood in a line one after the other, pierced the hill behind them and sped downwards to the nethermost hell, whence again it returned and dropt into the quiver at Ráma's side, from which it had been taken.

2 *Ararádhak*, 'a worshipper,' is for *árádhak*, from the root *rádh*, 'to propitiate,' with the intensive prefix á. In the Hindi glassary it is explained by *sevak*, 'a servant,' as if connected with *arara*.

delusion, and are not eternal realities. Báli is my greatest friend, by whose favour I have met you, O Ráma, destroyer of all sorrow; as when a man dreams that he has been fighting some one, and on waking and coming to his senses is ashamed of his illusion. Now, my lord, do me this favour, that I may leave all and worship you, night and day." When Ráma heard the monkey's devout speech, he smiled and said, with his bow in his hand: "Whatever I have said is all true; my words, friend, cannot fail." O Garúr, Ráma, as the scriptures say, is the juggler who makes us all dance like so many monkeys. Sugriva then took Raghunáth away with him, who went with bow and arrows in hand. Afterwards he sent Sugríva on ahead, who went up close and roared with all his might. Báli on hearing him, sprang up in a fury, but his wife clasped his feet in her hands and warned him: "Hearken, my lord, Sugríva's allies are two brothers of unapproachable majesty and might, the sons of the king of Kosala, Lakshman and Ráma, who would conquer in battle even Death himself."

Dohá 7.

Said Báli: "Hearken, timorous dame; Raghunáth is kind and the same to all; even if he kill me, he will still be my lord."

Chaupái.

So saying, he sallied forth in all his pride, thinking no more of Sugríva than of a blade of grass. The two joined combat; and Báli with a furious leap struck him a blow with his fist, which resounded like a clap of thunder. Sugríva at once fled in dismay; the stroke of his fist had fallen upon him as a bolt from heaven. "What did I say, O merciful Raghubír; this is no brother of mine but Death himself." "You two brothers are so much alike that for fear of mistake I did not shoot him." He then stroked Sugríva's body with his hands and his frame became as of adamant, and all his pain was gone. Next he put on his neck a wreath of flowers and sent him back with a large increase of strength. Again they fought in every kind of way, while Ráma watched them from behind a tree.

Dohá 8.

When Sugríva had tried every trick and put forth all his strength and had given up in despair, Ráma drew an arrow and struck Báli in the heart.

Chaupái.

Struck by the shaft, he fell in dismay to the ground. Again he sat up and saw the Lord standing before him, dark of hue, with his hair fastened up in a knot on his head, and his eyes inflamed as they were when he fitted the arrow to his bowstring. Again and again as he gazed upon him, he laid his soul at his feet and accounted his life blessed : for he recognized his lord. Though his heart was full of affection, the words of his mouth were harsh, as he looked towards Ráma and said : "You have become incarnate, sire, for the advancement of religion, and yet you take my life, as a huntsman would that of a wild beast. I, forsooth, am an enemy and Sugriva a friend; yet for what fault have you killed me, my lord ?" "Hearken, wretch ; a younger brother's wife, a sister, a daughter-in-law and an unwedded maid are all alike : whoever looks upon one of them with an evil eye may be slain without any sin. Fool, in your extravagant pride you paid no heed to your wife's warning. You knew that he had taken refuge under the might of my arm, and yet in your wicked pride you wished to kill him."

Dohá 9.

"Hearken Ráma ; I dealt craftily with my lord ; to-day, guilty as I am, I obtain, sire, at my death a place in heaven."

Chaupái.

When Ráma heard this most tender speech, he touched Báli's head with his hands : "I restore the soundness of your body ; retain your life." Said Báli ; "Hearken, All-merciful ; the saints are born again and again and labour throughout their life, and yet even to the last Ráma never comes near them. But he, the everlasting, by the virtue of whose name Sankara at Kási bestows heaven upon all alike, has come in visible form before my very eyes; can I ever, my lord, have such a chance again?

Chhand 1.

He has become visible to my eyes, whose praises the scriptures are all unequal to declare, to whom scarcely the saints attain after profound contemplation accompanied by laborious suppression of the breath,[1] abstraction of soul, and control of the senses. Seeing me the victim of excessive pride, the Lord has told me to retain my body. But who would be such a fool as to insist upon cutting down the tree of paradise and watering a wild *babul* tree? Now, my lord, look upon me with compassion and grant me the boon I beg; whatever the womb, in which it be my fate to be born, may I ever cherish a special devotion to the feet of Ráma. O my lord, take this my son Angad and grant him like discretion, power and prosperity; grasp him by the hand. O king of gods and men, and make him your servant."

Dohá 10.

After making a fervent act of devotion to Ráma's feet, Báli's soul left the body; as placidly as when a wreath of flowers drops from an elephant's neck without his knowing it;

Chaupái.

and Ráma dismissed him to his own heavenly mansion. All the people of the city ran together in dismay, and Tárá with dishevelled hair and tottering frame broke out into wild lamentation. When Raghurái saw her distress, he imparted to her wisdom and dispersed her delusion. "The

---

1 The eight means of mental concentration (according to Patanjali, the founder of the Yoga system of philosophy) are *Yama*, 'forbearance,' 'restraint'; *Niyama*, 'religious observances'; *Asana*, 'postures'; *Pránayáma*, suppression of the breath', or 'breathing in a peculiar way; *Pratyáhára* 'restraint of the senses'; *Dhárana*, 'steadying of the mind'; *Dhyána*, 'contemplation; and *Sámádhi*, 'profound meditation,' or rather, a state of religious trance.—*Monier Williams.*

body, which is composed of the elements, earth, water, fire, air and ether,[1] is of no value. The mortal frame, which you see before you, sleeps; but the soul is eternal; why then do you weep?" True understanding sprung up in her mind; she embraced his feet and received the boon that she asked, a perfect faith. O, Umá, the lord Ráma dances us all up and down like so many puppets. Then he gave orders to Sugríva and he performed all the funeral rites with due ceremony. Ráma next directed his brother to go and celebrate Sugriva's installation. He bowed his head at Raghupati's feet and went forth, he and all whom Ráma had commissioned to accompany him.

Dohá 11.

Lakshman immediately summoned the citizens and the council of Bráhmans, and invested Sugriva with the sovereignty and appointed Angad Prince Imperial.

Chaupái.

O, Umá, there is no such friend as Ráma in the world, neither guru, nor father, nor mother, nor kinsman, nor lord. It is the way with all other gods, men and saints, to make friends for selfish purposes; but the generous Raghubír, from mere natural kindness, made Sugríva king of the monkeys, when he was trembling all day and all night in such fear of Báli that there was no colour left in his face and his heart was burnt up with anxiety. I know this, that any man, who deserts such a lord, must needs be caught in the meshes of calamity. Ráma then sent for Sugríva and instructed him in all the principles of statecraft, and added: "Hearken, Sugriva, lord of the monkey race; I may not enter a city for fourteen years. The hot weather is now over and the rains have set in. I will encamp on the hills close by. Do you with Angad reign in royal state; but remain ever mindful of my interests."

1 Akása, 'ether,' is the subtle and ethereal fluid, supposed to fill and pervade the universe and to be the peculiar vehicle of life and of sound—*Monier Williams.*

Sugríva then returned to the palace, while Ráma remained in camp on mount Bravarshana.[1]

Dohá 12

The gods had beforehand made and kept for him a charming cave in the mountain, knowing that the all-merciful Ráma would come and stay there for some days.

Chaupái.

The magnificent forest was a most charming sight, with the trees all in flower and the swarms of buzzing bees gathering honey. From the time that the Lord came, every plant and fruit and every kind of agreeable foliage was forthcoming in profusion. Seeing the incomparable beauty of the hill, the Lord and his brother rested there. In the form of bees, birds and deer, the gods, saints and seers came and did service to their lord. From the time that Lakshmi's spouse took up his abode in it, the forest became a picture of felicity. There the two brothers sat at ease on the bright and glistening crystal rock, and the younger was told many a tale inculcating faith, self-governance, statecraft and wisdom. What with clouds that ever canopied the heavens and the frequent thunder, the season of the rains seemed a most delightful time.

Dohá 13.

"See, Lakshman, how the peacocks dance at the sight of the clouds, like a householder, enamoured of asceticism, who rejoices when he finds a true believer in Vishnu.

Chaupái.

Clouds gather in the sky and thunders roar; but my darling is gone and my soul is in distress.[2] The lightning flashes fitfully amid the darkness, like the friendship of the vile which never lasts. The pouring clouds cleave close to

1 In the Sanskrit Rámáyana the hill is called Prasravana; but the two words bear much the same meaning. The text might also be translated, 'remained on the hill during the early rains.'

2 In England a cloudy sky is associated with gloomy ideas, and the bright sunshine with everything that is cheerful. But in India it is the reverse. When the clouds gather and thunder is heard, every one rejoices at the prospect of rain.

the ground, as sages stoop beneath accumulated lore. The mountain endures the buffeting of the storm, as the virtuous bear the abuse of the wicked. The flooded streamlets rush proudly along, like mean men puffed up with a little wealth. The water by its contact with the earth becomes as muddy as the soul when environed by delusion. The lakes swell gradually and imperceptibly, like as when the quality of goodness developes in a good man; and the rivers flow into the bosom of the ocean, like as the soul, that has found Hari, is at rest for ever.

Dohá 14.

The green earth is so choked with grass that the paths can no longer be distinguished, like holy books obscured by the wrangling of heretics,

Chaupái.

On all sides there is a lively croaking of frogs, like a party of Bráhman students repeating the Vedas. All the trees put forth their new leaves, like pious souls that have come to matured wisdom. The *ák* and *jawása* plants lose their leaves: as in a well-governed realm the schemes of the wicked come to nought. Search as you like, the dusty footpath is no longer to be traced; like as when religion is put out of sight by passion. The earth rich with crops makes as goodly a show as the prosperity of benevolent. The fire flies glitter in the darkness of the cloudy night, like a mustered band of hypocritical pretenders. The ridges of the fields are broken down by the heavy rains, like women ruined by too much license. The diligent cultivators weed their lands, like philosophers who root up ignorance, vanity and pride. The *chakwá* and other birds are nowhere to be seen, like virtue that fled at the coming of the iron age. However much it may rain, no grass springs upon barren ground; so lust takes no root in the heart of Hari's worshippers. The earth gleams with swarms of living creatures of every kind; so the people multiply under good government. Here and there weary wayfarers stay and rest, like a man's bodily senses after the attainment of wisdom.

Dohá 15.

At times a strong wind disperses the clouds in all directions, like the birth of a bad son, who destroys all the pious practices of his family.

Chaupái.

Now the rains are over and the season of autumn has returned; see Lakshman, how exquisitely beautiful everything is. The whole earth is covered with the flowering *káns* grass, as though the rains had exposed its old age. The rising of Canopus[1] has dried up the water on the roads, like as greed is dried up by contentment. The surface of every river and lake is as pure and bright as is the soul of the saints devoid of all vanity and delusion; drop by drop their depths are diminished, like as the enlightened gradually lose all notions of self. The wagtails know the autumn season and come out once more, like virtuous deeds in an auspicious time. There is neither mud nor dust; the earth is as brilliant as the administration of a king who is well versed in state policy. The fish are distressed by the shrinking of the water, like improvident men of family by the loss of money. The unclouded sky shines as bright as a worshipper of Hari, who has discarded every other patron. Here and there is a slight autumn shower, like the faith of one who is not yet fully persuaded.

Dohá 16.

King and ascetics, merchants and mendicants, leave the city and go their way with joy, like men in any of the four stages of life,[2] who cease to labour when they have once attained to faith in Hari.

---

1 The heliacal rising of the constellation Agastya, *i.e.*, Canopus, takes place on the seventh day after the new moon of Bhádon, in the rainy season.

2 The four stages of life, through which every Bráhman should pass, are 1st, that of the Brahmachári, or student; 2nd, that of the Griha-stha, or householder; 3rd, that of the Vánaprastha, or anchorite; and 4th, that of the Bhikshu, or mendicant.

Chaupái.

Where the water is deep, the fish are as glad as men who have taken refuge with Hari and have not a single trouble. The lakes, with their flowering lotuses, are as beautiful as the immaterial Supreme Spirit when clothed with a material form. The garrulous bees make a wonderful buzzing, and the birds a charming concert of diverse sounds; but the *chakwá* is as sad of soul to see the night, as a bad man at the sight of another's prosperity. The chátak cries out from excess of thirst, like a rebel against Maháde v, who knows no rest. The moon by night subdues the autumnal heat of the sun, like as the sight of a saint expels sin. Flocks of partridges fix their gaze upon the moon, as Hari's worshippers look only to Hari. Mosquitoes and gadflies are driven away by the terrors of winter, like as a family is destroyed by the sin of persecuting Bráhmans.

Dohá 17.

Under the influence of the autumn, earth is rid of its insect swarms, as a man, who has found a good teacher, is relieved from all doubt and error.

Chaupái.

The rains are over and the clear season has come, but I have had no news, brother, of Síta. If I could only once anyhow get tidings of her, I would in an instant recover her out of the hands of even Death himself. Wherever she may be, if only she still lives, brother, I would make an effort to rescue her. Sugríva has forgotten all about me, now that he has got back his kingdom and treasure, his city and his queen. Fool that he is, I will to-morrow slay him with the selfsame arrow with which I slew Báli." He, by whose favour, Umá, pride and delusion are dissipated, could never even dream of being angry. Only enlightened saints can understand these actions of his, who have a hearty devotion to the feet of Raghubír. Lakshman believed his lord was angry, and strung his bow and took his arrows in his hands.

Dohá 18.

Then the all-merciful Raghupati instructed his brother, saying: " Frighten our friend Sugríva and bring him here."

Chaupái.

Now the Son of the Wind also had thought to himself, ' Sugríva has forgotten all about Ráma.' So he went near and bowed his head at his feet and reminded him of the four modes of making war.[1] As Sugríva listened, he became much alarmed: " Sensual pleasures have robbed me of all my understanding. Now, O Hanumán, despatch a multitude of spies, legions of monkeys, in every direction, and tell them that any one who is not back in a fortnight shall meet his death at my hands." Hanumán then summoned envoys, and showed them all special honour, making use of threats, blandishments and motives of policy. They all bowed their head at his feet and set forth. At that very time Lakshman entered the city. Seeing him to be angry, the monkeys all ran away.

Dohá 19.

He twanged his bow and cried ' I will burn the city to ashes.' Then came Báli's son, seeing the distress of the people,

Chaupái.

and bowed his head at his feet and made humble petition, till Lakshman assured him he had nought to fear. When the monkey king heard tell of Lakshman's wrath, he was terribly alarmed: " Hearken, Hanumán; take Tára with you and with suppliant prayers appease the prince." Hanumán; went with Tára and fell at his feet, and after hymning his lord's praises, respectfully conducted him to the palace and bathed his feet and seated him on a couch. The monkey king also bowed his head at his feet, but Lakshman took him by the hand and embraced him. " There is nothing, my lord, so intoxicating as pleasure;

1 The four *upayas*, or modes of making war, are, sowing dissension negotiation, bribery and open force.

in a single moment it infatuates even the soul of a saint." On hearing this humble speech, Lakshman was glad and said everything to reassure him, while Hanumán told him all that had been done and how a multitude of spies had already started.

Dohá 20.

Then Sugríva with Angad and the other monkeys went forth with joy, preceded by Lakshman, and arrived in Ráma's presence.

Chaupái.

With folded hands he bowed his head at his feet and cried: "My lord, it has been no fault of mine. Your delusive power, sire, is so strong that only Ráma's favour can disperse it. Gods and men, saints and kings are mastered by their senses; and I am but a poor brute beast, a monkey, one of the most libidinous of animals. A man who is invulnerable by the arrow of a woman's eye, who remains wakeful through the dark night of angry passion, and whose neck has never been bound by the halter of covetousness, is your equal, O Raghurái. It is a virtue not attainable by any religious observance; it is only by your grace that one here and one there can accomplish it." Then Raghupati smiled and said: "You are as dear to me as my own brother Bharat. Now take thought and make an effort to get tidings of Síta."

Dohá 21.

While they were yet thus speaking, the troops of monkeys arrived of all colours and from all parts of the world, a monkey host marvellous to behold.

Chaupái.

I, Uma, saw this army of monkeys; only a fool would try to count them. They came and bowed the head at Ráma's feet and gazing upon his face found in him their true lord. In the whole host there was not a single monkey to whom Ráma did not give separate greeting. This is no great miracle for the lord Raghurái, who is omnipresent and all pervading. They all stood as they were told, rank after rank, while Sugriva thus spoke and instructed them: "In Ráma's behoof and at my request, go forth ye monkey host in every direction. Make search for Janak's daughter, my brethren, and return within a month. Whoever comes back at the end of the time without any news shall die at my hands."

Dohá 22.

No sooner had they heard this speech than all the monkeys started at once in every direction. Sugríva then called Angad, Nila and Hanumán :

Chaupái.

"Hearken, Níla, Angad and Hanumán, and you, O staunch and sagacious Jámbaván ; go ye together, all ye gallant warriors, to the south, and ask every one for news of Síta. Strain every faculty to devise some way of accomplishing Ráma's object. The sun is content with back service and the fire with front, but a master must be served back and front alike, without any subterfuges.[1] Discard the unrealities of the world and consider the future ; so shall all the troubles connected with existence be destroyed. This is the end, brother, for which we were born, to worship Ráma without any desire for self. He only is truly discriminative, he only is greatly blessed, who is enamoured of the feet of Raghubír." After begging permission to depart and bowing the head at his feet they set out with joy, invoking Raghurái. The last to make obeisance was Hanumán. The lord, knowing what would happen, called him near and with his lotus hands touched his head and gave him his ring off his finger for he knew his devotion : "Say everything to comfort Síta, telling her of my might and my constancy, and come quickly." Hanumán thought

1 In this line there is no difference of reading in any of the MSS., but the precise meaning of the words is obscure and the Pandits interpret them in as many as 22 different ways. The translation given above exactly preserves the vagueness of the original. One of the alternative renderings is, 'as the flint nourishes fire in its bosom so should one serve a master ;' but I do not know of any parallelled passage where *bhánu píth* is used in the sense of 'a flint.'

himself happy to have been born and set forth, with the image of the all-merciful impressed upon his heart. Although the Lord knows everything, he observes the rules of statecraft in his character as the champion of the gods.

Dohá 23.

They went forth searching every wood, river, lake, and mountain cave, with their soul so absorbed in Ráma's concerns that they forgot all about their own bodily wants.

Chaupái.

Wherever it might be that they came across a demon, they took his life with a single blow. They looked into every recess of forest and hill, and if they met any hermit they all surrounded him. Overcome by thirst they were dreadfully distrest, and losing their way in the dense jungle, could find no water. Hanumán thought to himself " without water to drink we shall all die. He climbed a mountain peak and looking all round about, spied a strange opening in the ground ; with geese, herons and swans on the wing and all kinds of birds making their way into it. Then Hanumán came down from the mountain and took them all and showed them this cavern, and with him to lead the way they lost no time, but entered the chasm.

Dohá 24.

A grove and beautiful lake came in sight, with many flowering lotuses and a magnificent temple, where a holy woman[1] was sitting.

Chaupái.

From a distance they all bowed the head before her and made enquiry and explained their circumstances. She then said : " Take water to drink and eat at will of this luscious and beautiful fruit." They bathed and ate of the sweet fruit and then all came and drew near to her, and told her all their adventures. " I will now go to Raghurái ; close your eyes and so leave the cave ; you will recover Síta, do not fear." The warriors closed their eyes, and when they

1 In the Sanskrit Rámáyana her name is given as Swayamprabha, 'the self-shining.'

again opened them they were all standing on the shore of the ocean. But she went to Raghunáth and came and bowed her head at his lotus feet, and made much supplication. The lord bestowed upon her imperishable faith.

Dohá 25.

In obedience to the Lord's commands she went to the Badri forest, cherishing in her heart Ráma's feet, the adoration of the eternal Siva.

Chaupái.

Now the monkeys were thinking to themselves: "The appointed time has passed and nothing has been done." So they all came together and asked one another, "there is no news, brother; what are we to do?" Angad's eyes were full of tears as he replied: "It is death for us either way. Here we have failed to get tidings of Síta, and if we go home our king will slay us. After my father's death he would have killed me, had not Ráma protected me, no thanks to him." Again and again Angad told them all: "It is a case of death without a doubt." When the monkey chiefs heard Angad's words, they could make no answer, tears streamed from their eyes. For a moment they were overwhelmed with despair, but at last they all spoke and said "unless we get news of Síta we will not return, O sagacious prince." So saying the monkeys all went to the seashore, where they spread beds of *kusa* grass and sat down. But Jámbaván, seeing Angad's distress, addressed him with a discourse of appropriate admonition: "My son, do not imagine Ráma to be a man: know that he is the invisible god, unconquerable and from everlasting. All we who are his servants are most highly blessed in our love for the eternal God thus made incarnate.

Dohá 26.

Of his own free will the Lord has manifested himself on behalf of gods, Bráhmans, cows and Earth, and remains in bodily form among his worshippers, having abandoned all the joys of heaven."

Chaupái.

He exhorted him in this wise at great length, and Sampáti from his cave in the mountain heard him. When he came out and saw the multitude of monkeys, he cried : " God has provided me with a feast. I will eat them all up at once; I am dying for want of a meal these many days past. I have never yet had a good bellyful, but to-day God has supplied me for once and all." The monkeys trembled to hear the valture's words, 'we were right in saying to day we must die.' At the sight of him they all rose up, and Jámbaván was mightly disturbed at heart; but Angad, after thinking to himself, exclaimed : Glory to Jatáyu, there is none like him, who gave up his life in Ráma's service and, blessed beyond measure, has been translated to Hari's sphere in heaven." When the bird heard these words of mingled joy and sadness, he drew near to the monkeys in alarm and after assuring them of safety began to question them. They told him the whole history. When Sampáti heard of his brother's doings, he gave great glory to Raghupati.

Dohá 27.

" Take me to the sea-shore and make him an offering of sesamum seeds; with the help of my instructions you shall recover her whom you seek."

Chaupái.

When he had completed the funeral rites for his brother on the seashore, he told them his own history. " Hearken, monkey chiefs. We two brothers in our first youth mounted into the heaven, winging our way towards the sun. He could not endure its splendour and turned back, but I in my pride went closer. My wings were scorched by the excessive heat, and I fell to the earth uttering fearful cries. A saint, by name Chandrama,[1] was moved with compassion when he saw me, and instructed me in all kinds of knowledge and rid me of my inveterate pride. " In the Treta age God

1 In the Sanskrit Rámáyana he is called Nisákara, the night-maker, which also, like Chandrama, is a name for the moon.

will take the form of a man, and his spouse will be carried off by the king of the demons. The Lord will send out spies to search for her, and if you join them you will be purified. Your wings will sprout again, fear not, when you have found them Síta." The saint's prophecy has come true to-day. Hearken to my words and set about your lord's business. On the top of mount Trikút is the city of Lanká ; there lives Rávan in absolute security, and there, in a grove of Asoka trees, sits Síta, a prey to grief.

Dohá 28.

I see her, though you cannot ; a vulture's sight has no bounds. I am now old, or else I would have given you some assistance.

Chaupái.

If any one of you can leap over a hundred leagues of sea, he will do Ráma's business for him very cleverly. Look at me reassure yourselves ; see how my body has been restored by Ráma's favour. Any wretch, who invokes his name, is able to cross the vast and boundless ocean of existence, and you are his messengers; have then no fear, but with Ráma's image impressed upon your soul, concert your plans." So saying, Garúr, the vulture, left them, and their soul was in the greatest amazement. Each one vaunted his own strength, but doubted whether he could leap across. Said the king of the bears, "I am now too old and not a particle of my former strength is left in my body ; when Kharári took his three strides,[1] then I was young and full of vigour.

Dohá 29.

As he fettered Báli, the lord increased in stature to an indescribable size, but in less than an hour I ran round him seven times."

Chaupái.

Angad said : "I will leap across ; but I am rather doubtful about getting back again." Then said Jámbaván : You are quite competent ; but why should we send our

1 The allusion is to Vishnu's incarnation as a dwarf, which was the fifth in order, that as Ráma being the seventh.

leader ? Hearken, Hanumán," added the king of the bears, " why is our champion so silent ? You are the son of the wind and strong as your sire, a storehouse of good sense, discretion and knowledge : in all the world what undertaking is there so difficult that you, my son, cannot accomplish it ? and it is on Ráma's account that you have come down upon earth." On hearing this he swelled to the size of a mountain, with a body of golden hue and of dazzling splendour, as though a very monarch of mountains, and roaring again and again as it were a lion, he cried "I can easily spring across the salt abyss, and slay Rávan with all his army, and uproot Trikút and bring it here. But I ask you, Jámbaván, what I ought to do; give me proper instructions." " All that you have to do, my son, is to go and see Síta and come back with the news. Then the lotus-eyed, by the might of his own arm, taking with him merely for a show his hosts of monkeys.

Chhand 2.

With his hosts of monkeys Ráma will destroy the demons and recover Síta ; and gods and saints and Nárad and all will declare his glory, that sanctifies the three spheres." Any man attains the highest beatitude who hears, sings, tells or meditates upon the feet of Raghubír, lotus flowers which, like the bee, Tulsi Dás is ever singing.

Dohá 30.

If any man or woman will study the glories of Raghunáth, the panacea for all the ills of life, Siva will make him to prosper in everything that he desires.

Sorathá 2.

Hearken then to his praises, with his body dark of hue as the lotus, with more than all the beauty of a myriad Loves, the fowler who sweeps into his net all kinds of sin as it were so many birds.

[*Thus endeth the book entitled* " KISHKINDHYA," *composed by Tulsi Dás for the bestowal of pure wisdom and continence ; being the fourth descent ' into the holy lake of Ráma's deeds,' that cleanses from every defilement of the world.*]

BOOK V.

THE BEAUTIFUL.

THE BEAUTIFUL.

Sanskrit Invocation.

I ADORE, under his name RAMA, the passionless, the eternal, the immeasurable, the sinless; the bestower of the peace of final emancipation; the lord, whom Bráhma, Sambhu, and the Serpent-king incessantly worship; the theme of the Vedánta; the sovereign of the universe; the preceptor of the gods; Hari in the delusive form of man: the All-merciful; the princely son of Raghu; the jewel of kings.

O Raghupati, there is no other desire in my soul—I speak the truth and you know all my inmost thoughts—grant me, O Raghu king, a vehement faith, and make my heart clean of lust and every other sin.

I reverence the home of immeasurable strength, with his body resembling a mountain of gold; the fire that consumed the demons as it were the trees of a forest; the first name in the list of the truly wise: the store-house of all good qualities; the monkey chief; Raghupati's noble messenger, the Son of the Wind.

Chaupái.

On hearing Jámbaván speak so cheerfully, Hanumán was greatly rejoiced at heart. "Wait for me here, my friends, however great your discomfort, with only roots, herbs, and fruits for your food, till I return after seeing Síta; the task is one I am most pleased to undertake." So saying he bowed his head to them all and went forth with joy, having the image of Raghunáth impressed upon his heart. There was a majestic rock by the seashore; he lightly sprung on to the top of it; then, again and again invoking Raghubír, the Son of the Wind leaped with all his might. The mountain on which he had planted his foot sank down immediately into the depths of hell. Like Ráma's own unerring shaft, so sped Hanumán on his way.

Ocean had regard for Ramá's envoy and told Mainâka to ease his toil.[1]

Dohá 1.

But Hanumán merely touched him with his hand, then bowed and said, 'I can stop nowhere till I have done Ráma's business.'

Chaupái.

The gods saw Hanumán on his way and wished to make special trial of his strength and sagacity. So they sent the mother of the serpent-race, Surasá by name, who came and cried: "To-day the gods have provided me a meal.' On hearing these words, the Son of the Wind replied: "When I have performed Ráma's commission and have come back, and have given my lord the news about Síta then I will put myself into your mouth: I tell you the truth, mother, only let me go now." But, however much he tried, she would not let him go, till at last he said: 'You cannot get me into your mouth.' She opened her jaws a league wide; the monkey made his body twice that size. Then she stretched her mouth sixteen leagues. Hanuman at once became thirty-two. However much Surasá expanded her jaws, the monkey made his frame twice as large again. When she had made her mouth a hundred leagues wide, he reduced himself to a very minute form and went into her mouth and came out again: then bowed and asked permission to proceed. "The purpose for which the gods sent me, namely, to make trial of your wisdom and strength, I have now accomplished.

Dohá 2.

Your wisdom and strength are perfect; you will do all that Ráma requires of you." She then gave him her blessing and departed, and Hanumán went on his way rejoicing.

Chaupái.

A female demon[2] dwelt in the ocean, who by magic

---

1 Mainâka is a rock in the narrow strait between Lanká and the main land.

2 In the Sanskrit Râmâyana her name is given as Sinhikà, the mother of Ráhu.

caught the birds of the air. All living creatures that fly in the air as they look down upon the water cast a shadow upon it and she was able to catch the shadow, so that they could not fly away; and in this manner she always had birds to eat. She played this name trick on Hanumán; but the monkey at once saw through her craft and slew her, hero as he was, and all undismayed crossed over to the opposite shore. Arriving there, he marked the beauty of the wood, with the bees buzzing in their search for honey, the diverse trees all resplendent with simultaneous flower and fruit, and multitudes of birds and deer delightful to behold. Seeing a huge rock further on, he fearlessly sprang on to the top of it. But, Uma, this was not at all the monkey's own strength, but the gift of the Lord, who devours even Death himself. Mounted on the height, he surveyed Lanká a magnificent fortress that defies description, with the deep sea on all four sides around its golden walls of dazzling splendour.

Chhand 1.

Its golden walls studded with all kinds of jewels, a marvellously beautiful sight, with market-places, bazárs, quays, and streets, and all the other accessories of a fine city. Who could count the multitude of elephants, horses and mules, the crowds of footmen and chariots, and the troops of demons of every shape, a formidable host beyond all description. The woods, gardens, groves, and pastures, the ponds, wells and tanks were all superb: and the soul of a saint would be ravished at the sight of the fair daughters, both of men and Nágas, of gods and Gandharvas. Here wrestlers, of monstrous stature like mountains, were thundering with mighty voice and grappling with one another in the different courts, with shouts of mutual defiance. Thousands of warriors of huge bulk were sedulously guarding the city on all four sides; elsewhere horrid demons were banqueting in the form of buffaloes, men, oxen, asses and goats. Tulsi Dás for this reason gives them a few words of mention, because they lost their life by Ráma's hallowed shafts and thus became assured of entrance into heaven.

Dohá 3.

Seeing the number of the city guards, the monkey thought to himself, 'I must make myself very small and slip into the town by night.'

Chaupái.

Thereupon he assumed the form of a gnat[1] and entered Lanká after invoking Vishnu.[2] The female demon, by name Lankini, accosted him : "How dare you come here in contempt of me? Fool, do you not know my practice, that every thief in Lanká becomes my prey?" The monkey struck her one such a blow with his fist that she fell to the ground vomiting blood. Recovering herself again, she stood up and with clasped hands made this confident petition : "When Bráhma granted Rávan's prayer, the Creator gave me a sign before he left, 'When worsted by a monkey, know then that it is all over with the demons.' My meritorious deeds, my son, must have been very many that I have been rewarded with the sight of Ráma's messenger.

Dohá 4.

In one scale of the balance put the bliss of heaven and the final emancipation of the soul from the body, but it will be altogether outweighed by a fraction of the joy that results from communion with the saints.

Chaupái.

Enter the city and accomplish your task, ever mindful at heart of the lord of Kosala. Deadly poison becomes as

---

1 The word *masak*, which I translate 'gnat,' never, so far as I am aware, bears any other meaning. But in one glossary, with reference to this particular passage, it is explained by *bilar*, 'a cat,' only—as it would seem—because that is the animal mentioned in the Sanskrit Rámáyana. In both cases the poet has no sooner stated the transformation than he forgets all about it ; for all Hanumán's subsequent actions are described as if performed by him in his natural shape. He may be supposed to have resumed it as soon as he had passed the guard ; or the words may be taken to mean, "he made himself *as small as* a gnat." This latter view is confirmed by what follows on page 35, Vol. III.-

2 *Nara-hari* stands for the more common Nar-sinha—*hari* and *sinha* both meaning 'a lion'—and here denotes not that particular incarnation, but Vishnu generally.

ambrosia, foes turn friends, ocean shrinks to a mere puddle, fire gives out cold, and huge Sumeru is of no more account than a grain of sand for him whom Ráma deigns to regard with favour." In the tiny form that he had assumed, Hanumán entered the city with a prayer to God Carefully inspecting every separate palace, he found everywhere warriors innumerable. When he had come to Rávan's court, its magnificence was past all telling. The monkey saw him in bed asleep, but no trace of Síta in the room. He then noticed another splendid building, with a temple of Hari standing apart, its walls brilliantly illuminated with Rama s name too beautiful to describe, it fascinated every beholder.

Dohá 5.

The beauty of the chamber emblazzoned with Ráma's insignia was indescribable. At the sight of some fresh springs of tulsi, the monkey chief was enraptured.

Chaupái.

"Lanká is the abode of a gang of demons, how can the pious have any home here ?" While the monkey was thus reasoning within himself, Vibhíshan awoke and at once began to repeat Ráma's name in prayer. The monkey was delighted to find a true believer. "Shall I at once make myself known to him? A good man will never spoil any undertaking." Assuming the form of a Bráhman, he raised his voice in speech. As soon as Vibhíshan heard him, he rose to meet him, and bowing low, asked after his welfare, saying, "Tell me, reverend Sir, who you may be ; if a servant of Hari, you have my hearty affection ; if a loving follower of Rama, your visit is a great honour for me."

Dohá 6.

Hanuman then told him Ráma's whole history and his own name. At the recital and the recollection of his infinite virtues, both quivered all over the body, while their soul was drowned in joy.

Chaupái.

"Hearken, Son of the Wind; my condition here is like that of the poor tongue between the teeth. Yet do not suppose, Father, that I am friendless: the Lord of the Solar race will show me favour. The sinful body is of no avail, if the soul has no love for his lotus feet. But now, Hanumán, I have gained confidence: for it is only by Hari's favour that one meets a good man, and it is the result of his kindness that you have so readily revealed yourself to me." " Listen, Vibhíshan, to my experience of the Lord; he is ever affectionate to his servants. Say who am I and of what noble descent; a wanton monkey, of no merit whatever, a creature the mention of whose name in the early morning makes a man go fasting for the whole day.

Dohá 7.

So mean am I; yet hearken, friend; Raghubír has shown favour even to me." His eyes filled with tears as he recalled his perfection.

Chaupái.

"I know of a truth that any who turns aside in forgetfulness of such a lord may well be miserable." As he thus discoursed on Ráma's excellences, he felt an unspeakable calm. Vibhíshan then told him of all that had been going on and of Síta's mode of life, till Hanumán cried: "Hearken, brother; I would fain see the august Síta." Vibhíshan explained to him the whole mode of procedure, and the Son of the Wind then took his leave and proceeded on his way. Assuming the same form as at first he went to the Asoka grove, where Sita dwelt. As soon as he saw her, mentally prostrated himself in her presence. She had spent the first watch of the night sitting up, haggard in appearance, her hair knotted in a single braid on her head,[1] repeating to herself the list of Raghupati's perfections.

1 To twist the hair in a single braid is a sign of mouring for an absent husband.

Dohá 8.

Her eyes fastened on her own feet, but with her soul absorbed in the contemplation of the feet of her lord. Hanumán was mightly distrest to see her so sad.

Chaupái.

Concealing himself behind the branches of a tree, he mused within himself; "Come, sir, what ought I to do?" At that very moment Rávan drew near, with a troop of women in various attire. The wretch tried in every way to talk Síta over, by blandishments, bribes, threats and misrepresentations. "Hearken, fair dame," he cried," I will make Mandodari and all my other queens your handmaids, I swear it, if you only give me one look." Síta plucked a blade of grass, and with averted face, fondly remembering her own dear lord, replied: "Hearken, Rávan: will the lotus expand at the light of a glowworm? Ponder this at heart," cried Jánaki: "Wretch, have you no fear of Ráma's shafts? Even though absent, Hari will rescue me. Shameless monster, have you no shame?

Dohá 9.

I tell you, you are but a glowworm, while the very sun is only an image of Ráma." On hearing this bold speech he drew his sword and cried in the utmost fury:

Chaupái.

"Síta, you have outraged me; I will cut off your head with this bitting blade. If you do not at once obey my words, you will lose your life, my lady." "My lord's arms, Rávan, are beautiful as a string of dark lotuses and mighty as an elephant's trunk; either they shall have my neck, or if not, then your cruel sword. Hearken, wretch, to this my solemn vow. With your gleaming scimitar[1] put an end to my distress, and let the fiery anguish that I endure for Ráma's loss be quenched in night by the sharp blade of your sword: rid me, cried Síta, "of my burden of pain."

1 The word translated 'gleaming. scimitar' is *chandra-hás*, which means literally 'deriding the moon,' by reason, that is, of its own greater brilliancy.

On hearing these words he again rushed forward to kill her; but the daughter of Maya restrained him with words of admonition. He then summoned all the female demons and ordered them to go and intimidate Síta: 'if she does not mind what I say in a month's time, I will draw my sword and slay her.'

Dohá 10.

Rávan then returned to the palace, while the demonesses, assuming every kind of hideous form, proceeded to terrify Síta.

Chaupái.

One of them, by name Trijatá, was devoted to Ráma's service, prudent and wise. She declared to them all a dream, how that they for their own sake ought to show Síta reverence. "In my dream a monkey set fire to Lanka, and put to death the whole demon army, and set Rávan on an ass, naked, with his heads shorn and his twenty arms hacked off. In this fashion he went away towards the south,[1] while Vibhíshan succeeded to the throne of Lanká. The city resounded with cries for mercy in Ráma's name, till the Lord sent Síta among them. I deliberately warn you that four days hence this dream will be accomplished." Upon hearing her words they were all dismayed and went and threw themselves at Síta's feet,

Dohá 11.

after which they dispersed in every direction. But Síta was troubled at heart: 'At the end of a month[2] this vile monster will slay me.'

Chaupái.

With clasped hands she cried to Trijatá: "Mother, you are my helper in distress; quickly devise some plan that I may be rid of life, for this intolerable bereavement is no

1 The realm of Yama, the god of Death, is supposed to be in the south. For this reason a Hindu will never, when it is possible to avoid it, have the door of his house in that direction. Muhammadans even, at the present day, are much influenced by the same superstition.

2 As appears from what follows, it is not death that she dreads, but the long interval of a month, which has to elapse before her death takes place.

longer to be endured. Bring wood and erect my funeral pyre and then set fire to it. My affection, reverend dame, will thus be attested." Who could bear to listen to such an agonizing cry? When she heard her speech she clasped her feet and would fain comfort her by reciting the majesty and might and glory of her lord. "Hearken, fair lady; there is no fire to be had at night;" and so saying she went away home. Síta exclaimed: "Heaven is unkind; without fire my pain cannot be cured. I see the heaven all bright with sparks, but not a single star drops to the earth. The moon is all ablaze, but no fire comes from it, as if it knew what a poor wretch I am. Ye Asoka trees,[1] that hear my prayer, answer to your name and rid me of my pain; and you flame-coloured opening buds, supply me with fire to consume my body." A single moment seemed like an age to the monkey, as he beheld Síta thus piteously lamenting her bereavement.

Dohá 12.

After taking thought within himself he threw down the signet ring, as though a spark had fallen from the Asoka. She started up with joy and clasped it in her hand.

Chaupái.

When she had looked at the lovely ring, beautifully engraved with Ráma's name, she was all astonishment, for she recognized it, and her heart fluttered with mingled joy and sorrow. "Who can conquer the unconquerable Raghurái? This cannot be any trick of Maya." All sorts of fancies passed through her mind, till Hanumán spoke in honeyed accents and began to recount Rámchandra's praises. As Síta listened, her grief took flight. Intently she hearkened with all her soul as well as her ears, while he related the whole story from the very beginning. "The tale you tell is so grateful to my ears; why do you not show yourself, friend? Then Hanumán advanced and drew near. She turned and

---

1 The name Asoka is derived from *a* 'without' and *soka* 'pain.' The conceit cannot be preserved in an English translation.

sunk to the ground in bewilderment. "Noble Jánaki, I am Ráma's messenger; the Fountain of mercy himself attests my truth I have brought this ring, lady, which Ráma gave me for you as a token." "Tell me how can monkeys consort with man?" He then explained how they had come together.

Dohá 13.

On hearing the monkey's affectionate speech, her soul trusted him, and she recognized him as a faithful follower of the All-merciful.

Chaupái.

On perceiving him to be one of Hari's worshippers, she felt an intense affection for him; her eyes filled with tears, her body quivered with emotion. "O Hanumán, I was sinking in the ocean of bereavement; but in you, my friend, I have found a ship. Tell me now of their welfare, I adjure you; how is the blessed Kharári and how is his brother? Raghurái is tender-hearted and merciful, why, O monkey, should he affect such cruelty? The mere sound of his voice is a delight to his servants. Does he ever deign to remember me? Will my eyes, friend, be ever gladdened by the sight of his dark and delicate body?" Words failed, her eyes swam with tears. "Alas! my lord has entirely forgotten me." Seeing Síta thus distracted by her bereavement, the monkey replied in gentle and respectful tones: "Lady, your lord and his brother are both well, save that the All-merciful sorrows for your sorrow. Do not imagine, madam, that Ráma's affection is a whit less than your own.

Dohá 14.

Take courage now and listen to Ráma's message." So saying, the monkey's voice failed him and his eyes filled with tears.

Chaupái.

Then he proceeded to tell her of Ráma's forlorn condition "Every thing—says he—is changed into its opposite. The fresh buds upon the trees burn like fire; night seems as the night of death, and the moon scorches like the sun. A bed of lotuses seems a prickly brake, and the rain-clouds drop boiling oil. The trees only add to my pain, and the softest and most fragrant breeze is like the breath of a serpent. Nothing relieves my torture, and to whom can I declare it ? for there is no one who will understand. The essence of such love as yours and mine, my beloved, only my own soul can comprehend, and this my soul is always with you. Know such to be the profundity of my love." As the Videhan princess listened to Ráma's message, she became so absorbed in love as to have no thought for herself. Said the monkey: "Lady, compose yourself, remembering that Ráma is a benefactor to all who serve him. Reflect upon his might and, as you listen to my speech, discard all anxiety.

Dohá 15.

The demon crew are like moths and Raghupati's arrows as a flame ; be stout of heart, madam, and rest assured that they will all be consumed.

Chaupái.

If Raghubír only knew, he would make no delay. Ráma's shafts, like the rays of the rising sun, will scatter the darkling demon host. I would have carried you away at once myself, but, I swear to you by Ráma, that I have not received his order to do so. Wait patiently, madam, for a few days, and he will arrive with his monkeys, will slaughter the demons, and take you away, so that Nárad and the other seers will glorify him in all the three spheres of creation." "Are all the monkeys, my son, like you ? the demon warriors are very powerful, and my soul is sorely disquieted." On hearing this, the monkey showed himself in his natural form, his body in bulk like a mountain of gold, terrible in battle, and of vast strength ; then Síta took comfort at heart, and he again resumed a diminutive appearance.

Dohá 16.

"Hearken, lady; the monkeys have no great strength or wit of their own, but by the Lord's favour even a snake, small as it is, might swallow Garúr."

Chaupái.

As she hearkened to the monkey's speech, so full of glorious faith and noble confidence, her mind became easy, she recognized his love for Ráma and gave him her blessing: "May you abound, my son, in all strength and virtue; may neither age nor death affect your good qualities, and may you be ever constant in your devotion to Ráma, and may the Lord be gracious to you." Hearing these words, Hanumán became utterly overwhelmed with emotion; again and again he bowed his head at her feet, and with clasped hands spoke thus: "Now, lady, I am fully rewarded; for your blessing is known to be effectual. But hearken, madam, I am frightfully hungry and I see the trees laden with delicious fruit." "Know, my son, that this grove is guarded by most valiant and formidable demons." "I am not afraid of them, mother, if only you will keep your mind easy.

Dohá 17.

Seeing the monkey so strong and sagacious, Jánaki said: "Go, my son, and eat of this pleasant fruit, with your heart fixed on Hari's feet.

Chaupái.

He bowed his head and went and entered the garden and having eaten of the fruit began breaking down the trees. A number of stalwart watchmen were posted there; some he killed, the others went and called for help: "My lord, an enormous monkey has come and rooted up the Asoka grove; he has eaten the fruit and broken down the trees, and with many a blow laid the watchmen on the ground." On hearing this, Rávan despatched a number of his champions. At the sight of them Hanumán roared like thunder and overthrew the whole demon host; a few, more dead than alive, ran off shrieking. He then sent the young prince Aksha, who took with him an immense number of his best warriors. Seeing them approach he seized a tree, which he brandished and with an awful roar swept them down with it.

Dohá 18.

Some be hacked, some he crushed, some he laid low in the dust ; some got back and cried " My lord, this monkey is too strong for us."

Chaupái.

When he heard of his son's death, the king of Lanká was furious and he sent the valiant Meghnád. " Do not kill him, my son, but bind him ; I would fain see this monkey and where he has come from." Indrajit[1] sallied forth, a peerless champion, full of fury at the tidings of his brother's death. When the monkey saw this formidable warrior draw near, he ground his teeth, and with a roar rushed forward and tore up a tree of enormous size, with which he swept the prince of Lanká from his car. As for the mighty men of war who accompanied him, he seized them one by one and crushed them by his weight. Having finished them off, he closed with their leader. It was like the encounter of two lordly elephants. After striking him a blow with his fist, he went and climbed a tree, while for a moment a swoon came over his antagonist. But again he arose and practised many enchantments ; still the Wind god's son was not to be vanquished.

Dohá 19.

On his making ready Bráhma's magical weapon,[2] the monkey thought within himself, " If I do not submit to Bráhma's shaft, its infinite virtue will have failed."

---

1 Meghnád's name was changed by Bráhma to Indrajit, after his victory over Indra.

2 The weapon had been given to Meghnád by Bráhma with a promise that it should never fail. Hanumán therefore submits to it in order that Bráhma's promise might not be falsified.

Chaupái.

He launched the magic dart against the monkey, who overthrew a host as he fell. When he saw that he had swooned, he bound him with a running noose and carried him off. Observe, Bhaváni; the messenger of the god, by the repetition of whose name wise men cut the bonds of existence, himself came under bondage, or rather in his lord's service submitted to be bound. When the demons heard that the monkey had been bound, they all rushed to the palace to see the sight. The majesty of Rávan's court on the monkey's arrival there struck him as being beyond all description. The gods and regents of the air, standing humbly with clasped hands, were all in dismay, if they saw him frown But the monkey's soul was no more disturbed at the sight of his majesty than Garúr would be frightened by any number of snakes.

Dohá 20.

When Rávan saw the monkey, he laughed aloud and mocked him; then again he remembered his son's death and his soul grew sad.

Chaupái.

Said the King of Lanká: "Who are you, monkey, and by whose might have you wrought the destruction of the grove? What, do not you hear me? I see you are an uncommonly bold varlet. For what offence did you put the demons to death? Speak, wretch; as you value your life." "Hearken, Rávan; He by whose might Maya creates this universal sphere; by whose might Bráhma, Vishnu, and Siva produce, maintain and destroy the world; by whose might the thousand-headed serpent supports on his pate the mundane egg with its mountains and forests; who assumes various forms in order to befriend the gods, and to give a lesson to wretches like you; who broke Siva's stubborn bow and crushed your pride and that of the assembled kings: who slew Khara and Dúshan and Trisira and Báli, in spite of their matchless strength:

Dohá 21.

By the slightest exercise of whose might the entire mass of creation, animate and inanimate, exists ; he it is whose messenger I am, and it is his beloved spouse whom you have stolen away.

Chaupái.

I know your power; you had a fight with Sahasra-bhuj, and also gained renown in your conflict with Báli." He heard what the monkey said, but smiled as though he heard not. "I ate the fruit, my lord, because I was hungry, and then like a monkey began breaking the boughs. Every one, master, loves his life more than aught else ; those good-for-nothing fellows fell upon me, and I gave them blow for blow. Thereupon your son put me in bonds—bonds that I am in no way ashamed of—for my only object is to accomplish my master's business. Rávan, I implore you with folded hands, abandon your pride and attend to my advice. Have some consideration for your own family; cease to go astray and adore him, who relieves his worshippers from every anxiety. Never fight against him, for fear of whom Death trembles exceedingly ; even Death, who devours all else, gods and demons, animate and inanimate creation alike. Give up Síta, as I tell you.

Dohá 22.

Ráma is the protector of suppliants ; Kharári is a very ocean of compassion ; turn to him for protection, and the Lord will forget your offences and will shelter you.

Chaupái.

Take Ráma's lotus feet to your heart and reign for ever at Lanká. The glory of saint Pulastya[1] is stainless as the moon ; do not make yourself a spot on its brightness. Unless Ráma's name be in it, no speech has any charm : Think and see for yourself, apart from pride and vanity.

---

1 Pulastya was Rávan's grandfather.

Without her clothes, Rávan, a modest woman, however richly adorned with jewels, is a shameful sight; and so is wealth, or dominion, without Ráma, gone at once, gotten as if not gotten at all. Those rivers, that have no perennial source, flow only after rain and then soon dry up again. Hearken, Rávan; I tell you on my oath, if Ráma is against you, there is none who can save you. Siva, Seshnág, Vishnu and Bráhma cannot protect you, if you are Ráma's enemy.

Dohá 23.

Arrogance is a root fruitful of many thorns; abandon violence and pride, and worship Ráma, the prince of the Raghu race, the Ocean of Compassion, the Lord God."

Chaupái.

Though the monkey bespoke him in such friendly wise, in words full of faith and discretion, piety and sound judgment, he laughed and replied with the highest disdain: "What a sage adviser I have found, and in a monkey too! Wretch, you have come within an inch of death for daring to give me such vile counsel." "It will be contrariwise" said Hanuman; "you will acknowledge the error of your soul, I know well." On hearing the monkey's words, he ground his teeth in a fury. "Quick, some of you, and put an end to this fool's life." The demons obeyed and rushed forward to slay him, but Vibhíshan and his ministers advanced and bowing the head made humble petition: "It is against all statecraft: an ambassador must not be killed. Punish him in some other way, Sire." All exclaimed to one another, 'this is sound counsel, friend,' Rávan on hearing it, replied with a laugh: 'Let the monkey go then, but multilate him first.

Dohá 24.

A monkey is proud of his tail" (so he went on to say) "bind it with rags steeped in oil and then set fire to them.

Chaupái.

The poor tailless wretch can then go back and fetch his

master, and I shall have an opportunity of seeing his might, whom he has so extravagantly exalted." The monkey smiled to himself to hear this. 'Sárad, I know, will help me.' Obedient to Rávan's command the demons began making their foolish preparations. Not a rag was left in the city nor a drop of *ghi* or oil, to such a length the tail had grown. Then they made sport of him. The citizens crowded to see the sight, and struck him with their feet and jeered him greatly, and with beating of drums and clapping of hands they took him through the city and set fire to his tail. When Hanumán saw the fire blazing, he at once reduced himself to a very diminutive size, and slipping out of his bonds sprang on to the upper story of the gilded palace, to the dismay of the giants' wives.

Dohá 25.

That instant the forty-nine winds,[1] whom Hari had sent, began to blow; the monkey shouted with roars of laughter and swelled so big that he touched the sky.

Chaupái.

Of enormous stature and yet marvellous agility, he leaped and ran from palace to palace. As the city was thus set on fire, the people were at their wits' end; for the terrible flames burst forth in countless millions of places. "Alas! father and mother, hearken to my cry: who will save us now? As I said, this is no monkey, but some god in monkey form. This is the result of not taking a good man's advice; our city is burnt down as though it had no protector." The city was consumed in an instant of time, save only Vibhíshan's house; the reason why it

1 In the Veda, the Maruts, or winds. are said to be sixty-three in number, forming nine Ganas, or troops, of seven each. In post-Vedic literature they are described as the children of Diti, either seven, or seven times seven in number. After Diti's elder sons, the Asuras, had been subdued by Indra, their mother implored her husband Kasyapa, the son of Marichi, to bestow on her an Indra-destroying son. Her request was granted; but Indra, with his weapon Vajra, divided the child, with which she was pregnant, into forty-nine pieces, which commenced uttering grievous cries, till Indra in compassion transformed them into the Maruts, or Winds.—*Monier Williams sub-verbo.*

escaped, Bhaváni, was that he who sent the messenger had also created the fire. After the whole of Lanká had been turned upside down and given over to the flames, he threw himself into the middle of the sea.

Dohá 26.

After extinguishing his tail and recovering from his fatigue, he assumed his old diminutive form and went and stood before Jánaki, with hands clasped in prayer.

Chaupái.

" Be pleased, madam, to give me some token, such as Ráma gave me." She unfastened the jewel in her hair and gave it him.[1] The Son of the Wind received it gladly. " Salute him respectfully for me, my son, with these words: ' my lord, you never fail to fulfil desire and are renowned as the suppliant's friend; relieve me then from my grievous distress.' Repeat to him, friend, the story of Indra's son,[2] and remind my lord of the might of his arrows. If he does not come within a month, he will never find me alive. Tell me, monkey, how can I keep myself alive; for you now, my son, speak of going, and it is only the sight of you that has given me any comfort: henceforth day and night will seem to me both alike."

Dohá 27.

He did everything he could to console Síta and inspire her with confidence, and then bowed his head at her lotus feet and set forth to rejoin Ráma.

Chaupái.

As he went, he roared aloud with such a terrible noise that the wives of the demons, who heard it, were overtaken by premature childbirth. Crossing the sea with a bound, he arrived on this side and uttered a cry of joy for the monkeys to hear. At the sight of Hanumán, they were as

---

1 In both recensions of the Sanskrit Rámáyana, Síta gives Hanumán the jewel before he destroys the grove and sets the city on fire. The second interview is not mentioned at all in the up-country text.

2 The son of Indra, to whom allusion is here made, is Jayanta, who had attacked Síta in the form of a crow. *See* page 190, Vol 2.

delighted as if they have been given a new spell of life. "Your face is so glad and your whole body so radiant that you cannot but have accomplished Ráma's commission." All greeted him with as much delight as an expiring fish feels when it gets back into the water; and they set out with joy to rejoin Ráma, talking as they went of all that had lately occurred. When they had reached the Madhu-ban, with Angad's constent they began eating the luscious fruit; the watchmen tried to stop them, but were beaten off with fisticuffs. They then fled,

Dohá 28.

crying out that the prince had laid waste the garden. Sugríva rejoiced at the news: "The monkey must have returned, after successfully completing his master's business.

Chaupái.

If they had not got news of Síta, they would never have eaten the fruit of the Madhu-ban." While the king was thus reasoning within himself, Hanumán and his party arrived. They at once bowed the head at his feet, and he received them with all possible cordiality and asked of their welfare. "It is well with us now that we have seen your feet. By Ráma's favour the business has turned out excellently. Hanumán has accomplished his lord's purpose and has saved the life of us all." On hearing this, Sugríva again embraced him and then went on with the monkeys to where Ráma was. When Ráma saw them coming, he was greatly delighted at the completion of the business. The two brothers were seated on a crystal rock and all the monkeys went and fell at their feet."

Dohá 29.

Raghupati in his infinite tenderness greeted them all with much affection and asked of their welfare. "All is well with us, my lord, now that we have seen your lotus feet."

Chaupái.

Said Jámavant; "Hearken, Raghu-ráya; anyone, my lord on whom you show favour will always be prosperous for ever ; gods, men and saints will be gracious to him ; though victorious he will still remain modest and amiable, and his glory will irradiate all the three spheres of creation. By my lord's favour the task has been accomplished, and to-day we may well say that our life has been worth living. My lord, to tell the whole of Hanumán's doings would be too much for a thousand tongues " Jámavant then proceeded to inform Ráma of Hanumán's principal exploits. The All-merciful was charmed by the recital and again in his joy clasped Hanumán to his bosom. "Tell me, my son, how Jánaki is and how she keeps life in her body."

Dohá 30.

"Your name is sentinel over her by night and day ; her contemplation of you is as a prison-gate ; her eyes are the fetters for her feet ; how then is it possible for her life to flit away ?

Chaupái.

When I was leaving, she gave me this jewel from her hair." Raghupati took and clasped it to his heart, while his eyes overflowed with tears. "And did Síta send any message also ?" "Embrace the feet of my lord and his brother, crying, O friend of the poor, reliever of the suppliant's distress ; in heart, word and deed, I am devoted to your service; for what offence, my lord, have you deserted me ? Of one fault I am myself conscious, in that I still continue to live, though separated from you. But this, my lord, is the fault of my eyes, which prevent my soul from taking flight. In this furnace of bereavement which is fanned by my sighs, my body is as it were a heap of cotton and would be consumed in a moment, but my eyes drop such a flood in self-commiseration that it cannot catch fire. Síta's distress is so utterly everwhelming and you are so pitiful that it is better not to describe it.

Dohá 31.

O fountain of mercy, each single moment seems an age ere it passes. Set out at once, my lord, and with your mighty arm vanquish the miscreant crew and deliver her."

Chaupái.

On hearing of Síta's distress, the lotus eyes of the Lord, the abode of bliss, overflowed with tears. "When in thought, word and deed, a believer follows in my steps, what ought he to know of misfortune?" Said Hanumán: "There is no misfortune, my lord, except to forget you and your worship. Of what account are the demons to my lord, who can rout them at once and recover Síta." "Hearken, O monkey; neither god, nor man, nor saint that has ever been born into this world, has been such a benefactor to me as you. What return can I make you? There is none that occurs to my mind. Mark me, my son; I am not free from my obligation to you; I will think and see what I can do." Again and again as the deliverer of the gods gazed upon the monkey, his eyes filled with tears and his whole body quivered with emotion.

Dohá 32.

As he listened to his lord's words and looked upon his face, Hanumán was enraptured, and in an ecstasy of love fell at his feet, crying, 'save me, save me, O my Lord God.'

Chaupái.

Again and again his lord sought to raise him up, but he was so absorbed in devotion that he would not rise. (As he called to mind the Lord with his lotus hands thus placed on the monkey's head, Siva himself was overcome with emotion; but again, restraining his feelings, he proceeded with the charming narrative). After raising the monkey, the Lord embraced him and took him by the hand and seated him close by his side: "Tell me, O monkey, about Rávan's stronghold of Lanká, and how you were able in such an off hand way to burn down his fort." Seeing his lord so gracious, Hanumán replied in terms of singular modesty: "A monkey forsooth is a creature of singular prowess to skip about as he does from bough to bough. When I leaped across the sea, burnt down the golden city, routed the demon host and laid waste the grove, it was all done through your power, Raghurái ; it was no strength of mine, my lord.

Dohá 33.

Nothing is difficult for him to whom you are propitious; a mere shred of cotton, were it your pleasure, could burn up the whole submarine fire."[1]

Chaupái.

The Lord smiled much to hear these words, and recognized him as indeed a loving servant. "Ask of me a boon my son, some choice blessing ; to-day I will make you happy for ever." "Faith, my lord, is the greatest of blessings ; of your favour grant me this else unattainable boon." On hearing the monkey's pious request, the Lord, Bhaváni, responded : 'So be it.' O Umá, he who knows Ráma's true nature can take pleasure in nothing but his worship : and he who takes this truth to heart has attained to the virtue of faith in Ráma. When the assembled monkeys heard the Lord's reply, they cried 'glory, glory, glory to the All-merciful, the All-blessed.' Raghupati then summoned the monkey chief and told him to make preparations for the march : "What need now for any delay ? At once issue orders to the monkeys." The gods, who had witnessed the spectacle, rained down many flowers and returned with joy from the lower air to their own celestial spheres.

Dohá 34.

In obedience to Sugríva's summons all his hosts of captains came in, differing in colour, but all unequalled in strength, a vast multitude of monkeys and bears.

Chaupái.

They bowed the head at the Lord's lotus feet, those roaring bears and gigantic monkeys. Ráma beheld all the monkey host, and turned upon them the gracious glance of his lotus eyes. Each monkey chief was as much emboldened by his favour as Sumeru would be by the recovery of

---

1 *Badavánala*, the submarine fire, is represented in mythology as a being with a body of flame, but the head of a mare (badavá) which sprang from the thighs of the patriarch Urva and fell into the ocean.

his wings.[1] Ráma then sallied forth exulting, and many were the glad and auspicious omens that befell him. It was only befitting that his march should be attended by favourable omens, since in him abide all glory and auspiciousness. Jánaki knew of his departure, for her left side throbbed as if to tell her. Every good omen that befell her was converted into an omen of ill for Rávan. Who could adequately describe the army on the road, with the terrible roaring of the monkeys and the bears, how they marched, brandishing rocks and trees and with their talons for weapons, now in the heaven and now on earth, as the fancy moved them. They bellowed as if with the voice of a tiger; earth shook and the elephants of the eight quarters trembled.

Chhand 1—2.

The elephants of the eight quarters trembled, the earth reeled, the mountains tottered, and the ocean was agitated; the sun and the moon, gods, saints, Nágas, and Kinnars, all rejoiced to know that their troubles were over. Myriads upon myriads of enormous fighting monkeys pressed onwards, snapping, and snarling, singing glory to Ráma's conquering might and hymning the praises of Kosala's lord. The huge serpent king could not support the burden; he staggered again and again, but each time saved himself by clutching in his jaws the hard shell of the tortoise; as though he had mastered the stupendous theme of Raghubir's glorious expedition, and were inscribing it on the tortoise's back as the most imperishable material to be had.

Dohá 35. 36

In such wise the All-merciful marched onwards, till he arrived at the seashore, where the host of bears and fighting monkeys began to devour all the fruit they found.

1 This conceit has a very unmeaning sound when expressed in English. The allusion is to the legend which represents all the mountains as once having had wings, till they were clipped by Indra; while the word *paksha* which primarily means 'a wing' has also the secondary signification of favour.

Chaupái

On the other hand, the demons had been living in great fear, ever since the time the monkey had left, after burning down the city. Every one kept at home, thinking to himself: "There is no hope of safety for the demon race; if his messenger was so unspeakably powerful, how can the city escape when he comes himself?" When Mandodari was informed of what the people were saying, she was still more distrest, and with clasped hands fell at her lord's feet and thus besought him, in words full of sound judgment: "O my husband, cease to contend against Hari: take my words to your heart as most wholesome advice. His mere messenger did such deeds that our matrans, on hearing them, were overtaken by premature labour; if then you desire your own welfare, call your ministers and send him back his wife. As a frosty night comes upon a bed of lotuses, so has Síta come for the ruin of your race. Hearken, my lord; unless you give up Síta, neither Sambhu nor Bráhma can help you.

Dohá 36.

Ráma's arrows are like serpents, and the demon host so many frogs; delay not, but do the best you can before they have snapped you up."

Chaupái.

The monster heard her prayer and laughed aloud; his arrogance is known throughout the world. "A woman is naturally cast in a timorous mould, and even in prosperity has a mind ill at ease. If the monkey army comes, the poor wretches will all be eaten up by the demons. The very guardians of the spheres trembled for fear of me; it is quite absurd for my wife to be afraid." So saying he laughed and embraced her, and then full of inordinate conceit proceeded to the council-chamber. But Mandodari was sore troubled at heart, saying, 'Heaven is against my lord.' While he was sitting in court, he received intelligence that the whole army had crossed the sea. Then he enquired of his ministers, 'Tell me what you think best to be done.' They all laughed and replied, "Remain quiet. You have conquered gods and demons without any trouble; of what account can men and monkeys be?"

Dohá 37.

When these three, a minister, a physician and a spiritual adviser, use fair words, either from fear or hope of reward; dominion, religion and health are all three quickly destroyed.

Chaupái.

This was all the help that Rávan got; they did nothing but sound his praises. Perceiving his opportunity, Vibhíshan came and bowed his head at his brother's feet, then again bowing took his seat on his throne and after obtaining permission spoke thus: "As you graciously ask of me my opinion, I declare it, Sire, to the best of my ability. If you desire your own welfare and glory, with a reputation for wisdom, a prosperous issue and every other happiness, turn away from the face of another man's wife as from the moon on its fourth day.[1] Though a man were lord of the fourteen spheres, he cannot set himself to oppose the Universal. However amiable and accomplished a person may be, no one will speak well of him if he shows even the slightest covetousness.

Dohá 38.

Lust, passion, vanity, and covetousness are all paths that lead to hell: adjure them and worship Raghubír, whom all the saints worship.

Chaupái.

Ráma, my brother, is no mortal king, but the sovereign of the universe, the Fate of Fate itself, the Supreme Spirit, the imperishable and uncreated God, the benefactor of cows and of Bráhmans, of the earth and of the gods: who in his infinite mercy has assumed the form of humanity, to rejoice his votaries and to break the ranks of the impious; the

1 It is a Hindu superstition that it is unlucky to see the moon on the fourth day. Hence the proverb:—

"Jo dekh chauthe ká chanda, Bát chalat, láge pharphanda,"

champion of the Veda and true religion, the saviour of the immortals. Cease to fight against him and humbly bow the head. Raghunáth relieves the distress of every suppliant. O my lord, give him back Síta and worship him with disinterested affection. The lord has never abandoned any one who has fled to him for protection, though he were guilty of having ruined the whole world. Know of a truth, Rávan, that it is the lord, he who has for name 'the saviour from every calamity,' who has now appeared among us.

Dohá 39.

Again and again I lay my head at your feet and utter this my prayer: have done with pride, arrogance and conceit, and worship Ráma. These are the words which Saint Pulastya sent in a message to me, and I have at once taken this opportunity of repeating them to you, Sire."

Chaupái.

One of his wisest counsellors Mályaván, was greatly rejoiced to hear this speech. "Take to heart, my son, this admirable counsel which your brother Vibhíshan has given you." "These two villains who thus magnify my enemies, is there no one here who will rid me of them?" Mályaván thereupon returned home, but Vibhíshan with clasped hands spoke yet again: "In every one's breast, my lord, so the Vedas and Puránas declare, either wisdom or unwisdom finds a dwelling. Where wisdom dwells, there too is every kind of prosperity: and where unwisdom, there is final destruction. In your breast malignant unwisdom has established herself; you take your friends for enemies and your greatest enemy for a friend, being thus extravagantly enamoured of this Síta, who is the very night of Death for the whole demon race.

Dohá 40.

My brother, I clasp your feet and implore you to take my words in good part: restore Síta to Ráma; it will be much to your advantage."

Chaupái.

Though the words that Vibhíshan spoke were wise and prudent, and supported by the authority of the Vedas and Purános, the Ten-headed rose in a fury at hearing them: "Wretch, you are within an inch of your death. It is all owing to me, you villain, that you have been able to live at all; and yet, fool as you are, you take the side of my enemies. Can you tell me, wretch, of any one in the whole world, whom I have not conquered by the might of my arm. You live in my capital, but are in love with hermits; you had better go to them, if you want to preach." So saying, he spurned him with a kick; but he still continued to clasp him by the feet. "You are as it were my father; kill me, if you think proper; but, O my lord, to worship Ráma would be far better for you." This is the virtue of the saints, Umá, that they return good for evil. Taking his ministers with him, he went his way through the air, proclaiming aloud to them all:

Dohá 41.

"Ráma is the very soul of truth; your courtiers, my lord, are overpowered by fate; I will now take refuge with, Raghubír; lay no blame to me."

Chaupái.

After Vibhíshan had left with these words, it was all over with everyone of them. Disrespect to a saint, Bhaváni, brings speedy ruin on the most prosperous undertaking. As soon as Vibhíshan had left, Rávan lost all his glory and good fortune. But he rejoiced as he went to meet Ráma, and revolved in his mind many agreeable anticipation: "I am about to behold his lotus feet, so roseate, so soft, so beneficent to all who wait upon them; at whose touch the Rishi's wife was delivered from the cure, and the Dandaka forest was sanctified; feet that Síta cherished in her bosom, even while they ran to seize the delusíve deer; lotus feet in Siva's lake-like heart; how blest am I who am now about to see them!

Dohá 42.

"With these very eyes shall I this day behold the feet, whose shoes even Bharat clasped to his heart."

Chaupái.

With such loving fancies to occupy his mind, he quickly arrived on this side the ocean. When the monkeys saw Vibhíshan coming, they took him to be some special envoy. So they stopt him and went to their chief and told him all the circumstances. Said Sugríva: "Hearken, Raghurái; Rávan's brother has come to see you." The lord replied: "What do you advise, friend?" The monkey king rejoined: "Mark my words, Sire; the craft of these demons is past all telling. Why should he come thus of his own accord? The villain's object is to spy out our secrets. My idea is that we ought to keep him prisoner." "Friend, you have reasoned with much wordly wisdom; but I have a vow to befriend all suppliants. " Hanumán was delighted to hear these words from the Lord, the God who shows compassion on all who flee to him.

Dohá 43.

"The men who abandon a suppliant, from suspicion that he may be an enemy, are vile and criminal, and misfortune will keep her eye upon them.

Chaupái.

I would not abandon any one who had fled to me for protection, even though he had been guilty of the murder of a million Bráhmans Directly any creature appears before me, I blot out the sins of all his past lives. No one who is essentially wicked can delight in my service; if he is really bad at heart, how can he come into my presence? Only a man of pure soul can find me; I take no pleasure in hypocrisy, deceit and vice. Rávan may have sent him as a spy; but even so, O king, we need not fear any loss. All the demons, my friend, that the whole world contains, Lakshman could rout in a single moment. If he has come out of fear, to sue for mercy, I will protect him as I would my own life.

Dohá 44.

In either case bring him here." Thus spake the All-merciful with a smile. "Glory to the lord of mercy" cried the monkey as he went, taking with him Angad and Hanumán.

Chaupái.

The monkeys respectfully escorted him into the presence of the all-merciful Rama. He beheld from a distance the two brothers, the delight of all men's eyes, the givers of every blessing ; then looking again upon Ráma's perfect beauty, he stood stock still, with all his gaze intently fixed upon the long arms, the lotus eyes and dark-hued body of the suppliant's friend, his lion-like shoulders and magnificent broad chest and his charming face, that would ravish the soul of Kámadeva himself. With streaming eyes and trembling limbs he at last made bold to speak in accents mild. "My lord, I am Rávan's brother ; Champion of heaven, I have been born of demon race, with a savage temperament, as naturally prone to evil as an owl is partial to the night.

Dohá 45.

I have heard with my ears of your glory and have come ; O my lord, save me, save me ; you who are the deliverer from all life's troubles, the remover of distress, the friend of the suppliant, Raghubír.

Chaupái.

So saying he prostrated himself ; but at the sight the Lord arose in haste with much delight, being pleased to hear his humble address, and took him in his mighty arms and clasped him to his breast ; then with his brother seated him by his side, and to calm his votary's fears spake thus : "Tell me, prince of Lanká, is it all well with you and your family? Your home is in an ill place. How, my friend, can one practise the duties of religion, when encompassed day and night by wicked men ? I know all your circumstances, your proficiency in virtue, your aversion to evil. God keep us from evil communications : 'twere better, my son, to live in hell.' "Now that I have seen your feet, O Ráma, it is all well with me, since you have recognized me as one of your worshippers and have shown mercy upon me.

Dohá 46.

No creature can be happy, or even dream of rest to his soul, till he worship Ráma, after forswearing lust, that fountain of remorse.

Chaupái.

"So long as the heart is peopled by that villainous crew, avarice, sensuality, selfishness, arrogance and pride, there is no room there for Raghunáth, with his bow and arrows and quiver by his side. The intensely dark night of selfishness, so agreeable to the owl-like passions of love and hate, abides in the soul only until the rising of the sun-like lord. Now I am well, and all my fears are over, in that I have beheld your lotus feet. None of the threefold torments of life has any effect upon him, to whom you in your mercy show favour. I am a demon, utterly vile of nature, who have never observed any pious practices, and yet the lord, to whose vision even the saints have not attained, for all their profound meditation has been pleased to take me to his heart.

Dohá 47.

"Surely I am blessed beyond measure, and Ráma's grace is most beneficent, in that I behold with my eyes those lotus feet, which even Bráhma and Siva adore."

Chaupái.

"Hearken, friend; I will declare to you my characteristics, as known by Bhusundi, Sambhu and Umá. If a man who has been the curse of the whole world comes trembling and looks to me for protection, if he abjures all his pride and sensuality without guile or subterfuge; I make him at once like one of the saints. Father and mother; kinsfolk, children and wife; life and property; home, friends and establishment; in short, every object of natural affection is gathered up as the strands of a rope wherewith to attach his soul to my feet. He regards all things as alike, without any preference, and with a soul unmoved either by joy, sorrow, or fear. A saint like this is as fixed in my soul as money is in the heart of a miser. Good men like you are my friends, and it is only for their benefit that I have become incarnate.

Dohá 48.

"Virtuous and devoted believers, who are steadfast in uprightness, strict in pious observances, and who love and revere Bráhmans, are the men whom I regard as my own soul.

Chaupái.

"Hearken, Prince of Lanká; all these good qualities are yours, and you are therefore very dear to me." On hearing Ráma's speech, all the assembled monkeys exclaimed, 'Glory to the All-merciful!' But Vibhíshan, on hearing such ambrosial sounds, could not contain himself: time after time he clasped his lotus feet, his heart bursting with boundless joy. "Hearken, my God, lord of all creation, friend of the suppliant, reader of men's thoughts; I had at first another wish in my mind; but devotion to my lord's feet has come upon me like a torrent and swept it away: now in your mercy grant me such pure faith as that which ever gladdens Siva's soul." 'So be it,' said the Lord, the valiant in fight, and then at once called for water from the sea. "It was not part of your wish, friend, but the sight of me brings reward with it all over the world." So saying Ráma marked his forehead with the royal *tilak*: an infinite shower of flowers rained from heaven.

Dohá 49.

Thus did Raghunáth protect the humble Vibhíshan from Rávan's fiery wrath, fanned by the strong blast of his breath, and gave him secure dominion and all the good fortune which Siva had formerly bestowed upon the ten-headed Rávan.

Chaupái.

Men who forsake such a lord to worship any other are mere beasts without the tails and horns. All the monkeys were charmed with the Lord's amiability, who had recognized a servant and claimed him for his own. Then the All-wise, who dwelleth in the hearts of all, assuming any form at will, though himself formless and passionless, the champion of religion, the friend of men, and the destroyer of all the demon race, spoke and said: "Hearken monkey-king, valiant monarch of Lanká; how are we to cross the deep ocean, full of alligators, serpents and different kinds of sea monsters, of fathomless profundity and absolutely impassible." Vibhíshan replied: "Hearken, Raghu-náyak; your arrows could burn up a thousand seas, but still it would be better policy to go and make petition to the god of ocean.

Dohá 50.

For being your family priest,[1] my lord, he will take thought and suggest some scheme, by which the whole host of bears and monkeys may cross the deep without any trouble."

Chaupái.

"Friend, you have suggested a good idea; let us try it and may fortune be with us." This invocation did not please Lakshman; he was much annoyed at Ráma's words. "Why trust fortune, my lord? give vent to your indignation and dry up the ocean. It is the one resource of a coward in soul to sit still and pray fortune to help him." Raghu-bír laughed to hear this and said: "I shall do it all the same; but never you mind." So saying he went to the shore of the salt sea and there took his seat on grass that he had strewn. Now after Vibhíshan had joined Ráma, Rávan sent spies of his own,

Dohá 51.

who disguised themselves as monkeys, and so saw all

1 King Sagara, by whose sons the bed of the ocean was dug, which is thence called Ságar, was one of Ráma's ancestors.

that was going on. In their profound admiration of the Lord's generosity and his tenderness to suppliants,

Chaupái.

they loudly extolled his magnanimity and in the intensity of their devotion forgot their disguise. When the monkeys perceived them to be spies from the enemy, they seized them and took them to their chief. Said Sugríva. "Hearken, all you monkeys: just mutilate them and let them go." On receiving this command, the monkeys ran and paraded them in bonds all through the camp, ill-treating them in every possible way and refusing to let them go for all their prayers for mercy, till they cried: 'We adjure you by Ráma not to rob us of our nose and ears.' When Lakshman heard this, he called them all to him, and, being moved with compassion, smiled and had them at once set free: "Give this missive into Rávan's hands" and say 'Read, destroyer of your race, what Lakshman says.

Dohá 52.

Tell the fool also by word of mouth my emphatic command—'Surrender Síta and submit yourself, or it will be your death.'

Chaupái.

The spies bowed the head at Lakshma's feet and set out at once, praising his generosity. Still repeating Ráma's praises, they arrived at Lanká and prostrated themselves before Rávan. The Ten-headed with a smile asked them the news: "Tell me, Suka, I pray, of your own welfare, and then let me hear about Vibhíshan, to whom death has drawn very nigh. The fool left Lanká where he was a king; but now the wretched weevil must be crushed with the wheat. Tell me next what force these bears and monkeys muster, who have come here by command of their evil destiny though the poor old sea has been soft-hearted enough to spare their lives. Tell me finally about the hermits, whose soul trembles for fear of me.

Dohá 53.

"Did he meet you as a suppliant, or did he take to flight on hearing the report of my renown? Will you tell me nothing about the enemy's might and magnificence? Your wits seem utterly dazed."

Chaupái.

"Of your grace, my lord, be not wroth, but take a blunt reply to a blunt question. As soon as your younger brother joined him, Ráma bestowed upon him the mark of sovereignty. The monkeys, who had heard that we were your spies, put us in bonds and abused us shamefully. They were about to cut off our ears and nose, when we invoked the name of Ráma and they let us go. You ask, my lord, of Ráma's army; a myriad tongues would fail to tell it: such a host of bears and monkeys of diverse hue and gruesome visage, huge and terrible—the one who set fire to the city and slew your son is the very weakest of them all—champions with innumerable names, fierce and unyielding monsters of vast bulk, with the strength of unnumbered elephants.

Dohá 54.

"Dwivid and Mayand, Níla and Nala, Angad and Gada of the mighty sword, Dadhi-mukha and Kehari, the malignant Nisatha and the powerful Jámbaván.

Chaupái.

"Each of these monkeys is equal to Sugríva, and who could count all the myriads like them? By Ráma's favour their strength is unbounded; they reckon the three spheres of creation as of no more account than a blade of grass. I have heard say, O Rávan, that the monkey chiefs number eighteen thousand billions; and in the whole of the army, my lord, there is not a single monkey who would not conquer you in battle. They are all wringing their hands in excess of passion: 'Why does not Ráma give us some order, either to swallow the ocean with all its fish and serpents, or at least to fill it up with piles of trees and mighty mountains, and then crush Rávan and lay him low in the dust.' This is the language that all the monkeys hold. Utterly devoid of fear, they shout and leap about as if they would make Lanká a mere mouthful.

Dohá 55.

"All the bears and monkeys are born warriors, and, moreover, they have the lord Ráma at their head. O Rávan, they could conquer in battle even Death himself, a myriad times over.

Chaupái

"A hundred thousand Seshnágs would fail to declare all Ráma's glory and power and wisdom. With a single shaft he could burn up a hundred seas, yet so prudent is he that he took advice of your brother and, on hearing his reply, went to the sea and humbly asked the favor of a passage." On hearing this, the Ten-headed smiled: "Truly he showed as much sense then as when he took monkeys for his allies. He has put faith in the words of that arrant coward, my brother, and, like a spoiled child, begs of ocean what he will never get. Fool, you have been extolling a mere impostor: I have sounded the depth of my enemy's strength and skill. Where in the world could any one achieve the glory of a triumph, who had such a cowardly counsellor as Vibhíshan." The envoy waxed wroth at the wretch's speech, and thought it a good time to produce the letter. "Ráma's brother gave me this letter: have it read, my lord, and much good may it do you." Rávan smiled and took it with his left hand and told his minister, the wretch, to read it out.

Dohá 56.

"Fool, submit your soul to advice, and do not bring destruction upon all your race; you cannot escape from Ráma's displeasure, even though Vishnu, Bráhma and Siva be your protectors. Abandon your pride, and, like your younger brother, fly like a bee to the lotus feet of the lord, or like a moth you will be consumed in your wickedness, you and all your family, by Ráma's arrows of fire."

Chaupái.

The Ten-headed, as he listened, was terror-stricken at heart, but smiled with his lips and cried aloud for all to hear: "He who stretches out his hands to clutch the sky only falls to the ground; a devotee's idle talk is of small account." Said Suka: "My lord, every word is true; be wise and abandon your natural arrogance. Cease from wrath and hearken to my advice; make an end, Sire, of your feud with Ráma. Raghubír is exceedingly mild in disposition, though he is the sovereign of all the world. The Lord will be gracious to you directly you approach him, and will not remember even one of your offences. Restore to him Janak's daughter; this, Sire, is all I ask of you; do it." When he spoke to him of giving up Síta, the wretch spurned him with his foot; but he bowed his head to the ground before him and then went to join the all-merciful Ráma, and after due obeisance told him all that had happened. By Ráma's grace, he recovered his proper rank; for it was by the Rishi Agastyás curse, Bhaváni, that he had become a demon, though still retaining the intelligence of a saint. Now, once more in the form of a saint, after again and again prostrating himself at Ráma's feet, he went his way to his own hermitage.

Dohá 57.

Dullard Ocean made no answer to prayer, though three days had been spent; then cried Ráma in a fury: "He will do me no kindness, unless he frightened.

Chaupái.

"Lakshman bring me my bow and arrows: with my fiery darts I will dry up the deep. To use entreaties to a churl, to lavish affection upon a rogue, to deal liberally with a born miser, to discourse of divine wisdom with a man devoted to self, to speak of detachment from the world to the covetous, to tell of Hari to a man under the influence of passion or love, is all the same as sowing the sand in hope of a harvest." So saying, Ráma strung his bow, a proceeding that pleased Lakshman mightily. The Lord let fly the terrible shaft; a burning pain ensued in the bosom of ocean; the crocodiles, serpents and fish were all sore distrest. When Ocean perceived that these creatures were burning, he filled a golden dish with all kinds of jewels and humbly presented himself in the form of a Bráhman.

Dohá 58.

Though you may take infinite trouble in watering it, a plantain will not bear fruit, until it has been well trimmed; similarly, mark me, Garúr, a mean upstart heeds neither prayers nor compliments, but requires rougher treatment.

Chaupái.

Terrified Ocean clasped the Lord's feet: Pardon me, Sire, all my offences. Air, wind, fire, water and earth are all, my lord, naturally dull and slow to change. They have been produced by the delusive power that you sent forth with a view to creation - so all the scriptures declare—and as each has been fixed by the Lord's command, so it must remain, to secure its own happiness. My lord has done well in giving me this lesson; but still it was you who first fixed my bounds. A drum, a clown, a churl, a beast, and a woman are all fit subjects for beating. By my lord's favor, I shall be dried up, the army will cross over, and my glory will be at an end; the scriptures declare the word of the Lord to be unchangeable; do then at once what seemeth you good"

Dohá 59.

The Lord smiled to hear this exceedingly humble speech, and said, "Tell me, father, some device, how the monkey host may cross over?"

Chaupái.

"My lord, there are two monkey brothers, Nila and Nala, who from childhood have been instructed by a sage. The mightiest mountains touched by them will by your favor float upon the waves. I too, remembering your majesty, will assist to the best of my power. In this manner, my lord, you will bridge the sea and the glorious deed will be sung in earth, heaven and hell. With this arrow, Sire, slay the dwellers on my mothern shore, who are vile criminals." The All-merciful, on hearing Ocean's grievance, at once removed it, the valiant Ráma.[1] At the sight of his mighty vigour Ocean rejoiced and became easy of mind, and after telling him all that had taken place, bowed at his feet and took his leave.

Chhand 8.

Ocean returned home and Ráma approved his counsel. These his acts, which remove all the impurities of this sinful age, has Tulsi Dás sung to the best of his ability. The excellences of Raghupati are a treasure of delight, a panacea for all doubt, a purge for every sorrow, and they who are wise of heart will abandon all other hope and confidence and be ever singing them or hearing them sung.

Dohá 60.

The virtues of Raghu-náyak are the source of every blessing, and those who reverently hear their recital cross the ocean of existence without any need for a boat.

1 In the Sanskrit Rámáyana this curious incident is related rather more intelligibly. Ocean complains that the Abhíras of the north are such an impure race that he cannot bear to receive into his bosom any stream of which they have drunk. Thereupon, Ráma with his fiery arrow dries up every river in their land, but creates instead a deep chasm in the ground, with a constant supply of water, and blesses the riverless region with exemption from disease.

[*Thus endeth the book entitled 'the Beautiful,' composed by Tulsi Das, being the fifth descent into 'the holy lake of Ráma's deeds.'*]

BOOK VI.

LANKA.

LANKA.

Sanskrit Invocation.

I WORSHIP RAMA; the adored of Love's enemy; the dispeller of all the terrors of existence; the lion to destroy the mad elephant, Death; the lord of ascetics; accessible only by contemplation; the store-house of all good qualities; the invincible; the passionless; the unchangeable; above the influence of Mayá; the sovereign of the gods: the implacable destroyer of the wicked; the one god over Bráhma and all his fellows; the god incarnate in the form of an earthly king, lotus-eyed and lustrous as the jasmine.

I glorify the divine SANKARA; as glistening in hue as the conch shell or the moon; the all-beautiful in person, robed in tiger's skin; bedecked with horrible black snakes for ornaments, attended by the Ganges and the moon; the lord of Kási; the subduer of the flood of pollution that distinguishes this sinful age; a tree of Paradise to yield fruits of prosperity; the ever adorable lord of Párvati; the store-house of good qualities; the vanquisher of Love.

May Sambhu, who rewards the saints with eternal beatitude, difficult even for them to obtain, and who punishes the guilty; may that same Sankara grant me prosperity.

Dohá 1.

O my soul, why dost thou not worship Ráma, whose bow is Death and whose arrows are sharp, with whom the merest instant of time counts the same as an age and whose year is a cycle.

Sorathá 1.

After hearing Ocean's speech, the lord Ráma spoke and said to his ministers: "Why now delay? make the bridge, that the army may pass over." Jámbaván clasped his hands and replied: "Hearken, pride of the solar race; your name, my lord, is the bridge, by aid of which men cross the ocean of life.

Chaupái.

"What trouble then can there be about crossing this little stream ?" Hearing this, the Son of the Wind added : "By my lord's favour a fierce subterranean fire had before now dried up the depths of the sea, but it was filled again by the floods of tears shed by the widows of his foes, and that is what makes it salt." On hearing Hanumán's ingenious speech, the monkeys gazed with rapture on Ráma's person. Then Jámbaván spoke to the two brothers Nala and Níla and explained to them all the circumstances : "Keep your thoughts fixed on Ráma's power and begin building the bridge ; you will find no difficulty." Again he addressed himself to the whole monkey host : "Hearken, all of you ; I have one request to make ; only impress upon your soul Ráma's lotus feet ; and then you bears and monkeys will find the task a mere pastime. Away with you, my sturdy monkey troops, and bring hither heaps of trees and rocks." On hearing this, the monkeys and bears set forth hurrahing. 'Glory to Ráma and all his might !'

Dohá 2.

They plucked up and carried off in sport the biggest mountains and trees and brought them to Nala and Níla, who set to work to build the bridge.

Chaupái.

The enormous rocks, which the monkeys brought and gave them, were handled by Nala and Níla like mere pellets. When the All-merciful saw the charming construction of the bridge, he smiled and said : "This is a most exceedingly delightful spot : no words can tell its immeasureable dignity. I will set up here an image of Sambhu: I have a great desire at heart to do so." On hearing this, the monkey king sent a number of messengers to summon and fetch all the great saints. After moulding a lingam in the prescribed manner and worshipping it, "there is none other," he cried, "so dear to me as Siva. No man, though he call himself a votary of mine, if he offend Siva, can ever dream of really finding me. If he desire to serve me, in antagonism to Siva, his doom is hell; he is a fool of no understanding.

Dohá 3.

They who either out of attachment to Siva dishonor me, or who serve me but dishonor Siva, shall have their abode in the deepest hell till the end of the world.

Chaupái.

All who make a pilgrimage to Rámesvar will, on quitting the body, go direct to my sphere in heaven. Any one who takes and offers Ganges water there will be absorbed into the divine essence. To all who serve me unselfishly and without guile Siva will grant the boon of faith. Whoever makes a pilgrimage to the bridge that I have built will without any trouble cross the ocean of existence." Ráma's words gladdened the hearts of all, and the saints thereupon returned to their hermitages. This, Párvati, is Ráma's way; he is always gracious to the humble. Níla and Nala built the bridge so cleverly that by Ráma's favour they acquired brilliant renown. The rocks, which naturally sink themselves and cause other things to sink also, were like so many rafts; nor is this to be, ascribed to the power of the sea, or the virtue of the stone, or the action of the monkeys;

Dohá 4.

it was by the might of the blessed Ráma that the rocks made a way across the sea. How dull of soul then are they who leave Ráma to worship any other lord.

Chaupái.

When they had completed the bridge and made it thoroughly secure, the All-merciful was glad of heart at the sight. The passage of the host was beyond all telling, with the clamour of the multitude of warlike monkeys. The gracious Ráma mounted a spot near the bridge and gazed upon the mighty deep. Then all the creatures of the sea showed themselves, in their anxiety to behold the lord of compassion; every kind of crocodile, alligator, fish, and serpent, with bodies a hundred leagues in length and enormous bulk. After them were others, such that a single one could devour all the first swarm ; while they again trembled no less before one of the swarm that followed them. They could not take their eyes off the Lord, and in the general gladness of heart all were happy together. You could not see the water, so thickly they covered it, as they gazed in delight on the vision of Hari. At their lord's command the army marched on ; who can describe the magnitude of the monkey host ?

Dohá 5.

The bridge was so thronged with the crowd that some of the monkeys took to flying through the air, while others crossed over on the backs of sea monsters.

Chaupái.

When the two brothers had gazed awhile at the spectacle, the gracious Ráma smilingly advanced and crossed over with the host. The throng of monkey chiefs was more than I can describe. On the opposite shore the Lord pitched his tent, and told all the monkeys that they might go and feast on the goodly fruit and roots. On hearing this the bears and monkeys ran off in all directions. To please Ráma every tree was laden with fruit, whether it was in season or out of season, without any regard to the time of year. They devour the sweet fruit and shake the trees, and hurl masses of rock at the city of Lanká. If ever they found a straggling demon, they all hemmed him in and led him a pretty dance, and finally bit off his nose and ears with their teeth and so let him go, after making him hear of their lord's great deeds. Those who had lost their nose and ears went and told all to Rávan. When he heard of the bridging of the sea, the Ten-headed started up and cried in consternation :

Dohá 6.

" What ! he has bridged the sea, with all the springs and streams[1] that fall therein, the great deep with all its waters. Can it be true that ocean trembles, the lord of rivers, the store-house of the waters, the receptacle of the floods!"

Chaupái.

Then becoming conscious of the agitation he had displayed he turned with a smile to the palace, full of frantic imaginations. When Mandodari heard that the Lord had arrived and had made nothing of bridging the sea, she took her spouse by the hand and led him to her own apartment, and besought him in these humble and winning words, bowing her head at his feet and holding up the hem of her mantle [2] :—" Be not angry, my beloved, but hearken to my speech. You should fight, my lord, with one whom you may be able to subdue either by wit or strength. But the difference between you and Ráma is like that between a poor little fire-fly and the sun. He who slew the monsters Madhu and Kaitabha, who worsted Dit's valiant son, Hiranyáksha, who put Báli in bonds and slew Sahasrabáhu, he it is who has now become incarnate to relieve earth of its burdens. O my lord, do not fight against him, in whose hands are Death and fate and our very life.

Dohá 7.

Bow your head at Ráma's lotus feet and give him back Síta ; then resign your throne to your son and retire into the woods and there worship Raghunáth.

Chaupái.

He is pitiful to the humble, like a tiger, who will not devour a man who comes to meet him. All that you had to do you have done long ago ; you have vanquished gods and demons and all creation. The saints, O Rávan, have laid down this rule, that a king in his old age should retire to the forest. There, O my spouse, make your prayers to him, who is the creator, preserver and destroyer, even Ráma,

---

1 *Vana*, which ordinarily means 'a forest,' must be taken here in its very unusual signification of a stream.

2 This with women is a sign of the greatest humility. The corresponding action amongst men is to tie a cloth round their neck.

ever gracious to the humble ; put away your selflove and pride, my lord, and worship him. He for whom the greatest saints perform all their labours, for whom kings leave their throne to become hermits, is this very king of Kosala, this Ráma, who has come here to show mercy upon you. Only submit to my advice, and the glory of your renown shall spread through the three spheres."

Dohá 8.

So saying she clasped him by the feet, her eyes full of tears and trembling in every limb. "O my lord, worship Ráma, and your prosperity shall never be shaken."

Chaupái.

Rávan raised the daughter of Mayá from the ground and began, the fool, to boast of his own might. "Hearken, my beloved, you are disturbed by idle fears ; is there any warrior in the world my equal? Varuna, Kuver, the Wind-god, Yama, and Fate, and all the regents of the eight quarters, have been subdued by the might of my arm. Gods, demons and kinnárs are all in my power : what cause can have arisen for these fears of yours?" Having thus said everything that he could to comfort her, he again went and took his seat in the council. But Mandodari knew at heart that his arrogance was doomed to destroy him. In the council he enquired of his ministers : "In what way shall we fight the enemy?" They replied : "Hearken, demon-king ; why question us thus again and again? Consider now and say what there is to be afraid of ; men, monkeys and bears are our natural food."

Dohá 9.

But Prahasta, after listening to all they said, clasped his hands and cried—"Do not, my lord, act contrary to sound judgment ; your counsellors have mighty little sense.

Chaupái.

They have all spoken simply to please their master ; but good results do not come in that way. A single monkey leaped the ocean and came hither; what he did you all know by heart. What! were none of you hungry then, that you did not seize and devour him when he set fire to the city? Pleasant to hear but fraught with future trouble is the advice which your counsellors have given their lord. Come, sire, tell me now, is he a mere man that we can devour, who has bridged the sea without any trouble, and has crossed over to Suvelá with all his army? What they say is all idle boasting. Hearken, sire, with due respect to my prayer, and do not in your arrogance account me a coward. There are plenty of people in the world who are ready to make or listen to pleasant speeches; but few, my lord, who care either to hear or to give wholesome advice, if it sounds unpleasant. Hearken now to wise counsel; first send an envoy and, when you have restored Síta, do your best to make friends with him.

Dohá 10.

If he withdraws after recovering his wife, there will be no need of any further dispute; if otherwise, then, sire, face to face in the battle prepare for resolute encounter.

Chaupái.

In either case, my lord, if you accept my advice, you will have glory in the world." The Ten-headed answered his son in a fury: "Wretch, who has taught you to give such advice as this? From this time I have a doubt in my mind; can a bamboo root have produced such a mere reed?" On hearing his father's brutal and violent speech, he turned home, saying these bitter words: "Good advice is as much thrown away upon him as medicine on a man doomed to die." Seeing that it was now evening, Rávan proceeded to the palace, glancing with pride at his twenty arms. On the top of the Lanká rock was a hall with handsome court-yard, where he went and took his seat. A number of kinnars began to sing to the accompaniment of cymbals, drum and lute, while beauteous nymphs danced before him.

Dohá 11.

The delights that he here enjoyed exceeded a hundred-fold those of Indra: the most powerful enemy might threaten, but no fear nor anxiety could disturb his repose.

Chaupái.

Now the valiant Ráma had crossed over with his army to mount Suvelá. There having noted one specially lofty peak, beautiful and bright above all others, Lakshman with his own hands spread a couch of lovely flowers and fresh twigs, which he covered with a fine soft deer's skin; and here the All-merciful took his seat. The Lord's head rested in the lap of the monkey-king; to right and left of him were his bow and quiver; with his lotus hands he trimmed his arrows, while the prince of Lanká whispered texts of scripture in his ear. The highly favoured Angad and Hanumán caressed his lotus feet, while behind him Lakshman kept watch as a sentinel, with quiver by his side and bow and arrows in his hands.

Dohá 12.

Thus sat Ráma, a very store-house of benignity, beauty and all perfection. Blessed are they who with profound devotion ever contemplate him under this form.[1] As he looked towards the east, the Lord observed the risen moon and cried to them all: "See the moon, like some dauntless lion,

Chaupái.

that has its dwelling in a cave of the eastern range, pre-eminent in might, majesty and strength, rends asunder the darkness as it were the head of a wild elephant, and paces the plain of heaven, a lion-like moon. The stars scattered about the sky like pearls are the jewels of beauteous night. "But," said the Lord, "tell me, my friends, each one of you, your opinion as to the spots on the moon." Said Sugríva:

---

1 This scene affords a very favourite subject for Hindu painters; partly, no doubt, on account of the blessing which Tulsi Dás here promises to those who contemplate it.

Hearken, Ráma, it is only the shadow of the earth that is seen in the moon." Another said: "When Ráhu attacked the moon, its bosom became thus discoloured." A third suggested: "When Bráhma fashioned Rati's face, he stole from the moon a part of its essence, and this is the hole that you see in the moon's surface showing the shadow of the sky." Said the Lord: "The moon has a great liking for poison, and has given it a home in its very heart; thence darting abroad innumerable empoisoned rays, it tortures parted lovers."

Dohá 13.

But Hanumán cried: "Hear me, my Lord; the moon is your devoted slave, and it is your image enshrined in the moon's bosom that causes the darkness." The all-wise Ráma smiled to hear the speech of the Son of the Wind; then turning towards the south, the All-merciful spoke again.

Chaupái.

"Look Vibhíshan, to the southern quarter—to the gathering clouds and the flashes of lightning. A pleasant sound of distant thunder is heard amidst the gloom; there will be some rain, think you, or a storm of hail?' Vibhíshan, replied: "Mark me, Sire, there is neither lightning nor gathered cloud. On the top of the Lanká hill there is a palace, where Rávan witnesses the sports of the arena: the royal umbrella held above his head presents the appearance of a mighty mass of cloud: the jewelled ornament in Mandodari's ears emits the flashes, my lord, that you take for lightning; while the incomparable music of the cymbals and drums is the pleasant sound that you hear, O king of the gods." The Lord smiled and, perceiving his arrogance, strung his bow and fitted an arrow to the string.

Dohá 14.

A single shaft struck umbrella, crown and ear-drop; in the sight of all they fell to the ground, and none could explain the mystery. Having performed this startling feat,

Ráma's arrows returned and dropt into the quiver. But Rávan and the whole assembly were much disturbed when they saw this interruption to their revel.

Chaupái.

"There was no earthquake, nor wind to speak of, nor did we see a missile of any kind," thus they pondered each to himself. "It is certainly a most alarming ill omen." When Rávan perceived that the assembly had taken fright, he smiled and invented an ingenious answer: "Even when I lost my heads, I came to no harm; now, only my crowns have dropt off; what ill-luck is there in that? Go home all of you and go to sleep." They bowed and took their leave. But anxiety had settled in Mandodari's bosom the moment the jewel had dropt from her ear to the ground. With streaming eyes and hands clasped in prayer, she cried: "O lord of my life, hearken to my petition. O my husband, give over fighting against Ráma, and do not indulge your pride with the idea that he is a mere man.

Dohá 15.

The jewel of the line of Raghu, believe what I say, is the omnipresent God, in whose every limb, as the Vedas declare, is the fabric of a world.

Chaupái.

His feet are the infernal regions, his head the abode of Bráhma, and in every limb subsists some separate sphere; the play of his brows is the doom of fate, his eyes are the sun, his hair the dark thunder-cloud, his nostrils are the twin sons of Asvini, and the constant winking of his eyes the cause of day and night. His ears, as the Vedas declare, are the ten quarters of the heaven, his breath is the wind, and his articulate voice the scripture. His lips are greed and his teeth the terrors of death; his smile is Mayá; his arms the regents of the quarters; his face is the element of fire; his tongue, water; and his movements the creation, preservation and destruction of the universe. The hairs on his body are the trees and bushes that grow on the earth; his bones the mountains, and the net-work of his veins the rivers; his belly the sea, and his hinder parts hell. Everything may be called a manifestation of the omnipresent Lord,

Dohá 16.

who has Siva for his self-consciousness, Bráhma for his intelligence, the moon for his mind, and the great First Principle for his soul; who not only indwells in man, but also assumes the form of any animate or inanimate creature, the Lord God.[1] Hearken, my beloved, ponder upon this and cease to contend against the Lord; cherish a devotion to Ráma's feet, and then my happy estate shall never fail."

1 The terminology here employed is that of the Sánkhya philosophy according to which everything is evolved or produced from an original primordial *tattva*, or eternally existing essence, called Prakriti. From it proceed seven productions, which are also producers, and thence sixteen other principles, which are productions only, not producers. Soul *purusha*, the twenty-fifth essence, is neither a production nor a producer. The first production of Prakriti is *Buddhi*, commonly called intellect or intellectual perception, and variously termed *Mahat*, from its being the *Great* source, of the two other internal faculties, *Ahankara*, 'self-consciousness', and *Manas* or 'mind'. Third in order comes this *Ahankara*, the 'I-making faculty, that is, self-consciousness, or the sense of individuality [sometimes conveniently termed ego-ism] which produces the next five principles, called *Tan-matras*, or subtle elementary particles, out of which the grosser elements [*Mahá-bhúta*] are evolved. These are *ákàsa*, ether; *avayu*, air; *tejas* or *jyotis*, fire or light; *àpas*, water; and *prithivi* or *bhumi*, earth. In addition to the five *tan-màtras*, the third producer, Ahankára, produces also the eleven organs *viz*., the five organs of sense, *budhindriyáni*, the ear, skin, eye, nose and tongue; the five organs of action, *karmendriyáni*, the larynx, hand, foot and the excretory and generative organs; and an eleventh organ standing between these two sets, called *manas* 'the mind,' which is an internal organ of perception, volition, and action. Thus the eight producers, *viz*, Prakriti, Buddhi, Ahankàra, and the five tan-màtras, with the five grosser elements and the eleven organs, constitute the true elements of the phenomenal world; the most important—after the mere unintelligent original germ, *Prakriti*—being *Ahankàra*. (*See* Monier Williams' Indian Wisdom). It is tolerably clear that these categories were in the mind of Tulsi Dàs at the time of writing, but he has employed them in a loose and popular way. Thus *mahan*, which is strictly a synonym for *Ahankára*, seems in the text to stand rather for *Prakriti*. In Ráma Jasan's edition of the text the words are wrongly divided. As is frequently the case with native Sanskrit scholars when commenting on Hindi literature, the editor would seem to have read the passage too exclusively by the light of Sanskrit authorities. *Prakriti* may be explained as non-extended energy; unconscious life moving on towards consciousness; a latent ego destined to put forth conscious thought when the conditions of the environment allow of it. With increase of power there comes an increased *ahankára*, self-consciousness, or development of the ego into a personage, individual, self-balanced, master of its resources, characteristic, *sui generis*, himself.

Chaupái.

He laughed when he heard his wife's speech. "Wonderful, indeed, is the power of infatuation. The poets have truly described woman's nature. There are eight faults from which she is never free at heart; imprudence, falsehood, fickleness, infatuation, timidity, want of judgment, impurity, and illiberality. You have declared all the manifestations of the enemy and told me a most alarming story; but, my dear, I see through it at once and perfectly understand your kindness. I recognize your cleverness, my dear, for in this way you have exalted my power. Your words, fair dame, are obscure; but they are auspicious when understood, though they sound alarming.[1]" Then Mandodari perceived that her husband's infatuation was the fated forerunner of his ruin.

Dohá 17.

In such diverse ways did Rávan amuse himself until the dawn appeared, when the lord of Lanká, fearless by nature and further blinded by pride, entered the council chamber.

Sorathá 2.

Though the clouds rain ambrosia upon it, the bamboo neither flowers nor fruits; so the soul of a fool never learns, though he have Bráhma and Siva for his teachers.

Chaupái.

Now Ráma woke at break of day and summoned his ministers, to take counsel of them. "Quick, tell me what course should be adopted." Jámbaván bowed his head at his feet and said: "Hearken, omniscient observer of all men's hearts, perfection of wisdom, power, majesty, justice and every good quality. I thus advise you to the best of my ability: send the son of Báli as an ambassador." Every one heartily approved this good suggestion, and the All-merciful said to Angad: "Son of Báli, wise, strong and

1 The word *Bhaymochani* would seem to be here itself used in an obscure, sense as an illustration of the ambiguous language to which the speaker refers. Its ordinary signification would be 'delivering from fear;' but it may also be interpreted as 'letting loose,' that is, 'causing' fear, 'alarming.'

virtuous, go to Lanká, my son, in my service. Why should I give you any lengthy instructions? I am aware of your distinguished ability. Frame your address to the enemy in such a way that he will agree to my requirements."

Sorathá 3.

Obedient to his lord's command and bowing at his feet Angad arose, crying: "O, Ráma, any one on whom you show favour becomes possessed of every virtue. You have graciously granted me, my lord, your own good fortune for the accomplishment of this task of yours." At this thought the young prince exulted at heart and his whole body quivered with excitement.

Chaupái.

After prostrating himself at his feet and imprinting the image of his majesty on his soul, Angad bowed to the assembly and went forth, the delighter in battle, the gallant son of Báli, dauntless by nature and his heart all a glow with the might of his lord. As he entered the city, he came across Rávan's son, who was playing there. From words they proceeded to a struggle; both of unequalled strength and in the prime of their youth to boot. He raised his foot to kick Angad, who at once seized him by it and swung him round and dashed him to the ground. All the demons, even the stoutest warriors among them, who saw the deed, dispersed hither and thither, but dared not give the alarm; they did not even whisper to one another, but remained silent, when they saw his death. A rumour, however, was noised through the city: "The monkey who set Lanká on fire has come again; what has God in store for us now?" Thus they all pondered in excessive dismay. Without being asked they showed him the road: if he but looked at any one he withered away.

Dohá 18.

Then with his thoughts fixed on Ráma's lotus feet he entered the Council Hall, with the gait of a lion, glancing on this side and that, a bold and stalwart hero.

Chaupái.

One of the demons was immediately despatched to report the news to Rávan. On hearing it, the Ten-headed cried with a laugh : " Go and bring this strange monkey here." On receiving this order, a number of his messengers ran and fetched the monkey-chief. In Angad's eyes the Ten-headed appeared like the Black mountain endued with life; his arms like trees, his head a rocky peak, the hair on his body as it were all kinds of creepers, and his mouth, nose, eyes and ears like caves and chasms in the rock. Without the slightest trepidation of heart he entered the Court, the son of Bali ; most dauntless of heroes. The assembly rose at the sight of the monkey ; but in Rávan's heart was ungovernable fury.

Dohá 19.

As when a lion enters among a herd of mad elephants, so after bowing to the assembly he took his seat, his thoughts ever fixed on Ráma's power.

Chaupái.

Rávan asked : "Monkey, who are you ?" "I am an ambassador from Ráma, Rávan. There was friendship between you and my father ; and on that account, brother, I have come to you to do you a service. Of high descent, the grandson of Pulastya, you duly worshipped Siva and Bráhma, obtained your prayer of them accomplished all you undertook and conquered the guardians of the eight quarters and every earthly sovereign. Now under the influence of royal arrogance or some delusion you have carried off Síta, the mother of the world. Yet hearken to my friendly advoice and the Lord will still pardon you. Put a straw between your teeth and an axe to your throat, and with all your family and your own wife and with Janak's daughter placed respectfully at your head, go all of you in this wise without any alarm,

Dohá 20.

crying, ' O jewel of the race of Raghu, defender of the

suppliant, save now me, even me,' and when he hears your piteous cry the Lord will set your mind at rest."

Chaupái.

"Ah, you wretched monkey, take care what you are saying. Fool, do you not know that I am the declared enemy of the gods? Tell me your own name and your father's, friend, and through what relation you claim alliance." "My name is Angad; I am the son of Báli, with whom you once were on terms of friendship." On hearing Angad's reply, he was confused. "I admit, monkey, that it was so with Báli: but if Angad is that Báli's son, he has been born as a fire-brand for the destruction of his race. The womb that bare you, forsooth, was not pregnant for nothing; who with your own mouth confess yourself a hermit's envoy. Tell me now, is all well with Báli?" Angad laughed and replied: "Ten days hence go to Báli and embrace your old friend and ask him yourself of his welfare. He will tell you the kind of welfare that results from fighting against Ráma. Hearken, fool; he is a man divided against himself whose heart is closed to the divine Raghubír.

Dohá 21.

I, forsooth, am the destroyer of my race, while you, Rávan, are the preserver of yours. Who can say that you are blind or deaf while you have twenty eyes and twenty ears?

Chaupái.

What! I disgrace my family by acting as his ambassador whose feet Siva and Bráhma and all the gods and saints desire to serve: your heart should burst asunder for entertaining such an idea." When he heard the monkey's fierce rejoinder, Rávan glared at him and cried: "Wretch, I suffer all your abuse because I understand the maxims of statecraft and religion." Said the monkey: "I have heard of the piety and virtue you showed in stealing away another man's wife; and how you were so good and patient that you did not drown yourself at the sight of your messengers and watchmen, and from pious motives forgave the wrong when you saw your sister with her nose and ears cut off. Your piety and virtue are renowned throughout the world ; I am most fortunate in being able to see you."

Dohá 22.

"Prate no more, you stupid brute, but look at my arms, you impudent monkey, very Ráhus as they have proved to eclipse the full-moon-like might of the Lokpáls : while Sambhu and Kailás in the palm of my lotus hand were but as the stately swan in the heavenly lake.

Chaupái.

Hearken, Angad ; tell me what champion there is in all your army who is a match for me. Your lord has lost strength through pining for his bride ; his younger brother too is all sad and forlorn ; you and Sugríva are each the curse of your family ; while my brother is an utter coward. Your counsellor, Jámbaván, is so stricken in years that he can no longer enter the field of battle. Nala and Níla are good architects, and there is one monkey, no doubt, of exceptional strength, he who came first and set fire to the city." On hearing this Angad replied : "Tell me the truth now, O demon king ; is it a fact that a monkey burnt down your city ? A poor little monkey set Rávan's capital on fire ! Who, on hearing this said, could believe it true ? He, Rávan, whom you extol as so distinguished a champion, is only one of Sugríva's inferior runners. He is a good one to go, but no fighter : we only sent him to get news.

Dohá 23.

Is it true that a monkey set fire to the city without any order from his lord ? This is why he did not go back to Sugríva, but kept himself out of sight for fear. All that you have said, Rávan, is quite true, and I am not in the least angry at hearing it : there is not any one in our army who would be a fair match for you. Take your friends and enemies from among your equals is a good sound maxim : if a lion kills a frog, who thinks it a fine deed ? Though it is no glory to Ráma to kill you, however great your offence, still, mark me, Rávan, the fury of the Kshatriya clan is hard to withstand." The monkey foe set his heart on fire with the arrows of speech shot forth from the bow of sarcastic eloquence, and it was, so to speak, only with a pair of pincers that the dauntless Rávan could get out a rejoinder. At last he laughed and cried : " A monkey has, at all events, one good quality ; he will do anything to serve the man who feeds him.

Chaupái.

Bravo for a monkey who, regardless of shame, skips up and down in his master's service : dancing and jumping about to amuse the people, he does his duty by his employer right well. All of your race, Angad, are devoted to their lord ; it is quite natural for you to speak of your master's good qualities in the way you do. But I am too sagacious in appreciating merit to pay any attention to your insolent tirade." Said the monkey ; " Hanumán gave me a very true account of your generosity. Though he had laid waste your garden, killed your son and set fire to your city, still you would not do him any harm. It was in reliance upon your magnanimity, Rávan, that I have been thus outspoken. Now that I am here, I see that whatever a monkey may say will neither put you to shame nor excite you to anger or resentment." Your cleverness, monkey, is so great that it might well be the death of your father." So cried the Ten-headed and burst into a laugh. " After being the death of my father, I would now be the death of you too, had I not just thought of something. I look upon you as a monument of Báli's honour and renown, and that is why I do not slay you, you wretched braggart. Come, Raván, tell me how many Rávans there are in the world, or listen while I tell you how many I have heard of. One went down into hell to conquer Bali, where the children tied him up in the stable and made sport of him and buffeted him, till Bali took pity on him and let him go. Another again was discovered by Sahasra-báhu, who ran and secured him as a curiosity and took him home for a show, till Saint Pulastya came and rescued him.

Dohá 24.

Another, as I am ashamed to say, was held tight under Báli's arm. Do not be angry,[1] Rávan, but tell me the truth, which of all these are you?"

Chaupái.

"Hearken, fool; I am that mighty Rávan, the action of whose arms is well-known by Kailás and his valour by Siva; for him I worshipped not with flowers but with my own heads, which I took off with my own lotus hands times innumerable, when I worshipped Tripurari. The guardians of the eight quarters know the might of my arms; in their heart, you fool, is sore distress to-day. The elephants who support the world learnt also the hardness of my chest whenever I closed with them in conflict; their mighty tusks, though never broken before, snapt off like radishes when they struck against my front. As I moved, earth quivered like a small boat when a wild elephant steps into it. I am that glorious and renowned Rávan; have you no ears to hear, you lying chatterer?

Dohá 25.

This is the Rávan of whom you make light, while you exalt a mere man. Ah vile monkey, infamous wretch, are you at last beginning to understand?"

Chaupái.

On hearing this, Angad replied indignantly: "Give over talking, you pitiful boaster. He, whose axe was like a fire to consume Sahasra-báhu's mighty forest of arms; whose sword was like the tide of the salt sea, in which kings innumerable have been drowned time after time; and at the sight of whose majesty every one took to flight, how can he be accounted a man, you wretched Rávan? How can

---

1 *Mánkh* here stands for *másh*, which occurs elsewhere in the poem with the sense of 'anger.'

Ráma be a mere man, you arrogant fool? Is Kámadeva an ordinary archer; is the Ganges merely a river: the cow of plenty only a cow; the tree of Paradise only a tree; is charity only so much grain; is ambrosia any liquid; Garúr a mere bird; Seshnág a serpent, and the philosopher's stone, Rávan, only a stone? Hearken, O dull of understanding; is Vaikunth an ordinary world, or absolute faith in Ráma a common blessing.

Dohá 26.

Fool, how was it that the monkey Hanumán escaped, after trampling on the pride of you and your army, laying waste your garden, setting fire to your city and slaying your son?

Chaupái.

Hearken, Rávan; have done with conceit and worship Ráma, the all-merciful. If you are foolish enough to provoke Ráma, neither Brahma nor Rudra has the power to protect you. Do not puff yourself out with vain delusions; if you fight against Ráma, this will be your fate: smitten by Ráma's arrows, your many heads will fall to the ground, in front of the monkeys, and they and the bears will play polo with them, as if they were so many balls. When Ráma waxes wroth in battle, his arrows fly quick and terrible. Will you then persist in your vain boasting and not rather be wise and adore his clemency?" On hearing these words Rávan flared up afresh, like a blazing fire upon which butter has been cast.

Dohá 27.

"Have you never heard of my brother Kumbha-karn and my renowned son Indrajit and my own valour, by which I have conquered the whole universe?

Chaupái.

Fool, with the help of his monkey friends he has bridged the sea, but what is that to be proud of? Birds innumerable traverse the ocean, yet they are no heroes. Now mark me, monkey: my arms are like a sea filled with a flood of strength, beneath which many gods, men and heroes have been drowned. Who is there so strong that he can overcome these twenty unfathomable and boundless oceans? I even made the Dig-pals draw water for me. You have told me, poor wretch, of your king's renown, but if your lord is so valiant in battle as one would judge from the way in which you harp on his achievements, then why does he send an ambassador? Is he not ashamed to make terms with an enemy? Look at my arms, which could treat mount Kailás as a mere churning-stick, and then, foolish monkey, sing, if you will, the praises of your lord.

Dohá 28.

What hero is there equal to Rávan, who, with his own hands, cut off his own heads, and delighted to cast them into the fire, time after time, as Siva is witness.

Chaupái.

When I saw the skull burning, with the letters traced on my forehead by the Creator, and read that my death was to be at the hands of a man, I laughed, for I knew the divine prophecy to be untrue. When I remember this, I have no fear: Bráhma must have written when he was old and stupid. Are you not then ashamed, you fool, to keep boasting of any warrior's strength as compared with mine?" Angad replied: "There is no one in the whole world, Rávan, so shamefaced as you. Your modesty is so innate that you never speak of your own merits. You are always thinking of the old story of your heads and the mountain,[1] and that is the reason why you tell it me twenty times over. Bury deep in your heart the remembrance of that strength of arm by which you overcame Sahasra-báhu and Bali and Báli; but hearken, O dull of soul, make the business complete; if a man who cuts off his head is a hero, what a hero a juggler must be, who with his own hands cuts his whole body to pieces.

1 That is to say, of how you cut off your ten heads as a sacrifice to Siva and how you uprooted mount Kailás.

Dohá 29.

A moth is infatuated enough to burn itself to death, and an ass bears any burden, but they are not called heroes : look, stupid, and understand.

Chaupái.

Boast no more in arrogant speech, but listen modestly to my advice. I have not come, Rávan, as an envoy to propose terms, but Raghubír has sent me from another motive. In his mercy he has said again and again, 'It is no honour for a lion to kill a jackal.' Pondering at heart on my lord's words, I have submitted, wretch, to your injurious speech ; otherwise, I would have broken your head and carried off Síta, the fair bride. I know all about your strength, vile enemy of heaven, how in Hari's absence you robbed him of his wife. Your pride, demon king, is great, but I am the messenger of Ráma's servants, and if I were not afraid of displeasing him, I would as soon as look at you make you a perfect spectacle.

Dohá 30.

After dashing you to the ground and routing your army and destroying your city, I would have carried off Síta with all the ladies of your household.

Chaupái.

If I had done so, it would still be no great matter; there is no valour shown in slaying the slain. Now an outcast, a man mad with lust, a miser, a destitute beggar, a man in disgrace, a man in extreme old age, one who is always ill or always in a passion, a rebel against Vishnu, a hater of religion and the saints, a man who thinks only of his own body, a scandal-monger and a man thoroughly vicious, these twelve even while they live are no better than corpses. On this account, wretch, I do not slay you, but do not provoke me further." On hearing this, the demon king cried in a fury :—"Though small of stature, you have spoken big words. O foolish monkey, he of whose might you vaunt so fiercely, has no might, or sense, or glory at all.

Dohá 31.

Seeing him to be of no worth or dignity, his father banished him, and this is a sorrow to him, as also is the loss of his wife ; while his terror of me oppresses him night and day. Proud as you are of his might, there are thousand of men like him, whom my demons devour every day and night. Cease your perverseness, fool, and come to your senses."

Chaupái.

When he thus abused Ráma, the monkey prince waxed wroth. Those who open their ears to attacks upon Hari and Hara are as guilty as if they had killed a cow. The huge monkey gnashed his teeth and taking him in his two arms hurled him furiously to the ground. The earth shook, the assembly quaked and took to flight as if driven by a hurricane of terror. Rávan raised himself from his fall and sat up, but his magnificent diadems had fallen to the ground ; part he took and re-arranged on his heads, part Angad despatched to his lord. When the monkeys saw the crowns coming, they ran away, crying --"Good God, here are stars falling in the day time, or Rávan in his fury has sent forth four thunderbolts that come with rushing speed." The Lord smiled and said :—"Fear not at heart ; here is no star, nor sword, nor either Ketu or Báhu ; those are Rávan's crowns, which come as despatched by the son of Báli"

Dohá 32.

The son of the Wind sprang forward and caught them in his hand and brought and laid them at his lord's feet : the bears and monkeys gazed in astonishment at the sight, for their brilliancy was like that of the sun. On the other hand, Rávan in his wrath cried furiously to one and all— "Seize the monkey, seize him and kill him." Angad heard and smiled.

Chaupái.

"In like manner sally forth in haste, all ye mighty men, and devour every bear and monkey wherever ye find one.

Go and leave not a single monkey in the whole world, but take alive the two hermit brothers." The prince replied indignantly :—" Are you not ashamed to bluster like this. Cut your throat and die, you reckless destroyer of your own family ; does not your heart crack at the sight of his power. Ah ! villainous woman-stealer, compound of all that is mean and impure, sensual dullard, though at death's door, you still babble abuse ; Fate has you in his toils, wretched cannibal. Hereafter you shall reap the fruit of this, when the bears and monkeys belabour you : but when you thus speak of Ráma as a man, I wonder your proud tongue does not drop off : and beyond a doubt it will drop off to the ground, head and all, in the battle.

Sorathá 4.

How can he be a mere man, Rávan, who slew Báli with a single arrow ? you are blind with all your twenty eyes ; a curse on your birth, you baseborn fool. Ráma's arrows are all athirst to drink your blood : for fear of him I spare you, insolent boaster, contemptible demon.

Chaupái.

I am quite able to smash your jaws, but Ráma has given me no order ; otherwise I am so enraged that I would cleave asunder your ten heads and take up Lanká and drop it in the sea. Your Lanká is like a fig on a gúlar tree, and you the unsuspecting insect that lives in it. I, like a monkey, would lose no time in eating the fruit, but the gracious Ráma has given me no order." On hearing this simile, Rávan smiled : —" Fool, where did you learn to tell such lies ; Báli never blustered like this ; intercourse with the hermits has made you such a boaster." " If I do not tear out your ten tongues, Twenty-arms, of a truth, I am a mere boaster." As he thought on Ráma's power, the monkey waxed wroth ; he planted his foot firm and offered the assembly this wager : —" If you can stir my foot, you wretch, Ráma will take to flight and I lose Síta." " Hearken, champions all," cried Rávan, " seize this monkey by the leg and throw him to the ground." Indrajit and the other men of valour in their different ranks all rose with joy, but though they fell upon him with their full strength and with many a trick, his foot did not stir, and they bowed their head and sat down again. Again the enemy of the gods rose to the contest; but the monkey's foot moved no more, Garur, than the standard of selfishness planted in the soul of a hypocrite, which there is no shaking.

Dohá 33.

Millions of warriors, Meghnád's peers, arose with joy and essayed the wrestle; but the monkey's foot did not stir, and they bowed the head and sat down again. The pride of the enemy was broken when they saw that the monkey's foot was moved from the ground as little as the soul of a saint abandons the maxims of morality, though assailed by a thousand difficulties.

Chaupái.

When they saw the monkey's strength, they were all discomforted at heart, till he himself arose to try the test. On his grasping his foot, Báli's son cried:—"There is no safety in clinging to my feet! why, fool, do you not go and clasp Ráma's feet?" On hearing this, he turned away full sorry at heart, robbed of all his dignity, and his majesty clean gone from him, as when the moon shows faintly in the day-time. With bowed head he took his seat on his throne, like one despoiled of all his possessions. How can there be any rest for an enemy of Ráma, the soul of the world, the lord of life? O Umá, the play of Ráma's eyebrows now creates a universe and now again destroys it. He makes a blade of grass into a thunderbolt and again a thunderbolt into a blade of grass; how could his messenger fail in his challenge? Again the monkey urged upon him sound advice in every possible way; but he would not listen; his time had drawn near. When he had sufficiently trampled on the pride of the enemy and exalted his master's fame, the son of king Báli left, saying "Why should I trouble myself any more about you now; I shall have the pleasure of killing you on the field." Rávan was despondent from the very first when he heard that the monkey had killed his son: but the demons, when they witnessed Angad's challenge, were all still more disturbed.

Dohá 34.

Having crushed the power of the enemy, the mighty monkey, the son of Báli, his body quivering with emotion and his eyes full of tears, clasped in delight Ráma's lotus feet. When he saw it was evening, Rávan returned sadly to the palace, where Mandodari again spoke and advised him:

Chaupái.

"Reflect, my husband, and abandon ill counsel; it is not well for you to fight against Ráma. His younger brother drew a little line,[1] and even this you could not cross: such is your strength? My beloved, you will never conquer him in battle, whose simple messenger has done such great acts. Having lightly leaped across the sea, the monkey like a dauntless lion entered your Lánka, killed your watchmen, laid waste your garden, slew Achha as soon as he looked at him, and then set fire to the whole of the city and reduced it to ashes. What place is now left you for pride of power? Cease, my spouse, from idle vaunts and take my words a little to heart. Do not suppose that Ráma is a mere earthly king, but recognize in him the lord of all animate and inanimate creation, of infinite power. Márícha confessed the force of his arrows; you, miserable wretch, regard not his voice. Janak's court was crowded with kings, you too were there in all your valour; but it was he who broke the bow and wedded Síta? why did you not conquer him in battle then? The son of Indra felt a little of his might when he had his life spared but

1 This line was drawn round Síta, as a barrier against the demons. The circumstance is told in the Sanskrit Rámáyana, and Tulsi Dás, who refers to it here, forgets that he had omitted to mention it in his own poem.

lost one of his eyes; and you have yourself seen Surpanakha's condition: yet still your heart continues absolutely uncowed;

Dohá 35.

Know, Rávan, that this is he who slew Virádha and Khara and Dúshan; who with the greatest ease killed Kabandh and disposed of Báli with a single arrow;

Chaupái.

who bridged the ocean as a mere pastime and with all his army crossed over to Suvéla. But the Glory of the Solar race is full of compassion, and out of regard to you sent first an envoy; and even he in the very midst of your court trampled on your power, like a lion let loose upon a herd of elephants. Seeing that Angad and Hanumán are his servants, such brave and lusty leaders of the fray, how can you, my spouse, persist in calling him a man; you are bewildered by the intoxication of pride and self-conceit. O my husband, when the quarrel is against Ráma, fate prevents reason from working in the soul. It is not with uplifted club that fate strikes, but by robbing a man of his religion, his strength, and his faculty of reason. Whenever, Sir, a man's fate is near at hand, he becomes infatuated, as you are now.

Dohá 36.

He has slain your two sons and set your city on fire; to-day, O my husband, let him have your answer. O my lord, adore the mercy of Ráma and thus win for yourself the highest renown."

Chaupái.

He heard out his wife's speech though it pierced like an arrow, and then arose and went into the council-chamber, for it was now dawn. As he took his seat on his throne, he swelled with excess of pride; all his terror was forgotten. On the other side, Ráma summoned Angad, who came and bowed his head at his lotus feet, but he, with the utmost courtesy, seated him by his side and then said, with a smile, the gracious Kharári :—"O son of Báli, I am full of curiosity, answer truly, my son, to what I ask you. Rávan is the chief of all the demon race, and the unbounded might of his arm is famous throughout the world—how then did you send me four of his crowns? Tell me, my son, by what device you secured them?" "Hearken, all-wise protector of the humble, they were not crowns, but the four prerogatives of a king—conciliation concession, subjugation, and division, which, as the Vedas say, abide in a king's soul. Having recognized the gracious feet of kingly polity and religion, they came of themselves to their sovereign.

Dohá 37.

Leaving the impious Rávan, the rebel against his lord, the death-doomed, his kingly prerogatives—mark me, monarch of Kosala—have come to you." On hearing this most ingenious fancy, the gracious Ráma smiled, and the son of Báli then proceeded to give him all the news from the fort.

Chaupái.

When Ráma had heard his report of the enemy, he called all his ministers to him. "Take counsel as to how we should attack the four great gates of Lanká." Then the king of the monkeys and the king of the bears and Vibhishan, with their hearts fixed on the Glory of the Solar race, took counsel and settled a plan and divided the monkey army into four companies. After exalting their lord's power, they issued their orders; and the monkeys no sooner heard them than they rushed forward, roaring like lions. First they bowed their head with joy at Ráma's feet and then the heroes sallied forth, with peaks of mountains in their hands, roaring and leaping, bears and monkeys alike, and shouting 'Glory to Raghubír, the sovereign of Kosala!' Though they knew that Lanká was a most formidable stronghold, they went on undismayed, in the strength of their lord, spreading like a cloud over the whole horizon, and with trumpets at their mouth making loud music.

Dohá 38.

"Glory to Ráma, glory to Lakshman, glory to the monkey chief, Sugríva!" such was the lion-roar of the great and valiant monkeys and bears.

Chaupái.

Lanká was full of the utmost confusion; but Rávan heard the news with his wonted arrogance. "See the impudence of these monkeys," he said with a smile and summoned his demon host. "These monkeys have come by the decree of fate; my demons wanted a meal"—so saying the wretch burst into a loud laugh—'and God has provided them with one, without their going abroad to seek it. Sally forth in every direction, my warriors all, and seize these bears and monkeys and devour them." O Umá, Rávan's conceit was as great as that of the sandpiper, when it goes to sleep with its legs in the air.[1] On receiving their orders, the demons, sallied forth, armed with slings and mighty javelins, clubs, maces and trenchant axes, pikes, swords, bludgeons and masses of rock. Like foul carnivorous birds that swoop down upon a heap of rubies which they have espied, and after breaking their beaks upon them find out their mistake, so these man-eating monsters rushed forth in their folly.

Dohá 39.

Taking bow and arrows and weapons of every description, myriads upon myriads of the stoutest and most valiant demons climbed up to the battlements of the fort.

Chaupái.

The battlements of the fort looked like the peaks of Meru amidst dense clouds Drums and other instruments of music sounded for the fray, and the soul of the warriors was stirred by their crash. The trumpets and clarions brayed so fiercely that even a coward on hearing them would forget his fear. The throng of monkeys could not

1 And thinks that they help to support the sky.

be seen for the mighty stature of the warrior bears. They rush on, making no account of the most precipitous passes, but tearing down the rocks and so clearing a way for themselves. Grinding their teeth and biting their lips in their excess of fury, myriads of warriors shout aloud, there calling upon Rávan and here upon Ráma. 'Glory and victory, the battle has begun.' If the demons cast down any mountain crag, the monkeys with a bound would seize it and hurl it back.

Chhand 1.

The furious monkeys and bears lay hold of the mountain crags and hurl them against the fort. They join in closer struggle, seizing an antagonist by one leg and dashing him to the ground, and if he takes to flight challenging him again to the combat. With a bold dash and a vigorous spring they bound up the heights of the fort ; and every palace, into which the bears and monkeys penetrated, resounds with songs in Ráma's praise.

Dohá 40.

Again, taking each a demon in his clutch, the monkeys ran off and then dropt to the ground with the enemy beneath and themselves on the top.

Chaupái.

Strong in the power of Ráma, the monkey host overcame the throng of demon warriors, and having climbed the fort, made it ring all over with shouts of glory to Raghubír, the sun of majesty ! The demons fled headlong, like thunder-clouds driven by a strong wind. There was a grievous wailing throughout the city, children crying and women in dire distress. All agreed in abusing Ravan the king, who had thus invited ruin. When he heard that his forces had been routed, the Lord of Lanká indignantly rallied his captains : " If I hear of any one turning his back in battle, I will slay him myself with my terrible sword. After devouring all my substance and feasting as you pleased, you now on the field of battle think of nothing but your own safety." On hearing these stern words, the chiefs were all frightened and ashamed. Working themselves into a fury they sallied forth again crying : 'It is the glory of a warrior to die with his face to the foe,' and all desire to live entirely left them.

Dohá 41.

Arming themselves with weapons of every description, the gallant chiefs pressed forward to the fray, challenging the enemy one after the other, and so wielding mace and javelin that they sorely discomfited the bears and monkeys.

Chaupái.

Overcome with terror, the monkeys began to fly, although, Umá, they had already won the victory. Said one: " Where are Angad and Hanumán ? where Nala and Nila and the stalwart Dwivid? "Hanumán heard that his troops were in distress, but the hero was kept at the western gate. There Meghnád led the defence, nor was it possible to force the gate, so great was its strength. Then the Son of the Wind waxed exceeding wroth of soul ; with a terrible roar, as though the end of the world had come, the hero made a bound and sprang upon the top of Lanká ; then seizing a rock he rushed upon Meghnád, shattered his chariot, hurled its driver to the ground, and struck the prince himself with his foot in the chest. Another charioteer, seeing him senseless, threw him on to his car and brought him home with speed.

Dohá 42.

When Angad heard that Hanumán had made his way into the fort alone, he too, the adventurous warrior, bounded forward to join in his monkey sports.

Chaupái.

Maddened by the battle and full of fury, the two monkeys, mindful at heart of Ráma's glory, rushed upon Rávan's palace, and shouting, 'The king of Kosala to the rescue !' overthrew the whole building, so that not a pinnacle was left standing. When the demon chief saw this, he was dismayed; while the women all struck their breasts crying, 'Now two of these pestilent monkeys have come.' After terrifying them with their monkey tricks, and proclaiming the praises of Rámchandra, they grasped each a golden pillar in their hand and cried, 'Let us now make a beginning of destruction.' With a roar, they rushed into the midst of the enemy's army, and began laying them low with mighty strength of arm, here a kick and there a blow; crying 'Worship Ráma or take the consequences.'

Dohá 43.

Overthrowing one after another they strike off their heads and hurl them away, so that they fall at Rávan's feet smashed in pieces like so many earthen pots.

Chaupái.

Whenever they caught any great chief, they seized him by the leg and threw him to their lord. Vibhíshan mentioned their names and Ráma assigned them his own sphere in heaven. Thus, man-eating monsters who had devoured even the flesh of a Bráhman, obtain a translation such as even devotees desire. O Umá, Ráma is tender-hearted and full of compassion and bestowed salvation upon them for this reason, that the demons had taken his name albeit in a spirit of enmity. Tell me, Bhaváni, who else would be so merciful. Dull of heart indeed and utterly wretched are the men who, on hearing of such a lord, do not abandon their errors and worship him. Angad and Hanumán—thus cried the lord of Avadh—have forced their way into the fort and Lanká with the two monkeys makes a sight like the sea churned by two Mount Merus.

Dohá 44.

After crushing the host of the enemy with the might of their arm, they perceived that it was now the close of day, and forgetting all their fatigue they both came bounding into the presence of their lord.

Chaupái.

They bowed the head at their lord's lotus feet, and he was glad at heart to see his champions again. Graciously he looked upon them both, and at once their fatigue passed away and they were completely refreshed. On learning that Angad and Hanumán had gone, many warriors among the bears and monkeys turned from the field; while the demons, recovering their strength at nightfall, made a fresh onset, crying 'Raván to the rescue!' At the sight of the demon army, the monkeys turned again; there was everywhere gnashing of teeth as the heroes closed in the fray. In both gallant armies, the leaders impatiently challenged the foe, and fought as those who will not hear of defeat. The valiant demons were all black of hue; the huge monkeys of many different colours. Both armies were equal in strength, with equally matched champions, the passion with which they fought was a sight to see; as when in the rains, or the autumn, masses of cloud are driven against one another by the force of the wind. When the line began to break, the chiefs Akampan and Atikáya had recourse to jugglery, and all in a minute it became pitch dark, and there was a shower of blood, stones and dust.

Dohá 45.

Seeing the dense darkness all round, the monkey host became perplexed; it was impossible to see one another; there was everywhere a great shouting.

Chaupái.

Ráma understood the secret of it all and called to Angad and Hanumán and explained to them what was going on. The mighty monkeys had no sooner heard than they rushed forth in a fury; but the All-merciful with a smile drew his bow and at once let fly a fiery arrow. Light shone forth, and there was no darkness anywhere; as when at the dawn of intelligence all doubts disappear. Having recovered the light, the bears and monkeys forgot all their fatigue and alarm and pressed on exultingly. Hanumán and Angad thundered aloud on the field of battle, and at the sound of their roaring the demons fled; but the bears and monkeys, seizing them in their flight, dashed them to the ground, performing prodigies of valour, or catching them by the leg hurled them into the sea, where alligators, serpents, and fish snapped them up and devoured them.

Dohá 46.

Some were killed outright, some were wounded, some fled back to the fort; the bears and monkeys shouted for joy over the rout of the enemy's strong force.

Chaupái.

Seeing that it was now night, the four divisions of the monkey host returned to the lord of Kosala. As soon as Ráma cast his gracious glance upon them, all their fatigue was at once forgotton. On the other hand, Raván summoned his ministers and told them all how his champions had been killed; " the monkeys have destroyed half my army; tell me at once what counsel should be adopted." Thereupon Málγaván a very aged demon, who had been the sagacious adviser of Raván's father and mother, delivered himself of a speech of the soundest policy: " Hearken, my son, to a few words of instruction from me. Ever since you carried off Síta and brought her here, there have been omens of ill, more than I can tell. No advantage can be gained by opposing him, whose glory is the theme both of Veda and Purána.

Dohá 47.

He is the incarnation of the compassionate Lord God, who slew Hiranyáksha, with his brother Hiranya-kasipu, and Madhu and the monster Kaitabha. Who can fight against him whom Siva and Bráhma adore, full of all grace and wisdom, but like the angel of death, a very fire to consume the forest of wickedness?

Chaupái.

Have done with quarrelling; give back Síta and worship the All-merciful with loving devotion." His words stung like arrows: "Away, wretch, with your abominable suggestions; if it were not for your age, I would have killed you; but do not appear in my sight again." He thought within himself, 'He wishes to be killed by the All-merciful,' and so rose and departed, uttering words of reproof. Then Meghnád cried in a fury: "See what a sight I will show you to-morrow; though I do not say much, I do a great deal." On hearing his son's speech Raván's confidence returned and he took him lovingly into his lap. While they were still consulting, the day broke, the monkeys again assailed the four gates and fiercely encompassed the precipitous citadel. There was a confused noise in every part of the town, as the demons snatched up their weapons of every description and hurried forward and began hurling down masses of rock from the ramparts.

Chhand 2.

Thousands of them hurl down masses of rock: missiles of every kind are sent flying; the shock is as when a bolt falls from heaven and the thunderous noise like that of the clouds on the last day. The monstrous monkeys join in close combat; their bodies are hacked in pieces, but though mangled they faint not; they seize the rocks and hurl them against the fort wherever the demons are.

Dohá 48.

When Meghnád heard that they nad again come and seized the fort, he gallantly left his stronghold and sallied forth with beat of drum to meet the enemy face to face.

Chaupái.

"Where are the two brother princes of Kosala, those archers so famous throughout the universe? Where are Nala and Níla, Dwivid and Sugríva, Angad and Hanumán, most powerful of all? Where is Vibhíshan, his brother's curse, that I may slay the wretch at once, this very day?" So saying, he made ready his terrible arrows, and in vehemence of passion drew the string to his ear. The multitudinous shafts that he left fly sped forth like so many winged serpents. Everywhere you might see monkeys falling to the ground; at that time there was not one that dared to face him. Everywhere bears and monkeys were taking to flight, and every wish to fight was clean forgotten. Not a bear or a monkey was to be seen on the field but those who had left their life there.

Dohá 49.

At each flight he sent forth ten arrows; the warriors all bit the dust: with the roar as of a lion, Meghnád shouted aloud in the strength of his might.

Chaupái.

When Hanumán saw the distress of the army, he rushed forth terrible as death and quickly tearing up an enormous rock, hurled it at Meghnád with the utmost fury. Seeing it come, he mounted up into the air; chariot, driver, and horses were all lost to sight. Again and again Hanumán defied him to combat; but he came no nearer and he then understood the mystery. Meghnád had approached Ráma, and after assailing him with every kind of abuse, aimed at him weapens and missiles of every description; but the Lord with the utmost ease snapped them asunder and stopt them. On seeing this display of power the fool was sore vexed and began to put in practice all kinds of magic; as if a poor little snakeling were to mock Garur and frighten him by snapping at him.

Dohá 50.

The demon in the foolishness of his soul displayed his supernatural powers before him whose mighty magic subdues Síva and Bráhma and all both great and small.

Chaupái.

Mounting up into the air, he rained down a shower of firebrands while floods of water broke out from the earth. Goblins and witches of diverse form danced with uproarious shouts of "kill him, tear him in pieces." Now a shower of excrement, pus, blood, hair and bones, and now an overwhelming downfall of stones and ashes. The dust-storm made it so dark that if you held out your own hand you could not see it. The monkeys were dismayed at the sight of these apparitions and thought 'at this rate we must all of us perish.' But Ráma smiled at the idle show; seeing, however, that all the monkeys were alarmed, he with a single arrow cleft asunder the delusion, as when the sun disperses the thick darkness. With a glance of compassion, he looked upon the bears and monkeys; at once they waxed so strong that there was no holding them back from the field of battle.

Dohá 51.

Having obtained Ráma's permission, Lakshman, taking with him Angad and the other monkeys, marched forth in fury, with bow and arrows in hand—

Chaupái.

With blood-shot eyes[1] and mighty chest and arms and his body of reddish hue like Mount Himálaya. On the other side Rávan sent out his champions, who took up their armour and their weapons[2] and hastened forth. With mountains and huge trees for missiles, the monkeys rushed to meet them, shouting 'victory to Ráma.' They all closed in the fray, equally matched one with another, and both equally sanguine of success. After hurling the rocks and mountains at the foe, the monkeys next fell upon them with blows of the fist and kicks, and rendings of the teeth: 'seize, seize, seize, kill, kill, kill, strike off his head, rend off his arm,' such were the cries which filled the nine continents of the world, while headless bodies still full of fury kept running to and fro. From the heaven above, the

1 In Rám Jasan's edition, the one I habitually use, the reading is *chhatajanayan*, which may be translated 'with blood-shot eyes,' an epithet which appears appropriate to the context. In other editions is substituted the more common expression *jalaja-nayan*, with lotus eyes.'

2 Here the reading that I translate is *giri-sila*, 'the rocks and mountains' mentioned above as the monkeys' missiles. Rám Jasan reads *jaya-sila*, which would mean 'triumphant.'

gods beheld the spectacle now in dismay and now in rapture.

Dohá 52.

Every hollow in the ground was filled full of blood, with clouds of dust overhead, like as when the smoke of a burning corpse spreads over the ashes of a pyre :

Chaupái.

while the wounded heroes resembled so many *dhák* trees in flower. The two champions Lakshman and Meghnád grappled with one another in excess of fury. Neither could singly conquer the other ; the demon by force and by feint showing himself so wicked. At last the incarnation of Seshnág became mad with rage, and with one blow he crushed both the chariot and its driver. He so smote him in various ways that the demon was left barely alive. Then the son of Rávan thought within himself — 'I am in a strait, he will take my life,' and he let fly his spear, the destroyer of heroes, which struck Lakshman in the breast with full force. So great was the shock that he swooned away. Then he went and drew near, no longer afraid.

Dohá 53.

A hundred myriad warriors like Meghnád essayed to lift him ; but how could Seshnág the supporter of the world be thus lifted ? they retired in dudgeon.

Chaupái.

Hearken, Bhaváni ; who can conquer him in battle, the fire of whose wrath would consume in a moment the fourteen spheres of creation, whom gods and men and all things animate and inanimate adore ? Only he can understand this mystery, on whom rests the favour of Ráma. As it was now evening, both armies left the field and began to muster their several forces. The All-merciful, the ubiquitous Supreme Spirit, the invincible lord of the universe, asked 'Where is Lakshman ?' Hanumán then brought him forward. When the Lord saw his younger brother, he was much distrest. Jámbaván said : "The physician

Sushena is at Lanká, send some one to fetch him." Hanumán at once assumed a diminutive form and went and brought him, house and all.

Dohá 54.

Sushena came and bowed his head at Ráma's lotus feet and told Hanumán to go and bring herbs from a certain mountain that he mentioned.

Chaupái.

With Ráma's lotus feet impressed upon his heart, the Son of the Wind started in confident assurance. On the other side, a spy gave information. So Rávan went to the house of Kála-nemi and told him. When he had heard the news, Kàla-nemi beat his head again and again, crying, "Who can stop his path who burnt your city before your very eyes. Have come regard for your own welfare and worship Ráma and desist, sire, from henceforth from these vain endeavours. Cherish in your heart the delight of all eyes, whose body is dark and beautiful as the blue lotus. Have done with pride, conceit, and arrogance, and rouse yourself from this slumber in a night of delusion. Is it possible that any one should ever dream of conquering him for whom the serpent, Time, is mere food to devour?"

Dohá 55.

When the Ten-headed heard this, he was exceedingly wroth and Kálá-nemi reasoned to himself: "It will be better for me to die at the hands of Ràma's messenger, and not for this wretch to kill me."

Chaupái.

So saying he went and by the power of magic constructed on the wayside a lake, temple and fine garden. Hanumán espied the charming spot and thought to himself. 'After asking the holy man's leave, I will drink of the water and rest.' For the demon showed himself in a false attire, and sought to delude the messenger even of the king of delusion. So the son of the wind went and bowed the head before him; and he began to recite Ráma's praises, saying—"A great battle is raging between Rávan and Ráma, but Ráma will win the day; of this there is no doubt. Though I have not moved from here, I have seen it all, my friend; my intelligence is remarkably clear-sighted." On his asking for water, he gave him some in a cup; the monkey said—"That is not enough to satisfy me." "Go then and bathe in the tank and quickly come back, and I will then bestow upon you a gift, by which you may attain to understanding."

Dohá 56.

As he stepped into the tank, a fish seized the monkey by the foot. In his alarm he killed it. Whereupon it assumed a divine form, and mounting a chariot ascended into the heaven.

Chaupái.

"By the sight of you, O monkey, I have become freed from guilt, and the curse of the great saint has been removed. This is no hermit, but a fierce demon; doubt not the truth of my words." So saying, the heavenly nymph went her way, and the monkey at once returned to the demon. Said the monkey—"Holy sir, first receive my offering and after that tell me the charm." He then twisted his tail round his head and threw him down. At the moment of his Death he appeared in his proper form, and with a cry of Ráma, Ráma!" breathed his last. On hearing this Hanumán went on his way, glad of heart. He found the mountain, but could not recognize the herbs; so without any hesitation he tore up the hill by the root and went off with it. As he rushed through the night air with the mountain in his grasp, he passed over the city of Avadh.

Dohá 57.

Bharat saw him, and thinking him to be some most monstrous demon, drew his bow to his ear and shot him with a headless arrow.

Chaupái.

Struck by the dart he fell in a swoon to the earth, crying ' O Ráma, Ráma, prince of Raghu's line ! " On hearing this grateful sound, Bharat started up and ran, and in the utmost haste drew nigh to the monkey. Seeing him wounded, he clasped him to his bosom and tried in every way to revive him, but without success. With a disconsolate face and sore grief at heart he made this prayer while his eyes streamed with tears : " God who made me Ráma's enemy, has now caused me this additional distress If in thought, word and deed, I have a sincere affection for Ráma's lotus feet, and if Ráma is kindly disposed to me, may your pain and fatigue, O monkey, all pass away." At the sound of these words, the monkey chief arose and sat up, crying, " glory, glory to the king of Kosala."

Sorathá 5.

With quivering limbs and eyes full of tears, he took and clasped the monkey to his bosom, invoking Ráma, the crown of the line of Raghu, in a transport of affection, which was more than his soul could contain.

Chaupái.

" Tell me friend, is all well with the Fountain of joy and with his brother and the revered Jánaki." The monkey told him in brief all that had taken place. He became sad of heart and began to lament : Alas, my fate, why was I born into the world, if in nothing I can help my lord." But seeing the unfitness of the time he mastered his feelings the gallant prince, and again addressed the monkey : " Sir, you will be delayed in your journey, and your task will come to nought, for the day is now breaking. Mount my arrow, mountain and all, and I will send you straight into the presence of the all-merciful." On hearing this, the monkey's pride was aroused : " How can his arrow fly with my weight ? " But again reflecting on Ráma's power, he bowed at his feet and cried with clasped hands :

Dohá 58.

"O my lord, I have only to cherish the thought of your majesty in my soul in order to travel quickly." So saying, Hanumán took leave and after bowing at his feet set forth. As he went, the Son of the Wind again and again extolled to himself the mighty arm and the amiable disposition of Bharat and his boundless devotion to his lord's feet.

Chaupái.

Meanwhile, Ráma was watching Lakshman and using language after the fashion of a man. When half the night was spent, and still the monkey had not returned, Ráma raised his brother and clasped him to his heart. "O my brother, once you could not endure to see me in sorrow, your disposition was ever so affectionate. On my account, you left father and mother and exposed yourself to the forest, the cold, the heat and the wind. But where is now your old love, my brother, that you do not stir in response to my distress? If I had known that exile involved the loss of my brother, I would never have obeyed my father's commands [1] Sons, riches, wives, house and kinsfolk come again time after time in a life, but a real brother is not so to be had; remember this, brother, and awake to life. As a bird is utterly wretched without wings, a serpent without its head-jewel, or an elephant without its trunk, so is my life without you, my brother. If cruel fate preserves me alive, with what face can I show myself at Avadh, after sacrificing a dear brother for the sake of a woman. I would rather have endured the social

1 This lament over his want of foreknowledge and other similar passages, in which Ràma is represented as subject to human infirmities, are frequently quoted in Missionary polemics as fatal to the idea of his being a divine person and as clear evidences, even on the showing of the Hindu narrative itself, that he was only an ordinary human being. But it is very unwise to adopt such a line of argument, which might be retorted with equal force against the inspired records of Christianity. From the Hindu point of view, the answer given by Tulsi Dàs sufficiently covers the difficulty and corresponds precisely with the explanation of S. Jerome: "Non quod personam Domini separemus, sed quod opera ejus inter Deum hominemque divisa sint."

disgrace; for, after all, the loss of a wife is no such great matter, and my heart is so hard and unfeeling that it can bear the sight even of this your anguish. Your mother's only son, my brother, you are the sole support of her life, but she took you by the hand and entrusted you to me, knowing what a comfort and what a friend I should find you. What answer can I go and give her? Why do you not rise and advise me, brother?" Thus grievously sorrowed the healer of sorrow and his lotus eyes streamed with tears; but Umá, Ráma is one and unchangeable, and it was only in compassion to his worshippers that he exhibited the manners of a man.

Sorathá 6.

All the monkeys were in distress on hearing their lord's lamentation, till Hanumán arrived, like an heroic strain in the midst of an elegy.

Chaupái.

Ráma received him with exceeding joy, for the Lord is most grateful and supremely wise. Then quickly the physician concocted his remedies, and Lakshman gaily arose and sat up. The Lord affectionately clasped his brother to his heart and all the bears and monkey were rejoiced. The physician was then conveyed home again in the same manner as he had been brought away. When Rávan heard of these proceedings, he was greatly disturbed and began beating himself on the head. In his agitation, he went to Kumbhakarn and with much trouble succeeded in waking him When the monster was roused, he showed like Death itself in visible form. He asked, "Tell me, brother, why is your face so sad." He told him the whole history of how in his pride he had carried off Síta. "Brother, the monkeys have killed all the demons and routed my stoutest warriors, Durmukha and the man-devouring Sura-ripu; Atikaya and Akampan, those mighty champions, together with Mahodara and other valiant heroes, who have fallen on the field of battle."

Dohá 59.

On hearing Rávan's report, Kumbha-karn cried out; "Wretch, you have carried off the mother of the universe and yet expect to prosper!

Chaupái.

You have done ill, O demon king; and now why have you come and awakened me? At once, brother, abandon your pride and worship Ráma; so shall you prosper. How, Ten-heads, can Ráma be a man, when he has such a servant as Hanumán. Alas, brother, you have acted foolishly; why did you not come and wake me before? You have rebelled against the god who is adored by Siva and Bráhma and every other divinity. The knowledge which the sage Nárad imparted to me, I now declare to you; for the time has come. Embrace me, my brother, for I go to rejoice my eyes with the sight of the dark hued, the lotus-eyed, the healer of every sorrow!"

Dohá 60.

As he contemplated Rama's beauty and perfection, he was for a moment unconscious, then demanded of Rávan a million jars of wine and a whole herd of buffaloes.

Chaupái.

After he had eaten the buffaloes and drunk the wine, he roared aloud with a voice of thunder and sallied forth from the fort without any escort, maddened with drink, the war-loving Kumbha-karn. Vibhíshan, on seeing him, came forward and fell at his feet and said who he was. He raised his brother and took him to his heart, delighted to find him a worshipper of Ráma. "Brother, that wretch Rávan struck me with his foot for giving him the best possible advice. Resenting such treatment, I came to Ráma, and the Lord was glad at heart to see me his servant." "Mark me, brother, Rávan is under the influence of fate and will listen to no advice, however good. Thrice blessed are you, Vibhíshan, the glory of all the demon race; you have shed a lustre on all your kinsfolk by your worship of Ráma, that ocean of beauty and felicity.

Dohá 61.

You have guilelessly worshipped the heroic Ráma in thought, word and deed. But go, I cannot distinguish here between friend and foe." The warror's death was doomed.

Chaupái.

On hearing his brother's words, Vibhíshan turned and presented himself before the Glory of the three spheres "My lord, Kumbha-karn approaches; a warrior huge of stature as a mountain." The monkeys waited to hear no more, but ran off jabbering, the stoutest of them, and plucked up trees and rocks, which they hurled against him, gnashing their teeth the while. Millions upon millions of mountain peaks did the bears and monkeys cast upon him one after another; but neither did his courage fail, nor did he stir from his position; like an elephant pelted with flower-seeds. At last the Son of the Wind struck him with his fist; he fell to the ground and beat his head in dismay. Rising again, he gave Hanumán such a blow that he spun round and fell at once to the earth. Next he overthrew upon the plain Nala and Níla and dashed down the chiefs, hurling them this side and that. The monkey host scattered and fled in an utter panic, nor were there any to rally.

Dohá 62.

Having rendered insensible Angad and the other monkeys and Sugríva as well, he clapped the king of the monkeys under his arm and went off, in his illimitable might.

Chaupái.

O Umá, when Ráma plays the part of a man, it is like Garúr sporting in company with snakes. If he but knit his brows, he annihilates Death himself, how then can he condescend to such a combat as this? The answer is that the fame of it, when spread abroad, tends to the redemption of the world, and mortals, who make it their song, emerge safely from the ocean of existence. When his swoon had passed off, the Son of the Wind awoke and began at once to look for Sugríva. But he, on recovering from his swoon, slipped out of Kumbha-karn's clutches, who had taken him for dead. Having bitten off his nose and ears, he with a shout ascended into the air; but the giant saw him and caught him by the foot and dashed him to the ground. With wonderful agility he rose and struck him back and then betook himself—the hero—to the presence of his lord, crying, 'Glory, glory, glory to the Fountain of Mercy.' But he, when he became sensible of his mutilated nose and ears, turned in a fury and with sore distress of soul. The monkey host were horrorstricken when they saw the terrible warrior thus earless and noseless.

Dohá 63.

Raising a shout of 'victory to Ráma,' the monkeys rushed forward, and all at once hurled upon him a volley of rocks and trees.

Chaupái.

Maddened with the rage of battle, Kumbha-karn advanced, awful as Death, and seized and devoured myriads of the monkeys, like locusts swallowed up in a mountain cave; myriads of others he crushed with his body, and myriads he ground to powder between his hands. But many of the bears and monkeys escaped, by the passage of his mouth, or nostrils or ears. Drunk with the madness of battle, the demon was as boastful as though the whole universe had been made over to him to ravage. Every champion took to flight, and there was no turning them back; they could neither see with their eyes nor hear any cry. When they learnt that Kumbha-karn had routed the monkey host, the demons all rallied. But Ráma saw his army in distress and the forces of the enemy coming on in full array.

Dohá 64.

" Hearken, Sugríva and Vibhíshan, and you my brother,

collect your troops and let me test the might of these miscreants:" thus cried the lotus eyed.

Chaupái.

With bow in hand and quiver fitted to his side, Raghunáth went forth to scatter the ranks of the enemy. The Lord gave his bow a preliminary twang; the hosts of the foe were deafened by the din. Then he let fly a million of arrows, he, the god ever faithful to his promise; the winged shafts sped like serpents of death. The terrible bolts flew in all directions; the mighty demon warriors were cut to pieces. Feet, trunk, head, and arms were shorn away: many a hero was cut into a hundred pieces The wounded reel and fall to the ground, but gallantly recover themselves and rise again to renew the fight. The arrows as they strike give a thud like thunder: many fled when they saw how terrible they were. Headless bodies rush madly on; the cry resounds, 'Seize, seize, kill, kill.'

Dohá 65.

In a moment the lord Raghubír's arrows cut to pieces the terrible demons; and they his shafts all came back into the quiver.

Chaupái.

When Kumbha-karn saw and perceived that the demon host had been routed in a minute, the mighty warrior waxed exceeding wroth and roared aloud with the voice of a lion. In his fury, he tore up mountains by the root and hurled them upon the throng of monkey chiefs. The lord saw the monstrous rocks coming and with his arrows shattered them into dust. Again Raghunáyak indignantly strung his bow and let fly a volley of his terrible shafts. As they entered and passed through his body, they seemed like flashes of lightning stored in a dense thunder-cloud. The streams of blood on his black frame resembled rivers of red ochre on a mountain of soot. Perceiving his distress, the bears and monkeys rushed forward; he laughed when he saw them draw near.

Dohá 66.

Roaring aloud with a terrible voice, he seized myriads and myriads of the monkeys, and dashed them to the ground like a lion, invoking the name of Rávan.

Chaupái.

The bears and monkeys all fled, like a flock of sheep at the sight of a wolf; and in their flight, Bhaváni, they cried aloud in their distress with a piteous voice: "This demon is for the monkey race like a sore famine that threatens to devastate a whole country. O Ráma, Kharári, rain-cloud of mercy, ever ready to relieve the distress of the suppliant, have mercy upon us, have mercy upon us." When the Lord God heard their piteous cry, he took his bow and arrows and went forth. His army he checked in the rear and went forth in his own might, full of indignation. He drew his bow and fitted a hundred arrows to the string; they flew forth and entered into his body. At their stroke he rushed forth in a fury—the mountains reeled, the earth staggered—and tore up a rock, but Ráma shot away his arm. Again he rushed on, with a rock in his left hand; but that arm too Ráma cut off, and it fell to the ground. The monster thus robbed of his arms resembled mount Mandara without its wings. With savage eyes he glared upon the Lord, as though ready to devour the whole universe.

Dohá 67.

With a most terrible shriek he rushed forward with open mouth. The saints and gods above cried out in their terror, 'alas, alas, alas.'

Chaupái.

When the All-merciful saw the alarm of the gods, he drew his bow with its string to his ear. The flight of arrows filled the demon's mouth, yet he was so strong that he did not fall to the ground. With his mouth full of arrows he still rushed upon the foe, like a living quiver of death. Then the Lord in his wrath took his sharpest arrow and struck his head right off his body. The head fell at the feet of Rávan, who was as dismayed at the sight as a snake that has dropt its crest jewel. The ground sunk beneath the weight of the trunk, as it still ran madly on: till the Lord cut it in two. Then it fell to the earth like a mountain from the sky, crushing beneath it monkeys, bears, and demons. His soul entered the Lord's mouth, to the astonishment of gods, saints, and all. The gods in their delight sound the kettle-drum and hymn his praise, and rain down flowers in abundance. After paying homage, all the gods went their way. At that time came also the divine sage, Nárad, and extolled above the heaven Hari's infinite perfection. The Lord's soul was pleased by his stirring heroic strain. 'Make haste to destroy these miscreants' were the saint's words as he left. Ráma remained in his glory on the field of battle.

Chhand 3.

All-glorious shone forth Raghupati on the field of battle, in his immeasurable might and manifold beauty, with the drops of toil on his lotus face, with his lovely eyes and his body specked with blood, while in both hands he brandished his bow and arrows, with the bears and monkeys grouped all around him. Not Seshnág with his many tongues could tell all his beauty, so says Tulsi Dás.

Dohá 68.

Though the demons were so vile and very mines of impurity, he translated them to his own sphere. O Umá, how dull of understanding are the men who do not worship the divine Ráma.

Chaupái.

At the close of the day both armies retired; the battle had thoroughly exhausted the stoutest warriors. But by Ráma's favour the monkey host gathered fresh strength, like as a fire blazes up when fed with straw; while the demons wasted away day and night, like the merit of a man's good deeds when he tells them himself. Rávan made great lamentation, again and again taking his brother's head in his lap. His wives also wept and beat their breast with their hands, while they told of his pre-eminent majesty and strength. At this juncture Meghnád arrived and with many words consoled his father: "Be witness to-morrow of my prowess; what need now of boastful speeches? I have received from my patron divinity a chariot of strength, the virtue of which I have never yet shown you, father." While they were thus talking, the day broke and swarms of monkeys assailed the four gates. On the one side were the bears, and monkeys terrible as death; on the other the demons; fiercest of warriors. Valiantly they fight, each thirsting for victory; the battle, Garúr, baffles all description.

Dohá 69.

Meghnád mounted his magic car and ascended into the air with a laugh like the roar of thunder, which struck the monkey army with terror.

Chaupái.

Spears, lances, swords, and scymetars were plied, with weapons and missiles of every description; axes, hatchets, clubs and stones, and then a shower of innumerable arrows. The heaven was as dark all round with arrows as when the constellation Maghá[1] pours down its torrents. 'Seize, seize, kill, kill,' were the cries that sounded in their ears, but none could tell who it was that struck them. Snatching up rocks and trees, the monkeys sprang into the air; but they could not see him and returned disappointed. Ravines, gorges, roads, and mountain-caves were turned by his magic power into arrowy cages. The monkeys were confounded and knew not where to turn, and fell to the ground like the mountains fallen in bondage to Indra.[2] Hanumán, Angad,

1 Maghná is reckoned as the tenth of the Nakshatras and is in the ascendant in the month of Bhádon, at the height of the rains. Hence the saying *mata ke parase aur Magha ke barase.*

2 Indra, the wielder of the thunderbolt, is represented as the mountains' master, or jailor. The word *bandi* here is not the participle of the verb 'to reverence,' but the noun meaning a captive or 'slave.'

Nala, Níla, and every other warrior he sorely distressed; then he assailed with his shafts Lakshman, Sugríva and Vibhísban, piercing their bodies through and through again. Lastly he joined in combat with Ráma himself and let fly his arrows, which as they struck turned to snakes. Kharári was rendered powerless by the serpents' coils, he the great free agent, the everlasting, the one unchangeable, who like a juggler performs all sorts of dolusive actions, but is ever his own master, Ráma, our Lord. It was only to enhance the glory of the battle that he allowed himself to be bound by the serpents' coils; but the gods were in a panic.

Dohá 70.

O Umá, is it possible for him to be brought into bondage, by whose name when repeated in prayer the saints free themselves from the bonds of existence; who is the omnipresent centre of the universe?

Chaupái.

O Bhaváni, the actions of the incarnate Ráma are beyond the range of thought, or human strength, or speech. This is the reason why the wisest ascetics discard theological speculations and simply adore. Having thus thrown the army into confusion, Meghnád at last manifested himself with words of reviling. Jámbaván shouted: 'Wretch, keep your place.' On hearing this, his fury waxed still greater. 'Fool, I only spared you on account of your age. I think scorn of your challenge.' So saying, he let fly his terrible trident; Jàmbaván caught it in his hand and then rushed on and gave Meghnád such a blow on the chest that he, the scourge of heaven, fell swooning to the ground. Then in his wrath he caught him by the foot and swung him round and dashed him on the earth as a display of his strength. But he by virtue of the divine boon died not for all his killing; so he took him by the foot and tossed him into Lanká, while the gods and saints sent Garúr, who came in haste to Ráma,

Dohá 71.

and seized and devoured the whole swarm of false serpents. The delusion was dispelled, and all the monkey host rejoiced again. Tearing up with their claws the trees and rocks of the mountain, they rushed forward, while the demons fled in utter confusion and climbed up into the fort.

Chaupái.

When Meghnád recovered from his swoon, he was greatly ashamed to look his father in the face, and arose and went in haste to a cave in the mountain, intending to perform a sacrifice that would ensure victory. But Vibhíshan gave the caution: "Hearken, O king of unbounded might and generosity, Meghnád is preparing an unholy sacrifice—wretched sorcerer and scourge of heaven as he is—and if he bring it to completion, Sire, it will not be easy to conquer him." On hearing this, Raghupati was highly pleased and said to Angad and the other monkeys: "Go, my brothers, you and Lakshman, and put a stop to his sacrifice. It is for you, Lakshman, to fight and slay him; I am distressed to see the terror of the gods. Kill him, either by open force or by stratagem; one way or another—mark me, brother—the demon must be got rid of. But you three, Jámbaván, Sugríva and Vibhíshan, remain with the army." When Raghubír had finished his commands, the hero girt his quiver by his side and took his bow, and with the glory of his lord impressed upon his heart cried aloud with a mighty voice as of thunder: "If I return to-day without slaying him, may I be no longer called Ráma's servant; though a hundred Sivas give him help, I will slay him yet, in the name of Ráma."

Dohá 72.

After bowing his head at Ráma's feet, the incarnation of Seshnág went forth at once and with him Angad, Níla, Mayanda, Nala, and the valiant Hanumán.

Chaupái.

When the monkeys arrived, they found him making an oblation of blood and buffalo's flesh. They all tried to interrupt the ceremony, but he would not sir; they then took to praising him.[1] When still he did not rise, they went and pulled him by the hair, upon which he kicked out so fiercely that they ran away. He pursued them with his trident as they fled, till they joined Lakshman. He came on in the wildest fury, striking out and shouting again and again with a terrible roar. Hanumán and Angad rushed fiercely forward, but he struck them on the breast with his trident and beat them to the ground. Then he shot forth his mighty spear against the Lord, but he warded it off and broke it in two. Meanwhile the Son of the Wind and the prince had risen again and smote him furiously; but his wounds had no effect upon him. The heroes fell upon him once more, but their enemy was not to be killed; again he came on with a terrible shriek. Then Lakshman made up his mind; 'I have played with this miscreant long enough,' and seeing him advance, furious as hell, he let fly his terrible shaft. When he saw the arrow coming on like a thunderbolt, the wretch at once disappeared from sight and continued fighting under various disguises, now visible and now invisible. The monkeys thought him invincible and trembled. Then the incarnation of the serpent-king became exceeding wroth, and directing his intention to the glory of the lord of Kosala, fitted an arrow to the string and with all his might let it fly. It struck him full in the breast. In the moment of death he abandoned all falsehood,

Dohá 73.

and invoking the names of Lakshman and Ráma drew his

1 That is, they enlarged upon his strength and courage and wondered why he should turn from fighting to sacrifice.

last breath. 'Blessed indeed is thy mother' cried Angad and Hanumán.[1]

Chaupái.

Without an effort Hanumán took up his body and put it at the gate of the city and returned. When they heard of his death, the gods and Gandharvas mounted their chariots and came thronging the heaven, showering down flowers and beating drums and hymning the spotless renown of the divine Raghubír. 'Glory to Seshnág, glory to the world-supporter; You, O Lord, are the Saviour of all the gods.' Having thus hymned his praises, the gods and saints withdrew, while Lakshman went and presented himself before the All-merciful. When the Ten-headed heard of his son's death, he swooned away and fell to the ground; Mandodari made grievous lamentation, beating her breast and ever calling upon his name; the citizens too were all sorrowful and dismayed and with one consent reviled Rávan.

Dohá 74.

Then the Ten-headed set to comforting his wives in every way he could: "See and consider at heart how transitory is everything in this world."

Chaupái.

Rávan gave them sound advice; though a dullard himself, his counsel was good and wholesome. There are many men who excel in giving advice, but the people who put it in practice are not very plentiful. When the night had passed and the day broke, the bears and monkeys again beset the four gates. Rávan summoned his captains and thus addressed them: "If any one's heart fail him in facing the battle, he had better withdraw now and not incur disgrace by running away in the midst of the engagement. Relying on the strength of my own arm, I have continued the struggle, and can give an answer to any enemy

1 For giving birth to such a gallant warrior and one who showed such faith in the hour of death.

who may challenge me." So saying, he made ready his chariot, swift as the wind, while every instrument of music sounded forth a strain of deadly combat. His champions marched on in their peerless might, like the march of a whirlwind of blackness. At that time occurred numberless omens of ill, but he heeded them not, in the overweening pride of the strength of his arm.

Chhand 4.

In his overweening pride he took no heed of omens, good or bad : weapons dropt from the hand ; warriors fell from their cars ; horses, frightened by the trumpeting of the elephants, ran out of the line ; jackals, vultures and huge packs of dogs made a frightful clamour, and owls, like messengers of death, uttered their most lugubrious notes.

Dohá 75.

How was it possible for him to have prosperous omens of good fortune, or even to dream of peace of mind, when he was so infatuated that he desired the ruin of the whole world and was set upon opposing Ráma.

Chaupái.

The demon host marched on in countless number ; elephants and chariots, foot and horse, line after line ; equipages of every description, wagons and cars, with banners and standards of diverse colour; innumerable troops of infuriated elephants like autumn clouds when driven by the wind ; battalions of savage demons of different colours, inspired with all the phrenzy of martial heroes ; an army magnificent in every respect, like the mustered array of the gallant god of spring. As the host marched, the elephants of the eight quarters reeled, the ocean was stirred from its depths, the mountains shook. The dust rose in clouds that obscured the sun, the wind failed, and the earth was troubled. Drums and other instruments of music made an awful din, like the crash of thunder-clouds on the last day. Clarions, trumpets, and hautboys sounded the martial strain that gladdens the souls of heroes. With on accord they shouted as with the voice of a lion, each extolling his own strength and manhood. Rávan cried: "Hearken, my warriors; do you attack the common herd of bears and monkeys; I myself will slay the two brother princes." So saying, he ordered the army to advance to the front. When the monkeys heard the news, they all rushed on, crying 'Ráma to the rescue.'

Chhand 5.

The gigantic and terrible bears and monkeys rushed on like death; flying through the air like so many winged mountains of diverse colours. With talons and teeth and rocks and enormous trees for weapons they all feel no fear, singing the glory of Ráma, the lion-like vanquisher of the wild elephant Rávan.

Dohá 76.

With a shout of 'victory, victory,' raised from both sides, the heroes selected each his match and closed in combat, these calling on Ráma and those on Rávan.

Chaupái.

When Vibhíshan observed that Rávan was in a chariot and Ráma on foot, he became anxious; his extreme affection made him doubtful of mind, and falling at his feet he cried tenderly: "My lord, you have neither a chariot nor shoes to your feet, how can you conquer so powerful a warrior?" "Hearken, friend," replied the All-merciful, "a conqueror has a different kind of chariot. Manliness and courage are his chariot wheels; unflinching truthfulness and morality his banners and standards; strength, discretion, self-control and benevolence his horses, with grace, mercy and equanimity for their harness: prayer to Mahádeva his unerring charioteer; continence his shield, contentment his sword, alms-giving his axe, knowledge his mighty spear, and perfect science his stout bow. His pure and constant soul stands for a quiver, his pious practices of devotion for a sheaf of arrows, and the revenue he pays to Bráhmans and his guru is his impenetrable coat of mail. There is no equipment for victory that can be compared to this, nor is there any enemy, my friend, who can conquer the man who takes his stand on the chariot of

Dohá 77.

religion. He who has such a powerful chariot as this is a warrior who can overcome even that great and terrible enemy, the world ; hearken, friend, and fear not." When he had heard his lord's exhortation, Vibhíshan clasped his feet in his joy and cried—" O Ráma, full of mercy and kindness, you have used this parable to give me a lesson." On the one side Rávan's rabble, on the other Angad and Hanumán, the demons against the bears and monkeys, had joined in battle, each swearing by his own lord.

Chaupái.

Bráhma and the other gods, with all the saints and sages, mounted their chariots to watch the fray, from the heaven above. I too, Umá, was with them, beholding Ráma's exploits on the field of battle. On both sides the leaders were maddened with martial phrenzy, but the monkeys were triumphant through the might of Ráma. With shouts of defiance they close in single combat, each mauling his foe and beating him to the ground. They strike, they bite, they clutch, they fell ; they tear off heads and use them for missiles ; they rip up bodies, wrench off arms, and seizing by the leg dash to the ground. The bears bury the demon warriors in the earth and pile over them heaps of sand ; the sturdy monkeys raging in the fight were like so many monstrous images of ravenging death to look upon.

Chhand 6.

The monkeys, their bodies all streaming with gore, stood forth like multiplied images of the god of death, crushing the mightiest warriors of the demon host and roaring with a voice of thunder. They strike, the buffet, they tear with the teeth, they crush beneath the feet, uttering fierce cries, both bears and monkeys, and employing strength and stratagem alike, by which to reduce the miscreants. They seize and tear open their cheeks, they rip up the belly and take the entrails and hang them round their own necks, as though the lord of Prahlád (Narsinh) had assumed a multiplicity of forms, and were disporting himself on the field of battle. 'Seize, strike, tear, overthrow,' were the savage cries, with which earth and heaven resounded. Glory to Ráma, who can make a straw a thunderbolt and again reduce a thunderbolt to a straw.

Dohá 78.

When Rávan saw his troops in confusion, he mounted his chariot, with his twenty arms and ten bows, and essayed to rally them, crying ' turn, turn.

Chaupái.

The Ten-headed rushed forth in wild fury, and the monkeys with a whoop advanced to meet him. Taking in their hands trees, crags and mountains, together they all hurled them upon him. The masses of stone no sooner struck on his adamantine frame than they were at once shattered in pieces, while he flinched not, but stood firm as a rock and stayed his chariot, he, Rávan, maddened with the battle and terrible in his fury. This side and that he scattered and battered the monkey chiefs in the fierceness of his wrath. Bears and monkeys all took to flight, crying, "Help, help, Angad, Hanumán; save, save, O lord Raghubir; this monster, as sure as death, will devour us all. When he saw the monkeys in flight, he fitted an arrow to each of his ten bows.

Chhand 7.

He strung his bow and let fly a volley of arrows; they flew and lodged like serpents; the heaven and the earth were full of arrows; the monkeys fled in all directions. There was a terrible uproar, the monkey host and the bears were panic-striken and cried in dismay—" O Raghubir, fountain of mercy ; O Hari, friend of the forlorn, saviour of mankind."

Dohá 79.

Seeing the distress of his troops, Lakshman slung his quiver by his side, took his bow in his hand and sallied forth in a fury, after bowing his head at Ráma's feet.

Chaupái.

" Ah ! vile wretch, you kill bears and monkeys ; but now look at me, I am your death." "I have been searching for you, you murderer of my son, and to-day I will gladden my soul by your destruction." Thus he cried and let fly a storm of arrows ; but Lakshman shivered them all into a hundred pieces. Then Rávan hurled upon him myriads of missiles, but he warded them off as though they had been tiny sesamum seeds, and in turn assailed him with his own shafts, smashing his chariot and killing his charioteer. Each of his ten heads he transfixed with a hundred arrows, which seemed like serpents boring their way into the peaks of a mountain. With a hundred arrows more he struck him full in the breast : he fell senseless to the ground. When the swoon had passed off, he rose again in his strength and let fly the bolt given him by Bráhma

Chhand 8.

The mighty bolt, the gift of Bráhma, smote the incarnate Seshnág full in the breast ; the hero fell fainting ; the Ten-headed essayed to lift his body, but his immeasurable bulk stirred not. In his folly Rávan thought to carry him off, not knowing him to be the lord of the three spheres, who supports on one of his heads the whole created universe, as though it were a mere grain of sand.

Dohá 80.

When the Son of the Wind saw this, he rushed forward with a furious cry ; but as the monkey came on, he struck him a violent blow with his fist.

Chaupái.

The monkey dropt on the knee but did not fall to the

ground and, on recovering himself, arose full of exceeding wrath, and smote him one blow : he fell like a mountain struck by a thunderbolt. When he recovered from the swoon, he marvelled greatly at the monkey's mighty strength. "Shame on my manhood, shame on myself, if you remain alive, you plague of heaven." So cried the monkey, as he carried Lakshman away. At this sight Rávan was sore amazed. Said Raghubír, on finding his brother still alive : "You are indeed the destroyer of death and the saviour of the gods." On hearing these words, the Benignant arose and sat up, and the terrible bolt vanished into the heaven. Then again they took bow and arrows and rushed forward with the utmost impetuosity to meet the enemy.

Chhand 9.

Again, by their impetuous attack, they put him to confusion, smashing his chariot and slaying his charioteer. Rávan fell fainting to the ground, his heart transfixed by a hundred arrows. Another charioteer threw him on his car and carried him to Lanká, while Lakshman in all his glory prostrated himself at Ráma's feet.

Dohá 81.

On the one hand Rávan, on recovering, began to make preparations for a sacrifice ; fool to oppose Ráma and yet hope to prosper ; obstinate and ignorant indeed !

Chaupái.

On the other hand, Vibhíshan, on learning the news, went at once and told Raghupati :—"My Lord, Rávan is engaged in a sacrifice ; if he completes it, the wretch will never die. Despatch your valiant monkeys, sire, in all speed, to cut short his life." As soon as it was day, the lord sent out his warriors. Hanumán, Angad, and all started forth. Bounding with glee, the monkeys climbed Lanká and boldly entered Rávan's palace. Finding him engaged in the sacrifice, they all became furious :—"You run away home without shame from the battle and on getting here practise this hypocrisy !" [1] So saying, Angad gave him a kick, but the wretch took no notice, so absorbed was he in his own purpose.

Chhand 10.

As he took no notice, the monkeys in a fury tore him with their teeth and kicked him with their feet ; his wives, too, they seized by the hair and dragged out of doors, till the poor wretches screamed again. Then at last he rose, terrible as death, and caught a monkey by the leg and hurled him away : but seeing that the monkeys had thus succeeded in interrupting the sacrifice, his heart failed him.

Dohá 82.

Rejoicing at having spoilt his sacrifice, the monkeys returned to Raghupati ; while the demon went off in a fury, abandoning all hope of life.

Chaupái.

Fearful omens of ill met him as he went, for vultures flew and settled on his heads. Fated to die, he paid no heed, but gave the order to sound the onset. There seemed no end to the demon host as it marched on, with its many elephants, chariots, foot-soldiers and horsemen. The miscreants hastened to confront the Lord, like a swarm of gnats when they fly into the fire. On the other hand, the gods raised songs of praise : –" He has caused us grievous trouble ; play with him no longer, O Ráma, for Síta is in sore distress." On hearing the prayer of the gods, Ráma smiled[2] and rose and trimmed his arrows. His hair was tightly bound in a knot on his forehead, beautiful with the flowers that had here and there been caught (as they fell upon him from heaven). With his bright eyes and his body dark of hue as a raincloud, rejocing the sight of every created sphere, he girded

1 *Vak-dhyán*, literally, 'the contemplation of a crane,' *i.e*, the affectation of being absorbed in divine contemplation, while really thinking only of worldly interests ; like the crane, which seems lost in abstraction, but is only waiting for a fish to pounce upon.

2 Knowing that the gods were chiefly anxious on their own account, though they professed to be only thinking about Síta.

on his quiver with its belt about his lions and took in his hand his mighty bow, the bow of Vishnu.

Chhand 11.

With his bow Saranga in his hand and his beautiful quiver full of arrows slung by his side, with his muscular arms and fine broad chest adorned with the print of the Bráhman's foot, when the Lord—says Tulsi Dás—began to handle his bow and arrows, the elephants that support the world, the tortoise, the serpent and the earth itself with its mountains and seas, all reeled.

Dohá 83.

The gods rejoiced at the sight of his splendour and rained down flowers in abundance, singing 'Glory, glory, glory to the All-merciful, the storehouse of beauty, strength and perfection.'

Chaupái.

Meanwhile the demon hosts came rolling on in infinite number. The monkey warriors at the sight advanced to meet them, like the thunder clouds gathered at the last day. Spears, lances and swords flashed again like gleams of lightning from every quarter of the heaven. The awful din of elephants, chariots and horses was like the thundering of a frightful tempest. The monkeys' huge tails as they stretched across the sky were like the uprising of a magnificent rainbow. The dust was borne aloft like a cloud, and the arrows fell like a copious shower. The mountains hurled from either side were like the crash of repeated thunderbolts. When Rama in his wrath poured forth his arrows, the demon crew were sore smitten. At the smart of his shafts the warriors screamed with pain, and everywhere reeled and fell to the ground. The rocks streamed as it were with cascades in a river of blood, the terror of cowards.

Chhand 12.

A most loathsome river of blood, striking cowards with terror, rolled on between the two armies for its banks, with chariots for sand and wheels for eddies—a frightful flood—with elephants, foot-soldiers, and horses for its aquatic birds, and vehicles of every kind, more than one could count, for its reeds and grasses; with arrows, spears and lances for its snakes, bows for its waves, and shields for its shoals of tortoises.

Dohá 84.

The fallen heroes are the trees on its bank, the marrow of their bones its scum. Cowards tremble at the sight, but the gallant are dauntless of soul.

Chaupái.

Those who bathe in it are imps, demons and goblins, monstrous ghouls and horrible vampires. Crows and vultures fly off with human arms, which they tear from one another and seize and devour. Says one 'At such a time of plenty, you wretch, is your hunger still unsatisfied?[1] Wounded warriors, fallen on the edge of the field, utter groans like the dying left half in and half out of the water.[2] Vultures sit on the bank and tear the entrails of the dead, like fishermen intent on their roads. Many bodies float down with birds upon them, as if they were boating in a river. Witches draw water in skulls; other female demons and goblins dance in the air, clashing the skulls of warriors for cymbals, while the infernal goddesses sing song after song. Herds of jackals snarl and growl and scamper about devouring till they are gorged. Thousands of headless bodies roam the plain, while the heads fallen to the ground still shout 'victory, victory.'

Chhand 13.

The heads cry 'victory, victory,' while the headless trunks rush wildly about. Swords and skulls are inextricably involved, hero against hero, fighting and overthrowing. The monkeys crushed the demon crew and triumphed

1 That you must come and steal from me instead of foraging for yourself.
2 By *arddha jal*, 'half in the water,' is meant a dying man who has been taken by his friends and laid on the very edge of the river, so that he may breathe his last in the sacred stream.

through the power of Ráma. Smitten by Ráma's arrows the leaders are conspicuous on the field of battle.

Dohá 85.

Rávan thought within himself—"The demons are routed; I am alone, the bears and monkeys are many; I must put forth all my magic power."

Chaupái.

When the gods saw that the Lord was on foot, they were exceedingly disturbed in mind, and Indra at once despatched his own chariot. Mátali brought it gladly, a splendid chariot, divine, incomparable; the king of Kosala rejoiced as he mounted it. Its four beautiful and high-mettled steeds, deathless and ever young, flew swift as thought. When they saw Raghunáth mounted on a car, the monkeys rushed forward with renewed vigour. Their onset was irresistible. Then Rávan exerted his magic power. Raghubír knew it to be a mere delusion, but Lakshman and the monkeys took it for real. They saw among the demon host many Rámas and as many Lakshmans.

Chhand 14.

Seeing these multiplied Rámas and Lakshmans, the monkeys and bears were greatly dismayed; wherever they looked, they saw him standing, as in a picture, and Lakshman with him. The Lord of Kosala smiled to see the perplexity of his troops: Hari made ready his bow and in a moment scattered the delusion; the monkey host rejoiced again.

Dohá 86.

The Ráma looked round about him and cried with a mighty voice:—"Watch now the combat between us two, for my captains are all a-wearied."

Chaupái.

So saying, Raghunáth urged forward his chariot, after bowing his head at the Bráhmans' lotus feet. Then was the king of Lanká full of fury and rushed to meet him, challenging him with a voice of thunder:—"As for the warriors you have defeated in battle, mark me, hermit, I am not like them. The glory of Rávan's name is known throughout the world, and how he cast into prison the regents of the spheres. You forsooth have slain Khara and Dúshan and Virádha and killed poor Báli, lying in ambush for him like a huntsman. You have routed the leaders of the demon host, and put to death Kumbha-karn and Meghnád. But to-day I will make an end of all this fighting ; unless, indeed, you save yourself by flight from the field. To-day, wretch, I will give you in charge to Death ; you have now to deal with the mighty Rávan." On hearing this abusive speech, the All-merciful, knowing him to be death-doomed, smiled and answered:—"True, true, I have heard all about your greatness ; but no more boasting words, let me see your strength.

Chhand 15.

Do not destroy your reputation by boasting, but pardon me if I give you a lesson. In this world there are three kinds of men, resembling respectively the dhák, the mango, and the bread-fruit tree. The one has flowers, the second flowers and fruit, and the third fruit only. The one talks ; the second talks and does ; the third does, but says not a word."

Dohá 87.

On hearing Ráma's speech, he laughed and said:— "Now you are for teaching me wisdom. You did not fear to challenge me ; but at last you begin to hold your life dear."

Chaupái.

Having uttered this taunt, Rávan in a fury began to let fly his arrows like so many thunderbolts. The shafts sped forth, of many shapes, and on all sides around the heaven and earth were filled with the cloud of them. Raghubír discharged an arrow of fire, and in a moment the demon's bolts were all consumed. He ground his teeth and hurled forth his mighty spear ; the Lord turned it with an arrow and sent it back. Then he cast against him thousands of discs and tridents ; but the Lord without an effort snapped and turned them aside. Rávan's artillery was as unavailing as are always the schemes of the wicked. Then with a hundred arrows at once he struck the charioteer, who fell to the ground, crying 'victory to Ráma.' So the Lord had compassion upon him and raised him up again : but a terrible fury then possessed him :

Chhand 16.

Full of fury and raging in the battle, Raghupati's very arrows were ready to jump out of his quiver. At the sound of the awful twang of his bow all creation was seized with terror. Mandodari's heart quaked : the sea, the great tortoise, the earth and its supporter trembled ; the elephants of the eight quarters squealed and grasped the world tight in their jaws, while the gods laughed to see the sport.

Dohá 88.

He drew the bowstring to his ear and left fly his terrible darts ; they cleft the sky, quivering like so many serpents.

Chaupái.

The arrows sped forth like winged serpents and at once laid low the charioteer and his horses, breaking the car and snapping the flagstaff. Though inwardly his courage failed him, he roared aloud and quickly mounted another car, and grinding his teeth let fly weapons and missiles of every description. But all his efforts were as fruitless as the thoughts of a man who delights only in mischief. Then Rávan hurled forth ten spears, which struck the four horses and brought them to the ground. Ráma was furious : he raised the horses and then drew his bow and let fly his arrows. The edge of Raghubír's shafts swept off Rávan's heads as though they had been lotuses. He smote each of his ten heads with ten arrows : the blood gushed forth in torrents. Streaming with gore, he rushed on in his strength ; but the Lord again fitted arrows to his bow and let fly thirty shafts ; his heads and arms all fell to the ground. Again Ráma smote away his arms and heads ; for they had grown afresh after being cut off. Time after time the Lord struck off his arms and heads, but they were no sooner smitten off than they were again renewed. Again and again the Lord shred off his heads and arms. The king of Kosala mightily diverted himself. The whole heaven was full of heads and arms, like an infinite number of Ketus and Ráhus ;[1]

Chhand 17.

As though a multitude of Ráhus and Ketus streaming with gore were rushing through the air ; for Raghubír's arrows had such force, that after hitting their mark they could not fall to the ground. Each arrow transfixing a set of heads seemed, as it flew through the sky, like a ray of the angry sun strung all over with moon troublers.[2]

Dohá 89.

As quickly as the Lord struck off his heads, they were renewed again without end ; like the passions of a man devoted to the world, which increase ever more and more.

Chaupái.

When Rávan saw this multiplication of his heads, he thought no more of death and waxed still more furious. He thundered aloud in his insance pride, and rushed forward with his ten bows all strung at once, raging wildly on the field of battle, and overwhelmed Ráma's chariot with such a shower of arrows that for a moment it was quite lost to sight, as when the sun is obscured by a mist. The gods cried 'alack, alack' ; but the Lord wrathfully grasped his bow and parrying the arrows smote off his enemy's heads, which flew in all directions, covering heaven and earth.

1 The demon Ráhu, having disguised himself as one of the gods, succeeded in securing a draught of the nectar which they had churned out of the ocean. The sun and moon, who had detected the impostor, gave information to Vishnu, who thereupon cut off the monster's head and two of his four arms. As he could not rob him of the immortality that the nectar had conferred, the severed head and tail were metamorphosed into heavenly bodies, under the names of Ráhu and Ketu, or the ascending and descending node : of which the former still wreaks vengeance on the sun and moon by now and again swallowing them.

2 *Vidhun-tuda*,—literally 'the moon-troubler,' is another name for Ráhu.

Severed as they were, they flew through the sky, uttering hideous cries of "victory, victory! where is Lakshman, where Sugríva and Angad; where Ráma the prince of Kosala?

Chhand 18.

Where now is Ráma?" cried the heads as they sped through the air. The monkeys saw and turned to flight: but the Jewel of the race of Raghu, with a smile, made ready his bow and with his arrows shot the heads through and through; as though the goddess Káli, with a rosary of skulls in her hand and accompanied by all her attendants, had bathed in the river Blood and come to worship at the shrine of Battle.

Dohá 90.

Again Rávan in his fury hurled forth his mightiest spear: like the bolt of death it flew straight for Vibhíshan.

Chaupái.

When he saw the awful spear coming, he cried 'my trust is in him who ever relieves the distress of the destitute,' and Ráma at once put Vibhíshan behind him and exposed himself to the full force of the missile. When it struck, the Lord swooned for a while, a mimicry which filled the gods with dismay. When Vibhíshan saw his lord fainting, he seized his club in his hand and rushed on in a fury:—" Ah, ill-starred wretch, fool, dull of understanding, enemy alike of gods, men, saints and Nágas; inasmuch as you devoutly offered your head to Siva, you have received a thousand for one in return. This is the only reason why as yet you have escaped; but now death is dancing on your pate. Fool, to oppose Ráma and yet hope to triumph." So saying he struck him on the chest with his club.

Chhand 19.

At the terrible stroke of the mighty club on his chest he fell to the ground; but, his ten heads all streaming with blood, he again picked himself up and came on full of fury. The two closed with all their might in savage wrestle;

each mauling the other : but Vibhíshan was inspired with the strength of Ráma, and fell upon him as though he were of no account whatever.

Dohá 91.

O Umá, Vibhíshan would not have dared of himself to look Rávan in the face ; but now in the might of Ráma he closed with him like very death.

Chaupái.

But Hanumán saw that Vibhíshan was sorely exhausted and rushed forward with a rock in his hand, with which he crushed chariot, horses and driver, and gave the demon himself a kick in the ribs. He stood erect but trembled all over, and Vibhíshan escaped into the presence of the Saviour of the world. Then Rávan fell upon the monkey, who spread his tail and flew into the air. He laid hold of the tail and so was borne aloft with the monkey, the mighty Hanumán, who again turned and closed with him. The well-matched pair continued fighting overhead, each furiously bruising the other, and putting forth all his strength and skill ; as though mounts Anjan and Sumeru had come into collision in the heaven. The demon was so astute that there was no throwing him, till the Lord came to the support of the Son of the Wind.

Chhand 20.

Supported by Raghubír, the valiant monkey struck Rávan a violent blow. He fell to the ground, but rose again to fight, so that the gods shouted 'victory' to both. Seeing Hanumán in such a strait, the monkeys and bears advanced in furious passion : but Rávan, battle-mad, crushed all their stoutest champions with the might of his terrible arm.

Dohá 92.

Rallied by Raghubír, the bold monkeys came on again. Seeing them to be so strong, he had recourse to magic.

Chaupái.

In a moment he became invisible and then again showed

himself in a multitude of forms. Every bear and monkey in Ráma's army saw a separate Rávan confronting him. At the sight of such an infinity of Rávans, the bears and monkeys fled in all directions. Not one of them had the courage to stay, but all fled crying 'Help, Lakshman ; help, Raghubír'. Myriads of Rávans pursued them on every side, thundering aloud with hoarse and terrible cries. The gods were all panic-stricken and betook themselves to flight saying:—"Now, brother, abandon all hope of victory. A single Rávan subdued the heavenly host, andn ow there are many of them—make for the caves in the mountain." Only Bráhma and Sambhu and the wisest of the saints stood fast, who had some understanding of their lord's might.

Chhand 21.

They who understood his power remained fearless; but the monkeys took the apparitions for real enemies and fled, monkeys and bears alike, crying in their terror 'Help, god of mercy.' Only Hanumán, Angad, Níla and Nala, the leaders of the host, fought bravely on against the delusive growth of giants and crushed thousands upon thousands of Rávans.

Dohá 93.

The king of Kosala smiled to see the panic of the gods and monkeys, and stringing his bow dispersed with a single arrow the whole host of Rávans.

Chaupái.

In a moment the Lord dispersed the whole phantom scene, as when the darkness is scattered at the rising of the sun. Seeing only one Rávan, the gods turned again with joy and showered down many flowers upon the Lord. Ráma then raised his arms aloft and rallied the monkeys, who turned again, each shouting to his neighbour. Inspired by the might of their lord, the bears and monkeys went forth, and with renewed vigour re-entered the arena. When Rávan saw the gods exulting, he muttered:—"They think I am now reduced to one; fools, you have ever been my prey." So saying, he made a savage spring into the air, and as the gods fled screaming, he cried—'Wretches, whither can you go from my presence?' Seeing their dismay, Angad rushed forward and with a bound seized him by the foot and threw him to the ground.

Chhand 22.

Having seized and hurled him to the ground, the son of Báli gave him a kick and then rejoined his lord. The Ten-headed, on recovering himself, rose again and shouted terribly with a voice of thunder. Proudly he strung his bow, and fitting ten arrows to the string, he let fly many volleys, wounding all his enemies: at the sight of their confusion he gloried in his might.

Dohá 94.

Then Raghupati cut off Rávan's heads and arms, his arrows also and his bow; but they all sprouted again, like sins committed at a holy place.

Chaupái.

Seeing the multiplication of their enemy's heads and arms, the bears and monkeys were mightily indignant and rushed on in a fury, crying—"Will the wretch never die, with his heads and arms all cut off?" The son of Báli, with Hanumán, Nala and Níla, the monkey king Sugríva and the valiant Dwivid, hurled upon him trees and mountains; but he caught each mountain and tree and threw them back upon the monkeys. One tore the enemy's body with his claws, another would run past and kick him. But Nala and Níla clambered up on to his heads and set to tearing his face with their talons. When he saw the blood, he was sore troubled in soul and put up his arms to catch them; but they were not to be caught and sprang about over his hands, like two bees over a bed of lotuses. At last with a savage bound he clutched them both and dashed them to the ground, twisting and breaking their arms. Then in his fury he took his ten bows in his hands and with his arrows smote and wounded the monkeys, so that Hanumán and all were rendered senseless. The approach of night had invigorated him. Seeing all the monkey chiefs in a swoon, the valiant Jámbaván rushed forward, and with him the bears, armed with mountains and trees, which they began hurling upon him. The mighty Rávan was enraged, and many of the heroes he seized by the leg and dashed to the ground. Their king was wroth to see such havoc among his troops and gave him a savage kick on the breast.

Chhand 23.

The blow smote him so heavily on the breast that he fell fainting from his chariot to the ground, grasping a bear in each of his twenty hands, like bees hiding by night in the folds of the lotus. Seeing him senseless, the king of the bears again struck him with his foot and then rejoined the Lord As night had now come, the charioteer lifted Rávan on to the car and made off as best he could.

Dohá 95.

On recovering from their swoon, the bears and monkeys all appeared before Ráma; while all the demons crowded round Rávan in the utmost consternation.

Chaupái.

During the night Trijatá went to Síta and told her the whole story. When Síta heard of the multiplication of the enemy's heads and arms, she was sorely dismayed and thus addressed Trijatá, with downcast face and much anxiety of soul:—"Why do you not tell me, mother, what is to be done, and how this plague of the universe can be put to death? He will not die even though Raghupati's arrows have shorn off his heads; of a truth, God is making everything turn out perversely. It must be my ill-luck which gives him life; for I too survive, though separated from Ráma's lotus feet. The same fate that created the false phantom of the golden deer is still cruel to me. The god that enables me to support such insupportable anguish; which made me speak crossly to Lakshman; which keeps me alive under such pain, pierced through and through as

I am with the poisoned arrows of Ráma's loss, arrows with which Love has smitten me: it is this god, I swear, that keeps him alive." With many such words did Jánaki make piteous lamentation, as she re-called to mind the All-merciful. Trijatá replied :—"Hearken, royal maid, the enemy of the gods will die if an arrow strike him in the breast. But the Lord will not smite him there, because the image of Síta is imprinted on his heart.

Chhand 24.

Jánaki dwells in his heart and in Jánaki's heart is my home; in my heart are all the spheres of creation; if an arrow lodge there all will be undone." On hearing this explanation, she was somewhat comforted; but seeing her still uneasy in mind, Trijatá continued :—"Now this is the way the monster will be killed; hearken, fair lady, and cease to be so greatly disquieted.

Dohá 96.

In the pain of having his heads cut off your image will be forgotten and the sagacious Ráma will then smite him in the heart."

Chaupái.

With such words, having done all she could to comfort her, Trijatà returned home again But Síta, reflecting on Ráma's amiability, was a prey to all the anguish of bereavement and broke out into reproaches of the night and the moon :—"The night will never be spent, though it has seemed already an age long." In her heart of hearts she made sore lamentation, sorrowing for Ráma's loss. When the pangs of bereavement were at their very height, her left eye and arm throbbed. Considering this to be a good omen, she took courage :—'I shall now see again the gracious Raghubír.' Meanwhile Rávan had woke at midnight and began abusing his charioteer :—"Fool, to bring me away from the field of battle; a curse on you for a vile dullard." He laid hold of his feet and deprecated his wrath; and he, as soon as it was dawn, mounted his chariot and sallied forth again. When they heard of Rávan's approach, the monkey army was greatly excited, and tearing up mountains and trees on every side the terrible warriors rushed to the onset, gnashing their teeth.

Chhand 25.

The huge monkeys and terrible bears rushed on, with mountains in their hands, which they hurled forth with the utmost fury; the demons turned and fled. When they had thus scattered the ranks, the valiant monkeys next closed around Rávan, buffetting him on every side and tearing him with their claws, so that his whole body was mangled.

Dohá 97.

Seeing the monkeys so powerful, Rávan took thought, and in a moment became invisible and created a magic illusion.

Chhand Tomara.

By the magic that he wrought terrible beings were manifested; imps, demons and goblins with bows and arrows in their hands, witches clutching swords and in one hand a human skull, from which they quaff draughts of blood, dancing and singing many a song. Their horrible cries of 'seize and kill' echo all around, while dogs with open mouth[1] run to and fro. Then began the monkeys to flee; but wherever they turn in flight, they see a blazing fire. Monkeys and bears were both in dismay. Then there fell upon them a shower of sand. They were routed on all sides and the Ten-headed roared again Lakshman, they monkey-king and all tho chiefs were at their wits' end. The bravest of them wrung their hands, crying 'alas, Ráma, alas, Raghunáth.' After crushing all their might in this fashion, he next practised another kind of magic. A host of Hanumáns were manifested, who rushed forward with rocks in their hands and encircled Ráma in a dense

1 For *mukh báyá*, 'with open mouth,' some books read *makh báyá*, which would mean 'having scattered the sacrifice.' As no sacrifice has been mentioned, the former seems preferable: though the latter may also be understood as a general image of horror.

mass on every side. With gnashing teeth and up-turned tail, they shouted 'kill, hold fast, never let him go'; their tails making a complete circle all around with the king of Kosala in the midst.

Chhand 27-28.

In their midst the dark-hued king of Kosala shone forth as resplendent in beauty as a lofty *tamál* tree encircled by a hedge of gleaming rainbows. As they gazed upon the Lord, the heart of the gods was moved with mingled joy and grief, while they raised the cry of 'victory, victory.' In a moment and with a single arrow Raghubìr indignantly dispelled the delusion. As the phantoms vanished, the monkeys and bears rejoiced and all turned again, with trees and rocks in their hands. Ráma shot forth a flight of arrows and Rávan's heads and arms again fell to the ground Though a hundred Seshnágs' Sáradas and Vedic bards were to spend many ages in singing the various achievements of Ráma in his battle with Rávan, they would never come to the end of them.

Dohá 98.

Tulsi Dás, poor clown, who would tell even the least part of his glory, is like a gnat who thinks himself strong enough to fly up into heaven. Though his heads and arms were cut off again and again, the mighty king of Lanká was not killed. Sages, saints and gods were confounded by the agonizing sight, the pastime of their lord.

Chaupái.

No sooner were his heads cut off than a fresh crop grew, like covetousness increased by gain.[1] For all his toil the monster died not and Ráma then turned and looked at Vibhíshan. O Umá, the lord, whom fate and death obey, thus tested the devotion of one of his creatures. "Hearken, omniscient sovereign of all things animate and inanimate, defender of the suppliant, delight of gods and saints, it is

1 In a covetous man no sooner is one desire cut off or satisfied than other desires spring up to take its place.

only, sire, by virtue of the nectar that abides in the depth of his navel that Rávan lives." On hearing Vibhíshan's speech the All-merciful was pleased and took his terrible arrows in his hand. Many omens of ill then began to present themselves: asses, jackals and packs of dogs set up a howling; birds screamed over the distress of the world and comets appeared in every quarter of the Heaven; fierce flames broke out on every side, and though there was no new moon, the sun was eclipsed. Mandodari's heart beat wildly and statues flowed with tears from their eyes.

Chhand 29.

Statues wept, thunder crashed in the air, a mighty wind blew, the earth quaked, the clouds dropt blood, hair and dust: who could recount all the portents? At the sight of such unspeakable confusion the gods of heaven in dismay uttered prayers for victory. Perceiving their distress, the merciful Raghupati set arrows to his bow;

Dohá 99.

and drawing the string to his ear he let fly at once thirty-one shafts. The bolts of Raghu-náyak flew forth like the serpents of death.

Chaupái.

One arrow dried up the depth of his navel, the others struck off his heads and arms, and with such violence that they carried heads and arms away with them. The headless and armless trunk still danced upon the plain. The earth sunk beneath the weight of the body as it rushed wildly on, till the Lord with his arrows smote it in twain. At the moment of death he thundered aloud with a fierce and terrible yell: 'Where is Ráma, that I may challenge and slay him?' The earth reeled as Rávan fell; the sea, the rivers, the elephants of the eight quarters and the mountains were shaken. The two halves lay full length upon the ground, thronged by a crowd of bears and monkeys. But the arrows deposited the heads and arms, before Mandodari and then returned to the lord of the universe and dropped again into the quiver. Seeing this, the gods sounded their kettle-drums. His soul entered the Lord's mouth ; Siva and Bráhma rejoiced to see the sight. The whole universe resounded with cries of "victory, victory : glory to Raghubír, the mighty of arm ; glory to the All-merciful : glory to Mukunda ; " while throngs of gods and saints rained down flowers.

Chhand 30 - 31.

" Glory to Mukunda, the fountain of mercy, the subduer of rebellion, our refuge, our health-giving lord ; the scatterer of the ranks of the impious, the great First Cause, the compassionate, the ever Supreme." All the gods in their joy showered down flowers and the kettle-drums sounded aloud, while on the field of battle Rama's every limb displayed the beauty of a myriad Loves. The crown on his coil of hair all besprinkled with blossoms emitted rays of splendour like flashes of lightning gleaming amidst the star-lit peaks of a dark mountain. With bow and arrows brandished in his arms, his body, spangled with specks of blood, seemed like a swarm of spotted amadavads joyously perched on a tamál tree.

Dohá 100.

With a shower of gracious glances the Lord dispelled the fears of all the gods ; and bears and monkeys shouted in their joy ' glory to Mukunda, the abode of bliss.'

Chaupái.

When Mandodari saw her lord's heads, she fainted in her grief and fell to the ground. Her bevy of weeping maidens sprang up in haste and supported her and brought her to Rávan's body When she saw her lord's condition she set up a shriek, her hair flew loose, and there was no strength left in her body Wildly beating her bosom and weeping, she recounted all his glory : -- " At your might, my lord, the earth ever trembled ; fire, moon, and sun were bereft of splendour. The great serpent and tortoise could not bear the weight of your body, which now lies on the ground, a mere heap of ashes. Varuna, Kuver, Indra, and the Wind-god had never the courage to face you in battle. By the might of your arm, O my lord, you conquered death and fate; but to-day you have fallen like the poorest creature. Your magnificence was renowned throughout the world; while the strength of your son and your kinsmen surpassed description. But you withstood Ráma and this is now your condition; not one of your stock is left even to make lamentation. The whole sphere of creation was in your power, my lord, and the frighted regents of the eight quarters ever bowed their heads before you; but now jackals devour your heads and arms; and rightly so, seeing that you opposed Ráma. Death-doomed, my lord, you heeded not my words, and took the sovereign of all things animate and inanimate for a mere man.

Chhand 32.

"You took for a man, Hari, the self-existent, that fire to consume the forest of devildom; and you worshipped not, O my spouse, the All-merciful, to whom Siva and Bráhma and all the gods do reverence. From your birth you have delighted to injure others, and this your body has been a very sink of sin, and yet Ráma has now raised you to his own abode: I bow before the blameless God.

Dohá 101.

"Ah my lord, there is none other so gracious at Raghunáth, the great God, who has given you a rank, to which the company of saints can with difficulty attain."

Chaupái.

When they heard Mandodari's speech, gods, saints and sages were all enraptured. Bráhma, Siva, Nárad, Sanatkumára and all the great seers who have preached the way of salvation, gazed upon Raghupati with eyes full of tears and were overwhelmed with devotion. Seeing all the women making lamentation, Vibhíshan went to the spot, his heart heavy with grief, and was sorely pained to see his brother's condition. Then the Lord gave an order to

Lakshman, who did all that he could to console him. At last Vibhíshan betook himself to the Lord, who looked upon him with an eye of compassion and said 'Make an end of sorrow and perform the funeral rites.' In obedience to his command he celebrated the obsequies, wisely bearing in mind the circumstances of time and place.

Dohá 102.

Mandodari and the others presented the dead with the prescribed handfuls of sesamum seed and the queen then returned to the palace, recounting to herself all Raghupati's excellences.

Chaupái.

Again Vibhíshan came and bowed his head. Then the All-merciful called his younger brother and said, " Do you and the monkey prince and Angad and Nala and Níla, with Jámbaván and the sagacious Son of the Wind, go all together in company with Vibhíshan and make the arrangements for his coronation ; " thus cried Raghunáth ; " I by reason of my father's commands may not enter the city, but I send the monkey and my younger brother to take my place " The monkey started at once, on receiving his lord's order, and went and made ready for the installation. With due reverence they seated him on the throne, and after marking his forehead with the royal sign, they sang a hymn of praise and with clasped hands all bowed the head before him. Then with Vibhíshan they returned to the Lord, and Raghubír addressed the monkeys with such gracious words as made them all glad.

Chhand 33.

He made them glad with words that were sweet as nectar:—" It is by your might that the enemy has been defeated and that Vibhíshan has acquired the kingdom ; your glory will live for ever throughout the universe. Whoever with sincere devotion shall sing your glorious deeds in connection with me shall cross without an effort the boundless ocean of existence."

Dohá 103.

The monkey host would never have been tired of listening to their lord's words; again and again they all bowed the head and clasped his lotus feet.

Chaupái.

The Lord next addressed Hanumán. "Go to Lanka," said the god, "and tell Jánaki the news and bring me back word of her welfare." When Hanumán entered the city, the demons and demonesses no sooner heard of it than they ran to meet him and showed him every possible honour and pointed out Síta to him. From afar off the monkey prostrated himself. She recognized Ráma's messenger. "Tell me, friend, of my gracious lord, and of his brother; is he well, and all the monkey host?" "All is well, madam, with the king of Kosala; he has conquered Rávan in battle; Vibhíshan has been placed in secure possession of the throne." On hearing the monkey's reply, joy was diffused over her soul.

Chhand 34.

Síta's soul was overjoyed, her body thrilled and her eyes streamed with tears, as again and again she cried:— "What can I give you, monkey? there is nothing in the three spheres of creation to be compared to your tidings." "Hearken, madam; to-day of a truth I have already obtained the undisputed sovereignty of the world, when I see and adore Ráma with his brother triumphing over the ranks of the enemy."

Dohá 104.

"Hearken, my son Hanumán; every virtue finds a home in your heart: may you live and prosper for ever in the service of Kosala's king.

Chaupái.

But now, friend, devise some plan by which I may see with my own eyes his dark but comely form." Hanumán then returned to Ráma and told him of Síta's welfare. When the Glory of the solar race heard her message, he said to prince Vibhíshan :—" Go you with Hanumán and respectfully escort Síta here." They all went at once to the place where Síta was. The demon ladies humbly do her service and, being sharply ordered by Vibhíshan attend her to the bath with all formality and adorn her with ornaments of every description. Then they make ready and bring up a handsome palanquin, which she mounted with joy, thinking ever of Ráma with the deepest affection. On all four sides were guards, with staves in their hands, who marched with the greatest gladness of soul. The bears and monkeys all came to look, but the guards in a fury rushed to keep them back. Said Raghubir—" Attend to what I say; bring Síta on foot, friend ; let the monkeys see her as they would their own mother." Thus said the great Raghunáth and smiled. The bears and monkeys were delighted to hear his commands, and from heaven the gods rained down a profusion of flowers. To begin with, he placed Síta in the fire, for he wished the internal witness to be revealed.[1]

Dohá 105.

For this reason the All-merciful spoke with seeming harshness. All the demonesses, when they heard it, began to make lamentation.

Chaupái.

But Síta bowed to her lord's command—pure as she was in thought, word and deed—and said " Lakshman, be you the celebrant of this rite; show me the fire and be quick." When Lakshman heard Síta's words, so full of detachment, discretion and piety, his eyes filled with tears and he clasped his hands in prayer but could not speak a word to his lord. Seeing that Ráma was displeased, he ran and kindled a fire with a quantity of wood that he brought. Síta beheld the fierceness of the flame, but was glad of heart

1 The meaning of the words *Antara Sákhi*, the internal witness, or witness of the soul, would not be very obvious without a reference to the Sanskrit text, in which Síta makes her prayer to the Fire-god, addressing him thus: " Thou, O Fire, knowest the secrets of the hearts (*sarirantara gocharah*) of all living creatures; be thou my witness (*sákshi*); assume a visible form and save me, O best of gods."

without a particle of fear. "If neither in thought, word or deed I have ever abandoned Ráma or cherished any other, may the fire, which tests all men's actions, become as cooling as sandal-wood."

Chhand 35.

The flame was cool as sandal-wood, as Síta entered it, meditating on her lord:—"Glory to the king of Kosala, for whose feet, ever worshipped by Siva, I cherish the purest devotion." Her shadow and the stain of social disgrace were alone consumed in the blazing fire. Such an action on the part of the Lord had never been seen before: gods, saints and sages all stood at gaze. The Fire assumed a bodily form and took her by the hand and led and presented her to Ráma, the very Lakshmi celebrated alike in the Vedas and the world, who erst arose as Indirá from the sea of milk. Resplendent with exquisite beauty she shines forth as the left side of Ráma's body, like the blossom of a golden lily beside a fresh blue lotus.

Dohá 106.

The gods in their delight rain down flowers and make music in the air, while the Kinnaras sing and the nymphs of heaven dance, all mounted on their chariots. The beauty of Janak's daughter reunited to her lord was beyond all measure and bound; the bears and monkeys, in rapture at the sight, shouted 'glory to Ráma the beneficent.'

Chaupái.

Then came Mátali, having obtained Ráma's permission, and bowed his head at his feet. The gods, too, selfish as ever, came and made this seemingly pious prayer:—"Friend of the destitute, gracious Raghurái, a god yourself, you have shown mercy to the gods. This sensual wretch, who delighted to harass the whole world, has perished by his own wickedness in his sinful course. You are the supreme spirit, one and everlasting, ever unchangeable and unaffected by circumstances, without parts or qualities, uncreated, sinless, all perfect, invincible, unerring, full of power and compassion: incarnate as the fish, the tortoise, the boar, the lion-man, and the dwarf; as Parasu-rám also and now as Ráma; whenever, O lord, the gods have been in trouble, you have taken birth in one form or another to put an end to it: but this impure wretch, the persistent plague of heaven, given up to sensuality, greed, pride and passion, this monster of monsters, has been promoted to your sphere and thereat we marvel greatly. We gods are high masters, but in our selfishness we have forgotten the worship of our lord, and thus we are ever involved in the flood of worldly passions; but now, O lord, have mercy upon us, for we come to you for refuge."

Dohá 107.

With clasped hands the gods and saints stood all round about him, thus making supplication; and—his whole body quivering with excess of devotion—Bráhma at last broke out into this hymn of praise.

Chaupái.

"Glory to the immortal Ráma, the blissful Hari, the prince of Raghu's line, with his bow and arrows; the lionlike lord to rend in pieces the elephant of earthly existence; the ocean of perfection, the all-wise, the all-pervading; in whose body is concentrated the incomparable beauty of a myriad Loves; whose virtues are sung by bards, saints and sages. Hero of spotless renown, who in thy wrath didst seize Rávan, as Garúr might seize some monstrous serpent; delight of mankind; destroyer of grief and fear; ever unmoved by passion; lord of supreme intelligence; beneficent incarnation of illimitable perfection; loosener of earth's burdens; very wisdom; everlasting, all-pervading, ever one, without beginning; I rapturously adore thee, O Ráma, fountain of mercy. Glory of the line of Raghu, slaying Dúshan and making a king of the ever faithful Vibhíshan: storehouse of virtue and wisdom; incomprehensible and from everlasting; I constantly adore thee, O Ráma, the passionless, the supreme. Mighty of arm, strong in renown, exterminator of the hordes of the sinful; pre-eminent in auspiciousness; friend and protector even of the undeserving suppliant; I worship the perfection of beauty, the spouse of Lakshmi. Deliverer from the burden of mortality, extern to cause and effect, soul-created destroyer of hideous sin; wielder of the arrows and bow and lovely quiver; lotus-eyed paragon of kings; temple of bliss, Lakshmi's beautiful consort; subduer of pride, lust, lying and selfishnes; irreproachable, imperishable, transcendent; all forms alike and yet no determinate form; like the light of the sun—thus the Vedas have declared,[1] it is no mere quibble of speech—which is separate from it and yet not separate. How fortunate, my lord, are all these monkeys who reverently gaze upon thy face. A curse, Hari, on the life we gods enjoy; without devotion to you we have all gone astray in the world. Now, as thou art compassionate to the suppliant, have compassion upon me; a lion to destroy the elephant-like inconstancy of my purpose; may I practise the reverse of my former way and live happy, esteeming that a happiness which was before a pain. Mercy, destroyer of the wicked, beautiful jewel, whose lotus feet are cherished by Sambhu and Umá. O king of kings, grant me this boon, the blessing of a constant devotion to thy lotus feet."

Dohá 108.

As Bráhma made this prayer, his whole body quivered with excess of devotion, and his eyes beholding the ocean of beauty refused to be satisfied.

Chaupái.

Then too came Dasarath and, when he beheld his son, his eyes were flooded with tears. The Lord and his

---

1 *Nadanti* may be taken as the third person plural of the present tence of the verb *nad*, 'to declare,' like *vadanti* from *vad* and Ràm Jasan, from the way that he has divided the words in the text, evidently so regarded it. But perhaps it is better to divide thus, *na dánti-katha*, instead of *nadanti kathá*; 'danti-katha' being a common colloquial expression for a verbal quibble, or an argument unsupported by authority.

brother made obeisance before him and their father gave them his blessing. "It is all due, sire, to your religious merit that the invincible demon king has been conquered." On hearing his son's words, his affection increased still more ; his eyes streamed and every hair on his body stood erect. Seeing his father thus overcome by love, Raghupati, after first taking thought, bestowed upon him absolute wisdom. He did not receive the boon of deliverance from existence, Umá, for this reason, that Dasarath has grasped the mystery of faith. Worshippers of the incarnate are not rewarded with annihilation, but Ráma gives them devotion to himself. Having again and again prostrated himself before the Lord, Dasarath proceeded with joy to his abode in heaven.

Dohá 109.

The Lord, the king of Kosala, rejoiced together with his brother and Jánaki. At the charming sight the king of the gods in his delight chanted this hymn of praise.

Chhand Tomar[1] 37.

"Glory to Ráma, the home of beauty, the merciful, the refuge of the suppliant; equipt with quiver and bow and arrows, triumphing in his mighty strength of arm. Glory to the foe of Dúshan, the foe of Khara, the destroyer of the demon host ; when my lord slew this last monster all the gods were happy again. Glory to the remover of earth's burdens, whose greatness is indeed vast and unbounded. Glory to Rávan's merciful foe, the discomforter of the demons. Outrageous was the pride of the king of Lanká, who had reduced to subjection gods and gandharvas ; who relentlessly pursued saints and sages, men, birds and serpents ; a malignant and implacable monster ; but who now—the wretch—has obtained his reward. Hearken now, protector of the suppliant, with the large lotus eyes ; my pride was inordinate, there was no one to equal me. Now after

1 In the Tomar metre each line of the quatrain should consist of an anapæst followed by two amphibrachs ; but many licenses are allowed.

seeing thy lotus feet, the arrogance that caused me so much misery has passed away. Let others adore the unembodied Supreme, the primary existence, whom the Vedas hymn; but my desire is the king of Kosala, the divine Ráma, visible and material. Together with Síta and Lakshmán, make my heart thy abode. O spouse of Lakshmi, recognize me as thy servant, and grant me faith.

Chhand 38.

Grant me faith, O spouse of Lakshmi, soother of terror, consoler of the suppliant. Thee I adore, O blissful Ráma, prince of the house of Raghu, beautiful as a myriad Loves. Delight of the hosts of heaven, queller of strife; in form as a man of incomparable strength; object of the adoration of Bráhma, Sankara and all the gods; I worship thee, O Ráma, the gracious, the benign.

Dohá 110.

Now in thy mercy, O most merciful, look upon me and direct me what to do." On hearing this tender appeal the Protector of the poor made answer :—

Chaupái.

"Hearken, king of the gods; my bears and monkeys, who lie on the ground slain by the demons, have lost their life on my account: restore them all to life, wise king of heaven." Hearken, Garúr, this request of the Lord's is a mystery that only the greatest sages can apprehend. The Lord could himself destroy and re-create the three spheres of creation; only he wished to do Indra honour. With a shower of ambrosia he restored the bears and monkeys to life. They arose with joy and all betook them to the Lord. The shower of ambrosia fell on both armies; but the bears and monkeys came to life, not the demons. The image of Ráma was imprest upon the demons' soul; thus they were loosed from the fetters of existence and became absorbed in the divinity. The bears and monkeys were partial incarnations of the gods and were really all alive; but it was the will of Raghupati. Who is there so kind to the destitute as Ráma, who granted final deliverance even to the host of demons, while that filthy and sensual monster Rávan obtained translation to the same sphere as the holiest of saints.

Dohá 111.

After showering down flowers, the gods mounted their splendid chariots and withdrew. Then seeing his opportunity the sagacious Sambhu drew near to Ráma Most lovingly, with clasped hands, his lotus eyes full of tears and his body quivering all over, Tripurári uttered this prayer with chocking voice :—

Chhand 39.

"Save me, O prince of the house of Raghu, equipt with thy strong bow and graceful arrows in thy hand; dispeller of the murky clouds of delusion ; fire to consume the forest of doubt ; delight of the gods ; unembodied yet embodied ; glorious shrine of perfection ; sun of vehement splendour to disperse the darkness of error ; a very lion to attack the elephantine monsters, lust, anger and pride ; take up thy abode for ever, as in some forest, in the heart of thy servant. Stern frost for the lotus growth of sensual desires ; gracious beyond all conception ; a mount Meru to churn up the ocean of life ; dweller of the highest sphere; avert from me the stormy waves of the world or transport me across them. O king Ráma, dark-hued and lotus eyed, protector of the poor, soother of the sorrows of the distrest, dwell for ever in my heart with Lakshman and Jánaki, delight of the saints, glory of the terrestrial sphere, uprooter of every terror, Tulsi Das's own lord.

Dohá 112.

When your coronation, O my lord, takes place at Kosala, I will come to see the glorious ceremony, O greatly compassionate."

Chaupái.

When Sambhu had finished his prayer and gone away, then

Vibhíshan approached the Lord. Bowing his head at his feet he cried in pleading tones :--" Hearken to my prayer, O lord, with bow in hand. You have slain Rávan with all his kindred and all his army and made your unsullied glory known throughout the three spheres. On me, your vile servant, without either sense or breeding, you have in every way shown compassion ; now, sire, honour your servant's house and bathe and refresh yourself after the toil of the battle. Inspect my treasure, my palace, and my wealth, and by this condescension make all the monkeys happy. Consider, my lord, everything that I have as your own, and moreover take me with you to Avadh." When the All-merciful heard this affecting speech, both his great eyes filled with tears.

Dohá 113.

" Hearken, brother; all you say is true ; your house and treasure are as my own ; but thinking of Bharat's condition every minute seems to me an age. In penitential attire, with emaciated body, he is ever repeating my name in prayer. I entreat you, friend, to make an effort so that I may soon be able to see him again. If at the end of my time I go and find him no longer alive "—at the remembrance of his brother's affection, the Lord's body quivered all over—" but may you reign for ages, your soul ever mindful of me, and at the last enter into my sphere, where all the good go."

Chaupái.

When Vibhíshan heard Ráma's words, he was overjoyed and clasped the feet of the All-merciful. All the bears and monkeys with equal joy clasped the Lord's feet and recited his glorious merits. Then Vibhíshan proceeded to the palace and loaded the chariot with jewels and attire. When he had brought the car Pushpaka and set it before the Lord, the All-merciful smiled and said :—" Hearken, friend Vibhíshan ; step into the car, and when you have risen high into the air, throw down the dresses and jewels." Accordingly Vibhíshan mounted aloft into the heaven and scrambled the raiment and jewels among them all. The monkeys picked up anything they fancied, cramming the precious things into their mouth: while Ráma and his wife and brother laughed ; so full of playfulness is the All-merciful.

Dohá 114.

He, to whom the saints cannot attain by contemplation, whom the Veda itself fails to fathom, even he in his infinite compassion made merry with the monkeys. O Umá, abstraction, prayer, charity, penance, the different forms of fasting, sacrifice and vows,—all move Ráma's compassion less than simple love.

Chaupái.

After securing the dresses and ornaments, the bears and monkeys clothed themselves with them and appeared before Ráma. The king of Kosala laughed again and again to see the monkeys in their motley attire. As he looked upon them all, he was moved with pity, and said in gracious phrase: " It is by your assistance that I have killed Rávan and thus secured the throne for Vibhíshan. Now return all of you to your several homes ; remember me and fear no one." On hearing these words the monkeys were overcome with affection, and all with clasped hands thus reverently addressed him :—" What you say, my lord, is all to your honour ; but we are confused on hearing such words. Knowing the low estate of us monkeys, you gave us a leader : you, O Raghunáth, are the sovereign of the universe. When we hear our lord's words we die of shame : is it possible for a gnat to assist the mighty Garúr ?" The monkeys were so charmed as they gazed on Ráma's face that in the depth of their devotion they had no desire for their own home.

Dohá 115.

When the Lord had dismissed them, the bears and monkeys all went their way, cherishing Ráma's image in their heart, exulting with joy and making frequent prayer. The monkey king, Níla, the king of the bears, Angad, Nala, Hanumán, Vibhíshan also and all the other valiant monkey chiefs were so overcome by their feelings that they could not speak a word, while their eyes, streaming with tears, were fixed upon Ráma's person so intently that they had no time to wink.

Chaupái.

When Ráma perceived the strength of their affection, he took them all up into his chariot and, after mentally bowing his head at the Brahmans' feet, he directed the car towards the north. A tumultuous noise accompanied the car on its way, all shouting 'glory to Raghubír!' The throne on which the Lord and his consort were seated was very lofty and magnificent; there Ráma and his bride shone resplendent, like a dark cloud on the peak of Sumeru with attendant lightning. The beauteous car sped swiftly on its way, while the gods in their joy rained down showers of flowers. A delightful breeze breathed soft, cool and fragrant; the water of the sea and the Ganges was without a speck; omens of good fortune occurred on every side: the heart was glad and all the expanse[1] of ether clear. Said Raghubír:—"See, Síta, the field of battle; here Lakshman slew Megh-nád; here the huge demons that strew the plain were slaughtered by Angad and Hanumán; here fell the two brothers Kumbha-karn and Rávan, that plague of gods and saints.

Dohá 116.

Here the bridge was built and the symbol of the blessed Mahádeva adored:" the All-merciful and Síta here both

1 *Asa* here is not the common word *ása*, hope (from *á-sans*), but is derived from the root *as* and has the meaning of 'space, region, expanse.'

made obeisance to Sambhu. Every place in the forest wherever the gracious god had taken up his abode or rested, he pointed out to Janaki and told her the names of them all.

Chaupái.

Forthwith the chariot arrived at the charming Dandaka forest, and Ráma visited the hermitage both of Agastya and all the other great saints. After receiving the blessing of all the holy men, the Lord of the world came to Chitrakút. After gratifying the hermits there, the chariot again sped swiftly on. Ráma next pointed out to Síta the noble Jamuná, that washes away all the impurities of this sinful age. After this he espied the holy Ganges and said, "Síta, do it homage. See also the queen of all holy places, Prayág, the sight of which puts away all the sins committed in a thousand births. See again the most holy Tribeni, the antidote of sorrow, the ladder of heaven. See also the sacred city of Avadh, which heals all the three kinds of pain and every disease in life."

Dohá 117

The gracious god and Síta both did reverence to Avadh. With streaming eyes quivering limbs Ráma's joy was unbounded. Then went the Lord and with much delight bathed at Tribeni and bestowed gifts of all kinds on the Bráhmans and on the monkeys also.

Chaupái.

The Lord then spoke and enjoined Hanumán :—"Take the form of a young Bráhman and go into the city. Tell Bharat of my welfare, and come back here yourself with the news." The Son of the Wind was off at once. Then the Lord visited Bharadvája. The saint received him with all possible honour and after hymning his praises, gave him his blessing. The Lord prostrated himself at his feet, with his hands clasped in prayer, and then mounted his chariot and went on again. When the Nishád heard that the Lord had come, he cried 'a boat, a boat,' and summoned his people. The chariot crossed the sacred stream and then stopt on the bank, obedient to the Lord's command. Then Síta worshipped the divine Ganges and again and again threw herself at its feet. In gladness of soul the Ganges gave her this blessing:—"Fair lady, may your happiness be without a break." On hearing the news, Guha ran in a transport of love and drew near, bewildered with excess of joy. At the sight of Síta and the Lord, he fell flat upon the ground quite out of his senses. When Ráma perceived the vehemence of his love, he was glad and raised him up and took him to his bosom.

Chhand 40.

The all-merciful and all-wise Ráma, the spouse of Lakshmi, took and clasped him to his heart and seated him close by his side and asked of his welfare. He was all humility:—"Now is all well with me, for I have seen thy lotus feet, the adoration of Bráhma and Sankara: O Ráma, abode of bliss, fulfiller of desire, thee, thee only do I worship." Though he was only a poor low Nishád, Hari clasped him to his bosom, as though he were Bharat himself. Dull of soul, says Tulsi Dás, is he, who is so infatuated as to forget such a lord. Gods, saints and sages sing with delight these achievements of Ravan's foe, for they have a sanctifying effect, ever inspire devotion to Ráma's feet, destroy lust and other evil passions and inculcate true wisdom.

Dohá 118.

The wise, who listen to the achievements of Ráma and his victory in the battle, God rewards for ever with victory, wisdom and renown. This sinful age is the very home of impurity; think well on it and understand that if you abandon the blessed name of Ráma, there is no other saviour.

[Thus endeth the book entitled LANKA, *the bestower of pure wisdom ; being the sixth descent into the holy lake of Ráma's deeds, that cleanses from every defilement of the world.]*

BOOK VII.

THE SEQUEL.

THE SEQUEL.

Sanskrit Invocation.

I ADORE without ceasing the glorious lord of Síta, the noblest of the sons of Raghu, even Ráma as he appeared when mounted on the car Pushpaka, bright of hue as the neck of a peacock ; marked with the print of the Bráhman's lotus foot, which declared him the greatest of the gods : all beautiful ; yellow attired ; lotus-eyed ; ever gracious ; with bow and arrows in hand ; attended by a host of monkeys and served by his brother.

Beautiful are the lotus feet of the lord of Kosala, worshipped by Bráhma and Siva, caressed by the tender hands of Janaki, ever clustered about by the beelike souls of the devout.

I worship Sankara, the annihilator of Love ; beautiful with the brightness of the jasmine, the moon and the conch-shell : the lord of Ambiká : the granter of desired success, the compassionate lotus-eyed.

Dohá 1.

There remained only one day of the appointed term ; the people of the city, men and women alike, sorely distrest in mind and wasted in body by sorrow for Rama's absence, were everywhere despondent. Auspicious omens of every kind occurred ; at once every heart was glad and the city itself brightened up all round, as if to announce the lord's coming. Kausalyá and the other royal dames were all as happy as if that minute expecting to be told 'the Lord is here, and with him Síta and Lakshman.' Bharat's right eye and arm throbbed again and again. Recognizing this as a good sign, he was glad at heart and yet began to ponder deeply.

Chaupái.

" The one day that now only remains of the fixed time is my last chance ; as I think thereon, my soul is full of anxiety. What is the reason that my lord has not returned? God saw my evil nature when he passed me over. Ah! how blessed and truly fortunate is Lakshman in his devotion to Ráma's lotus feet. The lord knew me to be false and perverse, and therefore he did not take me with him If the lord were to consider my actions, there would be no redemption for me in a hundred million of ages. But the Lord never regards offences of his servants, being a very brother to the destitute and most tender-hearted. I am firmly persuaded of soul that Ráma will come; the omens are so favourable. But if my life holds out after the term once expires, I shall be a more despicable wretch than any in the world."

Dohá 2.

While Bharat's soul was thus sinking in the sea of Ráma's bereavement, the Son of the Wind, disguised in form as a Bráhman, came like a boat to his rescue. Seeing him seated on a mat of sacred grass, with matted hair for a crown, his body all wasted away, his lips muttering the names 'Ráma, Ráma, Raghupati,' and his eyes streaming with tears:

Chaupái.

At this sight Hanumán was overjoyed, every hair on his body stood erect and his eyes rained torrents; he felt at heart an indescribable satisfaction and addressed him in words that were as ambrosia to his ear: "He, for whose loss you sorrow night and day, the catalogue of whose virtues you are incessantly reciting, the glory of the line of Raghu, the benefactor of the pious, the deliverer of gods and saints, has arrived safely. After conquering the foe in the battle, with the gods to hymn his praises, the Lord is now on his way with Síta and his brother." On hearing these words he forgot all his pain, like a man dying of thirst who finds a stream of nectar. "Who are you, Sir, and whence have you come, who have told me such glad tidings?" "I am, the son of the Wind, a monkey,

Hanumán by name, O fountain of mercy, a servant of the beneficent Raghupati." On hearing this, Bharat rose and respectfully advanced to meet him. The affection with which he embraced him was too great for heart to contain; his eyes streamed with tears and his body quivered all over. "O monkey, at the sight of you all my sorrows are gone, to-day I have embraced a friend of Ráma's." Again and again he asked of his welfare: "Hearken, brother; what is there I can give you? after taking thought, I find nothing in the whole world to match this news. Otherwise, I should be your debtor. Now tell me of my lord's adventures." Then Hanumán bowed his head at his feet and told him all Raghupati's great doings. "Tell me, monkey, did the gracious god ever remember me as one of his servants?

Chhand 1.

Did the glory of the race of Raghu ever make mention of me his servant?" On hearing Bharat's modest speech, the monkey was in a rapture and fell at his feet. How can he be otherwise than humble and holy and an ocean of virtue, whose praises Ráma, the lord of all animate and inanimate creation, himself recites with his own mouth?

Dohá 3.

"My lord, you are as dear to Ráma as his own life; that is the truth, Sir." Again and again he embraced Bharat, and his joy was more than his heart could contain.

Sorathá 1.

After bowing his head at Bharat's feet, the monkey returned in haste to Ráma and told him that all was well. Then the Lord mounted his chariot and joyfully set forth.

Chaupái.

Bharat too returned in joy to Ayodhyá and told his *guru* all the news, then published the fact in the palace, that Ráma was approaching the city and was safe and sound. At these tidings all the dowager queens started up in haste; but Bharat spoke and assured them of their lord's welfare.

When the citizens heard the news, men and women all ran out in their joy, the ladies formed in procession with stately gait, singing and bearing golden salvers laden with curds, *dub* grass, the sacred yellow pigment, fruits and flowers and fresh sprigs of the tulsi plant, all things of good omen. Each ran out just as she happened to be, without stopping to bring either children or old folk. Every one was asking his neighbour, 'Friend, have you seen the gracious Ráma?' Directly it knew the Lord was coming, the whole city of Avadh became a quarry of delights. The water of the Sarju flowed clear as clear could be; the air was deliciously soft, cool and fragrant.

Dohá 4.

Bharat went forth to meet the All-merciful, full of joy and affection, accompanied by his *guru*, the citizens, his younger brother and a throng of Bráhmans. Many of the women mounted the upper stories of the houses to look for the chariot in the sky and, when they espied it, raised their sweet voices in auspicious songs of joy. As the waves of ocean rise and swell at the sight of the full moon, so poured forth the women of the city with a tumultuous noise at the sight of Ráma.

Chaupái.

On the other hand, the Sun of the lotuses of the solar race was pointing out the beauties of the city to the monkeys; "Hearken, Sugriva, Angad and Vibhíshan: this city is so holy and the country is so charming, that although all men speak of Vaikunth, which is indeed famous in the Vedas and Puránas and celebrated throughout the world, still it is not so dear to me as the city of Avadh: only here and there one can be found to comprehend this saying. Here is the delightful city, my birth-place, and to the north the sacred Sarju, where every man that bathes obtains without further trouble a home near me. The dwellers here are very dear to me; the city makes them my fellow-citizens both here and hereafter and is altogether blessed." The monkeys rejoiced to hear the Lord's words: what a glory for Avadh to be praised by Ráma!

Dohá 5.

When the all-merciful Lord God saw all the people coming out to meet him, he urged on his chariot close up to the city and there alighted on the ground. Having dismounted, he directed Pushpaka to return to Kuver.[1] On receiving Ráma's order it went its way, full of mingled joy and sorrow at parting.

Chaupái.

With Bharat came the whole population, all emaciated in body by their mourning for Ráma. When the Lord saw Vámadeva and Vasishtha, greatest of sages, he dropt his bow and arrows on the ground and ran to clasp his *guru's* lotus feet, both he and his younger brother, with every hair on their body erect. The great sage embraced them and asked of their welfare. "By your favour all is well with us." Then the champion of the faith, the king of the Raghu race, made obeisance to all the Brahmans. Next Bharat embraced the Lord's lotus feet, ever worship by Sankara, Bráhma and all the gods and sages. He fell to the ground and refused to rise, till the All-merciful by force took and pressed him to his bosom, every hair standing erect on his dark-hued body, and his lotus eyes all streaming with tears.

Chhand 2.

His lotus eyes streamed with tears and his beauteous body quivered with emotion, as he lovingly clasped his brother to his heart, even he, the Lord the sovereign of the three spheres. There is no similitude by which I can express the beauty of the meeting between the Lord and his brother; it was as though Love and Desire in bodily form had met together in a rapturous embrace. When the All-merciful asked of his welfare, it was with difficulty

1 The car Pushpaka had originally belonged to Kuver and had been stolen from him by Rávan.

that Bharat found words to reply. Hearken, Umá; such joy can only be felt, it is beyond speech or intelligence. "Now is all well with me, O Lord of Kosala; seeing your servant's distress, you have revealed yourself to him and have taken me by the hand, O All-merciful, when I was sinking in the deep waters of bereavement."

Dohá 6.

As when a thief going gaily along the road, with stolen property still about him, is suddenly seized at the waistbelt by the man he has robbed, so felt Sugríva and Vibhíshan at the sight of the meeting between Ráma and Bharat.[1] Then the Lord smilingly embraced Satrughna and took him to his bosom, while Bharat embraced Lakshman, his heart overflowing with love.

Chaupái.

After that Satrughna and Lakshman embraced, remembering no more the intolerable sorrow of separation. Finally Bharat bowed his head at Síta's feet, both he and his younger brother, with an intensity of delight. The citizens were so glad at the sight of the Lord, that all the sorrow caused by his absence was at once forgotten. Seeing all the people so agitated by affection, the gracious Kharári practised an illusion and appearing at one and the same time in multiplied form, was thus in his benignity enabled to salute every one with due ceremony. The look of compassion, with which Raghubír regarded them, made every man and woman supremely happy. In a single moment the God embraced them all; this, Umá, is a mystery that none can comprehend. When Ráma, the perfection of amiability and every virtue, had on this manner made them all happy, he went on his way. Kausalyá and the other royal dames ran out to meet him, like a cow that has lately calved at the sight of its little one.

---

1 In the midst of their joy, the sight of such fraternal affection reminded them painfully of the very different treatment they had experienced from their own brothers, Bali and Rá-an. Or perhaps more simply, they were forced to recognize Bharat's superior claim, and knew that they would have to give up Ráma to him.

Chhand 3.

Like a cow that has been driven by force to graze in the woods, leaving its little one at home, when it draws near to the village at the close of the day, hurries on lowing and with dripping teats, so did all the matrons haste to embrace the Lord with the utmost affection, lavishing upon him every term of endearment. The cruel pangs of parting had past away and were replaced by unutterable happiness and delight.

Dohá 7.

Sumitrá embraced her son, remembering his devotion to Ráma's feet; Kaikeyi too embraced Ráma, but with a heart sadly ill at ease. Lakshman embraced the royal dames one and all and with joy received their blessing; but though he embraced Kaikeyi again and again, her anguish of soul still continued.

Chaupái.

Síta saluted each of her mothers-in-law and rejoiced greatly to kiss their feet. They asked of her welfare and invoked upon her the blessing: "May your happy wedded life last for ever." All gazed on Raghupati's lotus face and out of regard for the auspiciousness of the day checked the tears that rose in their eyes. They waved above his head their golden salvers and sacrificial lamps and again and again contemplated his divine person. They scatter all round about him every kind of offering, their heart full of supreme felicity. Time after time Kausalyá fixed her gaze on Ráma, so pitiful and so valiant, and kept pondering within herself: "How can he have killed the king of Lanká? my two boys are so daintily delicate, is it possible they can have slain the demon's doughtiest champions?"

Dohá 8.

As she looked upon the Lord and upon Lakshman and Síta, her maternal heart was overwhelmed with felicity and her every limb quivered with emotion.

Chaupái.

Vibhíshan, Sugríva, Nala and Níla, Jámbavan and the generous Angad, with Hanumán and all the other monkey chiefs assumed beautiful human forms. With most reverent devotion, every one told the tale of Bharat's loving disposition, his penance and vow. When they saw the citizens' mode of life, they extolled them also for their attachment to their Lord's feet. Then Ráma summoned all his comrades and bade them kiss the feet of the saint. "The *guru* Vasishtha is highly to be reverenced by all my race; it is by his favour that we slew the demons in the battle. But hearken, holy Sir, all these my comrades were the raft that bore me safely out of the waves of the battle. For my sake they lost their lives and they are more dear to me even than Bharat." On hearing the Lord's words, all were greatly overcome. Every moment gave birth to some new rapture.

Dohá 9.

Then they bowed the head at Kausalyá's feet, who rejoiced to give them her blessing, saying "You are as dear to me as Ráma." The heaven was obscured with the showers of flowers as the Root of joy took his way to the palace, while all the fairest ladies in the city mounted the tops of the houses to see him.

Chaupái.

They made ready all kinds of golden bowls, which they took and set every one at her own door. They busied themselves with wreaths of flowers, flags and banners, all to make a glad show. The roads were all watered with perfumes, and innumerable mystic squares were drawn and filled in with the finest pearls. Every kind of festive preparation was taken in hand; the city was *en fête* and all sorts of music were heard. In different places women scattered their offerings on his path, invoking blessings upon him with their hearts full of joy. Girls wave over his head their golden salvers and sacrificial lamps, singing sweetly the while, salvers for him the salve of every ill, the

Sun of the lotus growth of Raghu's line. The beauty, the wealth, the magnificence of the city would be a theme for the Vedas, or Seshnág, or Sárada; but the spectacle was too much even for them; how then can any man, Umá, be able to describe its glory?

Dohá 10.

Ráma's absence, like the heat of the sun, had withered the lily-like fair in the Avadh lake; at sunset they blossomed again, at the sight of the moon-god Ráma. Every conceivable auspicious omen occurred and music resounded in the sky, as the Lord God moved to the palace, a father restored to his people.

Chaupái.

The lord knew Kaikeyi was ashamed and went to her house first, Bhaváni. After comforting her and putting her thoroughly at ease, Hari went on to his own apartments. The All-merciful entered the palace, and every man and woman in the city was happy once more. The *guru* Vasishtha then called the Bráhmans. "The day and the hour are now most auspicious: give the glad order, all ye Bráhmans, that Rámchandra to-day take his seat upon the throne." On hearing Vasishtha's gracious address, the Bráhmans were all highly pleased, and the multitude of them made seemly response, "Ráma's inauguration is the desire of the whole world. Now, best of saints, make no delay, but sign the king with the sign of sovereignty."

Dohá 11.

The saint thereupon ordered Sumantra, who no sooner heard than he went with joy and quickly got ready a multitude of chariots, elephants and horses. Then he despatched messengers in every direction to borrow stores of all good things, and lastly came himself with joy and bowed his head at Vasishtha's feet.

Chaupái.

When the city of Avadh had been decorated, the gods rained down a continuous shower of flowers. Ráma called and directed his servants, "Go first and assist my comrades at their bath." On receiving this order, his people ran in every direction and quickly bathed Sugríva and the rest. Next the all-merciful Ráma summoned Bharat and with his own hands untied his knotted coil of hair ; the Lord then proceeded to bathe all his three brothers, even he the gracious Raghu-raí, the cherisher of all pious souls. The blessedness of Bharat, the meekness of the Lord, not a hundred myriads of Sesh-nágs would be able to declare. Finally Ráma unloosed his own matted hair and, after receiving the *guru's* permission, himself bathed. After his bath the Lord put on his ornaments ; the beauty of his every limb outshining a myriad Loves.

Dohá 12.

Forthwith Jánaki was attended in the bath with all reverence by her mothers-in-law, who attired her in heavenly apparel with rich jewels for every part of her body. As she shone forth on Ráma's left side, the Goddess Lakshmi herself, full of beauty and goodness, the royal dames were all overjoyed at the sight and thought their life had been well worth living. Hearken, Garur; upon this occasion Bráhma, Siva and all the gods and saints mounted their chariots and came to have a sight of the Blessed one.

Chaupái.

The soul of the sage was enraptured as he gazed upon the Lord. He sent at once for a gorgeous throne. Then Ráma took his seat, after bowing his head to the Bráhmans, his glory effulgent as the sun, defying description. As they looked upon Ráma and Síta, the whole saintly throng was overjoyed. Then the Bráhmans repeated their Vedic incantations ; while in the heaven above the gods and saints shouted 'Victory.' The sage Vasishtha first himself made the *tilak* and then ordered the other Bráhmans to do the same. His mother rejoiced as she looked upon her son and again and again waved the sacrificial lamp above his head. All kinds of presents were made to the Bráhmans and not a beggar remained with a want unsatisfied. At the sight of the lord of the three spheres seated on his throne, the gods beat their kettle-drums.

Chhand 4.

Drums sounded in the sky, the hosts of Gandharvas and Kinnars sang and all nymphs of heaven danced before the enraptured assembly of gods and saints. Bharat and his other brothers, with Vibhíshan and Angad and Hanumán and the rest, were there to be seen, some with umbrellas and chaurise and fans, and some with bows, swords, shields and spears. With Síta by his side, the glory of the Solar race outshone the beauty of unnumbered Loves ; the soul of the gods was fascinated by his exquisite cloud-dark form in its yellow apparel, his diadem and bracelets and all the other ornaments that bedecked his limbs, his louts eyes and stalwart chest and arms, a blessed vision indeed for man to behold.

Dohá 13.

The magnificence of the sight and the delight of the assembly are past all telling, Garur ; Sarasvati, Sesh-nág and the Veda may tell it in part, but only Mahádeva has learnt all the sweetness of it. After they had all severally hymned his praises, the gods departed each to his own sphere. Then came the Vedas, in the disguise of bards, into the presence of the divine Ráma. The omniscient and compassionate Lord received them with all honour, nor did any one penetrate the mystery as they thus recited his panegyric :

Chhand 5.

" Hail, visible manifestation of the invisible, incomparable in thy beauty, jewel of kings ; who by the might of thy arm hast slain Rávan and the other terrible demons, monsters of iniquity ; who, incarnate as a man, hast loosed the burdens of the world and put an end to its grievous affliction ; hail, protector of the suppliant, lord of compassion, thee we worship, and with thee thy spouse. O Hari, gods and demons, Nágas[1], men, and all creation, animate and inanimate, have been overcome by thy marvellous delusive power, wearily wandering night and day in the paths of life, full of the mysteries of fate and necessity. If there be any, O lord, whom thou regardest with compassion, they at once are freed from all their troubles; so prompt to cut short the weariness of existence; have mercy upon us, O Ráma, we implore thee. They, O Hari, who intoxicated with the pride of learning, despise that faith in thee which overcomes the world, may attain to a rank which even the gods might fail to secure, and yet I have seen them fall from it again. They who confidently abandon every other hope and continue thy disciples, by repeating thy name cross the ocean of life without any difficulty; this is the lord whom we invoke. O Mukunda, Ráma, spouse of Lakshmi, we ever adore thy lotus feet, object of the worship of Siva and Bráhma; by touching the dust of which the sage's wife obtained salvation; from beneath the nails of which flows the Ganges, reverenced by the saints, sanctifier of the three spheres; feet that bear the marks of the flag, the thunderbolt, the elephant-goad and the lotus, sorely pierced by the thorns during thy wanderings in the forest. We adore the uncreated tree, whose root is the primordial germ; whose bark is fourfold as the Vedas and Puránas declare; whose boughs are six in number and branchlets twenty-five; with innumerable leaves and abundant flowers; whose fruits are of two kinds, bitter and

---

1 "Many tribes assumed in modern and ancient times the name of snakes (Nágas) whether in order to assert their autochthonic right to the country in which they lived, or because, as Diodorus supposes, the snake had been used as their banner, their rallying sign or crest. At the same time Diodorus points out, people may either have chosen the snake for their banner, because it was their deity, or it may have become their deity because it was their banner. At all events, nothing would be more natural than that people who, for some reason or other, called themselves snakes should in time adopt a snake for their ancestor, and finally for their god. In India the snakes assume, at an early time, a very prominent part in epic and popular traditions. They soon became what fairies or bogies are in our nursery tales, and they thus appear in company with Gandharvas, Apsaras, Kinnaras &c., in some of the most ancient architectural ornamentations of India."—*Max Muller's Hibbert Lectures.*

sweet; with a single creeper ever clinging to it; full of buds and blossoms and fruit, the everlasting tree of creation. [1] Let them preach in their wisdom, who contemplate thee as the Supreme Spirit, the Uncreate, the inseparable from the universe, recognizable only by inference and beyond the understanding; but we, O lord, will ever hymn the glories of thy incarnation. O merciful lord god, mine of every perfection, this is the boon we ask, that in thought, word and deed, and without any variableness we may maintain a devotion for thy feet."

Dohá 14.

When, in the sight of all, the Vedas had uttered this glorious prayer, they became invisible and returned to their home with Bráhma. Hearken, Garur; then came Sambhu to Raghubír and with a choking voice and every hair on his body erect he thus made supplication:

Totaká.[2]

"Hail to thee, Ráma, the spouse of Lakshmi, the pacifier; have mercy on thy servant, harassed with the terrors and troubles of existence. Glorious lord, sovereign of Avadh, sovereign of heaven, Lakshmi's sovereign, have mercy on the suppliant, who has fled to thee for refuge. Destroyer of the ten-headed and twenty-armed, remover of earth's sore burden, consumer of the moth-like demon host in the fierce flame of thy fiery arrows; most beauteous ornament of the terrestrial sphere; noblest of all that handle bow, arrows and quiver; radiant as the sun to disperse the thick darkness of the night of pride, ignorance

---

1 The four coats of bark are the four Vedas; the six boughs are thought to be the six stages of existence, *viz.* conception, birth, childhood, manhood, old age and death; or else the six natural impulses, *viz.*, hunger, thirst, excretion of both kinds, sleep, and sexual intercourse. The twenty-five branchlets are Prakriti, Buddhi, Ahankára, the five Tan-mát-ras, the five Mahábhutas, the ten Indriyas, Manas and Purusha (see Note to Book VI., Dohá 16). The two fruits are pleasure and pain, and the creeper Mayá.

2 In the Totaka, or Trotaka metre, each line in the quatrain consists of four anapæsts. Thus:—

Jáyà Ráma Ramá-rámànam sámànam.
Bhàvà-tàpà-bhàyàkula páhi janam.

and ego-ism; thou hast vanquished the God of Love,[1] who like a huntsman had smitten all men to the heart with the arrows of evil desire as though they were herd of deer; now, O lord Hari, have mercy on us destitute wretches, who have gone astray in the wilderness of sensuality. The many diseases and bereavements, with which the people are stricken, are the fruit of this disregard for thy holy feet. The bottomless ocean of existence overwhelms all who cherish no love for thy lotus feet. Poor indeed and vile and wretched for ever are they who have no affection for thy lotus feet. They who take delight in making mention of thy name, have the saints as their constant, friends for ever, are eternally exempt from passion, greed and arrogance, and regard prosperity and adversity as both alike. Thus it is that thy servants are so happy; the saint abandons for ever all confidence in mortification and making simply a vow of perpetual love serves thy lotus feet with a pure heart. O Raghu-bir, mighty and invincible hero, indwilling as a bee in the lotus-like soul of the saints, thy name, O Hari, I repeat in prayer and adore, destroyer of vanity and pride, which are the diseases of life. Humbly I adore without ceasing the spouse of Lakshmi, the supreme abode of goodness, generosity and compassion. O sun of Raghu, extirpate every animosity; O king of earth, regard thy humble servant.

Dohá 15.

Again and again I beg of thee a boon—be gracious and grant it O Sriranga[2]—an unwavering faith in thy lotus feet and constant communion with saints." After thus hymning Ráma's praises, Síva returned with joy to Kailás. The Lord then assigned the monkeys most delightful residences

1 *Manujád*, 'man-eaters,' or 'demons,' is the word in the text; but, as it seems impossible to fit it into the rest of the passage, I propose to read instead *manoját*, the 'mind-born,' *i.e.*, Káma-deva, the god of love.

2 Srîranga, Holy Ranga, is one of Vishnu's epithets, and gives its name to the city of Seringapatam (Srirangapattana), where is a great temple dedicated to the divinity under this title.

Chaupái.

Hearken, Garur; this sacred legend annihilates all the distresses and sins of the world. Any one who hears this narrative of the royal installation obtains self-control and discretion. They who lovingly sing it, or hear it sung, obtain every kind of happiness and prosperity; after enjoying in this world a bliss, to which the gods can scarce attain, they are admitted after death into Ráma's own presence. The finally emancipated, the detached from the world and the worldly, who hear it, obtain respectively faith, absorption into the divinity and ever-increasing prosperity. O Garur, this history of Ráma that I have repeated is the delight of a good understanding: a remedy for anxiety and sorrow; a confirmation of detachment, discretion and faith; a splendid raft on which to cross the river of delusion. In the city of Kosala was ever some new delight; the people were all happy, from the highest to the lowest. All felt an evergrowing affection for Ráma's lotus feet, the adored of Bráhma, Siva and the saints. The poor had clothes given them in abundance and the Bráhmans were presented with offerings of every description

Dohá 16.

The monkeys were drowned in a joy like that of heaven; all were devoted to the Lord's feet; day and night passed unnoticed till now six months had been spent.

Chaupái.

They had forgotten their homes so absolutely as never even to dream of them, like as the idea of injuring another never enters the soul of a saint. At last Raghupati summoned all his comrades before him. They came and made reverent obeisance. He seated them by his side with the greatest kindness and thus addressed them in gracious terms, which might well gladden their pious souls: "You have done me excellant service; but how can I praise you to your face? I hold you all most dear for having left the comforts of your home solely on my account. My younger brother, my crown ; my fortune, my wife, my life, my home and loving kinsmen are none of them so dear in my sight as you are. I tell you no falsehood ; these are my real sentiments. It is the ordinary rule for a man to cherish his own adherents, but I have a special affection for my servants.

Dohá 17.

Now, my comrades, return to your homes; there worship me with steadfast faith and maintain your fervent devotion, knowing me to be the eternal and omnipresent benefactor of the universe."

Chaupái.

When they heard the Lord's words, all were so overcome that they forgot who they were, or where they were, or where they had come from. With clasped hands and fixed gaze they stood before him, unable to speak from excess of devotion. The Lord perceived the intensity of their love and said all he could to teach them resignation. In his presence they could not answer a word, but still turned their eyes to his lotus feet. Then the Lord called for jewels and robes of honour, of many colours, incomparably beautiful, and first Bharat with his own hands made ready a dress, with which he invested Sugríva. By the Lord's command Lakshman next invested the king of Lanká, to Ráma's great contentment. But Angad remained seated and did not stir, Seeing his love, the Lord did not speak to him ;

Dohá 18.

but proceeded with the investiture of Jámbaván and Níla and the rest, who with Ráma's image impressed upon their heart after bowing their head at his feet withdrew. Then Angad arose and made obeisance and with weeping eyes and clasped hands uttered his humble petition, impregnate as it were with the very essence of devotion.

Chaupái.

"Hearken, all-wise, all-merciful and all-blessed, commiserator of the destitute, succour of the distressed ; Báli, my lord, in his last moments placed me in your charge. To be the helper of the helpless is the character you support; benefactor of the faithful, do not abandon me. You, Sire, are my spiritual guide, my father and my mother; where can I go, if I leave your lotus feet? Consider yourself and tell me, O king of men; apart from my lord, what is my home to me? Extend to me your protection, a mere child as I am without knowledge, wisdom, or strength, and regard me as one of the humblest of your servants. Let me perform the most menial office in your palace, if only I may see your lotus feet and thus traverse the ocean of existence." So saying, he fell at the Lord's feet, "O Sire, do not again tell me to go home."

Dohá 19.

On hearing Angad's piteous prayer, the all-merciful lord Ráma raised him from the ground and clasped him to his bosom, his lotus eyes streaming with tears. He clothed the son of Báli in his own robe and jewels and the chain from his own neck, and then the Lord dismissed him with many words of exhortation.

Chaupái.

Bharat with his brother Satrughna and Lakshman proceeded to escort him, being greatly moved by his devotion. But Angad's heart was so overflowing with love that he turned again and again for one more look at Ráma. Time after time he prostrated himself upon the ground, crying, 'Thus would I stay, if Ráma would only let me.' Treasuring up in his mind Ráma's look and voice and gait, his smile too and his embrace, with a last glance at his face and many words of fervent praper, he went forth, cherishing his lotus feet in his heart. After escorting all the monkeys with the utmost respect, Bharat and his brother returned. Then Hanumán clasped Sugríva by the feet and earnestly besought him: "Let me spend ten days more in Ráma's service and then I will return to your feet, my master."

" O son of the Wind, great is your piety; go, serve the All-merciful.'' So saying, the other monkeys went their way, but Angad cried: " Hearken, Hanumán:

Dohá 20.

With clasped hands I beg of you to present my service to the Lord and frequently remind him of me." So saying, the son of Báli started on his way, while Hanumán returned and told the Lord of his devotion: the great god was overjoyed. Now hard as adamant, now soft as the petal of a flower, such, Garur, is Ráma's heart; who can comprehend it?

Chaupái.

Next the All-merciful summoned the Nishád and graciously presented him with jewels and raiment. "Return to your home, but ever remember me, and in heart, word and deed observe all the ordinances of religion. You, my companion, are as much my brother as Bharat; you must always be backwards and forwards here." On hearing these words he was greatly delighted and fell at his feet, his eyes full of tears. With the image of his lotus feet impressed upon his heart, he returned home and declared the Lord's generosity to all his kinsfolk. The citizens, on beholding Ráma's actions, shouted again their *vivas* to his blessed name. Under Ráma's sway the three spheres were full of joy, all sorrow was at an end, no one had a grudge against another, every variance was extinguished under Ráma's auspices.

Dohá 21.

Devoted to religion, the people walked in the path of the Vedas, each according to his own caste and stage of life,[1] and enjoyed perfect happiness, unvexed by fear, or sorrow, or disease.

1 The *asramas*, or 'stages of life,' are not to be confounded by the English reader with what would be ordinarily designated 'states of life.' They are four in number: 1st, that of the Bráhmachári, or student; 2nd, that of the Griha-stha, householder; 3rd, that of the Vana-prastha, or anchorite; and 4th, that of the Bhikshu, or mendicant.

Chaupái.

In the whole of Ráma's dominions there was no one who suffered from trouble of any kind, whether of the body or from the visitation of heaven or the attacks of enemies. Every one was in charity with his neighbour and contented with the state of life to which he had been born, conformably to the teaching of Scripture and sound morality. The four pillars of religion[1] were established throughout the world; on one even dreamt of sin. Men and women alike were devoted to Ráma's worship and enjoyed all the blessedness of highest heaven. There was no premature death and no sickness even, but every one was comely and sound of body. No one was in poverty, in sorrow, or distress; no one ignorant or unlucky. All were unaffectedly good and pious, clever and intelligent. Every one appreciated the merits of his neighbour and was himself learned and wise; every one was grateful for kindnesses and guilelessly prudent.

Dohá 22.

Hearken, Garur; during Ráma's reign there was not a creature in the world, animate or inanimate, that suffered from any of the ills that ordinarily result from time or past conduct or personal temperament and character.

Chaupái.

The world encircled by its seven seas had only one king, Ráma, the lord of Kosala. This was no great matter for him, every hair on whose body is one of the countless spheres of creation. To a man who rightly understands the greatness of the Lord, this description will seem highly disparaging. But those who understand his divine majesty, Garúr, are the very persons who take a delight in these actions of his. They are the special rewards of such knowledge; so declare the greatest of sages and ascetics[2]

Not even Sesh-nág or Sáradá could describe the happiness and prosperity of Ráma's reign. Every one was

1 The four pillars of religion are truth, purity, mercy and charity.

2 For *barad susila*, given in Rám Jasan's edition, the preferable reading seems to be *bar dam-silá*.

generous and kindly disposed to his neighbour and submissive to the Bráhmans. Every husband was faithful to his single wife and every wife was devoted to her husband.

Dohá 23.

A rod was never seen, save in the hand of a Religious; the words 'to beat' had no meaning except to mark the time for a dancer on the stage; and the only victory known was self-conquest, throughout all Ramchandra's realm.

Chaupái.

The trees of the forest were ever full of flowers and fruit; the elephant and the lion dwelt peaceably together. Birds and deer forgot their instinctive animosities and lived in the greatest harmony with one another. The cooing of the birds and the many herds of deer fearlessly roaming the woods made a charming scene. The air was cool, fragrant and exquisitely soft; bees laden with honey made a pleasant humming. Every creeper and tree yielded its sweetness on being asked and the cows in sheer lightness of heart dropt their milk on the road. The earth was ever clothed with crops and every feature of the Golden Age was repeated in the Age of Silver. Mines of jewels of every description were disclosed in the mountains and the world acknowledged its king to be in truth the Universal Spirit. Every river flowed with an abundance of water, cool, pure and pleasant to the taste. The sea remained within its bounds, casting forth pearls on its shore for men to gather. The ponds were all thick with lotuses and every quarter and section of the world was supremely happy.

Dohá 24.

The earth was suffused with the radiance of the moon, the heat of the sun was greater than circumstances required, and the clouds dropt rain whenever asked, in the days when Ráma was king.

Chaupái.

The Lord celebrated millions of horse-sacrifices and

conferred innumberable gifts upon the Bráhmans, approving himself the defender of scriptural usage, the champion of religion, perfect in every virtue and the sworn foe of all sensuality. Síta was ever obediant to her lord, incomparable in her beauty, her virtue and her meekness, sensible of the majesty of the All-merciful and devotedly attached to his lotus feet. Though there were many man-servants and maid-servants in the palace, all well-skilled in their work, she discharged every domestic duty with her own hands, waiting on Ráma's orders. Any service that might give pleasure to the All-merciful she herself studied to perform. Without the slightest pride or conceit she attended on Kausalyá and the other queen dowagers in the palace. O Umá, Lakshmi, the object of the adoration of Bráhma and all the divinities, the mother of the universe, the ever blameless.

Dohá 25.

The slightest glance of favour from whose eye is coveted by the gods, practised this devotion to Ráma's lotus feet, for such was her nature.

Chaupái.

Though she waited diligently on all the brothers, her devotion to Ráma was most conspicuous. She never ceased to watch his lotus face on the chance that he might be pleased to speak to her. Ráma on his part was most affectionate to his brothers and instructed them on all points of morality. The citizens lived happy, each enjoying a felicity to which the gods might scarce attain. Day and night they made their prayer to God for a fervent devotion to Ráma's holy feet. Two comely sons were born to Síta, Lava and Kusa; so the Vedas and Puránas have declared; both glorious in battle, modest and accomplished and so beautiful that they seemed the very image of Hari. The other brothers also had each two sons, pre-eminent in beauty, virtue and all good qualities.

Dohá 26.

The Supreme Spirit that transcends all intelligence,

speech and perception; that is from everlasting; unaffected by material phenomena, or the workings of mind or the properties of things, even he it was who thus exhibited the actions of exalted humanity.

Chaupái.

In the early morning after bathing in the Sarju he sat in his court, in the midst of Bráhmans and sages, while Vasishtha recited the Vedas and Puránas; Ráma listening attentively, though he knew them all of himself. He took his meals with his brothers: the royal matrons looking on with the utmost satisfaction. Then Bharat and Satrughna, the two brothers, would take Hanuman to some grove, where they would sit down and ask him all about Ráma's doings, and he would reply out of the depth of his wisdom. It was such a delight to them to hear the glorious narrative that they would beg him to repeat it again and again. In every single house the sacred legend was told of Rama's marvellously holy deeds. Men and women alike joined in hymning his praises, and day and night passed unheeded.

Dohá 27.

Not a thousand Sesh-nágs could tell all the happiness and prosperity of the city of Avadh, when Ráma reigned as king.

Chaupái.

Nárad and Sanat-Kumára and all the great sages came every day to Ayodhyá to have a sight of the king of Kosala. The appearance of the city made them forget all their asceticism. The balconies encrusted with gold and jewels, the splendid pavements laid in diverse colours, the magnificent forts on every side of the city with their brightly painted battlements, as though the nine planets had been mustered in array to beleaguer Indra's capital, Amaravati; the floors so beautifully inlaid with coloured crystal that the soul of any saint would be distracted at the sight; the glistening palaces reaching to the sky with pinnacles that put to shame the brightness of sun and moon; the lattices gleaming with jewels and the jewelled lamps that shone in every room.

Chhand 6.

Beneath the light of jewelled lamps the houses were resplendent with their thresholds of coral and pillars of precious stone and golden walls, such as the Creator himself might have fashioned, all inlaid with emeralds and gems. The stately palace-courts were lovely with inworked crystal, and every gate was fitted with folding doors of gold embossed with diamonds.

Dohá 28.

In every house was a beautiful and well-furnished picture gallery, where Ráma's achievements were so set forth that the soul of a saint would be ravished at the sight.

Chaupái.

Every one had a flower garden trimmed with the greatest care, adorned with every kind of choice creeper, and blossoming with perpetual spring. There was ever a pleasant sound of the buzzing of bees, and the air was delightfully cool, soft and fragrant. Birds of all kinds, the children's pets, sweet of note and graceful in flight, peacocks, swans, herons and pigeons, made a charming show on the tops of the houses, cooing and dancing in high glee at the sight of their own shadow. Other children were teaching parrots and *mainas* to speak and repeat the names of Ráma, Raghupati, Saviour. The palace gates were most magnificent, and the roads, squares and bazárs all elegantly laid out.

Chhand 7.

The elegance of the bazárs was beyond all description, and things could be had without price. How is it possible to sing the riches of the city where the spouse of Lakshmi reigned as king? The cloth-merchants, money-changers and grain-dealers sat at their shops like so many Kuvers.

Every one was happy, every one well-conducted and comely, men and women, young and old, all alike.

Dohá 29.

To the north flowed the deep and pellucid stream of the Sarju, with a line of handsome ghâts and no muddy bank anywhere.

Chaupái.

At some distance was a fine spacious ghát, where all the horses and elephants went to drink. There were also elaborate gháts for the citizens' drinking water, where no one was allowed to bathe. The most beautiful of all was the king's ghát, which was frequented by men of all four castes. All along the banks were temples to the gods surrounded by pleasant groves. Here and there on the river bank hermits, sages and anchorites dwelt and meditated; and many bushes of the fragrant tulsi were there, planted by different holy men. The beauty of the city surpassed all description; its outskirts also were most picturesque. Every sin was effaced by a sight of it, with its woods and groves, its lakes and ponds.

Chhand 8.

Its matchless lakes and ponds and large and beautiful wells were so charming, with their elegant flights of steps and limpid water, that gods and saints were fascinated by the sight. The many-coloured lotuses, the cooing of the numerous birds and the buzzing of the bees made the spot a delightful one, where the parrots by the clamour seemed to be inviting travellers to halt.

Dohá 30.

How is it possible to describe the city, of which Lakshmi's lord was king? Animá and the other fairies had diffused through the whole of Avadh every happiness and prosperity.

Chaupái.

Everywhere men were singing Ráma's praises and as they sat thus exhorted one another: "Worship Ráma, the defender of the suppliant ; the home of beauty and goodness, of comeliness and virtue; the lotus-eyed and dark-complexioned ; who protects his servants as the eyelid does the eye equipt with lovely bow and arrows and quiver; the champion of the battle; a very sun to rejoice the lotus-like company of the saints; a Garur to consume the terrible serpent Death; whose loving kindness is over all who unselfishly worship Ráma ; a huntsman to scatter the deer-like herd of ignorance and greed ; a lion to quell the wild elephant, Love ; the giver of happiness to his people; a sun to scatter the thick darkness of doubt and sorrow ; a fire to consume the dense forest of demons ; who can refuse to worship Raghubír and Síta, seeing that he is the breaker of earth's burdens ; the frost that kills the insect swarm of manifold desires ; the ever uniform; the uncreated and imperishable; the delight of the saints ; the breaker of earth's burdens; Tulsi Dás's own gracious Lord ?"

Dohá 31.

In such wise the city sang Ráma's praises, while on his part the All-merciful was ever to them most gracious.

Chaupái.

From the time, Garur, of the uprising of the glorious sun of Ráma's power the three spheres were all suffused with light: many were happy, but many also were sad. First to enumerate the sorrowful: to begin with, the night of Ignorance was at an end; owl-like Sin slunk away out and of sight; Lust and Anger, like gamblers, were ashamed to show themselves; Formalism,[1] Phenomenal Existence,

1 By *Karma*, which I here translate 'Formalism,' is meant ceremonial as opposed to contemplative religion: the ordinary routine of fasts, sacrifices, ablutions and other outward observances as distinct from the interior and purely spiritual exercises of the soul, which it is the main object of this poem to recommend. It may also be taken in a wider sense as Necessity, the inexorable sequence of cause and effect, by which the whole world is governed. The ultimate result is the same; for the practice of external religious observances for the sake of the minor prizes attached to them—minor, that is, as compared with the reward promised to interior faith—is only one illustration of the belief in the general law, though the most important to Tulsi Dás, writing as a theologian.

Time and Nature, were as ill at ease as the *chakor* ; Envy, Pride, Infatuation and Conceit were like thieves, with nowhere a chance to display their skill. But the ponds of Piety blossomed with the lotuses of Knowledge and Understanding ; while Happiness, Contentment, Self-control and Discretion were like so many *chakwas* and *chakwis* when their sorrow is over.

Dohá 32.

When this glorious sun illumines any man's heart, the last-named qualities grow and increase, the first mentioned die away.

Chaupái.

One day Ráma with his brothers and his special favourite Hanumán went to visit a beautiful grove, where every tree was bright with flowers and fresh leaves. Sanat-Kumára and the others noted their opportunity and came also ; a glorious band of pre-eminent virtue and goodness, ever absorbed in the rapture of transcendental felicity, and still youthful to look at despite their immemorial years. One in appearance and without any distinctive mark, as it might be the four Vedas in bodily form, the saints had but this one hope, desire and ambition, to hear the recital of Ráma's actions. The stopt, Bhaváni, at the same place as the learned sage Agastyá, who repeated to them the whole of Ráma's history, the source of true wisdom, as friction is of fire.

Dohá 33.

When Ráma saw the sages approaching, he rejoiced and prostrated himself before them ; then after giving them welcome, the lord of the yellow robe made them sit down.

Chaupái.

His three brothers made their obeisance also and were greatly delighted, as also Hanumán. The saints, as they gazed on Ráma's incomparable beauty, were beside themselves with rapture. With clasped hands they bowed the head before him and could not close their eyes for a moment, so intensely were they fixed on the shrine of beauty, the conqueror of the world, with his lotus eyes and dark-hued frame. When Raghubír perceived their condition, his eyes streamed with tears and his body quivered with emotion. He took them by the hand and made them sit down and addressed them in these most gracious words: "Hearken, reverend Sirs; to-day I am indeed blessed; at the sight of you sin is annihilated. The fellowship of the saints is the greatest of blessings; it at once effects a severance from the world.

Dohá 34.

To consort with the saints leads to final beatitude, but with the sensual to endless transmigrations: so say the saints themselves, the greatest of the poets, the Vedas, the Puránas and all the Scriptures."

Chaupái.

The four sages were rejoiced to hear the lord's words and with quivering body they raised this hymn of praise: "Glory to the Lord God, the everlasting, the unchangeable, the sinless, the multiform, the One, the All-merciful. Glory to the unembodied; glory, glory to the universal embodiment, the palace of bliss, the beautiful in his comeliness. Glory to the spouse of Lakshmi; glory to the supporter of the earth, peerless in his splendour; the uncreated, of whom there is no beginning: the fountain of wisdom; the immeasurable;[1] the bestower of honour; whose holy fame is the theme of the Vedas and Puránas; the all-wise, the all-generous; the destroyer of ignorance; the many-named, the name-less; the emotionless; the universe itself, the universal spirit; the indweller of every heart. Abide with us and protect us for ever, O Ráma; dwell in our heart, tearing

1 *Amán* is capable of two meanings: either 'immeasurable,' from the root *má*, 'to measure;' or 'without pride,' from the root *man*, to think.' Either will suit the context equally well, and the jingle between it and the following word *mána-prad* is probably what chiefly suggested it to the poet.

asunder the bonds of the world and its miserable contentions and destroying our sensuality and conceit.

Dohá 35.

O holy Ráma, all-blessed and all-merciful, fulfiller of every desire of the soul, bestow on us the boon of constant love and devotion.

Chaupái.

Grant us, O Raghupati, that purifying faith which annihilates every distress and worldly conceit. Be propitious and grant us this boon, O our Lord, a very cow of heaven, or tree of paradise to satisfy the desires of the suppliant. O Raghu-náyak, the Agastya of the ocean of mundane existence, the bestower of blessings which only your servants find it easy to acquire ; destroyer of the destroying tortures of love ; friend of the friendless : diffuser of equanimity ; preventer of hope and fear, of envy and all evil passions ; bestower of meekness, discretion and detachment ; jewel of earthly kings ; glory of the world ; grant us devotion to thee, the only raft on which to cross the floods of existence ; immortal swan in the Manas lake of saintly souls ; whose lotus feet are adored by Bráhma and Siva ; standard of the line of Raghu ; bridge for the recovery of the Scriptures ; annihilator of time, destiny, nature and phenomenal existence ; ark of salvation ; healer of every sorrow ; glory of the three spheres ; Tulsi Das's own lord."

Dohá 36.

Having again and again hymned his praises and lovingly bowed the head, Sanat-Kumára and his companions returned to Bráhma's sphere, after obtaining the boon they had so vehemently coveted.

Chaupái.

When Sanat-Kumára and his companions had gone their way to Bráhma's sphere, the three brothers bowed their head at Ráma's feet, but being too diffident themselves to put the question to the Lord, they looked to Hanumán, wishing to hear from the Lord's own mouth an explanation which would terminate all their doubts. The reader of the heart understood this perfectly and said, "What is it you wish to know, Hanumán?" Then replied Hanumán with clasped hands: "Hearken, all-merciful Lord God; Bharat, Sire, wishes to ask something, but is too diffident to speak out." "Monkey, you know my feelings; there are no secrets between me and Bharat." On hearing the Lord's words Bharat clasped his feet: "Hearken, my lord, reliever of all the anxieties of the suppliant;

Dohá 37.

I have no doubts whatever, Sire; not a shadow of disquietude or distrust; and this all of your mercy, O all-merciful and all-blessed.

Chaupái

But if I may presume on your loving-kindness—for I am your servant and you the benefactor of your faithful people—the Vedas and Puránas, O Raghurái, have sung in various ways the greatness of the saints; you too have exalted them by your own holy mouth, declaring that the Lord has a special affection for them. I would fain hear, Sire, their distinctive marks, O gracious discerner of character and understanding. Instruct me, protector of the suppliant, in the notes that distinguish the good from the wicked." "Hearken brother; the notes of the good as told in the Vedas and Puránas are innumerable. The conduct of the good to the wicked is like that of the sandal-tree to the axe, for—see, brother—the fragrant wood imparts its perfume to the very iron that fells it.

Dohá 38.

For this reason sandal-wood is the desire of the world and has the honour of being put on the head of gods; while the axe, for its punishment, has its edge heated in the fire and is well hammered.

Chaupái.

Without attachment to sensual objects; store-houses of virtue and generosity; sorrowing in the sorrow of others and finding joy in their joy; equable, devoid of animosity; sober, passionless: conquerors of greed and impatience, joy and fear; tender of heart, compassionate to the poor; with a guileless devotion to me in thought, word and deed; giving honour to all, but claiming none for themselves; such, Bharat, are dear to me as my own life; unselfish, devoted to my name; happy abodes of tranquillity, continence and humility; models of contentment, simplicity, benevolence, piety and devotion to the Bráhmans. Verily, brothers, any heart in which these qualities abide is ever the heart of a saint. They are never disturbed in their quietude, their self-control, their religious observances or their moral principles; they never utter a harsh word;

Dohá 39.

they regard praise and blame as both alike, in their exclusive devotion to my lotus feet; such are the treasurers of virtue, the compendiums of bliss, who are the good, and whom I love as my own soul.

Chaupái.

Hear now the characteristics of the bad, with whom one should carefully avoid any dealings. Their company always leads to trouble, as when an ill-conditioned cow gets a gentle companion beaten like itself. The heart of the wicked is a consuming fire, which is ever rekindled at the sight of another's prosperity: but whenever they hear a neighbour abused, they are as glad as if they had picked up a treasure on the road. Devoted to sensuality, choleric, arrogant and greedy; censorious, treacherous, perverse and impure; cherishing causeless animosities against every one: disliking anything that others like; false in taking, false in giving, false in great matters and false in small; speaking plausible words, but ruthless of heart, like the peacock that devours the biggest snake.

Dohá 40.

Injurious to their neighbour, covetous of his wife and

wealth and gloating over his misfortunes; men thus vile and abominable are ruthless incarnate fiends.

Chaupái.

Coveting dress, coveting bed; addicted to lust and gluttony; with no fear of the realm of Yama before their eyes; catching their breath, as though they had got the ague when they hear of any one's advancement; but as glad as though they had been made kings of the world, when they see their neighbour in distress; devoted to their own selfish interests, quarrelsome to their kinsfolk, dissolute, avaricious and choleric; disobedient to father and mother, to guru and Bráhman: dragging down others into the same ruin with themselves; infatuated workers of other's ill; taking no pleasure in the company of the good or in discourse about Hari: oceans of immorality, dull of understanding, lascivious, revilers of the Vedas, masterful with other men's goods, special torment of the Bráhmans and the gods, with deceit and treachery in their heart, though outwardly fair seeming.

Dohá 41.

No such vile wretches of man existed in the first and second age, and only a few in the third, but in the fourth there are swarms of them.

Chaupái.

O my brother, there is no religion like charity and no meanness like malevolence. What I now declare to you is the sum of the Vedas and Puráns and the verdict of the philosophers. Men who in the body cause suffering to others undergo an enormous series of transmigrations. Men are so infatuated that in their devotion to their own selfish interests they commit many sins and ruin their prospects for the next world. I reveal myself to them, brother, as their destiny and assign them the reward of their deeds, whether good or evil. The truly wise consider the matter thus and worship me, regarding the world only as a burden; they discard action with its result, good or bad, and devoutly adore me, the king of gods and men and saints. Thus have I declared the characteristics of the good and the bad; they who remember them will not be submerged in the flood of existence.

Dohá 42.

Hearken, brother; the multitudinous forms of merit and demerit are all the products of Mayá : greatest merit is to notice neither: to notice them is an imperfection of knowledge."

Chaupái.

On hearing this utterance of the divine mouth, the brothers rejoiced and their heart overflowed with love. Again and again they paid him profound homage, while a boundless delight filled the soul of Hanumán also. Ráma then withdrew to the private palace ; but every day there was some new incident of the same character. The sage Nárad came time after time and hymned Ráma's holy acts, every day finding something new to record. He then went to Bráhma's realm and there ricited the whole story. The Creator on hearing it was so highly pleased that he urged him to repeat it again and again. Sanat-Kumara and the others marvelled at Nárad; and the saints, though absorbed in the contemplation of the Supreme Spirit, forgot their abstraction on hearing his hymn of praise. The highest powers listened reverently.

Dohá 43.

Though exempted from mundane existence and intent on the contemplation of the Supreme, they interrupted their meditations in order to hear his lay. Truly theirs must be a heart of stone who take no delight in Rám a's history.

Chaupái.

One day by Ráma's invitation all the gurus and Bráhmans and people of the city came together, and when the priests and nobles had taken their seat in the assemly, the Comforter of the pious made them this speech : " Hearken to my words, all ye people of the city : I speak without any selfish motive at heart, neither wronging another nor aggrandizing myself; listen and act as may seem good to you. He is my servant and he my best beloved, who accepts my commands. If I say anything that is wrong, brother, do not be afraid to correct me. All the Scriptures declare that it is great good fortune and a great difficulty surmounted to be born with the body of a man, which is a store-house of opportunities, a gate of deliverance ; and those who have received it and still attain not to heaven.

Doha 44.

They, I say, reap torment in the next world and beat their head in despair, wrongly attributing the blame to time, fate and God.

Chaupai.

But materialism, brother, is not the proper object of the human body ; it is happiness for a very brief period, but ends in misery. The possessor of a human body who gives himself up to materialism is like a fool who chooses poison in preference to ambrosia. He is one of whom none can speak well ; he throws away the philosopher's stone to pick up a pepper-corn. Such a creature drifts for ever among the four modes of birth and the eighty-four lakhs of living species, perpetually changing at the will of Mayá and encompassed by Time, Fate, Nature and Phenomena. At some time or another God of his mercy, and without any reason for the favour, gives him a human body, a raft on which he may cross the ocean of existence, with my grace as a fair wind to speed him on his course ; with pious teachers at the helm he easily procures all the equipment of a stout ship, which would else be beyond him.

Doha 45.

If thus equipt he fails to cross the sea, he is an ungrateful wretch, bent on his own destruction.

Chaupai.

Whoso desires happiness in this world and the next will hearken to my words and imprint them deeply in his heart.

It is an easy and a pleasant road, brother, that of my service, at the Vedas and Purános declare. Knowledge is difficult and beset with impediments; its appliances are cumbrous and it has no grasp on the soul. Though a man endures endless tortures, without faith he is no friend of mine. Faith is all-powerful and a mine of every blessing; but men cannot attain to it except by the fellowship of the saints. The saints are not won except by meritorious deeds; their fellowship is the end of mundane existence. Now there is no other meritorious deed in the whole world but this one, to worship Bráhmans in thought, word and deed. Seers and gods are all in his favour who eschews guile and devotes himself to the Bráhmans.

Dohá 46.

One other mysterious dogma I with clasped hands impress upon you all; without prayer to Siva no one can attain to the faith that I require.

Chaupái.

Tell me what are the difficulties in the way of faith; neither abstract meditation is necessary, nor sacrifice, prayer, penance nor fasting; only simplicity of character, a mind void of frowardness and absolute content whatever may befall. If one who is called a worshipper of mine trust in man, tell me where is his trust in me? But why protract my discourse to such a length? these are the practices, brother, by which I am won: avoidance of enmity and rancour, of hope and fear; a constant atmosphere of perfect repose; passionless, homeless; without pride and without sin; placid, provident and wise; ever devoted to the fellowship of the saints; lightly esteeming every object of sense and even heaven and final deliverance from the body; persistent in faith, innocent of wickedness, a stranger to impious scepticism.

Dohá 47.

Devoted to my name, which is the sum of all my perfections; devoid of selfishness, conceit and vain imagination;

such a man's happiness, be assured, is the very sum of transcendental felicity."

Chaupái.

On hearing the gracious Ráma's ambrosial speech, they all embraced his feet : " Fountain of mercy, you are our father, our mother, our spiritual guide and our brethren, and are dearer than our life. You, O Ráma, have blessed us in body, substance and house, and have removed all the sorrows of your suppliants. No one but you could teach us this lesson ; for even father and mother are self-interested. The only two disinterested friends in the world are you yourself and your servants, O conqueror of the demons. Every friend in the world has his own object in view : no one, Sire, ever dreams of the highest object." When Raghunáth heard them all speak in such terms of devotion, he was rejoiced at heart ; and they on receiving his permission returned to their several homes, making the Lord the glorious theme of all their talk.

Dohá 48.

O Umá, every man and woman among the inhabitants of Avadh was the picture of satisfaction ; the supreme felicity of heaven suffused the whole city when Ráma was king.

Chaupái.

One day saint Vasishtha came to visit the blessed and glorious Ráma. The prince of the house of Raghu received him with the most profund respect and washed his feet and drank of the water. " Hearken, Ráma," cried the sage, clasping his hands, " Ocean of mercy, I have a request to make. After seeing your deeds, a boundless bewilderment possesses my soul. Your immeasurable greatness is beyond the comprehension of the Vedas, how then can I tell it ? The business of a family-priest is very contemptible ; the Vedas and Puránas and all the Scriptures make small account of it. At first I refused it, but the Creator said to me, ' You will be a gainer hereafter, my son. Bráhma, the

Supreme Spirit, will be born in human form as a king, the glory of the race of Raghu.'

Dohá 49.

Then I thought to myself, I shall thus attain to him who is the object of all contemplation, penance, charity and sacrifice ; what better course can I pursue ?

Chaupái.

Prayer, penance, pious observances, and doing one's duty in life are different good actions based on the Scriptures. But knowledge, mercy, self-control, bathing at holy places and all the religious practices inculcated by revelation, as also the study of the Vedas and sacred traditions and numerous Purános are only means to a glorious end, *viz.*, a constant devotion to your lotus feet. Can dirt be removed by cleansing with dirt ? is *ghi* to be obtained by churning water ? Except, O Raghu-rái, by the water of faith and love, the interior stain can never be effaced. He is all-wise, he the philosopher, the scholar, the thoroughly accomplished, the irrefutable doctor, the truly judicious and the possessor of every auspicious attribute, who is devoted to your lotus feet.

Dohá 50.

My lord, I would ask one boon ; grant it, O Ráma, in your clemency : in all my future births may my love for my lord's lotus feet never diminish."

Chaupái.

So saying, Saint Vasishtha returned home and the All-merciful was greatly pleased at heart. Then, being ever gracious to his servants, he took with him Hanumán and Bharat and his other brothers and in his benignity went outside the city, where he ordered up the elephants, chariots and horses. After inspecting them, he praise them all and then distributed th person the one that he wished. The Lord, tl weariness, was himself a weary and repaired grove, where Bharat spread his own raiment on the ground, and there the Lord took his seat, with all his brothers in attendance, while the Son of the Wind fanned him. At this his body quivered with emotion and his eyes filled with tears. There is no one so blessed as Hanumán, nor any so devoted to Ráma's feet, whose love and devotion, O Umá, have again and again been told by the Lord with his own mouth.

Dohá 51.

At that time came the Saint Nárad, with his lute in his hand, and began to hymn Ráma's glorious renown, that pregnant theme.

Chaupái.

"Look upon me, O lotus-eyed, merciful of aspect, liberator from delusion; dark of hue as the blue lotus; conqueror of love; bee of the perfumed lotus of the soul; Hari, breaker of the might of the demon host; delight of the saints and the pious; exterminator of sin; beneficent to Bráhmans as a rain-cloud to the new crops; help of the helpless; befriender of the humble; by the might of whose arm earth's grievous burden has been broken; ingenious destroyer of Khara and Dúshan and Viradh; Rávan's antagonist; incarnation of beauty; noblest of kings. Glory to the moon of the lotus house of Dasarath, whose glory is renowned in the Puránas, the Vedas and all the Scriptures, and sung by gods and patriarchs and all the company of the saints. O merciful lord, destroyer of falsehood and pride, infinitely glorious, glory of Kosala, whose name corrects all the impurities of this sinful age and puts an end to the delusions of self, have mercy upon your humble adorer, even me Tulsi Dás."

Dohá 52.

When the venerable Nárad had completed his loving recital of Ràma's praises, he clasped the Ocean of beauty to his heart and withdrew to the realm of Bráhma.

Chaupái.

Hearken, Umá, to this glorious legend, the whole of which I have now told to the best of my ability. But Ráma's acts are hundreds of millions in number and beyond all reckoning: not even the Vedas or Sárada could recount them all. Ráma is infinite and his virtues are infinite; infinite are his incarnations, his actions and his names. You may count the drops in a shower of rain or the dust on the earth, but Ráma's doings defy enumeration. This holy story ensures translation to Hari's own sphere; whoever hears it acquires an imperishable devotion. The whole of the delectable history, which Bhusundi repeated to the king of the birds, has now, Umá, been told you. I have mentioned only a fraction of Ráma's virtues; tell me, Bhaváni, what I am to tell you next." Umá rejoiced to have heard the glorious narrative and in modest and gentle accents thus replied: "Blessed, yea thrice blessed am I, Purári, to have heard the virtues of Ráma, that put an end to all the terrors of life.

Dohá 53.

By your clemency, O most clement, I have attained my desire and am no longer in doubt: I know the glory of Ráma, that he is the Lord, the sum of all knowledge and joy. Your mouth, Sire, flows like the moon with the nectar of Ráma's praises; my soul drinks them in through the pitchers of my ears, but refuses to be satisfied, O resolute of purpose.

Chaupái.

They who can be satiated with hearing Ráma's deeds do not relish their peculiar savour. The great sages, who have been liberated from mundane existence, listen for ever to Ráma's virtues. Whoever desires to traverse the ocean of life finds in Ráma's history a sure ship. Even the worldly accept the praises of Hari as pleasant to the ear and grateful to the soul; for is there any one in the world with ears to hear who takes no pleasure in Ráma's history: they must be dull of soul indeed and self-destroyers, to whom Ráma' history gives no pleasure. While you have been reciting your Ráma lay, I have listened, my lord, with boundless delight. But this delectable story that you have repeated was declared by Káka-bhusundi to Garur.

Dohá 54.

Now I marvel greatly how any one in the form of a crow could be a votary of Ráma's, and possess such self-control and knowledge and wisdom and such staunch devotion to his feet.

Chaupái.

Hearken, Purári ; among a thousand men there may be one who is steadfast in the practices of his religion ; among a million religious people there may be one who loathes sensuality and delights in asceticism ; among a million ascetics—so the Scriptures declare—there may be one who attains to perfect knowledge ; among a million of the truly wise, one may be liberated from mundane existence ; among a thousand of these it is difficult to find the perfect bliss of philosophic absorption into the Supreme Spirit. But beyond the religious, the ascetic, the wise, the exempt from transmigration and the absorbed in the divinity, beyond all these persons, O king of the gods, there is one yet more

Dohá 55.

difficult to find, a devoted believer in Ráma, superior to all vanity and illusion of the senses. Tell me, lord of the universe, how a crow could attain to such faith Tell me, Sire, if he were devoted to Ráma, enamoured of wisdom, full of all good qualities and resolute of purpose, what was the reason that he had the body of a crow ?

Chaupái.

Be pleased to inform me where the crow learnt this holy and delectable history of the lord's doings. Tell me also, O conqueror of Love, the strange mystery of how you heard it. Garur again is very wise and accomplished and one of Hari's most intimate disciples, what was his reason for leaving a company of saints and going to a crow to hear this story? Describe to me the nature of the interview between these two servants of Hari, the crow and the serpent-eater." On hearing Gauri's artless and charming speech Siva was glad and made reverent reply: "A blessing, Sati on your sanctifying scheme! great indeed is your devotion to Ráma's feet. Hearken then to the all-holy story, the hearing of which puts an end to every sorrow and delusion; for from it there springs up an implicit faith in Ráma's feet and without any difficulty man crosses the abyss of existence.

Dohá 56.

This was the very question which the king of the birds, went and put to the crow, as I will reverently explain to you in full: hearken, Uma, with all attention.

Chaupái.

Beautiful and bright-eyed deliverer from the world, listen to the account of how and I heard the story. You first took birth in the house of Daksha and the name you then bore was Sati. At Daksha's sacrifice you were slighted and in the violence of your indignation yielded up your life. My servants then broke up the sacrifice; but all this is a story that you know already. Afterwards I was sorely troubled at heart, sorrowing for the loss of you, my beloved, and wandered among the beautiful woods, and hills and rivers and lakes, admiring the scene, but a sworn ascetic. Far away to the north among the heights of Sumeru is a huge and magnificent purple peak with four glittering pinnacles of gold, so lovely that my soul was enraptured. On each stood one enormous tree, a banyan, a pipal, a pákar and a mango, and on the top of the mountain was a glorious lake, with jewelled steps which it was a delight to behold:

Dohá 57.

Its water cool, pure and sweet; its lotuses abundant and of many colours; while flocks of swans murmured their melodious notes and the bees made a delicious buzzing.

Chaupái.

On this fair height dwelt a crow, outliving even the end of the world. All the virtues and vices that are produced of Mayá, together with Delusion, Love and the others errors of judgment, which permeate the whole world, never came near this mountain. Hearken, Umá, with tender affection, while I tell how the crow passed his life here in the worship of Hari. Under the *pipal* tree he practised meditation; under the *pákar*, prayer and sacrifice; in the shade of the mango he mentally performed the temple ritual, having no other occupation whatever save the worship of Hari; and under the banyan he recited the story of Ráma's adventures, which countless birds flocked to hear. With loving reverence he sung the varying cycle of Ráma's deeds, in the hearing of all the pure-souled swans that ever dwell in that lake. When I arrived there and saw the sight, an intense joy sprang up in my heart.

Dohá 58.

Assuming for a time the form of a swan, I took up my abode there and after reverently listening to Ráma's praises again returned to Kailás.

Chaupái.

I have thus told you, Girijá, the full account of the circumstances under which I visited the crow. Hearken now to the explanation of the reason for Garur's going to see him. When Raghunáth exhibited the battle phantasm, though I understood his action, I was ashamed that he should allow himself to be bound by Meghnád. Nárad the sage then despatched Garur, who cut his bonds and came back, the serpent-eater, but a grievous dejection possessed his soul, as he thought over the Lord's bonds and pondered the matter to himself: "The omnipresent and passionless Supreme Spirit, the lord of speech, who is absolute master over the vanities of illusion, has I hear taken birth in the world; but I see no signs of his majesty.

Dohá 59.

Can this be Ráma, by the repetition of whose name men escape from the bonds of existence, if a wretched demon can bind him in snakey coils?"

Chaupái.

Though he did all he could to re-assure himself, his understanding was not enlightened; error overshadowed his soul. Distracted by doubt and full of mental questionings, he became as subject to delusion as you yourself were. In his perplexity he went to the Rishi of the gods and told him the difficulty that he had in his mind. On hearing his tale, Nárad was moved with a great compassion: "Hearken, O bird; Ráma's delusive power is very strong. When he robs the wise of their sense, he makes their infatuation superlative. The same spectre that has often disturbed me has now, O king of the birds, affected you. The mighty error that has taken root in your soul will not be readily removed by any words of mine. You must go to Bráhma, and do whatever he enjoins you."

Dohá 60.

So saying the teacher of the gods went his way chanting Ráma's praises, again and again in his infinite wisdom insisting on the might of Ráma's delusive power.

Chaupai.

The king of the birds then went to the Creator and told him his difficulty. On hearing his story, Bráhma bowed the head to Ráma and, as he thought on his majesty, his heart was filled with love, and he thus mused within himself: "Poets and the wisest of philosophers are subjects to delusion. The might of Hari's deceptive power is unbounded; many a time has it made me its puppet, though all things animate and inanimate are of my creation, no wonder then that it has beguiled the king of the birds." Then said Bráhma in gracious accents: "Siva understands Ráma's power. Go to him, O son of Vinata, and ask no questions of any other. There you will find the solution of your doubts." On hearing Bráhma's advice, the bird went his way.

Dohá 61.

Then came the king of the birds in the utmost distress to me. At that time, Umá, I was on my way to the palace of Kuver, and had left you at Kailás.

Chaupái.

He reverently bowed his head at my feet and then told me his difficulty. On hearing his humble petition, I lovingly responded, Bhavání: "You have met me, Garur, on the road; how can I instruct you? Your doubts will not be settled till you have been for a long time in the company of the saints. There you must listen to the delightful story of Ráma, as sung in diverse manners by the seers, in which the beginning, middle, and end is the adorable lord, the great God Ráma. I will send you, brother to a place where the story of Ráma is told without ceasing; go there and listen. As you hear it, all your doubts will vanish; you will have a vehement affection for Ráma's feet.

Dohá 62.

Except in the company of saints there is no talk about Ràma; without that there is no overcoming delusion; till delusion is dispersed, there is no firm affection for Ráma's feet.

Chaupái.

Without affection there is no finding Ráma, though you have recourse to meditation, prayer, sacrifice, and asceticism. In the region of the north is a beautiful purple mountain, where lives the amiable Káka-bhusundi, supremely skilled in the method of Ráma's worship, wise and full of all good qualities and very aged. He unceasingly recites Ráma's history and all the noblest of the birds reverently listen. Go there and hear all Ráma's excellences; your distress born of delusion will then be removed." After I had given him full instructions, he bowed his head at my feet and set out with joy. I did not myself instruct him, Uma, for I understood the mystery of Ráma's grace. Perhaps he had shown pride on some occasion and the All-merciful wished that he should cure himself of this defect. There was also another reason why I did not detain him; being a bird he understood bird language. The Lord's delusive power, Bhaváni, is great; who is so wise as not to be fascinated by it?

Dohá 63.

Even the vehicle of the lord of the three spheres, the very crown of philosophers and saints, was overcome by its deceptive influence; wretched man may well have his doubts. It fascinates Siva and Bráhma; why speak of other poor creatures? The saints know this at heart, when they worship the great God, Mayá's master.

Chaupái.

Garur went to Bhusundi's abode, that sturdy-hearted and indefatigable votary of Hari's. At the sight of the rock his heart rejoiced; the trouble caused him by Mayá's wiles all passed away. After bathing in the lake and drinking of the water, he went under the banyan tree with exulting soul. There assembled flocks upon flocks of birds to hear of Ráma's glorious doings. He was just on the point of beginning to recite, when the king of the birds arrived. All were glad to see him approach, the crow no less than the rest of the assembly. They received him with the utmost politeness and asked of his welfare and conducted him to a seat. Then the crow, after doing him loving homage, addressed him in these winning words:

Dohá 64.

"Now am I content, O king of the birds, in that I have see you; whatever you may order me, I am ready to do: what is the object of your visit, my lord?" "You have ever been the image of content," replied Garur in gracious phrase, "seeing that Siva with his own mouth is ever reverently singing your praises.

Chaupái.

Hearken, father ; the object for which I came was attained as soon as I saw you. Directly I beheld your most holy hermitage, my delusion was at an end with all my distracting doubts. Now, father, repeat to me with all solemnity the most sanctifying story of Ráma, which is ever delightful and a remedy for every ill : this, my lord, is what I urgently beg of you." On hearing Garur's prayer, so humble, sincere and affectionate, so graceful and pious, a supreme joy was diffused over his soul and he began the recital of Raghupati's glory. First, Bhaváni, he expounded with fervent devotion the motive of Ráma's acts. Then he told of Nárad's extraordinary delusion and of Rávan's incarnation. After this he sang the story of the Lord's birth and then carefully recounted his doings as a child.

Dohá 65.

After telling all the details of his childish performances with the utmost rapture of soul, he next told of the Rishi's coming and of Raghu-bír's " marriage.

Chaupái.

Then came the narrative of Ráma's coronation, of the king's vow and abdication of royal state, the sorrow of the citizens at parting, the colloquy between Ráma and Lakshman, the journey to the forest, the devotion of the boatman, the passage of the Ganges and the stay at Prayág. He described also the Lord's meeting with Válmíki and how the god dwelt at Chitra-kút, the coming of the Minister, the death of the king in the city, the arrival of Bharat and the greatness of his affection, how after performing the king's obsequies both Bharat himself and the citizens had gone to join the Lord blessed for ever, and how after he had said all he could to console them Bharat took his sandal back with him to Avadh. Next he related Bharat's mode of life, the action of the son of Indra and the Lord's interview with Atri.

Dohá 66.

Then he told of Virádh's death, of how Sarabhanga dropped his body, of Sutikshná's devotion and the Lord's pious intercourse with Agastya.

Chaupái.

He told him also of the purification of the Dandaka forest, of the friendliness of the vulture, of the Lord's stay in the woods of Panchavati, and how he put an end to the fears of all the saints. Then came the incomparable exhortation to Lakshman and the story of Surpa-nakhás mutilation. After this he narrated to him the death of Khara and Dúshan, and how Rávan penetrated the myster and all the particulars of his talk with Márícha. Then he described the rape of the fictitious Síta and gave an idea of Ráma's bereavement. After this he told how the Lord performed the vulture's funeral rites and slew Kabandh and gave salvation to Sabari. He told also of Raghu-bír's mourning and how he went to the shore of the lake.

Dohá 67

Of his interview with Nárad, his meeting with Hanumán, his alliance with Sugriva and his taking Báli's life; of his making the monkey king and taking up his abode on the rock during the rains. He described also the rains and the autumn and Ráma's indignation and the monkey's alarm.

Chaupái.

How the monkey king sent out monkeys, who ran in every direction search for Síta; how they entered the cave and found Sampáti; how Hanumán, when he had heard all the circumstances, jumped over the mighty ocean; how he made his way into Lanká and bade Sita be of good cheer: how he laid waste the garden, and lectured Rávan and set fire to the city and leaped over the sea again. How the monkeys all rejoined Ráma and told him of Síta's welfare; how Raghu-bír with his army went and encamped on the sea-shore; how Vibhíshan came to meet him, and how the sea was put in check;

Dohá 68.

How the bridge was built and the monkey host crossed over to the opposite side, and how the valiant son of Báli went as an envoy. He described the various battes between the demons and the monkeys, the might and valour of Kumbha-karn and Meghnád and their destruction;

Chaupái.

The different deaths of all the demons, the fight between Báma and Rávan, the death of Rávan, the mourning of Mandodari, the enthronement of Vibhishan and the satisfaction of the gods; the meeting also of Ráma and Síta and how the gods with clasped hands hymned their praises; how the all-merciful Lord with the monkeys mounted the car Pushpaka and set out for Avadh; and how Ráma arrived at his own city; all these glorious doings were sung by the crow. Then he told of Ráma's coronation and described the city and all its kingly polity. The entire history did Bhusundi tell, as I have told it to you, Bhaváni. When the king of the birds had heard it all, his soul was in raptures and he cried:

Sorathá 5.

" My doubts are gone, now that I have heard Ráma's full history. By your favour, O best of crows, I feel a devotion to Ráma's feet. A mighty bewilderment possessed me when I saw the Lord bound in the battle: if Ràma be the sum of all knowledge and bliss, what can embarrass him?

Chaupái.

Seeing all his ways so entirely consistent with humanity, a very grievous doubt arose in my soul. But now I understand that my error was a favour which the All-merciful was pleased to bestow upon me. To appreciate the blessing of a shady tree, one must first have suffered from the sun. If this delusion had not befallen me, how should I have met you, father, and how should I have heard the delightful story of Ráma which you have told me so fully in all its details ? This is the doctrine of the Purános and all the Scriptures, the unhesitating assertion of all the seers and sages, that the company of good and holy men can only be attained by one on whom Ráma has looked with an eye of favour. By Ráma's favour I have had sight of you, and by your grace all my doubts are gone."

Dohá 69.

On hearing Garur's modest and affectionate speech, the crow was greatly rejoiced at heart; every hair on his body stood erect and his eyes streamed with tears. O Uma, when a good man finds and intelligent and well-disposed listener, who is pious and fond of religious reading and a worshipper of Hari, he reveals to him hidden mysteries.

Chaupái.

Then answered Káka-bhusundi, who had no slight affection for the king of the birds : " My lord, you are in every way entitled to my respect, as a vessel of Hari's grace. You had no doubts, infatuation, or delusion; it was only a pretext, Sire, for doing me a kindness. By sending you. Garur, as a victim of delusion, Raghu-pati has conferred an honour upon me. Yet there is nothing wonderful, Sir, in that delusion of yours of which you tell me; for Nárad, Siva, Bráhma, Sanat-Kumára and his brethren, with all the great saints who discourse of the soul, is there one of them whom delusion has not blinded, or whom Love has not made a puppet of, whom Desire has not maddened, or whose heart choler has not inflamed ?

Dohá 70.

Is there any philosopher, ascetic, or hero in the world, or any learned and accomplished bard, whom Greed has not beguiled; whom the pride of wealth has not rendered wanton; whom power has not made deaf; or whom the glance of beauty has not smitten as an arrow?

Chaupái.

Is there any whom success has not paralyzed; who has effectually discarded vanity and pride; whom the fever of youth has not overcome; whose glory has not been ruined by self-conceit; whom envy has not besmirched; whom the blast of sorrow has not shaken; whom the serpent of care has not bitten; or whom delusion has not affected? Is there any so well seasoned of frame that he has not been attacked by desire, as a plank by the weevil? The desire of family, of wealth and of renown is a threefold temptation; whose soul has it not sullied? These all are Mayá's suite; who can describe in full her illimitable might? Since Siva and Bráhma stand in awe of her, why speak of other creatures?

Dohá 71.

Mayá's formidable army is spread over the whole world; Love and the other Passions are her generals; Fraud, Deceit and Heresy her champions. Being the servant of Raghu-bír, though known to be a delusion, she can only be dispersed by his favour; this, my lord, I assert with the utmost confidence.

Chaupái.

This Mayá, that sets the whole world a-dancing and whose actions no one can understand, is herself set dancing with all her troupe, like an actress on the stage, O king of the birds, by the play of the Lord's eye-brows. For Ráma is the totality of existence, knowledge and bliss,[1] the uncreated the all-wise the home of beauty and strength; the

[1] For *Ghan Ràma* some books read *Ghan-Syáma*, which, however, would seem to be only an evasion of the difficulty. *Ghan* by itself, meaning literally 'solid, material, substantial,' might be intended to denote the visible world of phenomena, which is the converse of the ideal world indicated by the term *sachchidánand*. But it is simpler to take *sachchidànand-ghan* as one compound and translate as in the text.

permeator and the permeated ;[1] the indivisible, the eternal; the insoluble, the unerring ; the primal energy, the Godhead ; of whom no qualities can be predicated and no deceit ; beyond the range of speech or perception ; all-seeing,[2] irreproachable, unconquered ; without personal interests, without form, without illusion : deathless, passionless, blessed for ever ; trascending nature : the Lord that indwelleth in evey heart ; the Supreme Spirit, effortless, passionless, imperishable ; in him delusion finds no sphere ; does darkness ever attack the sun ?

Dohá 72.

For the sake of his faithful people, the very God, our lord Ráma, has become incarnate as a king and for our supreme sanctification has lived as it were the life of any ordinary man. As an actor in the course of his performance assumes a variety of dresses and exhibits different characters, but himself remains the same ;

Chaupái.

Such, Garur, is Ráma's divertissement, a bewilderment to the demons, but a delight to the faithful. Sensual libertines in their dulness of soul impute the delusion to the Lord, like as when, Sir, a man whose eyesight is in fault says that the moon is of a yellow colour ; or when mistaken as to the points of the compass, affirms that the sun has risen in the west ; or as one on boardship, who deludes himself with the idea that he is standing still and that the land is moving. When children in play turn round and

---

1 The words in the text are *vyápaka*, *vyápaya*, which are technical terms in the *Nyáya* philosophy, meaning 'the pervader,' or 'invariably pervading attribute 'and 'invariably pervaded.' They are employed in making a universal affirmation, or in affirming universal distribution ; as, for example. 'Wherever there is smoke, there is fire ;' 'Wherever there is humanity, there is mortality.' In such cases an Indian logician always expresses himself by saying that there is an invariably pervading concomitance of fire with smoke and of mortality with humanity ; thus fire and mortality would be called the pervaders, *vyápakas* ; smoke and humanity the pervaded, *vyápya* See *Monier Williams' Indian Wisdom.* As employed by Tulsi Dás, the words might be adequately rendered by 'cause and effect,' 'subject and predicate,' or by any other similar phrase which would be equally inclusive.

2 For *sab-darsi*, all-seeing,' another reading is *samdarsi*, 'seeing alike,' *i.e.*, 'impartial.'

round, the house, or whatever else it may be, does not turn round, it is only their idle fashion of talking. In this way only, O Garur, can error be ascribed to Hari ; never even in a dream is he really subject to delusion. The wretched dullards, who succumb to Máyá, have a thick veil over their soul, and these are the obstinate fools who raise doubts and lay their own ignorance on Ráma.

Dohá 73.

How can these clowns understand Raghu-pati, addicted as they are to lust, choler, pride and greed, absorbed in domestic affairs, pictures of misery, at the bottom of a well of darkness ? The unembodied phase of the Godhead is easy to understand, but who can comprehend its incarnation ? the soul of a saint is bewildered on hearing of all his actions, both natural and supernatural.

Chaupái.

Hearken, Garur, I will tell you to the best of my ability an agreeable story, in illustration of Ráma's power ; declaring to you in full all the particulars of a delusion which befell myself. You, Sire, are a vessel of Ráma's grace and cherish a special affection for Hari's actions, and are moreover my greatest benefactor ; I will therefore conceal nothing from you in this exposition of a great and excellent mystery. Hearken ; Ráma's natural disposition is such that he never tolerates pride in his servants. Pride has its root in worldliness and is the cause of many pains and every kind of vexation. Therefore the All-merciful does away with it, in the greatness of his affection for his servants : in the same way, Sire, as when a child has a boil on its body, its mother with seeming cruelty cuts it open.

Dohá 74.

At first the poor child cries with the pain, but the mother pays no attention to it, her object being to cure the disease. In like manner Raghupati cures his servants of pride, doing it all for their good. Ah, Tulsi Dás, who would not forswear error and worship such a lord as this ?

Chaupái.

I will now tell you the story, Garur, of Ráma's grace and my own stupidity; listen attentively. Whenever Ráma assumes human form and goes through his series of mimic actions in the behoof of his votaries, I always betake myself to Avadh and delight to watch his boyish doings. I go and attend the rejoicings at his birth and am glad to stay for five years. The child Ráma is my patron divinity, beautiful in form as a myriad Loves Ever gazing on the face of my own lord, O Garur, I give my eyes a treat indeed, and being in the trivial shape of a crow I keep close to Hari and observe all his child-like sports.

Dohá 75.

Whenever he rambles in play, I flutter about close at hand, and for my food I pick up the crumbs in the court-yard that fall from his table. One day Raghu-bír played a very quaint frolic. At the remembrance of his lord's playfulness, every hair on his body stood erect with rapture.

Chaupái.

Bhusundi continued: "Hearken, king of the birds, to my story of Ráma's actions, which are ever the delight of his servants. The king's palace was exquisitely beautiful; of gold studded with precious stones of every kind. The pleasantness of the court-yard, where the four brothers were always playing, surpasses description. Here Ráma roamed about, to the delight of his mother, diverting himself with childish amusements; his tender frame dark of hue as a sapphire, with the beauty of unnumbered Loves in every limb; his soft rosy feet like lotus buds, with lustrous nails that outshone the brightness of the moon, decorated with the four-fold stamp of the thunderbolt, the lotus, the elephant-goad and the flag, and circled with pretty bangles that made sweet music. Melodious, too, the pretty belt about his waist fashioned of gold and bossed with jewels.

Dohá 76.

With a belly creased in the three lines of beauty, a navel shapely and deep, and a broad chest gleaming with all the ornaments that befit a child's attire;

Chaupái.

With roseate hands and lovely nails; with long and richly raceleted arms and the shoulders of a young lion; with dimpled neck and rounded chin and face the perfection of beauty; with lisping speech and ruddy lips and two dear little pearly teeth above and below; with chubby cheeks and a darling nose and a smile as winsome as that of the moon; with lotus eyes that loose earth's ties and forehead gleaming with the mark of yellow pigment; with arched eye-brows and pretty ears; with curly hair black and beautiful; with a thin yellow jacket to set off his body, he fascinated me with his merry glance, as he sported in all his loveliness in the king's courts, dancing at the sight of his own shadow, and having all sorts of antics with me, which I blush to tell. When he laughingly ran to catch me, I flew away; then he showed me a piece of cake.

Dohá 77.

I came near and the Lord laughed. I flew away again and he fell a-crying. I approached to lay hold of his feet, and he ran off, again and again turning round to look at me. Seeing him play like an ordinary child, I was overcome by bewilderment. Can these be the actions of the Lord who is the totality of intelligence and bliss?

Chaupái.

This was what came into my mind, Garur, for Ráma had sent forth his delusive power to entangle me. But this delusion was in no way harmful to me. I was not so affected by it as other creatures. A special cause, my lord, was here at work, which I wish you, Garur, to observe attentively. Ráma alone is absolute intelligence; every creature, animate, or inanimate, is subject to Mayá. If all had the same perfect intelligence, tell me what would be the difference between God and his creature? The creature in his pride is subjected to Mayá. Mayá with all its phenomena is subject to God. The creature is dependent on others, the Deity is self-dependent; the creature is manifold, Ráma is one. Though the distinctions made by Mayá are false, without Hari's help they cannot be dispersed, whatever you may do.

Dohá 78.

The wisest of men, who hopes for salvation without prayer to Ráma, is like a beast without tail and horns. Though sixteen full moons were to rise and all the starry host and the forests on every mountain were set on fire, night would not yield except to the sun.

Chaupái.

In like manner, Garur, without prayer to Hari, the troubles incident to existence cannot be dispersed. Ignorance has no power over a servant of Hari's; knowledge emanating from the Lord pervades his whole being. Therefore, O best of birds, there is no destruction for a believer: his faith as of a servant in his master is ever growing. Ráma smiled to see me reel in error, and hear what a strange course he adopted. The secret of this diversion neither his brother nor his father or mother ever knew. As he crawled on his hands and knees in a hurry to catch me—with his body so dark of hue and his rosy hands and feet—I took to flight, Garur, and he stretched out his arms to lay hold of me. High as I flew into the air, I still saw his arms as close to me as ever.

Dohá 79.

I mounted even to Bráhma's sphere, but when I looked back in my flight, two fingers' breadth, Sir, was all the distance between me and Ráma's arms. I cleft the seven folds of the universe and mounted to the utmost height that I could reach, but still I saw the Lord's arms; then was I dumbfounded.

Chaupái.

In my terror I closed my eyes, and when I opened them again I found myself at Ayodhyá. Ráma looked at me with a smile, and as he laughed I jumped down his throat. In his belly (hearken, king of the birds) I saw multitudinous universes, with many strange worlds, each more wonderful than the other; with myriads of Bráhmas and Sivas; stars and suns and moons innumerable; innumerable Lokpàls and images of Death and Times: innumerable mountains and vast plains of earth; seas, lakes, rivers and forests without end, and all the complex machinery of creation; with gods, sages, saints, serpents and kinnars and the four classes of living things, both moving and motionless.

Dohá 80.

Such as eye has not seen, nor ear heard, nor has entered into man's mind to conceive, were all the marvels that I saw; how is it possible to describe them? In each universe I stayed a hundred years and in this manner made the round of all the multitudinous globes.[1]

Chaupái.

Each world had its own separate Creator, its own Vishnu, Siva, and Manu and its own Regents of the spheres; with men, Gandharvas, imps and evils spirits, kinnars and demons, cattle, birds and serpents, all the tribes of gods and giants, and every living creature, but differing in form; with lands, rivers, seas, lakes, and mountains, and the whole mechanism of creation also quite distinct. Each mundane egg had its own peculiar aspect and in all its manifold details was wonderful to behold. In each world was a separate city of Avadh with its own Sarju; its own men and women,

1 *Anda-katàha*, which I translate 'globes,' is simply a synonym for *Bráhámánda*, which occurs in the previous lines. It would be more precisely rendered 'half-globe,' *katàha* here standing for the common Hindi *karàha*, a large shallow iron vessel used for boiling sugar, &c.

with Dasarath and Kausalyá and the other queens, and Bharat and his brothers, each in their proper form. Each sphere had its own incarnate Ráma with all his child-like sports for me to see.

Dohá 81.

O Garur, I saw every part of the pageant separately repeated, but in my round of the innumerable worlds I saw no other Lord Ráma. The same child like ways, the same beauty, the same gracious Raghu-bír were what I saw in each successive world that I visited, driven on by the blast of delusion.

Chaupái.

Imagine a hundred cycles to have been spent in my wanderings through the different spheres. At last after all my travels I came to my own hermitage and there I stayed some little time. When I heard of my lord's birth at Avadh, I started up in an overwhelming ecstasy of devotion and went and witnessed the rejoicings at his nativity as I have already described to you. In Ráma's belly I saw many worlds, but what I saw is past all telling. Then again I saw the all-wise Ráma, the lord of Mayá, the merciful God, and much I questioned within myself, for my understanding was obscured by the mists of delusion. In two hours I saw everything; I was a-weary and my soul was bewildered entirely.

Dohá 82.

Seeing my distress, the all-merciful Raghu-bír laughed, and as he laughed I issued from his mouth; hearken, O firm of faith. Rama again began his childish pranks with me. I reasoned with myself in every way I could; but my mind had no peace.

Chaupái.

Seeing this miracle and weighing its transcendency I lost my senses. I fell to the ground and no word came to my mouth, but 'Save me, save me, O saviour of all distrest believers.' When the Lord saw my agony of devotion, he at once checked the influence of his delusive power. The Lord placed his lotus hands upon my head and—ever merciful to the poor—healed me of all my pain. Ráma, the gracious benefactor of his servants, thus dispelled my infatuation. As I reflected on his mighty power, there first arose in my heart a great transport of delight; and seeing his loving-kindness to his worshippers my bosom heaved with an unutterable love. With streaming eyes and quivering frame and hands clasped in prayer, I again and again made humble petition.

Dohá 83.

Hearing my loving words and seeing me to be his own devoted servant, he made me this gracious, profound and tender speech; "Káka-bhusundi, ask of me a boon, for know that I am highly pleased with you; be it the supernatural powers of the saints, or fabulous wealth, or deliverance from further transmigration, the sum of all bliss;

Chaupái.

or knowledge and wisdom, self-restraint and philosophy, qualities which as all the world knows scarce the gods can attain unto. To-day I will grant you anything; doubt not, but ask whatever your soul desires." On hearing the Lord's words I was greatly moved and began to reason thus within myself; "The Lord, it is true, has promised to give me every blessing, but has not said he would give me faith. Without faith what are any virtues or blessings? like any quantity of condiments without salt. Of what avail is any good without prayer?" Having thus considered, O Garur, I made reply: "If it be your good pleasure, my lord, to grant me a boon and if you wish to do me a favour and kindness, I will ask the boon, Sire, which my soul desires; you are generous and know the secrets of the hearts.

Dohá 84.

A steadfast and sincere faith, such as the Vedas and Puránas describe, such as the greatest ascetics and saints search after, but few only find and that by the Lord's grace: O my lord Ráma, tree of Paradise to the pious, friend of the suppliant, all-merciful, all-blessed, of your clemency grant me this faith."

Chaupái.

"So be it," said the prince of the house of Raghu and then continued in these most gracious words: "Hearken, O crow; you are very sagacious, and therefore no wonder that you ask this boon. You crave faith, the source of every blessing; there is none in the world so highly favoured as you; for the saints cannot grasp it after all their labours, though they consume their whole body in the fire of prayer and meditation. I am pleased to see your sagacity; your prayer for faith is most agreeable to me. Hearken, now, O bird, to the favours I bestow upon you; every good quality shall dwell in your bosom; faith, knowledge, divine, wisdom, self-governance, the practice of mystic abstraction and all the secrets of esoteric love. You shall understand the mysteries of every science and with my favour shall need no other help.

Dohá 85.

None of the errors that arise from Máyá shall hence forth affect you; you know me to be the Supreme Spirit, without birth or beginning, the immaterial root-of all matter. Remember, O crow, that every believer is dear to me; hearken to my words, and in thought, word and deed maintain an unalterable devotion to my feet.

Chaupái.

Attend now to this most holy exposition of mine, which is both simple and true and is implied in the Vedas and other Scriptures. I will reveal to you my own peculiar doctrine: apply your mind to listen and worship me only, abjuring all others. The world is the product of my delusive power, with all its varieties of life, both moving and motionless. I love them all, for all are my creatures; but man is the creature that delights me most. Of men, Bráhmans ; of Bráhmans, those who study the Vedas ; of these, such as follow the precepts of the sacred texts ; of these again celibates are my favourites, and yet more the wise ; of the wise I love best the spiritually wise, and of these the best beloved of all are my own servants, who come to me and have no other hope. Again and again I tell you of a truth there are none so dear to me as my own disciples. If Bráhma himself had no faith in me, he would be no dearer to me than any other creature ; while the meanest creature 'that breathes, if possessed of faith, is as dear to me as my own soul ; this is my doctrine.

Dohá 86.

Tell me how is it possible that a pure, well-disposed and intelligent servant should not be held dear ? hearken, O crow, with attention to the principle laid down both in the Vedas and Puránas.

Chaupái.

A father has a number of children, each different in character, temper and occupation. One is a student, another a philosophic ascetic, another an accumulator of wealth, an open-handed soldier, a clever man of the world, or a devotee ; the father feels the same affection for them all. Another, again, is in thought, word and deed entirely devoted to his father, never even dreaming of any other duty ; and this is the son whom the father loves as his own soul, though he be a perfect ignoramus. In like manner all animate and inanimate beings, including brute beasts, gods, men and demons, in short the entire universe that I have created, is viewed by me with equal compassion ; but, amongst them all, if there be one who forswears vanity and delusion and worships me only in thought, word and deed,

Dohá 87.

whether he be man, eunuch, or woman, whether animate or inanimate, if with all his soul he sincerely worships me, he is my best-beloved.

Sorathá 3.

O crow, I tell you of a truth that an honest servant is as dear to me as my own life. Remember this and worship me only, abjuring every other hope and assurance.

Chaupái.

Time shall have no power over you, so long as you remember to worship me without ceasing." I should never have tired of listening to my lord's ambrosial discourse; my body quivered all over and my soul rejoiced exceedingly. My mind and my ears experienced a delight, which it is beyond the power of tongue to tell. My eyes had the bliss of beholding my lord's beauty, but how can they declare it? they have no voice. After he had gladdened me by his manifold exhortations, he again began to sport like a child. With streaming eyes and mouth a little awry, he looked at his mother as if he were very hungry. Seeing this she started up in haste and ran and spoke to him with caressing words and clasped him to her bosom; then holding him in her lap she gave him to suck, singing the while of Ráma's charming deeds.

Sorathá 4.

The citizens of Avadh were ever flooded with that joy, to attain which the blessed Siva assumes his unsightly garb. They who have once realized even in a dream the least atom of that joy, think nothing, O Garur, if they are good and sensible, of the joys of heaven.

Chaupái.

After this I stayed some little time at Avadh, a spectator of his delightful boyish play. Then, by Ráma's blessing, having obtained the boon of faith, I kissed my lord's feet and returned to my hermitage. Since then no delusion has ever affected me, after I had joined Ráma. I have now told you the whole of this strange story of how I was bewitched by Hari's delusive power. From my own experience I warn you, Garur, that without prayer to Hari your troubles will not yield. Hearken, king of the birds; without Ràma's grace, there is no understanding his power; without understanding there is no confidence; without confidence there is no affection; without affection there is no consistency in faith; it slips away, Garur, like oil on water.

Sorathá 5.

How can there be knowledge without a teacher? how can there be knowledge without self-control, or (as the Vedas and Puránas declare) how can man attain to happiness without devotion to Hari? Without innate content, Sire, none can find peace: a boat will not float without water, though you strain every nerve, enough to kill yourself.

Chaupái.

Without content there is no cessation of desire; so long as desire continues, it is vain to dream of ease. Can desire be subdued without prayer to Ráma; can a tree ever take root without soil? Can equanimity be attained without knowledge, or can you have space without the ether? Without faith their is no religion, as there can be no scent without earth? Can fame spread without penance, any more than there can be moisture in the world without water? Can virtue be acquired without attendance on the wise, any more than vision can exist, Sir, without light? Can the mind be at rest when ill at ease, any more than the sense of touch is possible without air?[1] Without confidence there is no exercise of supernatural powers, and without prayer to Hari there is no conquest over the terrors of existence.

Dohá 88.

Without confidence there is no devotion; without devotion Ráma is not moved; without the grace of Ráma no creature can dream of peace.

Chaupái

Thus consider, O stout of heart, and abjuring scepticism

---

1 The five elements, ether, earth, water, light and air and their several properties are here enumerated.

and every doubt, worship Ráma, the heroic son of Raghu, fountain of mercy, the beautiful, the beneficent.

Chaupái.

Thus have I declared to you, king Garur, according to my ability, the greatness of the Lord's power; nor have I anywhere had recourse to studied invention, for I have seen it all with my own eyes. Ráma's greatness, his names, his glory, beauty and perfection, are all boundless and infinite. The saints sing his praises, according to their several ability, but not the Vedas, Sesh-nág or Siva could declare them fully. There is no winged creature, from yourself down to a gnat, who can reach to the end of the heaven in his flight. In like manner, Sire, the greatness of Raghupati is unfathomable; none can sound the bottom of it. Ráma is beautiful of body as a myriad Loves; irresistible in the destruction of his foes as a myriad Durgás; jocund as a myriad Indras; immeasurable in expanse as a myriad firmaments.

Dohá 89.

As masterful in might as a myriad winds; as bright as a myriad suns; as cooling as a myriad moons, soothing all the terror of existence; as impracticable, inaccessible and interminable as a myriad deaths; as irrepressible as a myriad fires, our very God,

Chaupái.

The Lord is as unfathomable as a myriad Hells; as inflexible as a myraid Yamas; as immeasurably holy as a myraid places of pilgrimage whose name obliterates any accumulation of sin. Raghu-bír is as immoveable as a myriad Himálayas; as profound as a myriad seas; as liberal in the fulfilment of every desire as a myriad cows of plenty, and is our very God. As illimitable in eloquence as a myriad Sáradás; as skilful in creation as a myriad Bráhmas; as potent to save as a myriad Vishnus; as potent to destroy as a myriad Sivas; as abounding in wealth as a myriad Kuvers; as fertile in phenomena as a myriad

Mayás; a supporter of the world like a myriad Sesh-nágs; the illimitable, incomparable Lord, the sovereign of the universe.

Chhand 9.

Incomparable indeed; for, as the Vedas declare, Ráma alone is Ráma's peer, none else can compare with him. If one should compare the sun to a hundred myriads of fire-flies, it would be utterly inadequate. In like manner the great sages have exercised their ingenuity in describing Hari, and the Lord, appreciating their intention, has of his great clemency listened kindly and approved.

Dohá 90.

Ráma is an unfathomable ocean of perfection, who can sound it to the bottom? I can only tell you the little I have myself heard from the saints.

Sorathá 7.

Abjure all selfishness, vanity and pride, and ever worship Síta's spouse, the great God who is moved by sincere devotion, the all-blessed, the all-merciful."

Chaupái.

On hearing Bhusundi's delectable discourse, the king of the birds rejoiced and preened his wings. His eyes streamed and his soul was overcome with delight as he meditated on the might of the divine Ráma. He was ashamed to think of his former delusion, when he had taken the everlasting and Supreme Spirit for a mere man. Again and again he bowed his head at the crow's feet, whom in the greatness of his affection he regarded as a second Ráma. "Without a spiritual guide none can traverse the ocean of existence, though he be the equal of Bráhma or Siva. Doubt like a serpent had crushed me in the painful coils of wordy scepticism; but Ráma appeared in your form as an antidote and restored me to life, beneficent as he is to all his votaries. By your favour I have overcome my delusion and have learnt the incomparable mystery of Ráma."

Dohá 91.

After eulogizing him in every possible way and bowing the head before him with clasped hands, Garur proceeded in these humble, affectionate and winning terms : " In my ignorance, O my lord and master, I would ask you a question. In your infinite compassion be pleased to instruct me, regarding me as your own peculiar servant.

Chaupái.

You are all-wise ; a perfect philosopher ; intelligent, amiable and upright in your dealings : a store-house of knowledge, sobriety and spiritual intuition ; and one of Ráma's favourite servants : what, then, is the reason, Sire, for your having received such a form ? Explain this to me in full. Tell me also, venerable bird, where you learnt this excellent history of Ráma's deeds. Further, my lord, I have heard from Siva that you do not perish at the time of the destruction of all things. The god never utters an idle word, and therefore my mind is in doubt. For the whole universe, my lord, with all creatures moving and motionless, serpents, men and gods, is but a mouthful for Death. Death has swallowed up worlds without end and is ever irresistible and strong.

Sorathá 8.

What is the reason that so terrible a monster as Death has no effect upon you ? be pleased to inform me whether it be the power of your intellect or the virtue of your mystical devotion.

Dohá 92.

Further, my lord, be so kind as to explain to me how it was that my delusion vanished directly I approached your hermitage."

Chaupái.

When he heard Garur's question the crow was pleased and answered him, Umá, with the greatest possible kindness : " A blessing on your wit, Garur ; your questions are most agreeable to me. As I listen to your affectionate and becoming enquiries, the recollection of many previous births comes back to me. I will tell you the whole of my history; listen, Sire, with full and reverent attention. Prayer, penance, sacrifice, sobriety of mind, self-control, acts of devotion, charity, chastity, knowledge, mystical meditation and spiritual wisdom, all have their fruit in the love for Ráma's feet, without which none can attain to happiness. It was in this body that I learnt devotion to Ráma, and therefore I have a special liking for it. Every one likes that by means of which he has gained his object.

Sorathá 9.

O Garur, this is a maxim approved by the Vedas and declared by the pious that love should be shown to the meanest creature, if you know it to be your friend. Silk is the product of a worm, but from it is made beautiful apparel; therefore, vile as the worm is, every one tends it with the most sedulous care.

Chaupái.

The highest object of every living creature is the love of Ráma. The holiest and comeliest of bodies is the one in which he has been worshipped. An enemy of Ráma's, though in bodily appearance he rival Bráhma, will never be extolled by any intelligent poet. It was in my present bodily form that my devotion to Ráma first took root, and on that account, Sire, I have a great affection for it. Though I can die when I like, I do not give up my body, for without a body, as the Vedas declare, I could not pray. At first delusion led me greatly astray; having Ráma against me, I was never happy even in my sleep. In different births I practised different courses of action, essaying mystical contemplation, prayer, fasting, sacrifice and almsgiving. Is there any womb in which I have not at some time taken birth, during my peregrinations of the universe? In all my experience, Sire, I was never so happy as I am at present; and yet, my lord, I recollect many previous existences, in which, by the blessing of Siva, no delusion oppressed my understanding.

Dohá 93.

Hearken, king of the birds; I will now tell you the story of a former birth. To hear it will increase your devotion to the Lord, which is the remedy for every ill. In a former Kalpa,[1] my lord, there was an iron age of the utmost impurity; man and woman were devoted to impiety and all rebelled against the Veda.

Chaupái.

In that iron age I went to the city of Kosala and was there born as a man of the servile class, a devoted worshipper of Siva, but a scornful reviler of all the other gods, intoxicated with the pride of wealth, outrageously boastful, savage of purpose and with a heartful of arrogance. Although I lived in Ráma's capital, I had at the time no knowledge of his greatness. Now I understand the virtue of Avadh, as it has been sung by the Vedas, Puráns and all the Scriptures, that every one who in any birth has lived at Avadh will eventually become a disciple of Ráma's. A man then knows the virtue of Avadh, when Ráma with bow in hand takes up his abode in his heart. It was an age, Garur, of terrible wickedness; every man and woman was bent on crime.

Dohá 94.

The sinfulness of the age had stifled religion; the sacred books were all neglected and false teachers had published endless heresies, which they had invented out of their own imagination. The people were all over-mastered by delusion and greed had stifled all acts of piety. Hearken, most wise Garur, while I describe some of the religious practices of those evil times.

Chaupái.

No regard was paid to caste or the four stages of life;

---

1 A *Kalpa* is a period of time comprising a thousand *mahá-yugas*. Each *mahá-yuga* is the aggregate of four *yugas*, or ages of gradually diminished duration, named respectively Krita, or Satya; Tretá; Dwápara and Kali; giving together a total of 4,320,000 years. The length of a Kalpa is thus 4,320,000,000 years. When it is over, the existing world is annihilated and another begins to run its course, and so on to all eternity.

every one was bent upon attacking the Scriptures. Bráhmans sold the Veda; kings devoured their subjects; no one regarded the injunctions of revelation. The right road was any that most took the fancy; the greatest Pandit was the one who talked the loudest. Any who indulged in false pretences and hypocrisy was universally styled a saint. A wise man was he who plundered his neighbour; every boaster was thought a fine fellow, every liar a wit and was spoken of as a man of parts in those evil days. A reprobate who denied the doctrines of revelation was an enlightened philosopher; and any one with unkempt hair and nails was celebrated in that debased age as a model of mortification.

Dohá 95.

To assume the loathsome rags and properties of a mendicant and feed indiscriminately on any kind of food was to be an ascetic, a saint, an object of veneration in that age of iniquity.

Sorathá 10.

All kinds of evil-doers were held in honour and respect, and the idlest babblers were accepted as preachers in those miserable days.

Chaupái.

The man was everywhere subject to the woman and played the buffoon like a dancing monkey. Súdras instructed the twice-born in theology and assuming the Bráhmanical cord took their infamous gains. Every one was addicted to sensuality, avarice and violence, and flouted the gods, the Bráhmans, the Scriptures and the saints. Wives deserted their husbands, however handsome and accomplished, and adored instead any wretched stranger. Married women appeared without any ornaments, widows were bedecked with jewels. Teachers and pupils were of no more account than the deaf and blind; the one would not listen, the other had never read. A teacher who takes his pupil's money but does not rid him of his doubts falls into an awful abyss of hell. Father and mother call up their children and teach them the duty of filling their belly.

Dohá 96.

People who are devoid of spiritual knowledge never say anything but this. In their greed they would kill a Bráhman or their own guru to gain a cowrie. Súdras dispute with the twice-born, "Are you any better than we are? any one who understands theology is as good as the best of Bráhmans:" thus they insolently scoff.

Chaupái.

Lecherous after their neighbour's wife, clever only in trickery, clasped about with ignorance, violence and selfishness, these are the men who are reckoned as theologians and philosophers. I have seen the practice of the Kali yuga. Falling themselves and dragging down others who were keeping the path of virtue, they who trouble the world by their glosses on the Scriptures spend a whole Kalpa in each abyss of hell. People of low caste, such as oilmen, potters, dog-feeders, kiráts, kols, and distillers of spirituous liquors, who on the death of their wife or loss of their household goods shave their heads and turn religious mendicants, and make Bráhmans bow down at their feet; such men by their deeds ruin themselves both for this world and also for the next. A Bráhman is unlettered, greedy and sensual, dissolute, stupid and the husband of an outcast. A Súdra practises prayer, fasting and all the other duties of religion and taking the highest seat expounds the Puránas. Every one practises the duties of some other state of life than his own, and the endless perversions of morality are beyond all description.

Dohá 97.

In the Iron Age different castes are confounded together and every one is a law to himself. Men practise sin and reap its reward in trouble, terror, sickness, sorrow, and bereavement. Overcome by delusion, they walk not in the path of Hari's service, such as is approved by the Scriptures and conjoined with sobriety and discernment, but invent diverse ways of their own.

Chhand Tomar.

Devotees build themselves costly houses and are carried away by sensuality, forgetful of self-mortification. Ascetics amass wealth, mendicants become householders; the absurdities of the Iron Age, Sir, are beyond all description. They turn out a well-born and virtuous wife and bring home a servant-girl in violation of family usage. A son obeys his father and mother so long only as he sees not a woman's face; as soon as he takes a fancy to his wife's kinsfolk, he looks upon his own family as his enemies. Kings, devoted to criminal courses and with no regard for religion, oppress their subjects with unrighteous judgments. The meanest churl, if he is rich, is accounted noble; a Bráhman is known only by his cord, and any naked wretch is an ascetic.

Any one in the Iron-Age who rejects both Vedas and Puránas is held a worshipper of Hari and a veritable saint. The world neither rewards nor even listens to a poet; a guru is universally reviled and there is not a single wise man to be found. In the Iron Age famines are of frequent occurrence and the people perish miserably for want of food.

Dohá 98.

Hearken, Garur; in the Iron Age the whole universe is saturated with hypocrisy, violence, pride, enmity, heresy, arrogance, ignorance, sensuality and every other evil passion. Men worship the powers of darkness with prayers, fasting, sacrifice, vows and alms-giving: the gods rain not upon the earth and the rice is sown but does not germinate.

Chhand.

A woman's only ornament is her hair and she is sorely a-hungered; the poor are in distress, but are intensely selfish, Fools desire happiness, but have no regard for religion; their narrow mind is hardened and knows no compassion.

Men burdened with disease find no rest anywhere, but only self-conceit and causeless wrangling. Life is short; man's age is only fifteen years, yet in their pride they reckon on outliving creation. The Iron Age has so unsettled mankind, that no one shows any obedience, neither younger sister nor daughter. There is no contentment, nor consideration, nor repose; every caste is degraded to the condition of an importunate beggar; the world is full of envy, censoriousness and greed; placidity of temper is obsolete. Every one is smarting with sorrow and bereavement; all thought of the duties connected with caste and stage of life is abandoned. Men are so niggardly that they ignore all self-denial, charity and kind-heartedness; torpor and dishonesty are multiplied exceedingly. Men and women alike all pamper their body and slanderers are sown broadcast.

Dohá 99.

Hearken, Garur; the Iron Age is a mine of impurity and iniquity; but it has one enormous advantage, escape from it is easy. In the Ages of Gold, Silver, and Brass solemn worship, sacrifice and mystical meditation were the appointed means; in the Iron Age those who attain salvation do so only by Hari's name.

Chaupái.

In the Golden Age every one was spiritual and wise and crossed the ocean of existence by meditating on Hari. In the Silver Age men performed many sacrifices and dedicating their actions to the Lord so accomplished their course. In the Age of Brass men had no other expedient save the worship of Ráma's feet In the Iron Age men sound the depths of existence simply by chanting Ráma's praises. In the Iron Age neither spiritual abstraction, sacrifice, nor knowledge is of any avail; man's only hope is in hymning Ráma. Any one who abjures all reliance in every other and prays devoutly to Ráma and sings his praises shall assuredly escape further mundane existence. The power of his name is the special revelation of the Iron Age. It is its one sanctifying influence by which the soul is purified and sin destroyed.

Dohá 100.

There is no age to compare with the Age of Iron : in it, if a man has only faith and devotes himself to singing Ráma's holy praises, he escapes from existence without further trouble. Religion has been revealed with four feet ; in the Iron Age one is of the most importance ; to whomsoever God has given, let him practise almsgiving and prosper.

Chaupái.

Every Age has its special characteristic, infused into the soul by Ráma's delusive power. Purity, truth, equanimity and wisdom, combined with joy of soul, are recognized as the outcome of the Golden Age. A great devotion to truth—though with some admixture of passion—and general happiness are the note of the Silver Age. Much passion, little truth and some ignorance, with mingled joy and terror of soul, are the note of the Brazen Age. Great ignorance, less passion and universal antagonism are the outcome of the Iron Age. The wise understand the proper virtue of each age and forswearing iniquity devote themselves to religion. The influence of the Iron Age has no effect on him who cherishes a love for Ráma's feet. A juggler, Garur, may practise the most wonderful deceptions, but they do not impose upon his own servants.

Dohá 101.

The good and evil, which are the creation of Hari's delusive power, can only be dispersed by prayer to Hari : know this and worship Hari, forswearing all sensuality. In that particular Iron Age I lived, Garur, for many years at Avadh, till a famine occurred which compelled me to go to another country.

Chaupái.

I went to Ujaiyin—mark me, Garur—a miserable outcast, poor and wretched. After some time I acquired wealth and as before practised devotion to Sambhu. There was there a Vedic Bráhman, who constantly worshipped Siva and had no other occupation; a very saintly man, learned in divine truth, who served Sambhu, but at the same time showed no disrespect to Hari. I hypocritically attended upon this benignant philosopher, and he, Sir, seeing me outwardly so submissive, instructed me as his own son, teaching me the Saiva incantations and giving me every kind of good advice. I went to a temple of Siva and repeated the spells with a heart full of pride and self-conceit.

Dohá 102.

Wretch that I was, with a soul full of impurity, low-born and enthralled by delusion, I flew into a passion if I saw any Bráhman a worshipper of Hari and I persecuted Vishnu.

Sorathá 11.

My teacher was distressed to see my manner of life and was always admonishing me; but I became exceedingly angry. Is pride ever pleased by sober counsel?

Chaupái.

One day the Guru called me and instructed me at length in the principles of morality: "The reward, my son, for serving Siva is a steadfast faith in Ráma. Siva and Bráhma both worship Ráma; why speak then of miserable man? Do you hope to secure happiness, you luckless wight, by persecuting him whose feet even Siva and Bráhma adore?" When I heard the Guru speak of Siva as a worshipper of Hari, my heart, Garur, was all on fire. Being such a low-born churl, after receiving education I became like a snake that has been fed on milk. Arrogant, perverse, ill-starred and ill-bred, I worried my Guru day and night. But he was too tender-hearted to be angry and still continued his wise admonitions. The very person from whom a churl obtains promotion is the first for him to destroy. Hearken, friend; smoke is produced by fire, and yet when promoted to cloudship it puts the fire out. Dust while it lies on the road is held in contempt and submits to be trodden under foot of every one. If the wind carries it aloft, it first darkens that and then gets into king's eyes or sullies his crown. Hearken, Garur, and thus understand my parable; sensible people have no dealings with the mean. The wisest of the poets have declared this maxim, it is good neither to quarrel with a churl nor to be friends with him; never have anything to do with him at all, Sir; let him alone, like a dog. Churl as I was, with a heart full of falsehood and perversity, I paid no heed to the Guru's friendly admonition.

Dohá 103.

One day I was in a temple of Siva saying his rosary when the Guru came in, and in my conceit I did not rise to salute him. He was too gentle to say anything, neither did he feel the slightest atom of resentment, but the grievous sin of slighting a spiritual teacher was more than Siva could tolerate.

Chaupái.

A heavenly voice proceeded from the shrine: "You miserable, conceited churl, though your Guru shows no resentment, being so tender-hearted and of such sublime intelligence, yet I must pronounce a curse upon you, you wretch: I cannot endure such a breach of morality. If I were not to punish you for your wickendness, my scriptural ordinance would be violated. Villains who bear malice against their Guru are cast for a million ages into the most awful abyss of hell; then they take birth in the brute creation and suffer affliction in a myriad successive existences. As for you, you guilty wretch, whose soul reeks with impurity, since you kept your seat, as it were some unwieldy boa-constrictor,[1] you shall become a snake; enter into the hollow of some huge forest tree and there remain, vilest of the vile, in the form of the vilest of creatures."

Dohá 104.

Alas! alas! cried the Guru, as he heard Síva's terrible curse; and seeing me all in a tremble, a profound compassion moved his soul. Devoutly prostrating himself in Siva's presence, with his hands clasped and his voice choked with emotion as he reflected on my awful fate, he uttered this prayer:

Chhand Bhujanga-prayát.[2]

"I adore the lord of lords; the embodiment of salvation; the omnipresent and all-pervading Supreme Spirit; the image of the Veda. I worship the absolute; the unqualified; the unconditioned the unwiseful; who dwelleth in the heavens and who has heaven for his soul. I bow before the formless germ of the mystic incantation OM; the transcendental; the lord that is beyond all speech, understanding, or faculty of the senses; the Himálayan king, terrible and the death of tyrant Death; and yet the all-merciful; the grace-abounding refuge of the world. Rugged and stern as the Snowy Mountains, yet radiant with the beauty of a myriad Loves; with the bright waters of the Ganges springing from thy head, with the crescent moon gleaming on thy brow and snakes on thy neck, with tremulous ear-rings and large eyes and shaggy brows, with benignant face and deep-stained throat, O all-merciful, robed in a tiger's skin, with a necklet of skulls, I worship thee, the universal Lord, even Sankara, whom I love. I adore thee, the vehement, the exalted, the intrepid, the

1 The *aja-gar*, here translated 'boa-constrictor,' is supposed to be too unwieldy to move, and devours only such animals as of themselves fall into its mouth. Hence the popular couplet of Malúk Dás:—

Ajagar kare na chákari, pachchhi kare na kám.
Dás Malúka yon kahe, sab ka dáta Rám.

2 In the metre called *Bhujanga-prayát*, which means literally 'snake-like montion,' each line consists of four Bacchics, or, to use the language of Hindi prosody, four *yaganas*.

supreme lord; the indivisible, the unbegotten, whose glory is that of a myriad suns; tearing up by the root every kind of trouble with the trident in thy hand; Bhavâni's lord, accessible only by meditation. Unchangeable and ever-blessed Purári, consummator of earth's cycles, constant bestower of blessings on the pious, sum of all knowledge and felicity, dispeller of delusion, Conqueror of Love have mercy, O my lord, have mercy. So long as they worship not the lotus feet of Umá's lord, neither in this world nor in the next is there any happiness for men, nor peace, nor cessation of misery; O my lord, clothed about with all the elements, have mercy. I know nothing of meditation, or prayer, or ritual. but at all times and in all places I bow before thee, O Sambhu. Have mercy, O my lord, on a wretch so sorely afflicted by old age and life's flood of troubles;[1] for thee only I worship, O my lord Sambhu."

Sloka 4.

Any one who devoutly repeats this hymn to Siva, as uttered by the Bráhman in his propitiation, upon him will Siva show favour.

Dohá 105.

When the omniscient Siva heard the Bráhman's prayer and saw his devotion, a heavenly voice again sounded in the temple: "Best of Bráhmans, ask a boon." "If my lord is well pleased with me and will show favour to his servant, grant me first devotion to thy feet and then yet another boon. Overcome by thy delusive power, ignorant creatures ever wander astray: be not then wroth with him, O merciful Lord God. Gracious Sankara, be merciful to him. After a little time may thy curse be a kindness,

Chaupái.

and the highest blessings attend him; bring it thus to pass, O fountain of mercy." On hearing the Bráhman's speech so pregnant with charity, the heavenly voice replied. "So

---

1 *Tátapyamánam* is the participle of the frequentative verb from the root *tap*, and thus signifies 'suffering excessive pain.'

be it. Although he has committed a grievous sin, and I in my wrath have cursed him, yet seeing your goodness I will visit him with a special favour. Bráhmans who are of a forgiving disposition and charitable to their neighbours are as dear to me as Kharári himself. Yet my curse, father, cannot be in vain; he shall of a certainty have a thousand lives. But the insupportable misery of birth and death shall not have the slightest effect upon him. In no birth shall his knowledge fail. Hearken, Sudra, to my judgment. You have been born in Ráma's capital and, further, you have done me service. By the blessing of the city and by my favour a devotion to Ráma shall spring up in your bosom. Now hearken, friend, to my solemn declaration: the way to please Hari is by fasting and ministering to the Bráhmans. Never again insult a Bráhman; regard the saints in the light of the Everlasting. Indra's thunderbolt, my mighty trident, the rod of Death and Vishnu's terrible discus, by all these a man may be smitten yet not die; but a Bráhman's wrath is a fire which shall burn him to ashes. Cherish this counsel at heart and there is nothing in the world too difficult for you to obtain. One other blessing I have still to bestow; your goings shall never be impeded."

Dohá 106.

On hearing Siva's promise, the Guru rejoiced and cried Amen. Then after admonishing me, he returned home, with the image of Sambhu's feet impressed upon his heart. Driven by my fate, I went to the Vindhya mountains and then became a snake, and again after some time quietly dropped that form. Whatever body I assume, Garur, I readily drop again, like a man who puts off his old clothes and takes to him new. Siva observed the ordinances of the Veda, while I suffered no pain; thus I assumed many different forms, but my understanding, Garur, never left me.

Chaupái.

Whatever body I assumed, whether of beast, god or man, I invariably retained the practice of prayer to Ráma. The one regret that never left me was in the remembrance of the Guru's mildness of temper and disposition. At last I took birth in the holy form of a Bráhman, a rank to which —as the Vedas and Puránas declare—it is difficult even for a god to attain. So joining in play with other children, I enacted all Ráma's boyish sports. When I grew bigger, my father gave me lessons; but I neither understood nor attended, nor gave my mind to anything; every other inclination clean deserted me and I was wholly absorbed in my devotion to Ráma's feet. Tell me, king of the birds, is there any one so foolish as to abandon the cow of plenty to tend a she-ass? I was so overwhelmed with love that naught else pleased me and my father was quite tired of trying to teach me. After my parents had succumbed to fate, I went into the forest, there to adore the Saviour of his people. Wherever I discovered any great saints living in the woods, I frequently visited their hermitage and bowed before them, asking them all about Ráma's excellences and listening. Garur, with delight to what they told me. I went about everywhere hearing the tale of Hari's goodness, for by the blessing of Sambhu there was no check to my movements. The three kinds of evil concern[1] had left me and I had only one great longing at heart: 'When I shall behold Ráma's lotus feet, then I shall account my life to have been worth living.' Every sage, whom I questioned, told me thus: "The Lord is present in all his creatures." This religion of the impersonal did not satisfy me; I felt an overpowering devotion towards the incarnation of the Supreme.

Dohá 107.

Remembering the Guru's words and with my mind fixed

1 The three kinds of excessive concern relate to family, wealth and worldly reputation.

on Ráma's feet, I wandered about, hymning his praises, and my love every moment grew yet more and more. On one of the peaks of Mount Meru, under the shade of a *bar* tree, sat the Seer Lomas. On seeing him I bowed my head at his feet and addressed him in most humble strain. No sooner, Garur, had the beneficent sage heard my meek and submissive address than he graciously enquired: "Say, O Bráhman, with what purpose you have come." Thereupon I replied: "Fountain of mercy, you are omniscient and allwise; teach me, Sire, how to worship the incarnate God."

Chaupái.

Thereupon, Garur, the great saint spoke. briefly though reverently, of Ráma's virtues; then, being himself a philosopher devoted to the mystery of the transcendental and thinking that I had fully mastered the subject, he began a sermon on Bráhm, the unbegotten, the indivisible, the immaterial, the sovereign of the heart; unchangeable, unwishful, nameless, formless; approachable only by analogy, indestructible, incomparable: beyond the reach of thought or sense, spotless, immortal, emotionless, illimitable, blessed for ever; identical with yourself, you and he being as absolutely one as a wave and its water: so the Vedas declare. The saint gave me the fullest possible instruction, but the worship of the impersonal laid no hold of my heart. Again I cried, bowing my head at his feet: "Tell me, holy father, how to worship the Incarnate. Devotion to Ráma, O wisest of sages, is like the element of water and my soul—which is as it were a fish—how can it exist without it? Of your mercy so instruct me that I may see Ráma with my own eyes. When I have seen my fill of the lord of Avadh, then I will listen to your sermon on the Unembodied." Again the saint discoursed of the incomparable Hari and demolishing the dogma of the incarnation expounded him as altogether passionless. But I rejected the theory of the abstract and with much obstinacy insisted on his concrete manifestation. For every answer I had a rejoinder ready. The saint at last showed signs of anger. Mark me, Sir; I was so disrespectful that resentment was aroused even in the breast of a philosopher. An excessive amount of friction will strike fire even out of sandal-wood.

Dohá 108.

Again and again the saint angrily expounded his theory, while I sat still and argued the matter from every point of view in my own mind : "Can there be anger without duality, or duality without ignorance ? Can a soul, dull, circumscribed and subject to delusion be identified with divinity ?

Chaupái.

Can pain under any circumstances be the same as pleasure ? Can the possessor of the philosopher's stone suffer poverty ? Can an oppressor be free from anxiety or a sensualist remain without reproach ? Can a man's family prosper if he persecute Bráhmans ? Can religious observances be practised by a man careful only for bodily comfort ? Can sound doctrine be acquired by intercourse with the wicked ? Can an adulterer attain to the felicity of the Blessed ? Can a searcher after the Supreme Spirit escape from transmigration ? Can a reviler of Hari be ever happy ? Can a kingdom stand without a knowledge of statecraft ? Can sin coexist with a recital of Hari's virtues ? Can spotless renown be acquired without religious merit ? Can any one be disgraced except by sin. Is there any gain like devotion to Hari, as hymned by the Vedas, the saints and the Puránas ? Is there any loss, Sire, in the whole world like that of being born as a man and yet not worshipping Hari ? Is there any other sin so bad as detraction, or any virtue, Garur, so great as charity ?" Thus I reasoned to myself with much ingenuity and could not listen with patience to the saint's instruction. Again and again I maintained the doctrine of the Incarnation, till at last the saint uttered these angry words :

"Fool, I have given you the most advanced teaching, but still you are not convinced and persist in your replies and rejoinders. You have no confidence in my veracious discourse but like a crow suspect everything. Wretch, as your soul is so exceedingly self-opinionated, you shall at once be changed into an unclean bird."[1] I took the curse on my head, but was neither alarmed nor humbled.

Dohá 109.

Immediately I was turned into a crow. Then again I bowed my head at the saints feet and mindful of Ráma, the jewel of the line of Raghu, I joyfully flew away. O Umá, they who devote themselves to Ráma's feet and abjure lust, pride and choler, they see their lord present in everything: with what then can they quarrel?

Chaupái.

Hearken, king of the birds; the saint was no way in fault; it was Ráma who had stirred his soul. The All-merciful had confounded his intellect and thus made trial of my love. When the Lord God had proved the thoroughness of my devotion, he restored the saint his senses. On beholding my great amiability and pre-eminent confidence in Ráma, the holy man was much astonished and sorely repented him and courteously called me near. After consoling me in every possible way, he gladly taught me the spell by which Ráma is invoked, and in his infinite compassion told me how to meditate on the blessed child. The beauty and sweetness of this cult pleased me well. I told you all about it at the beginning. The saint kept me there some little time and recited the whole of the poem, entitled 'the Lake of Ráma's deeds. When he had reverently completed the narrative, he finally adressed me in these gracious words: "By the blessing of Sambhu, my son, I discovered this secret and delectable fountain of song; I know you to be one of Ráma's most devoted servants and

1 There is here a play on the words *sva pachchh*, 'self-opinionated,' and *pachhi*, 'a bird' which cannot be preserved in an English translation.

therefore I have told it all to you. Never repeat it, my son, in the presence of any whose heart is void of Ráma's love." The saint reiterated his instructions again and again, and I lovingly bowed my head at his feet. He touched my head with his lotus hands and gladly gave me his blessing: " Henceforth by my favour an unalterable devotion to Ráma shall dwell for ever in your heart.

Dohá 110.

Be for ever Ráma's favourite ; an illimitable; store-house of all good qualities ; changing your form at will and choosing your own time for death ; a treasury of knowledge and asceticism. May every hermitage, where you hereafter abide and make your prayer to the blessed God, be unapproachable by the spirit of ignorance for the space of a league all round.

Chaupái.

May neither time nor fate, merit, demerit nor circumstance ever cause you any vexation. May the unspeakably delightful mysteries of Ráma, the esoteric as well as the exoteric doctrines of the Chronicles and Puránas, be all comprehended by you without any difficulty, and may your affection for Ráma's feet increase day by day. May every desire you form in your mind by the blessing of Hari be ever easy of attainment." On hearing the saint's benediction—mark me, O firm of faith—this solemn response of Bráhma's came from heaven: " May your words come to pass, O wisest of sages: he is my votary in thought, word and deed.' When I heard the heavenly voice I rejoiced and was so drowned in love that all my doubts vanished. After making humble petition I received the saint's commands, and bowing again and again at his lotus feet I took my leave and arrived with joy at this hermitage, having obtained by my lord's favour an inestimable boon. During my stay here mark me, king of the birds, seven and twenty cycles have elapsed. I incessantly repeat Ráma's praises, and the birds in their wisdom reverently listen. Whenever

Rughu-bír in behoof of his votaries takes upon him the form of a man at the city of Avadh, I go and stay at his capital and delight myself with the spectacle of his childish sports. Again, cherishing in my heart the image of the child Ráma, I return, Garur, to my own cell. I have now told you the whole history of the reason for which I was changed into a crow and have replied, Sir, to all your questions. The efficacy of faith in Ráma is truly marvellous.

Dohá 111.

Therefore I love this form, in which my devotion to Ráma's feet has been exhibited, in which I have been favoured with the sight of my lord and all my doubts have been removed. For my obstinacy in upholding the doctrine of faith I was cursed by the seer, but eventually I obtained a boon which even the saints find difficult : see the efficacy of prayer.

Chaupái.

They who knowingly reject such devotion and labour merely for wisdom are fools, who would leave at home the cow of plenty and go out to look for *ák* plants to give them milk. Hearken, Garur; all who abandon the worship of Hari and seek to prosper by any other means are wretched blunderers who would try to swim across the ocean without a boat. On hearing Bhusundi's speech, Bhaváni, Garur was glad and said in gentle accents : " By your favour, my lord, every doubt, anxiety, error and delusion has been removed from my breast. Through your clemency I have heard the holy tale of Ráma's achievements and have gained peace. There is still one matter, Sir, about which I would ask; in your infinite compassion be pleased to enlighten me. The saints and sages, the Vedas and Puránas, all say there is nothing so difficult of attainment as wisdom. But the saint told you, father, that there is nothing so estimable as faith. Explain to me, most gracious lord, all the difference between faith and wisdom." The sagacious crow was pleased to hear Garur's question and courteously replied : There is no difference between faith and wisdom ; both put an end to the troubles incident ; to existence. There is no discrepency, Sir, in the saint's doctrine ; give me your attention, O noblest of birds, while I explain the matter. Wisdom, asceticism, abstraction and science—mark me, Garur—are all masculine. Now the masculine character is altogether strong, while the feminine is weak and naturally inferior.

Dohá 112.

The man who can forswear woman must be self-restrained and resolute ; not a sensual voluptuary without any regard for Hari's feet.

Sorathá 12.

Even such a saint and philosopher, Garur, is distracted at the sight of a woman, with her fawn-like eyes and moon bright face. Now creation's bride is manifested as Mayá.

Chaupái.

Here I maintain no private theory of my own. I only declare the doctrine of the Vedas, Puránas and the saints. Delusion is not feminine, though of feminine appearance ; this, Garur, is a strange proceeding. But observe ; Mayá and Faith are both of the faminine gender, as every one knows. Again, Faith is beloved of Ráma, while he regards Mayá as a mere dancinggirl. Ráma being thus amiable to Faith, Mayá is greatly afraid of her. Ráma's Faith is incomparable and illimitable, and he in whose heart she abides is ever blessed. Mayá at the sight of her is confounded and can do nothing of her own power. Knowing this, the most enlightened sages attest Faith to be the source of every blessing.

Dohá 113.

This mystery of Raghunáth's no one can grasp all at once ; whoever, by his favour, does comprehend it is never even in sleep subject to any delusion. Further now, hearken with your best intelligence to the distinction between

Wisdom and Faith, by the hearing of which is induced an imperishable devotion to Ráma's feet.

Chaupái.

Attend, my son, to this unutterable utterance, which is in truth incapable of expression though it may be mentally conceived. The soul is a particle of the divinity, immortal, intelligent, pure and naturally, blissful. But, Sir, being overcome by Mayá, it is caught, as it were a parrot or monkey.[1] The enfeebled intellect is bound with a knot, which though imaginary is difficult to untie. Thus the soul becomes worldly; there is no loosing the knot and it knows no happiness. The Vedas and Purános have declared many remedies; but there is no getting free, the entanglement is rather increased. The interior of the soul is full of the darkness of delusion and it cannot see how the knot can be untied. When God brings about such a complication, escape is problematical. If by Hari's favour a spirit of sincere piety like a beautiful cow comes and dwells in the heart, the prayers, penance and fasts and all the religious observances and acts of devotion which the Vedas have inculcated as meritorious practices are, as it were, a green pasture for the cow to graze in. The calf which fills her teats with milk is love; the heel-rope with which she is bound is the spirit of quietism, the milk-bowl faith, and the herdsman who tends her a spotless soul. After drawing off the milk of sound religion, it is set to boil on the fire of continence. Forbearance then cools it with the breath of patience; and perseverance is the

1 The allusion is to two modes of catching parrots and monkeys, which, whether ever really practised or not, have at all events passed into a proverb. A stick with a bait at the end and a string attached to it is so set in the ground that it revolves from the weight of the parrot when it lights upon it, and the bird confused by the motion fancies it is entangled in the string, though it is really loose and might fly away if it tried. For the monkey a large jar with a narrow mouth is sunk in the ground full of grain; the monkey puts in his paw and clutches a handful, but being unable to draw out his closed fist on account of the smallness of the jar's mouth, he fancies himself caught, though if he opened his hand he could extricate it immediately. Two apt illustrations are thus afforded of the way in which man allows himself be caught by delusive phenomena.

rennet that coagulates it into curds. Contentment is the maid who churns it in the bowl of discretion, with self-restraint for the stick, and truth and good words for the cord. By such churning is produced the butter of pure, excellent and holy asceticism.

Dohá 114.

After kindling the flame of meditation and applying actions both good and bad, Intelligence allows the *ghi* of wisdom to cool, but burns all the scum of selfishness in the fire. Then Intelligence, master of highest wisdom, takes absolutely pure ghi, and filling with it the lamp of the soul sets it on the stand of equanimity. Then extracting from the cotton the soul's three conditions[1] and the three properties, it works up the clean fibre of the fourth state and fashions it into an excellent candle.

Sorathá 13.

In this manner is kindled a splendid torch of science and the gnat-like swarms of vanity and other vices on approaching it are consumed by it.

Chaupái.

The unalterable persuasion of the identification of the soul with God is its pre-eminently brilliant flame, and the happiness that results from this knowledge of self is the light it diffuses, by which it destroys the erroneous distinctions which are born of the world. Delusion and all the other forms of darkness that attend upon tyrant Ignorance are utterly dispersed. Thus Intelligence having procured a light[2] sits in the chamber of the heart and tries

1 According to the Vedantists the three ordinary conditions of the soul are waking, dreaming and profound dreamless sleep. The fourth is the state of abstraction in which it is permanent indistinguishable from the Supreme Spirit. When awake, it has to do with the visible and material world ; while asleep with the world of illusion ; and when in dreamless sleep, it is temporarily enfolded as it were in the soul of the universe.

2 This is a paraphrase of a passage in the Vedánta-Sára. " When the understanding, free from the four hindrances (mental inactivity, distraction passion and propensity to pleasure) and motionless as a lamp sheltered from the wind, thus becomes the infinite intelligence only, then is realized that which is called undifferentiated meditation.

to loosen the knot; should he succeed in untying it, the soul obtains its object. But when Mayá, O Garur, sees him loosening the knot, she creates many difficulties and sends forth, Sir, innumerable elves and fairies to excite his concupiscence. In some way or other, by force or by fraud, they get near and try to put out the lamp by a side puff. If Intelligence is altogether wise, he perceives their hostile intent and will not look at them. Should he escape free from this danger, the gods then proceed to attack him. The faculties of sense are so many portals, at each of which a god sits on guard. When they see any sensual air stirring, they at once throw the doors wide open. If the blast penetrates the chamber of the soul, it forthwith extinguishes the lamp of knowledge. When its light is put out, there is no untying the knot, for Intelligence is undone by this blast of sensuality. Neither the senses nor the gods approve of wisdom; they are always inclined to sensual enjoyment. When Intelligence has been thus fooled by the breath of sensuality, who can light the lamp again as before?

Dohá 115.

Then the soul is again subjected to all the manifold miseries of transmigration. O Garur, Hari's delusive power is a trackless ocean that none can traverse. Wisdom is difficult to describe, difficult to understand, difficult to master, and if by any lucky chance a right judgment be formed, still many impediments block the way.

Chaupái.

The path of wisdom is like the edge of a scimitar; for those who fall on it, Garur, there is no escape. If any traverse the path in spite of its difficulty, they attain to the supreme sphere of beatitude. But this exalted felicity is immensely hard of attainment, as is declared by the saints, the Puránas, the Vedas and all the Scriptures. By the worship of Ráma, Sir, salvation comes freely of its own accord. As water cannot stay without some support, however much you may try to make it; in like manner, mark me, Garur, the joy of final salvation cannot be secured without the worship of Hari. The wisest of Hari's worshippers know this, and thinking lightly of the soul's deliverance from the body crave rather for faith. By faith, without any trouble or difficulty, the ignorance that arises from mundane existence is utterly abolished. Eating is for the sake of satiety, but it is the heat of the belly that digests what is eaten; in like manner the worship of Hari gives immediate relief. A man must be a fool indeed who does not delight in it.

Dohá 116.

Except by the good favour of the worshipped, it is not possible, Garur, for any worshipper to escape from existence; worship then the lotus feet of Ráma, knowing this to be the end of all theology. With Raghunáth is the power to make the living dead and the dead alive; blessed are the souls that worship him.

Chaupái.

I have thus stated and expounded the theory of Science; hear now the virtue of the jewel Faith. Faith in Ráma is a glorious philosopher's stone; in whose-ever heart it dwells, Garur, there night and day is an infinite splendour, a lamp that never requires to be fed with oil. Delusion and poverty come not near; no blast of covetousness ever extinguishes it. The gloom of overpowering ignorance is dispersed; the swarms of gnats are all destroyed. Neither vile lust nor any other vice approaches the soul in which faith abides. It changes poison to ambrosia, enemies to friends, and without this jewel no one can attain to happiness. Those grievous mental diseases, by the influence of which all living creatures are rendered miserable, have no effect upon him in whose heart is the jewel of Faith; not even in a dream can he feel the slightest atom of pain. They are truly paragons of wisdom in the world who labour persistently to secure this jewel. Though it be revealed on earth, without Ráma's grace none can find it. There is an easy device for finding it, but luckless wights go on wrangling. The Vedas and Purânas are the holy mountain, the legends of Ráma its many glorious mines : the pious are the discoverers, and good counsel is their pick-axe, while wisdom and asceticism, Garur, are their eyes. Any creature who searches with a will can find the jewel, faith ; in itself a mine of every blessing. I have in my mind persuasion of this, Sir, that one of Ráma's servants is greater than Ráma himself. Ráma is the sea, the good and pious are the rain-clouds. Hari is the sandal-tree and the saints are the winds that diffuse its perfume. Faith in Hari is a delight and the crown of all desire, but it cannot be had without the saints. Any one, Garur, who understands this and communes with the saints will find faith in Ráma easy of attainment.

Dohá 117.

The Supreme Spirit is the ocean, wisdom is mount Mandara and the saints are the gods, while the sacred legends are the nectar which they churn out having faith for its sweetness. Again, self-control is the shield, and wisdom the sword, with which faith in Hari slays his enemies, Pride, Greed and Delusion, and wins the victory ; take thought, O king of the birds, and see if it be not so."

Chaupái.

Garur asked further in loving tones : "Since, my lord, you are pleased to be gracious to me, acknowledge me as your disciple and resolve me these seven questions. Tell me first, O staunchest of the faithful, what form is the most difficult of all to obtain. Next consider and explain briefly what is the greatest pain and the highest pleasure. Tell me also the essential characteristics both of the good and of the evil, for this is a secret you understand. Tell me further what is the highest religious merit as made known in the Scriptures, and what the most awful sin. In your infinite wisdom and supreme compassion explain to me also the diseases of the soul." "Listen, my son, with the greatest reverence and devotion, while I briefly expound this scheme of doctrine. The human form is the most excellent of all, and the desire of every living creature, whether moving or motionless. It is the ladder that connects hell and heaven and final emancipation and is the bestower of the blessings of wisdom, continence and faith. Men who have attained to this form and yet do not worship Hari show themselves, in their infatuation for the world, greater fools than any fool living, clutching at bits of glass while they throw away the philosopher's stone which they had in their hands. There is no pain in the world so great as poverty and no pleasure like that which results from communion with the saints. It is an essential characteristic of the good, Garur, to be charitable to others, in thought, word and indeed. The good take pains to help their neighbours, but wicked wretches to trouble them. The good in their compassionateness resemble the birch tree[1] and constantly submit to the greatest distress in order to benefit others. The wicked, like the hemp, have their skin flayed off and perish in agony, merely to supply cords to bind people. Observe, Garur; the wicked do mischief, even when they have no object of their own to gain, like a serpent or a rat. They would kill themselves to ruin another's prosperity, like the hail which dissolves after destroying the crops. The rising of the wicked is as much a cause of calamity to the world as that of the famous planet Ketu is known to be. The rise of the good is ever productive of happiness, as when the moon rejoices the world by scattering the darkness. The highest religious merit as declared in the Scriptures is to do no harm to any creature; and there is no sin so heinous as the abuse of another. He who abuses Hari or his Guru becomes a frog and is born a thousand times in that form. He who abuses a Bráhman, after suffering

1 The bark of which is employed as paper and for other useful purposes and after being torn off the tree is again renewed.

in many Hells, will be born into the world in the form of a crow. They who have the presumption to abuse the gods or the Scriptures will fall into the hell called Kaurava. They who delight to abuse the saints will be changed into owls, as loving the night of error and hating the sun of knowledge. The fools who abuse every one will be born again as bats. Hearken now, my son, to the diseases of the soul from which all people suffer pain. Delusion is the root of all ailments and from these again spring many pains. The flatulence of lust, the phlegm of insatiable greed, and the bile of passion constantly inflame the breast, and when these three combine, Sir, there results a miserable paralysis of the whole system. Who can tell the names of all the diseases represented by the various obstinate sensual cravings? Such are the leprosy of selfishness, the itch of envy, the rheumatic throbs of joy and sorrow, the consumption that burns at the sight of another's prosperity, the horrible open sore of a malignant spirit, the excruciating gout of egoism, the sciatica of heresy, hypocrisy, vanity and pride, the terrible leprosy of greed, the violent tertian ague of the three kinds of covetousness,[1] the two fevers of jealousy and indiscrimination; but why continue the interminable list of diseases?

Dohá 118.

A man dies even of one disease; but these incurable diseases which constantly harass the soul are many in number, how then can it find rest? Pious and religious observances penance, meditation, sacrifice, prayer and almsgiving are so many different remedies; [2] but the disease, Garur, does not abate.

1 The three things not to be coveted are another man's wife, wealth and good name.

2 The pessimistic views, as expressed above, have been revived in an exaggerated form by Schopenhauer and the modern European Buddhists, who hold that life is necessarily a state of suffering. For the only reality is Will, *i.e.* a blind force pervading the universe, the Greek *avarky*. This is primarily unconscious and only manifested in the species by actions, which

Chaupái.

Thus every creature in the world is diseased, destracted alternately by sorrow and joy, by fear and love. I have mentioned only some of the diseases of the soul; they touch every one, but few only detect them. On detection the wretches diminish somewhat, but these tormentors of the faithful are not completely destroyed. They spring up even in the soul of a saint, if fed on the unwholesome diet of materialism ; how much more in that of an ordinary man ? By the grace of Ráma every disease is extirpated, if the treatment is conducted in the following manner, with a holy teacher for physician, faith for a prescription, contempt of the world for regimen, devotion to Hari for life-giving drug and a soul full of faith for the vehicle in which it is administered. By this treatment the disease is easily subdued : otherwise all your efforts go for nothing. You may know, Sir, that the mind is free from disease as soon as it gains strength in self-control, with a daily increasing appetite for good resolutions and disappearance of the weakness of material hopes. After bathing in the pure stream of divine knowledge, the whole soul is suffused with faith in Ráma. This, O king of the birds, is the doctrine of Siva, Bráhma, Sukadeva, Sanat-Kumára, Narad and all the sages, who have been eminent in theological speculation ; 'Practise devotion to Rama's lotus feet.' The Vedas and Puránas and all the Scriptures declare that without faith in Ráma there is no happiness. It would

tend to the conservation of the individual and serve to prolong the life of the species. Will is thus the will to live ; life being that for which everything pants and labours. To will is, therefore, to strive, and to strive is to suffer. Our nature is thus a kind of insatiable thirst, a struggle for existence with the certainty of being vanquished. Hence the deductions, first, that all pleasure is merely negative, suffering alone positive ; and second, that increased intelligence is simply increased capacity for pain ; the world being the worst possible world ; if it were worse, it would cease to exist. The will to live ought therefore to be rooted out, and the means to this (as Tulsi Dás also says) are voluntary poverty, chastity, and the various practices of asceticism. But the spiritual faith and devotion, upon which the Hindu theologian insists as the crowning step in the process, are necessarily ignored by the modern school, with whom not only is the world of experience an unreality, but the idea of God also is a mere dream.

be easier for water to stay on the back of a tortoise, or for the son of a childless woman to be slain, or for flowers of every description to bloom in the air, than for any creature to be happy in opposition to Hari. Sooner shall thirst be satisfied by drinking of a mirage, or horns sprout on the head of a hare, or darkness extinguish the sun, than any creature finds happiness if he has Ráma against him. Sooner shall fire appear out of ice than any one oppose Ráma and yet find happiness.

Dohá 119.

Sooner shall butter be produced by churning water, or oil come out of sand, than the ocean of existence be traversed without prayer to Hari : this is an indisputable conclusion. The Lord can change a gnat into Bráhma, or make Bráhma himself even less than a gnat. A wise man will consider this and discard all doubt and worship Ráma.

Sloká 5.

I declare to you as an established truth, and I have nothing to say as against it, that they who worship Hari can alone traverse the impassable.

Chaupái.

I have told you, my lord, Hari's unparalleled achievements, in full or in brief as my ability served me, and this Garur, is the crowning dogma of the Scriptures to abandon sensuality and worship Ráma. Whom else can you serve if you forsake the Lord Raghupati, who was compassionate even to such a wretch as myself. You are wisdom itself and superior to delusion, but you showed me, my lord, a great kindness in that you asked me for Ráma's history, which is so holy that it delights the soul even of Sukadeva and Sanat-Kumára and Sambhu. The company of the good is hard to get in the world, even for once only and for a single moment. See, Garur, and consider for yourself ; I am now a master in the worship of Raghu-bír ; though I was the vilest of birds and in every way abominable, the Lord has made me famous as a purifier of the world.

Dohá 120.

Blessed, blessed indeed am I to-day not withstanding my meanness; for Ráma has acknowledged me as one of his own servants and has admitted me to the communion of the saints. I have spoken, my lord, according to my ability and have concealed nothing; but Ráma's doings are a very ocean; who can find the bottom of them ?"

Chaupái.

As he pondered on Ráma's manifold perfections, the all-wise Bhusundi was yet more and more enraptured. "He, whose greatness the Scriptures have declared to be unutterable, whose might and majesty and dominion are unbounded, whose feet are adored by Siva, and Bráhma, even he Raghu-rái, has in his infinite compassion shown favour to me. Never have I seen or heard of such benignity; to whom, O Garur, can I compare Ráma ? Miracle-working saints, deified anchorites, inspired bards and rigid ascetics, spiritualists, doctors, self-mortified divines and the wisest and most religious of philosophers, can none of them escape but by serving my lord; again and again and yet again I bow myself before Ráma. I worship the Immortal, with whom all who take refuge are sanctified, though even guiltier than I.

Dohp 121.

He whose name is an elixir of life, the healer of every kind of trouble, may he in his mercy remain ever gracious both to me and to thee." Hearing Bhusundi's words and perceiving his admirable devotion to Ráma's feet, Garur replied in loving tones and with every doubt at an end :

Chaupái.

"By your discourse I have attained my end, now that I have learnt the delectable doctrine of faith in Ráma. My love to his feet increases ever more and more, and the trouble created by Mayá is clean gone. You have been my raft in the sea of delusion and have bestowed on me, my lord, the most exquisite delight. I can in no way requite you; but again and again I prostrate myself at your feet. Full to overflowing with love for Ráma you are so blessed, Sire, that none can equal you. Saints, trees, rivers, mountains and the earth, all operate for the good of others. The heart of the saints is like butter; so the poets say, but they say not well; for butter melts when itself is tried by the fire, but the saints are so good that they melt at others' trials. Now has my life become worth living, for by your favour my doubts have disappeared. Regard me ever as your servant." Again and again, O Umá, thus spake the noblest of birds.

Dohá 122.

After affectionately bowing his head at his feet, Garur proceeded to Vaikunth, with Ráma's image impressed upon his heart. O Girijá, there is no blessing like that of communion with the saints; it is attainable only by Hari's grace; so the Vedas and Puránas declare.

Chaupái.

I have now finished the all-holy history, by the hearing of which the bonds of existence are loosened, a very tree of Paradise abounding in mercies for all who approach it and stimulating a devotion to Ráma's lotus feet. Sins engendered of thought, word and deed are all absolved in those who listen attentively to this legend. Pilgrimages to shrines, recourse to all the means of grace, meditation, self-control, perfection in wisdom, works of religious merit, devotional practices, fasting and almsgiving, continence, temperance, prayer, penance and manifold sacrifices, tender-heartedness to all living creatures, ministering to Bráhmans and Gurus, learning, morality and exalted intelligence, in short all the forms of discipline, which the Vedas have recommended, have but one aim, Bhaváni, *viz.*, devotion to Ráma. To such devotion—as the Scriptures describe it—scarce any has attained and then only by Ráma's favour.

Dohá 123.

But though the patriarchs found it scarce attainable, any one can now easily acquire it, by the repeated hearing of this history, if only he believes.

Chaupái.

He is all-wise, he is an accomplished scholar, he is renowned throughout the world for learning and beneficence, he is truly pious and his kinsfolk's saviour, whose soul is enamoured of Ráma's feet. He is perfect in morality and supremely intelligent ; he has a thorough understanding of scriptural doctrine ; he is an inspired bard and a man of fixed purpose, who without hypocrisy worships Raghu-bir. Blessed is the land where the Ganges flows ; blessed is the wife who is faithful to her husband ; blessed is the king who governs justly ; blessed is the Bráhman who swerves not from his duty ; blessed is the wealth which is used to the best advantage ; blessed is the creed which most conduces to works of piety ; blessed is the hour which brings communion with the saints : blessed is the life which is staunch in devotion to the twice-born.

Dohá 124.

Blessed is the family, yea—mark me, Umá – worthy of veneration throughout the world and truly holy, in which is born a humble worshipper of the divine Raghu-bír.

Chaupái.

Though at first I kept it secret, I have now to the best of my ability told you the whole story. I saw the extreme devotion of your soul, and it is for this reason that I have declared to you Ráma's history. It is not to be repeated to any perverse wretch, who will not give his mind to understand the tale of Hari's sportive manifestations, nor to any covetous, choleric or sensual person, who worships not the lord of all animate and inanimate creation. Neither must it ever be told to a persecutor of the Bráhmans, even should he be as great a king as Indra. They are fit for instruction in Ráma's history, who dearly love the communion of the saints, who have a great affection for the feet of their Guru and the precepts of morality and are submissive to the Bráhmans : these are fit recipients. But he will derive a special delight from it who loves Ráma as he loves his own life.

Dohá 125.

Whoever wishes to love Ráma's feet or to attain to final deliverance should devoutly fill the pitchers of his ears with the water of this legend.

Chaupái.

The story of Ráma, as I have now told it you, O Umá, has power to subdue the impurity of this evil age and to remove all the impurities of the soul. It is a healing remedy for every disease of life, as is declared by those learned in the Veda. It has seven beautiful ghâts, being so many steps towards faith in him. Only he to whom Hari shows special favour can set his feet on this road. They who guilelessly recite this history obtain success in everything their soul desires. They who hear, or repeat and gladly assent to it, traverse the depths of existence as they would a mere puddle." Umá was greatly pleased to have heard the whole history and cried in joyous tones : "By my lord's favour my doubts have been dispelled, and my love for Ráma's feet has sprung up anew.

Dohá 126.

Through your grace, O lord of the universe, I have now attained my desire ; a firm faith in Ráma has resulted and all my troubles are at an end."

Chaupái.

This glorious dialogue between Sambhu and Umá is fruitful in blessings and destructive of sorrow ; it breaks the bonds of existence, refutes scepticism ; delights the believer and is dear to all good men ; there is nothing in the world equally dear to a worshipper of Ráma. By Raghupati's favour I have sung to the best of my ability his holy and gracious deeds. In this the last age of the world there is no other means of salvation, neither abstraction, sacrifice, prayer, penance, the paying of vows, nor religious ceremonial. Think only of Ráma, sing only of Ramá, give ear only to Ráma's infinite perfections. Let the soul give over its perversity and worship him whose special characteristic it is to sanctify the fallen, as is declared by saints and seers, by Veda and Puránas: is there any one who has worshipped Ráma and not found salvation?

Chhand 12.

Hearken, O dull of soul; is there any creature who has worshipped Ráma, the purifier of the fallen, and not found salvation? The wretches whom he has redeemed are countless, such as the harlots Pingalá and Ajámil, the huntsman Valmíki, the vulture Jatáyu and the elephant.[1] An Abhír, a foreigner, a Kirát, a Khasia, are an outcast, embodiments of pollution as they are purified if they but once repeat his name; O Ráma, I adore thee. Any one who reads, or hears, or recites this history of the glorious son of Raghu washes out the stains of the world and the stains of his own soul and without any trouble goes straight to Ráma's sphere in heaven. Any one who, appreciating their beauty, learns by heart five or six stanzas is delivered by the blessed Raghubír from all the disturbances created by the five[2] over whose councils the monster Ignorance presides. Ráma alone is all-beautiful, all-wise, full of compassion and of loving-kindness for the destitute, disinterested in his benevolence and the bestower of final deliverance; whom else can I desire? There is no other lord like Ráma, by whose favour, however slight, even I, the dullwitted Tulsi Dás, have found perfect peace.

---

1 See page 23 Note 1.

2 In this antithesis between the five stanzas and the five members of council, who are not specifically designated, the latter would seem to stand for five senses.

Dohá 127.

There is no one so poor as I am and no one so gracious to the poor as you, O Raghu-bír: remember this, O glory of the race of Raghu, and rid me of the grievous burden of existence. As a lover loves his mistress and as a miser loves his money, so for ever and ever may Ráma be beloved by me.

[*Thus endeth the Book entitled* THE SEQUEL, *a provocative to steadfast faith in Hari, being the seventh descent into the holy lake of Rama's deeds, that cleanses from every defilement of the world*].

[THE END.]

Printed by RAMZAN ALI SHAH at the National Press, Allahabad.